EXPLORATIONS IN PRAGMATIC
ECONOMICS

D1483964

To Janet L. Yellen: The Light of my Life

Explorations in Pragmatic Economics

SELECTED PAPERS OF GEORGE A. AKERLOF
(AND CO-AUTHORS)

OXFORD

UNIVERSITY PRESS

OXFORD

UNIVERSITY PRESS

Great Clarendon Street, Oxford OX26DP

Oxford University Press is a department of the University of Oxford.
It furthers the University's objective of excellence in research, scholarship,
and education by publishing worldwide in

Oxford New York

Auckland Cape Town Dar es Salaam Hong Kong Karachi Kuala Lumpur
Madrid Melbourne Mexico City Nairobi New Delhi Shanghai Taipei Toronto
With offices in

Argentina Austria Brazil Chile Czech Republic France Greece
Guatemala Hungary Italy Japan South Korea Poland Portugal
Singapore Switzerland Thailand Turkey Ukraine Vietnam

Published in the United States by Oxford University Press Inc., New York

British Library Cataloguing in Publication Data

Data available

Library of Congress Cataloging in Publication Data

Data available

ISBN 0–19–925390–0 (hbk.)
ISBN 0–19–925391–9 (pbk.)

1 3 5 7 9 10 8 6 4 2

Typeset by Kolam Information Services Pvt. Ltd, Pondicherry, India
Printed in Great Britain
on acid-free paper by
Biddles Ltd., King's Lynn, Norfolk

Contents

Part II.   Macroeconomics

Introduction: Explorations in Pragmatic Economics[1]

Y20

It is easier to describe a French garden than an English garden. But each type of garden has an order of its own kind, so that French gardens are not inherently any more orderly than English gardens. A collection of papers is like a garden. Both should have order and focal point, as both also should be well-weeded of the extraneous. This collection is an English, not a French, garden. There is no immediately apparent grand design. Like an English garden, it is an attempt to re-create nature, indeed to punctuate the type of order that nature itself creates, rather than an attempt to impose some pre-ordained order on it.

This collection has two parts, microeconomic and macroeconomic. The microeconomic part begins with **'The Market for "Lemons,"'** which examined, perhaps for the first time, the economic consequences of asymmetric information for markets. The macroeconomic part begins with 'Relative Wages and the Rate of Inflation,' which examined the effects of overlapping contracts with nominally fixed wages for the duration of the contract (or overlapping price setting, with nominally fixed prices). Each of these papers is an example of the English-garden approach that pervades this collection. They are both motivated by empirical examples. They use these examples to assay some detail of economic life, and then they demonstrate its economic consequences. In the microeconomic section these consequences are on the scale of markets; in the macroeconomic section they are on the scale of the macroeconomy.

Milton Friedman's (1953) essay, 'The Methodology of Positive Economics,' opines that economics should be done differently. Instead, he says, economists should not use detailed information to model the economy. He says that the exact realism of the model, the correspondence of the model to the details of economic transactions, should not matter. The test of the model, instead, is whether it is rejected (or not) by statistical testing. For example, it may seem to the observer that the economy is monopolistically competitive, but a model of *perfect competition* may fit the data better. In that case we

[1] Many of the ideas in this introduction came from ongoing work and conversations with Rachel Kranton. I also wish to thank Janet Yellen and Robert Akerlof for many helpful comments and suggestions.

should ignore what observers think they see: the economy behaves *as if* it were perfectly competitive.

While such 'positive' methodology might be good for fields (such as physics, perhaps), where experiments are tolerably easy, it cannot be good methodology in a field like economics where hypothesis testing is close to impossible. I can hardly imagine a worse prescription for how to do *economics*. Economists, of course, now do experiments, but typically such experiments would not be acceptable by Friedman's methodological strictures. The situations in all experiments are specially contrived. Also, experimental subjects are rarely a random sample of the relevant population. The nature of economic statistics from the wild adds further to the difficulty of hypothesis testing. The use of statistical data to test economic theories always suffers from the looseness of connection between theory and the specification of econometric tests. Even tests with just a single endogenous variable involve a great deal of independent choice for the econometrician: for example, with any time series test he must specify the dependent variable, at least one independent variable, leads and lags, the period of estimation, the functional form, and the autocorrelations of the error term. Theory typically pins down these forms so little that he is likely to have multiple choices in each of these categories. Indeed, with four possible choices in each category, the econometrician will have more than 4,000 separate possible specifications. In the absence of a natural experiment, identification typically requires estimating a system of simultaneous equations with many endogenous variables. If the typical endogenous variable has approximately m specifications and n such variables are being determined simultaneously, the number of possible specifications is on the order of magnitude of m^n. We have already seen that m is likely to be large, so that in most practical cases m^n is huge. It should be no surprise that practical economists, as represented by the business press (*e.g. The Economist*) and official reports (*e.g. The Economic Report of the President*) are remarkably sparse in their presentation of estimates of key economic parameters.

In the face of such difficulties in hypothesis testing, economists must be opportunists. In my view the formal positivist methodology wantonly throws away the best information available to us. Of course we should pursue the standard formal methods of hypothesis testing and estimation of parameters (*e.g.* econometrics), but we must also be heedful of the inherent ambiguity of the enterprise. That means we should also take every other advantage we can get, since the official methodology of hypothesis-testing, insofar as it works at all, requires more judiciousness than we would ideally like.

Economists typically impute to others considerable ability to extrapolate from the anecdote of their experience to the broader context how they are affected by economic markets and conditions. The standard assumption of rational expectations indeed assumes that the public acts as if it perfectly understands all aspects of the economy's behavior, except for the value of current unknowable shocks. Almost surely this assumption overestimates the public's ability to estimate the true model of the economy. But surely the common assumption that trained economists have *no judgment whatsoever* in connecting anecdote and experience to economic structure must be an understatement on the other side. The papers in this volume are all based on such judgment. They all rely on the ability of the author and the reader to connect the relation between the telling incident and the nature of economic structure.

Thus it is no coincidence that the initial paper in the macroeconomic section, as well as many of the other papers that follow, bases its model of the macroeconomy on monopolistic competition. Friedman's essay on positive economics is not just a general statement about the nature of proper economic methodology, but it is also a particular warning to the misguided that even though the economy 'appears to be' monopolistically competitive, perfect competition should be the economic model. I am proud to be among the misguided. The use of monopolistic competition is just one example of the pragmatic approach to economics everywhere in this collection.

In contrast to Friedman, who urges us to consider models that are constructed without concern for 'realism,' except insofar as their predictions can be rejected by statistical testing, I suggest that, on the contrary, economists should restrict their attention to models that are consistent with the detail of microeconomic behavior. Friedman may be correct that such methodology does not conform to the positivist ideal, but that does not make it 'unscientific.' On the contrary, I perceive most science as inferring macro behavior from micro structure. To a remarkable degree the progress of science since the discovery of the microscope has been the inference of the large from the structure of the very small.

Because nature duplicates itself at the level of the very small, it is inherent that the study of the microscopic generates an understanding of the macroscopic. Nature duplicates itself at the atomic level, at the molecular level, and, in biology, even at the level of the organism. Thus much (but not all) science involves the study of micro structures and the interpretation of the implications of those structures for larger aggregates.

To me, the most dramatic example of the relation between the small and the large is the structure of life itself. Crick and Watson[2] conjectured correctly that if they could describe the crystalline structure of a single DNA molecule they would have unlocked the secret of life. The duality between the structure of the DNA molecule and the way in which organisms are generated and reproduced is one of most beautiful findings of human knowledge. It indicates the sense in which Crick and Watson were, indeed, profoundly correct.

But what are the implications for social science? Standard economic methodology, with its emphasis on statistical analysis of *populations*, would suggest that the intensive study of a single molecule would be an all but worthless 'case study.' In the case of DNA, we know that the exact opposite is true: because DNA is a template that determines all of the cells of the organism, and also its reproduction, one molecule may not tell all, but it does tell a great deal.

Is there some reason to believe that economic behavior and economic units are any different? Economic decisions may not be as duplicable as biological processes, but the basic reason why science intensively studies the microscopic applies to economics as well. The individual economic unit, be it a firm, a consumer, or an employee, behaves

---

[2] As dramatically described by Watson (1969).

the way it does *for a reason*. Therefore it makes sense to discover the reasons why these units behave as they do.

Standard economic methodology says that it is impossible to infer motivation of individual actors from intensive case studies. But shouldn't this question be decided empirically, rather than *a priori*? Anthropologists and sociologists listen carefully to individuals in case studies because, as in a lie detector test, people find it hard to cover up the real reasons for their actions, even when they want to hide them. If that is the case, the best information on the behavior of populations probably comes from close observation of individual units, rather than from analysis of statistical populations. There is good reason to follow the methodology of Truman Bewley (1999) in his detailed interview study of Connecticut wage setters. But, such methodology is not considered *pukka*.

The link behind all of the papers in this English-garden collection is their common exploration of the way in which the duplication of the small affects the nature of the large. With these prefatory remarks, it is now time to make a tour of the collection, to see each of the articles in turn. I shall conclude with a few remarks, returning to the difference between the methodology in these papers and the standard view of how economics should be done.

MICROECONOMICS

Information Asymmetries

The collection begins with **'The Market for "Lemons"'** [3], which concerns the question how product quality is ensured when buyers and sellers have different information. The used car market, where the seller of a used car is likely to know more about its quality than potential buyers, is used to illustrate the problem. If good and bad cars are sold at the same price, owners are more likely to offer a bad car for sale than a good one. Potential buyers of used cars suspect that the cars on the market are bad. Accordingly they reduce the price they are willing to pay, reducing further the incentive to put a good car up for sale. In a vicious circle such interactions between the buyers and the sellers may even cause a total market collapse.

The used car example especially reflects the method of these essays, which is to explore the consequences of economic features that are sufficiently pervasive that their validity is obvious. Most adults in the developed world understand the problems of buying and selling a used car from their own personal experience. In a recent retrospective the New York *Times* even recently asserted that in the 1960s, when 'Lemons' was written, cars were as much a part of American culture as rock and roll music. The behavior of this market (and the role of asymmetric information in it) would therefore have been personally familiar to every reader.

Of course, the problem of buyers in the used car market takes place at least to some lesser degree in every other market. Buyers of products in every market must somehow establish that product quality at least roughly corresponds to their expectations. How

---

[3] Articles in this collection will be named in boldface when initially mentioned.

quality is guaranteed is an essential problem that must somehow be answered in every market.

Why had economic analysis ignored a problem of such significance? My personal view is that the underlying innovation in 'The Market for "Lemons" ' was its methodology, which was highly unusual in the mid 1960s. 'Lemons' constructs models explicitly designed to capture the common structure in a class of examples. Only a handful of economists, who included those who had discovered monopolistic competition, had such a naturalistic approach to economic theory at the time. The standard theoretical methodology was instead to do economic analysis by making *ad hoc* changes to models of perfect competition. In addition, economists were fundamentally interested in quantity and price; it was simply assumed that, somehow, in some unspecified way, the problem of quality could be independently addressed. Since that time, first with further analysis of asymmetric information, but then with the introduction of games that are tailored to correspond to economic structure, the methodology of constructing theory to conform to examples has become more common, at least in microeconomic theory.

The difference in mind-set between 'The Market for "Lemons" ' (together with all the other papers in this volume) and the economic theory of the time can be gauged by the difference between my view and the view of other economists toward the proof of existence of equilibrium in the competitive model (Debreu (1959)). To some economists (see, for example, Lindbeck (1985)) this was a keystone in economic theory. In my view that accomplishment was only the dotting of the last *i* in a theory that was *already* well understood. In addition, the theory has also been used inappropriately. In my view most attempts to analyze the economy through the perfectly competitive general equilibrium model are forced: they usually involve an attempt to impose economists' conception of order on economic systems without sufficient attention to observation of the system itself. The difference between economic theory like 'lemons' and that like *The Theory of Value* is the English gardens/French gardens dichotomy from the very introduction.[4]

The basic message of 'The Market for "Lemons" ' was that asymmetric information made it difficult to conduct business. Markets where there could have been possible gains from trade in the absence of asymmetric information might even collapse. Welfare can be improved by government intervention if markets are seriously impacted, as with government-supplied medical insurance for the elderly and with securities regulation. In addition, a variety of private-market institutions such as guarantees and repeat business may serve to ensure quality, but also such institutions entail problems that arise from market power.

I wrote 'The Market for "Lemons" ' in 1966–1967, which was my first year at Berkeley, and submitted it for publication at the end of the year to *The American Economic Review*, which in short order rejected it. The editor returned it without any referee reports (perhaps a case of asymmetric information). His letter said that *The American Economic Review* did not publish articles so trivial. I spent the academic year 1967–1968 in India,

---

[4] In graduate curricula this dichotomy also conforms to the standard division of the first-year graduate microeconomics sequence between the game theory/information theory course and the course in general-equilibrium/classical economics.

where I revised the paper, incorporating some examples from economic development. I sent the new version, first to *The Review of Economic Studies* and then to *The Journal of Political Economy*. They also both rejected it. These editors indicated that if this was economics, then *economics* would be something very different. Only on a fourth try, in 1968, did I finally obtain acceptance of the article, at *The Quarterly Journal of Economics*.

Caste and Identity

The next article in the collection, '**The Economics of Caste and of the Rat Race and Other Woeful Tales**,' reflects the difficult reception of 'Lemons' in several ways. The rocky reception of 'Lemons' had made me slow to follow up on its implications. First, my priority from 1967 to 1969 had been to get the original paper accepted and suitably revised. Second, although I did see that the introduction of asymmetric information to markets was a notable change in economic theory, the lack of enthusiam of the editors and referees was also demoralizing. But, also, I thought that the lack of acceptance by others gave me the luxury of continuing this research at my own pace. I did not predict that by the time I wrote my model of the rat race in the fall of 1971, Michael Spence would have already produced his analysis of signaling models, with greater sophistication. What I call an *indicator* in my article, Spence had called a *signal*. But there is an innovation in 'Caste and the Rat-Race,' which is the notion of a caste equilibrium. At the time, as I also see in re-reading the article in preparation of this collection, I knew that its inclusion in an article on the role of signals was forced. Here too is further indication of the lesson I had learned in my previous difficulty in publishing 'Lemons.' I suspected that 'caste equilibrium' could only be published as an addendum to an article where it was not ostensibly the major theme. Today as I write this review I still believe that the truths we see from caste regarding economic equilibrium are as fundamental as those in 'Lemons.'

The key idea underlying the caste equilibrium is that codes of caste behavior can trump the marginal decisions that people would make as individuals to maximize their economic welfare. As a result equilibrium may occur where supply (as determined solely by economic considerations) will not equal demand (as determined solely by economic conditions). The caste codes themselves are also major factors in determining the economic equilibria. The challenge to economic theory is to answer why obedience to caste codes that are contrary to the economic benefit of their practitioners do not break down because of self-interest. The reasoning in the paper regarding how the caste equilibrium is maintained is at least marginally acceptable in modern game theory: those who fail to enforce the caste code against those who disobey it are themselves disobeying the caste code and should themselves be outcasted. Thus it pays everyone to enforce the caste code against one other, and no one will disobey it. In practice, except in extraordinary circumstances, such as the worst witch hunts (see Mui (1999)), I am dubious that the punishment of the higher order breakers of the code (who *fail* to punish) will occur. These higher order punishments are difficult to enforce because it is hard to establish clearly that someone should have punished the breaking of the caste code but failed to do so.

It is interesting to note the difference between the methodology of this article and of most other economic theory. Most economists want to make their assumptions as parsimonious as possible. Indeed Friedman suggests such parsimony as the criterion of a good model. In contrast, I see the primary objective of a good model as the correct description of the nature that it wants to portray. Since I see caste codes as being important independent determinants of behavior, I therefore think it would be scientifically *wrong* to leave them out of the model.

The caste-code equilibrium concept led in two directions. The first direction, which is the possibility of gap between demand and supply, provided a possible explanation for unemployment. In due course that line of argument evolved into efficiency wage theories, as I shall describe below in reviewing the macroeconomics papers in this collection. But, more directly, the caste model led to the question as to what enforces the codes to be obeyed in equilibrium. The equilibrium in the original article was particularly shaky. Someone obeyed the caste code when it was contrary to her interests because she would be punished if she met someone who also obeyed the caste code. That person delivered that punishment, because she would be punished in turn if she did not also obey the caste code. The caste code demanded that she should punish the original offender against it. Such an equilibrium is especially shaky since a small group of people can form their own separatist society and trade with each other while disobeying the caste code. In American history the Pilgrims and the founders of the Massachusetts Bay Colony did just that. But the experience of these intrepid settlers in the Massachusetts wilderness illustrates a much higher cost of separatism than implied by the original model.

'Discriminatory, Status-Based Wages among Tradition-Oriented, Stochastically Trading Coconut Producers' repairs this problem; it presents a model that greatly weakens the conditions necessary for caste-code equilibria. In this model separation typically entails forgoing *positive* idiosyncratic gains from trades with one's best trading partner. That contrasts with Walrasian models, where there is no gain from trade with one's best partner over the next best alternative. The model also makes the further assumption that the best trading partner, who confers these positive benefits, is randomly drawn from the whole population. It follows Peter Diamond's (1982) model of an economy with a significantly smaller number of traders than in Walrasian equilibrium. A caste code is then much easier to uphold. The individual follows the caste code because she realistically fears that her random trading partner will boycott her if she disobeys it. Thus even if there were a large number of agents who wanted to disobey the caste code themselves and who would not punish anyone else who did, the potential breaker of the code may still not want to do so. I believe that this model describes the enforcement of caste codes in rural areas, especially the Jim Crow customs of the United States South.

'Economics and Identity,' with Rachel Kranton, constitutes yet a further effort to explore the economic consequences of the idea that codes of how people should behave play a role in determining their actual behavior. Rachel Kranton played the major role in bridging the intellectual chasm between 'Caste and the Rat-Race' and 'Economics and Identity.' The new paper draws on the significant literature in sociology and psychology where subjects take on group values. In the classic Robbers Cave experiment by Sherif *et al.* (1961) normal 11-year-old boys who were isolated into two groups in a state park in Oklahoma quickly established fierce loyalty to their own group, and also antagonism to the other. Tajfel (1978) and his followers have shown that group attachment occurs even under the most minimal conditions, where subjects know that their group assignment is only a randomly chosen label.[5] The concepts of *identity* and *social category* are perhaps as fundamental in sociology as the concepts of supply and demand in economics. In this view people divide themselves and others into social categories with which they identify. These social categories have ideal types that exemplify how people in those social categories *should* behave.[6]

'Economics and Identity' uses the concepts of identity, social category, prescriptions, and ideal type to introduce five new ideas into economics. First, people's tastes for action depend upon the social categories to which they belong. Second, these tastes also depend on the prescriptions for behavior corresponding to those social categories. Thus because people identify with these *prescriptions* (which I would have earlier described as caste codes), they tend to be obeyed. But, third, there are also externalities. People lose identity utility if someone else of their social category disobeys the prescriptions as to how they should behave and sometimes they can (at least partially) restore their identity by some response, often in punishment of the offender. This yields a much more natural reason for the punishment of those who disobey the caste code than in the earlier article. It is simpler, and also truer to life. Fourth, in many contexts people have some choice over their social category. Indeed, these may be the most important life choices that any of us ever make. And then, fifth, but perhaps no less important, people may also manipulate others' identity.

'Economics and Identity' also shows the relevance of identity in analyzing important features of the labor market. In an identity model of gender discrimination the fundamental bias comes from typing of some jobs or tasks as female rather than male (or vice-versa). Women (men) then are not supposed to undertake male (female) tasks or jobs. An identity model also gives an explanation that is new to economics on the nature of discrimination against African-Americans in the United States, with explanation for the high rates of drug addiction, crime, and out-of-wedlock birth. Following the major theme in Black studies, we interpret the worst effects of racial discrimination in the United States as due to natural African-American adoption of a low-reward counter-cultural identity in response to White rejection. In further application of the identity model, Akerlof and Kranton (2003) shows the role of identity in organization theory: successful organizations assign people to *offices* (jobs) with which they identify. This identification means that job-holders wish to live up to an ideal behavior of their assigned office. In the successful organization employees have such identification, which causes them to fulfill organizational goals. The analysis can also be applied to schools, which are just one special form of organization. It explains why some schools

---

[5] For a review of this literature see Haslam (2001).
[6] How they should behave may not be universal for all people in a given category: it may also depend upon personal characteristics and social background.

succeed while others fail (Akerlof and Kranton (2002)). Following education scholars, we view schools' success, when it occurs, as mainly due to widespread student acceptance of an academic ideal type.

Economics of Income Redistribution and Family Structure

The previous three papers take one approach to social problems, such as discrimination and the economics of the disadvantaged, by describing equilibria that are influenced by social norms. But the economics of information, the starting point in these essays, also has implications for the handling of social problems. The 'Economics of "Tagging" ' describes the economic costs and benefits of government aid to the disadvantaged. Evaluating the costs of aiding the disadvantaged by the expenditures of programs to aid them mis-estimates the costs of transfers to the poor. Those costs are not the dollars that go to the recipients, but instead are the deadweight losses that arise because of the high rates of marginal taxation that come from giving such aid.

A simple formula indicates how very large such distortions may be. With a linear negative income tax, the marginal rate of taxation must be the sum of two terms. The first term is the ratio of government revenues relative to income (a number which is typically about 1/3). The second term is the ratio of the minimum support level to per-capita income. Typical levels of welfare support suggests that this term might also be about 1/3. As a result the marginal rate of taxation with a suitably generous negative income tax program is likely to be as high as 2/3. Such high marginal rates occur because high marginal tax rates are needed to tax back the support that income-earners would receive if they had no earnings at all. They have been the Achilles heel of negative income tax proposals.

But in the US the poor do receive significant welfare payments and marginal tax rates are also considerably less than 2/3 for most of the population. How is this achieved? If the government knew what individual earnings would be in the absence of taxes, the problem could be solved easily: it could then give lump sum transfers to those with low incomes. But, there is a problem of asymmetric information, because, of course, the government cannot know incomes *a priori*. So it does the next best thing. It 'tags' groups of people who are especially likely to be needy (for example, those who fail to meet a wealth test) and it gives them a tax schedule that is more favorable than it gives to the rest of the population. By 'tagging' people in this way the government avoids the high marginal rates of taxation entailed by a need to claw back the immense losses in revenue from giving minimum support to everyone. In comparison to a negative income tax 'tagging' thus allows higher levels of support to the poor and lower marginal tax rates to the rest of the population. In this article I claim that in fact the US system of welfare is a hodgepodge constructed from such principles. We allow the distortions and inequity of our system (for example from the eligibility requirements for welfare) in a compromise that yields lower marginal tax rates and higher levels of support for those tagged as disadvantaged.

This theory of income support naturally argues in favor of the earned income tax credit. For those who receive the credits the tax incentives are positive, but the higher marginal tax rates to the rest of the population because of the tax credits is extremely small, since, luckily, there are relatively few people with incomes so low that they qualify. David Ellwood (1988) has especially appreciated the benefits of the Earned Income Tax Credit, which I had not seen in the original article. The increase in the EITC was one of the most successful policy initiatives of the 1990s.

There are two major sources of poverty in the United States. One source is low earnings due to low skill and other misfortune. But family structure is also important. The poverty rate of single-parent families is many times that of two-parent families. Thus the natural accompaniment to 'Tagging,' which concerns the nature of the optimal welfare system, is an examination of single-parenthood. Not only are female-headed single-parent families common, but also out-of-wedlock birth rose dramatically in the United States in the 1960s and 1970s. In the conservative view (see Murray (1984)) these changes were the result of increased generosity in welfare benefits. In this view poor women merely responded to the incentives that were offered: they had children out of wedlock. But other reasons can also account for the change. It is well known that in this period the stigma attached to out-of-wedlock births also declined precipitously.

'An Analysis of Out-of-Wedlock Childbearing in the United States,' with Janet Yellen and Michael Katz, discusses the connection between this decline in stigma and the rise in out-of-wedlock births in the US. Empirically we are motivated by statistics that show that the near simultaneous legalization of abortion and introduction of the pill for unmarried women were also accompanied by significant declines in the shot-gun marriage rate. The shot-gun marriage rate is the fraction of pregnant women who get married in the nine months prior to the birth of the child. These statistics support the view of Kristin Luker (1991) that in the old days young men and young women may have had sex out of wedlock, but typically they also had an understanding that if the woman got pregnant the man would marry her. With the advent of the pill, and also of legalized abortion, sex out of wedlock began earlier in such relations. Also there was much less need for such a mutual understanding. Legalized abortion meant that the pregnant woman did not need to have the child. And with the pill available, pregnancy was also less arguably the 'man's fault.' In a mutually reinforcing feedback loop, as out-of-wedlock births became more common the stigma attached to them declined, further exacerbating the trend in births out-of-wedlock.

This paper explains the increase in the problems that welfare systems with 'tagging' are supposed to ameliorate. It also contradicts the claims of conservatives regarding the role of welfare. The conservatives have claimed that the simultaneous rise in welfare benefits and out-of-wedlock births suggests that the changes in welfare benefits were causal. But, on the contrary, our paper suggests that there was a shock in the secularization of sexual relations. That shock also caused the disappearance of the social custom for the boy to marry the girl if she got pregnant. In such circumstances the rise in welfare was a life-saver. The women and children left out in the cold were given a much-needed helping hand. Our theory suggests that cutting welfare benefits to poor single mothers is unlikely to cause great changes in out of wedlock births, but such cuts will seriously decrease the income and welfare of unfortunate mothers and children.

The rise in single parenthood and also in out-of-wedlock births has further implications for social welfare in the United States, as explored in **'Men without Children.'** It is no coincidence that if women are marrying later, or not at all, that men will be doing the same. In 1964 by the age of 25, only 20 percent of men with just a high school diploma had never married; by 1989 that figure had more than doubled, to 50 percent. For women in 1964, only 10 percent had not married by the age of 25, but that fraction had tripled to 30 percent in 1989. The changes in fatherhood are also striking. In 1965 roughly one third of male 25-year-olds with 12 years of education were in childless households; by 1993 roughly two thirds were living without children. These changes in family structure may have affected the behavior of young males, who typically 'settle down' with marriage and fatherhood. The change in family structure may have played a significant role in the epidemic of drug addiction and crime that accompanied the changes in sexual customs of the 1960s.

The analysis of social problems in these last two papers ('Out-of-Wedlock Childbearing' and 'Men without Children') has a common basis. Note that both emphasize the role of changing norms. The conservative argument is basically price-theoretic: the increase in out-of-wedlock births occurred because the monetary rewards to them increased. In contrast, in our view out-of-wedlock births increased initially because at the margin there were changes in 'technology,' with the advent of birth control and the legalization of abortion, but then they increased much more because of the feedback between the rise in out-of-wedlock births and their destigmatization (a change in the norms). Similarly, we think that a major reason for the increase in crime and drug addiction in the 1960s and 1970s is a change in the ideal type for young men in the United States. The ideal young man in his mid-twenties in the early 1960s was married with children; by the late 1970s he was a swinging single.

Economics and Psychology

Economics has changed greatly since these essays were begun. The economics of the 1960s was all but devoid of serious consideration of information and the externalities that it causes. It was also devoid of sociology and psychology. Before Kahneman and Tversky, decision-making was assumed to be based on unbiased use of information. While perhaps a good description of some decision-making, this assumption also excludes everything of interest to a psychologist. Most of psychology describes wrong decisions due to cognitive and emotional bias.

In **'The Economic Consequences of Cognitive Dissonance'** with William Dickens and in **'The Economics of Illusion'** people choose their beliefs as a compromise between the economic losses that result from mistakes in decision-making due to erroneous beliefs and the gain in happiness from beliefs that make them comfortable.[7] In this fashion 'Cognitive Dissonance' accounts for a number of economic phenomena, especially lapses in adherence to safety standards. 'The Economics of Illusion' shows the consequences for public finance from beliefs chosen for comfort. In a democracy the loss

---

[7] In work by Benabou and Tirole individuals choose their preferences to bolster their confidence.

to an individual from her own incorrect beliefs about public issues is of measure zero (corresponding to a negligible chance of her being the marginal voter); but the gain to herself from beliefs that make her happier will be significant. The voting public therefore has no reason to inform itself regarding public concerns, beyond what would maximize individuals' own comfort regarding their ignorance. Thus voter expertise regarding public policy may be extremely low.

It is useful to compare 'Cognitive Dissonance' and 'Economics of Illusion' with the later paper, 'Economics and Identity.' The basic mechanism in the two earlier papers is biased beliefs, because people choose their beliefs, in part, to make themselves comfortable. In contrast, in 'Economics and Identity,' instead of choosing *beliefs* people choose their *identity*. They choose who they want to be and their view of how they should behave. But identities are not only associated with changes in utility, they are also associated with biased beliefs. When Tajfel's subjects were knowingly divided randomly into groups, they identified with their own groups. This identification is revealed in preferences to give rewards to members of their own group. But the identification was also revealed in biased use of information. Subjects also believed that members of *their own* group were superior.

Identity gives added precision regarding how beliefs will be biased, as can be illustrated by the interpretation of culture in 'The Economics of Illusion.' That paper cites as an example of such bias Clifford Geertz' (1973) shaggy dog tale of cultural misunderstanding in 1909 backwater Morocco between a French lieutenant, a Jewish trader, and a local sheikh. The French lieutenant could not understand that the Jewish trader took 500 sheep in compensation after the sheikh's tribe had killed his guest in a raid on his tent. The lieutenant jailed the trader since he could only imagine that he had acquired the sheep by force. 'The Economics of Illusion' interprets this action as due to cultural bias. This interpretation is correct as far as it goes, but the concept of identity allows more precise explanation of the lieutenant's error. The lieutenant, who identifies with being French, has an ideal for how the trader and the sheikh should have behaved (as proper Frenchmen, of course). Imputing such motivation to both of them, he cannot imagine an honest transaction whereby the sheikh gave the sheep to the trader. Similar cognitive bias occurs in a different context. Paul Willis' (1977) 'lads,' who are working class youth in a grammar school in a British industrial town, get drunk on the day before they are to graduate from grammar school. The teachers wonder why the lads had not waited to get drunk until the next day, after graduation. With their middle-class identities, the teachers cannot imagine that the lads' motivation is different from their own.

The concept of identity allows deeper explanation than in these papers on biased beliefs from the 1980s, because it allows a characterization why people are more comfortable with some beliefs than with others. 'Identity' thus gives one natural source for bias. With identity, people want to behave like the ideal type of their respective social category. When they have different identifications from others, their natural bias is to impute their own motives to others. The French lieutenant and Willis' teachers both illustrate bias of this form.

In retrospect, 'The Economics of Illusion' could have been written differently. The key protagonists in the basic model in this paper are fishermen, who are deciding how to vote on an optimal tax on fish, which are a scarce resource. Each fisherman obtains significant loss in happiness if he believes that every fish he catches depletes the fish supply. In contrast, his marginal benefit from correct belief, which would induce his political support for the optimal tax, is negligible: since his vote will not affect the tax. As a result, in the model, the fishermen collectively choose beliefs that make themselves comfortable; and they eschew a tax. Now Rachel Kranton and I would tell the same story differently. We would say that the ideal type for the fisherman is someone who contributes to the common good. He does not deplete the stock of fish. Since the fisherman loses identity if he believes that he is responsible for reducing the stock of fish, he chooses his beliefs accordingly. But then he fails to support the optimal tax.

As a further foray in psychology, the volume also includes '**Procrastination and Obedience**.' The article fits in this collection, but it was much less original than I thought at the time of publication since unfortunately I had been unaware of the earlier literature on present bias.[8] 'Procrastination and Obedience' shows some potential applications of such present bias, which is now called 'beta-delta discounting.'[9] Since that time its implications have been explored by many authors, and, especially by David Laibson (1997). My paper showed that relatively minor biases in terms of evaluating the present relative to the future can result in continued procrastination. For example, people fail to save in the present because the benefits of present consumption are especially salient, and therefore they defer consumption until tomorrow. But then tomorrow again vanishes into the future, so that there is never a time to save.

I believe that many of the phenomena that people now attribute to such time-inconsistent behavior could also be captured by other models that are algebraically very different. Writing about 'self-control,' the psychologist Howard Rachlin (2000) points out the connection between hyperbolic discounting and identity. He cites Strike, who is the drug-dealing protagonist in Richard Price's (1992) novel *Clockers*. Following Rachlin, Strike's actions are determined by his desire of the moment, which explains the curious title of the book: Strike is a 'clocker,' which means that he lives by and for the moment. But in another representation of the same phenomenon Strike has an *identity* as a drug dealer (Rachel Kranton and I would call it a countercultural or 'Red' identity), and one of the imperatives of that identity is to live for the moment. Thus the phenomenon of procrastination could be represented by an alternative model. I see this as illustrative of one of the current failures in psychology and economics. This field has broadened the vision of economists, but its range of models and modes of explanation are still too narrow. Economists and psychologists should be more willing than at present to develop multiple views for the same phenomenon.

---

[8] This literature included, among others, the economics papers of Strotz (1956), Phelps and Pollak (1968), Thaler and Shefrin (1981), and Loewenstein (1987). The work on hyperbolic discounting in psychology, as summarized by Ainslie (1992).

[9] The term beta-delta discounting comes from the assumption that the present rate of discount, given by the product of beta and delta, is greater than all future rates of discount, which are given by delta.

The Economics of Looting

The 'microeconomics' section of the collection concludes with a foray into the economics of finance: '**Looting: The Economic Underworld of Bankruptcy for Profit**' with Paul Romer. According to this paper small errors in accounting rules and regulations can open up massive opportunities for exploitation. Stigler has demonstrated the ability of market forces to undermine government regulations.[10] In our paper market incentives are similarly powerful, with similar ill consequence. The paper shows the mischief that can be spawned by divergence between accounting definitions and economic definitions of profits. We show the possibility that owners or managers may take the money from their companies and run. In the simplest case, if accounting rules allow it, they will pay dividends in the first period that exceed the economic value of the firm, which will later go bankrupt. Such a strategy results in extremely perverse incentives: once it is clear that the firm will be bankrupt it pays the owners to make whatever payments they can to themselves from the firm's resources irrespective of the cost to the firm. In simple language they loot it. The managers have such an incentive since their return from a marginal dollar of the firm's revenues, once it is bankrupt, is exactly zero. With this example and many like it this paper thus demonstrates the sensitivity of the economic system to its accounting rules.

By demonstrating the ways in which firms are able to take advantage of accounting rules that are at even small variance with the optimal economic definitions, this paper is in the spirit of the rest of this volume. It gives one more example that the nature of the underlying micro structure can have surprisingly large effects at the macro level. In the case of 'looting' these large effects occur because market forces create incentives to take advantage of accounting discrepancies.

MACROECONOMICS

Staggered Price Setting and Money-Demand with Target-Threshold Monitoring

As mentioned earlier, the macroeconomic collection begins with a model of staggered price and wage setting, '**Relative Wages and the Rate of Inflation.**' New at the time of publication, variants of this model are now a work-horse of Keynesian economics. Firms are monopolistic competitors. Most importantly, they have staggered price setting, as represented by two sets of firms that alternate in making price changes over a two-period interval. In the most parsimonious model, no labor is needed in the production of output and firms stagger price setting. In a less parsimonious, more realistic model, prices are a mark-up over labor cost and there is staggered wage setting, rather than staggered price setting.

The three basic assumptions, that firms are monopolistically competitive, that wage setting (or price setting) is staggered, and that wages are determined by bargains between firms and workers, stands as the best answer to the assertion of classical economists that foreseen changes in the money supply have no effect on equilibrium

---

[10] See Peltzman (1993) for an excellent review of Stigler on regulation.

output or employment. As discussed further below, classical economics suggests that predicted increases in the money supply will be neutral because they will be matched by equal changes in wages and prices that leave no real variable unchanged. The classical assertion of monetary neutrality will be correct in the total absence of money illusion. But this model shows that only a small amount of money illusion is sufficient to make it false. The source of money illusion in this model is only the constancy of prices (or wages, in the more complicated version) for the two-period interval for which they are respectively set.

Indeed, Friedman had been remarkably prescient in sensing that monopolistic competition would provide the basis for a challenge to his version of macroeconomics. In later developments, Taylor (1981) greatly simplified the mathematics of my model with better notation; he also added rational, rather than adaptive, expectations. Calvo (1983) further noted that the mathematics could be further simplified by assuming that a firm would change its price randomly in a given interval of time. Both of these developments have brought this model up to date.

The paper was written before the challenge to macroeconomics that arose from rational expectations. For that reason it must appear a bit quaint today. If I were to rewrite it now, I would emphasize the implications of the model for the short-run trade-off between inflation and unemployment, even where there are rational expectations. Indeed that is precisely the stance later taken by Taylor. My assertion of the existence of a long-run trade-off between inflation and unemployment in the paper is wrong in my current view, since I view that trade-off as extremely small in the model. In the model, at zero inflation the long-run marginal trade-off between output and inflation is exactly zero. Only later, Bill Dickens, George Perry and I (see below) discovered how similar models would produce significant long-run trade-offs between inflation and unemployment, especially when inflation is low.

The next two papers represent the beginning of another significant strand in current Keynesian macroeconomics. They are similar in spirit to staggered price and wage setting. We have seen that staggering of wage and price setting changes macro-dynamics. The alternative model of wage and price setting, where they are only changed when they reach some threshold level, should also change macro-dynamics because it introduces staggering of a different form. For example, if I adjust the price of my product only when its deviation from the optimum reaches some upper or lower threshold, it is highly unlikely that my competitors will have hit their threshold at the exact same time. That means that I am setting my price when my competitors' prices are fixed, just as they are setting their prices when my price (and also the prices of their other competitors) are also fixed. That, of course, is the reason why staggered contracts affects macro-dynamics, causing monetary policy to be effective in changing income. And so we should expect the staggered-contract systems and target-threshold systems to have very similar macrodynamics.

In the 1970s and early 1980s Robert Barro (1972) and Katsuhito Iwai (1981) worked on such systems. Barro (1972) made his careful analysis of price adjustment with monopolistic competition and menu costs. Iwai wrote his path-breaking (and much underappreciated) *Disequilibrium Dynamics: A Theoretical Analysis of Inflation and*

Unemployment. Since that time this theme has been taken up first by Caplin and Spulber (1987) and then by Caplin and Leahy (1991).[11] These papers show that, except in the special case where the optimum price only increases or decreases, price setting responds sluggishly to shocks (such as changes in the nominal supply of money).

If the demand for a commodity is also determined by targets and thresholds, responses to shifts in demand are similarly sluggish. I have examined the demand for money when there are menu costs to buying and selling other assets. The first of the two papers in this volume on this subject analyzes the nature of money demand when bank balances are monitored by target-threshold rules; if money holdings fall to a lower threshold (perhaps zero), they are adjusted to a higher level target; if they reach an upper threshold they are adjusted to a lower level target. In such a regime money demand does not just depend upon the policies for monitoring it, which are the targets and the thresholds, but it also depends upon the autonomous flows into and out of bank accounts. 'The Microfoundations of a Flow of Funds Theory of the Demand for Money' indicates the ways in which positive flows of funds into bank accounts, given the targets and thresholds, will increase money demand, just as negative flows into bank accounts will reduce it. Thus the demand for money is at least partially determined by the flow of funds. This adds to the equilibration mechanisms in standard Keynesian models of the demand for money to the supply.

Considerations of target-threshold demands for money have further payoff beyond establishing the role of flow of funds in determining aggregate money demand and therefore equilibrium output. 'Irving Fisher on His Head' explains why fiscal policy and monetary policy are both effective in changing aggregate demand in the short run. The traditional quantity theory of the demand for money assumes that peoples' strategy for managing their money balances will respond only slowly to the opportunity cost of money holding. That opportunity cost is the rate of interest, or the return on non-monetary assets. The traditional quantity theory also assumes that as income rises the demand for money will increase proportionately *in the short run* if people have made no adjustments in their management of their cash balances. 'Irving Fisher on His Head,' shows that if money holdings are managed by target-threshold monitoring, the short-run proportionality of money demand to income is exactly wrong. There is no change in money demand as income changes if the targets and the thresholds that control the level of money balances are constant. As a result, there is a low short-run interest elasticity to money demand because the targets and thresholds are slow to change, but there is also a low short-run income elasticity for that same reason.

Thus, changes in fiscal policy will affect income in the short run. The usual argument that interest rate rises choke off fiscal stimulus with an interest inelastic short-run demand for money turns out to be in error. Contrary to standard assumption, an increase in income does not cause a significant short-run increase in money demand, resulting in a rise in interest rates that crowds out the effects of the fiscal stimulus. The most common form of lagged money demand function has such a functional form that exactly

---

[11] Ricardo Caballero (for example (1993)), sometimes with other co-authors has also written about the role of target-threshold monitoring in causing slow adjustments.

conforms to this theory. Stock adjustment money demands have both low short-run interest and income elasticities.[12] The theory is thus consistent with the usual characterization of the data. Monetary policy will also be effective in the short-run, even with such short-run inelasticity, since large changes in interest rates (and therefore in asset prices) are necessary to get people to hold either more, or less, money.

Unemployment

Probably the most fundamental question in macroeconomics is how there can be 'involuntary unemployment.' After all, why should wages not equilibrate the demand and supply of labor, as indeed prices on commodity exchanges (wheat and stocks, for example) equate demand to supply. Again, following the theme of every one of the papers in this collection, we explain this phenomenon by the detailed nature of jobs and employment.

A neoclassical explanation shows why workers may not be able to get a job at any wage, no matter how low. For example, it would be false economy to hire a worker with habitually dirty hands to restore a valuable 14th Century painting, no matter how low his wage. If capital is sufficiently scarce, poor workers who use capital inefficiently will not be given capital to work with—even if they are willing to work for nothing.[13] They will then be unemployed if some capital is necessary to produce output. Ricardo had a similar explanation why the least productive land would be idle. 'Jobs as Dam Sites' is based on this basic idea, but it also incorporates an important feature of the workplace into the analysis. It models the work-place as consisting of a set of jobs. Even at a zero wage, it will be a false economy to allocate a job to a low-skilled worker with sufficiently low productivity. The explanation is implicit in the title of the paper, 'Jobs as Dam Sites.' The construction of a low quality dam at a prime dam site, no matter how cheap the dam may be, is uneconomic, because it underutilizes the dam site. Similarly, unemployment in this paper occurs among low-skilled workers, because their employment sufficiently underutilizes the employer's jobs, which are a scarce resource like the dam site.

Are there other explanations for involuntary unemployment? 'Labor Contracts as Partial Gift Exchange' is a somewhat shaky first attempt at demonstrating the existence of involuntary unemployment as due to firms' concerns about morale. 'The Fair Wage-Effort Hypothesis and Unemployment' with Janet Yellen follows the same line of reasoning, but with a model of much greater elegance. In these two papers firms do not reduce their wages to market-clearing levels because there is a loss to them from reducing their wages. The gap between the supply of labor and the demand for labor at these wages in excess of market-clearing constitutes involuntary unemployment. Both of these papers emphasize the relation between wages and worker morale. The first paper pictures the firm and its workers as engaged in a partial gift exchange: the firm gives a 'gift' of wages in excess of market-clearing to the worker; the worker works

---

[12] See for example Goldfeld (1973).
[13] See Akerlof (1969).

willingly, even when she is not fully supervised. In the second paper firms pay wages above market-clearing in order to conform to workers' notions of pay equity. If workers do not consider their wages to be fair, they reduce their work-effort.

Truman Bewley's (1999) interviews of participants in compensation decisions in Connecticut strongly support the view that firms' failure to cut wages in recessions is caused by such concerns about morale. Bewley (1999, p.2) summarizes his findings: 'worker behavior ... is not always completely rational, though reasonable and understandable. A model that captures the essence of wage rigidity must take into account the capacity of employees to identify with their firm and to internalize its objectives.'

The joint emphasis in the papers in this collection and in Bewley (1999) on the twin themes of morale and identity is no coincidence. My view that unemployment is mainly caused by wages in excess of market clearing because of morale considerations grew out of 'Caste and the Rat Race.' 'A Theory of Social Custom, of Which Unemployment May Be One Consequence' (Akerlof (1980)) directly modeled unemployment as due to non-market clearing in parallel to the caste equilibrium model; 'Gift Exchange' and 'The Fair-Wage Effort Hypothesis,' both of which emphasize the role of morale, come from further metamorphosis of the original idea. But 'Caste and the Rat-Race' is also the intellectual forerunner of 'Economics and Identity.' Both the morale-based efficiency wages and the identity papers emphasize the consequences of people's sense of self. This sense of self causes them to behave contrary to their *economic* interests because they have an ideal for how they and others *should* behave. Such a 'model' makes sense of Bewley's assertion that worker behavior is "not always completely rational, though reasonable and understandable." In the presence of such worker response, it may pay firms to maintain wages above market clearing for the sake of worker morale. Bewley shows that such considerations prevented firms in the Connecticut recession of the early 1990s from cutting money wages.

In the two papers reproduced here we show that wages may exceed *market clearing*. But Bewley has probably expressed the reasons for involuntary unemployment better. At times of very high demand most workers with more than minimal skills appear to be able to find jobs fairly quickly. The leading question then is why is there unemployment in recessions, or following Bewley's title: 'Why Don't Wages Fall During a Recession?' According to the standard Keynesian answer, wages are *slow* to adjust to gaps between supply and demand because workers resist money wage cuts. That is exactly what Bewley finds: that due to considerations of morale, managers are slow to change wages. They think that the ill-effects of reducing wages in recessions will result in relatively little direct savings to the firm, and will greatly alienate their work force. Even if workers do not immediately retaliate because of lack of alternative jobs when the cuts are made, they are likely to remember the lack of loyalty of the firm and retaliate later when the economy recovers and they can get even. Of course explaining why wages are slow to change—in the formal terms of differential equations, explaining why they are a state variable—is at the heart of Keynesian economics. Such behavior is reflected in a Philips Curve where the *rate of change* of wages, not *the level* of wages, depends on the level of unemployment (as well as other arguments).

Nature of Equilibrium and the Effectiveness of Monetary Policy

The next two papers in the collection concern the nature of macroeconomic equilibria. The two papers on unemployment show that involuntary unemployment can be a well-defined concept since employers may have reasons to pay their workers more than the market-clearing wage. Establishing the meaningfulness of involuntary unemployment is a first step in explaining how output and employment vary over the course of the business cycle. But classical economics poses a further problem for the theory of the business cycle. It suggests that changes in the supply of money should have no effect on economic equilibria, and therefore no effect on output or employment. Consider an economy initially in equilibrium with a given money supply. A change in the money supply that is matched with a change in all wages and all prices in the exact same proportion will preserve the equilibrium. No real demand or supply will be changed since all relative prices and relative wages are constant. There will then be no change in any real outcome, including no change in real output or employment. In such a world changes in the quantity of money matched by such corresponding wage and price changes, have no effect whatsoever. Monetary policy is ineffective.

Two papers show why classical economics may be wrong about such monetary neutrality. The first of these papers ('**A Near Rational Model of the Business Cycle with Wage and Price Inertia**,' with Janet Yellen) shows that if monopolistically competitive firms are slow to change their prices in response to changes in the optimum, their profits will only be slightly less than if they had adjusted their prices instantaneously. Suppose that the money supply changes by a proportion $\in$, which realistically might be a small fraction like .05. Those firms that were optimizing before the change but that respond only slowly lose only negligibly because of their sluggishness. Because their profits were being maximized before, those losses from failing to maximize are proportional to the square of their error, and are thus approximately proportional to the square of $\in$. If $\in$ is realistically about .05, its square is about .0025. However, if a fraction of firms are similarly sluggish in their price response, the change in the real equilibrium variables will be proportional to $\in$. Thus the effect on the economy due to sluggish prices will be an order of magnitude larger than the losses incurred by the firms because of their slow response. The change in the macroequilibrium from such slow response is likely to cause changes in real output and employment of the same magnitude as business cycle fluctuations, which in the US typically result in changes in the unemployment rate of 2 to 5 percentage points. In summary, money neutrality may occur then if all firms and workers respond totally rationally to changes in the money supply, but even a small amount of sluggishness of response will result in significant changes in equilibrium due to changes in the quantity of money.[14]

---

[14] There are other problems with the classical neutrality proposition: especially since it assumes complete foresight regarding everybody else's reactions to the change in the money supply, including the reactions to the reactions. Departure from the stringent expectations in the classical model and sluggish adjustment because of the small size of losses reinforce each other, making it especially likely that the quantity of money will affect output and employment.

The next paper ('**The Macroeconomics of Low Inflation**,' with William Dickens and George Perry) addresses the applicability of a second neutrality proposition from classical economics. According to this proposition, as long as expected bargains are made in real terms, the level of inflation, so long as it is anticipated, will have no effect on the long-run equilibrium of the economy, including its level of output and employment. In the long-run, expected inflation and actual inflation should coincide. Phillips Curve estimates show short-run trade-offs between output and inflation. But this neutrality proposition says that those short-run trade-offs should disappear in the long run. The long-run Phillips curve is vertical.

Our paper shows that a small amount of money illusion, where firms are responsive to workers' dislike of money wage cuts, will result in a significant long-run trade-off between inflation and unemployment when inflation is low. Both simulated and estimated models of the United States economy show that there are significant losses in employment (on the order of magnitude of two percentage points) from permanent reduction of inflation from three percent to zero. Natural rate theories of unemployment, where long-run unemployment is at the same 'natural rate' independent of long-run inflation, are therefore quite sensitive to their assumption of the absence of money illusion.

Natural rate theories also fail to fit the facts. They predict that in severe depressions, when unemployment is significantly above its long-term 'natural rate,' expected and actual inflation will mutually chase each other in an interactive downward spiral. In the United States' Great Depression the unemployment rate was extremely high for more than a decade, yet no such deflationary spiral occurred. Indeed, from 1932 to 1942 the price level was approximately constant. Such behavior, however, accords with the predictions of both our estimated and simulated model, but it is contradictory to natural rate theory.

The two preceding papers demonstrate yet again the basic proposition that underlies all of the papers in this collection. That proposition is that the exact nature of the microeconomic structure determines the properties of the macroeconomic equilibrium. In one case a small amount of price and/or wage sluggishness has an effect on the macroeconomic equilibrium that is an order of magnitude larger than the losses of those who engage in the behavior. In the second case a small amount of downward wage rigidity produces significant trade-offs at low inflation between inflation and unemployment, even in the long-run with valid expectations.

Behavioral Macroeconomics and Macroeconomic Behavior

The last paper in the volume is my Nobel Lecture, '**Behavioral Macroeconomics and Macroeconomic Behavior**.' It argues that if there is any subject in economics that should be behavioral, it is macroeconomics. If the economy were perfectly competitive, the questions of conventional macroeconomics would be moot. There would be no failure to fully utilize resources. Except for the very unskilled (as in 'Jobs as Damsites') unemployment would only be suffered by those who would rather stay home at the existing wages than work. Thus, macroeconomic questions only become meaningful if the economy departs from the standard perfect competition model. This essay explains how behavioral macroeconomics, including some of the papers in this collection, have answered some of these questions regarding the reasons for underutilization of resources due to unemployment.

Conclusion

The papers in this collection all deviate from the economics of my youth. They also deviate from the standard for economics in many circles today. That economics is characterized by perfect competition, profit maximizing by firms, and maximization by consumers with only economic concerns. In contrast, the models in these papers are derived from close observation. These observationally determined models then give our null hypotheses regarding economic behavior.

Why should the null hypothesis matter? It seems odd to argue over what should or should not constitute a proper null hypothesis. In a world with powerful tests—that reject the null a large fraction of the time when an alternative hypothesis is true—the nature of the original null hypothesis will not much matter. Wrong hypotheses will be rejected, as correct hypotheses will fail to be rejected, by tests that have power to reject hypotheses that are in error.

But the very nature of economics dictates that true hypotheses can only be formulated with considerable generality. Indeed, such generality underlies both the beauty and practicality of standard Marshallian economics, centered as it is on supply and demand. Supply curves always slope upwards, and demand curves always slope downwards, except in graduate micro theory's pedantic exception of upward sloping demand for Irish potatoes. Thus the qualitative effects of changes that variously affect only a supply curve or a demand curve are remarkably robust.

This lack of specificity makes most null hypotheses in economics almost impossible to refute. Economic hypotheses are like those earth-born warriors from Greek mythology, who, when slain, cause new ones to arise full armed in their place. How many times have readers of this volume gone to a fine empirical seminar only to hear the refutation of the initial hypothesis followed by demands to consider new forms of the null hypothesis, with different assumptions about selection bias, autocorrelation of errors, etc. As the null hypothesis is rejected, new versions arise from the ground.

But failure to reject all possible versions of the null does not mean that it is the correct model. Indeed I believe that *by nature* most interesting economic hypotheses are so multiple-faceted and are so inherently lacking in specificity that they can only rarely be rejected by statistical methods. Given the difficulty of refuting a null hypothesis, we should use our information opportunistically, not turning away any. As Bayesians we should simultaneously use informal sources, detailed nonstatistical studies, and statistical observations.

That then is the pragmatic spirit of all of the work in this volume. We build models that we believe are fully consistent with statistical findings, but that are motivated also by close observation, which other economists have been far too quick to pejoratively label as *anecdote*. I believe that the imagination of economists and the lack of power of tests against all the variants of the null hypothesis make it all but impossible to refute most economic null hypotheses with statistical data. Thus, contrary to Friedman, and his interpretation of positive economics, I find myself ready to entertain models based upon observation, and to do so even before I have seen definitive rejection of the perfectly competitive model (as a null).

Because of lack of power, failure to reject the perfect competition general equilibrium model does not make it right. If anecdotal evidence seems to refute this model, and also to suggest an alternative, that is where I think that the economic theorist should turn. Indeed lack of power has given too much credence to a version of economics that is sometimes insightful, but also all too often ridiculously at odds with our simple powers of observation. If everyone assumes that the emperor must wear clothes, then they will fail to see it if he does not. Indeed, it is only a child who sees when the emperor is, indeed, naked. In that spirit I offer you these child-like explorations.

References

Referenced papers that are in this volume (in order of review):

Akerlof, George A., 'The Market for "Lemons": Quality Uncertainty and the Market Mechanism,' *The Quarterly Journal of Economics*, Vol. 84, No. 3. (Aug., 1970), pp. 488–500.

——, 'The Economics of Caste and of the Rat Race and Other Woeful Tales, *The Quarterly Journal of Economics*, Vol. 90, No. 4. (Nov., 1976), pp. 599–617.

——, 'Discriminatory Status-Based Wages among Tradition-oriented Stochastically-Based Coconut Producers,' *The Journal of Political Economy*, Vol. 93, No. 2. (Apr., 1985), pp. 265–276.

——and Rachel E. Kranton, 'Economics and Identity,' *The Quarterly Journal of Economics*, Vol. 115, No. 3. (Aug., 2000), pp. 715–753.

——, 'The Economics of "Tagging" as Applied to the Optimal Income Tax, Welfare Programs and Manpower Planning,' *The American Economic Review*, Vol. 68, No. 1. (Mar., 1978), pp. 8–19.

——, Janet L. Yellen and Michael L. Katz, 'An Analysis of Out-of-Wedlock Childbearing in the United States,' *The Quarterly Journal of Economics*, Vol. 111, No. 2. (May, 1996), pp. 277–317.

——, 'Men without Children,' *Economic Journal*, Vol. 108, No. 447. (March, 1998), pp. 287–309.

——, and William T. Dickens, 'The Economic Consequences of Cognitive Dissonance,' *The American Economic Review*, Vol. 72, No. 3. (Jun., 1982), pp. 307–319.

——, 'The Economics of Illusion,' *Economics and Politics*, Vol. 1, No. 1. (Spring 1989), pp. 1–15.

——, 'Procrastination and Obedience,' *The American Economic Review*, Vol. 81, No. 2, Papers and Proceedings of the Hundred and Third Annual Meeting of the American Economic Association. (May, 1991), pp. 1–19.

——, and Paul M. Romer, 'Looting: The Economic Underworld of Bankruptcy for Profit,' *Brookings Papers on Economic Activity*, Vol. 1993, No. 2. (1993), pp. 1–60 and 70–73.

——, 'Relative Wages and the Rate of Inflation,' *The Quarterly Journal of Economics*, Vol. 83, No. 3. (Aug., 1969), pp. 353–374.

——, 'The Microfoundations of a Flow of Funds Theory of the Demand for Money,' *Journal of Economic Theory*, Vol. 18, No. 1. (June, 1978), pp. 190–215.

——, 'Irving Fisher on His Head: The Consequences of Constant Target-Threshold Monitoring for the Demand for Money,' *The Quarterly Journal of Economics*, Vol. 93, No. 2. (May, 1979), pp. 169–187.

——, 'Jobs as Dam Sites,' *The Review of Economic Studies*, Vol. 48, No. 1. (Jan., 1981), pp. 37–49.

——, 'Labor Contracts as Partial Gift Exchange,' *The Quarterly Journal of Economics*, Vol. 97, No. 4. (Nov., 1982), pp. 543–569.

—— and Janet L. Yellen, 'The Fair-Wage Effort Hypothesis and Unemployment,' *The Quarterly Journal of Economics*, Vol. 105, No. 2. (May, 1990), pp. 255–283.

—— and Janet L. Yellen, 'A Near-Rational Model of the Business Cycle, with Wage and Price Inertia,' *The Quarterly Journal of Economics*, Vol. 100, Supplement. (1985), pp. 823–838.

——, William T. Dickens and George L. Perry, 'The Macroeconomics of Low Inflation,' *Brookings Papers on Economic Activity*, Vol. 1996, No. 1. (1996), pp. 1–59 and 74–76.

——, 'Behavioral Macroeconomics and Macroeconomic Behavior,' *The American Economic Review*, Vol. 92, No. 3. (June, 2002), pp. 411–433.

Referenced sources that are not in this volume:

Ainslie, George. *Picoeconomics*. Cambridge: Cambridge University Press, 1992.

Akerlof, George A., 'Structural Unemployment in a Neoclassical Framework,' *The Journal of Political Economy*, Vol. 77, No. 3. (May -Jun., 1969), pp. 399–407.

——, 'A Theory of Social Custom, of Which Unemployment May Be one Consequence,' *The Quarterly Journal of Economics*, Vol. 94, No. 4. (Jun., 1980), pp. 749–775.

——, and Rachel E. Kranton, 'The Economics of Organizations,' mimeo, Berkeley, CA, September, 2003.

——, and ——, 'Identity and Schooling: Some Lessons for the Economics of Education,' *Journal of Economic Literature* 40:4, December 2002, pp. 1167–1201.

Barro, Robert J., 'A Theory of Monopolistic Price Adjustment,' *The Review of Economic Studies*, Vol. 39, No. 1. (Jan., 1972), pp. 17–26.

Benabou, Roland and Jean Tirole, 'Self-Confidence and Personal Motivation,' *The Quarterly Journal of Economics*, Vol. 117, No. 3. (Aug., 2002), pp. 871–915.

Bewley, Truman F., *Why Wages Don't Fall During a Recession*. Cambridge, MA: Harvard University Press, 1999.

Caballero, Ricardo J., 'Durable Goods: An Explanation for their Slow Adjustment,' *The Journal of Political Economy*, Vol. 101, No. 2. (Apr., 1993), pp. 351–384.

Calvo, Guillermo A., 'Staggered Prices in a Utility-Maximizing Framework,' *Journal of Monetary Economics*, Vol.12. No. 3. (Sept., 1983), pp. 383–98.

Caplin, Andrew S. and John Leahy, 'State-Dependent Pricing and the Dynamics of Money and Output,' *The Quarterly Journal of Economics*, Vol. 106, No. 3. (Aug., 1991), pp. 683–708.

——, and Daniel F. Spulber, 'Menu Costs and the Neutrality of Money,' *The Quarterly Journal of Economics*, Vol. 102, No. 4. (Nov., 1987), pp. 703–726.

Debreu, Gerard, *Theory of Value: An Axiomatic Analysis of Economic Equilibrium*. New Haven: Yale University Press, 1959.

Diamond, Peter A., 'Aggregate Demand Management in Search Equilibrium,' *The Journal of Political Economy*, Vol. 90, No. 5. (Oct., 1982), pp. 881–894.

Ellwood, David T., *Poor Support: Poverty in the American Family*. New York: Basic Books, 1988.

Friedman, Milton, 'The Methodology of Positive Economics,' pp. 3–43 in Milton Friedman, *Essays in Positive Economics*. Chicago: University of Chicago Press, 1953.

Geertz, Clifford, *Interpretation of Cultures*. New York: Basic Books, 1973.

Goldfeld, Stephen M., 'The Demand for Money Revisited,' *Brookings Papers on Economic Activity*, Vol. 1973, No. 3. (1973), pp. 577–646.

Haslam, S. Alexander, *Psychology in Organizations: The Social Identity Approach*. Thousand Oaks, CA: Sage Publications, 2001.

Iwai, Katsuhito, *Disequilibrium Dynamics: A Theoretical Analysis of Inflation and Unemployment*. New Haven: Yale University Press, 1981.

Laibson, David I., 'Golden Eggs and Hyperbolic Discounting,' *The Quarterly Journal of Economics*, Vol. 112, No. 2, In Memory of Amos Tversky (1937–1996). (May, 1997), pp. 443–477.

Lindbeck, Assar, 'The Prize in Economic Science in Memory of Alfred Nobel,' *Journal of Economic Theory*, Vol. 23, No. 1. (March, 1985), pp. 37–56.

Loewenstein, George. 'Anticipation and the Valuation of Delayed Consumption.' *Economic Journal*, Vol. 97, No. 387. (Sept., 1987), pp. 666–84.

Luker, Kristin, 'Dubious Conceptions: The Controversy over Teen Pregnancies,' *The American Prospect*, Vol. 2, No. 5. (Spring, 1991), pp. 73–83.

Mui, Vai-Lam, 'Information, Civil Liberties, and the Political Economy of Witch-Hunts,' *Journal of Law, Economics, and Organization*, Vol. 15, No. 2. (July, 1999), pp. 503–25.

Murray, Charles A., *Losing ground: American social policy, 1950–1980*. New York: Basic Books, 1984.

Peltzman, Sam, 'George Stigler's Contribution to the Economic Analysis of Regulation,' *Journal of Political Economy*, Vol. 101, No. 5. (Oct., 1993), pp. 818–832.

Phelps, Edmund S. and Robert A. Pollak. 'On Second-Best National Saving and Game-Equilibrium Growth,' *Review of Economic Studies*, Vol. 35, No. 2. (April, 1968), pp. 185–99.

Price, Richard, *Clockers*. New York: Houghton Mifflin, 1992.

Rachlin, Howard, *The Science of Self-Control*. Cambridge, MA: Harvard University Press, 2000.

Sherif, Muzafer, and O. J. Harvey, B. Jack White, William E. Hood, and Carolyn W. Sherif, *Intergroup Conflict and Cooperation: The Robbers Cave Experiment*. Norman, OK: University of Oklahoma Book Exchange, 1961.

Strotz, Robert H. 'Myopia and Inconsistency in Dynamic Utility Maximization,' *Review of Economic Studies*, Vol. 23, No. 3. (Jan., 1956), pp. 165–80.

Tajfel, Henri, 'Interindividual Behavior and Intergroup Behavior,' pp. 27–60, in H. Tajfel, ed. *Differentiation between Social Groups: Studies in the Social Psychology of Intergroup Behavior*. London: Academic Press, 1978.

Taylor, John B., 'Staggered Wage Setting in a Macro Model,' *The American Economic Review*, Vol. 69, No. 2, Papers and Proceedings of the Ninety-First Annual Meeting of the American Economic Association. (May, 1979), pp. 108–113.

Thaler, Richard H. and Herschel M. Shefrin, 'An Economic Theory of Self-Control,' *The Journal of Political Economy*, Vol. 89, No. 2. (Apr., 1981), pp. 392–406.

Watson, James D., *The Double Helix: A Personal Account of the Discovery of the Structure of DNA*. New York: New American Library, 1969.

Willis, Paul R. *Learning to Labour: How Working Class Kids Get Working Class Jobs*. Westmead, Farnborough, Hants., England: Saxon House, 1977.

PART I

MICROECONOMICS

1

The Market for 'Lemons': Quality Uncertainty and the Market Mechanism[*]

GEORGE A. AKERLOF[†]

I. INTRODUCTION

This paper relates quality and uncertainty. The existence of goods of many grades poses interesting and important problems for the theory of markets. On the one hand, the interaction of quality differences and uncertainty may explain important institutions of the labor market. On the other hand, this paper presents a struggling attempt to give structure to the statement: 'Business in underdeveloped countries is difficult'; in particular, a structure is given for determining the economic costs of dishonesty. Additional applications of the theory include comments on the structure of money markets, on the notion of 'insurability,' on the liquidity of durables, and on brand-name goods.

There are many markets in which buyers use some market statistic to judge the quality of prospective purchases. In this case there is incentive for sellers to market poor quality merchandise, since the returns for good quality accrue mainly to the entire group whose statistic is affected rather than to the individual seller. As a result there tends to be a reduction in the average quality of goods and also in the size of the market. It should also be perceived that in these markets social and private returns differ, and therefore, in some cases, governmental intervention may increase the welfare of all parties. Or private institutions may arise to take advantage of the potential increases in welfare which can accrue to all parties. By nature, however, these institutions are nonatomistic, and therefore concentrations of power—with ill consequences of their own—can develop.

The automobile market is used as a finger exercise to illustrate and develop these thoughts. It should be emphasized that this market is chosen for its concreteness and ease in understanding rather than for its importance or realism.

[*] This work was previously published as George Akerlof (1970), 'The Market for "Lemons": Quality Uncertainty and the Market Mechanism', *Quarterly Journal of Economics* 1970. Copyright © The MIT Press. Reproduced by kind permission.

[†] The author would especially like to thank Thomas Rothenberg for invaluable comments and inspiration. In addition he is indebted to Roy Radner, Albert Fishlow, Bernard Saffran, William D. Nordhaus, Giorgio La Malfa, Charles C. Holt, John Letiche, and the referee for help and suggestions. He would also like to thank the Indian Statistical Institute and the Ford Foundation for financial support.

II. THE MODEL WITH AUTOMOBILES
AS AN EXAMPLE

A. *The Automobiles Market*

The example of used cars captures the essence of the problem. From time to time one hears either mention of or surprise at the large price difference between new cars and those which have just left the showroom. The usual lunch table justification for this phenomenon is the pure joy of owning a 'new' car. We offer a different explanation. Suppose (for the sake of clarity rather than reality) that there are just four kinds of cars. There are new cars and used cars. There are good cars and bad cars (which in America are known as 'lemons'). A new car may be a good car or a lemon, and of course the same is true of used cars.

The individuals in this market buy a new automobile without knowing whether the car they buy will be good or a lemon. But they do know that with probability q it is a good car and with probability $(1-q)$ it is a lemon; by assumption, q is the proportion of good cars produced and $(1-q)$ is the proportion of lemons.

After owning a specific car, however, for a length of time, the car owner can form a good idea of the quality of this machine; i.e., the owner assigns a new probability to the event that his car is a lemon. This estimate is more accurate than the original estimate. An asymmetry in available information has developed: for the sellers now have more knowledge about the quality of a car than the buyers. But good cars and bad cars must still sell at the same price—since it is impossible for a buyer to tell the difference between a good car and a bad car. It is apparent that a used car cannot have the same valuation as a new car—if it did have the same valuation, it would clearly be advantageous to trade a lemon at the price of new car, and buy another new car, at a higher probability q of being good and a lower probability of being bad. Thus the owner of a good machine must be locked in. Not only is it true that he cannot receive the true value of his car, but he cannot even obtain the expected value of a new car.

Gresham's law has made a modified reappearance. For most cars traded will be the 'lemons,' and good cars may not be traded at all. The 'bad' cars tend to drive out the good (in much the same way that bad money drives out the good). But the analogy with Gresham's law is not quite complete: bad cars drive out the good because they sell at the same price as good cars; similarly, bad money drives out good because the exchange rate is even. But the bad cars sell at the same price as good cars since it is impossible for a buyer to tell the difference between a good and a bad car; only the seller knows. In Gresham's law, however, presumably both buyer and seller can tell the difference between good and bad money. So the analogy is instructive, but not complete.

B. *Asymmetrical Information*

It has been seen that the good cars may be driven out of the market by the lemons. But in a more continuous case with different grades of goods, even worse pathologies can exist. For it is quite possible to have the bad driving out the not-so-bad driving out the medium driving out the not-so-good driving out the good in such a sequence of events that no market exists at all.

One can assume that the demand for used automobiles depends most strongly upon two variables—the price of the automobile p and the average quality of used cars traded, μ, or $Q^d = D(p, \mu)$. Both the supply of used cars and also the average quality μ will depend upon the price, or $\mu = \mu(p)$ and $S = S(p)$. And in equilibrium the supply must equal the demand for the given average quality, or $S(p) = D(p, \mu(p))$. As the price falls, normally the quality will also fall. And it is quite possible that no goods will be traded at any price level.

Such an example can be derived from utility theory. Assume that there are just two groups of traders: groups one and two. Give group one a utility function

$$U_1 = M + \sum_{i=1}^{n} x_i$$

where M is the consumption of goods other than automobiles, x_i is the quality of the ith automobile, and n is the number of automobiles.

Similarly, let

$$U_2 = M + \sum_{i=1}^{n} 3/2 x_i$$

where M, x_i, and n are defined as before.

Three comments should be made about these utility functions: (1) without linear utility (say with logarithmic utility) one gets needlessly mired in algebraic complication. (2) The use of linear utility allows a focus on the effects of asymmetry of information; with a concave utility function we would have to deal jointly with the usual risk-variance effects of uncertainty and the special effects we wish to discuss here. (3) U_1 and U_2 have the odd characteristic that the addition of a second car, or indeed a kth car, adds the same amount of utility as the first. Again realism is sacrificed to avoid a diversion from the proper focus.

To continue, it is assumed (1) that both type one traders and type two traders are von Neumann-Morgenstern maximizers of expected utility; (2) that group one has N cars with uniformly distributed quality x, $0 \leq x \leq 2$, and group two has no cars; (3) that the price of 'other goods' M is unity.

Denote the income (including that derived from the sale of automobiles) of all type one traders as Y_1 and the income of all type two traders as Y_2. The demand for used cars will be the sum of the demands by both groups. When one ignores indivisibilities, the demand for automobiles by type one traders will be

$$D_1 = Y_1/p \qquad \mu/p > 1$$
$$D_1 = 0 \qquad \mu/p < 1.$$

And the supply of cars offered by type one traders is

$$S_2 = pN/2 \qquad\qquad p \leq 2 \tag{1}$$

with average quality

$$\mu = p/2. \tag{2}$$

(To derive (1) and (2), the uniform distribution of automobile quality is used.)
Similarly the demand of type two traders is

$$D_2 = Y_2/p \qquad\qquad 3\mu/2 > p$$
$$D_2 = 0 \qquad\qquad 3\mu/2 < p$$

and

$$S_2 = 0.$$

Thus total demand $D(p, \mu)$ is

$$D(p, \mu) = (Y_2 + Y_1)/p \qquad\qquad \text{if } p < \mu$$
$$D(p, \mu) = Y_2/p \qquad\qquad \text{if } \mu < p < 3\mu/2$$
$$D(p, \mu) = 0 \qquad\qquad \text{if } p > 3\mu/2.$$

However, with price p, average quality is $p/2$ and therefore at no price will any trade take place at all: in spite of the fact that *at any given price* between 0 and 3 there are traders of type one who are willing to sell their automobiles at a price which traders of type two are willing to pay.

C. *Symmetric Information*

The foregoing is contrasted with the case of symmetric information. Suppose that the quality of all cars is uniformly distributed, $0 \leq x \leq 2$. Then the demand curves and supply curves can be written as follows:
Supply

$$S(p) = N \qquad\qquad p > 1$$
$$S(p) = 0 \qquad\qquad p < 1.$$

And the demand curves are

$$D(p) = (Y_2 + Y_1)/p \qquad\qquad p < 1$$
$$D(p) = (Y_2/p) \qquad\qquad 1 < p < 3/2$$
$$D(p) = 0 \qquad\qquad p > 3/2.$$

In equilibrium

$$p = 1 \qquad\qquad \text{if } Y_2 < N \qquad\qquad\qquad (3)$$

$$p = Y_2/N \qquad\qquad \text{if } 2Y_2/3 < N < Y_2 \qquad\qquad (4)$$

$$p = 3/2 \qquad\qquad \text{if } N < 2Y_2/3. \qquad\qquad\qquad (5)$$

If $N < Y_2$ there is a gain in utility over the case of asymmetrical information of $N/2$. (If $N > Y_2$, in which case the income of type two traders is insufficient to buy all N automobiles, there is a gain in utility of $Y_2/2$ units.)

Finally, it should be mentioned that in this example, if traders of groups one and two have the same probabilistic estimates about the quality of individual automobiles—though these estimates may vary from automobile to automobile—(3), (4), and (5) will still describe equilibrium with one slight change: p will then represent the expected price of one quality unit.

III. EXAMPLES AND APPLICATIONS

A. *Insurance*

It is a well-known fact that people over 65 have great difficulty in buying medical insurance. The natural question arises: why doesn't the price rise to match the risk?

Our answer is that as the price level rises the people who insure themselves will be those who are increasingly certain that they will need the insurance; for error in medical check-ups, doctors' sympathy with older patients, and so on make it much easier for the applicant to assess the risks involved than the insurance company. The result is that the average medical condition of insurance applicants deteriorates as the price level rises—with the result that no insurance sales may take place at any price.[1] This is strictly analogous to our automobiles case, where the average quality of used cars supplied fell with a corresponding fall in the price level. This agrees with the explanation in insurance textbooks:

Generally speaking policies are not available at ages materially greater than sixty-five.... The term premiums are too high for any but the most pessimistic (which is to say the least healthy) insureds to find attractive. Thus there is a severe problem of adverse selection at these ages.[2]

The statistics do not contradict this conclusion. While demands for health insurance rise with age, a 1956 national sample survey of 2,809 families with 8,898 persons shows that hospital insurance coverage drops from 63 per cent of those aged 45 to 54,

---

[1] Arrow's fine article, 'Uncertainty and Medical Care' (*American Economic Review*, Vol. 53, 1963), does not make this point explicitly. He emphasizes 'moral hazard' rather than 'adverse selection.' In its strict sense, the presence of 'moral hazard' is equally disadvantageous for both governmental and private programs; in its broader sense, which includes 'adverse selection,' 'moral hazard' gives a decided advantage to government insurance programs.

[2] O. D. Dickerson, *Health Insurance* (Homewood, Ill.: Irwin, 1959), p. 333.

to 31 per cent for those over 65. And surprisingly, this survey also finds average medical expenses for males aged 55 to 64 of $88, while males over 65 pay an average of $77.[3] While noninsured expenditure rises from $66 to $80 in these age groups, insured expenditure declines from $105 to $70. The conclusion is tempting that insurance companies are particularly wary of giving medical insurance to older people.

The principle of 'adverse selection' is potentially present in all lines of insurance. The following statement appears in an insurance textbook written at the Wharton School:

There is potential adverse selection in the fact that healthy term insurance policy holders may decide to terminate their coverage when they become older and premiums mount. This action could leave an insurer with an undue proportion of below average risks and claims might be higher than anticipated. Adverse selection 'appears (or at least is possible) whenever the individual or group insured has freedom to buy or not to buy, to choose the amount or plan of insurance, and to persist or to discontinue as a policy holder.'[4]

Group insurance, which is the most common form of medical insurance in the United States, picks out the healthy, for generally adequate health is a precondition for employment. At the same time this means that medical insurance is least available to those who need it most, for the insurance companies do their own 'adverse selection.'

This adds one major argument in favor of medicare.[5] On a cost benefit basis medicare may pay off: for it is quite possible that every individual in the market would be willing to pay the expected cost of his medicare and buy insurance, yet no insurance company can afford to sell him a policy—for at any price it will attract too many 'lemons.' The welfare economics of medicare, in this view, is *exactly* analogous to the usual classroom argument for public expenditure on roads.

B. *The Employment of Minorities*

The Lemons Principle also casts light on the employment of minorities. Employers may refuse to hire members of minority groups for certain types of jobs. This decision may not reflect irrationality or prejudice—but profit maximization. For race may serve as a good *statistic* for the applicant's social background, quality of schooling, and general job capabilities.

---

[3] O. W. Anderson (with J. J. Feldman), *Family Medical Costs and Insurance* (New York: McGraw-Hill, 1956).

[4] H. S. Denenberg, R. D. Eilers, G. W. Hoffman, C. A. Kline, J. J. Melone, and H. W. Snider, *Risk and Insurance* (Englewood Cliffs, N. J.: Prentice Hall, 1964), p. 446.

[5] The following quote, again taken from an insurance textbook, shows how far the medical insurance market is from perfect competition:

'...insurance companies must screen their applicants. Naturally it is true that many people will voluntarily seek adequate insurance on their own initiative. But in such lines as accident and health insurance, companies are likely to give a second look to persons who voluntarily seek insurance without being approached by an agent.' (F. J. Angell, *Insurance, Principles and Practices*, New York: The Ronald Press, 1957, pp. 8–9.)

This shows that insurance is *not* a commodity for sale on the open market.

Good quality schooling could serve as a substitute for this statistic; by grading students the schooling system can give a better indicator of quality than other more superficial characteristics. As T. W. Schultz writes, 'The educational establishment *discovers* and cultivates potential talent. The capabilities of children and mature students can never be known until *found* and cultivated.'[6] (Italics added.) An untrained worker may have valuable natural talents, but these talents must be certified by 'the educational establishment' before a company can afford to use them. The certifying establishment, however, must be credible; the unreliability of slum schools decreases the economic possibilities of their students.

This lack may be particularly disadvantageous to members of already disadvantaged minority groups. For an employer may make a rational decision not to hire any members of these groups in responsible positions—because it is difficult to distinguish those with good job qualifications from those with bad qualifications. This type of decision is clearly what George Stigler had in mind when he wrote, 'in a regime of ignorance Enrico Fermi would have been a gardener, Von Neumann a checkout clerk at a drugstore.'[7]

As a result, however, the rewards for work in slum schools tend to accrue to the group as a whole—in raising its average quality—rather than to the individual. Only insofar as information in addition to race is used is there any incentive for training.

An additional worry is that the Office of Economic Opportunity is going to use cost-benefit analysis to evaluate its programs. For many benefits may be external. The benefit from training minority groups may arise as much from raising the average quality of the group as from raising the quality of the individual trainee; and, likewise, the returns may be distributed over the whole group rather than to the individual.

C. *The Costs of Dishonesty*

The Lemons model can be used to make some comments on the costs of dishonesty. Consider a market in which goods are sold honestly or dishonestly; quality may be represented, or it may be misrepresented. The purchaser's problem, of course, is to identify quality. The presence of people in the market who are willing to offer inferior goods tends to drive the market out of existence—as in the case of our automobile 'lemons.' It is this possibility that represents the major costs of dishonesty—for dishonest dealings tend to drive honest dealings out of the market. There may be potential buyers of good quality products and there may be potential sellers of such products in the appropriate price range; however, the presence of people who wish to pawn bad wares as good wares tends to drive out the legitimate business. The cost of dishonesty, therefore, lies not only in the amount by which the purchaser is cheated; the cost also must include the loss incurred from driving legitimate business out of existence.

[6] T. W. Schultz, *The Economic Value of Education* (New York: Columbia University Press, 1964), p. 42.
[7] G. J. Stigler, 'Information and the Labor Market,' *Journal of Political Economy*, Vol. 70 (Oct. 1962), Supplement, p. 104.

Dishonesty in business is a serious problem in underdeveloped countries. Our model gives a possible structure to this statement and delineates the nature of the 'external' economies involved. In particular, in the model economy described, dishonesty, or the misrepresentation of the quality of automobiles, costs $1/2$ unit of utility per automobile; furthermore, it reduces the size of the used car market from N to 0. We can, consequently, directly evaluate the costs of dishonesty—at least in theory.

There is considerable evidence that quality variation is greater in underdeveloped than in developed areas. For instance, the need for quality control of exports and State Trading Corporations can be taken as one indicator. In India, for example, under the Export Quality Control and Inspection Act of 1963, 'about 85 per cent of Indian exports are covered under one or the other type of quality control.'[8] Indian housewives must carefully glean the rice of the local bazaar to sort out stones of the same color and shape which have been intentionally added to the rice. Any comparison of the heterogeneity of quality in the street market and the canned qualities of the American supermarket suggests that quality variation is a greater problem in the East than in the West.

In one traditional pattern of development the merchants of the pre-industrial generation turn into the first entrepreneurs of the next. The best-documented case is Japan,[9] but this also may have been the pattern for Britain and America.[10] In *our* picture the important skill of the merchant is identifying the quality of merchandise; those who can identify used cars in our example and can guarantee the quality may profit by as much as the difference between type two traders' buying price and type one traders' selling price. These people are the merchants. In production these skills are equally necessary—both to be able to identify the quality of inputs and to certify the quality of outputs. And this is one (added) reason why the merchants may logically become the first entrepreneurs.

The problem, of course, is that entrepreneurship may be a scarce resource; no development text leaves entrepreneurship unemphasized. Some treat it as central.[11] Given, then, that entrepreneurship is scarce, there are two ways in which product variations impede development. First, the pay-off to trade is great for would-be entrepreneurs, and hence they are diverted from production; second, the amount of entrepreneurial time per unit output is greater, the greater are the quality variations.

D. *Credit Markets in Underdeveloped Countries*

(1) Credit markets in underdeveloped countries often strongly reflect the operation of the Lemons Principle. In India a major fraction of industrial enterprise is controlled by managing agencies (according to a recent survey, these 'managing agencies' controlled 65.7 per cent of the net worth of public limited companies and 66 per cent of total

---

[8] *The Times of India*, Nov. 10, 1967, p. 1.

[9] See M. J. Levy, Jr., 'Contrasting Factors in the Modernization of China and Japan,' in *Economic Growth: Brazil, India, Japan*, ed. S. Kuznets, *et. al.* (Durham, N. C.: Duke University Press, 1955).

[10] C. P. Kindleberger, *Economic Development* (New York: McGraw-Hill, 1958), p. 86.

[11] For example, see W. Arthur Lewis, *The Theory of Economic Growth* (Homewood, Ill.: Irwin, 1955), p. 196.

assets).[12] Here is a historian's account of the function and genesis of the 'managing agency system':

The management of the South Asian commercial scene remained the function of merchant houses, and a type of organization peculiar to South Asia known as the Managing Agency. When a new venture was promoted (such as a manufacturing plant, a plantation, or a trading venture), the promoters would approach an established managing agency. The promoters might be Indian or British, and they might have technical or financial resources or merely a concession. In any case they would turn to the agency because of its reputation, which would encourage confidence in the venture and stimulate investment.[13]

In turn, a second major feature of the Indian industrial scene has been the dominance of these managing agencies by caste (or, more accurately, communal) groups. Thus firms can usually be classified according to communal origin.[14] In this environment, in which outside investors are likely to be bilked of their holdings, either (1) firms establish a reputation for 'honest' dealing, which confers upon them a monopoly rent insofar as their services are limited in supply, or (2) the sources of finance are limited to local communal groups which can use communal—and possibly familial—ties to encourage honest dealing *within* the community. It is, in Indian economic history, extraordinarily difficult to discern whether the savings of rich landlords failed to be invested in the industrial sector (1) because of a fear to invest in ventures controlled by other communities, (2) because of inflated propensities to consume, or (3) because of low rates of

---

[12] *Report of the Committee on the Distribution of Income and Levels of Living*, Part I, Government of India, Planning Commission, Feb. 1964, p. 44.

[13] H. Tinker, *South Asia: A Short History* (New York: Praeger, 1966), p. 134.

[14] The existence of the following table (and also the small per cent of firms under mixed control) indicates the communalization of the control of firms. *Source*: M. M. Mehta, *Structure of Indian Industries* (Bombay: Popular Book Depot, 1955), p. 314.

Distribution of Industrial Control by Community			
	1911	1931 (number of firms)	1951
British	281	416	382
Parsis	15	25	19
Gujratis	3	11	17
Jews	5	9	3
Muslims	—	10	3
Bengalis	8	5	20
Marwaris	—	6	96
Mixed control	28	28	79
Total	341	510	619

Also, for the cotton industry see H. Fukuzawa, 'Cotton Mill Industry,' in V. B. Singh, editor, *Economic History of India, 1857–1956* (Bombay: Allied Publishers, 1965).

return.[15] At the very least, however, it is clear that the British-owned managing agencies tended to have an equity holding whose communal origin was more heterogeneous than the Indian-controlled agency houses, and would usually include both Indian and British investors.

(2) A second example of the workings of the Lemons Principle concerns the extortionate rates which the local moneylender charges his clients. In India these high rates of interest have been the leading factor in landlessness; the so-called 'Cooperative Movement' was meant to counteract this growing landlessness by setting up banks to compete with the local moneylenders.[16] While the large banks in the central cities have prime interest rates of 6, 8, and 10 per cent, the local moneylender charges 15, 25, and even 50 per cent. The answer to this seeming paradox is that credit is granted only where the granter has (1) easy means of enforcing his contract or (2) personal knowledge of the character of the borrower. The middleman who tries to arbitrage between the rates of the moneylender and the central bank is apt to attract all the 'lemons' and thereby make a loss.

This interpretation can be seen in Sir Malcolm Darling's interpretation of the village moneylender's power:

It is only fair to remember that in the Indian village the money-lender is often the one thrifty person amongst a generally thriftless people; and that his methods of business, though demoralizing under modern conditions, suit the happy-go-lucky ways of the peasant. He is always accessible, even at night; dispenses with troublesome formalities, asks no inconvenient questions, advances promptly, and if interest is paid, does not press for repayment of principal. He keeps in

---

[15] For the mixed record of industrial profits, see D. H. Buchanan, *The Development of Capitalist Enterprise in India* (New York: Kelley, 1966, reprinted).

[16] The leading authority on this is Sir Malcolm Darling. See his *Punjabi Peasant in Prosperity and Debt*. The following table may also prove instructive:

	Secured loans (per cent)	Commonest rates for—Unsecured loans (per cent)	Grain loans (per cent)
Punjab	6 to 12	12 to 24 (18 ¾ commonest)	25
United Provinces	9 to 12	24 to 37 ½	25 (50 in Oudh)
Bihar		18 ¾	50
Orissa	12 to 18 ¾	25	25
Bengal	8 to 12	9 to 18 for 'respectable clients' 18 ¾ to 37 ½ (the latter common to agriculturalists)	
		15 for proprietors	25
Central Provinces	6 to 12	24 for occupancy tenants 37 ½ for ryots with no right of transfer	
Bombay	9 to 12	12 to 25 (18 commonest)	
Sind		36	
Madras	12	15 to 18 (in insecure tracts 24 not uncommon)	20 to 50

Source: Punjabi Peasant in Prosperity and Debt, 3rd ed. (Oxford University Press, 1932), p. 190.

close personal touch with his clients, and in many villages shares their occasions of weal or woe. *With his intimate knowledge of those around him he is able, without serious risk, to finance those who would otherwise get no loan at all.* [Italics added.][17]

Or look at Barbara Ward's account:

A small shopkeeper in a Hong Kong fishing village told me: 'I give credit to anyone who anchors regularly in our bay; but if it is someone I don't know well, then I think twice about it unless I can find out all about him.'[18]

Or, a profitable sideline of cotton ginning in Iran is the loaning of money for the next season, since the ginning companies often have a line of credit from Teheran banks at the market rate of interest. But in the first years of operation large losses are expected from unpaid debts—due to poor knowledge of the local scene.[19]

IV. COUNTERACTING INSTITUTIONS

Numerous institutions arise to counteract the effects of quality uncertainty. One obvious institution is guarantees. Most consumer durables carry guarantees to ensure the buyer of some normal expected quality. One natural result of our model is that the risk is borne by the seller rather than by the buyer.

A second example of an institution which counteracts the effects of quality uncertainty is the brand-name good. Brand names not only indicate quality but also give the consumer a means of retaliation if the quality does not meet expectations. For the consumer will then curtail future purchases. Often too, new products are associated with old brand names. This ensures the prospective consumer of the quality of the product.

Chains—such as hotel chains or restaurant chains—are similar to brand names. One observation consistent with our approach is the chain restaurant. These restaurants, at least in the United States, most often appear on interurban highways. The customers are seldom local. The reason is that these well-known chains offer a better hamburger than the *average* local restaurant; at the same time, the local customer, who knows his area, can usually choose a place he prefers.

Licensing practices also reduce quality uncertainty. For instance, there is the licensing of doctors, lawyers, and barbers. Most skilled labor carries some certification indicating the attainment of certain levels of proficiency. The high school diploma, the baccalaureate degree, the Ph.D., even the Nobel Prize, to some degree, serve this function of certification. And education and labor markets themselves have their own 'brand names.'

---

[17] Darling, *op. cit.*, p. 204.

[18] B. Ward, 'Cash or Credit Crops,' *Economic Development and Cultural Change*, Vol. 8 (Jan. 1960), reprinted in *Peasant Society: A Reader*, ed. G. Foster *et al.* (Boston: Little Brown and Company, 1967). Quote on p. 142. In the same volume, see also G. W. Skinner, 'Marketing and Social Structure in Rural China,' and S. W. Mintz, 'Pratik: Haitian Personal Economic Relations.'

[19] Personal conversation with mill manager, April 1968.

V. CONCLUSION

We have been discussing economic models in which 'trust' is important. Informal unwritten guarantees are preconditions for trade and production. Where these guarantees are indefinite, business will suffer—as indicated by our generalized Gresham's law. This aspect of uncertainty has been explored by game theorists, as in the Prisoner's Dilemma, but usually it has not been incorporated in the more traditional Arrow-Debreu approach to uncertainty.[20] But the difficulty of distinguishing good quality from bad is inherent in the business world; this may indeed explain many economic institutions and may in fact be one of the more important aspects of uncertainty.

UNIVERSITY OF CALIFORNIA, BERKELEY
INDIAN STATISTICAL INSTITUTE—PLANNING UNIT, NEW DELHI

---

[20] R. Radner, 'Équilibre de Marchés à Terme et au Comptant en Cas d'Incertitude,' in *Cahiers d'Econometrie*, Vol. 12 (Nov. 1967), Centre National de la Recherche Scientifique, Paris.

2

The Economics of Caste and of the Rat Race and Other Woeful Tales[*]

GEORGE AKERLOF[†]

I. INTRODUCTION

There is a standard model of economic behavior, the Arrow-Debreu general equilibrium model of perfect competition. While this model may not be entirely adequate as a description of economic reality, it is most useful as a standard of comparison. For in equilibrium in this model, subject to the careful qualifications of Pareto optimality, peoples' lives are as pleasurable as they possibly can be, given their tastes and productive capabilities. Consequently, to understand why peoples' lives are not as pleasurable as they might be (in the Pareto sense), it is necessary only to know why the real world fails to correspond to the Arrow-Debreu utopia.

In the real world, contrary to the assumptions of Arrow and Debreu, information is neither complete nor costless.[1] On the contrary, given the cost of information and the need for it, people typically make predictions about the behavior of the economy and the behavior of individuals based upon a limited number of easily observable characteristics. We say that such a prediction is based upon an *indicator*, an econometrician would

[*] This work was previously published as George Akerlof (1976), 'The Economics of Caste and of the Rate Race and Other Woeful Tales' *Quarterly Journal of Economics* 1976. Copyright © The MIT Press. Reproduced by kind permission.

[†] The original version of this paper was written in the summer of 1971 and presented in seminars at Nuffield College, Oxford and Essex Universities. Sections I, II, III, and IV are taken from that original paper. Since that time some of this work has been duplicated. See Michael Spence, 'Job Market Signaling,' this *Journal*, LXXXVII (Aug. 1973), 355–79. Section V, on the theory of caste and its applications, was written in the summer of 1975. The author would like to thank Marcelle Arak and Daniel McFadden for valuable help and the National Science Foundation for financial support. He would also especially like to thank Michael Rothschild, the Guest Editor of this Symposium, for his many invaluable editorial comments.

[1] Other approaches to the difficulties encountered by the A-D model in explaining labor markets are given by the 'new' labor economics. See, for example, Doeringer, P. B. and Piore, M., *Internal Labor Markets and Manpower Analysis* (Lexington, Mass.: Heath, 1971); G. Becker, *Human Capital* (New York: Columbia University Press, 1964); and E. S. Phelps, *et al.*, *The Macroeconomic Foundations of Employment and Inflation Theory* (New York: W. W. Norton, 1970).

call it a prediction using the method of instrumental variables. This paper shows the distortions caused to examples of the A-D (Arrow-Debreu) model by the introduction of *indicators*.

There are two types of examples of the use of *indicators* in the models that follow. One sort of *indicator* owes its existence to the potentially useful economic information provided. In the example of *sharecropping* the output produced is used as *indicator*; it serves the useful function of differentiating between farmers who have expended different levels of effort in tilling the crop. In the example of *work conditions* the speed of the assembly line predicts the ability of workers on that assembly line, and therefore differentiates workers of different ability. In contrast, in the following two examples the *indicators* owe their existence purely to social convention. In the example of *statistical discrimination*, under conditions described, all persons of the same race are predicted to have equal ability. In the example of caste the behavior of one member of society toward another is predicted by their respective caste statuses.

In this second type of example, introduction of *indicators* into the A-D model brings with it a second previously missing aspect of reality, the panoply of cultural characteristics used by anthropologists and sociologists to describe a society. For, by definition, culture consists of 'regularities in the behavior, internal and external, of the members of a society, excluding those regularities which are purely hereditary.'[2] Since culture concerns regularities in behavior and since subcultural membership is easy to observe, members of society, as well as visiting anthropologists and sociologists, can predict individual behavior from subcultural membership. By definition, such predictions are based on *indicators*, typical examples being predictions of behavior or ability of an individual based on his caste, class, race, sex, organizational membership, religion, friends, possessions, personal appearance, or job.

The examples are presented in detail below; each one shows the possibility, given the values of the members of the society, of an equilibrium that is not Pareto optimal. But before this presentation, we should also mention, at least parenthetically, another role of *indicators* in shaping society. The *indicators* by which men judge each other may warp their values and distort their goals. The anthropologists give accounts such as those of the Kwakiutl Indians, among whom the chief who, at feast-time, burned the greatest number of blankets as the mark of the most conspicuous consumption, received the greatest honor.[3] The economists Galbraith and Veblen see similarity in our own consumption rites.[4]

---

[2] Quoted by Arnold Toynbee, *A Study of History, A New Edition, Revised and Abridged* (London: Oxford University Press, 1972), p. 43; from P. Bagby, *Culture and History* (London: Longmans), pp. 84 and 95.

[3] Benedict, R., *Patterns of Culture* (Boston: Houghton Mifflin Co., 1944).

[4] Veblen, T., *The Theory of the Leisure Class* (New York: Modern Library, 1934); and J. K. Galbraith, *The Affluent Society* (Boston: Houghton Mifflin Co., 1958).

II. SHARECROPPING

The first example of *indicators* deals with the simplest phenomenon. Several economists have asked why sharecropping is a common form of land system.[5] After all, since the sharecropper is much poorer than the landlord and much less liquid as well (not owning land that can be mortgaged), it would be more natural for the landlord rather than the tenant to bear the risk of crop failure. This would be accomplished if the landlord paid the tenant a wage and sold the crops (perhaps even selling some of it back to the tenant).

There is also evidence that fixed wage payments are more 'natural' than sharecropping. A recent study of sharecropping in the United States South concludes that immediately following the Civil War 'the wage payment system was, from all indications universally attempted.'[6] Travelers' accounts seem to show that at the end of the Civil War sharecropping was viewed as an 'experiment'.[7]

There is, however, a very simple reason for a preference for sharecropping over a wage-payment system. There are two components to the sharecropper's input: the time he puts in and the effort expended. While the first is easy to observe, and can be paid a fixed wage, the second cannot be observed without careful supervision of the labor.

Suppose that the input of the sharecropper depends upon his time at work and his effort; suppose further that his effort can be measured and called e. With a wage system the sharecropper should receive an income w dependent on e and t:

$$w = w(e, t).$$

Without supervision the landlord cannot determine the effort put in; and the wage paid to the individual worker will depend on the average effort of the average worker, $\bar{e}$: thus

$$w = w(\bar{e}, t).$$

This leaves no incentive to the worker for any effort beyond the minimum necessary to be paid for his time. If he dislikes effort, he will minimize it.

In contrast, in sharecropping, the farmer is paid for the effort that he puts in as well as for his time; but this effort and time are estimated imperfectly from another characteristic—the output produced. The equilibrium is distorted by this procedure, since the risk-averse farmer remains unprotected from the natural randomness inherent in agriculture.

The basic stylized facts of this model conform with the conditions of sharecropping. In traditional agriculture the hard-working farmer usually receives yields that are considerably greater than the yields of the average farmer. A Punjabi peasant, who prided himself on yields greater than those of his neighbors, once listed for me 'the

[5] Cheung, S. N. S., 'Private Property Rights and Sharecropping,' *Journal of Political Economy*, LXXVI (Nov./Dec. 1968), 1107–22. For an approach similar to that taken here, see J. E. Stiglitz, 'Incentives and Risk in Sharecropping,' *Review of Economic Studies*, XLI (April 1974), 219–58.

[6] Ransom, R. and Sutch, R., *What Was Freedom's Price?* (New York: Cambridge University Press, forthcoming), Ch. 4.

[7] *Ibid.*, Ch. 5.

seven things which a good farmer does, which a poor farmer does not do.' It is significant that many of these seven things involve arduous work and much patience; many are also difficult to observe.[8] A similar story has been told by John Mellor in his study of farms in a village of Uttar Pradesh.[9] Hard work generated significantly higher yields even with the use of only traditional farming methods.

The division of crops between those grown on a wage-payment system and those grown on shares is also consistent with our explanation. Where supervision is needed for reasons other than determination of effort, the model predicts that wages rather than shares will be paid. In India, for example, as an excellent rule of thumb, capital-intensive plantation crops are grown on a wage-payment system.[10] And these crops need supervision to insure proper cultivation.

III. WORK CONDITIONS: THE RAT RACE

The second example of the use of *indicators* concerns the choice of occupation and work conditions for the selection of workers. Workers who are willing to work at a fast speed (or, equivalently for the model, under difficult work conditions) are judged to have superior abilities. The model is a complicated analog of the rat race. In the rat race the chances of getting the cheese increase with the speed of the rat, although no additional cheese is produced. In our model, unlike the rat race, workers produce more output at faster speeds; but, like the rat race, the private return for additional speed exceeds the additional output produced (faster speed results in a higher wage to the individual, not only from the return from his added production, but also because of the greater estimate of his individual ability). Furthermore, as in the rat race, the individual worker is goaded on by the knowledge that at slower speeds he must share his output with workers of lesser ability (being judged the same); similarly, he is spurred on by the knowledge that at faster speeds he will share the output of workers of greater ability.

'Speed' in our model stands for 'work conditions' and educational attainment.[11] In real life, wage differentials do induce persons to work under harder working conditions, and also to increase their levels of education. Likewise, it is also plausible that workers' willingness to work under harsh conditions or to obtain education is correlated

---

[8] The list included the following:
  [1] Planting on time.
  [2] Using the proper inputs—seeds, fertilizers.
  [3] Smoothing the ground carefully before sowing, both to preserve moisture and to make irrigation easier; this involved going over the fields as many as five times with a bullock and plowboard.
  [4] Drilling the seed to the right depth and planting in straight lines with rows of proper width. This also involved hard work with a wooden plow and considerable manual dexterity.
  [5] Irrigation and proper use of water.
  [6] Weeding often.
  [7] Harvesting quickly.
[9] Mellor, J., *The Economics of Agricultural Development* (Ithaca, N.Y.: Cornell University Press,), Ch. 8.
[10] Buchanan, D. H., *The Development of Capitalist Enterprise in India* (New York: Macmillan, 1934).
[11] The role of education in screening is mentioned by T. W. Schultz, *The Economic Value of Education* (New York: Columbia University Press, 1964).

positively with their productivity. (In some professions this could be reversed; good workers may demand good work conditions so that they can perform their task more satisfactorily. Perhaps chess is an example.)

A model is made to illustrate these points in the following way: good workers have a greater tolerance for poor working conditions than poor workers. Surrealistically, we picture all workers at work on some assembly line; the assembly lines, however, can work at different speeds—with three consequences: (1) the faster assembly lines require harder work and are therefore distasteful; (2) faster assembly lines produce more output; and (3) workers are faceless and nameless (in our surrealistic picture). The organization that runs the assembly line cannot tell the difference between good and bad workers, but it can perceive the average difference in quality of workers who adhere to assembly lines working at different speeds. Note that the assumption is quite realistic if unions or feelings of fairness severely restrict firms' ability to treat workers on an assembly line according to their real merit.

In our model there are N different classes of workers, numbered from 1 to N. All classes have equal population. The utility of workers of class n depends upon the goods they consume G, and the speed at which they work S. This is given by the function

$$U_n = G - S - 3/8 \, (S - n)^2, \quad n = 1, \ldots, N.$$

Utility depends positively on the goods consumed and negatively on the speed of the assembly line. Higher grade workers are more willing to trade output for speed. The reason for the seemingly arbitrary fraction '$\frac{3}{8}$' in the utility function results from a desire to have an equilibrium with all workers of the same class working at the same speed.

Output per worker on an assembly line depends upon its average grade of worker and also the speed at which it operates. The simplest such production function can be written

$$Q = \bar{\alpha} + S,$$

where Q is output per worker, $\bar{\alpha}$ is the average grade of worker on the assembly line, and S is the speed of the assembly line.

Capital is no constraint; and assembly lines can work at speeds S corresponding to any integer. The wage paid to each worker in equilibrium is equal to the output per worker on that assembly line.

To summarize, this is the complete specification of the economy. There are N classes of workers; there are assembly lines potentially operating at any integral speed. The solution to the economy consists of matching workers with assembly lines operating at different speeds. In equilibrium no worker will wish to move from the assembly line where he is working to an assembly line operating at a different speed.

Equilibrium. This model has the following equilibrium: Workers of type n, $n = 2, \ldots, N$, will be working at speed $n + 1$; workers of type 1 will be working at speed 1. No worker will wish to move to an assembly line working at any other speed.

George A. Akerlof

Proof. The proof is given in three parts. Part I shows that a worker of index n, $n \geq 3$ has no incentive to move from an assembly line of speed $n + 1$. Part II shows that a worker of index $n = 1$ has no incentive to move from an assembly line of speed 1. Part III shows that a worker of index $n = 2$ has no incentive to move from an assembly line of speed 3.

Part I

A worker of index n, $3 \leq n \leq N - 1$ has no incentive to move. The northwest quadrant of Table 2.1 shows the utility of a type-n worker at equilibrium speed and if he moves to

Table 2.1. *Utility of worker by type of worker on assembly lines at equilibrium and one unit faster and one unit slower than equilibrium*

Type of worker	Speed	Average quality	Utility	Type of worker	Speed	Average quality	Utility
	n	$n-1$	$n-1$		N	$N-1$	$N-1$
$3 \leq n \leq N-1$	$n+1$	n	$n-3/8$	N	$N+1$	$N+1$	$N-3/8$
	$n+2$	$n+1$	$n-1/2$		$N+2$	N	$N-3/2$
	0	1	5/8		2	11/8	11/8
1	1	1	1	2	3	2	13/8
	2	1	5/8		4	3	12/8

assembly lines one unit faster than the equilibrium $(n + 2)$, and to speeds one unit slower than equilibrium (n). Speeds more than one unit faster or slower than equilibrium can easily be shown to be outside the range of consideration. The northwest quadrant of Table 2.1 shows that a worker of type n has highest utility at speed $n + 1$. Table 2.1 is derived by applying the formula

$$U_n = G - S - \tfrac{3}{8}(S - n)^2 = \bar{\alpha} - \tfrac{3}{8}(S - n)^2.$$

The northeast quadrant of Table 2.I is analogous for workers of class N. Labor of index N receives maximum utility working at speed $N + 1$.

Part II

A worker of type 1 has no incentive to move from assembly lines of speed 1. The southwest quadrant of Table 2.1 shows the utility of type 1 if he moves to speeds 0 or 2 and if he remains at speed 1. Maximum utility is obtained at $S = 1$.

Part III

A worker of type 2 has no incentive to move. If he moves to speed 2, workers of type 1 will move onto these assembly lines until the utility of type 1 workers is the same on assembly lines of speeds 1 and 2. This will occur if the average quality on assembly lines of speed 2 is 11/8. Thus, the southeast quadrant of Table 2.1 gives the utility that a worker of Type 2 will enjoy at equilibrium speed $S = 3$, and at speeds one unit faster and slower. His utility is maximized at speed $S = 3$.

Comment on Equilibrium

It is clear that in this solution everyone except type 1 workers is working at speeds faster than the optimum. In the absence of workers of other grades, each type of worker n would work at speed n, receiving utility in amount n. The solution is nonoptimal because each grade of worker (except for the lowest) works at a faster speed than in the absence of other workers—since each grade of worker wishes to avoid sharing its output with workers of lower grade. Workers increase their speed so as to winnow out poorer grades.

If the government places a tax on assembly lines of one unit per worker per unit speed, all workers will work at speed n. (This is easy to see by reconstruction of Table 2.1 with workers of type n working at speed n and a tax on work at speed n equal to n. For $n \leq N - 1$, workers of type n receive 0 utility at speed n. If they move to assembly lines one unit faster or one unit slower, they receive utility $-\frac{3}{8}$.) Since any redistribution of the taxes collected will leave the social rate of transformation of goods for speed equal to the marginal rate of substitution of goods for speed for each worker, such redistributions are Pareto optimal.

IV. STATISTICAL DISCRIMINATION

In the first two examples the *indicators* chosen have arisen for reasons of technology and production. They are used for natural economic reasons, given the utility functions, the production functions and the technology of obtaining information. In the next two examples the *indicators* chosen are based instead on social groupings whose existence is totally independent of utility functions, production functions, or information technology. The first two examples showed how *indicators* of natural origin caused distortions to marginal principles. The next two examples show how *indicators* of social origin may lead the economy into a low-level equilibrium trap.

We begin with Arrow's model[12] of *statistical discrimination* (perhaps already familiar to the reader). In this example, under some circumstances, employers use the average quality of a given race to predict the quality of individuals of that race. It is easy to see that if such an *indicator* is used, it will destroy all incentive for self-improvement for that race, since all individuals of the race are judged the same and therefore paid the same wage irrespective of individual merit. In this way prejudice may produce a lower

---

[12] Arrow, K. J., 'Models of Job Discrimination,' and 'Some Mathematical Models of Race in the Labor Market,' Chs. 2 and 6, in A. H. Pascal, ed., *Racial Discrimination in Economic Life* (Lexington: Heath, 1972). The model here is different in important detail from the original by Arrow, who does not consider the two equivalent. I am sure that he would agree that, however the mathematics differ, the economic spirit of the two models is the same.

level equilibrium trap: if a race is deemed by prejudice to be unqualified, no incentive is given to become qualified, and the prophecy is self-fulfilling.

The Model

In this model there are just two types of jobs, one requiring qualified labor and the other requiring either qualified or unqualified labor. It is costly to test workers individually to see whether or not they are qualified. The change in proportion of qualified workers depends upon the incentives for self-improvement, which are differences in wages for qualified and unqualified workers of that race.

With slight modification of Arrow's notation and also of his equations, these assumptions lead to the following model. Let f_u be the marginal product of unqualified labor; f_q be the marginal product of qualified labor; let P_R be the proportion of race R predicted to be qualified. Let r be the cost spent per period to determine whether an individual worker is qualified. Let $\dot{P}_R$ be the change in the proportion of qualified workers of race R. The newly qualified of race R depends upon the differential in wages paid to qualified and unqualified workers of that race. The rate of retirement of that race is λ, so we can write $\dot{P}_R$ as

$$\dot{P}_R = \phi(w_{qR} - w_{uR}) - \lambda P_R,$$

where w_{qR} is the wage paid to qualified members of race R, and w_{uR} is the wage paid to unqualified members of race R.

If the expected costs of testing a worker of a given race exceed the difference in marginal products of qualified and unqualified workers, no worker will be tested, and all workers of that race will be used in unqualified jobs. Thus, competitive firms, earning zero profits, will pay wages

$$w_{qR} = max\,(f_q - r/P_R, f_u)$$
$$w_{uR} = f_u,$$

and $\dot{P}_R$ becomes

$$\dot{P}_R = \phi(\,max\,(f_q - r/P_R - f_u,\,0)) - \lambda P_R.$$

If $\phi(0)$ is small (i.e., less than $\lambda r/(f_q - f_u)$), P_R has a locally stable low level equilibrium equal to $\phi(0)/\lambda$.

There are, however, some difficulties in applying this model to real-world racial discrimination. The costliness of testing workers' qualifications suggests that the traits necessary for qualification must also be difficult to observe.[13] Arrow is specific in this

---

[13] There is also the possibility that tests that are available for whites are not available for blacks. A recent Berkeley Ph.D. thesis reports that, although a group of blacks were more consistent in their answers to a long questionnaire than a group of whites, nevertheless, their IQ scores were significantly lower. See L. Dunn, 'Labor Supply for Southern Industrialization,' Ph.D. thesis, University of California, Berkeley, 1974, pp. 298 and 301.

regard: 'I am thinking here not of the conventional type of education or experience, which is easily observable, but more subtle types the employer cannot observe directly: the habits of action and thought that favor good performance in skilled jobs, steadiness, punctuality, responsiveness, and initiative.'[14] Indeed, there is considerable evidence of the importance of these four qualities for job success.[15] But is it also true, as implied by the equation for $\dot{P}_R$, that these 'habits of thought and action' are acquired in response to wage differentials? Psychologists seem to believe that most fundamental personality traits are learned at an early age.[16] If they are correct, the low-level trap will occur only if schooling and child-rearing techniques are responsive to wage incentives.

V. CASTE AND GROUP ORGANIZATIONS

Whether or not statistical discrimination in the fashion of Arrow is directly applicable to racial discrimination, his model is appealing in at least one respect. It differs fundamentally from the previous models of Becker[17] and Welch,[18] in which discrimination is explained by tastes. In these models any individual with positive taste for discrimination will receive positive economic rewards for reducing this taste. Thus in the Becker-Welch models discrimination persists despite economic incentives. In contrast, in Arrow's example discrimination exists at least partially because of economic incentives.

It may appear that the tastes of persons in discriminating societies are so overwhelmingly biased in favor of discrimination that, relatively, the positive or negative effects of economic incentive are of only minor moment. But this ignores the broad historical perspective, which attempts to explain the stability (or disappearance) of institutions over a long period of time. For there are a fair number of cases where opportunities have arisen for deviants to break the caste code and make economic profits, with consequent rise in their social position and erosion of the caste taboos. Consider three diverse examples of this phenomenon. In Japan as merchants have become more economically successful, so too have the taboos against trade and manufacture been reduced.[19] Even in caste-bound India caste status rises with the economic success of the caste, although, typically, newly successful castes also adjust their social customs, at least partially, to reflect their higher status.[20] The best example of economic success reducing taboos is,

[14] Arrow, *op. cit.*, p. 97.

[15] The essays in the book edited by Peter Doeringer, *Programs to Aid the Disadvantaged* (Englewood Cliffs, N.J.: Prentice-Hall, 1969), repeatedly and emphatically mention the importance of punctual and steady job attendance. E. Banfield in *The Unheavenly City* (Boston: Little, Brown and Company, p. 143) cites the findings of the Coleman Report that for blacks, *attitude* was the most important determinant for school success.

[16] See Erik Erikson, *Childhood and Society* (New York: W. W. Norton, 1956, 1963).

[17] Becker, G., *The Economics of Discrimination* (Chicago: University of Chicago Press, 1969).

[18] Welch, F., 'Labor-Market Discrimination: Extrapolation of Income Differences in the Rural South,' *Journal of Political Economy*, LXXV (Aug. 1967), 584–96.

[19] See, for example, Marion Levy, 'Contrasting Factors in the Modernization of China and Japan,' in S. Kuznets *et al.*, eds., *Economic Growth: Brazil, India, Japan* (Durham, N.C: Duke University Press, 1955).

[20] See M. N. Srinivas, *Social Change in Modern India* (Berkeley: University of California Press, 1967), pp. 7–8. For a detailed description of the upgrading of one caste and its links with economic opportunity, see Oscar Lewis, *Village Life in India* (New York: Vintage Books, 1965), pp. 70–7. It is clear that this caste would have found it much more difficult to upgrade its caste status in the absence of economic opportunities outside its village.

most probably, the elimination of the sanctions against collection of interest. The usurer of the Middle Ages has turned into the banker of today.

This section introduces a new class of models in which, as in Arrow's statistical discrimination equilibrium trap, those who break caste customs suffer economically. This class of models depends upon an important facet of caste societies missing in previous models of discrimination. In previous models current transactions (so long as they are legal) do not result in changed relations with uninvolved parties in subsequent transactions.[21] For example, if farmer X makes a contract for sale of wheat to speculator Y, his subsequent dealings with speculator Z will be unaffected. On the contrary, in a caste society any transaction that breaks the caste taboos changes the subsequent behavior of uninvolved parties toward the caste-breakers. To take an extreme example, consider what would happen if a Brahman should knowingly hire an outcaste cook: the Brahman would be outcasted, and the cook would find subsequent employment almost impossible to obtain.

The possible intervention of third parties in a transaction allows for a richer class of *indicators* than that given by Arrow's statistical discrimination—typically, the use of *indicators* in caste societies being less narrowly technological. Generally, in a caste society if a member of caste A relates to a member of caste B in a given way, he can predict from knowledge of the relations between caste A and caste B how members of all castes will relate to him in future transactions. Such predictions can lead to an equilibrium in which all expectations are met and economic incentives favor obedience to the caste code—even in the extreme case where tastes are totally neutral regarding the observance of caste customs.

The following three conditions describe marriage customs in India.[22]

1. Society is divided into mutually exclusive groups (called castes).
2. A code of behavior dictates how members of these castes should behave. Regarding marriage there are complicated rules as to who may marry whom, payment of the dowry, the timing and performance of the marriage rites, etc. The caste rules dictate not only the code of behavior, but also the punishment for infractions: violators will be outcasted; furthermore, those who fail to treat outcastes as dictated by caste code will themselves be outcasted.
3. Caste members predict that those who do not follow the caste code will be made outcastes and will receive the treatment of the average outcaste. An outcaste in India is permitted to hold only scavenging (or other polluting) jobs. He is not allowed to eat with caste members, to touch them, or to touch their food, which in the case of someone outcasted includes his own parents and siblings. Of course, his own children will be outcastes and will suffer the same prohibitions.

---

[21] Note that one aspect of magic and taboo is that persons or events uninvolved in the Western sense, may be involved by *contagious or homeopathic magic.* See Sir James G. Frazer, *The Golden Bough* (New York: St. Martins, 1936).

[22] A good account of caste marriage customs is given in J. H. Hutton, *Caste in India* (Oxford University Press, Fourth Edition, 1961).

Why should these three conditions describing marriage customs in India be of interest to the economist? First, note that those who fail to follow, or even to enforce the caste customs do not gain the profits of the successful arbitrageur but instead suffer the stigma of the outcaste. If the punishment of becoming an outcaste is predicted to be sufficiently severe, the system of caste is held in equilibrium irrespective of individual tastes, by economic incentives; the predictions of the caste system become a self-fulfilling prophecy.[23]

Second, the recent extensions of the model of supply and demand to discrimination, household organization, crime and marriage show that the boundaries between sociology and economics are by no means clear; if economic models can explain sociological phenomena, so also the process can work in reverse with sociological models describing economic phenomena. With appropriate adjustment, the model of marriage in India explains both economies pathologically different from the A-D utopia, and also special pathologies in economies in which perfect competition, or slight deviations therefrom, are the norm.

Finally, the formal model of caste equilibrium works spontaneously without direction of any individual or organization. But in this model it is also natural to have the exact same economic structure with some arbiter of the caste code. Indeed the model is therefore useful in indicating how individuals and organizations can yield great powers—quite possibly, as in some of the later examples, with considerable abuse.

Formal Model of Caste Equilibrium

This subsection presents a formal model of caste equilibrium. Caste equilibrium is defined as a state of the economy in which caste customs are obeyed, yet no single individual, by behaving differently, can make himself better off. The first concern is, of course, to describe this equilibrium. However, since there are also coalitions of individuals who by acting together can make themselves better off than in equilibrium, it is also of interest to know the relative ease or difficulty of forming such a coalition. For this purpose we also look at the size and nature of the smallest equilibrium-breaking coalition.

Four sets of assumptions describe the economy; those describing technology, market structures, tastes, and the social system. The assumptions describing the social system are laid out in parallel with the earlier description of marriage in India. In general this model is extremely simple, subject to one complication. By its very nature the caste system involves trade and the division of labor. If outcastes could set up their own economy independent of caste members, the caste system would fall apart. Therefore, three assumptions are inserted that lead individuals to trade with one another; laborers can produce only one product; firms produce only one product; and tastes are such that persons will wish to purchase more than one good.

---

[23] Note that this is the 'terrorist' model of economic activity. One good example is the terrorist regime of Henry V of England, described by G. Mattingly, *Catherine of Aragon* (New York: Random House Paperback, 1960). Note also that this model describes the college 'honors' systems.

Technology T1. There are three types of jobs: skilled jobs, unskilled jobs, and scavenging jobs. (Subscripts *sk, u,* and *sc* refer to *sk*illed, *u*nskilled and *sc*avenging, respectively.)

T2. There are *n* different products, labeled $i = 1, \ldots, n$.

T3. The production of each product depends upon the quantity of labor employed and the jobs performed by the labor. Let θ_{sk}, θ_u, and θ_{sc} denote the output of one unit of labor in producing any product in a skilled job, unskilled job, or scavenging job, respectively. The production function of good *i* is then

$$q_i = \sum_j \theta_j n_{ij},$$

where
  $j = sk, u, sc, i = 1, \ldots, n$
  q_i = output of product *i*, and
  n_{ij} = quantity of labor employed in job type *j* in production of good *i*.
Of course,

$$\theta_{sc} < \theta_u < \theta_{sk}. \tag{1}$$

T4. Because of economies due to specialization workers can work on the production of only one product.

Market Structures. All firms are competitive profit maximizers. These firms can produce only one product. They hire labor and sell output on the market. A firm is willing to bid for labor the expected marginal value product of that labor.

Tastes. All persons have the same utility function *U*, which is independent of the caste code.

$$U = \sum_{i=1}^{n} \min(x_i, \alpha), \tag{2}$$

where x_i is consumption of good *i* and α is a parameter of the utility function.

Social Structure S1. By birth there are just two castes divided into a dominant caste *D* and a nondominant caste *N*. Labor of both castes *D* and *N* can be outcasted. Outcastes, if any, form a third group.

S2. The caste code dictates that *D* labor may work in only skilled jobs; *N* labor may work in only unskilled jobs; and outcaste labor may only hold scavenging jobs. The caste code also says that all persons who purchase from firms not using labor according to the caste code will themselves be outcasted.

S3. Persons predict that breakers of the caste code will be outcasted and receive the wages bid for outcaste labor.

Caste Equilibrium. Let the economy be described as above. Let w_k, $k = D, N$ denote the wage of caste *k*. Let p_i denote the price of good *i* produced by firms that use labor according to the caste code. Let good 1 be the numeraire good, with price equal to 1. Assume parameter values

$$\alpha < (\theta_u - \theta_{sc})/(1 - \theta_{sc}/\theta_{sk}) \tag{3}$$

and

$$n > \theta_{sk}/\alpha. \tag{4}$$

The following describe an equilibrium with fulfilled expectations:

1. $w_D = \theta_{sk}$, $w_N = \theta_u$.
2. The price of all goods produced by firms using labor according to caste code is 1.
3. There are no outcastes. N labor works at unskilled jobs. D labor works at skilled jobs.
4. Utility of D labor is θ_{sk}; utility of N labor is θ_u.
5. The highest wage bid for outcaste labor is θ_{sc}.

A coalition of k^* firms, producing k^* different products and using outcaste labor in skilled jobs, can break this equilibrium if

$$k^* > (\theta_u - \theta_{sc})/\alpha(1 - \theta_{sc}/\theta_{sk}).$$

Proof. It is obvious that the described equilibrium is feasible. We need show only that no new firm can make zero or positive profits and bid a higher wage either for N labor or for outcaste labor.

N Labor. Suppose that a new firm bids a higher wage for N labor than θ_u. It must use some of this labor in skilled jobs. In this case its profits per laborer will not exceed

$$p\theta_{sk} - \theta_u,$$

where p is the price received for its product. If profits are nonnegative,

$$p \geq \theta_u/\theta_{sk}.$$

But at a price as great as θ_u/θ_{sk} this firm will have no customers. Consider a prospective customer. This customer will be outcasted because N labor is used in skilled jobs. Therefore, his expected wage is θ_{sc}. He will maximize expected utility by purchasing α units at a price p and $(\theta_{sc} - \alpha p)$ units of other goods from other firms that use labor according to the caste code.

His total utility will therefore be

$$\theta_{sc} - \alpha p + \alpha \leq \theta_{sc} - \alpha\theta_u/\theta_{sk} + \alpha. \tag{5}$$

But by (1) and (3) the right-hand side of (5) is less than θ_u.

Since the customer of this firm receives utility at least as large as θ_u if he does not purchase from the caste-breaking firm, the demand for the firm's products will be zero.

Outcaste Labor. No firm can bid a wage higher than θ_{sc} for outcaste labor and receive a profit if this bid is accepted. For a firm to pay a higher wage than θ_{sc}, it must employ outcaste labor in skilled or unskilled jobs. Its profits per laborer will not exceed

$$p\theta_{sk} - \theta_{sc}.$$

If profits are nonnegative,

$$p \geq \theta_{sc}/\theta_{sk}.$$

But at a price as great as θ_{sc}/θ_{sk} the firm will have no customers: any prospective customer will be outcasted and expect to receive a wage θ_{sc}. Consider this customer. He will buy α units from this firm at a price p and will purchase $(\theta_{sc} - \alpha p)$ units of other goods from other firms. Therefore, his utility will be no greater than

$$\theta_{sc} - \alpha\theta_{sc}/\theta_{sk} + \alpha. \tag{6}$$

But since (6) is less than θ_u by (3), this firm will have no customers. Hence the maximum bid for outcaste labor will be θ_{sc}.

Equilibrium-Breaking Coalition

Finally, a coalition of k^* firms, $k^* > (\theta_u - \theta_{sc})/\alpha(1 - \theta_{sc}/\theta_{sk})$ can break the equilibrium. Such firms can offer a wage bid θ_{sc} for outcaste labor, and offer to sell their output at a price θ_{sc}/θ_{sk}. The expected utility of a person purchasing from these firms will be

$$\min (\theta_{sk}, \theta_{sc} - k^*\alpha\theta_{sc}/\theta_{sk} + k^*\alpha),$$

which is greater than θ_u if $k^* > (\theta_u - \theta_{sc})/\alpha(1 - \theta_{sc}/\theta_{sk})$. Thus the coalition of firms will be able to attract customers; and since workers will be better off receiving θ_{sc} in wages and purchasing from firms that break the caste code, these firms will also be able to attract workers.

Comments on Caste Equilibrium

1. The equilibrium described has two types of distortions due to caste structure. The equilibrium is not Pareto optimal, since in a Pareto-optimal equilibrium N workers would work in skilled jobs, for which they are fully qualified. Also, income distribution is skewed along caste lines, since in the absence of caste all workers would receive the same wage.
2. There is another equilibrium, also with fulfilled expectations, in which all workers work in skilled jobs and receive a wage θ_{sk}. The price of all goods is 1.

3. The smallest equilibrium-breaking coalition is the smallest group that can set themselves up as a separate subsector and be as well off as in equilibrium while trading with caste members on the terms of trade granted to outcastes.

In situations where this coalition must be large, where trade with the caste economy is necessary, or where the cost of forming a coalition is high, the threat to equilibrium of such a coalition is small. These principles are illustrated in the examples that follow.

Three Examples of Caste Equilibrium

Example 1.   Racial Discrimination. Racial discrimination is implicit in the model; the major difference between the caste model and those of Becker, Welch, and Arrow[24] being in the assumption that persons use race to predict how everyone else will react to hiring persons of different races in different jobs. Their predictions result in a lower level equilibrium trap in which all predictions are met.[25]

Example 2.   Government-Business Groups. Allegedly many government-business groups, including the military-industrial state, governmental regulator-regulatee nexuses and political machines are held together by a caste-outcaste structure similar to that of our model. By nature the important operations of these groups are usually secret[26] or too technical for unambiguous assessment; but there are some recent and exceptional accounts of the detailed operation of particular political machines.[27]

The example of Robert Moses, the construction boss of New York City of long duration, illustrates especially well the applicability of the model. The story of Moses, as all such tales of powerful men, is in many ways unique—but his system of control through outcasting exactly corresponds to our model. There were a large variety of statuses in the Moses machine (from personal aide to Mayor of New York City); but it was clear to all concerned that disobedience to the boss' dictates regarding construction would lead to outcasting from the machine. For the politician, this meant loss of campaign funds and of the construction pork barrel and, consequently, the almost certain loss of his next election; for engineers it meant loss of job. Furthermore, it is reported, persons who failed to respect the outcaste status of those in Moses' disfavor

---

[24] Arrow, *op. cit.*; Becker, *op. cit.*; Welch, *op. cit.*

[25] Certainly our model gives a good first approximation to the apartheid system in South Africa. A. Lewis, 'South Africa: The End Is Inevitable But Not Predictable,' *New York Times Magazine*, September 21, 1975.

[26] A recent incident epitomizes bureaucratic attitudes toward public disclosure. Alexander Butterfield, the bureaucrat whose own disclosure toppled the Nixon administration, wrote a memorandum to Haldeman regarding A. Ernest Fitzgerald, the government cost accountant who was fired after disclosing the Lockheed C-5A cost overruns. 'Let him bleed a little,' wrote Butterfield. According to the *New York Times Magazine*, Butterfield felt justified because 'he considered Fitzgerald disloyal for not confining his reports to Air Force channels.' A. R. Smith, 'The Butterfield Exchange,' *New York Times Magazine*, July 20, 1975.

[27] See T. Harry Williams, *Huey Long* (New York: Knopf, 1969); R. A. Caro, *The Power Broker: Robert Moses and the Fall of New York City* (New York: Knopf, 1974); and paperback, (New York: Vintage, Random House, 1974).

were in turn threatened, becoming themselves the subjects of Moses' abuse and threats.[28] The uniqueness of Moses lay largely in his perfection of the system—mainly in his use of interlocking jobs to threaten the elected officials responsible for his reappointments and also in his use of the Triborough Bridge Authority (whose files, by a Moses-engineered legal quirk, were closed to public scrutiny) to maintain secret dossiers.

While the Moses example is extreme, it shows that in cases where public authority is delegated and cannot be easily scrutinized from outside, a caste-outcaste mechanism can arise that keeps the use of the authority secret while the resources are used for private aims. Because of the secrecy of such operations ipso facto, the importance of such misallocations for the distribution of income and of power is impossible to assess.

Example 3. Professional Groups. A final example (or set of examples) of the caste-class equilibrium occurs in professional groups. The public often delegates authority to professional organizations to police their own members—the most prominent of these being bar and medical associations. In turn, the members are expected to maintain professional conduct. Since cooperation with others in the profession is a necessary part of the job, the same outcasting mechanism used by caste, races, and government-business cliques enforces a professional unanimity that gives the profession more than its fair share of economic power.

VI. CONCLUSIONS

Our four woeful tales have described the ways in which the use of *indicators* can distort equilibrium. In so doing, we have also answered two challenges to economic theory.

The standard individualistic theories of income distribution and resource allocation are notable by the absence of variables describing social structure, except insofar as these variables affect exogenously given tastes or the initial allocation bundles. The absence of these variables poses the first challenge: to construct an individualistic theory in which income distribution and resource allocation reflect, to some extent, the divisions of society as described by the sociologists. The most common *indicators* are based upon the standard subcultural divisions of a society. And, as a result, the use of *indicators* makes equilibrium income distribution and resource allocation dependent on these divisions; and the first challenge is answered.

The second challenge to economic theory concerns the relation between marginalism and social custom. As long as most persons have positive utility for obeying social customs, and as long as activities are pursued up to the point where marginal costs equal marginal benefits, there will be rewards to breaking social customs insofar as they fail to promote economic efficiency. While such rewards occur sometimes, and they may also

---

[28] See Caro's rather blunt description of Moses' style of operation: 'Within a remarkably brief time after Moses entered the City Administration word spread through City Hall and the Municipal Building that any time anyone got in Moses's way Moses kicked him in the.... So the men who worked in the two buildings were in general exceedingly careful not to get in his way, they went to great lengths to do exactly what he wanted—when he wanted.'

be spectacular, I would tend to believe that usually the greatest returns go to those who do not break social customs. Archetypically, they join the proper fraternity, work for the proper law firm, and may even marry the boss' daughter. In a segregationist society, such persons discriminate; in a caste society they follow the caste code. While not denying the possible returns to the arbitrageur and social deviant, the models of statistical discrimination and caste explain why economic rewards may favor those who follow prevailing social custom; and in so doing, they give economic reasons why such social customs may endure.

University of California, Berkeley

3

Discriminatory, Status-based Wages among Tradition-oriented, Stochastically Trading Coconut Producers[*]

GEORGE A. AKERLOF
University of California, Berkeley

J71
J15
J20

A robust model of discrimination is presented; even if there is a significant minority without a taste for discrimination and even if there is capital transfer among entrepreneurs with different tastes for discrimination, no entrant can profit by violating the discriminatory custom. The key innovation in this model of discrimination is that markets are in some sense smaller than the Walrasian market. All traders have a chance of trading with one another. And at the time of trade there is no other equally satisfactory alternative trading partner. This assumption corresponds to empirical sociological studies that similarly find markets to be small.

This paper presents a model of discrimination in which trade in goods occurs in random encounters between agents. The assumption of Becker (1957) that trade occurs in Walrasian markets is altered, making it easier to explain wage differentials for labor of a preferred type (*W*-labor) relative to an unpreferred type (*B*-labor) of equal quality.

There are two reasons why such differentials are not explained by Becker's model (see Arrow 1972). First, the proportion of nondiscriminatory entrepreneurs and nondiscriminatory purchasers of goods need be no greater than the proportion of the unpreferred labor type for the disappearance of the equilibrium wage differential.

I would like to thank Pranab Bardhan, Peter Diamond, James Heckman, Michael Reich, James Tobin, Eric Wanner, and Janet Yellen for helpful comments. In addition, I would also like to thank the National Science Foundation for financial support under research grant no. SES 81-19150, administered by the Institute of Business and Economic Research of the University of California, Berkeley.

Second, in an equilibrium in which the marginal entrepreneur hiring *B*-labor has a positive taste for discrimination, those who hire *B*-labor could profitably buy the capital of entrepreneurs who hire *W*-labor with resultant decreases in the wage differential. These properties of Becker's model occur because those who 'make the market' for *B*-labor and *B*-produced goods are those with the least discriminatory tastes: the least discriminatory entrepreneurs hire *B*-labor because they are willing to pay the highest wages to *B*-labor; and the least discriminatory purchasers of *B*-produced goods are willing to pay the highest prices for such goods. In contrast, this paper constructs a model in which *all* individuals, not just the least discriminatory, are potential traders with firms that use *B*-labor. And, as a result, even with a significant minority of nondiscriminatory traders, a nondiscriminatory entrant may not be able profitably to disobey prevailing social customs.

I. THE MODEL EXPLAINED

A model, following Diamond (1982), is constructed with the key feature that trading partners are those who randomly meet in a search process. This contrasts with the Walrasian model in which trading partners are any pair of agents, with the buyer willing to pay at least the market price and the seller willing to accept at least the market price. In Diamond's model, because trading occurs only when partners meet, the loss of any potential trading partner has a cost, since an agent boycotted by any particular agent will not be able to sell immediately at the market price. Because any agent is a potential trading partner and the loss of a trading partner is costly, every purchaser with a high discrimination coefficient imposes a cost on an entering firm that disobeys discriminatory social customs.

The next section will describe the equilibrium of a model in which there is a universally followed discriminatory custom in production that is inefficient in its use of labor and consequently raises production costs. It is then asked whether a maverick entering firm could profitably break the social custom when a fraction of traders will boycott the firm that has broken the social custom. (In Becker's framework these *boycotters* would have high buying-discrimination coefficients.)

The differences for discrimination between the Walrasian model and the random-trade model are illustrated in Figures 3.1*a* and 3.1*b*, which plot the cost of production plus sales as a function of the fraction of boycotting traders. In both models the costs of production are lower for the nondiscriminatory entrant than for the discriminatory entrepreneurs. But in the Walrasian case the cost of sales is independent of the number of boycotters as long as the nonboycotters are a larger share of the market than the entrant's production. If the entrant is sufficiently small, his cost of sales rises only as the number of boycotters approaches 100 percent. In this case he must pay a sales premium equal to the discrimination coefficient of the least discriminatory boycotter. This is pictured in Figure 3.1*a*; the cost of production and sales of a nondiscriminatory entrant into a market with all goods produced according to the discriminatory custom is plotted as a function of the percent of boycotters. This maverick has lower costs than the discriminatory firms if the fraction of boycotters is less than 100 percent.

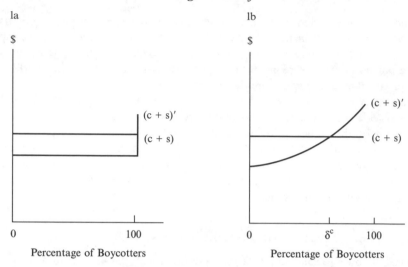

Figure 3.1. *Cost of production and sales for nondiscriminatory entrant and discriminatory firm in Walrasian (1a) and random-trade (1b) models. In both 1a and 1b, (c + s) represents the combined cost of production and sales of a firm that follows the discriminatory custom as a function of the percentage of boycotting buyers. Similarly, (c + s)′ represents the cost of production and sales of a nondiscriminatory entrant as a function of the percentage of boycotters. In the Walrasian model (c + s)′ is flat up to 100 percent boycotters. In the random-trade model (c + s)′ rises continuously with the percentage of boycotters. If the percentage of boycotters exceeds δᶜ in fig. 1b, nondiscriminatory entrants make lower profits than firms that follow the discriminatory custom.*

In contrast Figure 3.1*b* plots the cost of production plus sales for an entrant into the same market in a model with random trade. If the fraction of boycotters is zero, then the costs of the entrant are lower than the costs of the discriminatory firms, because the entrant uses labor efficiently in production. But as the number of boycotters rises, the search time to make a sale by the entrant increases and, consequently, so do sales costs. As a result, the entrant's total costs of production plus sales may, as pictured in Figure 3.1*b*, rise in excess of the total costs of a discriminatory firm. Even with a significant minority of buyers with no taste for discrimination (i.e., a minority smaller in proportion than $1 - \delta^c$ in fig. 1*b*) an entrant even of size zero cannot profitably break the social custom. Furthermore, unlike Becker's model, there is no excess profit to be made by entrepreneurs with no taste for discrimination. And entrepreneurs with a low taste for discrimination cannot profitably purchase the capital of those with a high taste for discrimination.

The Assumption of the Random Appearance of Trading Partners

The model of trade that occurs between partners each of whom values the other's patronage because the market is fairly small corresponds to an empirical view of markets consistent with sociological studies. Work on 'weak ties' following Granovetter (1973) has shown that many exchanges in both factor and product markets occur through mutual contacts. According to Macaulay (1963), engineering firms value their customers, and as a result most business transactions are on a less than strictly contractual basis; many transactions that are costly to one party and beneficial to another (such as the cancellation of orders) are performed without consideration. Rendering of such services to 'valued customers' could be profitable only in a market in which alternative trading partners were scarcer than in the Walrasian model.

II. THE FORMAL MODEL

Diamond's (1982) model will be revised for the purpose of parsimoniously demonstrating the possibility of discriminatory equilibria. As in Diamond's model, economic activity occurs on a tropical island and consists of picking and marketing coconuts. There are N carts (i.e., firms, each of which owns one unit of capital) on the island. The length of time to fill a cart with coconuts depends on the number of labor efficiency units in two types of jobs, numbered type 1 and type 2. A cart working with N_1 labor efficiency units in type 1 jobs and N_2 labor efficiency units in type 2 jobs can be filled in length of time $N_1^{-\frac{1}{2}} N_2^{-\frac{1}{2}}$. Carts leave the coconut groves after they have been filled for a market area where other carts with the similar purpose of trading coconuts will be randomly encountered.

The islanders search for others carts with which to trade coconuts because they have utility for coconuts, but there is a taboo against the consumption of coconuts gathered by one's own firm. The islanders are also quite traditional: firms that break the social custom of the island by hiring men or women in different proportions from other firms will be shunned by some fraction of the traditional firms (i.e., some firms that obey the traditional hiring practices will not trade with other firms that depart from the tradition).

Production

There are two distinct groups of people in this model, men and women. There are L men and L women. One-half of the men, appropriately named type 1 men, have a comparative advantage in type 1 jobs. They contribute one labor efficiency unit in a job of type 1 and β labor efficiency units in a job of type 2, where β is less than one. Type 2 men, who are also $L/2$ in number, have the opposite comparative advantage: type 2 men contribute $\beta(< 1)$ labor efficiency units in jobs of type 1 and one labor efficiency unit in jobs of type 2.

Women's productive abilities are exactly like men's. One-half of all women are of type 1. These women, like type 1 men, contribute one labor efficiency unit to type 1 jobs but only $\beta(< 1)$ units to type 2 jobs. Symmetrically, the other half of all women are of type 2: they contribute $\beta(< 1)$ labor efficiency units in type 1 jobs and one labor efficiency unit in type 2 jobs.

Trading: Probability of Meeting

Carts are met at a rate proportional to the number of carts in the marketplace. Any individual cart is either in the marketplace trying to sell a load of coconuts or else in the coconut groves being loaded with coconuts. Any two carts in the marketplace will meet randomly with probability $(1/\gamma)dt$ in a short period of time dt. The probability of a particular cart's meeting another in the marketplace is $[(S - 1)/\gamma]dt$ when there are S carts in the marketplace. We assume that one is sufficiently small relative to S that it is suppressed in the rest of the paper.

Trading: Discrimination in Trade

If two carts meet in the marketplace but one cart has used male and female labor in jobs 1 and 2 in different proportions from the norm, only with probability $1 - \delta(0 < \delta < 1)$ will a trade occur. The variable δ may be dependent on the deviation in proportions of men and women in jobs 1 and 2; it may also be dependent subtly on the social customs in rather complicated ways. For the purpose of the demonstration here of the existence of discriminatory equilibrium, it is assumed that if the proportions are *at all* different from the norm, then δ is a positive constant.

The Nature of the Bargain between Two Trading Carts

When carts meet they trade (except in the case of discrimination against an innovator). The barter price of coconuts is indeterminate unless a bargaining solution is specified. I assume an axiom of symmetry. If the carts are in exactly symmetric positions the trade of coconuts will be one-to-one. However, if the trade has more value to one cart than another, the cart for which the trade has more value is in a weak bargaining position. Trade will occur at less than a one-to-one rate for the disadvantaged cart.

The Market for Labor

Labor supply of both men and women is totally inelastic. There is no discount rate in this economy. Both labor and owners of carts want to maximize the undiscounted value of their income in terms of coconuts. Thus, cart owners maximize the expected returns on carts per unit time; the competitive wage rate is the marginal product of a laborer of a given type in production on his own cart. A competitive labor market is assumed, so that this is the wage actually received.

III. THE NONDISCRIMINATORY EQUILIBRIUM

Note that the model described in the previous section would exactly correspond to the standard neoclassical model if the coefficients of N_1 and N_2 summed to less than unity, which is a matter of no importance, and if γ were zero, which is a matter of great importance. If it takes length of time $N_1^{-\alpha_1} N_2^{-\alpha_2} (\alpha_1 + \alpha_2 < 1)$ to fill a cart, then $N_1^{\alpha_1} N_2^{\alpha_2} N^{1-\alpha_1-\alpha_2}$ is a neoclassical production function for output. With $\gamma = 0$ the only equilibrium possible in this model is the neoclassical equilibrium with labor and capital receiving their respective marginal products.

Factor Allocations

Let us consider a natural nondiscriminatory equilibrium of this model. Jobs 1 and 2 will be filled by men and women in equal number, with jobs of type 1 divided equally between type 1 men and women and jobs of type 2 similarly divided between type 2 men and women.

Division of Carts between Production and Trade

Let θ denote the proportion of carts engaged in selling; $(1 - \theta)$ will then be the proportion of carts engaged in production of coconuts. It is possible to discover what the value of θ must be in this natural nondiscriminatory equilibrium. Having solved for the equilibrium value of θ, denoted θ^*, it will then be possible to describe all the key variables in this economy: wages for men and women of types 1 and 2, and also profits.

The ratio $(1 - \theta^*)/\theta^*$ will be equal to the ratio of the time to fill a cart to the time it takes to sell a cartful of coconuts once they have been taken to market. In this nondiscriminatory equilibrium the length of time to fill a cart must be

$$\left(\frac{L}{N}\right)^{-\frac{1}{2}} \left(\frac{L}{N}\right)^{-\frac{1}{2}} = \left(\frac{L}{N}\right)^{-1}, \tag{1}$$

as can be found by substitution into the earlier formula of the number of labor efficiency units in type 1 and 2 jobs. The time to sell a cartful of coconuts is

$$\frac{\gamma}{S} = \frac{\gamma}{\theta^* N}. \tag{2}$$

Thus in equilibrium

$$\frac{1 - \theta^*}{\theta^*} = \frac{\left(\frac{L}{N}\right)^{-1}}{\frac{\gamma}{\theta^* N}}. \tag{3}$$

Equation (3) is a quadratic equation with a positive solution for θ^*.

$$\theta^* = \frac{-1 + \sqrt{1 + 4x}}{2x}, \tag{4}$$

where $x = N^2/\gamma L$. A bit of calculus shows the relation between θ^* and x according to (4). For $x = 0$, by L'Hospital's rule, $\theta^* = 1$. For $x = \infty$, $\theta^* = 0$. And for x between zero and infinity, $d\theta^*/dx < 0$.

Wages and Profits

In the nondiscriminatory equilibrium, the length of time to produce and sell a cartful of coconuts is

$$\left(\frac{L}{N}\right)^{-1} + \frac{\gamma}{\theta^* N}.$$

(5)

Accordingly, output per cart per period is the reciprocal of (5) or

$$\frac{1}{\left[\left(\frac{L}{N}\right)^{-1} + \frac{\gamma}{\theta^* N}\right]}.$$

(6)

The wage of type 1 workers w_1 is

$$\frac{\partial}{\partial J_1} \frac{1}{J_1^{-\frac{1}{2}} J_2^{-\frac{1}{2}} + \frac{\gamma}{\theta^* N}} \Bigg|_{\substack{J_1 = J_2 = L/N \\ \theta^* = RHS\ of\ (4)}} = \frac{\frac{1}{2}\left(\frac{L}{N}\right)^{-2}}{\left[\left(\frac{L}{N}\right)^{-1} + \frac{\gamma}{\theta^* N}\right]^2},$$

(7)

where J_i represents the number of labor efficiency units in a job of type i, $i = 1, 2$. A type 1 worker embodies one labor efficiency unit. By symmetry the wage of type 2 workers is the same as that of type 1 workers and is also given by the right-hand side of (7). The share of profits can be calculated using the definition of profits as production net of labor costs and is equal to

$$\frac{\frac{\gamma}{\theta^* N}}{\left(\frac{L}{N}\right)^{-1} + \frac{\gamma}{\theta^* N}},$$

(8)

an expression that is always between zero and one, as theory suggests it should be.

These explicit calculations of productivity (6), wages (7), and profit share (8) will allow comparison with the discriminatory equilibrium described in the next section.

It should be obvious that if the allocation of labor across jobs is as described above no firm could enter, pay higher wages using labor in different proportions, and earn positive profits even in the total absence of discrimination (i.e., with $\delta = 0$), since, given wages, labor is used in the most profitable fashion. Therefore, provided δ is at all less than one for an innovating firm, profitable innovative entry will not be possible in this equilibrium.

IV. A DISCRIMINATORY EQUILIBRIUM

Factor Shares

The preceding nondiscriminatory equilibrium is to be contrasted with discriminatory equilibria in which men and women receive different wages, although not in the same jobs. Consider an equilibrium in which *all* women and all type 2 men work in type 2 jobs. Type 1 men work in type 1 jobs. Given what wages of men and women of the two types must be for such an equilibrium, it will be shown that values of δ can be chosen so that no innovative firm can profitably hire men and women in different proportions.

In this equilibrium output per cart per period must be

$$\frac{1}{\left(\frac{1}{2}\frac{L}{N}\right)^{-\frac{1}{2}}\left(\frac{L}{N}+\frac{\beta}{2}\frac{L}{N}\right)^{-\frac{1}{2}}+\frac{\gamma}{S}}. \tag{9}$$

The first term in the denominator of (9) represents the length of time to fill a cart, given $L/2N$ labor efficiency units in jobs of type 1 (from type 1 men) and $(L/N)+(\beta/2)(L/N)$ labor efficiency units in type 2 jobs: L/N of these efficiency units come from type 2 men and women together; $(\beta/2)(L/N)$ of these come from type 1 women working in type 2 jobs at efficiency β. The second term of the denominator of (9) represents the length of time to sell the output of a cart.

Number of Carts Engaged in Marketing

As before it is possible to solve for S. Let θ^{**} be the proportion of carts engaged in selling, so that $S = \theta^{**}N$, and, as before,

$$\frac{1-\theta^{**}}{\theta^{**}} = \frac{\left(\frac{1}{2}\frac{L}{N}\right)^{-\frac{1}{2}}\left(\frac{L}{N}+\frac{\beta}{2}\frac{L}{N}\right)^{-\frac{1}{2}}}{\frac{\gamma}{\theta^{**}N}}. \tag{10}$$

This yields a root for θ^{**},

$$\theta^{**} = \frac{-1+(1+4x)^{\frac{1}{2}}}{2x}, \quad x = \frac{N^2}{\gamma L(\frac{1}{2})^{\frac{1}{2}}\left(1+\frac{\beta^{\frac{1}{2}}}{2}\right)}. \tag{11}$$

Relative to the nondiscriminatory equilibrium, the denominator of x has decreased so that the proportion of carts that are selling has also decreased. It takes longer to sell output.

Wages and Profits

The wage rate per efficiency unit in type 1 and type 2 jobs is found by taking the derivatives with respect to J_1 and J_2, respectively, of expression (12) for output per unit time or the derivative of

$$\frac{1}{J_1^{-\frac{1}{2}}J_2^{-\frac{1}{2}}+\frac{\gamma}{\theta^{**}N}}, \tag{12}$$

evaluated with $J_1 = L/2N$, $J_2 = L[1 + (\beta/2)]/N$, and θ^{**} given by (11).

Doing this algebra yields an expression for the wage of type 2 labor that is unambiguously smaller than in the nondiscriminatory equilibrium. There are three reasons: in the new equilibrium the number of substitute labor efficiency units in type 2 jobs has risen, the number of complementary labor efficiency units in type 1 jobs has fallen, and the length of time to sell the product has risen. The wage per efficiency unit in type 1 jobs changes ambiguously. The number of substitute labor efficiency units in type 1 jobs has fallen, and the number of complementary labor efficiency units in type 2 jobs has risen. Both of these effects should raise wages in type 1 jobs, but the length of time in selling has risen, and this may more than counteract the other two effects.

Profit share in the discriminatory equilibrium is given by a formula analogous to (8) and is calculated in similar fashion. Profits per cart are

$$
\frac{\frac{\gamma}{\theta^{**}N}}{\left\{ \left(\tfrac{1}{2}\tfrac{L}{N}\right)^{-\frac{1}{2}} \left[\left(1+\tfrac{\beta}{2}\right)\tfrac{L}{N}\right]^{-\frac{1}{2}} + \frac{\gamma}{\theta^{**}N} \right\}^2 } . \tag{13}
$$

It is of use later that this expression is always positive. (Note also that it is easy to show, using [9], [13], and $S = \theta^{**}N$, that profit share is between zero and one.)

Choice of δ So That Innovative Entry Cannot Be Profitable

Now consider whether an innovator might use women of type 1 in jobs of type 1 and thereby make a profit, given the existing wage structure. Remember, however, that a fraction δ of noninnovative carts will not trade with the maverick. Can a lower bound be found so that for any higher level of δ, profitable entry cannot occur? That is the question of this subsection.

Before answering this key question, let me first deal with a technical issue concerning the bargaining between the traders. Among the traders previously described in this equilibrium all are alike: therefore trades of coconuts will occur at a rate of one-to-one. The maverick firm will have lower production costs but a longer wait for potential buyers, since some fraction δ of all buyers will refuse to trade. Therefore the innovators are in a weaker bargaining position, since the cost of failing to make a trade is greater to them than to noninnovators, and therefore they will barter their coconuts on a less than one-for-one basis. Let the expected barter rate be $p < 1$.

Let the innovator hire N_1^I, N_2^I (I for innovator) workers in jobs 1 and 2 on his cart. He will hire women of type 1 in jobs of type 1. Such women receive a wage of w_2 per labor efficiency unit in type 2 jobs; they supply only β labor efficiency units. Thus their wage is βw_2. In type 2 jobs the innovator can arbitrarily decide the proportion of men and women of type 2, paying each w_2, or he can hire women of type 1 paying βw_2 for β labor efficiency units. The entrepreneur's profits Π^I are

$$\Pi^I = p\frac{1}{(N_1^I)^{-\frac{1}{2}}(N_2^I)^{-\frac{1}{2}} + \frac{\gamma}{(1-\delta)\theta^{**}N}} - \beta w_2 N_1^I - w_2 N_2^I. \tag{14}$$

It is possible, but involves very complicated formulae, to calculate the optimal N_1^I, N_2^I given w_2 and δ and find an exact formula for the critical level δ^c; for values of δ above this critical level innovative entry is not profitable; for values below this critical level innovative entry is profitable. For the crude purpose of establishing an upper bound for this δ^c, let us make a very crude approximation. Note that

$$\Pi^I \le \frac{1}{\frac{\gamma}{(1-\delta)\theta^{**}N}}, \tag{15}$$

using (14), $p < 1$, $N_1^{-\frac{1}{2}}N_2^{-\frac{1}{2}} \ge 0$, $\beta w_2 N_1^I \ge 0$, and $w_2 N_2^I \ge 0$. It follows using (15) that the profits of noninnovators (given by [13]) will be greater than the left-hand side of (15), provided

$$\delta > 1 - \frac{\left(\frac{\gamma}{\theta^{**}N}\right)^2}{\left[\left(\frac{1}{2}\frac{L}{N}\right)^{-\frac{1}{2}}\left(1 + \frac{\beta}{2}\frac{L}{N}\right)^{-\frac{1}{2}} + \frac{\gamma}{\theta^{**}N}\right]^2}. \tag{16}$$

The right-hand side of (16) gives a crude upper bound on the critical value δ^c. The crudeness of this bound is directly related to the crudeness of (15) as a bound on the profits of the innovating firm. Nevertheless, it has been demonstrated that suitable values of δ can be chosen so that innovative firms cannot profitably enter in the posited discriminatory equilibrium.[1]

V. CONCLUSION

A model of discrimination has been presented that is robust; even if there is a significant minority without a taste for discrimination and even if there is capital transfer among entrepreneurs with different tastes for discrimination, no entrant can profit by violating the discriminatory custom. The key innovation in this model of discrimination is that markets are in some sense smaller than the Walrasian market. All traders have a chance of trading with one another. And at the time of trade there is no other equally satisfactory alternative trading partner. This assumption corresponds to empirical sociological studies that similarly find markets to be small.

---

[1] One discriminatory equilibrium was analyzed. Clearly, many discriminatory equilibria are possible. If, as posited, avoidance depends on departure from the status quo use of the different sexes, there are four symmetric discriminatory equilibria. The roles of men and women can be symmetrically reversed, as can the roles of jobs 1 and 2. Furthermore, there is no reason why equilibria must of necessity be a corner solution, as in the example, with all women and type 2 men in type 2 jobs. There are whole continua of possible equilibria in which there is avoidance of those who depart from the status quo.

References

Arrow, Kenneth J. 'Models of Job Discrimination.' In *Racial Discrimination in Economic Life*, edited by Anthony H. Pascal. Lexington, Mass.: Heath, 1972.

Becker, Gary S. *The Economics of Discrimination*. Chicago: Univ. Chicago Press, 1957.

Diamond, Peter A. 'Aggregate Demand Management in Search Equilibrium.' *J.P.E.* 90 (October 1982): 881–894.

Granovetter, Mark S. 'The Strength of Weak Ties.' *American J. Soc.* 78 (May 1973): 1360–80.

Macaulay, Stewart. 'Non-contractual Relations in Business: A Preliminary Study.' *American Soc. Rev.* 28 (February 1963): 55–67.

DII
J7I
JI5
DI3
I32

67-99
['00]

4

Economics and Identity*

GEORGE A. AKERLOF AND RACHEL E. KRANTON[†]

I. INTRODUCTION

This paper introduces identity—a person's sense of self—into economic analysis. Identity can account for many phenomena that current economics cannot well explain. It can comfortably resolve, for example, why some women oppose 'women's rights,' as seen in microcosm when Betty Friedan was ostracized by fellow suburban housewives for writing *The Feminine Mystique*. Other problems such as ethnic and racial conflict, discrimination, intractable labor disputes, and separatist politics all invite an identity-based analysis. Because of its explanatory power, numerous scholars in psychology, sociology, political science, anthropology, and history have adopted identity as a central concept. This paper shows how identity can be brought into economic analysis, allowing a new view of many economic problems.[1]

* This work was previously published as George A. Akerlof and Rachel E. Kranton (2000), 'Economics and Identity', *Quarterly Journal of Economics*, 115,3. Copyright © The MIT Press Reproduced by kind permission.
† The authors especially wish to thank Abdeslam Maghraoui for his continued help and insights and Michael Ash, Jennifer Eichberger, and Cyd Fremmer for invaluable research assistance. Henry Aaron, William Dickens, Claudia Goldin, Edward Glaeser, Lawrence Katz, Robert Merton, Anand Swamy, and an anonymous referee made extensive comments on earlier drafts for which the authors are particularly grateful. They also thank Robert Akerlof, Abhijit Banerjee, Kaushik Basu, Paul Beaudry, Samuel Bowles, Robert Boyd, Gary Burtless, Alessandra Casella, Catherine Eckel, Stuart Elliott, Gary Fields, Pierre Fortin, James Foster, Richard Harris, Victoria Hattam, Peter Howitt, Aurora Jackson, Kevin Lang, George Loewenstein, Glenn Loury, Michael Kremer, David Laibson, Janet Pack, Matthew Rabin, Francisco Rodriguez, Paul Romer, Eric Verhoogen, Eric Wanner, Kent Weaver, Robin Wells, Janet Yellen, and Peyton Young for help and comments. George Akerlof is grateful to the Canadian Institute for Advanced Research, the MacArthur Foundation, the Brookings Institution, and the National Science Foundation, under research grant number SBR 97-09250, for financial support. Rachel Kranton expresses her gratitude to the Russell Sage Foundation where she was a Visiting Scholar for 1997–1998.

[1] Previous economic literature on identity includes Folbre (1994) who discusses the importance of gender identity for collective action that preserves male privilege. Our general model of utility allows for this outcome, as well as many other sources of gender inequality. Sen (1985) mentions identity as an influence on goal achievement, but does not incorporate identity into a utility function or models of specific economic settings. 'Identity' also has other connotations: Landa (1994) and Kevane (1994) consider how identity, defined as membership in a particular group, affects economic transactions when individual members are subject to group sanctions. Bowles and Gintis (1997) likewise consider cooperation within a community.

We incorporate identity into a general model of behavior and then demonstrate how identity influences economic outcomes. Specifically, we consider gender discrimination in the labor market, the household division of labor, and the economics of social exclusion and poverty. In each case, our analysis yields predictions, supported by existing evidence, that are different from those of existing economic models. The Conclusion indicates many other realms where identity almost surely matters.

Our identity model of behavior begins with social difference. Gender, a universally familiar aspect of identity, illustrates. There are two abstract social categories, 'man' and 'woman.' These categories are associated with different ideal physical attributes and prescribed behaviors. Everyone in the population is assigned a gender category, as either a 'man' or a 'woman.' Following the behavioral prescriptions for one's gender affirms one's self-image, or identity, as a 'man' or as a 'woman.'[2] Violating the prescriptions evokes anxiety and discomfort in oneself and in others. Gender identity, then, changes the 'payoffs' from different actions.

This modeling of identity is informed by a vast body of research on the salience of social categories for human behavior and interaction. We present in the next section a series of examples of identity-related behavior. These examples, and other evidence, indicate that (1) people have identity-based payoffs derived from their own actions; (2) people have identity-based payoffs derived from others' actions; (3) third parties can generate persistent changes in these payoffs; and (4) some people may choose their identity, but choice may be proscribed for others.

The concept of identity expands economic analysis for at least four corresponding reasons.

First, identity can explain behavior that appears detrimental. People behave in ways that would be considered maladaptive or even self-destructive by those with other identities. The reason for this behavior may be to bolster a sense of self or to salve a diminished self-image.

Second, identity underlies a new type of externality. One person's actions can have meaning for and evoke responses in others. Gender again affords an example. A dress is a symbol of femininity. If a man wears a dress, this may threaten the identity of other men. There is an externality, and further externalities result if these men make some response.

---

[2] We use the word *prescriptions* rather than *norms* because previous usage in economics has given the latter term connotations that would be misleading in the context of this paper. Here, agents follow prescriptions, for the most part, to maintain their self-concepts. In contrast, in much of the economics literature, a norm is obeyed because failure to do so results in punishment (e.g., Akerlof (1976), Kandori (1992), and Cole, Mailath, and Postlewaite (1992)). Other authors, however, see norms as something similar to our prescriptions. In Montgomery's (1997) game-theoretic model of social roles, agents adopt strategies that norms assign their roles because otherwise they 'would not recognize themselves.' Elster (1989) writes that social norms are sustained by strong feelings of embarrassment, anxiety, and guilt suffered from violating them. Huang and Wu (1994) also consider social norms sustained by people's emotions, which in the view of this paper would result from a person's sense of self.

Third, identity reveals a new way that preferences can be changed. Notions of identity evolve within a society and some in the society have incentives to manipulate them. Obvious examples occur in advertising (e.g., Marlboro ads). As we shall explore, there are many other cases, including public policies, where changing social categories and associated prescriptions affect economic outcomes.

Fourth, because identity is fundamental to behavior, choice of identity may be the most important 'economic' decision people make. Individuals may—more or less consciously—choose who they want to be. Limits on this choice may also be the most important determinant of an individual's economic well-being. Previous economic analyses of, for example, poverty, labor supply, and schooling have not considered these possibilities.

Our analysis proceeds as follows. In the next section we propose a general utility function that incorporates identity as a motivation for behavior. It introduces the vocabulary and theoretical framework used throughout the paper. This section also justifies our inclusion of identity in a utility function, presenting a series of examples of identity-related behavior. Section III then constructs a prototype game-theoretic model of identity that mirrors standard psychological theory. This model of two social categories—Green and Red—contains the essential elements of social differentiation, identity, and economic interaction. Sections IV, V, and VI consider gender discrimination in the labor market, the economics of poverty and social exclusion, and the household division of labor, respectively. Section VII concludes and indicates directions for future research.

II. UTILITY FUNCTION AND EVIDENCE OF IDENTITY-RELATED BEHAVIOR

This section proposes a utility function that incorporates identity as a motivation for behavior. We draw on extensive work in psychology and discuss specific examples of behavior that support our framework.

A. *A Utility Function with Identity*

In our utility function, identity is based on social categories, C. Each person j has an assignment of people to these categories, c_j, so that each person has a conception of her own categories and that of all other people.[3] Prescriptions P indicate the behavior appropriate for people in different social categories in different situations. The prescriptions may also describe an ideal for each category in terms of physical characteristics and

---

[3] An individual j's mapping of another individual k into categories need not correspond to k's own mapping. In addition, social categories need not be mutually exclusive, and an individual may be mapped into several social categories (e.g., individual j is both a 'woman' and a 'professional').

other attributes. Categories may also have higher or lower social status. We use the word identity to describe both a person's self-image as well as her assigned categories.

Gender identity, as indicated earlier, could be formalized as follows. There is a set of categories **C**, 'man' and 'woman,' where men have higher social status than women. c_j describes j's own gender category as well as j's assignment for everyone else in the population. **P** associates to each category basic physical and other characteristics that constitute the ideal man or woman as well as specifies behavior in different situations according to gender. E.g., the ideal woman is female, thin, and should always wear a dress; the ideal man is male, muscular, and should never wear a dress, except perhaps on Halloween.

We propose the following utility function:

$$U_j = U_j(a_j, a_{-j}, I_j).$$ (1)

Utility depends on j's identity or self-image I_j, as well as on the usual vectors of j's actions, a_j, and others' actions, a_{-j}. Since a_j and a_{-j} determine j's consumption of goods and services, these arguments and $U_j(\cdot)$ are sufficient to capture the standard economics of own actions and externalities.

Following our discussion above, we propose the following representation of I_j:

$$I_j = I_j(a_j, a_{-j}; c_j, \varepsilon_j, P).$$ (2)

A person j's identity I_j depends, first of all, on j's assigned social categories c_j. The social status of a category is given by the function $I_j(\cdot)$, and a person assigned a category with higher social status may enjoy an enhanced self-image. Identity further depends on the extent to which j's own given characteristics ε_j match the ideal of j's assigned category, indicated by the prescriptions **P**.[4] Finally, identity depends on the extent to which j's own and others' actions correspond to prescribed behavior indicated by **P**. We call increases or decreases in utility that derive from I_j, *gains or losses in identity*.[5]

In the simplest case, an individual j chooses actions to maximize utility (1), taking as given c_j, ε_j, and **P** and the actions of others. We use the verb 'choose' advisedly. We do not presume one way or another that people are aware of their own motivations, as in standard utility theory which is agnostic as to whether an individual shopper is aware or not of the reasons for her choices.[6]

---

[4] In the case of a category with high (low) social status, a person j may gain when own characteristics are close to (far from) from the ideal.

[5] Since an individual's self-concept may be formed by seeing oneself through the eyes of others (Gleitman 1996, p. 343), these gains or losses may also depend on how others interpret i's actions. The opinions of others may be revealed through actions a_{-j}; the individual may also care about others' categorizations c_{-j}.

[6] Sen (1997) makes the analogy that light does not know that it is minimizing distance, but behaves as if it does. This notion follows Friedman's (1953) dicta for the methodology of positive economics. Whether or not j consciously realizes she is maximizing a utility function such as (1), she does so nevertheless. In our setting, in particular, the motivations for behavior may be unconscious.

Beyond actions, to some extent an individual may also choose the category assignment c_j. Social categories may be more or less ascriptive, and in general, the individual is likely to have some choice over identity, as indeed people may even have some choice over their gender. Again, this 'choice' may be more or less conscious.

Individual actions may also affect the prescriptions **P**, the set of social categories **C**, as well as the status of different categories reflected in $I_j(\cdot)$. With respect to gender, for example, status differences between men and women have diminished over time, and prescribed behavior and physical ideals have changed. Gender categories themselves have become varied and complex. There may be no universal agreement about social categories and prescriptions. Indeed, they are the subject of much debate and controversy.

B. *Psychology and Experiments on Group Identification*

The prominence of identity in psychology suggests that economists should consider identity as an argument in utility functions. Psychologists have long posited a self or 'ego' as a primary force of individual behavior. They have further associated an individual's sense of self to the social setting; identity is bound to social categories; and individuals identify with people in some categories and differentiate themselves from those in others.[7]

While experiments in social psychology do not show the existence of a 'self' or this identification per se, they do demonstrate that even arbitrary social categorizations affect behavior.[8] Consider the Robbers Cave experiment. In its initial week, two groups of boys at a summer camp in Oklahoma were kept apart. During this period, the boys developed norms of behavior and identities as belonging to *their* group. When they met for a tournament in the second week, the eleven-year-old equivalent of war broke out, with name-calling, stereotyping, and fighting. Later experiments show that competition is not necessary for group identification and even the most minimal group assignment can affect behavior. 'Groups' form by nothing more than random assignment of subjects to labels, such as even or odd. Subjects are more likely to give rewards to those with the same label than to those with other labels, even when choices are anonymous and have no impact on own payoffs. Subjects also have higher opinions of members of their own group.

Our modeling of identity exactly parallels these experiments. In the experiments, as in our utility function (1), there are social categories; there is an assignment of subjects to those social categories; finally, subjects have in mind some form of assignment-related prescriptions, else rewards would not depend on group assignment.

---

[7] For discussion of the 'self,' see Thomas (1996), Breger (1974), or Gleitman (1996). For a review of the social psychology of identity, see Brown (1986) and Wetherell (1996), and especially the work of Tajfel and Turner (1979).

[8] For discussion of social psychology experiments, see Brown (1986, pp. 541–66) and Wetherell (1996, pp. 203–16).

C. Examples of Identity-Related Behavior

We next present a set of 'real-world' examples of four different ways, outlined in the introduction and formalized in our utility function, that identity may influence behavior.

Our *first* set demonstrates that people have identity-related payoffs from their own actions. The impact of an action a_j on utility U_j depends in part on its effect on identity I_j.

Self-Mutilation. The first of these examples is perhaps the most dramatic: people mutilate their own or their children's bodies as an expression of identity. Tattooing, body-piercing (ear, nose, navel, etc.), hair conking, self-starvation, steroid abuse, plastic surgery, and male and female circumcision all yield physical markers of belonging to more or less explicit social categories and groups.[9] In terms of our utility function, these practices transform an individual's physical characteristics to match an ideal.[10] The mutilation may occur because people believe it leads to pecuniary rewards and inter-actions such as marriage. But the tenacity and defense of these practices indicate the extent to which belonging relies on ritual, and people have internalized measures of beauty and virtue.[11]

Gender and Occupations. Female trial lawyer, male nurse, woman Marine—all conjure contradictions. Why? Because trial lawyers are viewed as masculine, nurses as feminine, and a Marine as the ultimate man. People in these occupations but of the opposite sex often have ambiguous feelings about their work. In terms of our utility function, an individual's actions do not correspond to gender prescriptions of behavior. A revealing study in this regard is Pierce's (1995) participant-observer research on the legal profession.[12] Female lawyers thought of themselves as women, yet being a good lawyer meant acting like a man. Lawyers were told in training sessions to act like 'Rambo' and to 'take no prisoners.' In the office, trial attorneys who did not 'win big' were described as 'having no balls.' Intimidation of witnesses was 'macho blasts against the other side.' A Christmas skit about two partners dramatized the gender conflict:

(O)ne secretary dressed up as Rachel and another dressed up as Michael. The secretary portraying Michael...ran around the stage barking orders and singing, 'I'm Michael Bond, I'm such a busy

---

[9] See Khatibi (1986) for analysis of how marking the body, by circumcision and tribal tattoos, marks the self.

[10] An alternative explanation is that these practices are signals of some unobserved economically relevant attribute. However, it is hard to imagine why individual costs of these signals would be correlated with these attributes.

[11] In a study of sexuality in rural Egypt, Khattab (1996) reports that women consider female circumcision a beautifying practice. It accentuates the difference between the sexes: 'We don't want to look like a man with a protruding organ' (p. 20). Bumiller (1990) reports an example of female defense of female self-sacrifice. Both men and women journeyed to pay their respects after a young woman committed *sati* in a Rajasthani village in 1987. *Sati* is the practice of the widow burning to death on her husband's funeral pyre. One devotee expressed her admiration: 'If I had known she was going to do this I would have touched her feet. Now I will give her a place in my house and worship her every day.' This respect is no less diminished by admirers' doubts that they would have had the same courage or by their ignorance of the pressure on the widow from her in-laws.

[12] For a study of nurses and Marines, see Williams (1989).

man. I'm such a busy man.' The other secretary followed suit by barking orders and singing, 'I'm Rachel Rosen, I'm such a busy man, I mean woman. I'm such a busy man, I mean woman....' Michael responded to the spoof in stride.... Rachel, on the other hand, was very upset (Pierce, 1995, p. 130).

Female lawyers expressed their ambivalence in many discussions. 'Candace,' another partner, told Pierce: 'I had forgotten how much anger I've buried over the years about what happened to the woman who became a lawyer.... To be a lawyer, somewhere along the way, I made a decision that it meant acting like a man. To do that I squeezed the female part of me into a box, put on the lid, and tucked it away' (Pierce 1995, p. 134).

Alumni Giving. Charitable contributions may yield a 'warm glow' (Andreoni 1989), but how do people choose one organization over another? Charity to the organization with the highest marginal return would maximize its economic impact. Yet, at least for higher education, contributions may well reflect identity. Graduates give to *their own* alma mater. Alumni giving could enhance the value of a degree by maintaining an institution's reputation. But this explanation suffers from the collective action problem. And it does not account for student loyalty and identification with an institution, as expressed in such lyrics as 'For God, for country, and for Yale.'

Mountaineering. Why do people climb mountains? Loewenstein (1998) argues that facing the extreme discomfort and danger of mountaineering enhances an individual's sense of self.

Our *second* set of examples demonstrates that people have identity-related payoffs from others' actions. The effect of an action a_{-j} on utility includes an impact on I_j.

Gender and Occupations. A woman working in a 'man's' job may make male colleagues feel less like 'men.' To allay these feelings, they may act to affirm their masculinity and act against female coworkers. In her study of coal handlers in a power plant, Padavic (1991) interpreted the behavior of her male coworkers in this way. On one occasion, they picked her up, tossed her back and forth, and attempted to push her onto the coal conveyer belt (jokingly, of course). In the case of another worker, no one trained her, no one helped her, and when she asked for help, she was refused assistance that would have been routine for male coworkers.[13]

To further assay the reasons for such behavior, we took a random-sample telephone survey relating a vignette about a female carpenter at a construction company who was 'baited and teased' by a male coworker. We see in Table 4.1 that among the six possible explanations, 84 percent of the respondents said it was 'somewhat likely,' 'likely,' or 'very likely' that the male worker behaved in this way because he felt less masculine.[14]

---

[13] Levine (1997) also found that men often refused to train women and sabotaged their work. In addition, women in men's jobs were subject to sexual innuendo. For a collection of such examples see Schultz (1998).

[14] Differences in response by gender were negligible. The survey included three other vignettes, two of which described a man (woman) contemplating a switch to a predominantly female (male) occupation. Responses indicate that gender could be of concern in such a decision. The responses were uninformative, however, when the switch was otherwise undesirable so that any gender conflict would be moot. Responses to the last vignette strongly suggest that identity considerations are a major reason for taking the time to vote. Our sample was half male, half female, and 60 percent college graduates.

George A. Akerlof

Table 4.1. *Vignette concerning harassment and evaluation of possible explanations*

Vignette: Paul is a carpenter for a construction company. The company has just hired Christine, its first female carpenter, for 3 dollars *less* per hour than it pays Paul and the other carpenters. On Christine's first day of work, Paul and two of his coworkers bait and tease Christine, making it difficult for her to do her job.

Try to imagine why Paul behaved as he did. Rate each of the following explanations for Paul's behavior as not-at-all likely, not likely, somewhat likely, likely, or very likely.

Explanation	Fraction somewhat likely, likely, or very likely[a,b]	Average score[c]
Paul put Christine down because he is afraid that by hiring a woman the company can lower his wage.	.36 (.06)	2.5 (.12)
Paul put Christine down because he does not feel that it is fair that Christine is getting a lower wage.	.13 (.04)	1.7 (.12)
Paul put Christine down because he feels less masculine when a woman is doing the same job.	.84 (.04)	3.4 (.12)
Paul put Christine down because he feels he and his friends will not be able to joke around if a woman is present.	.84 (.04)	3.6 (.12)
Paul put Christine down because he is afraid that other men will tease him if a woman is doing the same job.	.76 (.05)	3.3 (.13)
Paul put Christine down because he is afraid that people will think that his job requires less skill if a woman is doing the same job.	.64 (.06)	2.9 (.12)
Paul put Christine down because he is afraid that if he does not, then his male coworkers will start to tease him.	.80 (.05)	3.4 (.13)
Paul put Christine down because he feels that it is wrong for women to work in a man's job.	.77 (.05)	3.2 (.14)

[a] Sample size is 70 households. Households were selected randomly from the Fremont, CA phonebook.
[b] Standard errors are in parentheses.
[c] Average with not-at-all likely = 1, not likely = 2, somewhat likely = 3, likely = 4, very likely = 5.

This explanation was one of the most popular, and more than three-quarters of the respondents thought that a woman in a man's job 'frequently' or 'almost always' faces such treatment.

Manhood and Insult. For a man, an action may be viewed as an insult which, if left unanswered, impugns his masculinity. As in the example above, an action a_{-j} impacts I_j which may be countered by an action a_j. Psychologists Nisbett and Cohen (1996) have detected such identity concerns in experiments at the University of Michigan. These experiments, they argue, reveal remnants of the white antebellum Southern 'culture of honor' in disparate reactions to insult of males from the U. S. South and North.[15] Their experiments involved variations of the following scenario: an associate of the experimenters bumped subjects in the hallway as they made their way to the experiment. Rather than apologizing, the associate called the subject 'asshole.' Insulted Southerners were more likely than insulted Northerners and control Southerners to fill in subsequent word-completion tests with aggressive words (for example, g-un rather than f-un) and had raised cortisol levels.

Most revealing that the insult affected identity, insulted Southerners were also more likely to fear that the experimenter had a low opinion of their masculinity. They will probably never meet the experimenter or the hallway accomplice again; their encounter in the experiment is otherwise anonymous. Their concern about the experimenter then can only be a concern about how they feel about themselves, about their own sense of identity, as perceived through the 'mirror of the opinions and expectations of others' (Gleitman 1996, p. 343). We see the same psychology in other examples.

Changing Groups or Violating Prescriptions. Because of j's *identification* with others, it may affect j's identity when another person in j's social category violates prescriptions or becomes a different person.[16] A common response is scorn and ostracism, which distances oneself from the maverick and affirms one's own self-image. Such behavior occurs daily in school playgrounds, where children who behave differently are mocked and taunted. Those who seek upward mobility are often teased by their peers, as in *A Hope in the Unseen* (Suskind 1998), which describes Cedric Jennings' progress from one of Washington's most blighted high schools to Brown University. The book opens with Cedric in the high-school chemistry lab, escaping the catcalls of the crowd at an awards assembly. Those who try to change social categories and prescriptions may face similar derision because the change may devalue others' identity, as for the housewives in Betty Friedan's suburb.

Our *third* set of examples demonstrates that to some extent people choose their identity; that is, c_j may be partially a choice. Many women in the United States can choose either to be a career woman or a housewife (see Gerson (1986)). Parents often choose a school—public versus private, secular versus parochial—to influence a child's

---

[15] For a description of this 'culture of honor,' see also Butterfield (1995). 'Gentlemen' reacted to insult by engaging in duels. Those of lower class fought with hands and fists with no holds barred, so that fights extended to such extremities as eyes, ears, and nose.

[16] We discuss the psychology of *identification* and its implications further in the next section.

self-image, identification with others, and behavior.[17] The choice of where to live at college can both reflect and change how students think of themselves. Fraternities, sororities, African-American, or other 'theme'-oriented dorms are all associated with social groups, self-images, and prescribed behavior.[18] The list can continue. The choice for an immigrant to become a citizen is not only a change in legal status but a change in identity. The decision is thus often fraught with ambivalence, anxiety, and even guilt.

Identity 'choice,' however, is very often limited. In a society with racial and ethnic categories, for example, those with nondistinguishing physical features may be able to 'pass' as a member of another group. But others will be constrained by their appearance, voice, or accent.

Our *fourth* set of examples demonstrates the creation and manipulation of social categories C and prescriptions P.[19]

Advertising. Advertising is an obvious attempt to manipulate prescriptions. Marlboro and Virginia Slims advertisements, for example, promote an image of the ideal man or woman complete with the right cigarette.[20]

Professional and Graduate Schools. Graduate and professional programs try to mold students' behavior through a change in identity. As a 'one-L' Harvard Law School student said: ' "They are turning me into someone else. They're making me different" ' (Turow 1977, p. 73). In medicine, theology, the military, and the doctorate, a title is added to a graduate's name, suggesting the change in person.

Political Identity. Politics is often a battle over identity.[21] Rather than take preferences as given, political leaders and activists often strive to change a population's preferences through a change in identity or prescriptions.[22] Again, examples abound. Fascist and populist leaders are infamous for their rhetoric fostering racial and ethnic divisions, with tragic consequences. Symbolic acts and transformed identities spur revolutions. The ringing of the Liberty Bell called on the colonists' identities as Americans. Gandhi's Salt March sparked an Indian national identity. The French Revolution changed subjects into *citizens*, and the Russian Revolution turned them into *comrades*.

---

[17] Catholic schools in the United States at the end of the nineteenth century were a bridge between immigrants' old European identities and their new American selves (Bryk, Lee, and Holland 1993, p. 27). Muslim schools, whose enrollment is currently growing, are partly refuges from public school systems, but parents also choose them to instill in their children a Muslim identity and respect for behavioral prescriptions, and to counter what many view as a distorted image of Muslims and Islam in America (Sachs 1998).

[18] For an anthropological study of identity, fraternities, and prescriptions for brothers' behavior, see Sanday (1990).

[19] The social evolution and construction of group distinctions and social categories is the subject of much research. For a survey, see Wetherell (1996, pp. 219–27).

[20] See de Grazia's (1996) volume for historical studies of advertising and other influences on gender and consumption.

[21] For theory and analysis of political identity, see Norton (1988).

[22] Romer (1994) has considered the possibility that politicians can manipulate voters' emotions, in particular their 'anger,' and thereby affect political outcomes.

III. ECONOMICS AND IDENTITY:
A PROTOTYPE MODEL

In this section we construct a prototype model of economic interaction in a world where identity is based on social difference. In addition to the usual tastes, utility from actions will also depend on identity. Identity will depend on two social categories—Green and Red—and the correspondence of own and others' actions to behavioral prescriptions for their category.

A. *A Prototype Model*

We begin with standard economic motivations for behavior. There are two possible activities, Activity One and Activity Two. There is a population of individuals each of whom has a taste for either Activity One or Two. If a person with a taste for Activity One (Two) undertakes Activity One (Two), she earns utility V. An individual who chooses the activity that does not match her taste earns zero utility. In a standard model of utility maximization, each person would engage in the activity corresponding to her taste.

We next construct identity-based preferences. We suppose that there are two social categories, Green and Red. We assume the simplest division of the population into categories; all persons think of themselves and others as Green.[23] We add simple behavioral prescriptions: a Green should engage in Activity One (in contrast to Reds who engage in Activity Two). Anyone who chooses Activity Two is not a 'true' Green— she would lose her Green identity. This loss in identity entails a reduction in utility of I_s, where the subscript s stands for 'self.' In addition, there are identity externalities. If an i and j are paired, Activity Two on the part of i diminishes j's Green identity. j has a loss in utility I_o, where the subscript o denotes 'other.' After i has committed Activity Two, j may 'respond.' The response restores j's identity at a cost c, while entailing a loss to i in amount L.[24]

Figure 4.1 represents an interaction between an individual with a taste for Activity One ('Person One') and an individual with a taste for Activity Two ('Person Two'). Person One chooses an activity first.[25]

This model can be expressed by ideas central to the psychodynamic theory of personality, found in almost any psychology text.[26] In personality development, psychologists agree on the importance of *internalization* of rules for behavior. Freud called this process the development of the *superego*. Modern scholars disagree with Freud on the importance of psychosexual factors in an individual's development, but they agree on

---

[23] Of course, it is possible that not everyone thinks of herself as Green. We discuss the possibility of different identities and other extensions to the model below.

[24] In Rabin's (1993) theory of fairness, agents are willing to pay to be 'mean' to those who are 'mean' to them. The similarity is probably no coincidence. A likely reason for such a response is preservation of self-image.

[25] Since Person One never chooses Activity Two in a subgame perfect equilibrium, we suppress this branch of the tree.

[26] See, for example, Gleitman (1996, Chapter 17), Thomas (1996), and Breger (1974).

George A. Akerlof

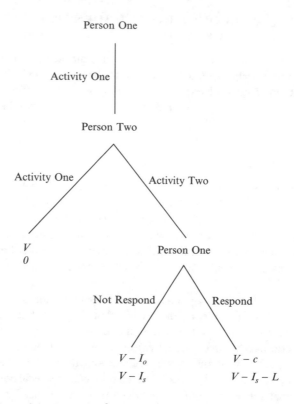

Figure 4.1. *Game tree of interaction between person one and person two.*

the importance of *anxiety* that a person experiences when she violates her internalized rules. One's *identity*, or *ego*, or *self*, must be constantly 'defended against anxiety in order to limit disruption and maintain a sense of unity' (Thomas 1996, p. 284). In terms of our model, Person Two's internalization of prescriptions causes her to suffer a loss in utility of I_s if she chooses Activity Two. To avoid this anxiety, she may refrain from that activity.

Identification is a critical part of this internalization process: a person learns a set of values (prescriptions) such that her actions should conform with the behavior of some people and contrast with that of others. If Person One has internalized prescriptions via such identifications, another person's violation of the prescriptions will cause anxiety for Person One.[27] In our model, this anxiety is modeled as a loss in utility of I_0. Person One's response, in our language, restores her identity, and in terms of the psychology

---

[27] The violation arouses emotions that Person One has repressed in the process of internalizing the behavioral rules. The psychoanalytic theory, then, suggests unconscious motivations for behavior.

textbook relieves her anxiety and maintains her sense of unity. Person One no longer loses I_o, although she does incur c.[28]

B. *Equilibrium Outcomes*

There are four possible subgame perfect outcomes of the game in Figure 4.1.

(i) Person One deters Person Two from engaging in Activity Two, when $c < I_o$ and $I_s < V < I_s + L$.

(ii) Person One responds but does not deter Person Two from engaging in Activity Two, when $c < I_o$ and $I_s + L < V$.

(iii) Person One does not respond, and Person Two engages in Activity Two, when $c > I_o$ and $I_s < V$.

(iv) Person Two does not engage in Activity Two regardless of Person One's response, when $I_s > V$.

This simple model affords three lessons. First, as discussed earlier, the model establishes the connection between economic interactions and the psychology of identity, especially the implications of *identification*. Second, the model allows a comparative static analysis on identity-related parameters. Finally, the elementary assumptions of the model suggest extensions that entail greater realism and further implications of identity for economic interaction.

C. *Comparative Statics*

Comparative statics show how traditional economic policies can affect behavior in this setting. For example, a 'tax' T on the response to Activity Two will affect the equilibrium outcome in case (i). For a sufficiently high tax ($T > I_o - c$), Person One's response to Activity Two is no longer credible, and Person Two will switch from Activity One to Activity Two. This policy benefits Person Two at the expense of Person One. Total utility changes from V to $2V - I_s - I_o$, a positive change if V exceeds $I_s + I_o$.[29] A policy with the opposite effect is a tax on Activity Two itself. This policy would benefit Person One at the expense of Person Two in cases (ii) and (iii). In the first (second) case, a tax in excess of $V - I_s - L$ ($V - I_s$) induces Person Two to desist from Activity Two. This policy would increase total utility, in the first case, if $V < c + I_s + L$, and, in the second case, if $V < I_o + I_s$. Finally, policies may change the prescriptions themselves. A rhetorical campaign, for example, may make Activity Two more loathsome to Greens, leading to higher values of I_s and I_o and greater conformity to the prescriptions. Of course, a different campaign could have the opposite effect.

---

[28] Another basis for the model is the psychology of cognitive dissonance. When Person Two engages in Activity Two, she challenges the validity of Person One's beliefs, and Person One suffers from cognitive dissonance. To remove this dissonance, Person One may act against Person Two.

[29] Of course, such a 'welfare analysis' is subject to the usual caveats concerning interpersonal comparisons and the measurability of utility.

These policies are identity examples of the conflict of the Paretian Liberal (Sen 1970). It is not possible to protect Person One against the externalities caused by Person Two's choice of Activity Two and at the same time protect Person Two from Person One's response. There is a conflict between protecting individuals who engage in certain activities and suppressing these same activities that may cause others discomfort and anxiety.

D. *Extensions to the Model and the Definition of 'Situations'*

Different assumptions about identity, pairings, and information all yield potentially interesting extensions to the model. As in the basic model, individual behavior would depend on what sociologists would call the 'situation'—who is matched with whom and in what context.[30] In the basic model, everyone shared the same identity and prescriptions, but there could be, more realistically, many identities among the population. Activities One and Two could have different meanings for different people. For example, by choosing Activity Two, a person could affirm her identity as a Red. People could also choose—more or less consciously—their identities as well as their activities. These choices could depend on the probability of different matchings, or situations.[31] We will explore this possibility below in our study of poverty and social exclusion.

Furthermore, pairings need not be exogenous, nor tastes and prescriptions known. In fact, much conflict occurs because people with different prescriptions or identities come into contact. To avoid conflict and losses in utility, people may want to match with those who share the same identity or for whom actions have the same meaning. Thus, the matching process itself—the 'situations' in which agents find themselves—can be endogenous, driven by prescriptions and identities. We will see this outcome below in our first, and perhaps most obvious application.

IV. IDENTITY, GENDER, AND ECONOMICS IN THE WORKPLACE

An identity theory of gender in the workplace expands the economic analysis of occupational segregation. As recently as 1970, two-thirds of the United States' female or male labor force would have had to switch jobs to achieve occupational parity. This measure of occupational segregation remained virtually unchanged since the beginning of the century. Yet, in twenty years, from 1970 to 1990, this figure declined to 53 percent.[32] An identity model points to changes in societal notions of male and female as a major cause.

[30] When an individual's identity is associated with multiple social categories, the 'situation' could determine, for example, which categories are most salient.

[31] Choice could also depend on frequency of certain actions. Kuran (1998) considers ethnically symbolic activities in a model where people care about belonging to an ethnic group. When greater overall resources are devoted to an ethnic activity, an individual's marginal utility from this activity can increase, leading to an 'ethnification' cascade.

[32] See Goldin (1990*a*, Chapter 3) for historical measures of occupational segregation. See Blau, Simpson, and Anderson (1998), who use Census Bureau three-digit classifications of occupations, for 1970–1990 figures.

The model we propose captures the 'auras of gender' (Goldin 1990a) that have pervaded the labor market. Occupations are associated with the social categories 'man' and 'woman,' and individual payoffs from different types of work reflect these gender associations. This model can explain patterns of occupational segregation that have eluded previous models. It also directly captures the consequences of the women's movement and affords a new economic interpretation of sex discrimination law.

Identity also provides a microfoundation for earlier models. The 'distaste' of men for working with women, as in the crudest adaptations of racial discrimination models (Becker 1971; Arrow 1972), can be understood as due to loss in male identity when women work in a man's job. Similarly women's assumed lower desire for labor force participation (as in Mincer and Polachek (1974), Bulow and Summers (1986), and Lazear and Rosen (1990)) can be understood as the result of their identity as home-makers.[33]

A. The Model[34]

There are two social categories, 'men' and 'women,' with prescriptions of appropriate activities for each. A firm wishes to hire labor to perform a task. By the initial prescriptions, this task is appropriate only for men; it is a 'man's job.' Relative to a 'woman's job,' women lose identity in amount I_s by performing such work.[35] In this situation, male coworkers suffer a loss I_o.[36] They may relieve their anxiety by taking action against women coworkers,[37] reducing everyone's productivity.

To avoid these productivity losses, the firm may change gender-job associations at a cost. The firm is likely to create a 'woman's job' alongside the 'man's job,' rather than render the whole task gender neutral, when a new job description can piggyback on existing notions of male and female.[38] A well-known historical example illustrates. In the nineteenth century, Horace Mann (as Secretary of Education for Massachusetts) transformed elementary school teaching into a woman's job, arguing that women were 'more mild and gentle,' 'of purer morals,' with 'stronger parental impulses.'[39] Secondary school teaching and school administration remained jobs for men.

The model also indicates why gender-job associations may persist. If associations are sectorwide or economywide, and not firm-specific, perfectly competitive firms will

---

[33] In Bergmann (1974), male employers are averse to hiring women for particular jobs and may collude to keep women out of high paying occupations, reserving the gains for other males. In our theory, the source of occupational segregation is empirically motivated—the maintenance of gender identity on the part of employees.

[34] An appendix with complete specification of the model is available from the authors upon request.

[35] Blau and Ferber (1986, Chapter 7) also discuss the 'psychic costs' incurred by a woman (man) working in a job requiring 'masculine' ('feminine') traits.

[36] Goldin (1990b) considers a model where men lose 'status' when women work on their jobs because the jobs are revealed to be less difficult or physically demanding.

[37] We have already seen such emotions and behavior in Pierce's (1995) law firm and Padavic's (1991) power plant. Schultz (1998) relates a plethora of similar cases.

[38] A firm with market power will earn a further bonus from occupational segregation in the form of wage discrimination.

[39] See quotation of Mann in Sugg (1978, p. 74), and other *Annual Reports* by Mann.

underinvest in new job categories. Benefits would accrue to other firms. In the absence of market power or technological change, a shift in social attitudes and legal intervention would be necessary for changes in employment patterns.

The model easily extends to the decision to participate in the labor force. If women's identity is enhanced by work inside the home, they will have lower labor force attachment than men. Historically, female labor force participation rates, relative to male rates, have been both lower and more cyclically variable.

B. *Implications for Labor Market Outcomes*

This identity model explains employment patterns arising from associations between gender and type of work. These patterns go beyond what can be explained by women's assumed lower labor force attachment as in Mincer and Polachek (1974), where women work in occupations that require little investment in firm-specific human capital.[40]

In our model, women will dominate jobs whose requirements match construed female attributes and inferior social status; men eschew them. Historically, three occupations illustrate: secretaries (97.8 percent female in 1970[41]) have often been called 'office wives,' and elements of sexuality are inscribed in the working relationship (boss = male, secretary = female) (MacKinnon 1979; Pringle 1988). Secretaries are expected to serve their bosses, with deference, and to be attentive to their personal needs (Davies 1982; Kanter 1977; Pierce 1996). Elementary school teachers (83.9 percent female), in contrast to secondary school teachers (49.6 percent female), are supposed to care for young children. Nurses (97.3 percent female) are supposed to be tender and care for patients, as well as be deferential to doctors (Fisher 1995; Williams 1989).

In our model, women do not enter male professions because of gender associations. Historically, many male professions have required similar levels of education and training to female professions and could have been amenable to part-time and intermittent work. Contrast nursing and teaching with accounting and law. All require college degrees and certification, and sometimes have tenure and experience-based pay. Only the very top of these professions have required continuity in employment and full-time work.

Rhetoric surrounding job shifts from male to female further demonstrates the salience of gender-job associations. The recruitment of women into 'men's jobs' during World War II, for example, was accompanied by official propaganda and popular literature picturing women taking on factory work without loss of femininity (Milkman 1987;

---

[40] The empirical evidence for this human capital explanation is mixed (see Blau, Simpson, and Anderson (1998) for review). Other theories based on low workplace attachment of women include Lazear and Rosen (1990), where occupational segregation is a form of statistical discrimination; workers in the male occupations, i.e., with high labor force attachment, are targets for promotion, and those in the female occupations are not. In Bulow and Summers (1986), primary-sector firms must pay women higher wage premiums to prevent them from shirking because women are more likely to quit their jobs. These firms, therefore, prefer hiring men to women.

[41] See Blau, Simpson, and Anderson (1998, Appendix A-1) for these and following figures. All figures here are for 1970.

Honey 1984; Pierson 1986). In addition, the jobs were portrayed as temporary; only the wartime emergency excused the violation of the usual gender prescriptions.

C. *Effects of the Women's Movement*

The model gives a theoretical structure for how the women's movement may have impacted the labor market. The movement's goals included reshaping societal notions of femininity (and masculinity) and removing gender associations from tasks, both in the home and in the workplace. In the model, such changes would decrease women's gains (men's losses) in identity from homemaking, and decrease the identity loss I_s of women (men) working in traditionally men's (women's) jobs, as well as the accompanying externalities I_o. These shifts would increase women's labor force participation and lead to a convergence of male and female job tenure rates. More women (men) would work in previously male (female) jobs.

All these outcomes are observed coincidental with and following the women's movement.[42] Gender-job associations diminished, reflected in changes in language (e.g., firemen became firefighters). In 1998 the median job tenure of employed women over 25 was 0.4 years lower than that of men; in 1968 that gap had been 3.3 years.[43] Changes in sex composition within occupations accounted for the major share of decline in occupational segregation from 1970–1990 (Blau, Simpson, and Anderson, 1998). Of the 45 three-digit Census occupations that were 0.0 percent female in 1970, only one (supervisors: brickmasons, stonemasons, and tile setters) was less than 1 percent female twenty years later.[44] Many incursions of females into male-dominated professions were very large. Consider again accounting and law. In 1970 (1990) females were 24.6 (52.7) percent of auditors and accountants, and 4.5 (24.5) percent of lawyers. Not only did the proportion of women in men's jobs increase, but so did the proportion of men in women's jobs (albeit much less dramatically).[45] Of the triumvirate of explanations for such increases—technology, endowments, and tastes—elimination makes tastes the leading suspect, since there was no dramatic change in technology or endowments that would have caused such increased mixing on the job.[46] Legal initiatives discussed next reflect such changes in tastes.

D. *Gender-Job Associations and Sex Discrimination Law*

Legal interpretations of sex discrimination correspond to earlier economic models as well as our own. Title VII of the Civil Rights Act of 1964 makes it unlawful for an

---

[42] *The Feminine Mystique* was published in 1963, and the National Organization for Women was founded in 1966.

[43] 3.8 years for men versus 3.4 for women in 1998 (United States Department of Labor, 1998); 7.1 years for men versus 3.8 for women in 1968. (*Source:* calculation from Table A, U. S. Department of Labor, Special Labor Force Report 112, *Job Tenure of Workers, January 1968.*) The figures for the two years are not strictly comparable; in 1968 the question asked for the time elapsed since the beginning of the current *job*, in 1998 since the current *employer*. Median male job tenure has also been considerably affected by shifts in the age distribution of the workforce, both because of demographic shifts and also early retirement.

[44] *Source:* Blau, Simpson, and Anderson (1998, Appendix A-1).

[45] See Blau, Simpson, and Anderson (1998, Table 3 and Appendix A-1).

[46] Computers are used intensively in few of the occupations with major changes in mix.

employer to discriminate 'against any individual...with respect to...compensation, terms, conditions...of employment' or 'to (adversely) limit, segregate, or classify his employees...because of...sex.'[47] At its most basic, this law prohibits a discriminatory exercise of 'tastes' against women (analogous to Becker (1971) and Arrow (1972)). Courts also interpret Title VII as outlawing statistical discrimination by sex or criteria correlated with sex, even when women on average lack a desirable job qualification. Discriminatory hiring because of women's presumed lower workplace attachment, as in Lazear and Rosen (1990), was precisely the issue addressed in *Phillips v. Martin-Marietta.*[48]

Our model, where sex discrimination occurs because jobs have gender associations, corresponds to a wider interpretation of Title VII. This interpretation is at the forefront of current legal debate and is supported by a number of precedents. In *Diaz v. Pan American World Airways,*[49] the Court outlawed sex bans in hiring. The airline originally pleaded for their prohibition of male flight attendants because women were better at 'the nonmechanical aspects of the job.' But this association of gender with the job was disallowed on appeal since feminine traits were deemed irrelevant to the 'primary function or services offered' (cited in MacKinnon (1979, p. 180)). *Price Waterhouse v. Hopkins*[50] set a precedent for workers already hired. The plaintiff had been denied a partnership after negative evaluations for her masculine deportment. The Supreme Court ruled that 'an employer who objects to aggressiveness in women but whose positions require this trait places women in an intolerable and impermissible Catch 22' (cited in Wurzburg and Klonoff (1997, p. 182)). Cases have also involved harassment of women working in men's jobs as, in the terminology of our model, male coworkers protect themselves from loss of identity I_o. *Berkman v. City of New York*[51] reinstated a firefighter who had been dismissed because of substandard work performance. The Court ruled that the interference and harassment by her male coworkers made it impossible for her to perform her job adequately (Schultz 1998, p. 1770). This expansive interpretation of a 'hostile work environment,' a category of sexual harassment which is in turn a category of sex discrimination, has been exceptional. Judges have viewed sexual desire as an essential element of sexual harassment. However, Schultz (1998) and Franke (1995) argue that any harassment derived from gender prescriptions has discriminatory implications (as depicted in our model) and are thus violations of Title VII.

[47] 42 U.S.C. §§ 2000e–2000e17 (1982), Sections 703(a)(1) and 703(a)(2).

[48] 442 F. 2d 385 (5th Cir. 1971), *cert. denied,* 404 U.S. 950 (1971). *Griggs v. Duke Power,* 401 U.S. 424 (1971), a race discrimination case, is an important precedent outlawing test results and other criteria correlated with race or gender as employment screens.

[49] 442 F.2d 385 (5th Cir.) *cert. denied,* 404 U. S. 950 (1971).

[50] 490 U. S. 228 (1989).

[51] 580 F. Supp. 226 (E.D.N.Y. 1983), *aff'd,* 755 F. 2d 913 (2d Cir. 1985). *Berkman* followed the expansive view in *McKinney v. Dole,* 765 F. 2d 1129 (D.C. Cir. 1985), that 'any harassment or unequal treatment of an employee or group of employees that would not occur but for the sex of the employee or employees may, if sufficiently patterned or pervasive, comprise an illegal condition of employment under Title VII' (cited in Schultz (1998, p. 1733)).

V. IDENTITY AND THE ECONOMICS OF
EXCLUSION AND POVERTY

This section will consider identity and behavior in poor and socially excluded communities. In an adaptation of the previous model of Greens and Reds, people belonging to poor, socially excluded groups will choose their identity. Greens identify with the dominant culture, while those with Red identity reject it and the subordinate position assigned to those of their 'race,' class, or ethnicity.[52] From the point of view of those with Green identities, Reds are often making bad economic decisions; they might even be described as engaging in self-destructive behavior. Taking drugs, joining a gang, and becoming pregnant at a young age are possible signs of a Red identity. This aspect of behavior has not been explored in previous models, but it is implicit in Wilson's account of black ghetto poverty (1987, 1996). It also is implicit in every study that finds significant dummy variables for 'race,' after adjustment for other measures of socioeconomic status. The Green/Red model of this section offers an explanation for the significance of such dummy variables. Furthermore, it yields a less monolithic view of poverty than current economic theories that emphasize conformity (e.g., Akerlof (1997) and Brock and Durlauf (1995)).

A. *Motivation for Model*

Our model reflects the many ethnographic accounts of 'oppositional' identities in poor neighborhoods. MacLeod's (1987) study of teenagers in a Boston area housing project, for example, contrasts the murderous and alcoholic Hallway Hangers to their obedient and athletic peers, the Brothers. In *Learning to Labour* Willis (1977) describes the antagonism between the unruly 'lads' and the dutiful 'earholes' in a working-class English secondary school. Similarly, Whyte's (1943) description of Boston's Italian North End circa 1940 contrasts the Corner Boys to the College Boys. Yet earlier, turn-of-the century accounts of the Irish in the United States contrast the 'lace curtain' Irish of poor districts to their neighbors (see, e.g., Miller (1985)).

Our model further evokes the psychological effects of social exclusion in the colonial experience analyzed by Bhabha (1983) and Fanon (1967), and in the context of African-Americans in the United States by Anderson (1990), Baldwin (1962), Clark (1965), DuBois (1965), Frazier (1957), Hannerz (1969), Rainwater (1970), Wilson (1987, 1996), and others. In these settings, individuals from particular groups can never fully fit the ideal type, the ideal 'Green,' of the dominant culture. Some in excluded groups may try to 'pass' or integrate with the dominant group, but they do so with ambivalence and limited success.[53] A series of autobiographies tells of the pain and

---

[52] Much literature on identity and social exclusion argues that dominant groups define themselves vis-à-vis 'other(s),' and members of the dominant (excluded) groups benefit (lose)—materially and psychologically—from the differentiation. For discussion of different approaches to the study of social difference and racism, see Wetherell (1996).

[53] Indeed, the word *passing* itself is pejorative and evokes a penumbra of reactions to being other than one's 'true' self.

anger of discovering that one is not really 'Green.' Former *New York Times* editor Mel Watkins (1998) titles the chapter on his freshman year at Colgate as 'stranger in a strange land.' Gandhi (1966), Fanon (1967), Fulwood (1996), Staples (1994), and Rodriguez (1982) all relate strikingly similar experiences of perceived or real rejection and alienation. This social exclusion may create a conflict: how to work within the dominant culture without betraying oneself. As Jill Nelson (1993, p. 10) explains her exhaustion after a long day of interviewing for a job at *The Washington Post*:

I've also been doing the standard Negro balancing act when it comes to dealing with white folks, which involves sufficiently blurring the edges of my being so that they don't feel intimidated, while simultaneously holding on to my integrity. There is a thin line between Uncle-Tomming and Mau-Mauing. To fall off that line can mean disaster. On one side lies employment and self-hatred; on the other, the equally dubious honor of unemployment with integrity.

These reactions, it must be emphasized, reflect how dominant groups define themselves by the exclusion of others. The creation and evolution of such social differences are the subject of much historical research. Said (1978) documents the emergence of the Western idea of the 'Oriental,' a concept that had significant implications for colonialism. In the United States Roediger (1991) and other historians show how workers of European descent in the nineteenth century increasingly were defined as 'white.' Prior to Emancipation, this identity evoked the contrast between white freedom and African-American enslavement. In the model we construct, the key interaction is between such social differences and the adoption of oppositional identities by those in excluded groups.

Lack of economic opportunity may also contribute to the choice of an oppositional identity. Wilson (1987, 1996) underscores the relation between the decline in remunerative unskilled jobs, the loss of self-respect by men who cannot support their families, and the rise in inner city crime and drug abuse. This process is illustrated in microcosm by 'Richard' in *Tally's Corner* (Liebow 1967). Unable to find decent-paying work, he abandoned his family and joined Tally's group of idlers on the street corner. By adopting a different identity, Richard no longer suffered the guilt of a failed provider.[54]

Red activities have negative pecuniary externalities. Richard's wife and children had to find alternative means of support. The prime goal of the 'lads' in Willis' secondary school was to get a 'laff,' through vandalism, picking fights, and returning drunk to school from the local pub. Running a school with lads is difficult. The situation corresponds to the externalities in Bénabou's (1993, 1996) models of high schooling costs in poor neighborhoods. Further externalities accrue from drug dealing, crime, and other 'pathological' behavior.

In our model, there are also identity-based externalities. A Red is angered by a Green's complicity with the dominant culture, while a Green is angered by a Red's 'breaking the rules.' Again consider Willis' lads and earholes. As the lads define

---

[54] See Montgomery (1994) for an interpretation of Richard's behavior in terms of cognitive dissonance.

themselves in contrast to the earholes, the earholes define themselves in contrast to the lads. The earholes are even more proestablishment than the teachers—feeling that the teachers should be stricter. The lads, in turn, bait the earholes. This situation is just one (relatively tame) example of how interaction between the two groups generates antagonism on both sides.

B. *Identity Model of Poverty and Social Exclusion*

As in the prototype model, there are two activities, One and Two. Activity One can be thought of as 'working' and Activity Two as 'not working.' There is a large community, normalized to size one, of individuals. The economic return to Activity One for individual i is v_i which we assume is uniformly distributed between zero and one, to reflect heterogeneity in the population and to ensure interior solutions. The economic return to Activity Two is normalized to zero.

As for identity, there are two social categories, Green and Red. A Green suffers a loss in identity r, representing the extent to which someone from this community is not accepted by the dominant group in society. Those with the less adaptive Red identity do not suffer this loss. Behavioral prescriptions say that Greens (Reds) should engage in Activity One (Two). Thus, a Green (Red) loses identity from Activity Two (One) in amount $I_s^G(I_s^R)$.[55] Because Reds reject the dominant Green culture, they are also likely to have lower economic returns to Activity One than Greens.[56] A Red individual i will only earn $v_i - a$ from Activity One, as well as suffer the loss I_s^R. There are also identity externalities when Greens and Reds meet. A Green (Red) suffers a loss $I_o^G(I_o^R)$. In addition, Reds who have chosen Activity Two impose a pecuniary externality k on those who have chosen Activity One.

Each person i chooses an identity and activity, given the choices of everyone else in the community. We assume that people cannot modify their identity or activity for each individual encounter. Rather, individuals choose an identity and activity to maximize expected payoffs, given the probabilities of encounters with Greens who choose Activity One, Greens who choose Two, Reds who choose One, and Reds who choose Two.

C. *Equilibria and Interpretation*

Equilibria of this model show how social interaction within the community and social exclusion from the dominant group determine the prevalence of Red identities and Activity Two behavior.[57] An *All-Green Equilibrium* (everyone is Green and engages in

---

[55] We discuss below the possibility of a Red identity where individuals can both reject the dominant culture and at the same time do not lose I_s^R from Activity One.

[56] Wilson (1996, Chapter 5) documents the difficulties that employers perceive in hiring employees from the inner city. From the vantage point of our model, it does not matter whether the perceived problems, parameterized by a, reflect real differences in productivity or those that are merely imagined because of the mismatch of the employers' and the employees' attitudes.

[57] Full analysis of the model is available from the authors upon request. In the analysis we make the simplifying assumption that $I_s^G > k$ so that anyone who chooses a Green identity will choose Activity One. We also assume that all parameters are strictly positive and less than unity and that $I_s^R + a + k < 1$.

Activity One) exists, if and only if the loss in Green identity, r, from exclusion from the dominant group is smaller than the difficulty of being Red in a community of Greens, I_o^R. Figure 4.2 shows this condition in the area above the 45° line from the origin. For higher levels of r, equilibria must involve some in the community adopting a Red identity. The nonexistence of the All-Green equilibrium reveals a difference in the predictions of this model and previous models of behavior in poor neighborhoods. Here, social exclusion ($r > 0$) will lead some people in the community to adopt an oppositional identity and Activity Two behavior, even in the absence of conformity-generating externalities (i.e., $I_o^R = I_o^G = k = 0$).

In a *Mixed Equilibrium* of our model, some in the community choose Activity One and a Green identity, but others choose Activity Two and Red identities. This equilibrium arises for intermediate levels of r (in the area between the two upward-sloping lines in Figure II).

The equilibrium adoption of Red identities and Activity Two behavior captures the self-destructive behavior of the underclass central to sociological study, but contrary to standard economic thinking. Rainwater (1970, p. 3) summarized his classic study of ghetto poverty: 'white cupidity creates structural conditions highly inimical to basic

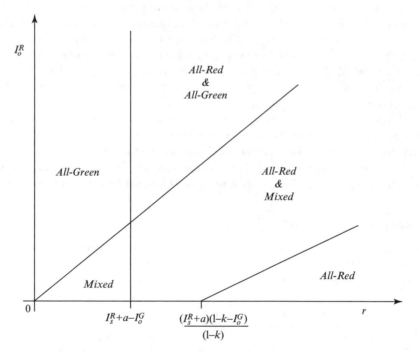

Figure 4.2. *Equilibria in model of poverty and social exclusion.*
This figure shows ranges of parameter values for three different equilibria: All-Green where everyone is Green and chooses Activity One; Mixed where Greens choose Activity One and Reds choose Activity Two; All-Red where everyone is Red and some choose Activity One and others choose Activity Two.

social adaptation to which Negroes adapt by social and personal responses which serve to sustain the individual in his punishing world but also to generate aggressiveness toward the self and others which results in suffering directly inflicted by Negroes on themselves and on others.' While Activity One is maximizing to someone with a Green identity, it is not maximizing to someone with a Red identity. The 'self-destructive' Red behavior is not the result of individual 'irrationality,' but instead derives from low economic endowments and a high degree of social exclusion.

Comparative statics of the mixed equilibrium captures Wilson's (1987, 1996) analysis of ghetto poverty. An out-migration of the middle class (those with high returns v_i in the model) will result in further adoption of Red identities among the remaining population. Also, when work disappears, there will be a downward shift in distribution of payoffs from Activity One. This shift will also increase the incidence of Activity Two and Red identities.

In an *All-Red Equilibrium*, some individuals choose Activity One and conform with the dominant group in terms of economic behavior, but all choose an oppositional Red identity. This equilibrium arises when a high loss from being Green in an all-Red community, I_o^G, complements high levels of social exclusion, r (in the area to the right of the vertical line in Figure 4.2).[58] This equilibrium is also achieved with a low value of I_s^R and, thus, provides an interpretation of social movements that may arise from exclusion. Some separatist leaders, such as Malcolm X and Louis Farrakhan, have advanced an oppositional Red identity but at the same time have tried to change associated prescriptions, resulting in a lower I_s^R. In these movements, Activity One does not imply complicity with the dominant group. Rather, self-restraint, education, and employment are a means for individual advancement and community liberation.

D. *Further Lessons from the Model*

The model and its solution also afford interpretations of policies designed to reduce poverty and the effects of social exclusion.

First, the model indicates why residential Job Corps programs may succeed while other training programs fail (Stanley, Katz, and Krueger 1998). According to the model, taking trainees out of their neighborhoods would eliminate, at least for a time, the negative effects of interaction with those with Red identities. Moreover, being in a different location may reduce a trainee's direct loss r from being Green and pursuing Activity One. That is, this loss may be both individual-specific and situational, and leaving a poor neighborhood is likely to generate a lower r than otherwise. In a somewhat controlled experiment, the U. S. government tried to save money with JOBSTART, which preserved many of the features of Job Corps except the expensive housing of trainees. Follow-up studies of JOBSTART show little or no improvement in employment or earnings.[59]

---

[58] It overlaps the regions of other equilibria because this condition is independent of I_o^R, unlike those for the above equilibria where a Red would suffer the loss from interacting with Greens.

[59] The Center for Employment and Training in San Jose was the one remarkable exception.

Second, the model affords an interpretation of different education initiatives for minority students. Like Job Corps, the Central Park East Secondary School (CPESS) in East Harlem may succeed because it separates Green students from Red students. Students, for example, must apply to the school, indicating their and their parents' willingness to adopt its rules (see Fliegel (1993) and Meier (1995) for this and other details). Another interpretation of CPESS and other successes (e.g., Comer (1980) in New Haven) parallels the logic of the all-Red equilibrium where some people nonetheless pursue Activity One. The schools take measures to reduce the loss in identity of Red students, I_s^R, in activities such as learning Standard English.[60] Delpit's (1995) award-winning book *Other People's Children* proposes numerous ways to reduce the alienation that minority students may experience in school.

Finally, the model illuminates a set of issues in the affirmative action debate. Much of this debate concerns the success or failure of specific programs (see, e.g., Dickens and Kane (1996)). Yet, more is at stake. The rhetoric and symbolism of affirmative action may affect the level of social exclusion r. On the one hand, Loury (1995) argues that portraying African-Americans as victims, a portrayal necessary to retain affirmative action programs, is costly to blacks. In terms of the model, such rhetoric will increase r and the adoption of Red identities. On the other hand, affirmative action will decrease r, to the extent it is seen as an apology for previous discrimination and an invitation for black admission to the dominant culture. Reversal of affirmative action would negate this effect. To cite a recent example, our analysis suggests that removing affirmative action admissions criteria at the University of California and University of Texas Law Schools could have behavioral implications that far exceed the impact on applicants.

The identity model of exclusion, then, explains why legal equality may not be enough to eliminate racial disparities.[61] If African-Americans choose to be Red because of exclusion and if whites perpetuate such exclusions, even in legal ways, there can be a permanent equilibrium of racial inequality. The negative externalities and their consequences, however, would disappear when the community is fully integrated into the dominant culture, so that $r = a = 0$, and everyone in the community adopts a Green identity. This, of course, is the American ideal of the melting pot, or the new ideal of a mosaic where difference can be maintained within the dominant culture.

VI. IDENTITY AND THE ECONOMICS OF THE HOUSEHOLD

An identity model of the household, unlike previous models, predicts an asymmetric division of labor between husbands and wives. Theories based on comparative advantage (e.g., Becker (1965) and Mincer (1962)) predict that whoever works more outside

---

[60] Ogbu (1997) and Delpit (1995) find that African-American students in poor neighborhoods may be ambivalent about learning Standard English, whose use may be construed as 'acting white.'

[61] We see this distinction in the different conclusions of two recent studies of U. S. race relations. Thernstrom and Thernstrom (1997) urge an end to affirmative action, making the case that attitudes of whites toward blacks as well as the legal opportunities for blacks have changed since *The American Dilemma* (Myrdal 1944). In contrast, Shipler (1997) points out the many ways in which African-Americans and whites feel uncomfortable with each other and how blacks are still seen as different and not fully accepted.

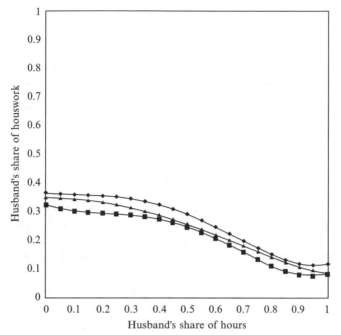

Predicted values from tobit estimation.
Quartic in husband's share of hours.
Full, demeaned controls.

—◆— No children —■— Youngest child 6-13 —▲—Youngest child 1-5

Figure 4.3. *Husbands' share of housework hours versus their share of outside work hours.*

the home will work less inside the home, whether it be the husband or the wife. Yet, the data we present below indicate a gender asymmetry. When a wife works more hours outside the home, she still undertakes a larger share of the housework.

Hochschild's (1990) study *The Second Shift* reveals the details of such asymmetries. One of the couples in her study found an ingenious way to share the housework. 'Evan Holt,' a furniture salesman, took care of the lower half of the house (i.e., the basement and his tools). His wife 'Nancy,' a full-time licensed social worker, took care of the upper half. She took care of the child. He took care of the dog.

Quantitative evidence from Hochschild's sample and our data analysis suggest that the Holts conform to a national pattern. Figure 4.3 shows the low average of husband's share of housework and its low elasticity with respect to their share of outside work hours. The figure plots shares of housework reported by married men[62] in the Panel Study of Income Dynamics,[63] as computed from answers to the question(s): 'About how much time do you (your wife) spend on housework in an average week? I mean time

[62] Men's reports of housework shares matched almost exactly women's reports in Preston's (1997) study of 1,700 scientists.
[63] The unit of observation is a couple-year for the years 1983 to 1992. Couples were included in a given year, if they were married, neither member was retired, neither member was disabled, the couple had positive work hours, positive earnings, and positive hours of housework. In addition, they were only included if there

spent cooking, cleaning, and doing other work around the house?' The intent of the
question was to exclude child care. The figure plots men's share of housework as a
fourth-order polynomial of their share of outside hours, for households by age of
youngest child. When men do all the outside work, they contribute on average about
10 percent of housework. But as their share of outside work falls, their share of
housework rises to no more than 37 percent. As shown in the figure the presence of
children of different ages makes a small difference to the function.[64] Similar results
obtain when the independent variable is shares of income rather than shares of outside
work hours.

Existing theories do not predict this asymmetry. Consider the following variant based
on comparative advantage. Husband and wife both have the same utility function, which
is increasing in quantity of a household public good that derives from their joint
labor.[65] Utility is decreasing in own labor inputs in outside and home production.[66]
We assume equal bargaining power, so that each marriage partner enjoys the same level
of utility.[67] With this framework, returns to specialization explain the observed division
of labor when a wife has a comparative advantage in home production. Women who put
in less than half of the outside work hours put in more than half the housework, as seen
in the right-hand side of the graph of Figure 4.3. But this model is inconsistent with the
left-hand side of the graph.

Identity considerations can explain the high shares of housework of wives who
undertake a large share of outside work hours. Add to the above model two social
categories, 'men' and 'women.' Prescriptions dictate that 'men' should not do 'women's
work' in the home and 'men' should earn more than their wives. Hochschild's interviews
suggest that many men, and some women, hold these prescriptions. In the amended

were complete data from both members on earnings, work hours, housework hours, and number of children.
The final sample had slightly more than 29,000 couple-years of observations. We define a husband's share of
housework, $hswk$, as his share of the total performed by the couple. Thus, we capture the division of labor even
in households that hire outside workers. We estimate the following Tobit equation:
$hswk = a + \Sigma_{i=1, 2, 3}\{b_{1i}h_i + b_{2i}h_i^2 + b_{3i}h_i^3 + b_{4i}h_i^4\}+$ error, where h_i is the husband's share of outside
hours worked if in group i. The summation ($i = 1, 2, 3$) runs over three types of household: with no children
or youngest child over age 13, with youngest child 0 to 5, and with youngest child 6 to 13. Controls were
included for age of husband, and wife relative to population average, log of total income, and also total hours
of housework. Results were robust to different specifications and estimators, and substitution of share of
earnings for share of hours worked. The equations and confidence intervals are available upon request.

[64] Hersch and Stratton (1994) use the PSID to study whether husbands' higher wage incomes account for
their lower shares of housework. The estimation here, in contrast, evaluates the asymmetry in the relationship
between husbands' share of income and their shares of housework, and wives' shares of income and
housework.

[65] The public goods aspect of a marriage follows Lundberg and Pollak (1993), where the contributions of
each spouse are in 'separate spheres' that reflect gender roles. The first bargaining models of the household are
due to Manser and Brown (1980) and McElroy and Horney (1981).

[66] Utility of the wife is $U_f = U_f(\bar{g}, h_f^h, h_f^o)$, where $\bar{g}$ is the household public good, produced by both home
and outside labor, h_f^h is the wife's hours of housework, and h_f^o is her outside work. The husband's utility
function is, similarly, $U_m = U_m(\bar{g}, h_m^h, h_m^o)$, where U_f and U_m are assumed to be the same functions.

[67] We assume that a household maximizes the sum of utilities subject to the condition $U_f = U_m$. When
bargaining power derives from earning capabilities and control of financial resources, as assumed by Hersch
and Stratton (1994) and others, it only reinforces the conclusion that whoever works more outside the home
works less inside.

model, the husband loses identity when he does housework and when his wife earns more than half the household income. Equality of utility is restored when the wife undertakes more housework than her husband. Hochschild reports that in the 'Tanagawa' household, for example, 'Nina' earned more than half the family income, but she worked more than 'Peter' at home to assuage his unease with the situation. Eventually, she quit her job.

VII. CONCLUSION

This paper considers how identity affects economic outcomes. Following major themes in psychology and sociology, identity in our models is based on social difference. A person's sense of self is associated with different social categories and how people in these categories should behave. This simple extension of the utility function could greatly expand our understanding of economic outcomes. In a world of social difference, one of the most important economic decisions that an individual makes may be the type of person to be. Limits on this choice would also be critical determinants of economic behavior, opportunity, and well-being.

Identity affects economic behavior in our models through four avenues. First, identity changes the payoffs from one's own actions. We capture this possibility by a value I_s in our models. In our study of gender in the workplace, for example, a woman working in a 'man's' job suffers a loss in utility, affecting the labor supply. Second, identity changes the payoffs of others' actions. We capture this externality by a value I_o in our models. A 'Red' in our poverty model, for example, is harmed by a member of his own community who complies with the dominant culture. Third, the choice, or lack thereof, of different identities affects an individual's economic behavior. In our poverty model, while individuals could choose between Green or Red, they could never be a 'true' Green. The greater the extent of this social exclusion, the greater the possibility of equilibria in which individuals eschew remunerative activities. Finally, the social categories and behavioral prescriptions can be changed, affecting identity-based preferences. This possibility expanded the scope of employment policy in our model of gender in the workplace and of education policy in our study of social exclusion.

This paper has only scratched the surface of the economic implications of identity. A first tack in future research would be continued analysis of particular settings. Identity is likely to affect economic outcomes, for example, in areas of political economy, organizational behavior, demography, the economics of language, violence, education, consumption and savings behavior, retirement decisions, and labor relations.[68] As in this paper, models that incorporate well-documented existing social categories and prescriptions could yield new results. A second tack in this agenda is comparative, examining identity across space and time.[69] Researchers, for example, could consider why notions of 'class' or 'race' vary across countries; why might gender and racial integration vary across industries; what might explain the rise and fall of ethnic tensions. Such

---

[68] See a previous version of the paper for short versions of many of these applications.
[69] We are grateful to an anonymous referee for this list of comparative studies.

comparative studies would be a fruitful way to explore the formation of identity-based preferences.[70]

In peroration, this paper explores how to incorporate identity into economic models of behavior. Many standard psychological and sociological concepts—*self-image, ideal type, in-group and out-group, social category, identification, anxiety, self-destruction, self-realization, situation*—fit naturally in our framework, allowing an expanded analysis of economic outcomes. This framework is then perhaps one way to incorporate many different nonpecuniary motivations for behavior into economic reasoning, with considerable generality and a common theme.

UNIVERSITY OF CALIFORNIA AT BERKELEY AND THE BROOKINGS INSTITUTION
UNIVERSITY OF MARYLAND AT COLLEGE PARK

References

Akerlof, George A., 'The Economics of Caste and of the Rat Race and Other Woeful Tales,' *Quarterly Journal of Economics*, XC (November, 1976), 599–617.

——, 'Social Distance and Social Decisions,' *Econometrica*, LXV (September 1997), 1005–1027.

Altenbaugh, Richard J., *The Teacher's Voice: A Social History of Teaching in Twentieth-Century America* (London: The Falmer Press, 1992).

Anderson, Elijah, *StreetWise: Race, Class, and Change in an Urban Community* (Chicago: University of Chicago Press, 1990).

Andreoni, James, 'Giving with Impure Altruism: Applications to Charity and Ricardian Equivalence,' *Journal of Political Economy*, XCVII (December 1989), 1447–1458.

Arrow, Kenneth J., 'Models of Job Discrimination' and 'Some Mathematical Models of Race Discrimination in the Labor Market,' in Anthony H. Pascal, ed., *Racial Discrimination in Economic Life* (Lexington, MA: D. C. Heath, 1972).

Baldwin, James, *The Fire Next Time* (New York: The Dial Press, 1962).

Becker, Gary S., 'A Theory of the Allocation of Time,' *Economic Journal*, LXXV (September 1965), 493–517.

——, *The Economics of Discrimination*, second edition (Chicago: University of Chicago Press, 1971).

Bénabou, Roland, 'Workings of a City: Location, Education, and Production,' *Quarterly Journal of Economics*, CVIII (August 1993), 619–652.

——, 'Heterogeneity, Stratification, and Growth: Macroeconomic Implications of Community Structure and School Finance,' *American Economic Review*, LXXXVI (June 1996), 584–609.

Bergmann, Barbara R., 'Occupational Segregation, Wages and Profits When Employers Discriminate by Race or Sex,' *Eastern Economics Journal*, I (1974), 103–110.

Bhabha, Homi, 'Difference, Discrimination, and the Discourse of Colonialism,' in *The Politics of Theory*, F. Barker, ed. (London: Colchester, 1983).

---

[70] Some scholars have studied the formation of identity-based preferences from principles of optimization. Theories of evolutionary psychology, for example, posit that hostility toward 'outsiders' might be inherent to human nature as a result of an evolutionary process; survival depends on cooperation with insiders and hostility toward outsiders. Another functional explanation of identity derives from social cognition theory: stereotypes summarize information and compensate for human beings' limited cognitive abilities. (See Wetherell (1998, pp. 186–197) for review.) These theories, however, may find it difficult to accommodate the complexity of social categories and prescriptions and the variety of social categories across societies and across time.

Blau, Francine D., and Maríanne A. Ferber, *The Economics of Women, Men, and Work* (Englewood Cliffs, NJ: Prentice-Hall, 1986).

——, Patricia Simpson, and Deborah Anderson, 'Continuing Progress? Trends in Occupational Segregation in the United States over the 1970's and 1980's,' NBER Working Paper No. 6716, 1998.

Bowles, Samuel, and Herbert Gintis, 'Optimal Parochialism: The Dynamics of Trust and Exclusion in Communities,' mimeo, University of Massachusetts at Amherst, 1997.

Breger, Louis, *From Instinct to Identity: The Development of Personality* (Englewood Cliffs, NJ: Prentice-Hall, 1974).

Brock, William A., and Steven N. Durlauf, 'Discrete Choice with Social Interactions I: Theory,' NBER Working Paper No. 5291, 1995.

Brown, Roger W., *Social Psychology: The Second Edition* (New York: The Free Press, 1986).

Bryk, Anthony S., Valerie E. Lee, and Peter B. Holland, *Catholic Schools and the Common Good* (Cambridge, MA: Harvard University Press, 1993).

Bulow, Jeremy I., and Lawrence H. Summers, 'A Theory of Dual Labor Markets with Application to Industrial Policy, Discrimination and Keynesian Unemployment,' *Journal of Labor Economics*, IV (July 1986), 376–415.

Bumiller, Elisabeth, *May You Be the Mother of a Hundred Sons: A Journey Among the Women of India* (New York: Random House, 1990).

Butterfield, Fox, *All God's Children: The Bosket Family and the American Tradition of Violence* (New York: Avon Books, 1995).

Clark, Kenneth, *Dark Ghetto* (New York: Harper & Row, 1965).

Cole, Harold L., George J. Mailath, and Andrew Postlewaite, 'Social Norms, Savings Behavior and Growth,' *Journal of Political Economy*, C (December 1992), 1092–1125.

Comer, James P., *School Power: Implications of an Intervention Project* (New York: The Free Press, 1980).

Davies, Margery, *Women's Place Is at the Typewriter: Office Work and Office Workers, 1870–1930* (Philadelphia, PA: Temple University Press, 1982).

Davis, Fred, *The Nursing Profession: Five Sociological Essays* (New York: John Wiley & Sons, 1966).

de Grazia, Victoria, *The Sex of Things: Gender and Consumption in Historical Perspective* (Berkeley: University of California Press, 1996).

Delpit, Lisa, *Other People's Children: Cultural Conflict in the Classroom* (New York: The New Press, 1995).

Dickens, William T., and Thomas J. Kane, 'Racial and Ethnic Preference in College Admissions,' *Brookings Policy Brief No. 9* (Washington, DC: The Brookings Institution, November 1996).

Du Bois, William E. B., *The Souls of Black Folk* (Greenwich, CT: Fawcett Publications, 1965).

Elster, Jon, *The Cement of Society: A Study of Social Order* (Cambridge: Cambridge University Press, 1989).

Fanon, Frantz, *Black Skin, White Masks* (New York: Grove Press, 1967).

Fisher, Sue, *Nursing Wounds: Nurse Practitioners/Doctors/Women Patients/And the Negotiation of Meaning* (New Brunswick, NJ: Rutgers University Press, 1995).

Fliegel, Seymour, *Miracle in East Harlem: The Fight for Choice in Public Education* (New York: Random House, 1993).

Folbre, Nancy, *Who Pays for the Kids: Gender and the Structures of Constraint* (New York: Routledge, 1994).

Franke, Katherine M., 'The Central Mistake of Sex Discrimination Law: The Disaggregation of Sex from Gender,' *University of Pennsylvania Law Review*, CXLIV (November 1995), 1–99.

Frazier, Franklin, *The Black Bourgeoisie: The Rise of the New Middle Class in the United States* (New York: The Free Press, 1957).

Friedman, Milton, *Essays in Positive Economics* (Chicago: University of Chicago Press, 1953).

Fulwood III, Sam, *Waking from the Dream: My Life in the Black Middle Class* (New York: Doubleday, 1996).

Gandhi, Mohandas, *Autobiography* (London: Jonathon Cape, 1966).

Gerson, Kathleen, *Hard Choices: How Women Decide about Work, Career, and Motherhood* (Berkeley, CA: University of California Press, 1986).

Gleitman, Henry, *Basic Psychology* (New York: Norton, 1996).

Goldin, Claudia, *Understanding the Gender Gap: An Economic History of American Women* (New York: Oxford University Press, 1990a).

——, 'A Pollution Theory of Discrimination,' mimeo, Harvard University, 1990b.

Goodson, Ivor F., and Andy Hargreaves, *Teachers' Professional Lives* (London: The Falmer Press, 1996).

Hannerz, Ulf, *Soulside: Inquiries into Ghetto Culture and Community* (New York: Columbia University Press, 1969).

Hersch, Joni, and Leslie S. Stratton, 'Housework, Wages, and the Division of Housework Time for Employed Spouses,' *American Economic Association Papers and Proceedings*, LXXXIV (May 1994), 120–125.

Hochschild, Arlie, with Anne Machung, *The Second Shift* (New York: Avon, 1990).

Honey, Maureen, *Creating Rosie the Riveter: Class, Gender, and Propaganda during World War II* (Amherst: University of Massachusetts Press, 1984).

Huang, Peter H., and Ho Mou Wu, 'More Order without Law: A Theory of Social Norms and Organizational Cultures,' *Journal of Law, Economics, & Organization*, X (October 1994), 390–406.

Kandori, Michihiro, 'Social Norms and Community Enforcement,' *Review of Economic Studies*, LXIX (January 1992), 63–80.

Kanter, Rosabeth Moss, *Men and Women of the Corporation* (New York: Basic Books, 1977).

Kevane, Michael, 'Can There Be an "Identity Economics"?' mimeo, Harvard Academy for International and Area Studies, 1994.

Khatibi, Abdelkebir, *La Blessure du Nom Propre* (Paris: Denoël, 1986).

Khattab, Hind, 'Women's Perceptions of Sexuality in Rural Giza,' Reproductive Health Working Group, The Population Council, Monographs in Reproductive Health No. 1, 1996.

Kuran, Timur, 'Ethnic Norms and Their Transformation through Reputation Cascades,' *Journal of Legal Studies*, XXVII (Summer 1998, Part 2), 623–659.

Landa, Janet T., *Trust, Ethnicity, and Identity: Beyond the New Institutional Economics of Trading Networks* (Ann Arbor: University of Michigan Press, 1994).

Lazear, Edward P., and Sherwin Rosen, 'Male-Female Wage Differentials in Job Ladders,' *Journal of Labor Economics*, VIII (January 1990), S106–S123.

Levine, Judith A., 'It's a Man's Job, or So They Say: The Production of Sex Segregation in Occupations,' mimeo, Department of Sociology, Northwestern University, 1995.

Liebow, Elliott, *Tally's Corner: A Study of Negro Streetcorner Men* (Boston: Little-Brown, 1967).

Loewenstein, George, 'Because It Is There: The Challenge of Mountaineering...for Utility Theory,' mimeo, Carnegie Mellon University, 1998.

Loury, Glenn C., *One by One from the Inside Out* (New York: The Free Press, 1995).

Lundberg, Shelly, and Robert A. Pollak, 'Separate Spheres Bargaining and the Marriage Market,' *Journal of Political Economy*, CI (December 1993), 988–1010.

MacKinnon, Catharine A., *Sexual Harassment of Working Women* (New Haven, CT: Yale University Press, 1979).

MacLeod, Jay, *Ain't No Makin' It: Leveled Aspirations in a Low-Income Neighborhood* (Boulder, CO: Westview Press, 1987).

Manser, Marilyn, and Murray Brown, 'Marriage and Household Decision Making: A Bargaining Analysis,' *International Economic Review*, XXI (February 1980), 31–44.

Mason, Karen Oppenheim, 'Commentary: Strober's Theory of Occupational Sex Segregation,' Chapter 9 in Barbara Reskin, ed., *Sex Segregation in the Workplace* (Washington, DC: National Academy Press, 1984).

McElroy, Marjorie B., and Mary Jean Horney, 'Nash Bargained Household Decisions,' *International Economic Review*, XXII (June 1981), 559–583.

Meier, Deborah, *The Power of Their Ideas: Lessons for America from a Small School in Harlem* (Boston, MA: Beacon Press, 1995).

Milkman, Ruth, *Gender at Work: The Dynamics of Job Segregation by Sex during World War II* (Urbana: University of Illinois Press, 1987).

Miller, Kerby A., 'Assimilation and Alienation: Irish Emigrants' Responses to Industrial America,' in P. J. Drudy, ed., *The Irish in America: Emigration, Assimilation and Impact* (Cambridge, UK: Cambridge University Press, 1985).

Mincer, Jacob, and Solomon Polachek, 'Family Investments in Human Capital: Earnings of Women,' *Journal of Political Economy*, LXXXII (March 1974), S76–S108.

—— 'Labor Force Participation of Married Women: A Study of Labor Supply,' in *Aspects of Labor Economics*, Conference No. 14 of the Universities-National Bureau Committee for Economic Research (Princeton, NJ: Princeton University Press, 1962).

Montgomery, James D., 'Revisiting *Tally's Corner*: Mainstream Norms, Cognitive Dissonance and Underclass Behavior,' *Rationality and Society*, VI (1994), 462–488.

——, 'Towards a Role-Theoretic Conception of Embeddedness,' mimeo, London School of Economics, 1997.

Mottus, Jane E., *New York Nightingales: The Emergence of the Nursing Profession at Bellevue and New York Hospital 1850–1920* (Ann Arbor: University of Michigan Press, 1981).

Myrdal, Gunnar, *An American Dilemma: The Negro Problem and American Democracy* (New York: Harper and Row, 1944).

Nelson, Jill, *Volunteer Slavery: An Authentic Negro Experience* (New York: Penguin, 1993).

Nisbett, Richard E., and Dov Cohen, *Culture of Honor: The Psychology of Violence in the South* (Boulder, CO: Westview Press, 1996).

Norton, Anne, *Reflections on Political Identity* (Baltimore, MD: The Johns Hopkins University Press, 1988).

Ogbu, John U., 'Beyond Language: Ebonics, Proper English and Identity in a Black American Speech Community,' mimeo, University of California at Berkeley, Department of Anthropology, 1997.

Okuno-Fujiwara, M., and Andrew Postlewaite, 'Social Norms and Random Matching Games,' *Games and Economic Behavior*, IX (April 1995), 79–109.

Padavic, Irene, 'The Re-Creation of Gender in a Male Workplace,' *Symbolic Interaction*, XIV (1991), 279–294.

Pierce, Jennifer, *Gender Trials: Emotional Lives in Contemporary Law Firms* (Berkeley: University of California Press, 1995).

Pierson, Ruth Roach, *They're Still Women After All: The Second World War and Canadian Womanhood* (Toronto: McClelland and Stewart, 1989).

Preston, Anne, 'Sex, Kids, and Commitment to the Workplace: Employers, Employees, and the Mommy Track,' Russell Sage Foundation Working Paper No. 123, 1997.

Pringle, Rosemary, *Secretaries Talk: Sexuality, Power and Work* (New York: Verso, 1988).

Rabin, Matthew, 'Incorporating Fairness into Game Theory and Economics,' *American Economic Review*, LXXXIII (December 1993), 1281–1302.

Rainwater, Lee, *Behind Ghetto Walls: Black Families in a Federal Slum* (Chicago, IL: Aldine, 1970).

Reskin, Barbara, and Patricia Roos, eds., *Job Queues, Gender Queues: Explaining Women's Inroads Into Male Occupations* (Philadelphia, PA: Temple University Press, 1990).

Rodriguez, Richard, *Hunger of Memory: The Education of Richard Rodriguez* (New York: Bantam, 1982).

Roediger, David R., *The Wages of Whiteness* (New York: Verso Press, 1991).

Romer, Paul M., 'Preferences, Promises, and the Politics of Enlightenment,' mimeo, University of California at Berkeley, December, 1994.

Sachs, Susan, 'Muslim Schools in U. S. a Voice for Identity,' *The New York Times*, November 10, 1998, A1.

Said, Edward W., *Orientalism* (New York: Random House, 1978).

Sanday, Peggy Reeves, *Fraternity Gang Rape: Sex, Brotherhood, and Privilege on Campus* (New York: New York University Press, 1990).

Schultz, Vicki, 'Reconceptualizing Sexual Harassment,' *Yale Law Journal*, CVII (April 1998), 1683–1805.

Sen, Amartya K., 'The Impossibility of a Paretian Liberal,' *Journal of Political Economy*, LXXVIII (January 1970), 152–157.

——, 'Goals, Commitment, and Identity,' *Journal of Law, Economics, and Organization*, I (Fall 1985), 341–355.

——, 'Maximization and the Act of Choice,' *Econometrica*, LXV (July 1997), 745–779.

Shipler, David, *A Country of Strangers: Blacks and Whites in America* (New York: Knopf, 1997).

Stanley, Marcus, Lawrence Katz, and Alan Krueger, 'Impacts of Employment Programs: The American Experience,' mimeo, Harvard University, 1998.

Staples, Brent, *Parallel Time: Growing Up in Black and White* (New York: Pantheon, 1994).

Stinnett, T. M., *Professional Problems of Teachers* (New York: Macmillan, 1968).

Strober, Myra, 'Toward a General Theory of Occupational Sex Segregation: The Case of Public School Teaching,' Chapter 8 in Barbara Reskin, ed., *Sex Segregation in the Workplace* (Washington: National Academy Press, 1984).

Sugg, Redding S., *Motherteacher: The Feminization of American Education* (Charlottesville: University of Virginia Press, 1978).

Suskind, Ron, *A Hope in the Unseen* (New York: Broadway, 1998).

Tajfel, Henri, and John Turner, 'An Integrative Theory of Intergroup Conflict,' in *The Social Psychology of Intergroup Relations*, William G. Austin and Stephen Worchel, eds. (Monterey, CA: Wadsworth, 1979).

Thernstrom, Stephan, and Abigail Thernstrom, *America in Black and White: One Nation, Indivisible* (New York: Simon and Schuster, 1997).

Thomas, Kerry, 'The Defensive Self: A Psychodynamic Perspective,' in *Understanding the Self*, Richard Stevens, ed. (Thousand Oaks, CA: SAGE Publications, 1996).

Turow, Scott, *One L* (New York: Warner Books, 1977).

Watkins, Mel, *Dancing With Strangers: A Memoir* (New York: Simon and Schuster, 1998).

Wetherell, Margaret, 'Group Conflict and the Social Psychology of Racism,' in *Group Conflict and the Psychology of Racism*, Margaret Wetherell, ed. (Thousand Oaks, CA: SAGE Publications, 1996).

Whyte, William Foote, *Street Corner Society: The Social Structure of an Italian Slum* (Chicago: University of Chicago Press, 1943).

Williams, Christine, *Gender Differences at Work: Women and Men in Nontraditional Occupations* (Berkeley: University of California Press, 1989).

Willis, Paul R., *Learning to Labour: How Working Class Kids Get Working Class Jobs* (Westmead, Farnborough, Hants., UK: Saxon House, 1977).

Wilson, William J., *The Truly Disadvantaged* (Chicago, IL: University of Chicago Press, 1987).

——, *When Work Disappears: The World of the New Urban Poor* (New York: Knopf, 1996).

Wurzburg, Lynne A., and Robert H. Klonoff, in Hope Landrine and Elizabeth A. Klonoff, eds. *Discrimination Against Women: Prevalence, Consequences Remedies* (Thousand Oaks, CA: SAGE Publications, 1997), pp. 175–195.

5

The Economics of 'Tagging' as Applied to the Optimal Income Tax, Welfare Programs, and Manpower Planning*

BY GEORGE A. AKERLOF[†]

The advantages of a negative income tax are easy to describe. Such a tax typically gives positive work incentives to even the poorest persons. With some forms of the negative income tax there are no incentives for families to split apart to obtain greater welfare payments. Furthermore, individuals of similar income are treated in similar fashion, and therefore it is fair and also relatively cheap and easy to administer.

In contrast to these advantages of a negative income tax, the advantages of a system of welfare made up of a patchwork of different awards to help various needy groups are less easy to describe and also less well understood. Such a system uses various characteristics, such as age, employment status, female head of household, to identify (in my terminology to 'tag') groups of persons who are on the average needy. These groups are then given special treatment, or, as the economist would view it, they are given a special tax schedule different from the rest of the populace. A system of tagging permits relatively high welfare payments with relatively low marginal rates of taxation, a proposition which will be explained presently and discussed at some length.

I. INTRODUCTION

It is the aim of this paper to explore the nature of the optimal negative income tax with tagging and to compare this tax with the optimal negative income tax in which all groups are treated alike. I should emphasize at the outset, however, that I do not wish to defend one type of welfare system versus another—rather, I feel that if welfare reform is to be successful, the merits of different systems must be understood, especially the merits of the system which is to be replaced. The evidence is fairly strong that the proponents

* This work was previously published as George Akerlof (1978), 'The Economics of "Tagging" as Applied to the Optimal Income Tax, Welfare Programs, and Manpower Planning' *The American Economic Review*, 68, 1. Copyright © The American Economic Association. Reproduced by kind permission.

† Professor, University of California–Berkeley. I am indebted to George Borts and an anonymous referee for invaluable comments. I would also like to thank the National Science Foundation for research support under grant number SOC 75-23076, administered by the Institute of Business and Economic Research, University of California-Berkeley.

of welfare reform have failed to understand (or to face) the costs involved in going from a system of welfare based on tagging (such as we now have in the United States) to one which treats all people uniformly.

The role of tagging in income redistribution can be seen most simply in a very simple formula and its modification. Consider a negative income tax of the form $T = -\alpha \bar{Y} + tY$, where α is the fraction of per capita income received by a person with zero gross income, t is the marginal rate of taxation, and $\bar{Y}$ is per capita income. Summing the left-hand side and the right-hand side of this formula over all individuals in the economy and dividing by total income yields a formula of the form:

$$t = \alpha + g \tag{1}$$

where g is the ratio of net taxes collected to total income, and t and α come from the formula for the negative income tax.[1] Formula (1) indicates the fundamental tradeoff involved in income redistribution by a linear negative income tax. Higher levels of support α can be given, but only at the cost of higher marginal rates of taxation. Thus, if α is 40 percent and g is 15 percent, numbers which are not unrealistic, marginal tax rates are 55 percent.

Suppose, however, that it is possible to identify (tag) a group which contains all the poor people and that this group contains only a fraction β of the total population. By giving this tagged group a minimum support, which is a fraction α of average income and a marginal tax rate t, and by giving untagged persons a zero support level and the same marginal tax rate t, similar to formula (1), we find:[2]

---

[1] Define g as: $\Sigma T_i / \Sigma Y_i$, where g is net tax collections relative to total income. Formula (1) can be derived as follows: $T_i = -\alpha \bar{Y} + tY_i$ is the taxes paid by individual i. Summing over all i individuals (assumed to be n in number),

$$\sum_{i=1}^{n} T_i = \sum_{i=1}^{n} -\alpha \bar{Y} + \sum_{i=1}^{n} tY_i$$

$$\sum_{i=1}^{n} T_i = -\alpha n \bar{Y} + t \sum_{i=1}^{n} Y_i \quad (a)$$

Because $\bar{Y}$ is by definition, $(\Sigma Y_i)/n$, and because g is by definition, $\sum_{i=1}^{n} T_i / \sum_{i=1}^{n} Y_i$, a division of the left-hand and the right-hand sides of (a) by ΣY_i yields:

$$\frac{\Sigma T_i}{\Sigma Y_i} = -\alpha \frac{n\bar{Y}}{\Sigma Y_i} + t$$

whence: $g = -\alpha + t$, and $t = \alpha + g$.

[2] Formula (2) is derived in similar fashion to formula (1). Let n_p denote the number of poor people, with $n_p/n = \beta$. (Let poor people be numbered 1 to n_p.) Poor people pay a tax

$$T_i = (-\alpha \bar{Y} + tY_i) \quad i = 1, \ldots, n_p$$

whereas other people pay a tax

$$T_i = tY_i \quad i = n_p + 1, \ldots, n$$

Thus, total net revenues are:

$$\sum_{i=1}^{n} T_i = \sum_{i=1}^{n_p} (-\alpha \bar{Y} + tY_i) + \sum_{i=n_p+1}^{n} tY_i$$

$$t = \beta\alpha + g. \tag{2}$$

Formula (2) shows that tagging makes the tradeoff between levels of support and marginal rates of taxation more favorable by eliminating the grant to taxpayers, and thus allows greater support for the poor with less distortion to the tax structure.

Table 5.1 is taken from the 1974 *Economic Report of the President* (p. 168). This table indicates the scope and magnitude, and also the importance, of tagging in federal redistribution programs. Such programs as aid to the aged, the blind, and the disabled, and also Medicare (including such aid administered by the Social Security system), are examples of tagging. Such programs as aid to families with dependent children are less clearcut—but it must be remembered that this program began as Aid to Dependent Children, and assistance was given to families with children without able-bodied fathers.

Female-headed households have a particularly high incidence of poverty, and this criterion (despite its perverse incentive to families to split up) was therefore one of the most efficient techniques of tagging. Other programs, such as Medicaid and housing subsidies, represent a form of tagging most common in underdeveloped and Communist countries. Since poor people spend a greater fraction of their income on some items than others, the subsidization of items of inferior but utilitarian quality constitutes one method of income 'redistribution.' It is also an example of tagging. In sum, Table 1 shows, to a fairly good degree of accuracy, that U.S. federal redistribution schemes are, with some exceptions, based on tagging.

Furthermore, the record of the debate on welfare reform reveals that the central issues involve the tradeoffs between α, t, and β reflected in formulas (1) and (2). Recall that, in August 1969, President Nixon proposed the Family Assistance Plan. By this plan a typical welfare family would receive $1,600 per year if it earned no income at all (*New York Times*, Aug. 9, 1969). There would be no decrease in benefits for the first $720 earned, but thereafter a 50¢ decline in benefits for every dollar earned up to an income of $3,920. The debate on this proposal in Congress was long and discussed many peripheral questions, but one central issue stands out. On the one side were those, with

and

$$\sum_{i=1}^{n} T_i = -n_p \alpha \bar{Y} + t \sum_{i=1}^{n} Y_i$$

or using the definition of β, $n_p = \beta n$

$$(b) \quad \sum_{i=1}^{n} T_i = -\beta \alpha n \bar{Y} + t \sum_{i=1}^{n} Y_i$$

Dividing the left-hand and right-hand sides of (b) by ΣY_i yields:

$$\frac{\sum_{i=1}^{n} T_i}{\sum_{i=1}^{n} Y_i} = -\beta \alpha \frac{n\bar{Y}}{\sum_{i=1}^{n} Y_i} + t$$

or $g = -\beta\alpha + t$.

Table 5.1.　—*Federal government transfer programs, fiscal year 1973*

Program	Total Expenditure (millions of dollars)	Number of Recipients (thousands)	Monthly Benefits per Recipient[a]	Percent of Recipients in Poverty[b]
Social Security				
Old age and survivors insurance	42,170	25,205	$139	16
Disability insurance	5,162	3,272	132	24
Public Assistance				
Aid of families with dependent children	3,617	10,980	c	76
Blind	56	78	c	62
Disabled	766	1,164	c	73
Aged	1,051	1,917	c	60
Other Cash Programs				
Veterans' compensation and benefits	1,401	7,203	74	(4)
Unemployment insurance benefits	4,404	5,409	68	(4)
In Kind				
Medicare	9,039	10,600	71	17
Medicaid	4,402	23,537	c	70
Food stamps	2,136	12,639	14	92
Public housing	1,408	3,319	c	d
Rent supplements	106	373	24	d
Homeownership assistance (section 235)	282	1,647	14	d
Rental housing assistance (section 236)	170	513	28	d

[a] The number of recipients is for individuals, not families.
[b] Poverty is defined relative to money income and the size of the recipient's family. Money income includes money transfer payments but excludes income received in kind. All percents are estimated.
[c] Programs with federal-state sharing of expenses.
[d] Not available.

Senator Abraham Ribicoff as the leading protagonist, who considered the benefits too 'meager' (Ribicoff's phrase, *New York Times*, Apr. 21, 1970); on the other side was the administration, with a succession of secretaries of Health, Education, and Welfare as leading protagonists, who viewed any increase in these benefits as too 'costly' (Elliott Richardson's phrase, *New York Times*, July 22, 1971). By this it was meant that with such an increase the marginal tax rate t would have to be too great. No compromise was reached, and in March 1972 the bill was withdrawn by the administration. In the background, of course, was the current welfare system, whose tagging programs allow a better tradeoff between α and t—even though other incentives such as incentives to work and to maintain a family may be perverse.

Thus, formula (1) and its modification with tagging are instructive and pertain to real issues. These formulas are generally useful in showing the two-way tradeoff between welfare support and marginal rates of taxation, and the three-way trade-off between these two variables and tagging. It is fairly intuitive by consumer's surplus arguments that the cost of a tax is the 'dead-weight loss' due to the gap created between private and social marginal products, which in this case is the marginal rate of taxation itself; ideally, however, the welfare cost of a tax is endogenous and should be derived from basic principles of utility maximization and general equilibrium analysis.

Ray Fair and James Mirrlees have developed the theory of the negative income tax uniformly applied. Their approach is reviewed in the next section, because, with added complication, the tradeoffs may be applied to a model of the optimal negative income tax with tagging. Section III illustrates the proposition that tagging of poor people typically results in greater support levels to the poor. Section IV gives a complicated and generalized model of optimal income redistribution with tagging, of which Section III presented a simple but illustrative example. Section V discusses the relation between tagging and the estimation of costs and benefits of manpower programs. Section VI gives conclusions.

II. A SIMPLE EXAMPLE AND EXPLANATION OF MIRRLEES-FAIR

Following the example of Mirrlees and Fair, there is a population with a distribution of abilities a, according to the distribution function $f(a)$. Members of this population receive income dependent on their marginal products of the form $w(a)L(a)$, where $w(a)$ is the wage of a worker of ability of index a, and $L(a)$ is the labor input of such a worker. After-tax income is $w(a)L(a) - t(w(a)L(a))$, where $t(y)$ is the tax paid on gross income y. Members of this population have utility positively dependent on after-tax income and negatively dependent on labor input. Thus, utility of a person of ability a is

$$u(a) = u[w(a)L(a) - t(w(a)L(a)), L(a)] \tag{3}$$

The optimal tax is defined as maximizing the expected value of the utility of the population, denoted U,

$$U = \int u[w(a)L(a) - t(w(a)L(a)), L(a)]f(a)\,da \tag{4}$$

subject to the constraint that taxes equal transfers, or,

$$\int t(w(a)L(a))f(a)\,da = 0 \tag{5}$$

and also subject to the constraint that each individual chooses his labor input to maximize his utility, given the wage rate paid to persons of his ability, his utility function u, and the tax schedule $t(y)$, yielding the first-order condition:

$$\frac{\partial}{\partial L(a)} \{u[w(a)L(a) - t(w(a)L(a)), L(a)]\} = 0.$$

However complicated the equations or the mathematics, the basic tradeoff made in the choice of an optimal Mirrlees-Fair style income tax can be explained as follows. As taxes are raised and incomes are redistributed, there is a gain in welfare, because income is distributed to those who have greater need of it (higher marginal utility). But this gain must be balanced against a loss: as tax rates rise in relatively productive jobs and as subsidies rise in relatively unproductive jobs, workers are less willing to take the productive (and more willing to take the unproductive) jobs. Such switching, per se, results in a loss in U because each worker is choosing the amount of work, or the kind of job, which maximizes his private utility rather than the amount of work or kind of job which maximizes social utility. In general, the redistributive gains versus the losses caused by tax/transfer-induced switching is the major tradeoff in the theory of optimal income taxes and welfare payments—both with and without tagging.

III. A SIMPLE EXAMPLE OF OPTIMAL TAXES AND SUBSIDIES WITH TAGGING

Section I gave formula (2) which indicated that tagging improved the relation between the marginal tax rate and the minimum subsidy to *tagged* poor people. Loosely, it could be said that tagging will in consequence reduce the cost of income redistribution (since, with lower marginal tax rates, there is a smaller gap between social and private returns from work and therefore less loss of consumer's surplus due to redistribution-caused job switching). As a result, it is only natural that tagging increases the optimal transfers to poor people.

A. *The Rudimentary Mirrlees-Fair Model*

As implied by Mirrlees, there are no interesting easily solved algebraic examples of the optimal income tax with a continuum of abilities. There is no question that tagging, since it adds an additional degree of freedom, makes the problem still harder. Therefore, the example presented here is a much simplified version of the Mirrlees-Fair general case.

The example here is the most rudimentary model in which the optimal tax structure, both with and without tagging, is dictated by the tradeoffs between the dead-weight loss due to taxes and subsidies and the gains of redistribution from rich to poor. Instead of a continuum of workers (as in Mirrlees), there are just two types: skilled and unskilled; instead of a continuum of output dependent upon labor input, there are just two types of jobs: difficult jobs (denoted by subscript D) and easy jobs (denoted by subscript E). Instead of a marginal condition describing the optimal tax reflecting continua of both labor input and worker types and the corresponding use of the calculus of variations, the optimum tax is characterized by a binding inequality constraint, which results from the discrete calculus corresponding to the discrete number of job types and worker types.

It is assumed that there are an equal number of skilled and unskilled workers. Skilled workers may work in either difficult or easy jobs, but unskilled workers may work only in easy jobs.[3] The output of a skilled worker in a difficult job is q_D, which is a constant independent of the number of workers in such jobs. Similarly, the output of both skilled and unskilled workers in easy jobs is q_E, which is also a constant independent of the number of workers in such jobs. These data are summarized in Table 5.2, which gives the technology of the model. Of course, output in difficult jobs exceeds output in easy jobs, so that $q_D > q_E$.

The economy is competitive, so that pretax, pretransfer pay in each job is the worker's marginal product in that job. The utility of each worker depends upon after-tax, after-transfer income and upon the non-pecuniary returns of his job. The utility functions can be written as a separable function of the pecuniary and the nonpecuniary returns. Let t_D denote the taxes paid by workers in difficult jobs (with income q_D), and let t_E denote transfers to workers in easy jobs (with income q_E). After-tax income in difficult jobs is $q_D - t_D$; after-transfer income in easy jobs is $q_E + t_E$. The utility of skilled workers in difficult jobs is $u(q_D - t_D) - \delta$, and the utility of both skilled and unskilled workers in easy jobs is $u(q_E + t_E)$. The parameter δ reflects the nonpecuniary distaste of workers for difficult jobs due to the greater effort necessary. Of course, $u' > 0$, $u'' < 0$. It is further assumed that $u(q_D) - \delta > u(q_E)$; otherwise, easy jobs dominate difficult jobs, so that, at the optimum, all workers (trivially) work in easy jobs without paying taxes or receiving transfers. The preceding data are summarized in Table 5.3.

In the absence of tagging, the Mirrlees-Fair optimal income tax, as applied to this model, is obtained by choosing a tax on income in difficult jobs t_D and a transfer to income in easy jobs t_E, subject to the constraint that qualified workers will choose

Table 5.2. *Output of worker by type of worker by type of job*

Type of Worker (Percent of Workforce)	Type of Job	
	Difficult	Easy
Skilled (50%)	q_D	q_E
Unskilled (50%)	Not applicable	q_E

Note: $q_D > q_E$

---

[3] The model works out equivalently if unskilled workers can work in different jobs but have great distaste for the extra effort required.

Table 5.3. *Utility of workers by type of worker by type of job, with taxes t_D on persons with pretax income q_D, and transfers t_E to persons with pretax income q_E*

Type of Worker (Percent of Workforce)	Type of Job	
	Difficult	Easy
Skilled (50%)	$u(q_D - t_D) - \delta$	$u(q_E + t_E)$
Unskilled (50%)	Not applicable	$u(q_E + t_E)$

Note: $u(q_D) - \delta > u(q_E)$

skilled or unskilled jobs depending upon which one yields greater utility (after taxes), and also subject to the constraint that taxes equal transfers. In mathematical form this becomes the maximization problem to choose t_D and t_E to maximize U,

$$U = \frac{1}{2}\max\{u(q_D - t_D) - \delta,\, u(q_E + t_E)\} + \frac{1}{2}u(q_E + t_E) \tag{6}$$

subject to

$$t_D = t_E \text{ if } u(q_D - t_D) - \delta \geq u(q_E + t_E) \tag{7a}$$

$$t_E = 0 \text{ if } u(q_D - t_D) - \delta < u(q_E + t_E) \tag{7b}$$

It is convenient to denote optimal values with an asterisk. Thus the optimal value of U is U^*, of t is t^*, and of t_E is t_E^*.

The maximand (6) consists of the sum of the utilities of skilled and unskilled workers weighted by their respective fractions of the population. The utility of a skilled worker is $max\{u(q_D - t_D) - \delta,\, u(q_E + t_E)\}$ since skilled workers are assumed to work in difficult jobs if $u(q_D - t_D) - \delta \geq u(q_E + t_E)$, and in easy jobs otherwise. Equations (7a) and (7b) jointly reflect the balanced budget constraint. If skilled workers work in difficult jobs, the tax collection per skilled worker is t_D. If tax collections equal transfers, $t_D = t_E$ (which is (7a)). However, if skilled workers work in easy jobs, they must receive the same transfer as unskilled workers. As a result, the condition that taxes equal transfers implies that $t_E = 0$, which is (7b).

Tagging does not occur in this maximization, since skilled and unskilled workers alike receive the same transfer t_E if they work in easy jobs.

Two equations, (8) and (9), characterize the optimal tax-*cum*-transfer rates t_D^* and t_E^* which maximize U:

$$t_D^* = t_E^* \tag{8}$$

$$u(q_D - t_D^*) - \delta = u(q_E + t_E^*) \tag{9}$$

Table 5.4. *Taxes on difficult jobs and transfers to easy jobs in models with and without tagging*

	Model without Tagging	Model with Tagging
Tax on Difficult Job	t_D	T_D
Transfer to Easy Job (workers untagged)	t_E	T_E
Transfer to Easy Job (workers tagged)	Not Applicable	τ

Of course, (8) is the tax-equal-transfer balanced budget constraint. Equation (9) expresses the additional condition that, at the optimum, as much is redistributed from skilled to unskilled workers as possible, subject to the constraint that any greater redistribution would cause skilled workers to switch from difficult to easy jobs. (Any increase in t_D above t_D^*, or in t_E above t_E^*, results in a shift of all skilled workers into easy jobs.) As a result of this threatened shift, the deadweight loss due to a marginal increase in taxes or in transfers exceeds the returns from any redistributive gain.[4] Thus, our model, although rudimentary, has an optimal tax-*cum*-transfer schedule which reflects the tradeoffs of Mirrlees-Fair: the optimal tax/transfer policy being determined both by the gains from redistribution and the losses due to labor-supply shifts in response to changes in taxes and transfers.

B. *Tagging Introduced into Rudimentary Mirrlees-Fair Model*

Now consider how tagging will alter the Mirrlees-Fair maximization and its solution. Suppose that a portion β of the unskilled workers can be identified (i.e., tagged) as unskilled and given a tax/transfer schedule different from that of other workers. In the altered model with tagging, let T_D denote the taxes paid by untagged workers in difficult jobs; let T_E denote transfers (perhaps negative) paid to untagged workers in easy jobs; and let τ denote the transfer to tagged workers (all of whom work in easy jobs). Table 5.4 compares the tax/transfer schedule of the earlier model without tagging and the tax schedule of the current model with tagging.

Using Table 5.4, it is easy to construct Table 5.5, which gives the utility of workers by type of job after taxes and after transfers. Table 5.5 differs from Table 5.3 by addition of the bottom row, which represents the utility of tagged workers in easy jobs who receive the transfer τ.

---

[4] It also happens in this maximization that any further increase in taxes or in transfers at the margin causes such a large and discontinuous shift in the number of workers earning high incomes in difficult jobs that such an increase also decreases the revenues available for redistribution to unskilled workers.

Table 5.5. *Utility of worker by type of worker by type of job with tagging; untagged workers pay taxes T_D in difficult jobs and receive transfers T_E in unskilled jobs; tagged workers receive a transfer τ in unskilled jobs*

Type of Worker (Fraction of Workforce)	Type of Job	
	Difficult	Easy
Skilled (Untagged) (1/2)	$u(q_D - T_D) - \delta$	$u(q_E + T_E)$
Unskilled (Untagged) $((1 - \beta)/2)$	Not Applicable	$u(q_E + T_E)$
Unskilled (Tagged) $(\beta/2)$	Not Applicable	$u(q_E + \tau)$

Using the data in Table 5.5, it is easy to see that, with tagging, the optimum tax-*cum*-transfer policy is to choose the values (T_D, T_E, τ) that maximize U^{Tag}, where:

$$U^{Tag} = \frac{1}{2}\max\{u(q_D - T_D) - \delta,\ u(q_E + T_E)\}$$
$$+ \frac{1}{2}(1 - \beta)u(q_E + T_E) + \frac{1}{2}\beta u(q_E + \tau) \tag{10}$$

subject to the balanced budget constraints (11a) and (11b):

$$T_D = (1 - \beta)T_E + \beta\tau \text{ if } u(q_D - T_D) - \delta \geq u(q_E + T_E) \tag{11a}$$

$$(2 - \beta)T_E + \beta\tau = 0 \text{ if } u(q_D - T_D) - \delta < u(q_E + T_E) \tag{11b}$$

Again, denote the optimum values with an asterisk: T_D^*, T_E^*, τ^*, and U^{Tag^*}.

The maximand U^{Tag} is the sum of the utility of all three types of workers—skilled, untagged unskilled, and tagged unskilled—weighted by their respective fractions of the population. The utility of skilled workers is $u(q_D - T_D) - \delta$ or $u(q_E + T_E)$, dependent upon whether they choose difficult or easy jobs. Equations (11a) and (11b) are the tax-equal-transfer, balanced-budget constraints. The respective equation applies accordingly as skilled workers are in difficult or in easy jobs.

In the Appendix, it is shown that with $u(q_D) - \delta > u(q_E)$, for $0 < \beta \leq 1$, the optimal transfer to tagged workers τ^* exceeds the optimal transfer to untagged unskilled workers t_E^* in the model without tagging. With $\beta = 1$, complete equality of income is attained at the optimum. In this precise sense, tagging increases the optimum transfers to those who are identified as poor and given special tax treatment.

The difference between the tagging and the nontagging optimization is clear: with tagging, for a given increased subsidy to tagged people, there is a smaller decline in the income differential between difficult and easy work, since l_E need not shift, and there is therefore a smaller tendency for workers to shift from difficult to easy jobs with a given redistribution of income. As a result, optimal transfers to tagged workers are greater with tagging than in its absence.

An outline of the proof, which is given in the Appendix, illustrates the application of this logic more particularly. The proof shows that, at the optimum, the rate of taxation of workers in difficult jobs and the rate of transfer to untagged workers in easy jobs is taken up to the point that any further increase in either of those two rates will induce skilled workers to shift into easy jobs. This is reflected by the optimization condition (12), which is exactly analogous to the similar optimization condition (9) in the untagged case:

$$u(q_D - T_D^*) - \delta = u(q_E + T_E^*) \tag{12}$$

It is then shown by contradiction that τ^* (the optimal transfer to tagged workers) exceeds T_E^* (the optimal transfer to unskilled untagged workers). Suppose the contrary (i.e., $\tau^* \leq T_E^*$). In that case, a marginal decrease in T_E and a marginal increase in equal dollar amount in τ can cause no decrease in utility, while it allows some additional redistribution to be made from skilled workers in difficult jobs to other workers without inducing any skilled workers to switch from difficult into easy jobs. Since total utility U^{Tag} is sure to be increased by at least one of these two changes and not decreased by the other, the optimality of τ^* and T_E^* is contradicted. At the optimum, therefore, τ^* must be greater than T_E^*.

Knowing that $\tau^* > T_E^*$, as has been shown, knowing that T_D^* and T_E^* satisfy (12), and knowing that t_D^* and t_E^* satisfy the similar condition (9), $u(q_D - t_D^*) - \delta = u(q_E + t_E^*)$, the budget constraints can be used to show that $\tau^* > t_E^*$.

IV. GENERALIZED PROBLEM

In the example in the last section, there was no opportunity for people to change the characteristics by which they were tagged. Age, race, and sex are real life examples of such characteristics. However, there are also redistribution programs in which people, by some effort or with some loss of utility, may alter their characteristics, thereby becoming members of a tagged group. The most commonly cited example of this concerns families who allegedly have separated in order to obtain payments under the Aid to Dependent Children program (see Daniel Moynihan).

To consider the case more generally, in which group membership is endogenous, this section presents a general model. It then becomes an empirical (rather than a theoretical) question to determine what amount of tagging (and quite possibly the answer is none) will maximize aggregate utility U. There is no major theorem in general, unless it is the falsity of the proposition to which the previous section gave a counterexample, that a uniform negative income tax is always superior to a welfare system that gives special aid to people with special problems or characteristics.

In general, we may assume the goal is to choose functions $t_y(y_y)$ to maximize

$$U = \int u_x f(x) dx \tag{13}$$

where $f(x)$ denotes the distribution of people of type x, and where the utility of such a person depends on his after-tax income, his characteristics, and the group to which he belongs γ, or

$$u_x = u(y - t, x, \gamma) \tag{14}$$

In the real world, of course, tagging is not costless, one of the major complaints against the current welfare system being its cost of administration. Let Γ be the grouping of people into various subgroups of the population, and let $c(\Gamma)$ be the administrative cost of such tagging.

U is maximized subject to two constraints, the first being that taxes equal transfers plus administrative costs, or

$$\int_x t_\gamma(y(x), \gamma(x)) f(x) dx + c(\Gamma) = 0 \tag{15}$$

where $\gamma(x)$ is the group to which an individual of type x belongs, and the second being that an individual of type x chooses his labor input and the group to which he belongs to maximize

$$u[w(x, \gamma)L(x, \gamma) - t_\gamma(w(x, \gamma)L(x, \gamma)), x, \gamma] \tag{16}$$

where $w(x, \gamma)$ is the wage of a person of characteristic x belonging to group γ, and $L(x, \gamma)$ is the labor input.

In sum, this is the generalization of Mirrlees' (and Fair's) problem to taxation with tagging. I have taken the trouble to specify this general problem since it is important to note the potential endogeneity of the tagged characteristics and of administrative costs.

V. COST–BENEFIT EVALUATION OF MANPOWER PROGRAMS AND TAGGING

Another type of program in which tagging is important is manpower training programs. Typically, such programs in the United States have aimed at improving the skills of the disadvantaged and the temporarily unemployed. Because of formal eligibility requirements, and also because of the self-selectivity of the trainees, people in special need are identified (or tagged) by such programs.

There has been an intensive effort in the United States to evaluate the benefits and costs of such programs, so much so that there have been extensive 'reviews of the reviews' (see David O'Neill). The studies have typically (but with some exceptions) found that the benefits of manpower training programs, as conventionally accounted, have been less than the costs. But because of the value of tagging done by such programs, a benefit-cost ratio of less than unity is not sufficient reason for their curtailment.

This last point can be made formally in terms of the tagging models in Sections III and IV. A manpower program could be introduced into the model in Section III by assuming that, at a given cost per worker, an unskilled worker who is previously untagged can be made into a skilled worker. The costs of such a program, as usually accounted, are its costs of operation plus the wages foregone by workers while engaged in training. The cost of operation becomes an additional term in the balanced budget constraint (analogous to the term $c(\Gamma)$ in (15)). The benefits from the program are the increase in the pretax, pretransfer wages of the worker subsequent to training. It is easy to construct an example in which the benefits (thus accounted) are less than the costs (thus accounted), yet U^{Tag} is greater with the program than in its absence, because the program tags unskilled workers and makes income redistribution possible with relatively little distortion to the incentive structure.

An unrigorous calculation using consumer's surplus logic shows that the tagging benefits of manpower programs may be substantial. Consider two subgroups of the population, both of which are young and both of which have low current incomes. One group is skilled but has low current income because it is building up human capital; the other group is unskilled and has low current income for that reason; it also has low permanent income.

Let there be a manpower training program. At a cost of c dollars, the permanent income of a young unskilled worker can be raised by \$1. The costs of this program (as usually accounted) are c dollars, and its benefits are \$1. Considering consumer's surplus and assuming that there is a dead-weight loss of λ per dollar due to taxes to pay for the program, the cost of the program, inclusive of deadweight loss is $c(1 + \lambda)$.

Now compare the advantages of this training program to a negative income tax that gives lump sum transfers to all young workers, whether skilled or unskilled. Let unskilled workers be a fraction θ of the total population. To redistribute \$1 to an unskilled young worker, a total of $1/\theta$ dollars must be redistributed to all young people.

Which scheme—the manpower training program or the negative income tax—is the cheaper way of redistributing \$1 to unskilled workers? The cost, inclusive of dead-weight loss of the manpower program, is $c(1 + \lambda)$. The cost, inclusive of deadweight loss of the negative income tax, is the dead-weight loss on $1/\theta$ dollars, plus the \$1 redistributed, or $\lambda/\theta + 1$. Which scheme is cheaper depends upon whether $c(1 + \lambda)$ is greater or less than $(\lambda/\theta + 1)$.

Let λ be .05 and let θ be .1, numbers which are not unrepresentative of reasonable parameters for deadweight loss due to income taxation and the fraction of the population eligible for a typical manpower training program such as the Job Corps. If the benefit-cost ratio of the manpower program $(1/c)$ is less than .7, the negative income tax is the cheaper method of redistribution; if the benefit-cost ratio is greater than .7, the manpower program is preferable.

VI. SUMMARY AND CONCLUSIONS

This paper has identified the important tradeoffs in the design of institutions to redistribute income. Some types of programs, either by their eligibility requirements or by the self-selection of the beneficiaries, identify (tag) people who are in special need. With tagging, taxpayers (as opposed to beneficiaries) are denied the benefit of the transfer, so that in effect a *lump sum* transfer is made to tagged people.

In contrast, with a negative income tax, a grant is made to all taxpayers and this grant must be recovered to achieve the same net revenue. This recovery results in high marginal tax rates, whose disincentive effects are the major disadvantage of a negative income tax. This disadvantage, however, must be weighed against the disadvantages of tagging, which are the perverse incentives to people to be identified as needy (to be tagged), the inequity of such a system, and its cost of administration.

The problem of the optimal redistributional system, both with and without tagging, has been set up in the framework of the Mirrlees-Fair optimal income tax. It was shown in a special example that if a portion of the poor population could be identified (costlessly, in this example), total welfare U could be raised by giving increased subsidies to the tagged poor.

Finally, the consequences of tagging for manpower programs were discussed. Since tagging is a benefit of most manpower programs, benefit-cost ratios need not exceed unity to justify their existence. In fact, an example showed that benefit/cost ratios could be significantly less than one (.7 in the example), and a manpower program might still be preferable to a negative income tax as a method of income redistribution.

APPENDIX

Theorem 1: *Using the definitions of τ^* and t_E^* in Section III, and also the models in that section, if $u(q_D) - \delta > u(q_E)$ and $0 < \beta \leq 1, \tau^* > t_E^*$.*

Proof:

The proof proceeds by five propositions. Propositions 1 and 2 make variational arguments which show that at the maximum as much must be redistributed from skilled workers as possible without inducing them to switch into easy jobs. This yields the condition:

$$u(q_D - T_D^*) - \delta = u(q_E + T_E^*) \tag{A1}$$

It is similarly true without tagging that

$$u(q_D - t_D^*) - \delta = u(q_E + t_E^*) \tag{A2}$$

From (A1) and (A2) it can be easily shown (Proposition 3) that if $T_D^* > t_D^*, T_E^* < t_E^*$ (and vice versa).

Proposition 4 then shows that $\tau^* \geq t_E^*$. There are two cases. In one case, $T_D^* < t_D^*$. If $T_D^* < t_D^*$, by Proposition 3, $T_E^* > t_E^*$. Suppose $t_E^* \geq \tau^*$. A variational argument shows that this cannot be a maximum, for a decrease in T_E^* and an increase in τ^* can increase U^{Tag}. In the other case, $T_D^* \geq t_D^*$. But if $T_D^* \geq t_D^*$, by Proposition 3, $T_E^* \leq t_E^*$. It follows from the balanced budget constraints that if T_E^* is smaller than t_E^*, but also, T_D^* is larger than t_D^*, that τ^* must be larger than t_E^*. As a result, in both Case I and Case II, $\tau^* \geq t_E^*$. Proposition 5 shows that the inequality is strict.

Proposition 1: $u(q_D - T_D^*) - \delta \geq u(q_E + T_E^*)$.

Proof:
   Suppose otherwise. Then,

$$U^{Tag^*} = \frac{1}{2}\{(2 - \beta)u(q_E + T_E^*) + \beta u(q_E + \tau^*)\} \leq u(q_E) \tag{A3}$$

by the concavity of u and the constraint (11b) that $(2 - \beta)T_E^* = -\beta\tau^*$. Since $u(q_D) - \delta > u(q_E)$ by assumption,

$$u(q_E) < \frac{1}{2}\{u(q_D) - \delta + u(q_E)\}. \tag{A4}$$

Since $T_D = T_E = \tau = 0$ is a feasible tax/transfer vector (satisfying budget constraint (11)), and with

$$U^{Tag} = \frac{1}{2}\{u(q_D) - \delta + u(q_E)\} \tag{A5}$$

the optimality of U^{Tag^*} is contradicted by (A3), (A4), and (A5). By this contradiction,

$$u(q_D - T_D^*) - \delta \geq u(q_E + T_E^*). \tag{A6}$$

Proposition 2:

$$u(q_D - T_D^*) - \delta = u(q_E + T_E^*). \tag{A7}$$

Proof:
   Suppose that $u(q_D - T_D^*) - \delta > u(q_E + T_E^*)$. A variational argument shows that (T_D^*, T_E^*, τ^*) is not optimal.
   Let $T_D' = T_D^* + \varepsilon$

$$T_E' = T_E^* + \varepsilon/(1 - \beta)$$

$$U^{Tag}(T_D', T_E', \tau^*) = U^{Tag}(T_D^*, T_E^*, \tau^*) + \\ \varepsilon/2[-u'(q_D - T_D^*) + u'(q_E + T_E^*)] + o^2(\varepsilon) \tag{A8}$$

where $o^2(\varepsilon)$ is an expression with $lim_{\varepsilon \to 0}\, o^2(\varepsilon)/\varepsilon = 0$. But since $u(q_D - T_D^*)$ $-\delta > u(q_E + T_E^*)$ by assumption,

$$u'(q_D - T_D^*) < u'(q_E + T_E^*) \tag{A9}$$

by the concavity of u.

Therefore, by (A8), $U^{Tag}(T_D', T_E', \tau^*) > U^{Tag}(T_D^*, T_E^*, \tau^*)$ for ε sufficiently small, which contradicts the optimality of (T_D^*, T_E^*, τ^*). Therefore, $u(q_D - T_D^*)$ $-\delta \le u(q_E + T_E^*)$.

By Proposition 1, $u(q_D - T_D^*) - \delta \ge u(q_E + T_E^*)$. Therefore,

$$u(q_D - T_D^*) - \delta = u(q_E + T_E^*). \tag{A10}$$

Proposition 3: $T_D^* > t_D^*$ *if and only if* $T_E^* < t_E^*$.

Proof:

Suppose $T_D^* > t_D^*$. By Proposition 2

$$u(q_D - T_D^*) - \delta = u(q_E + T_E^*). \tag{A11}$$

By similar logic,

$$u(q_D - t_D^*) - \delta = u(q_E + t_E^*). \tag{A12}$$

If $T_D^* > t_D^*$, then

$$u(q_D - T_D^*) < u(q_D - t_D^*), \tag{A13}$$

whence

$$\begin{aligned}
&u(q_E + T_E^*)\\
=&u(q_D - T_D^*) - \delta < u(q_D - t_D^*) - \delta\\
=&u(q_E + t_E^*).
\end{aligned} \tag{A14}$$

$$T_E^* < t_E^*. \tag{A15}$$

Similarly, if $T_D^* < t_D^*$, $T_E^* > t_E^*$.

Proposition 4: $\tau^* \geq t_E^*$.

Proof:
  Suppose

$$\tau^* < t_E^*. \tag{A16}$$

It will be shown that the optimality of τ^* or of t_E^* is contradicted. Two cases will be analyzed:
  Case I: $T_D^* < t_D^*$
  Case II: $T_D^* \geq t_D^*$

Case I: By Proposition 3, if $T_D^* < t_D^*$,

$$T_E^* > t_E^* \tag{A17}$$

But then

$$
\begin{aligned}
U^{Tag}(T_D^*,\ T_E^* - \varepsilon,\ \tau^* + (1 - \beta)/\beta\ \varepsilon) \\
= U^{Tag}(T_D^*,\ T_E^*,\ \tau^*) \\
-(1 - \beta)\varepsilon/2\ u'(q_E + T_E^*) \\
+\beta\,\frac{1 - \beta}{\beta}\,\varepsilon/2\ u'(q_E + \tau^*) + o^2(\varepsilon)
\end{aligned}
\tag{A18}
$$

which last equation (A 18) for sufficiently small ε

$$> U^{Tag}(T_D^*,\ T_E^*,\ \tau^*) \tag{A19}$$

since $u'(q_E + T_E^*) < u'(q_E + t_E^*) < u'(q_E + \tau^*)$ by the concavity of u and by both the inequality (A17), $(T_E^* > t_E^*)$, and the supposition (A16), $(t_E^* > \tau^*)$. The inequality (A19) contradicts the optimality of $(T_D^*,\ T_E^*,\ \tau^*)$. Therefore, if $T_D^* < t_D^*$, $\tau^* \geq t_E^*$.

Case II: $T_D^* \geq t_D^*$.
  Suppose again

$$\tau^* < t_E^*. \tag{A20}$$

We will show a contradiction. By Proposition 3, if $T_D^* \geq t_D^*$,

$$T_E^* \leq t_E^*. \tag{A21}$$

By inequality (A21), $(T_E^* \leq t_E^*)$, the budget constraint (7a), $(t_D^* = t_E^*)$, and inequality (A20), $(\tau^* < t_E^*)$,

$$T_D^* \geq t_D^* = t_E^* > (1 - \beta)T_E^* + \beta\tau^*, \tag{A22}$$

which contradicts the budget constraint (11a), which states:

$$T_D^* = (1 - \beta)T_E^* + \beta\tau^*. \tag{A23}$$

Hence, if $T_D^* \geq t_D^*$, $\tau^* \geq t_E^*$.

Combining Cases I and II, it has been shown that $\tau^* \geq t_E^*$.

Proposition 5: $\tau^* > t_E^*$.

Proof:

It remains to show that $\tau^* \neq t_E^*$. Suppose the contrary, that $\tau^* = t_E^*$. A contradiction will be demonstrated. By Proposition 3, at the optimum

$$u(q_D - T_D^*) - \delta = u(q_E + T_E^*). \tag{A24}$$

and similarly,

$$u(q_D - t_D^*) - \delta = u(q_E + t_E^*). \tag{A25}$$

The optimum (T_D^*, T_E^*, τ^*) and (t_D^*, t_E^*) must also satisfy the budget constraints (7a) and (11a):

$$T_D^* = (1 - \beta)T_E^* + \beta\tau^* \tag{A26}$$

$$t_D^* = t_E^*. \tag{A27}$$

Add to the system (A24) to (A27) the assumption (A28):

$$\tau^* = t_E^*. \tag{A28}$$

An optimum with $\tau^* = t_E^*$ must satisfy the five relations (A24) to (A28). These five equations constitute a system of five equations in the five variables $(T_D^*, T_E^*, \tau^*, t_D^*, t_E^*)$, with unique solution with the property

$$T_D^* = T_E^* = \tau^* = t_D^* = t_E^*.$$

Let

$$T'_D = T^*_D + 2\varepsilon_1 \tag{A29}$$

$$T'_E = T^*_E - 2\varepsilon_2 \tag{A30}$$

$$\tau' = \tau^* + \frac{1-\beta}{\beta} 2\varepsilon_2 + \frac{1}{\beta} 2\varepsilon_1 \tag{A31}$$

with

$$\varepsilon_1 < \frac{u'(q_D - T^*_D)}{u'(q_E + T^*_E)} \varepsilon_2. \tag{A32}$$

Then,

$$
\begin{aligned}
U^{Tag}(T'_D, T'_E, \tau') = {}& U^{Tag}(T^*_D, T^*_E, \tau^*) \\
&- \varepsilon_1 u'(q_D - T^*_D) - (1-\beta)\varepsilon_2 u'(q_E + T^*_E) \\
&+ \beta \frac{\varepsilon_1}{\beta} u'(q_E + \tau^*) \\
&+ \beta \frac{1-\beta}{\beta} \varepsilon_2 u'(q_E + \tau^*) \\
&+ o^2(\varepsilon_1) + o^2(\varepsilon_2)
\end{aligned}
\tag{A33}
$$

Since $\tau^* = T^*_E$, for $(\varepsilon_1, \varepsilon_2)$ sufficiently small $U^{Tag}(T'_D, T'_E, \tau') > U^{Tag}(T^*_D, T^*_E, \tau^*)$, which contradicts the optimality of (T^*_D, T^*_E, τ^*). Hence, $\tau^* \neq t^*_E$. And, using Proposition 4, $\tau^* > t^*_E$.

References

R. C. Fair, 'The Optimal Distribution of Income,' *Quart. J. Econ.*, Nov. 1971, *85*, 557–79.

J. A. Mirrlees, 'An Exploration in the Optimal Theory of Income Taxation,' *Rev. Econ. Stud.*, Apr. 1971, *38*, 175–208.

D. P. Moynihan, 'The Negro Family: The Case for National Action,' in L. Rainwater and W. L. Yancey, eds., *The Moynihan Report and the Politics of Controversy*, Cambridge, Mass. 1967.

D. M. O'Neill, 'The Federal Government and Manpower: A Critical Look at the MDTA-Institutional and Job Corps Programs,' American Enterprise Institute for Policy Research, 1973.

New York Times, Aug. 9, 1969; Apr. 21, 1970; July 23, 1971.

U.S. Council of Economic Advisers, *Economic Report of the President*, Washington, 1974.

6

An Analysis of Out-of-Wedlock Childbearing in the United States*

GEORGE A. AKERLOF, JANET L. YELLEN
AND MICHAEL L. KATZ[†]

I. INTRODUCTION

When Daniel Moynihan wrote his famous report, *The Negro Family* [U. S. Department of Labor 1965] the black out-of-wedlock birth rate was 24 percent. Twenty-five years later this rate, defined as the percentage of births to unmarried women, had more than doubled, to 64 percent. Over the same period the white out-of-wedlock birth ratio experienced yet faster growth—albeit from a lower-level—more then quintupling, from 3.1 percent to 18 percent.[1] Rising out-of-wedlock birthrates are of social policy concern because children reared in single-parent households are more likely to be impoverished and to experience difficulties in later life.[2]

* This work was previously published as George A. Akerlof, Janet L. Yellen, and Michael L. Katz (1996), 'An Analysis of Out-of-Wedlock Childbearing in the United States', *Quarterly Journal of Economics*, 111, 2. Copyright © The MIT Press. Reproduced by kind permission.

[†] The authors thank Michael Ash, Halsey Rogers, and Neil Siegel for excellent research assistance. They are grateful to Lawrence Katz, John Baldwin, Nancy Chodorow, Curtis Eaton, Pierre Fortin, Claudia Goldin, Bronwyn Hall, Eugene Hamill, Joseph Harrington, Richard Harris, Elhanan Helpman, Edward Lazear, Ronald Lee, Richard Lipsey, Mark Machina, Carl Mason, Hajime Miyazaki, Preston McAfee, Daniel McFadden, James Montgomery, Fraser Mustard, Peter Nicholson, James Rauch, Christina Romer, David Romer, Paul Romer, Andrew Rose, Nathan Rosenberg, Edward Safarian, Andrei Shleifer, Tamara Springsteen, Judy Stacy, James Wilcox, Michael Wolfson, and anonymous referees for invaluable comments. They thank the Canadian Institute for Advanced Research and the National Science Foundation under research grant number SBR-9409426 for generous financial support. Janet Yellen is Governor of the Federal Reserve System. The views in this paper are those of the authors and do not represent the opinions of the Federal Reserve System.

[1] The simultaneous rise of out-of-wedlock births and other forms of social/economic distress such as crime, drug abuse, and poverty, especially in black urban ghettos, well documented by Anderson [1990], Wilson [1987], and others, is consistent with Moynihan's gloomy predictions.

[2] A substantial literature documents that single parenthood results in a variety of adverse consequences for children (see, for example, Manski, Sandefur, McLanahan, and Powers [1992]).

A major role in the increase in out-of-wedlock births has been played by the declining practice of 'shotgun marriage.' Until the early 1970s it was the norm in premarital sexual relations that the partners would marry in the event of pregnancy. The disappearance of this custom has been a major contributor to the increase in the out-of-wedlock birth ratio for both whites and blacks. In fact, about three-fourths of the increase in the white out-of-wedlock first-birth ratio, and about three-fifths of the black increase, between 1965–1969 and 1985–1989 are explicable by the decrease in the fraction of premaritally conceived first births that are resolved in marriage. By that we mean that if the fraction of premaritally conceived births resolved by marriage had been the same from 1985 to 1989 as it had been over the comparable period twenty years earlier, the increase in the white out-of-wedlock birth ratio would have been only a quarter as high, and the black increase would have been only two-fifths as high.[3]

Ethnographic studies describe shotgun marriage in the late 1960s. For example, Rubin [1969], who studied working-class whites in San Francisco in the late 1960s, found that courtship was brief and quite likely to involve sexual activity. In the event of pregnancy, marriage occurred. One of her subjects expressed the matter succinctly and with the absence of doubt with which many social customs are unquestionably observed: 'If a girl gets pregnant you married her. There wasn't no choice. So I married her.' The norms regarding pregnancy and marriage were apparently much the same among blacks, although perhaps with greater ambiguity and more doubt since out-of-wedlock birthrates for blacks were much higher than for whites.[4]

For whites the shotgun marriage ratio began its decline at almost the same time as the advent of female contraception for unmarried women and the legalization of abortion. In the late 1960s and very early 1970s, many major states including New York and California clarified their laws regarding abortion (significantly prior to Roe v. Wade in January 1973). At about the same time it became easier as well as more common for

---

[3] The data for this calculation are taken from retrospective marital and fertility histories of the Current Population Survey, with a shotgun marriage defined as one occurring within seven months prior to the birth of the baby. The data are described in the Appendix. The CPS fertility supplements were first used to estimate shotgun marriage ratios by O'Connell and Moore [1980] and O'Connell and Rogers [1984]. The proportion of the change in out-of-wedlock births due to the change in the shotgun marriage rate is calculated as follows. If oow_t and oow_{t+1} are the fractions of out-of-wedlock births, $bcoow_t$ and $bcoow_{t+1}$ are the fraction of births conceived out-of-wedlock, and sr_t and sr_{t+1} are the shotgun marriage rates at t and $t+1$, respectively, then the formula for the change in the out-of-wedlock birth ratio due to the change in the shotgun marriage ratio is $((1 - sr_{t+1})bcoow_{t+1} - (1 - sr_t)bcoow_{t+1})/(oow_{t+1} - oow_t)$. The denominator is the change in the out-of-wedlock birth ratio. The first term in the numerator is the fraction of out-of-wedlock births at $t+1$. The second term is what the fraction would have been at $t+1$ if the shotgun marriage ratio had been the same at $t+1$ as at t. The difference between the first and the second term of the numerator is the change in the out-of-wedlock birthrate due to the change in the shotgun marriage rate.

[4] Thus, in the very poor Pruitt-Igoe public housing project in St. Louis, Rainwater [1970] reports, 'marriage is considered the most attractive solution [to an unwanted pregnancy].' But the custom of marriage, at least in Pruitt-Igoe, was not unquestioned, for Rainwater also observes: 'But it [marriage] is not automatic; shotgun weddings are to be carefully considered, because if the couple is not compatible, they are not likely to stay married.'

unmarried people to obtain contraceptives. In July 1970 the Massachusetts law prohibiting the distribution of contraceptives to unmarried individuals was declared unconstitutional in the landmark case Eisenstadt v. Baird. (See Garrow [1994, p. 457].) This paper will explain why there might be a link between female contraception and the legalization of abortion and the declining shotgun marriage rate.

Why should there be such a link? Both the advent of female contraception and the legalization of abortion are analogous to technical change: each has shifted out the frontier of available choices. While the morality of using these options generates heated debate, family planners have viewed female contraception and abortion as welfare-improving for women: they have made women free to choose. But technological innovation creates both winners and losers. A cost-saving innovation almost invariably penalizes producers who, for whatever reason, fail to adopt it. The hand-loom weavers of Britain in the early nineteenth century are the classic illustration of this point. In the case of female contraception and abortion, women who want children, and women who, because of indecision or religious conviction have failed to adopt the new innovations, have lost disproportionately.[5] Technological change may also benefit those who are not directly affected. For example, the development of yield-increasing varieties of wheat will lower wheat prices and benefit consumers. Analogously, in the case of female contraception and abortion, men may have been beneficiaries. Finally, it is conceivable that technological innovation could even harm those who choose to implement it. For example, if wheat is inelastically demanded, the availability of a new variety that costlessly increases yields will benefit consumers; but the returns to farmers will decline as long as they plant the same wheat acreage.

The first task of this paper is to illustrate, through two theoretical models, how analogous mechanisms could operate with respect to increased availability of abortion and female contraception for women. These models will show how the legalization of abortion and the availability of female contraception could result in a decline in the competitive position of women relative to men—especially if they do not use contraception or abortion.

In the first model a decline in the cost of abortion (or increased availability of contraception) decreases the incentives to obtain a promise of marriage if premarital sexual activity results in pregnancy. Those women who will obtain an abortion or who will reliably use contraception no longer find it necessary to condition sexual relations on such promises. Those women who want children, who do not want an abortion for moral or religious reasons, or who are unreliable in their use of contraception, may want marriage guarantees but find themselves pressured to participate in premarital sexual relations without any such assurance. They have been placed at a competitive disadvantage: in this case analogous to farmers who do not switch to the new varieties of wheat.

---

[5] According to the 1982 National Survey of Family Growth, mothers of children born out of wedlock in 1970 reported that 19 percent of these children were wanted at the time; 65 percent were mistimed or neither wanted nor unwanted; 15 percent were unwanted. These numbers reflect the commonly perceived indecision of women giving birth out of wedlock and ambiguity as to whether the children are wanted or unwanted.

Sexual activity without commitment is increasingly expected in premarital relationships, immiserizing at least some women, since their male partners do not have to assume parental responsibility in order to engage in sexual relations.

A second model illustrates another reason why the previous support system could have been eroded by the advent of female contraception and legal abortion. The fact that the birth of the baby is now a *choice* of the mother has implications for the decisions of the father. The sexual revolution, by making the birth of the child the *physical* choice of the mother, makes marriage and child support a *social* choice of the father. This second model explores how the decisions of the father depend upon the decisions and options of the mother. The logic of this model corresponds to what one contributor to the Internet wrote to the Dads' Rights Newsgroup: 'Since the decision to have the child is solely up to the mother (see Roe v. Wade) I don't see how both parents have responsibility to that child.... When one person has the decision-making power, they alone have the responsibility to provide and care for that decision.'

In this second model, out-of-wedlock birth is the consequence of a sequence of decisions: about male-female relationships, about sexual activity, about the use of contraceptives, about abortion in the event of pregnancy, and about marriage in the event of birth. This work extends that of Becker [1981] by incorporating out-of-wedlock births and the sexual participation decision into a rational choice framework.[6]

The major economic theories for increased out-of-wedlock births are based on changes in job availability (see Wilson [1987]) and changes in welfare incentives (see Murray [1984]),[7] but as will be discussed, empirically neither of these factors explains more than a small fraction of the change. The alternative hypothesis offered in this paper thus fills a void. In the absence of any better theory, despite econometric evidence to the contrary, the welfare theory serves as the primary rationale for reducing welfare support. However, if the rise in out-of-wedlock births is mainly due to technical change or has occurred for yet some further reason, currently envisioned cuts in welfare will fall far short of their proponents' expectations.

This paper offers theoretical reasons why the technological shock of abortion and female contraception may have played a major role in the rise of out-of-wedlock childbearing. If the simplest versions of our models totally explained the data, then arguably the repeal of abortion and the denial of female contraception to unmarried women could reverse this trend. But the change in sexual customs and the subsequent rise in out-of-wedlock births have been accompanied by a decline in the stigma attached to out-of-wedlock childbearing. Because there is no reason to believe that destigmatization is reversible, it does not follow that the prohibition of abortion or of the pill and other contraceptive devices to unmarried women would be effective in reducing out-of-wedlock births. Instead of decreasing out-of-wedlock childbearing, the denial of choice would, in all likelihood, further increase the number of out-of-wedlock births as

---

[6] This paper also extends to premarital states the work on the distribution of returns between men and women in marriage. For a recent review see Lundberg and Pollak [1994].

[7] These are the two main theories reviewed by Ellwood and Crane [1990].

women who would have obtained abortions or used contraceptives instead give birth to unwanted babies.

If Humpty Dumpty cannot be put back together again, what can be done? In the old days a private system of contracting between sexual partners insured that children received the financial and emotional support of two parents. Although the old system may be impossible to reconstruct, social policy can still create incentives that make it costly for fathers to abrogate parental responsibility for their offspring. Ellwood [1988] has suggested administrative ways of making fathers pay. Such a system would not only directly contribute to the well-being of children born out of wedlock, but it would also tax men for fathering such children, thereby offsetting at least partially the technology-shock-induced change in terms between fathers and mothers.

II. BASIC TRENDS

Before presenting models of out-of-wedlock births, it is useful to describe some key facts concerning the magnitude and timing of out-of-wedlock births, total births, abortion, use of the pill, sexual experience as an indicator of sexual participation, shotgun marriage, and the living arrangements of children. These facts will serve as the relevant background both for the development of the models and for their inter-pretation. The Data Appendix describes the derivation of statistics dependent on our own calculations. Table 6.1 summarizes the trends in vital statistics, and Table 6.2 presents statistics concerning important decisions relating to women's fertility and childbearing histories.

Table 6.3 describes time series tests for jumps and changes in trends in the use of abortion and the pill, sexual participation, and the shotgun marriage ratio. All regres-sions were run in first-difference form after failure to reject unit roots in the underlying series, but not in their first differences. In each case we fit ARMA models to characterize the relevant time series processes including year dummies (the dummy in levels is 0 prior to the relevant year and 1 thereafter) to capture discrete changes in the level of a series at one or more dates or trend dummies (the dummy is 0 prior to the relevant data and increases by 1 per annum thereafter) to allow for changes in trends. In the case of abortion, use of the pill, and sexual participation, there was a jump in levels, rather than a change in trend, whereas in the case of the white shotgun marriage ratio there was a change in trend, rather than a jump in the series. The table reports our preferred specifications. Key findings concerning the presence and estimated magnitudes of changes in levels and trends are robust with respect to alternative specifications, including the inclusion of lagged dependent variables, further moving average and autoregressive errors, changes in the sample period, and alternative methods of con-struction of the underlying series.[8] Precise dating of shocks is typically more difficult for nonwhites than for whites. The reported benchmark equations pass standard tests for the absence of autoregressive errors and heteroskedasticity.

---

[8] See Akerlof, Yellen, and Katz [1994] for further details.

Table 6.1. *Vital statistics: births, fertility rates, marital status, out-of-wedlock births*

	1965–1969	1970–1974	1975–1979	1980–1984	1985–1989
Births (in thousands)[a]					
Total	3,599	3,370	3,294	3,646	3,809
White	2,990	2,760	2,660	2,915	3,001
Black	542	538	540	590	636
Birthrates per 1,000 married women 15–44[b]					
White	119.4	103.6	93.1	94.5	90.2
Black	129.1[f]	110.3	93.3	90.6	84.5
Birthrates per 1,000 unmarried women 15–44[c]					
White	12.7	12.6	13.7	18.9	24.1
Black	91.0[f]	94.6	85.5	81.7	84.4
Women married, 15–44 (in percent)[d]					
White	67.8	65.3	61.6	58.8	57.9
Black	55.9[f]	52.9	45.2	39.9	37.7
Men married, 15–44 (in percent)[d]					
White	60.9	58.7	54.9	52.1	51.4
Black	49.7[f]	46.5	42.1	36.8	35.6
Out-of-wedlock births (in 1,000s)[a]					
Total	322	406	515	715	911
White	144	166	220	355	485
Black	189[f]	230	280	337	393
Percent of births out-of-wedlock[e]					
Total	9.0	12.1	15.6	19.6	23.9
White	4.8	6.0	8.2	12.2	16.1
Black	34.9[f]	43.0	51.7	57.1	61.8

[a] *Source: Vital Statistics of the United States, 1989: Volume I—Natality*, Tables 1–76 to 1–79 and Current Population Series P-20.
[b] *Source: Vital Statistics of the United States, 1989: Volume I—Natality*, Tables 1–77.
[c] *Source: Vital Statistics of the United States, 1989: Volume I—Natality*, Table 1–76.
[d] *Source*: Current Population Reports, Series P-20, *Marital Status and Living Arrangements and Marital Status and Family Status.*
[e] *Source: Vital Statistics of the United States, 1989: Volume I—Natality*, Tables 1–77 and 1–78.
[f] Based only on 1969 figures.

A. *Out-of-Wedlock Births*

The fraction of children born out of wedlock increased at an accelerated pace beginning in the middle 1960s, for both whites and blacks. This trend has continued almost to the present time. In 1970 there were about 400,000 out-of-wedlock births (out of 3.7 million total births); in 1990 there were 1.2 million out-of-wedlock births (out of 4.0 million total).

Table 6.2. *Experience of unmarried women: sexual participation, use of pill, shotgun marriage, living arrangements of children, and adoptions*

	1965–1969	1970–1974	1975–1979	1980–1984
Women age 16 with sexual experience (percent)[a]				
White	13.8	23.2	28.1	32.8
Black	35.0	42.3	50.8	49.9
Unmarried women using pill on first intercourse (in percent)[b]	5.7	15.2	13.4	NA
Abortions of unmarried women 15–44 (1,000s)[c,d]	88	561	985	1,271[h]
Per 1,000 unmarried women 15–44	6.7	35.3	50.0	54.2
First birth shotgun marriage rate (percent)[e]				
White: marriage before birth	59.2	55.4	45.7	42.0
Marriage before first birthday	70.9	65.6	57.6	53.3
Black: marriage before birth	24.8	19.5	11.0	11.4
Marriage before first birthday	34.7	29.3	18.1	16.4
Children age 3 to 5 living with never married mother (percent)[f]				
White	NA	0.5[i]	1.5[i]	2.2
Black	NA	13.5[i]	23.4[i]	28.6
Children age 3 to 5 living with neither parent (percent)[f]				
White	NA	1.5[i]	1.9[i]	1.5[i]
Black	NA	5.0[i]	5.6[i]	6.5[i]
Adoptions (in 1,000s)[h]	158	156	129[j]	142[j]
Through agencies	83	69	48[j]	51[j]
By individuals	75	86	81[j]	91[j]
Ratio of adoptions to out-of-wedlock births (in percent)	49.0	38.4	29.0[j]	19.8[j]

[a] *Source*: Women in given year who had ever had intercourse from retrospective data in the 1982 National Survey of Family Growth.

[b] *Source*: Women using pill on first intercourse by year from retrospective data in the 1982 National Survey of Family Growth.

[c] *Source*: 1965–1972: abortions for women 15 to 44 from retrospective reports in the 1982 National Survey of Family Growth, adjusted for age truncation, adjusted to conform to the Alan Guttmacher series for years 1973–1981.

[d] *Source*: 1973–1984: *Abortion Factbook: 1992 Edition*, Alan Guttmacher Institute, Table 3, pp. 176–177.

[e] *Source*: Authors' calculations based on data from June 1980, 1982, and 1990 Fertility Supplements of the Current Population Survey.

[f] *Source*: Current Population Reports, Series P-20, *Marital Status and Family Status*.

[g] *Source: Adoption Factbook*. Washington, DC: National Committee for Adoption, 1989. Table 11, p. 99.

[h] Figure for 1983 is the average of 1982 and 1984.

[i] Adjusted for increased coverage after 1982. Children with neither parent includes those living in group quarters or not in families.

[j] 1975 to 1979 is based on 1975 adoption survey; 1980 to 1984 is based on 1982 adoption survey.

Table 6.3. *Time series properties of abortion, use of pill, sexual experience, and shotgun marriage*

Dependent variable	Years	Constant	Change in 1970 dummy	Change in 1971 dummy	MA(1)	AR(1)	AR(2)	Adjusted R^2
Change in abortions per 1,000 women 15 to 44[a]								
White women	1960–1987	−0.013 (0.45)	10.90*** (2.31)	—	−0.60*** (0.17)	—	—	0.55
Nonwhite women	1960–1987	−0.170 (0.28)	6.24** (2.87)	7.51** (2.86)	0.40 (0.29)	-1.07*** (0.22)	−0.46** (0.17)	0.55
Change in percentage of all women using pill on first intercourse[b]	1961–1980	−0.0038 (7.10)	9.60** (3.82)	—	−0.96*** (0.30)	—	—	0.58
Change in percentage of 16-year-old women with sexual experience[c]								
White women	1955–1981	0.41 (0.97)	10.20*** (3.58)	—	−1.00*** (0.12)	—	—	0.40
Black women	1955–1981	0.21 (1.29)	—	13.63** (6.27)	−0.94 (0.15)	—	−0.51*** (0.15)	0.45

Dependent variable	Years	Constant	1968 change in trend dummy	MA(1)	Adjusted R^2
Change in first-birth shotgun marriage ratio[d]					
White women	1955–1989	0.0083	−0.021**	−0.90***	0.48
		(0.0069)	(0.0089)	(0.11)	
Black women	1955–1989	−0.0037	−0.0057	−0.75***	0.40
		(0.013)	(0.017)	(0.13)	

[a] *Source:* Abortions per 1,000 women 15 to 44 from retrospective reports in the 1982 and 1988 National Survey of Family Growth, adjusted for age truncation, combined. See Data Appendix.
[b] *Source:* Percent of women using the pill on first intercourse by year of first intercourse from retrospective reports in the 1982 National Survey of Family Growth. See Data Appendix.
[c] *Source:* Percentage of 16-year-old women in the given year who had ever had intercourse from retrospective data in the 1982 National Survey of Family Growth. See Data Appendix.
[d] *Source:* Authors' calculations based on data from the June 1980, 1982, and 1990 Fertility Supplements of the Current Population Survey. The dependent variable is the percentage of women who conceived their first child out of wedlock and married within seven months prior to the birth of the child. A child is considered to be conceived out of wedlock if the mother was unmarried eight months prior to the birth. See Data Appendix.

Standard errors are in parentheses. *Significance at the 10 percent level. **Significance at the 5 percent level. ***Significance at the 1 percent level.

B. Fertility and Marriage Rates

The number of births per unmarried woman aged 15 to 44 roughly doubled for whites from the late 1960s to the late 1980s. In contrast, for blacks this rate declined by 5 to 10 percent over the same period. For both whites and blacks the fraction of unmarried women rose dramatically: by slightly more than 30 percent for whites and by slightly more than 40 percent for blacks. There were also rapid declines in the fertility rates of married women, by almost a third for blacks and a quarter for whites. The decline in the fertility rates of married women and the decrease in the fraction of married women contributed, along with the decline in the shotgun marriage ratio, to the rise in the out-of-wedlock birth ratio.[9]

C. Abortions

Abortions to unmarried women prior to legalization were fairly small in number; our estimates show them to be less than 100,000 per year in the late 1960s.[10] This compares with an annual average of 322,000 out-of-wedlock births from 1965 to 1969. Abortion, both in absolute and in relative terms, increased rapidly in the 1970s. From 1980 to 1984 abortions to unmarried women averaged more than 1.25 million, while out-of-wedlock births had risen to 715,000.

As shown in the preferred regression in Table 6.3, there appears to have been a discrete abortion shock in 1970 just at the time of legalization of abortion in New York and the liberalization in California under the Beilensen Act. Many other states liberalized their abortion laws at about this time (see Luker [1984, p. 272]).

D. The Pill

Use of the pill by unmarried women on first intercourse became a significant factor in the 1970s. According to retrospective self-reports in the National Survey of Family Growth, use of the pill on first intercourse averaged 15 percent from 1970 to 1974, more than double the fraction of the previous five years. The preferred regression equation (reported in Table 6.3) shows that a jump occurred between 1969 and 1970. Given the significant fraction of unmarried women using the pill on first intercourse, it is likely that a sizable fraction of all sexually active unmarried women were using the pill in the 1970s.

E. Sexual Experience

Our index of sexual experience—the fraction of women retrospectively reporting having had sexual intercourse prior to age sixteen—jumped in precisely 1970 for whites and possibly one year later for blacks as shown by the regression results in

---

[9] Nathanson and Kim [1989] have devised a decomposition that has shown the importance of decreasing marriage and increasing sexual experience for teenagers for the period 1971 to 1979.

[10] For a discussion of the accuracy of abortion statistics, see the Data Appendix.

Table 6.3. Due to greater noise in the black data than in the white data, however, this jump is more difficult to date for blacks.

F. *Shotgun Marriage*

The white shotgun marriage ratio began to fall in the late 1960s. In 1969 the first-birth shotgun marriage rate peaked at 0.61; by 1988 it had fallen to 0.35. There has been a similar fall in the black shotgun marriage ratio, beginning earlier, however, than the negative trend for whites. In the late 1960s the black shotgun marriage ratio was about 0.25; by the late 1980s it had fallen to about 0.085. If the shotgun marriage rate had remained at its 1965–1969 level, the rise in the out-of-wedlock first-birth ratio for whites would have been 85 percent smaller over the ensuing fifteen years, and 76 percent smaller over the ensuing twenty. The decline in the shotgun marriage ratio also played an important role in the increase in the out-of-wedlock first-birth ratio for blacks, although the corresponding contributions, 50 percent and 58 percent, respectively, are not as large.

G. *Births and Abortion*

There was a drop in births both to black and white teenage women in New York immediately following the legalization of abortion in New York in 1970. However, recent studies, which are discussed below, have surprisingly found a positive relation between teenage births and abortion availability.

H. *Living Arrangements of Children*

In the old days, prior to the 1970s, only a small fraction of children born out of wedlock were kept by mothers who never married. In contrast, today only a small fraction are put up for adoption or given to other relatives. Consider the disposition of the 360,000 out-of-wedlock children born in 1969, just before the technology shock. According to our own estimate, the mothers of 135,000 of these children married within the next three years.[11] Of the remaining 225,000 children, 65,000 were reported living with never married mothers three years later. Seventy thousand children in the 1969 cohort were reported in 1972 as living with neither parent, a figure that entails some double counting since not all of these children were born out of wedlock. These figures are roughly consistent with the high rate of adoption at the time. In 1969 there were 170,000 adoptions, including some children whose mothers had been married at the time of birth.[12] The fraction of children kept by the mothers who had not married within three years was roughly 0.28.

---

[11] We calculated an extended shotgun marriage ratio, defined as the fraction of births conceived out of wedlock resulting in marriage before the child's third birthday. Applying these rates to the number of out-of-wedlock births reported in Vital Statistics yielded estimates of the fraction of out-of-wedlock children whose mothers had married before the age of three.

[12] Because of reporting error, double counting, and children whose mothers were married at the time of birth, the sum of adoptions, children living with neither parent, children living with never married mothers, and children with mothers who later married do not add to the total number of out-of-wedlock births. Four

In contrast, fifteen years later a much larger fraction of children born out of wedlock were kept by their mothers. In 1984 there were 770,000 of these births. We estimate that the mothers of 200,000 of these children were married within three years. Of the remaining 570,000 about 320,000 were reported living with mothers who had never married three years later, and there were 60,000 with neither parent. Annual adoptions had fallen to 105,000. The ratio of children living with never married mothers to those born out of wedlock whose mothers had not married had doubled to 0.56.

III. A RUDIMENTARY MODEL OF FEMALE IMMISERATION

We shall now present a rudimentary model of shotgun marriage. In this model, prior to sexual relations, women may or may not ask for a promise of marriage in the event of pregnancy. If they ask for such a guarantee, they are afraid that their partners will seek other relationships. When the cost of abortion is low, or contraceptives are readily available, potential male partners can easily obtain sexual satisfaction without making such promises and will thus be reluctant to commit to marriage. Thus, women who, in the absence of contraception and abortion, would not engage in premarital sexual activity without assurance of marriage will feel pressured to participate in uncommitted relationships once contraception and abortion become available. In this model the implicit or explicit promise to marry is viewed as an enforceable contract. Men will, if necessary, meet their prior commitments.

Prior to sexual relations a woman may or may not ask for an implicit or explicit promise of marriage in the event of pregnancy. We saw that 25 years ago among white working-class youths in San Francisco such a promise was the norm.[13] Our own survey (described below) of University of California at Berkeley undergraduates in the summer of 1994 suggests that today premarital sexual activity does not usually entail such a commitment.

---

different sources of data were used, each with its own reporting error. The total number of out-of-wedlock births is from *Vital Statistics*. Estimates of the fraction of mothers who had married within three years of birth come from the Current Population Survey's Fertility Supplements, which contain retrospective questions regarding women's dates of marriage and birth dates of their children. The number of children living with never married mothers and the number of those with neither parent are from the annual March CPS surveys on living arrangements. Adoption statistics come from the National Committee for Adoption. The number of children in the one-year cohort living with a never married mother or living with neither parent was estimated as one-third of the children aged three to five in these respective categories. Those classified as living with neither biological nor adoptive parents correspond to the Census categories 'living in households with neither parent' and 'not in families.' Both the series on children living with never married mothers and those living with neither parent were adjusted for the change in coverage in 1982. Of course, children with neither parent and adoptions include some whose mothers had been married at the time of birth. Adoptees also include children whose parents have remarried and have been adopted by a new spouse.

[13] Luker [1991, p. 78] writes: 'Yet even these statistics [on the growth of teen sexuality from the 1950s to 1979–1981] do not capture how profoundly different [current] teen sexuality is from that of earlier eras. As sources such as the Kinsey Report suggest, premarital sex for many American women before the 1960s was "engagement" sex. The woman's involvement, at least, was exclusive and she generally went on to marry her partner in a relatively short period of time. Almost half of the women in the Kinsey data who had premarital sex had it with their fiances.'

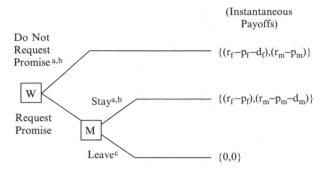

a. p_f takes on the two values $p_f^+ > 0$ and $p_f^- < 0$
b. with probability θ random mating occurs in the next period
c. with probability 1 random mating occurs in the next period

Figure 6.1. *Marriage request game tree with payoffs.*

A. *Decisions in the Game*

Figure 6.1 presents the tree for a simple game that focuses on the role of 'competition' as it affects the choices of women whether or not to exact a promise to marry as a condition for premarital sexual activity. The decision of the woman is whether or not to ask for such a promise. If she asks for this assurance, she runs the risk that her boyfriend will exit. The basic decision for the man is whether or not to leave the relationship when such a guarantee is the prerequisite for sexual relations with his current partner. We shall proceed to describe the payoffs to the woman and to the man.

B. *Payoffs to the Woman*

If the woman chooses to engage in premarital sex but does not exact the contingent marriage promise, she receives an instantaneous payoff $(r_f - p_f - d_f)$. p_f is the expected per period cost of pregnancy if there is a marriage promise prior to sexual relations. d_f is the expected per period additional loss if she does not obtain a promise of marriage from her partner. r_f is the per period value to her of her relationship with her partner. We assume that, if both parties have agreed to the relationship, then the relationship will continue in the next period with probability $1 - \theta$ and will terminate with probability θ. If the relationship terminates, there will be random pairing of available men and women in the next period. For tractability it is assumed that there are equal numbers of men and women.[14] The payoff to such a game will be v_f, the value of the game to this woman with random mating. In either event—if the woman begins a new relationship or if she continues the old—the future payoffs will be weighted with a discount factor γ.

[14] Other authors have emphasized that changes in the ratio of men to women will affect the equilibrium number of men who would rather marry than remain single. (See, for example, Willis [1994].)

To continue the discussion of the payoffs, if the woman asks for an assurance of marriage in the event of pregnancy, the man may then either remain in the relationship, or leave. If the man remains, the woman's payoff is $(r_f - p_f)$ in the current period. She keeps the relationship, whose per period return is r_f. She also continues to bear the potential costs of pregnancy, p_f, but without the extra costs of single motherhood because of the promise. Next period with probability $1 - \theta$ she will continue the same relationship with the same instantaneous payoffs, and with probability θ she will begin a new relationship with value v_f.

If the man leaves, the woman receives an instantaneous payoff of zero. She has forgone the relationship this period and, with it, the complications of a possible pregnancy. Next period she will begin another relationship whose expected value is v_f.

C. *Payoffs to the Man*

If the woman does not exact a promise prior to premarital sex, the man's instantaneous payoff is r_m, the per period value of the relationship. For convenience we assume that p_m, the man's pregnancy cost, is zero if he has not promised to marry the woman. As in the case of the woman, the relationship will continue with probability $1 - \theta$, and with probability θ the man will begin a new game with random mating of women seeking partners. The value of such a game to the man is v_m. If the woman exacts the promise and the man stays in the relationship, he receives an instantaneous payoff $(r_m - d_m)$. Again, with probability $1 - \theta$ the relationship will continue, and with probability θ he returns to the matching pool. Analogous to the notation for the woman's payoff, d_m is the expected per period cost of the promise of potential marriage. If the man leaves, in the next period he will begin a new game with value v_m. Of course, future returns are discounted by the factor γ.

D. *A Simple Example*

In principle, all of the payoffs, p_f, p_m, r_f, r_m, d_f, and d_m, have distributions across individuals. We shall make the minimal assumptions necessary to illustrate the earlier analogy with the hand-loom weavers. Such an illustration requires two types of women. One of these types will adopt the technologies of abortion or contraception or both when they become available, with a probable increase in welfare, while the other type will not adopt the new technologies and will consequently become impoverished. Men are all of the same type.

Women in this example fall into two classes depending on their expected costs of pregnancy. For a fraction α the expected cost of pregnancy is positive, denoted p_f^+. For these women pregnancies will be terminated by abortion if this option is available at sufficiently low cost. In order to model what we consider the norm in the old days, we shall assume that p_f^+ is not only positive but also less than r_f so that p_f^+ women would be willing to participate in sexual activity if their boyfriends promise to marry them. In addition, we shall assume that the sum $p_f^+ + d_f$ exceeds r_f so that, in the absence of contraception and abortion, p_f^+ women will not engage in sexual activity without an assurance of marriage.

In contrast to the women for whom a pregnancy without marriage would lead to a decrease in utility, we assume that there is a second group of women, a fraction $(1 - \alpha)$ of the population, for whom the cost of pregnancy, denoted p_f^-, is negative. We also assume that $r_f > p_f^- + d_f$, so that these women are willing to engage in premarital sex and bring the baby to term even without an assurance of marriage. d_f is also assumed to be positive. As a result, p_f^- women prefer a baby without a husband to neither baby nor husband, but, better yet, they would prefer both baby and husband.

While two types of women are necessary to illustrate the analogy with the hand-loom weavers, our example requires only one type of man. For simplicity, we shall assume that p_m is zero and that d_m, which is the same for all men, is positive but less than r_m. Men would prefer not to make a marriage promise, but they would be willing to do so if that is their only way to maintain their relationships.

E. *The Equilibrium*

We can now describe the equilibria in this model both before and after the technology shock. Before the technology shock it is clear that no woman with positive pregnancy costs will engage in sexual activity without a promise of marriage. There will always be an equilibrium in which women with negative pregnancy costs will also demand a promise of marriage before engaging in sexual activity. Indeed, this will be the unique equilibrium as long as α, the fraction of p_f^+ women, is sufficiently high. With α sufficiently high, even if *no* p_f^- women were demanding a promise of marriage, it would pay a man to stay with any p_f^- individual woman who decided to demand such a promise.[15] In this equilibrium p_f^+ women, who would be unwilling to bear children in the absence of marriage, demand a marriage assurance in the event of pregnancy, while p_f^- women, who would be willing to bear children even in the absence of marriage, demand the same, since they know the man will accept. For the man it is not worthwhile to seek another relationship because he would forfeit current utility and, ultimately, do no better.

Let us now see how this game and its equilibrium will be altered by the development of inexpensive and easily available contraception and abortion. Let us assume that the cost of abortion to p_f^+ women is less than the cost of pregnancy. For simplicity, let the cost of the abortion be zero. Empirically, the financial cost of an abortion is extremely low relative to the financial cost of raising a child. (Alternatively, we could assume that reliable contraception becomes available.) With the advent of abortion a p_f^+ woman has no need to request a promise in the event of pregnancy. And even if she were to ask for such a promise, her partner would know that he would have no cost in fulfilling it, since the woman would obtain an abortion rather than bring the baby to term. The payoff to the p_f^+ women becomes r_f, with the payoff to the man in such a

---

[15] The man's stay/leave decision will be affected by the ratio of promise/do not promise women to be encountered in the random mating process. This ratio in the next period's random matching, however, will always be greater than $\alpha/(1 - \alpha)$ since all p_f^+ women demand promises (of whom a fraction θ will be searching for new partners in the next period) and all the p_f^- women who are deserted by their partners and are therefore looking for new mates in the next period have decided on the demand-promise strategy.

relationship, symmetrically, r_m. In this example, the new technology enhances the welfare of p_f^+ women and their partners.

Let us now consider the decision of a p_f^- woman and of her partner. This woman may ask for a promise of marriage, but if she does, her partner may leave. With abortion and the range of p_f^+ and d_f in our example, we know that the man will get r_m next period if he encounters a p_f^+ woman. Indeed, he will always leave if parameter values are such that the random mating of the next period yields him a p_f^+ woman with sufficiently high probability and if his disutility of marriage and discount factor are also sufficiently high. Under these conditions, the p_f^- woman therefore will not ask the man for a promise because she knows he would leave, and the man will stay in the relationship without making a commitment since he will not fare better elsewhere. The consequence is that after abortion and contraception become easily available, there is a new equilibrium in which no woman—even if she wants children and marriage—asks for a promise of marriage. In this equilibrium if any woman did ask for such a promise, her partner would leave, and she would lose the relationship. The p_f^- women, like the hand-loom weavers, suffer a reduction in welfare.[16]

A slight modification of this example illustrates the possibility that all women, like the wheat farmers, could lose from implementing the new technology. Suppose that the advent of contraception/abortion decreases pregnancy costs without eliminating them. This may cause a switch from a unique equilibrium, with all women obtaining marriage commitments, to dual stable equilibria. In one equilibrium, as before, every woman obtains a marriage promise, and welfare is unchanged, but in the other equilibrium no woman obtains a marriage guarantee because each correctly foresees that such a demand would cause the breakup of her relationship. A move to this no-commitment trap is likely to reduce welfare for all women. In this example the gains from the advent of abortion and contraception accrue totally to the men.

Although we have used the model to analyze the effect of changes in abortion and contraceptive availability, other changes can easily be incorporated. Increases in welfare benefits payable only to single mothers will decrease the value of d_f, as will changes in the stigma of single motherhood. Better labor market opportunities for women, so that there is less dependence on male financial support, will likewise decrease the value of d_f. Higher wages for women will also increase the cost of pregnancy, p_f, because of the

[16] If α, the fraction of p_f^+ women, is sufficiently low, there will also be equilibria in which all p_f^- women ask men to stay, and no man paired with such a woman will leave. In addition, in this very simple model there may be mixed equilibria with some women demanding marriage promises and other women forgoing them over a wide range of parameter values. This occurs, however, for an implausible reason. If a large number of p_f^- women ask men for marriage promises but a significant fraction of those men leave, disappointed p_f^- women who ask men for a promise to marry may dominate the random pairings in the next period. A high probability of encountering such a partner in the next stage of the game can be sufficient inducement for a fraction of the men to stay even when asked for a marriage commitment. This fraction of men staying will in turn be the incentive for some women to ask for a promise of marriage. We believe that this flooding of the random pairings with women asking for commitments after the technology shock is only a curiosum. For simplicity, we assumed that the exogenous probability of the relationship's termination, θ, did not depend upon the type of relationship between the couples. It seems reasonable, however, that the probability of a breakup is higher for couples in 'uncommitted' relationships than for those in committed ones. As a result, with just a bit more realism, the equilibrium with no p_f^- women asking for marriage assurances is likely to be unique.

increased opportunity cost of own child care. Increased financial obligation by unmarried fathers for their biological offspring will increase p_m if the father does not marry the mother, and it will also decrease the value of d_m.

F. *Isomorphic Model of Sexual Participation*

Under a slight reinterpretation the previous game structure illustrates how increased competition may affect sexual participation. In this analogous model, women decide whether or not to engage in premarital sex at all, and men then decide whether to remain in relationships without sexual activity. This model is isomorphic to the previous one, with participate/do not participate substituting for promise/do not promise. Before the technology shock, abstinence would be the norm for all women. After the technology shock those women who would use contraception or would be willing to obtain an abortion in the event of pregnancy or both engage in premarital sexual activity. However, those women who are not willing to use contraception or obtain an abortion will also engage in sexual activity, since they correctly fear that if they abstain their partners would seek satisfaction elsewhere. The advent of contraception and abortion used by others may result in an unwanted increase in sexual participation for those who reject the new technology.

IV. SEXUAL PARTICIPATION, ABORTION, AND SHOTGUN MARRIAGE

The previous section illustrated the consequences of competition in games with only one major decision. In reality, however, shotgun marriage is the outcome of a sequence of decisions: about premarital sexual activity, abortion, and marriage. In this section we model this sequence of decisions, with one significant change from the previous game. In that model the promise to marry was considered enforceable. In contrast, we now assume the man's willingness to marry just prior to the birth of the child depends upon a comparison of his own cost of getting married with his perception of the cost to his partner of becoming a single mother.

The previous model showed that advances in reproductive technology could lead to the immiseration of women through increased competition. The model in this section illustrates another mechanism whereby the technology shock could lead to the feminization of poverty. In the old world, before the sexual revolution, women were less free to choose, but men were expected to assume responsibility for their welfare, an expectation that was more often fulfilled than breached. Nowadays women are freer to choose, but men are affording themselves the comparable option. In the model we present, the man reasons: 'If she is not willing to obtain an abortion or use contraception, why should I sacrifice myself to get married?' This model accurately predicts a decline in shotgun marriage: with abortion readily available, many relationships that previously ended in shotgun marriages now end in abortion. When, instead, the woman carries the baby to term, the man can also rationalize remaining single. The model also realistically predicts a decline in the fertility rate (see Wilson and Neckerman [1986])

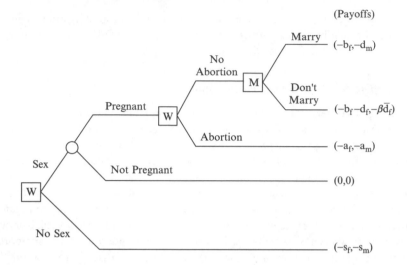

Figure 6.2. *Sequence of decisions and payoffs confronting a couple initiating a sexual relationship.*

and an increase in the out-of-wedlock birthrate. However, as shall be discussed later, we think that the factors emphasized in the last section are probably more important empirically in explaining the increase in out-of-wedlock births in the United States.

A. *Description of the Model*

Figure 6.2 is a tree diagram showing the sequence of decisions and their payoffs for a couple deciding whether or not to initiate a sexual relationship.[17] We omit from this model the value of the relationship to the woman and the man, r_f and r_m, respectively, but we shall describe in greater detail than in the previous model the sequence of decisions that each partner faces and then the payoffs attached to the various outcomes. In the beginning, the woman decides whether or not to initiate a sexual relationship with her partner. If she decides to have sex, there are potential future consequences. With probability q the woman becomes pregnant. This probability obviously depends on whether or not the partners use contraception, but for simplicity we ignore contraception and take q as fixed. If the woman becomes pregnant, we assume that she next chooses whether or not to have an abortion. If she chooses not to have an abortion, her partner must then decide whether or not to marry her (and she has to decide whether or not to marry him). Interestingly, a model in which the woman chooses whether or not to use contraception, rather than to obtain an abortion, is exactly isomorphic and yields results analogous to those obtained in the present model.

---

[17] The same decision tree is used by Lundberg and Plotnick [1990, p. 247] in their study of the effects of state policies on pregnancy, abortion, and marriage.

The payoffs corresponding to each path of the tree determine the equilibrium outcomes of the game, including the shotgun marriage rate. We first describe the payoffs to the woman and then to the man.

B. *Payoffs to the Woman*

For notational convenience we shall normalize the payoffs so that the woman's payoff if she engages in sex and does not become pregnant is 0. If she decides to forgo the relationship entirely, her payoff is $-s_f$. If the woman agrees to the sexual relationship and a pregnancy occurs, she has the further choice of whether or not to obtain an abortion. The financial and emotional cost of the abortion to the woman is a_f, so her payoff if she chooses an abortion is $-a_f$. If she does not choose to have an abortion, there are two possibilities: either her partner marries her, or she is left as a single mother. We let b_f be the cost of having a child even if she does get married, so that her payoff as a married mother is $-b_f$. In contrast to our previous model, we assume for simplicity that b_f is positive for all women, so that no women want children, even with marriage. If she does not get married, there is an additional cost (both financial and emotional) in the amount d_f, so that her payoff in this state is $-b_f - d_f$. (For simplicity, we assume that $d_f > 0$ so that all women prefer marriage to single motherhood. With $d_f < 0$, a woman prefers single parenthood to marriage to the partner, and the game tree must include the woman's decision whether or not to marry as well.)

C. *Payoffs to the Man*

We normalize the man's payoffs by assuming that the reward from sex is 0 if no pregnancy occurs. Assuming that the man gains enjoyment from sex equal to s_m, his payoff if the woman chooses not to initiate a sexual relationship is $-s_m$. In the event of a pregnancy the man's payoff depends on whether or not the woman chooses an abortion and, if not, whether the man marries her. To allow for the possibility that the woman's choice of an abortion may be costly to the man, we denote the man's payoff in the event that the woman chooses an abortion as $-a_m$. If the man's partner chooses not to abort, the man's payoff depends on whether or not he marries her. We assume for simplicity that marriage imposes a cost of d_m on the man, so that his payoff if he marries is $-d_m$. Survey research by Marsiglio [1988] suggests that the major costs which men attach to forming households with their partners as a consequence of unplanned pregnancy stem from the loss of interaction with friends and inability to date other women. Men also strongly believe that they would be required to obtain steady work. But to explain why men may nevertheless marry, we assume that there is also a cost to be borne in the event that the man fails to marry the mother of his child. We let this cost depend on the concern of the man with his partner's (and child's) well-being as reflected in the parameter β and on the amount of suffering that the man expects to impose on the woman by his failure to tie the knot, denoted $\bar{d}_f$, where $\bar{d}_f$ is the mean value of d_f in the population of women who choose not to have abortions following unplanned pregnancies. The man's payoff is thus $-d_m$ if he marries the woman and $-\beta \bar{d}_f$ if he does not. An important assumption is that the man's feeling of guilt depends on $\bar{d}_f$ and not on the woman's own d_f, which we assume is unobservable. The importance of guilt as a motive for marriage is consistent with Marsiglio's findings. In the words of one respondent: 'I wouldn't want to marry my girlfriend but since it was *my fault* I couldn't leave her in the cold' (italics added).

D. *A Simple Example*

In principle, virtually all of the payoffs along the tree differ among individuals, and therefore should be characterized by a joint distribution in the population. However, a simple example illustrates how the decline in the cost of abortion can induce a rise in the out-of-wedlock birthrate. We shall analyze the outcomes of this game in the simple case in which women differ only with respect to their values of d_f, the disutility of being single—rather than married—mothers, and men differ only with respect to d_m, the disutility of marrying. We assume that for all women, d_f is uniformly distributed from 0 to D_f^{max}. Because there is the possibility that some women—those with high values of d_f—may not engage in sex at all, the distribution of d_f for pregnant women may not occur over this entire range. We let D_f denote the maximum value of d_f for those women who engage in sex, with the possibility of pregnancy. We assume that d_m is uniformly distributed from 0 to D_m. The remaining parameters are assumed to be the same for all individuals. These include a_f, the cost of abortion; b_f, the cost of having a child; β, the man's degree of empathy; s_f and s_m, the returns to sex for the woman and man; a_m, the man's distaste for abortion; and q, the odds of pregnancy. This simple model allows a surprisingly rich description of the interactions between the woman's decision and the man's.[18]

E. *Equilibria of the Game*

If the cost of abortion is less than the cost of single motherhood, this game has a trivial solution: all pregnant women obtain abortions. Since in this case there are no births whatsoever, we focus on the more relevant case in which $a_f > b_f$. In this instance the

---

[18] Pairs for whom (d_f, d_m) are not in the positive orthant will reveal their true values of d_f and d_m prior to the abortion decision and therefore will separate themselves from the game that we are describing here. The minimum values of d_f and d_m at 0 correctly reflect the information structure of the game for pairs of men and women for whom $d_f > 0$ and men for whom $d_m > 0$. If the woman has a negative value of d_f, she has no reason not to reveal it to her partner prior to the abortion decision since she does not want to marry him in any case. She should then make up her mind whether or not to have a baby dependent upon whether $a_f > b_f$ or $a_f < b_f$ independent of the man's decision. If the man has a negative value of d_m, then he should reveal that to his partner prior to the abortion decision. If d_m is negative and d_f is positive, the couple should reveal their information and then get married if the woman does not prefer an abortion. The game we have described will take place, however, if both d_f and d_m are greater than 0. If $d_m > 0$, the man wants the woman to believe that d_m is as large as possible to maximize her willingness to obtain an abortion. Similarly, if $d_f > 0$, the woman wants the man to believe that d_f is as great as possible so he will marry her. In such a situation neither the man's statements about his value of d_m nor the woman's statements about her value of d_f are credible. In these circumstances our model correctly assumes that the man and the woman know the distribution of d_f and d_m, but not their values for their specific partners.

frequency of abortions, legitimate births, and out-of-wedlock births depend on parameter values.

With $a_f > b_f$, the game contains a basic simultaneity: abortion is sufficiently costly that any pregnant woman would prefer to carry her baby to term if she could be sure that her partner would marry her. But men differ in the disutility of marriage (d_m). Some will, and others will not, marry partners who forgo abortion. Thus, the woman's decision whether or not to abort depends on her perceived probability that the man will marry her if she carries the baby to term. For a given probability of marriage, those women with d_f in excess of a critical value, d_f^{crit}, choose to abort. For these women the disutility of single parenthood is too high to risk bearing a child. In contrast, women with d_f below d_f^{crit} carry their babies to term, gambling on the prospect that, having decided against abortion, their partners will legitimate the child. These decisions of the women determine the average d_f of those women choosing not to abort. This value is $\bar{d}_f$; with the uniform distribution assumed, $\bar{d}_f = d_f^{crit}/2$. The higher the probability of marriage, the higher is d_f^{crit}.

Simultaneity arises because the probability of marriage depends in turn on d_f^{crit}. The higher is d_f^{crit}, the more likely it will be that men will marry women who choose to forgo abortions. The decision of the men whether or not to marry, given their own distaste for it, depends on the perceived cost to their partners of single parenthood. Men marry if $d_m < \beta \bar{d}_f$. With d_m uniformly distributed from 0 to D_m, the odds of marriage, F, for women choosing not to abort is $\beta \bar{d}_f / D_m$. We assume that men have no information concerning the actual d_f of their partner but they do have an accurate assessment of the mean value of d_f of women choosing not to abort. Thus, their decision is positively conditioned on their estimated value of $\bar{d}_f$.

The rational expectations equilibrium requires that $\bar{d}_f$ must be the actual mean value of d_f of those women choosing not to abort. In consequence,

$$\bar{d}_f = d_f^{crit}/2. \tag{1}$$

Provided that d_f^{crit} is below its ceiling of D_f, it will be determined so that the marginal woman with $d_f = d_f^{crit}$ is exactly indifferent whether or not to abort. The payoff if a woman chooses abortion is $-a_f$, and the payoff if the woman chooses not to abort is $-b_f$ with probability F (which is $\beta \bar{d}_f / D_m$) and $-b_f - d_f$ with probability $1 - F$ (which is $1 - \beta \bar{d}_f / D_m$). The value of d_f^{crit} such that the woman is exactly indifferent to getting an abortion satisfies the equation,

$$\frac{b_f \beta \bar{d}_f}{D_m} + (b_f + d_f^{crit})\left(\frac{D_m - \beta \bar{d}_f}{D_m}\right) = a_f. \tag{2}$$

In the internal solution in which the limits on the value of d_f^{crit} are not binding, we can express $d_f^{crit}/2$ as a function of $\bar{d}_f$:[19]

---

[19] If $(a_f - b_f)/(1 - \beta \bar{d}_f / D_m) \geq D_f$, then the limits on d_f^{crit} are binding, and $d_f^{crit} = D_f$.

$$\frac{d_f^{crit}}{2} = \frac{a_f - b_f}{2(1 - \beta \bar{d}_f / D_m)}.$$ (3)

Equation (3) is a 'reaction function' that shows how the decision of women whether or not to abort depends on the mean value of d_f. As $\bar{d}_f$ rises, the odds of marriage rise, and thus d_f^{crit} rises, inducing more women to forgo abortion.

The equilibrium in this subgame is determined by the requirements that (1) and (3) be simultaneously satisfied. The solution sets are somewhat complex, largely because of ceilings and the possibility of multiple equilibria when D_f is sufficiently large, but the nature of the solutions can be summarized by a graph, which plots the equilibrium value(s) of $\bar{d}_f$ as a function of $a_f - b_f$.

Figure 6.3 shows that as the cost of abortion, a_f, falls, with the cost of bearing a child (b_f) constant, the equilibrium value of $\bar{d}_f$ will fall. A decrease in the cost of abortion raises both the abortion rate and the out-of-wedlock birthrate. With abortion less costly, the fertility rate is lower for sexually active women. With fewer women choosing to carry their babies to term, the mean disutility of single parenthood among women choosing to bear children declines, and there is a consequent decrease in the marriage rate (F). The out-of-wedlock birthrate therefore rises.

For each equilibrium plotted in Figure 6.3, the welfare (pay-offs) to women and to men can be easily calculated. Three comparative static results are obtained if we restrict our attention to 'internal equilibria.' First, as the cost of abortion falls, women who do not refrain from sexual activity and who will not obtain an abortion if they become pregnant will lose out, because their probability of marriage will decline. Second, the expected value of welfare for all women may rise, or decline, dependent on the distribution of women's attributes. Third, as long as the parameter a_m (the man's own disutility of abortion) is sufficiently low, men's welfare will rise with a decline in the cost of abortion.[20]

The model may be expanded to include AFDC payments which are paid only to single mothers. The simplest way in which to incorporate such payments is to let the payoff to the woman in the event of single motherhood be equal to $-b_f - d_f + w$, where w is the level of AFDC payments. The payoff to the man who does not marry, in this case, is $-\beta(\bar{d}_f - w)$. The effect of decreased stigma to out-of-wedlock birth is identical in the model to an increase in benefits to unwed mothers.

---

[20] In addition to 'internal' equilibria with a positive abortion rate, equilibria are also possible with $\bar{d}_f = D_f/2$, implying that no abortion occurs in spite of its availability. In such an equilibrium, there is, however, a positive out-of-wedlock birth rate. Figure 6.3 shows that this outcome may occur in two ways. (1) For costs of abortion in the range $\{b_f + D_f - (\beta D_f^2/2D_m) \le a_f \le b_f + D_m/2\beta\}$, there are dual equilibria. The two solutions correspond to the respective branches of equation (3)—one in which the ceiling on d_f^{crit} is binding, so that $\bar{d}_f = D_f/2$, and the other in which it is not, so that an internal equilibrium occurs. (2) For yet larger values of the cost of abortion, $(a_f > b_f + D_m/2\beta)$, the only equilibrium occurs with $\bar{d}_f$ at its ceiling of $D_f/2$. These solutions suggest that, as the cost of abortions fall, there may be discontinuous shifts in the levels of marriage and out-of-wedlock births. This discontinuity reflects the possibility of a rapid unraveling of men's willingness to marry due to their changing perception of the cost to women of their failure to do so—a process that may be triggered by a small change in the cost of abortion. Such a discontinuous fall in marriage and rise in out-of-wedlock births may in fact correspond to the abrupt decline in marriage and rise in the out-of-wedlock birthrates in the United States. These changes have occurred very rapidly in comparison with the usual sluggish pace of changes in family structure.

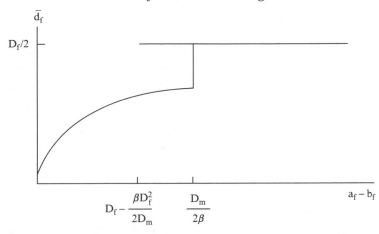

Figure 6.3. *The relationship between the cost of abortion and the mean disutility of single parenthood among women who bear children conceived out of wedlock.*

F. *The Decision to Engage in Premarital Sex*

Our discussion so far has focused on the determinants of fertility and out-of-wedlock births for those women choosing to engage in premarital sex. Following the game tree in Figure 6.2 back to its initial node, we can also analyze the determinants of the original decision: whether or not to engage in premarital sex. A decrease in the cost of abortion or increased availability of contraception is likely to result in an increase in premarital sexual activity.

V. DISCUSSION OF MODELS AND EXPERIENCE IN THE UNITED STATES

Neither of the leading economic theories, the welfare theory and the jobs theory, nor a third to be described, the mix-effect hypothesis, is capable of explaining either the magnitude or the timing of the change in out-of-wedlock births. In contrast, the technology shock explanation, particularly when realistically amended to include endogenous changes in stigma, is consistent with the facts documented in Section II concerning the magnitude and timing of changes in sexual participation, abortion, contraceptive use, shotgun marriage, and the living arrangements of children.

A. *Welfare Theory, Jobs Theory, and Mix Effect*

Despite their prominence in the literature, neither the welfare theory (see Murray [1984]) nor the job-shortage theory (see Wilson [1987]) can explain the size and timing of the increase in out-of-wedlock births. For example, Ellwood and Summers [1986] argue that AFDC could not have played a major role in the rise of out-of-wedlock births because AFDC rose a great deal in the 1960s and fell in the 1970s (when eligibility requirements also became more stringent), while out-of-wedlock births rose continually. Moffitt [1992, p. 29] reaches similar conclusions. He also finds that the effects of welfare benefits estimated with cross-section and panel data are too small to account for more than a very small fraction of the rise in the out-of-wedlock birth ratio.

Wilson's joblessness hypothesis has also been questioned. Mare and Winship [1991, p. 194], using cross-section data, estimate that at most 20 percent of the decline in marriage rates of blacks between 1960 and 1980 can be explained by decreasing employment. Jencks [1992, p. 133] has noted that the decline in the fraction of married unemployed black men aged 30 to 44 between 1960 and 1980 was only slightly higher (13 percent) than the decline in the fraction of married employed black men (11 percent).[21] In confirmation of these suspicions, Wood [1995] estimates that only 3 to 4 percent of the decline in black marriage rates can be explained by the shrinkage of the pool of eligible black men.

A third theory, which we term the mix-effect hypothesis, posits a relationship due to selection between the legalization of abortion and the out-of-wedlock birthrate. If anything, this theory fares worse than either the joblessness theory or the welfare theory. According to the mix-effect hypothesis, the shotgun marriage rate might have declined following the legalization of abortion because the type of couples who would have been especially likely to marry in the event of a premarital pregnancy prior to legalization would have been especially likely to obtain an abortion and avoid shotgun marriage after legalization. (O'Connell and Rogers [1984] suggest this explanation for the decline in the shotgun marriage ratio.) Akerlof, Yellen, and Katz [1994] test for such an effect through cross-section regressions of an individual's probability of terminating a premarital pregnancy by abortion after legalization on that individual's predicted probability of shotgun marriage in the pre-abortion era. Education, which would be correlated with a tendency to plan ahead, and measures of religious practice (Catholic/ non-Catholic, rate of attendance at services) were included in the various prediction equations.[22] Given the robust absence of any significant, positive association between the odds of shotgun marriage and abortion, it is unlikely that the mix effect played any serious role in the decline in shotgun marriage.

In sum, the failure of the job-shortage theory, the welfare theory, and the mix-effect hypothesis leaves a void in explaining the increase in out-of-wedlock births.

B. *Relative Magnitudes of Technology Shock and Out-of-Wedlock Births*

The models of the previous section have shown why the total impact of abortion and female contraception on the out-of-wedlock birthrate could have been positive— contrary to the natural supposition that the direct effects of abortion and contraception would dominate by reducing the number of unwanted out-of-wedlock babies. If the change in abortion and the use of female contraception were all quantitatively large relative to the number of births and relative to the number of unmarried women, it

---

[21] Also see Lerman [1988].
[22] For details see Akerlof, Yellen, and Katz [1994].

would then seem plausible that the technology shock could have been a very significant factor causing the large rise in out-of-wedlock births.

As we documented in Section II, both the use of the pill and the increase in the number of abortions were indeed very large relative to the numbers of unmarried women and out-of-wedlock births. The use of the pill at first intercourse by unmarried women jumped from 6 to 15 percent in just a few years, and the number of abortions to unmarried women, which were less than half the number of out-of-wedlock births in the 1960s, grew tenfold, or more. Indeed, the number of abortions grew yet faster than out-of-wedlock births over the 1970s so that, by the end of the decade, unmarried women had 75 percent more abortions than out-of-wedlock births.

The technology shock hypothesis thus meets the test that changes in the use of the technology are of sufficient magnitude to be a potential propagator of the subsequent and very substantial changes in out-of-wedlock births and family structure—provided that the effect has the right sign.

C. *The Technology Shock Explanation for Rising Out-of-Wedlock Childbirth*

A very simple theory, which builds on the models of the previous sections, suffices to explain not only the increase in the out-of-wedlock birthrate but also the related changes in family structure and sexual practice. According to this theory, the legalization of abortion, starting in the late 1960s, induced a large fraction of unmarried women, who were willing to obtain an abortion if pregnant, to engage in premarital sexual relations while forgoing the promise of marriage in the event of a premarital conception. Similarly, the invention of the pill and increased availability of contraception enhanced the willingness of unmarried women to participate in uncommitted, premarital sex by reducing the odds of a pregnancy in the first place. The technology shock thereby triggered the behavioral shifts depicted in our two static models. Women who wanted to bear children were immiserized because their competitive position, and thereby their ability to bargain for the marriage guarantee, deteriorated, as in our first model. Moreover, their partners' degree of empathy and willingness to marry after the fact, may also have declined once it was apparent that the woman herself was unwilling to obtain an abortion. This causation mechanism is illustrated by our second model.

The technology shock hypothesis, like Wilson's job shortage theory, relates the increase in out-of-wedlock childbearing to a decline in the supply of eligible males. However, this decline occurs because there are fewer men who are willing to get married, and not just because there is a shortage of jobs. The technology shock theory explains the reduced marriage rates of both educated men with low unemployment and uneducated men with high unemployment. The technology shock model also predicts, and our survey results described below confirm, a decline in intimacy between sexual partners, since relations are likely to be short term, reinforcing the unwillingness to marry.

The technology shock theory suffices to explain why there was such a large rise in the rate of retention of children born out of wedlock. In the old days, if the woman wanted a child, she was typically able to exact a promise that the man would marry her.

Thus, most premaritally conceived first births (about 60 percent for whites and 35 percent for blacks by our tabulations) resulted in marriage before the birth of the baby who was then, of course, kept by the woman. If the woman did not get married soon after the birth of the baby, the chances were less than 30 percent that the child would be kept. In the new world, however, after the legalization of abortion, there were two reasons why the baby would more likely be kept. First, unmarried women who wanted children would find it increasingly difficult to make (and also to enforce) a contract in which marriage was promised in the event of pregnancy. Since these women wanted children, they would naturally keep them. Furthermore, because women who would not want to keep a child born out of wedlock had easy access to contraception and the option to abort an unwanted pregnancy, a greater fraction of the children born out of wedlock would be wanted. It is then no surprise that, despite the very large rise in sexual participation, the number of agency adoptions was halved from 86,000 to 43,000 in the five years following the introduction of abortion, or that 1970, the year of our shock, was the peak year for adoptions.

The question remains why the decline in the shotgun marriage ratio, following the technology shocks of the early 1970s occurred gradually over time rather than abruptly and all at once. For example, the time series results reported in Table 6.3 indicate a significant change in the shotgun marriage trend for white women beginning around 1968. Starting in the late 1960s, the white shotgun marriage ratio began a long and steady decline.

There are two different factors that probably account for the gradual decline in the white shotgun marriage rate. The first is simply that, in reality, shifts between equilibria take time to complete. The second, complementary factor, is that the stigma associated with out-of-wedlock motherhood has declined endogenously.

Focusing first on the transition between equilibria in our models, it is easy to appreciate why such moves would, in actuality, be gradual. Consider, for example, the attitudes of p_f^- women in the first 'immiserization model'—those who would bring the baby to term with or without marriage—and their male partners. It would most likely have taken time for men to recognize that an implicit or explicit promise of marriage in the event of a pregnancy was too high a price to pay for sexual relations because men could fare better elsewhere. It may also have taken time for women to perceive the increased willingness of men to move if such marriage promises are demanded. As new expectations formed, social norms readjusted, and the shotgun marriage rate declined, albeit gradually. In the end, however, men who wanted sexual activity but did not want to promise marriage in case of pregnancy, were neither expected nor required to do so.

A second, important reason, why the decline in the shotgun marriage ratio occurred gradually, rather than abruptly, relates to stigma. Declining stigma of out-of-wedlock childbirth was a natural, endogenous consequence of the technology shock. A decline in stigma, represented in both models by a decrease in d_f, further reinforced the technology-driven causes for the decline in shotgun marriage and increased retention of out-of-wedlock children.

As we have documented, the norm of premarital sexual abstinence all but vanished in the wake of the technology shock. With premarital sex the rule, rather than the exception, an out-of-wedlock childbirth could no longer serve as a sign that society's sexual taboos had been violated. The stigma attached to out-of-wedlock childbearing thus gradually but, ultimately greatly, eroded. A reduction in d_f in our first model augments the willingness to engage in uncommitted premarital sex. In our second model, a reduction in d_f is an additional factor working to reduce the pressure on fathers to do their duty in the case of an unwanted pregnancy. Since out-of-wedlock childbirth no longer resulted in social ostracism, literally and figuratively, shotgun marriage no longer occurred at the point of the shotgun. Reduction in stigma provides an additional reason why women who, in previous times would have put up their baby for adoption, chose to keep the baby instead. As we have seen, in 1970 most children whose mothers did not get married in the first three years after their birth were put up for adoption (commonly by relatives). In contrast, by the late 1980s about two-thirds of these babies were kept by the mothers.

There can be little doubt that the stigma of out-of-wedlock childbearing has declined enormously. Even the name of the phenomenon has been changed over the last fifteen years: children born out-of-wedlock are no longer referred to as 'illegitimate.' The willingness of officials to ask, and of citizens to answer, questions about out-of-wedlock childbearing is a further indicator of the decline in stigma. For example, in the CPS fertility supplement, retrospectively questioned white mothers revealed 32 percent higher rates of out-of-wedlock first births when queried in 1990 than when queried ten years earlier (1980) about the very same births.[23] In former times high school students would quit school in the event of pregnancy. In 1958 the high school completion rate of mothers who became pregnant at seventeen or younger was 19 percent. By 1986 it was 56 percent. In 1972 Federal law made it illegal for schools to expel students for pregnancy or parenthood. The *New York Times* has described the transformation of attitudes underlying these changes:

In the 'old days' of the 1960s, 50s and 40s, pregnant teenagers were pariahs, banished from schools, ostracized by their peers or scurried out of town to give birth in secret. Today, pregnant teen-agers are even beginning to be viewed by their peers as role models. No longer are they shunned or ridiculed, but supported and embraced in their decisions to give birth, keep their babies, continue their education and participate in school activities [Williams 1993, p. C1].

A final paradox that requires explanation is why the black shotgun marriage ratio began to fall earlier than the white ratio and exhibits no significant change in trend around 1970. Here, welfare may play a role. For women whose earnings are sufficiently low that they are potentially eligible for welfare, an increase in welfare benefits has the same effect on out-of-wedlock births as a decline in the stigma to bearing a child out of wedlock. The difference in eligibility between whites and blacks and the patterns of change in welfare benefits—rising in the 1960s and falling thereafter—may then explain why the decline in the black shotgun marriage ratio began earlier than that

---

[23] These mothers may have had different recall bias in 1990 than in 1980 because of the lapse of time, but that recall bias would most likely have resulted in an increased number of forgotten children which would have decreased the number of out-of-wedlock births rather than increased them.

for whites. That blacks will be more affected by changes in welfare benefits than whites goes almost without saying because of their lower incomes. Ellwood [1988, p. 201] has calculated that a full third of black children will live in poverty more than 70 percent of the time, in contrast to only 3 percent of white children. As a result, the rise in welfare benefits in the 1960s may have had only a small impact on the white shotgun rate but resulted in a significant decrease in the black shotgun marriage rate.

D. *Survey Results*

Our technology shock theory posits two distinct mechanisms whereby the shotgun marriage norm eroded. The first model emphasizes the role of the new technologies in increasing the willingness of women to participate in uncommitted premarital sex. The second emphasizes the diminished sense of responsibility of men to care for women who have passed up available contraception and abortion options. Our guess, based partly on the qualitative results of a survey we conducted of University of California at Berkeley undergraduates, is that the first mechanism is more important than the second. We attempted to see whether students would agree with the logic of the second choice model regarding the effect of abortion availability on a man's responsibility to marry his partner.

Students were asked to gauge the responsibility of a man to marry his sexual partner in two vignettes: one in which abortion is 'easily available' and another in which abortion is 'illegal, as it was in this country until the 1970s.'[24] They were also asked to explain the reasoning underlying their responses. Differences in students' ratings of responsibility with and without easily available abortion had the expected sign, but were on average small—only 1.2 points on a scale of one to ten—a particularly surprising result given that the questionnaire had been designed to elicit such a reaction. In this sense, students implicitly conceded the logical point that abortion should have an impact on their responsibilities. Interestingly, however, not a single student volunteered any explanation whatever of the *difference* in his or her answer to the two different vignettes. In other words, no student commented on the availability of abortion as a factor governing the responsibility for marriage. Instead, students focused on the *level* of responsibility. The most common explanation, offered by both male and female respondents, was that the man is responsible to the child but not to the pregnant woman. Many emphasized the *financial* responsibility of the man for the child. Others explained that a forced marriage was likely to end in an early divorce, so that the child would suffer more in a shotgun marriage than if born out of wedlock. Perhaps this folk wisdom is right. Nevertheless, such a response implicitly assumes that the couples in the

---

[24] The first vignette concerned Michael, aged 20, and Sharon, aged 19, each of whom earns $15,000 per year and is a department store clerk. After going out with Michael for a year, Sharon becomes pregnant. Michael makes it clear that he would prefer not to get married and that he wants Sharon to get an abortion. Abortions are easily available in their area, but Sharon says she would like to get married and wants to bring the baby to term. The second vignette is exactly the same as the first vignette except for the conditions under which abortion can be obtained. Rather than being 'easily available,' on the contrary, 'abortion is illegal, as it was in this country until the early 1970s.'

vignettes—who had been going out together for a year and were clearly sexually intimate—would not be compatible. Consider the difference between Rubin's [1969] description of sexual and social mores in San Francisco 25 years earlier. Such a couple would surely have been considered sufficiently compatible to have gotten married even if the man had preferred to remain single. Indeed, sexual relations would have involved an implicit promise of marriage if the woman had become pregnant. We believe that the worldview of these UC Berkeley students in the summer of 1994 fits well with the description of behavior in our first model, in which unmarried partners have no commitment to marriage if a baby is the outcome of their sexual relations.

The students are probably a good gauge of the social mores regarding expectations of couples at the present time. If such questions had not arisen in a respondent's personal experience, he/she would still surely have heard numerous discussions of such matters. The respondents' implicit lack of enthusiasm for the second model as an explanation for the decline in shotgun marriage, however, should be viewed with some caution. An appreciation of social expectations regarding sexual and marital conduct five years prior to their own birth is likely to require unusual historic perspective, especially since those customs have, in fact, changed very greatly.

E. *Recent Studies of the Relation between Abortion and Motherhood*

Several recent studies have examined the relationship between abortion availability and births with surprising conclusions which support the basic tenet of this paper that the availability of abortion influences behavior, especially through sexual participation. If births decline less than one for one with the advent of abortion, then sexual participation or contraceptive use must be influenced by the availability of abortion. Jackson and Klerman [1993] and Levine, Trainor, and Zimmerman [1995] have shown that state restrictions of Medicaid funds for abortions have been associated with *declines* in birth rates. Kane and Staiger [1996] found that teen birthrates increase in a county when the distance to the nearest abortion provider declines.[25] These studies thus show that births decline at a much lower rate than one to one with the number of abortions.

VI. CONCLUSIONS

Over the last 25 years disturbing trends have occurred in the United States (and other Western countries as well). Just at the time, about 1970, that the permanent cure to poverty seemed to be on the horizon and just at the time that women had obtained the tools to control the number and the timing of their children, single motherhood and the feminization of poverty began their long and steady rise. As a result, United States poverty rates have been stubbornly constant for the last quarter century.

---

[25] These new results are particularly surprising in view of earlier studies that showed declines in teenage birthrates following the legalization of abortion—a decline in teenage birthrates in New York City after statewide legalization (see Joyce and Mocan [1980]) and a differential decline in out-of-wedlock birth ratios in states that legalized abortion in the late 1960s and early 1970s (see Sklar and Berkov [1974]).

It is important to understand why these changes in family structure have occurred. Quantitative work by economists and sociologists suggests strongly that the magnitude of these changes is simply too great to be explained by the increase in welfare eligibility and benefits (which occurred in the 1960s and not the 1970s). Nor can it be explained by the decline in jobs for the less educated. Despite the lack of ambiguity from econometric work, misperceptions persist. On the right it is commonly believed that welfare did it, and on the left, that the deterioration of male jobs is the culprit.

There is, in consequence, a need for another explanation. That other explanation, which is also popular, centers on the vague notion that single parenthood increased because of a change in attitudes toward sexual behavior. This paper endorses that view, and attempts to explain the mechanisms whereby those changes in sexual and marital customs occurred. Although doubt will always remain about the ultimate cause for something as diffuse as a change in social custom, the technology shock theory of this paper does fit the facts. The new technology was adopted quickly and on a massive scale. It is therefore prima facie plausible that it could have accounted for a comparably large change in marital and fertility patterns. The timing of the changes also seems, at least crudely, to fit the theory.

From a policy perspective, attempts to turn the technology clock backward by denying women access to abortion and contraception is probably not possible, and even if it were possible, it would almost surely be both undesirable and counter-productive. In addition to probably reducing the well-being of women who use the technology, along with that of men, such measures could lead to yet greater poverty. In the new equilibrium in which sexual abstinence is rare and the stigma of out-of-wedlock motherhood is small, denial of access would probably increase the number of children born out of wedlock and reared in impoverished single-parent families. On the contrary, efforts should be made to ensure that women can use the new technologies if they choose to do so. Finally, if the technology shock theory of this paper provides the correct explanation for the rise in single motherhood, cuts in welfare, as currently proposed, would only further immiserize the victims. Such cuts would have little impact on the number of out-of-wedlock children while impoverishing those already on welfare yet further. Instead, administrative measures, such as those suggested by Ellwood, to make fathers pay, deserve serious policy consideration.

DATA APPENDIX

Abortion, Sexual Experience, and Use of Pill

The time series on sexual experience, use of the pill, and abortion are derived from the 1982 and the 1988 panels of the National Survey of Family Growth. These surveys interviewed a nationally representative sample of women 15 to 44 of all marital statuses, with approximately 8,000 respondents in each panel. Women were asked retrospectively about their fertility histories: pregnancies and their outcomes, infertility, contraceptive use, childbearing plans, adoption, sex education, and family composition.

Abortions were tabulated from answers to questions about the date of each pregnancy and its respective outcome, with the abortion series computed as the number of pregnancies terminated by that method. We used the age distribution of abortions in our data set and data from Vital Statistics on the age distribution of the population to impute the abortion experience of women under 45 who were omitted from the sample in prior years because of age truncation. A single series was constructed from the two panels by using the data from the 1982 panel for the period 1960 to 1972, an average of the data in the 1982 and 1988 panels for the period 1973 to 1981, and the data from the 1988 panel thereafter. The later panel was omitted from the pre-1973 series because of the importance of age truncation. This series was used to perform the time series tests reported in Table 6.3. However, the NSFG contains considerable underreporting of abortion, in comparison with the complete tabulations from medical providers available from the Alan Guttmacher Institute after 1972. For example, from 1973 to 1982 the NSFG third and fourth panels reported only 31.3 percent of the abortions to unmarried women reported in the Alan Guttmacher Institute survey. The aggregate abortions statistics in Table 6.2 are based on the Alan Guttmacher data after 1972. Before 1973 the table uses abortions from the 1982 NSFG, adjusted for reporting error.

The fraction of women aged 16 with sexual experience was compiled from the 1982 panel of the National Survey of Family Growth from answers to the following two questions: 'At any time in your life, have you ever had sexual intercourse?' If yes, women were subsequently asked: 'When did you have sexual intercourse for the first time— what month and year was that? How old were you at that time?'

The series on the use of the pill is the fraction of unmarried women reporting using the pill on first intercourse by date of first intercourse from the 1982 panel.

Shotgun Marriage Rate

The shotgun marriage ratio, to recall, is the fraction of births conceived out of wedlock with marriage between conception and birth. To obtain an annual series and extended shotgun marriage ratios with marriage after the birth of the child, we followed the methodology of O'Connell and Moore [1980], O'Connell and Rogers [1984], and U. S. Department of Commerce [1991, p. 10, Table F]. The Fertility Supplements to the Current Population Survey taken in 1980, 1982, and 1990 asked women about the birth dates of their children and also their dates of marriage and divorce. The 1980 and 1990 surveys queried all women 15 to 65 about the first five births; the 1982 Supplement asked only about first births. The first birth shotgun marriage ratio is the fraction of *first* births taking place within seven months of marriage, where the mother was unmarried at the time of conception. We concentrate our analysis on first-births, since a first-birth is much more likely to be a defining event in a woman's life than a second (or subsequent) birth to an unmarried woman who is already a mother. The time series data used to estimate the change in trend in Table 6.3 are composite series consisting of the data from the 1980 and 1982 panels of the CPS Fertility Supplements up to 1979, and the 1990 panel thereafter. Because the shotgun marriage ratio estimated from the 1980 and 1982 CPS surveys for the exact same period as the

1990 CPS survey was 32 percent lower—presumably because of the decline in stigma attached to out-of-wedlock births—the entire pre-1979 series was adjusted upward to conform to the later reports concerning the same births.

UNIVERSITY OF CALIFORNIA AT BERKELEY AND THE BROOKINGS
INSTITUTION
BOARD OF GOVERNORS OF THE FEDERAL RESERVE SYSTEM
UNIVERSITY OF CALIFORNIA AT BERKELEY

References

Akerlof, George, A., Janet L. Yellen, and Michael L. Katz, 'An Analysis of Out-of-Wedlock Childbearing in the United States,' mimeo, University of California at Berkeley, 1994.

Anderson, Elijah, *StreetWise* (Chicago: University of Chicago Press, 1990).

Becker, Gary S., *A Treatise on the Family* (Cambridge: Harvard University Press, 1981).

Ellwood, David T., *Poor Support: Poverty in the American Family* (New York: Basic Books, 1988).

—— and Jonathan Crane, 'Family Change among Black Americans: What Do We Know?' *Journal of Economic Perspectives*, IV (1990), 65–84.

—— and Lawrence H. Summers, 'Poverty in America: Is Welfare the Answer or the Problem?' in *Fighting Poverty: What Works and What Doesn't*, S. Danziger and D. Weinberg, eds. (Cambridge: Harvard University Press, 1986).

Garrow, David J., *Liberty and Sexuality: The Right to Privacy and the Making of Roe v. Wade* (New York: Macmillan, 1994).

Jackson, Catherine A., and Jacob A. Klerman, 'Welfare, Abortion and Teenage Fertility,' mimeo, The RAND Corporation, 1994.

Jencks, Christopher, *Rethinking Social Policy* (Cambridge: Harvard University Press, 1992).

Joyce, Theodore, J., and Naci H. Mocan, 'The Impact of Legalized Abortion on Adolescent Childbearing in New York City,' *American Journal of Public Health*, LXXX (1980), 273–78.

Kane, Thomas, and Douglas Staiger, 'Teen Motherhood and Abortion Access,' *Quarterly Journal of Economics*, CXI (1996), 467–506.

Lerman, Robert I., 'Employment Opportunities of Young Men and Family Formation,' mimeo, Brandeis University, 1988.

Levine, Phillip B., Amy B. Trainor, and David J. Zimmerman, 'The Effect of Medicaid Abortion Funding Restrictions on Abortions, Pregnancies and Births,' NBER Working Paper No. 5066, 1995.

Luker, Kristin, *Abortion and the Politics of Motherhood* (Berkeley: University of California Press, 1984).

——. 'Dubious Conceptions: The Controversy over Teen Pregnancy,' *The American Prospect* (1991), 73–83.

—— and Robert D. Plotnick, 'Effects of State Welfare, Abortion and Family Planning Policies on Premarital Childbearing among White Adolescents,' *Family Planning Perspectives*, XXII (1990), 246–75.

—— and Robert A. Pollak, 'Noncooperative Bargaining Models of Marriage,' *American Economic Review*, LXXXIV (1994), 132–37.

Manski, Charles F., Gary D. Sandefur, Sara McLanahan, and Daniel Powers, 'Alternative Estimates of the Effect of Family Structure during Adolescence on High School Graduation,' *Journal of the American Statistical Association*, LXXXVII (1992), 25–37.

Mare, Robert D., and Christopher Winship, 'Socioeconomic Change and the Decline of Marriage for Whites and Blacks,' in *The Urban Underclass*, C. Jencks and P. E. Peterson, eds. (Washington, DC: Brookings Institution, 1991).

Marsiglio, William, 'Commitment to Social Fatherhood: Predicting Adolescent Males' Intentions to Live with Their Child and Partner,' *Journal of Marriage and the Family*, L (1988), 427–41.

Moffitt, Robert, 'Incentive Effects of the U. S. Welfare System: A Review,' *Journal of Economic Literature*, XXX (1992), 1–61.

Murray, Charles, *Losing Ground: American Social Policy 1950–1980* (New York: Basic Books, 1984).

Nathanson, Constance A., and Young J. Kim, 'Components of Change in Adolescent Fertility, 1971–1979,' *Demography*, XXVI (1989), 85–98.

O'Connell, Martin, and Carolyn C. Rogers, 'Out-of-Wedlock Births, Premarital Pregnancies, and Their Effects on Family Formation and Dissolution,' *Family Planning Perspectives*, XVI (1984), 157–62.

—— and Maurice J. Moore, 'The Legitimacy Status of First Births to U. S. Women Aged 15–24, 1939–1978,' *Family Planning Perspectives*, XII (1980), 16–25.

Rainwater, Lee, *Behind Ghetto Walls* (Chicago: Aldine, 1970).

Rubin, Lillian Breslow, *Worlds of Pain: Life in the Working-Class Family* (New York: Basic Books, 1969).

Sklar, June, and Beth Berkov, 'Abortion, Illegitimacy, and the American Birthrate,' *Science*, CLXXXV (September 13, 1974), 909–15.

U. S. Department of Commerce, *Fertility of American Women: June 1990*, Current Population Reports, Population Characteristics, Series P-20, No. 454 (Washington, DC: U.S. Government Printing Office, 1991).

U. S. Department of Labor, Office of Policy Planning and Research, *The Negro Family: The Case for National Action* (March 1965).

Williams, Lena, 'Pregnant Teen-Agers Are Outcasts No Longer,' *The New York Times*, Late Edition (December 2, 1993), C1.

Willis, Robert J., 'A Theory of Out-of-Wedlock Childbearing,' mimeo, University of Chicago and National Opinion Research Center, 1994.

Wilson, William J., *The Truly Disadvantaged* (Chicago: Chicago University Press, 1987).

—— and Katherine M. Neckerman, 'Poverty and Family Structure: The Widening Gap between Evidence and Public Policy Issues,' in *Fighting Poverty: What Works and What Doesn't*, S. Danziger and D. Weinberg, eds. (Cambridge: Harvard University Press, 1986), pp. 232–59.

Wood, Robert G., 'Marriage Rates and Marriageable Men: A Test of the Wilson Hypothesis,' *Journal of Human Resources*, XXX (1995), 163–93.

7

Men without Children*

GEORGE A. AKERLOF[†]

The chorus of family values that has rocked America over the last few years has focused on the impact of children growing up without fathers. In this lecture I shall address the obverse question: what is the impact on society of men neither marrying nor living with children. Between 1968 and 1993 the fraction of men 25 to 34 who are householders living with children declined from 66% to 40%.[1] I shall model marriage according to its traditional and conventional meaning as a rite of passage—a sacrament that marks the transition from one stage of life to another. I shall discuss what difference it might make that men are increasingly delaying this rite of passage with the implication that they are also delaying the transition that it symbolises.

In America over the past 30 years crime rates have risen, marriage rates have fallen and out-of-wedlock births have soared. Substance abuse has also risen dramatically as incarcerations, largely drug related, have more than doubled—exceeding one and one third million.[2] The conservatives (see Murray (1984)) have blamed most of these ill developments on the rise in welfare, a claim that does not stand up to econometric evidence since there is little correlation over time and across states between welfare payments and out-of-wedlock births (see Moffitt (1992), Ellwood and Summers (1986), and Ellwood and Crane (1990)). The liberals (see Wilson (1987, 1996)) have laid the blame on the loss of jobs, a claim that, again according to econometric evidence, is equally spurious, since there is little correlation between the decline in job availability for different persons and the decline in their respective chances of being married (see Wood (1995) and Jencks (1992)).

* This work was previously published as George Akerlof (1998), 'Men Without Children', *The Economic Journal* 108. Copyright © Royal Economic Society 1998. Reproduced by kind permission of Blackwell Publishing.

† The 1997 Harry Johnson Lecture. The author would especially like to thank Michael Ash and Jennifer Eichberger for invaluable research assistance and William Dickens, Sanders Korenman, Richard Lipsey, and Janet Yellen for invaluable comments. I am also grateful for the financial support of the Canadian Institute for Advanced Research and the National Science Foundation under Research Grant No. SBR-9409426.

[1] Source: Tabulations from the Current Population Survey.
[2] Freeman (1996, p. 1).

In this lecture I want to suggest another view of the changes in social pathology. Although I am quite sure that this new view will not explain all of the facts, it may give an adequate explanation for a sufficient portion of the changes that have occurred to cause a changed strategy for economic policy toward the poor and the disadvantaged. Indeed, I shall take a view so old that it is new—that welfare mothers are poor and unfortunate, and therefore deserving of decent support; furthermore, the growth of social pathology of crime and drugs have social, but, for the most part, not any clear economic cause such as a lack of jobs or a substitution of welfare for work. Even with some seemingly contradictory facts yet unexplained, I am hopeful that I can convince you of the possibility that *social* changes have played a major role in the rise in social pathology.

Since the early and mid 1960's marriage customs have changed dramatically. Perhaps they changed because of the technology shocks of the advent of female contraception and legalisation of abortion—so that the guy did not have to marry the girl who became pregnant. Perhaps they changed for other reasons regarding, for example, the destigmatisation of out-of-wedlock birth, that grew out of the more temperate attitudes associated with the culture shocks of the 1960's. Perhaps the same secularisation of society that allowed stores to be open on Sunday destigmatised out-of-wedlock birth so that the mothers felt free to keep their children. Whatever the reason for the change, the existence of that change is undeniable.

In the old days a young man who got his girlfriend pregnant was expected to marry her; and she was expected to marry him. (See Akerlof, Yellen and Katz (1996)). Most of the time that occurred in the event of an out-of-wedlock pregnancy. Sometimes premarital conception resulted in abortion, but abortions were illegal and, for unmarried women, also quite rare. If the couple did not marry after the birth of the baby, most likely the child was adopted—either by relatives or through formal adoption agencies. Only rarely was the child kept by a single mother. This system began to break down in the early 1960's among blacks and in the late 1960's and early 1970's among whites. Decreasingly would the boy marry the pregnant girlfriend. Mothers increasingly kept their babies. Adoptions fell from about one half of all out-of-wedlock births to one fifth.

To continue the contrast between old and new, previously, the young man who had married his pregnant bride, or perhaps married his girlfriend just after the birth of the child, was expected to settle down to support a family. Typically, the fathers were a few crucial years older than the mothers so they would not have to drop out of high school, although that sometimes did occur.[3] The pregnant woman, however, if sufficiently young, would almost surely drop out of high school. Lillian Rubin (1969) has documented the great pain caused by this system as immature men married equally immature women, both ill prepared for life and for each other.

This previous system has now all but disappeared. The destigmatisation of divorce has played a role—as men and women who entered shotgun marriages could end them almost as speedily as they had been begun. In the new world, also, of sexual freedom

---

[3] In 1965 the median age of grooms was 22.8 and, of brides, was 20.6 for first marriages. Source: *Statistical Abstracts of the United States.*

and of easily available abortion, the boyfriends feel a reduced responsibility to marry their girlfriends in the event of a pregnancy since, with abortion, the woman no longer has to give birth simply because of a pregnancy. Probably more important, because sexual relations are now occurring very early in relations, partners have so little acquaintance with one another that marriage in the event of pregnancy hardly seems practicable. For these reasons shotgun marriage is now, mainly, a custom of the past. I have written about this disappearance of the custom of shotgun marriage and its relation to the technology shock of the late 1970's in a previous paper with Janet Yellen and Michael Katz. Now I want to take the story one step further. At least in mind's eye I want to contemplate how the disappearance of this custom of early and frequent shotgun marriage will change the life course of young men. I want to contemplate how their lives will be different because they remain single.

What used to happen in the old days to this hypothetical couple and what happens now? In the old days, at least according to the norms, the man would settle down. Perhaps unwillingly and also perhaps unhappily, the young man would, according to the old norms, take on his new responsibilities of fatherhood and marriage. Since his friends would also be doing the same, the previous peer groups to which he belonged would break up. Insofar as they continued to meet, it would be in part to reminisce about their lives of a very different past.

Now, life has changed. The man will not be forced to live with the woman. He may cohabit with her (as has become increasingly common (see Moffitt, *et al.* (1995)), but on the average he assumes less of the responsibility of fatherhood and marriage than was expected in the past as indicated especially by the increases in the fraction of men who either have not had children and therefore incurred no responsibility or who have abandoned the children they have fathered. Indications of such increasing abandonment are the fraction of children living in single-parent female-headed households, which are the result of never marriage, separation and divorce. Even among the divorced middle class only a small minority of fathers assume significant responsibility for the children (see Wallerstein (1980)). For some men, this absence of current family responsibilities is an opportunity. The career of the single male is now more likely to evolve uninterruptedly for longer. For those who are pursuing long-term goals this translates into longer and more intensive education. For those without such commitments the result is likely to be a lengthier evolution of former peer group activities. There should be no presumption as to how that evolution will take place. Some single young men will become bored with the activities of their past—including whatever youthful indiscretions and misdeeds that past may have involved. Perhaps these are the young men who are most likely to be what is now the minority who are getting married and becoming full-time live-in fathers. For others the indiscretions, and worse, of the past will become the forerunners of greater misdeeds in their twenties. With delays in marriage this evolution has a lower hazard of interruption. The peer groups that used to be transformed into groups of old friends meeting but not hanging out together, now linger on—with more time to evolve. And because older brothers and older friends in their late teens or early twenties act as role models, teenage peer groups are copying role models that are engaged in escalating violence. Thus the marriage shock has intensified, and perhaps even, resulted in, the crime shock and the substance abuse shock, while, in turn, all of these shocks have fed one another—yielding to current youth ever higher standards of misconduct for the next generation of the very young to emulate.

This alternative story about the causes for the rise of social problems and the economic problems due to the feminisation of poverty takes as given the social changes that have occurred. It does not blame government for its role in increasing welfare. Instead welfare is seen as a useful stop-gap. And it fails to romanticise the old-style values, with their positive and their negative aspects. Fathers were present, but many were unhappy. In this view of welfare reform, the political demand for welfare reform is due to the disparities in equity between the working and the nonworking poor. The appropriate solution to the political problem of welfare is not to forsake the nonworking poor who are likely to have sufficient child care duties that there is not a great deal of gain to working but, instead, to increase the returns to the nonworking poor (see Rubin (1992) and Ellwood (1988)). In the United States this is currently accomplished by aid to the working poor through the earned income tax credit.

The preceding story about the causation of increasing crime and substance abuse has depended on the idea that men settle down when they get married: if they fail to get married they fail to settle down. There is no question that there is a very large difference in behaviour between single and married men. We shall present a raft of evidence showing a whole range of ways in which single and married men of approximately the same age differ. The difficult question, however, is not whether single and married men behave differently, as surely they do, but instead whether marriage is just a marker in the evolution of men's behaviour, rather than a shock that seriously alters this behaviour. The cross-section differences between the married and the unmarried may only be due to selection bias. The married may simply always be different from the single, or, if not permanently different they may be at different stages of their life cycle. We shall also present some fairly sophisticated evidence that on getting married men tend to change their behaviour. But even this evidence is subject to scrutiny because men may get married at the time that they are planning to change their behaviour. If they had married any earlier or any later their behaviour might be totally unchanged by those events. So just because single and married men, as we shall show, behave very differently, and just because men change their behaviour when they get married does not mean that the change in the average age of marriage should have any significant impact on what men do. I shall then give some evidence that attempts to take account both of the selection bias in marriage and also of the possible near simultaneity of life cycle changes and marriage.

In sum, I shall advance a simple explanation for the rise in crime and drug addiction. Social customs changed. What men would have done if they had remained single, they now do. That the rise in the marriage age could have such effects was apparently appreciated by Shakespeare. The demographic historian Lawrence Stone relates:

This rise of the companionate domesticated marriage was accompanied by a rise in the proportion of unmarried in the society, caused partly by the postponement of marriage to a later and later age, and partly by an increase in the proportion who never married at all. The problem of adolescence, and the nuisance it causes to society, were familiar enough to Europeans since the fifteenth century, especially as the time lag between sexual maturity and marriage got longer and longer. The shepherd in Shakespeare's *A Winter's Tale* must have struck a familiar chord when he remarked, 'I would there were no age between sixteen and twenty-three, or that youth would sleep out the rest; for there is nothing in the between but getting wenches with child, wronging the ancientry, stealing, fighting.' (Stone, 1979, p. 241)

This explanation is of course too simple. Because it can be difficult to tease the truth out of econometric evidence, whatever the truth may be, there may still have been an employment shock that has seriously affected marriage rates. There may have also been crime, drug, and welfare shocks in addition to the family shock, all interacting. But the family shock is, quite likely, also a significant part of the story. I have so far emphasised the differences between my hypothesis and Wilson's about the origins of the change in marriage rates, but we should not forget the equally important similarities. I follow Wilson in my hypothesis that low marriage rates will lead to increases in the social pathologies of hopelessness, such as crime and drug addiction. Curiously, those who have tested the 'Wilson hypothesis' have looked at the relation between employment and marriage, but have not examined the further relation emphasised in *The Truly Disadvantaged*—between low marriage rates and other social pathologies. Whatever the causes for the low marriage rate, we now turn to examining its consequences.

I. MODEL OF MARRIAGE

A common view in anthropology is that various rites of passage mark the beginning of new phases of life. Marriage is a sacrament in the Christian religion, and the wedding ceremony celebrates this important transition. According to *The Encyclopaedia Britannica* (1973, v. 14, p. 927), '[In Christianity], through the doctrine of the sacramental nature of marriage, it was elevated to the level of being a vehicle of divine grace. Marriage was thus endowed with the highest possible responsibility of the spouses to each other, to their offspring, and to the Lord.' We would expect that marriage will redirect the energies of the bride and the groom as suggested by this ideal and that after the wedding the life of the bride and of the groom will be changed. This can be modelled as a change in utility: with marriage the bride and the groom will have increased commitment toward each other, toward their offspring and, if religious, toward the Lord Himself. In some societies marriage also confers new responsibilities toward the community as well. As we shall see, this view of marriage corresponds to the empirical facts: it appears that marriage begins a period in which men devote themselves to the acquisition of human capital whose returns will later be used to support the marriage. Numerous statistical indicators shall suggest that marriage in fact does presage a change in behaviour in many different ways.

A rudimentary model captures this idea of marriage as a rite of passage very parsimoniously. A person has a utility function of the form

$$u = u(t_b, t_o, M), \tag{1}$$

where t_h is the fraction of time spent in home oriented activities, t_0 is the fraction of time spent in activities that are oriented outside of the home, and M is marital status. In the simplest classification M would have two values: m, ever married and s, single. Common classifications also distinguish the additional states: divorced, widowed and separated. The sum of the fraction of time oriented to the home and time spent oriented outside the home is 1. Marriage is complementary with time spent in the home and a substitute for time oriented outside the home. A decrease in the benefits of marriage relative to remaining single will cause a decrease in the fraction of people choosing m (married) rather than s (single). The net result will be a decrease in the complement of marriage, t_h, and an increase in the substitute to marriage, t_0. The basic idea of the model is that after the rite of passage, which in this case is the transition in M from s to m, the utility of time spent in different activities changes.

This model is, of course, a variation on the Becker-Mincer optimal allocation of time, but the emphasis is different. In their classic papers Becker (1965) and Mincer (1962) discuss the ways in which market time and home time are alternative inputs into production of utility-yielding services or commodities; they consider the products of the workplace and of the home as potentially close substitutes. In contrast, I focus on the ways in which goods produced by home oriented time and by outside oriented time are less than complete substitutes for each other and I also focus on the bias due to changes in marital status on the benefits of the two types of commodities. The model is formally similar to Laibson's model of cues: according to Laibson (1996) a person's utility may be altered because of a cue in the environment. Similarly, in the model behaviour changes after marriage. But the motivations in our model are fundamentally different from environmental cues: the wedding bells do not cue new behaviour—instead, they symbolise the adoption of a new identity by both the bride and the groom.[4]

The model above is, of course, only the first approximation to a much more realistic model. A more detailed model would also account for time allocations between spouses, for earning income to acquire commodities that complement the marriage, for the childbearing decision, and further changes in utility symbolised by further rites of passage, as at the time of childbirth. Despite its lack of detail, our model may still be useful if we can classify activities into those involving time oriented to the home and time oriented to outside activities. In general, t_h may be viewed not only as time literally spent in the home, but also as time spent earning the income to purchase goods complementary to household activities. We might expect, for example, that upon marriage people will be more likely to purchase a home, and they will also be more likely to bear children. They will spend considerable time taking care of the children, and also earning the income to buy the store bought goods for their feeding and care. As well, upon marriage, couples will spend time directly in the home, taking care of it, as well as more time outside of the home earning the money necessary for its purchase. Especially, with childbearing or homeownership, there will be greater need for present income relative to future income. Children need shoes, food, toys and space; houses, usually, have demanding mortgage payments as well as expensive upkeep. Children and

---

[4] I owe this observation to work that is currently in progress with Rachel Kranton.

houses also need time for their care that take time out of leisure. So we would expect that the married are more likely to have a higher trade-off of goods and of time for house/child care for leisure than the single. If t_h reductively represents not only time spent in home oriented activities including the time spent in earning the income for purchases that are home oriented, and if t_0 similarly represents not only time spent outside the home but also time earning the income for non-home oriented activities, then we would expect that marriage will increase the time spent in earning income for home-oriented purchases if it does not entail spending more time in the home itself. Both the demands for income and also for child/house care are likely to decrease the demand for education. Women are more likely to be engaged in childcare and less likely to pursue education or to be full time (or even part time) in the labour force; men are less likely to pursue education and are more likely to increase their income through on the job training. All of the family-oriented strategies to the division of time under marriage require a complete Becker-Mincer style model of time allocation, but nevertheless the model of (1) gives an approximation and rough predictions how a change in the benefits from marriage will affect time allocations between t_h and t_0.[5]

Two addenda will make this model more realistic and may also be needed to explain the facts. Stigler and Becker (1977) (or, similarly, Becker and Murphy (1988)) allow the utility function to change as a form of acquisition of human capital. In our application the differential behaviour initiated by marriage will cause further changes in the utility function that will further affect behaviour. In the language of Becker and his coauthors the spouses are building up marriage capital. The addition of such habituating behaviour may be useful in explaining the empirical results that are reported below that wage differentials build up over the course of a marriage.

As a further addendum to the model for the sake of realism, marriage may not be the only cue, or indeed the only rite of passage. To be specific, teenagers may copy their elders, in their twenties, so that when the fraction of singles in their twenties changes, and, in consequence their behaviour, teenagers may also change, as they copy their elder brothers or sisters. Such behaviour will give a multiplier to the effects due to the change in the marriage age so that changes of behaviour of young men in their twenties may affect the behaviour of boys in their teens.

II. MARRIED VS. SINGLE

According to our basic hypothesis the change in the age at marriage has been large and the behaviour of single and married men is quite different. This section will examine the changes in the age of marriage and differences between single and married men. As hypothesised, both of these magnitudes are large and sufficient to explain a significant fraction of the changes in United States crime rates. But correlation is not causation, especially in the case of differences between married and single, and so the next two sections will be devoted to estimation of the extent to which the correlation between

---

[5] I do not report this model here since the complication of the model overwhelmed the additional insight obtained from it.

married and single reflects the effects of marriage on behaviour, as in our rites-of-passage model.

2.1. *Change in the Age of Marriage*

Among men with exactly twelve years of education in the old days—for example, in 1965—three quarters of 24-year-old men had married, in contrast to only 40% 25 years later.[6] In 1965 almost one half of men 20 to 24 were already married, compared to 20% in 1990. Among men five years older, 25 to 29, in 1965 only 20% remained single, whereas 25 years later almost 50% were single.[7] Figs. 7.1*a* and 7.1*b* show the fraction of men and women with just 12 years of education who had married between 1964 to 1968 compared to those who had married between 1989 and 1993 as a function of age from 21 to 34. At age 21 there is about a 30% difference in the fraction of men married; the gap rises to a peak of 33% at age twenty five at first tapering off gradually. At age thirty it is down to 17%. With the change in marriage there was also a dramatic change in the fraction of men who had assumed the responsibilities of fatherhood. In 1965 only 37% of 25 year old men with exactly 12 years of education

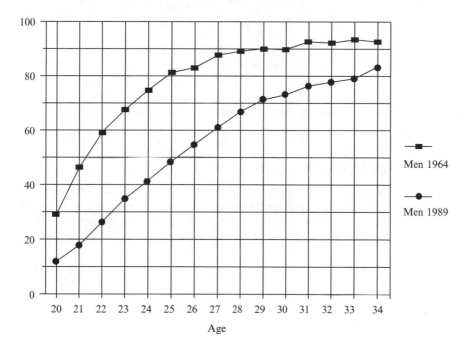

Figure 7.1a. *Percent married by age with high school diploma only. Source; computed using CPS data; percentages for 1964 are averages for years 1964–8; percentages for 1989 are averages for 1989–93.*

---

[6] Source: computations from the Current Population Survey.
[7] Source: *Statistical Abstracts of the United States.*

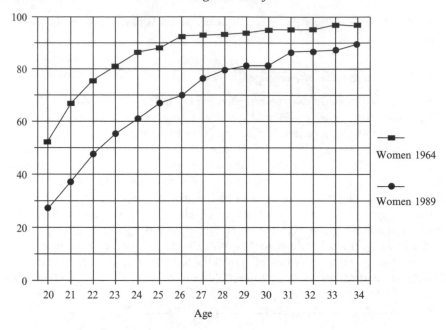

Figure 7.1b. *Percent married by age with high school diploma only. Source: computed using CPS data; percentages for 1964 are averages for years 1964–8; percentages for 1989 are averages for 1989–93.*

were living without children in their households. By 1993, the latest year for which we have data, that fraction had risen to 64%.

2.2 *Differences Between Married and Singles*

If the change in the marriage age has made a difference in the social outcomes, there should be differences in the characteristics of the married and the unmarried. I shall now present a battery of indicators that all show significant differences between married and unmarried men. We shall first look at the labour market, next at the incidence of crime victimisation and arrests, and then at the use of drugs and alcohol, and other social indicators. The crude statistics will all show large differences between married and unmarried men.

2.3. *Labour Force Activities*

Married and single men who are not in school are differentiated by five labour market attributes. They have higher wages, are more likely to be in the labour force, less likely to be unemployed because they had quit their job, have lower unemployment rates, are more likely to be full-time, and are less likely to be part-year workers. In each and every dimension the married men have stronger labour market attachment than the unmarried.

Table 7.1a. *Comparisons of single and married men: labour force characteristics*

	Ages 20–24		Ages 25–29	
	Ever married	Single	Ever married	Single
Not enrolled in school				
Wages per hour*	7.54	7.05	9.99	9.27
Out of labour force†	3.78	7.84	4.12	10.3
Unemployed‡	9.0	13.9	7.0	9.7
Work full time, full year†	65.6	48.0	73.6	59.8
Unemployed because quit last job‡	0.96	1.65	0.66	1.19
With Just 12th Grade Education				
Wages per hour*	7.59	6.84	9.34	8.18
Out of labour force†	3.0	9.7	3.1	8.7
Unemployed‡	7.8	13.8	7.8	11.5
Work full time, full year†	69.7	50.3	74.8	61.6
Unemployed because quit last job‡	0.94	1.43	0.6	1.23

Source: 1989 to 1993 CPS, five year average for all categories.
* In dollars.
† Percent of population with described characteristics.
‡ Percent of labour force with described characteristics.

These differences are tabulated in Tables 7.1a and 7.1b by age for 1993. The wages for the married men are slightly higher. For example, married men with just 12 years of education between 20 and 24 years of age and 25 and 29 have 11 and 14% higher wages than their respective single counterparts. The differences in labour force attachment are indeed dramatic. Single men 20 to 24 with this amount of education are more than three times as likely to be out of the labour force as married men. If in the labour force, a single man of that age and educational attainment is 75% more likely to be unemployed than a married man with similar traits. Similarly, the fraction of such men working full year full time if married is also almost 40% greater, 70% for the married, compared to 50% for the single. A single man 20 to 24 with just 12 years of education is 50% more likely than a comparable married man to be unemployed because he quit his last job.[8] Age 25 to 29, he is more than twice as likely.

2.4. Crime

Married men are also less likely than unmarried men to commit crimes as well as to be the victims. The probability of imprisonment is much larger for the single than for the married. Single men have almost six times the probability of being incarcerated as married men, and the multiple relative to the divorced is almost as large.

There are two ways in which young men get into trouble because of crime. Perpetrators may be caught, and the not always innocent bystanders may be victims.

---

[8] The fraction of men 21 to 24 with just 12 years of education who are unemployed because they quit their last job. Very few men of this age with only 12 years of education will be enrolled in school.

Singles are not only more likely to be perpetrators of crime as revealed by their higher imprisonment rate, they are also more likely to be victims. Unmarried men (undifferentiated by age except for being older than 12) have almost four times the chance of married men of being the victim of crimes of violence including almost five times the chance of being robbed.

2.5. *Use of Drugs, Alcohol, and Tobacco and Other Social Indicators*

There is also evidence that substance abuse differs by marital status. The NLSY shows that the fraction of married who report using marijuana in the last month is more than 35% less than the fraction for the unmarried; similarly the married are 6% less likely to have had more than six drinks at a time in the last month, after adjustment for age, survey year, labour force experience and experience squared, education, south, and urban.

Other social indicators give yet further proof of the large difference in lifestyle between the single and the married. Table 7.2 shows the differences in death rates for married and single for different age groups by different causes.

Table 7.1b. *Comparisons of single and married men: social characteristics*

	Married	Never Married
Ages 18–44		
Incarceration (state prisons)*†	2.6	17.6
Ages 12 and over		
Victimisation rates*‡		
Crimes of violence	30.1	111.9
Robbery	3.3	16.2
Ages 21–25		
Membership in literary or arts groups §‖	3.9	8.6
Visited art museum or gallery§‖	29.4	56.2
Attended classical opera§‖	0.0	19.4
Age 25		
Homeownership (living independently in 1976)§**	47	25

* Rate per thosand.
† U.S Department of Justice, Bureau of Justice Statistics. 1991. *Correctional Populations in the United States.* Table 4.1, p. 26. Divorced/separated/widowed are not included in these rates. Also not included in the rates is an estimate of those under 18 and over 44, who made up about 9% of the total state prison population. An assumption was made that the marital status for these age groups reflected that of the same age bracket in the general population, the numbers were reduced accordingly.
‡ U.S. Department of Justice. 1993. *Criminal Victimization in the United States.* Table 12, p. 20. Divorced/ separated/widowed victims are not included in these rates.
§ Percent of population with described characteristics.
‖ Data: 1972–94 General Social Survey; variables memlit, visitart, gomusic by marital status for men age 21–25, various years.
** *Data:* 1976 CPS; only those reported as householders were included

Table 7.2. *Deaths per 100,000 for married and single by cause, 1990*

	Ages 25–34		Ages 35–44	
	Single	Married	Single	Married
All causes	330	131	824	233
Diabetes mellitus	3	1	11	4
Diseases of heart	14	8	82	43
Cerebrovascular	3	2	13	6
Chronic obstructive pulmonary	1	0	5	1
Accidents	75	48	86	43
Motor vehicle	44	31	36	23
All other accidents	31	17	50	20
Suicide	34	20	41	21
Homicide	47	17	43	15

Source: U.S. Bureau of the Census. 1990. *Vital Statistics of the United States: Volume II-Mortality.* Table 1–34, pp. 387–400.

Over a wide range of causes the single have a higher chance of dying. Differences between married and single are clear in automobile accident rates. According to Canadian data, payments for single men 21 to 25 on auto insurance are 40% higher than for married men, and, in consequence, the NAIC Advisory Committee on insurance standards (1979) urges the use of marital status as a factor in auto premia.

Out of a concern for the causes of social problems I have so far emphasised pernicious differences that are likely to be intensified by prolongation of single careers. But the prolongation of these careers has beneficial results as well. According to tabulations from the General Social Survey, compared to the ever married, unmarried men, 21 to 25, were more than twice as likely to be a member of a literary or an art group, about twice as likely to have visited a museum or gallery, and much more likely to have attended a performance of classical music or opera, in the last year. They were also about 10% more likely to be a member of a service group.

In addition to acquiring children, the married are more likely than the single to make another major commitment, in buying their own home. Among those living independently, in 1976 the first year for which data were available, close to half—47%—of married men age 25 with just 12 years of education had become homeowners, in contrast to only 25% of the single. (This gap has narrowed considerably in recent years, perhaps because of reduced differences between married and singles as bachelorhood has become more common, or perhaps because of the increase in young men of this age who are not living independently but are still at home with their parents.)

2.6. *Summary*

To summarise, the marriage age changed over the past twenty-five years and there are noticeable differences in the lifestyle of married and unmarried men. Married men are more attached to the labour force; they have less substance abuse, they commit less crime, are less likely to become the victims of crime, have better health, and are less accident prone.

These statistics show the existence of significant differences between married and unmarried—sufficiently different that the change in the marriage age *could* have played a major role in the social changes that have occurred over the last quarter century. The news here is that the differences are large enough *potentially* to account for a significant portion of the change.

But the cross section differences between married and single may not occur *because* men develop different behaviour because of marriage. Two other explanations are also consistent with the data. The first explanation is selection bias: married and single men are just different. Marriage has no effect on their behaviour. This potential explanation for the differences between married and single behaviour can be tested by adding person-specific fixed effects to regression analysis of personal data. An alternative explanation for the differences in behaviour by marital status is more difficult to test: at some predetermined age men's behaviour changes. This age differs by individual. Marriage occurs at or near the time of that change. We shall also test for this explanation for the observed differences in behaviour by marital status.

A simple test suggests that selection bias in behaviour could be quite important. The more serious form of diabetes mellitus (insulin-dependent) is a genetically predisposed disease, which is believed to be triggered by a variety of conditions, such as viral infections from the mumps or Coxsackie B4 virus, toxic chemical agents or cytotoxins often with considerable lag after exposure (see Karam (1981, p. 735)). It seems unlikely from this etiology that the incidence of this disease would be much affected by marriage, so that differential morbidity by marital status serves as a diagnostic for the potential presence of selection bias by marital status. In fact, for this disease the death rates for married and single are dramatically different. For those aged 25 to 34 the death rate of the single was triple the death rate of the married. For those slightly older, 35 to 44 the death rate of the singles was more than double that of the married. These large differences suggest that significant differences between married and unmarried behaviour could be due to selection bias.

III. TESTS OF THE EFFECTS OF MARRIAGE ON HUMAN CAPITAL

Korenman and Neumark (1991) have used a fixed effects model to estimate the importance of selection bias as a determinant of the wage premium in the National Longitudinal Survey of Young Men. They do so by comparing the marriage premium in regressions with and without fixed effects for young men who have completed their education. There are two methods of doing so: one method just enters a dummy variable for married, spouse present and another for divorced, widowed, or separated. The alternative specification nests the other and has the additional independent variable of the number of years since marriage and its square. In this case the marriage dummy becomes fairly small and statistically significant, but at mean years of marriage (7.7 for the currently married) every year of marriage adds 0.9% to wage earnings. This is a remarkably large premium; in comparison, the growth in wages for workers because they are advancing in the life cycle is approximately 1.2% per year. (Workers who stay in the same job receive on average 1.2% higher wage increases than the average increase for the labour force as a whole (see Akerlof, Dickens and Perry (1996, p. 18))). In either specification of the fixed effects model, the fixed coefficient or the variable years specification, the fraction of the wage premium due to marriage, in the fixed coefficient model is 80 to 90% of the estimated marriage premium in the corresponding model without fixed coefficients. This suggests that most of the wage premium is due to the differential accumulation of human capital due to marriage rather than the selection bias of the married relative to the single.

The Korenman and Neumark findings correspond closely to similar findings by Kenny (1983) with a very different sample. Kenny used data from the Coleman Rossi Life History Study with a sample of somewhat older men—between the ages of 30 and 40. He calculated the difference in the growth of earnings for years of marriage and for years of not being married. He finds (1983, p. 229) that ten years of marriage will result in a 17 to 20% higher wage rate. In both of these studies it appears that married men have higher *growth* rather than higher levels of earnings. These findings both seem to suggest greater rates of accumulation of human capital beginning with marriage—a finding that is not consistent with selection bias as the major determinant of the wage premium. It is hard to explain why selection bias would yield increased growth in wages for the same man after marriage than before. A study, by Loh (1996), using the 1990 wave of the NLSY for white males and fixed effects confirms the Korenman and Neumark and Kenny findings of greater growth of earnings of men after marriage than before. On the other hand, recently it appears that the marriage wage premium is very much diminished, and quite possibly has even disappeared altogether. Blackburn and Korenman (1994) show that the marriage premium has greatly declined in CPS data. Gray (1997) confirms the findings of Korenman and Neumark regarding the marriage premium in the 1970's, but finds the premium in the 1990's to be small (only 1.4 percent) and statistically insignificant.

Using the NLSY data although a bit later wave, 1993, we show qualitatively the same results as Korenman and Neumark and Kenny. In contrast to Korenman and Neumark we used fewer controls such as occupation, industry and union status because we thought that upgrading of occupational status is one of the ways in which income would be increased with marriage. Our use of the NLSY panel data shows that in the cross section without fixed effects the married not only have somewhat higher wages, but also are much more likely to work full-time, on the average work more hours per week, are more likely to work year round, work more weeks, have fewer weeks of unemployment and have fewer weeks out of the labour force. Furthermore, upon marriage the probability of having had more than six drinks on one occasion in the last month and the probability of having smoked marijuana in the last year will also have declined. This impression, that sobriety and commitment to the labour force are enhanced by marriage, is confirmed by fixed effect regressions. Each and every one of these findings is confirmed in the fixed effect regressions although the size of the effect is smaller than in the cross section. The data seem to carry the message that behaviour changes after marriage. These results are reported in Tables 7.3 and 7.4.[9] Table 7.3 shows the effects of marriage on log wages, fulltime, hours per week, year round, weeks worked, weeks unemployed, weeks out of the labour force, use of marijuana in the last month, had six or more drinks in the last month. Table 7.4 repeats the same tabulations with the addition of years of marriage and years of marriage squared. Except for wages, our data do not show much growth in these variables after marriage. On the average it is the change at marriage that is statistically significant rather than marriage years.[10,11]

While, as already mentioned, Loh has confirmed the Korenman and Neumark and Kenny findings of greater growth of earnings of men after marriage than before, he also claims to refute the human capital interpretation. Loh cites the Becker-Mincer model of the division of labour and the accumulation of human capital within the household, as explaining the growth of the male wage marriage premium as due to the comparative advantage of men in market work and of women in home activities. In this model the man will have more time to build up his human capital after marriage rather than before marriage *if his wife stays home from work.* In this interpretation the marriage premium should depend upon whether or not the wife works; also the premium should begin with cohabitation, not with marriage. Loh shows that the premium does not depend upon whether or not the spouse works and also cohabitation has no effect on earnings. This may be a good refutation of the Mincer-Becker model of the division of work within the family, which is now a bit obsolete, but, in fact, it conforms to our interpretation that human capital changes with marriage. Consistent with Loh's findings the utility functions of men and women will change with marriage because, with marriage, men (and women) take on new identities that change their behaviour.[12]

---

[9] We have followed Korenman and Neumark both in our selection criteria of the sample, but we used the NLSY79 rather than the original NLS. Our econometric technique is similar, but again slightly different. We restricted the sample to white men who had completed their schooling by 1985 for whom all needed variables were available for all observations between years 1985 and 1992. We could determine education for 2,306 such men; 1,704 had completed all education by 1985. Of these, 1,023 had complete data for the 1985–1992 period. We deviate slightly from Korenman and Neumark (p. 291) in econometric technique. They use GLS to estimate their three-year panel. We estimate an eight-year panel both using OLS and also allowing an AR1 process for within-person error. The two methods give similar results.

[10] All regressions had controls for years of education, experience, experience squared, south, urban, year of survey, and eight years of birth.

[11] Two studies—one preceding and the other following Korenman and Neumark—purport to get different results (see Nakosteen and Zimmer (1987) and Cornwell and Rupert (1995)). They use instruments to predict marriage; and then use predicted marriage as a variable in the wage premium equation. This methodology solves the problem of selection bias, but the instruments chosen are very weak because there are few variables that predict marriage but not wage premia. The results are very high standard errors on the marital status dummies and are, in fact consistent with the fast build-up of human capital during marriage.

[12] Curiously, Loh offers another set of tests whose results he interprets in refutation of the Becker-Mincer model: that the marriage premium of self-employed men is negative. Interestingly these findings are exactly consistent with the Mincer model: marriage will allow the man to build up his human capital by engaging in self-employment, in which the low current income reflects the deferral of current income for future income. The tax laws alone provide incentives that the reported income of self-employed males will be understated.

Table 7.3. *Commitment to labour market and to sobriety by marital status**

Dependent variable	Cross-section Estimates[†]		Longitudinal Estimates[‡]	
	Coefficients on		Coefficients on	
	Marriage Dummy	Child Dummy	Marriage Dummy	Child Dummy
Log wages§	0.086 (0.018)	0.023 (0.018)	0.043 (0.018)	−0.003 (0.016)
Full-time dummy‖[**]††	0.371 (0.084)	0.259 (0.061)	0.345 (0.063)	0.100 (0.062)
Probability change†††	0.047	0.031	0.016	0.005
Hours per week§††	2.12 (0.540)	1.15 (0.395)	0.985 (0.533)	0.245 (0.366)
Year round dummy‖††‡‡	0.397 (0.060)	0.039 (0.044)	0.244 (0.047)	0.008 (0.044)
Probability change†††	0.115	0.011	0.054	0.002
Weeks worked§††§§	1.97 (0.487)	0.502 (0.355)	1.16 (0.487)	0.124 (0.336)
Weeks unemployed§§§	−0.769 (0.324)	−0.161 (0.237)	−0.155 (0.368)	0.109 (0.253)
Weeks out of labor force§§§	−1.36 (0.343)	−0.294 (0.248)	−1.01 (0.353)	−0.184 (0.245)
Marijuana use‖‖‖	−0.408 (0.073)	0.203 (0.085)	−0.153 (0.053)	−0.023 (0.058)
Probability change†††	−0.154	0.080	−0.058	−0.009
Overdrinking‖[***]	−0.238 (0.069)	−0.089 (0.071)	−0.127 (0.072)	−0.077 (0.070)
Probability change†††	−0.077	−0.029	−0.033	−0.020

* *Data*: Wage and Labour Force: White Males, 1985 to 1992 Panels of NLSY, reporting all needed data and who have completed their education by 1985.
  Marijuana use: White Males, 1979 to 1983 Panels of NLSY, reporting all needed data.
  Overdrinking: White Males, 1982, 1983, 1985, 1986, 1988, and 1989 Panels of NLSY, reporting all needed data and who have completed their education by 1982.
† *Controls*: experience, experience squared, and dummies for South, urban, year-of-birth, year-of-survey, divorced/widowed/separated spouse absent, and education.
‡ *Controls*: same as for Cross-section excluding the [nonvarying] education and year of birth dummies.
§ Method of Estimation: Generalised Least Squares with AR1 serially correlated errors for each individual
‖ Method of Estimation: probit, random effects probit for the longitudinal estimate.
** Dummy = 1 if worked more than 35 hours in average week.
†† Control for wife worked also included in cross-section.
‡‡ Dummy = 1 if worked more than 50 or more weeks in last calendar year.
§§ Control for working wife in both cross section and longitudinal.
‖‖ Dummy = 1 if smoked marijuana in the last year.
*** Dummy = 1 if had six or more drinks on single occasion in the last month.
††† Probability change is the effect of a change in the variable from zero to one, with all other variables held constant at their means across the sample.

In summary, the findings of Kenny, Korenman and Neumark, Loh and ourselves are exactly consistent with our model of marriage. Marriage involves a commitment. That commitment is perhaps an epiphany upon saying the words 'I do', perhaps a gradual change in experience leading to a penumbra of changes that ultimately result in the formation of human capital. The Mincer model is also on the right track but it tells us something different about the division of labour within a household. It explains why married women are much less apt than single women to be in the labour force, and, if so, to be in the labour force part-time. Thus our general view of what marriage means seems to be on the right track.

Table 7.4. *Commitment to labour market and to sobriety by marital status and by years of marriage*

Dependent variable	Cross-Section Estimates†			Longitudinal Estimates‡		
	Marriage Dummy	Coefficients on Years Married	Years Married Squared	Marriage Dummy	Coefficients on Years Married	Years Married Squared
Log wages§	0.034 (0.024)	0.028 (0.008)	−0.0016 (0.0006)	0.018 (0.020)	0.016 (0.007)	−0.0015 (0.0005)
Full-time dummy‖**††	0.314 (0.109)	0.022 (0.028)	−0.0012 (0.0019)	0.297 (0.080)	0.028 (0.026)	−0.0020 (0.0018)
Probability change	0.040	0.003	−0.00014	0.014	0.0013	−0.00009
Hours per week§††	0.953 (0.652)	0.575 (0.191)	−0.031 (0.014)	0.735 (0.575)	0.068 (0.159)	−0.009 (0.010)
Year round dummy‖††‡‡	0.258 (0.076)	0.049 (0.020)	−0.002 (0.001)	0.170 (0.058)	0.042 (0.019)	−0.002 (0.001)
Probability change	0.074	0.014	−0.0005	0.037	0.009	−0.0005
Weeks worked§††§§	1.04 (0.575)	0.458 (0.177)	−0.014 (0.013)	1.16 (0.524)	−0.182 (0.152)	0.002 (0.009)
Weeks unemployed§††§§	−0.198 (0.401)	−0.220 (0.111)	0.007 (0.008)	−0.122 (0.396)	0.029 (0.111)	0.002 (0.007)
Weeks out of labour force§††§§	−1.02 (0.395)	−0.192 (0.129)	0.004 (0.009)	−1.03 (0.378)	0.156 (0.115)	−0.003 (0.007)
Marijuana use‖‖‖	−0.067 (0.129)	−0.258 (0.084)	0.028 (0.011)	−0.126 (0.072)	−0.025 (0.049)	−0.0015 (0.0068)
Probability change	−0.026	−0.10	0.01	−0.048	−0.01	−0.001
Overdrinking‖***	−0.075 (0.108)	−0.079 (0.047)	0.004 (0.004)	−0.089 (0.098)	−0.024 (0.042)	0.0006 (0.004)
Probability change	−0.024	−0.025	0.001	−0.023	−0.006	0.0002

* *Data*: Wage and Labour Force: White Males, 1985 to 1993 Panels of NLSY, reporting all needed data and who have completed their education by 1985.
Marijuana use: White Males, 1979–1983 Panels of NLSY, reporting all needed data.
Overdrinking: White Males, 1982, 1983, 1985, 1986, 1988, and 1989 Panels of NLSY, reporting all needed data and who have completed their education by 1982.

† *Controls*: experience, experience squared, and dummies for South, urban, year-of-birth, year-of-survey, divorced/widowed/separated spouse absent dummy, and education.

§ Method of Estimation: Generalised Least Squares with AR1 serially correlated errors for each individual.

‖ Method of Estimation: probit, random effects probit for the longitudinal estimate.

** Dummy = 1 if worked more than 35 hours in average week.

†† Control for wife worked also included in cross-section.

‡‡ Dummy = 1 if worked more than 50 or more weeks in last calendar year.

§§ Control for working wife in both cross section and longitudinal.

‖‖‖ Dummy = 1 if smoked marijuana in the last year.

*** Dummy = 1 if had six or more drinks on single occasion in the last month.

††† For Marriage Dummy, probability change is the effect of a change from zero to one; for Years Married and Years Married Squared, probability change is the instantaneous effect. In both cases, all other variables are held constant at their means across the sample.

IV. CHANGE IN FIXED EFFECTS COINCIDENTAL
WITH TIMING OF MARRIAGE

There yet remains another problem with the fixed effects model by Korenman and Neumark as well as the empirical extension of their results. This problem will tend to result in overstatement of the effects on human capital formation of marriage. Suppose that people change their taste for human capital accumulation at the same time that they also decide to get married. Then the fixed effects are not constant in time, but change in time. The level of the fixed effect should also be correlated with marital status. By omitting the change in the fixed effect coefficient, which is correlated with the marital status dummy, the fixed effect regressions by Korenman and Neumark, and also by ourselves, have a specification error that is likely to raise the coefficient on the marital status dummy. It is thus possible that the results I have cited overstate the effects of marriage on human capital formation and other labour market behaviour. I shall now turn to some other methods therefore to try to see the relation between marital status and behaviour.

Korenman and Neumark have examined another set of data which, at least to some extent, resolves the problem. They examine the marriage differential in the wages reported in the personnel records of a large manufacturing firm in Massachusetts. This would totally solve the problem of the correlation of the change in the fixed effects and marital status, if in fact workers' change in life was coincidental with their beginning to work for this firm. Again they find a large marriage effect, which is apparently due to faster promotion of married than single employees. Adjusted for job grade, married and single employees get about the same earnings, but married employees have considerably higher chances of promotion. These chances of promotion are no greater when there is a control for job performance, but the job performance of married employees appears to be significantly better than the job performance of single employees: a fact consistent with the view of this paper that marriage is a rite of passage that marks a change in the way of life of the groom.

But there remains the possibility that, although marriage is a marker for change in life style for those who had joined the firm, this change would have occurred at about the same time even in the absence of marriage. We therefore have another test for the existence of changes in life after marriage. These are tests using macro data for the whole population. Aggregating to the whole population eliminates selection bias because the behaviour of the whole population will have no selection bias. As a result, we should expect that if marriage is causal, the incidence of marriage-induced behaviour should fall as the fraction married declines. We use this idea to estimate econometrically the effect of decreased marriage rates, with the identifying assumption that age cohorts with large decreases in the fraction of married men should also have large decreases in the types of behaviour associated with marriage.

We can aggregate and find

$$P_{A,\,at} = f_t \gamma_a [1 + (1 - f_{at})s]. \tag{2}$$

where $P_{A,at}$ is the aggregate rate of the activity for age group a at time t, where f_t is the rate of the activity at t for married men in the baseline age group, γ_a is the factor for age group a relative to the baseline, $1 + s$ is the factor for single relative to married men, and f_{at} is the fraction married of age group a at time t. As an approximation, with error term we get the econometric equation for estimation:

$$\ln P_{A,at} = \ln f_t + \ln \gamma_a + (1 - f_{at})s + \varepsilon_{at} \qquad (3)$$

where we have added the error term ε_{at}, which we assume to be independent and normally distributed.

The aggregate time series/cross-section regressions use (3) to estimate the parameters f_t, γ_a for different respective times and age groups and the value of s for different behaviours. We add a squared term in f_{at} for the possibility that as the fraction single goes up the premium s will go down, so that $s = c - d(1 - f_{at})$.

The model becomes just slightly more complicated if we think that the incidence of the fraction single of an age cohort is influenced by the fraction of the next oldest cohort—for example the homicide rate of teenagers may be affected by the amount of drug dealing by people in their twenties, which is likely to be higher if there are fewer married men, both because of a greater supply of potential dealers and also a greater demand for their product.

To test the hypothesis, we regressed the log of seven different statistics for five year averages on their respective fraction single and fraction single squared in that period for that age group with dummy variables for the time period and the age group. The inclusion of the square of the single fraction of the population allows for selection bias: as the fraction single becomes larger, we would expect the singles premium to decline, since, at least up to some point, the married and the single populations are becoming more alike. The seven statistics were death rate by homicide, arrest rate for violent crime, mortality rate in auto accidents, the fraction of those with just twelve years of education who were out of the labour force and with no work experience, and also the fraction of dropouts (with fewer than 12 years of education) in the same categories. The period of observation was 1965 to 1993,[13] and the age categories were 20 to 24, 25 to 29, 30 to 34, and 35 to 39.

The one message that comes through from the data with some clarity is the importance of selection bias. For six out of the seven characteristics—all but death by homicide—the coefficient on the square of the fraction of singles is negative. These results are shown in Table 7.5, which reports the coefficients on the age–time cohort of the fraction single and also the coefficient on its square. These results can be interpreted as a decline in the singles premium as the fraction single rises in each of these six categories. In all six cases the coefficient was significant at the 5% level. In each of these six cases the coefficient on the fraction of single men was also positive, although in none was it significant. In five out of the six the coefficient was sufficiently large that the

---

[13] The last period's observation for each age group averaged the observations for the four years 1990 to 1993 corresponding to the latest availability of data.

Table 7.5. *Relationship between different behaviour of age–time cohorts and fraction single*

| | Coefficients on | |
	Fraction single*	Fraction single squared
Out of labour force		
Only high school	1.58 (1.31)	−4.04(0.89)
Less than high school	0.94 (0.84)	−1.48(0.57)
No work experience in previous year		
Only high school	10.61 (1.14)	−8.96(1.58)
Less than high school	0.36 (0.96)	−2.36(0.65)
Violent arrest rate	0.76 (0.21)	−0.77(0.14)
Motor vehicle death rate	0.50 (0.29)	−0.54(0.19)
Homicide death rate	−1.43 (1.08)	3.37(0.74)
	Own fraction single† (Older than 20)	Own fraction single squared (Older than 20)	Fraction 20–24 single (Teenagers, 15–19)
Homicide death rate	−1.52 (1.14)	3.40 (0.79)	4.23 (0.80)

* 5 year ago cohorts 20–24, 25–29, 30–34, 35–39 and 5 year averages 1965–9, 1970–4, 1975–9, 1980–5, 1985–9 and 4 year average 1990–3, controls for age and time not reported.
† Same as above with inclusion of teenagers 15–19.

marginal effect of the singles ratio would be positive at the mean of the fraction singles ratio in the age-cohort populations in the regressions, although in some cases the marginal effect was quite small. For homicides the opposite was true. The coefficient on the linear term was negative, but on the squared term was large, positive, and significant. At the mean value of the fraction single the marginal effect of an increase in the singles ratio would cause an increase in the homicide ratio. The inclusion of teenagers, the 15 to 19 year old cohorts, into the homicide rate regressions shows that homicide rates for the more than 20's were sensitive to their own fraction single, but for the teenagers were sensitive to the fraction single of the next oldest cohort, as might be suspected if the activities of those in their early twenties, such as in drug-dealing or other crime affected teen age deaths.

Interestingly, the significant coefficients on the square of the fraction single, even if negative, are indicative of the fact that the fraction single does matter to behaviour. The null hypothesis whereby fraction single has no effect on aggregate behaviour would place a zero coefficient both on fraction single and also on the fraction single squared. The fact that as single behaviour becomes more normal the singles premium declines— whence the negative coefficient on singles squared—also suggests *ipso facto* the existence of a singles premium.

The good news from these results is that the significance of the marginal effect suggests that an important singles effect must be present. The bad news is that they also indicate that selection bias is quite important. As the fraction singles goes up, particularly for the older age groups, the difference between married and unmarried behaviour is likely to decline because the two populations become more similar. These results would also be consistent with the findings cited earlier by Blackburn and Korenman (1994) that the marriage premium has fallen significantly, and, yet more strongly by Gray (1997), that it has disappeared (ie is positive but quite small and statistically insignificant). Both of these findings support the view that as marriage becomes less common, employers are less likely to distinguish on the basis of marital status. Any conclusions from our own data exercise should be interpreted with a great deal of caution. Twenty-four data points—four age groups, for six time periods—are unlikely to be sufficient to estimate subtle cross-partial derivatives, such as the relative incidence of marriage-typical behaviour for groups with relatively higher fractions single. Biased changes in activities relative to age are likely to submerge any effect due to the increases in the fraction single. Perhaps, the data weakly support the hypothesis that marital status matters for aggregate activity, but the results themselves are not robust. Alternative specifications yield different results.

4.1. *Summary of Econometric Findings*

Econometric findings suggest that there is a difference between married and single behaviour, and some of those findings may even suggest that the differences are causal. The considerable consistency of the results under many different specifications suggest that the data is trying to speak to us. But the last test which would unambiguously solve the problem of selection bias suffers from the problem of omitted variable bias that means that the results are not robust to specification. Where the method might be expected to work best, on automobile accident rates it has the significantly wrong sign. Perhaps the data are trying to reveal a message, as in the cross section and the panel results, but nevertheless the possibilities of a myriad different specification errors as well as recent results concerning the fall in the marriage wage premium means the results should be treated tentatively and cautiously. Just possibly, Lawrence Stone and Shakespeare's shepherd got it right.

V. CONCLUSION

The conservative view on welfare (see Murray (1984)) claims that the major cause for increases in out-of-wedlock births has been the increases in the availability of welfare for young unmarried mothers. Murray's extreme prescription to end welfare has at least been partially adopted since cash welfare benefits have fallen by almost 50% in real terms in the last twenty-five years (although there have been increases in food stamps and in Medicaid).

This is the 150th anniversary of the great Irish potato famine (see Woodruff-Smith, 1962). The official British reaction to that famine was to limit the aid that was given. The prevailing economic theory of the time, like Murray's about welfare, was that public aid would crowd out healthy market responses to the lack of food. The provision of food to the poor would decrease their work incentive and would reduce the price of food in Ireland, thus crowding out the importation of supplies. Over the course of 1846, the second and most disastrous year of the famine, the British government had the policy of winding down its relief operations just as they were most needed. But the Irish peasants had no money for food and the private response did not materialise. Charles Trevelyan, the Assistant Secretary of the British Treasury, was in small measure correct: government provision of food to the Irish would undoubtedly have had some dampening response on the private provision of food. But as history shows, that response was small, and insufficient. The reaction to a great and unexpected natural disaster should have been to aid the victims.

The Potato Famine is an extreme example—extreme because any significant private response to the failure of the potato was impossible. British aid could have no significant crowding out effect. Today we face another problem, another type of disaster. That disaster is the failure of the family system in America, which has fallen apart not just for those who have ended up on welfare but to a significant but smaller degree for those higher in the distribution of economic and social rewards. Again the problem is to design a system that will not crowd out a healthy private response so that people will have as much incentive as possible to take care of their own problems, and not just rely on the government. For example, it has been alleged that women on welfare, who do not need to work, lose the discipline over the management of time. Another problem with the welfare system is that work incentives are so very low—keeping those who are on welfare from work, and alienating those who work for low wages.

By exploring causes for social pathology other than the welfare system itself this lecture has suggested that welfare is a response to poverty and not its cause. Insofar as poverty comes from causes other than the provision of welfare itself, the reduction of each dollar for the poor takes resources away from those who need it most. If the first reaction of the British Government to the natural disaster of the Potato Famine should have been to replace the food that had disappeared, the first reaction to the social disaster of the disintegrating family structure should be to replace the income that has disappeared. Each dollar reduction in welfare comes from the poorest families in America. The secondary, but still important, task, is to design that system of support so that the system itself will create the minimum disincentive and disruption.

This essay is one of several to explain aspects of the natural disaster that has occurred in America. By understanding these natural forces we hope to prevent the sacrifice of our children, as previous generations have done, to propitiate a nonexistent god.

University of California at Berkeley and the Brookings Institution

References

Akerlof, G. A., Dickens, W. T. and Perry, G. L. (1996), 'The macroeconomics of low inflation,' *Brookings Papers on Economic Activity*, vol. 1, pp. 1–76.

——, Yellen, J. L. and Katz, M. L. (1996), 'An analysis of out-of-wedlock childbearing in the United States,' *Quarterly Journal of Economics*, vol. 111 (May), pp. 278–317.

Becker, G. S. (1965), 'A theory of the allocation of time,' *Economic Journal*, vol. 75 (September), pp. 493–517.

Becker, G. S. and Murphy, K. M. (1988), 'A theory of rational addiction,' *Journal of Political Economy*, vol. 96 (August), pp. 675–700.

Blackburn, M. and S. Korenman (1994), 'The declining marital-status earnings differential,' *Journal of Population Economics*, vol. 7 (July), pp. 247–70.

Cornwell, C. and Rupert, P. (1995) 'Marriage and earnings,' *Federal Reserve Bank of Cleveland Economic Review*, (Quarter 4), pp. 10–20.

Ellwood, D. T. (1988), *Poor Support: Poverty in the American Family*, New York: Basic Books.

—— and Crane, J. (1990), 'Family change among black Americans: what do we know?' *Journal of Economic Perspectives*, vol. 4, pp. 65–84.

—— and Summers, L. H. (1986), 'Poverty in America: Is welfare the answer or the problem?' in *Fighting Poverty: What Works and What Doesn't*, (S. Danziger and D. Weinberg, eds), Cambridge, MA: Harvard University Press.

Freeman, R. B. (1996), 'Why do so many young American men commit crimes and what might we do about it?', National Bureau of Economic Research Working Paper 5451. Cambridge, MA: National Bureau of Economic Research.

Gray, J. S. (1997), 'The fall in men's return to marriage: declining productivity effects or changing selection?', *Journal of Human Resources*, vol. 32 (Summer), pp. 481–504.

Jencks, C. (1992), *Rethinking Social Policy*, Cambridge, MA: Harvard University Press.

Karam, J. H. (1981), 'Diabetes Mellitus, Hypoglycemia, and Lipoprotein disorders,' in (M. A. Krupp and M. J. Chatton, eds.), *Current Medical Diagnosis and Treatment 1981*. Los Altos, CA: Lange Medical Publications.

Kenny, L. W. (1983), 'The accumulation of human capital during marriage by males,' *Economic Inquiry*, vol. 21 (April), pp. 223–31.

Korenman, S. and Neumark, D. (1991), 'Does marriage really make men more productive?', *Journal of Human Resources*, vol. 26 (Spring), pp. 282–307.

Laibson, D. I. (1996), 'A cue-theory of consumption,' mimeo, Harvard University, September.

Loh, E. S. (1996), 'Productivity differences and the marriage wage premium for white males,' *Journal of Human Resources*, vol. 31 (Summer), pp. 566–89.

NAIC (1979), *Private Passenger Automobile Insurance Risk Classification: A Report of the Advisory Committee*, mimeo, May.

Moffitt, R. A. (1992), 'Incentive effects of the U.S. welfare system: a review,' *Journal of Economic Literature*, vol. 30, pp. 1–61.

——, Reville, R. and Winkler, A. E. (1995), 'Beyond single mothers: cohabitation, marriage, and the U.S. welfare system,' mimeo, July.

Mincer, J. (1962), 'Labour force participation of married women: a study of labour supply,' in *Aspects of Labour Economics*, Conference No. 14 of the Universities-National Bureau Committee for Economic Research, Princeton: Princeton University Press.

Murray, C. (1984), *Losing Ground: American Social Policy 1950–1980*, New York: Basic Books.

Nakosteen, R. and Zimmer, M. (1987), 'Marital status and earnings of young men,' *Journal of Human Resources*, vol. 22 (Spring), pp. 248–68.

Rubin, L. B. (1969), *Worlds of Pain: Life in the Working-Class Family*, New York: Basic Books.

—— (1992), *Families on the Fault Line*, New York: Harper Collins.

Stigler, G. J. and Becker G. S. (1977), 'De gustibus non est disputandum,' *American Economic Review*, vol. 67 (March), pp. 76–90.

Stone, L. (1979), *The Family, Sex and Marriage in England 1500–1800*, abridged edition. New York: Harper and Row.

Wilson, W. J. (1987), *The Truly Disadvantaged*, Chicago: Chicago University Press.

Wilson, W. J. (1996), *When Work Disappears: The World of the New Urban Poor*, New York: Random House.

Wallerstein, J. (1980), *Surviving the Breakup*, New York: Basic Books.

Wood, R. G. (1995), 'Marriage rates and marriageable men: a test of the Wilson hypothesis,' *Journal of Human Resources*, vol. 30, pp. 163–93.

Woodruff-Smith, C. (1962), *The Great Hunger: Ireland 1845–1849*, London: Hamish Hamilton.

8

The Economic Consequences of Cognitive Dissonance*

BY GEORGE A. AKERLOF AND WILLIAM T. DICKENS†

Since the publication of *The Wealth of Nations*, economists have built an entire profession on a single powerful theory of human behavior based on a few simple assumptions. That model has been fruitfully applied to a wide range of problems.

But, while economists have been elaborating their analysis, keeping their basic behavioral assumptions the same, sociologists, anthropologists, political scientists, and psychologists have been developing and validating models based on very different assumptions.

For most types of economic behavior, the economists' model is probably quite adequate.[1] The models developed by other social scientists are generally ill-suited for direct incorporation into economic analysis. Nevertheless, insofar as studies in these other disciplines establish that people do not behave as economists assume they do, economics should endeavor to incorporate these observations.

This paper presents an example of how this might be accomplished in one special case. Psychologists have devoted considerable attention to the theory of cognitive dissonance. This theory has been used earlier by Albert Hirschman (1965) to describe attitude changes toward modernization in the course of development. Our paper expands the economic applications of cognitive dissonance and analyzes its welfare consequences in a formal model.

---

* This work was previously published as George A. Akerlof and William T. Dickens (1982), 'The Economic Consequences of Cognitive Dissonance', *The American Economic Review*, 72, 3. Copyright © The American Economic Association. Reproduced by kind permission.

† University of California-Berkeley. We would like to thank Allen Berger, Robert Clower, Jack Hirshleifer, Bernard Saffran, and Janet Yellen for valuable comments.

[1] The approach of this paper to what economists might call the economics of 'irrational' behavior differs from that of Gary Becker (1962). Becker views irrational behavior as random deviations from economic rationality. We use the findings of the psychologists who view irrational behavior as predictable, and therefore not totally random. Welfare implications seem to follow from the predictability of such behavior.

I. AN OVERVIEW

A. *The Basic Premises*

To begin, we must translate the psychological theory into concepts amenable to incorporation into an economic model. We think the theory of cognitive dissonance can be fairly represented in economists' terms in three propositions: first, persons not only have preferences over states of the world, but also over their beliefs about the state of the world. Second, persons have some control over their beliefs; not only are people able to exercise some choice about belief given available information, they can also manipulate their own beliefs by selecting sources of information likely to confirm 'desired' beliefs. Third, it is of practical importance for the application of our theory that beliefs once chosen persist over time.[2]

In the next section we will give a brief summary of results from studies in social psychology which show that people in certain circumstances behave according to each of these three premises.

B. *The Fundamental Model*

The meaning of each of these premises and a practical application are illustrated by a model given in Section III. A great deal of anecdotal information suggests that workers in dangerous jobs are often quite oblivious to the dangers that are involved.[3] In this regard, interviews with benzene workers, some of whom denied that they were working with dangerous chemical substances, are typical (see Daniel Ben-Horin, 1979). Alternatively, Brian Main has related to us his experience in a nuclear plant where workers were given specially designed safety badges to collect information on radiation exposure in a weekly checkup. All workers in this plant, some of whom were Ph.D.s, failed to wear these badges; they were put in workers' desks and only brought out for the weekly checkup. Howard Kunreuther et al. (1978) related similar tales regarding failure for persons with high risk of flood or earthquake damage to purchase flood or earthquake insurance.

The model presented in Section III is constructed as an explanation for such phenomena. In that model, people prefer to believe that their work is safe. This corresponds to the first premise that workers have preferences over their states of beliefs. Workers make a choice about whether to believe the activity is safe or not safe. This accords with the second premise that workers have a choice about their beliefs. There is a benefit to believing that a job is safe, but also a cost. Those who choose to believe the job is safe do not experience the unpleasant feelings of constant fear or unsettling doubts about how wise it was to take such a dangerous job. On the

---

[2] Actually, these assumptions allow for a much richer type of behavior than simple cognitive dissonance. Some of the 'applications' in Section IV take advantage of this.

[3] Another possible explanation for this phenomenon is that workers have noisy estimates of the safety of different jobs. In that case, there will be a tendency for workers who take a job to be those who underestimate its danger. Some of the implications of such a model have been considered in Dickens (1981).

other hand, if they convince themselves the job is safe, they may make costly judgment errors due to the discrepancy between their beliefs and the true state of the world.

In our model the cost of believing that work is safe is the possibility of making a mistake in the choice of safety practice. The worker chooses his beliefs according to whether the benefit exceeds the cost, or vice versa. If the psychological benefit of suppressing one's fear in a particular activity exceeds the cost due to increased chances of accident, the worker will believe the activity to be safe. Otherwise he will believe it to be unsafe. (This model assumes that the worker's beliefs are totally plastic: he can believe whatever he chooses irrespective of the information available to him. Of course this is a polar case. More complicated and general models would endow persons with a set of beliefs that may be chosen given the available information. Given his total choice set the agent chooses beliefs, and other things, to maximize his utility.)

A model of such a decision process is presented in Section III. It is analyzed with respect to how wages and labor supply will respond to the introduction of new safety equipment. The effects of safety legislation are also considered, as are the conditions under which such legislation will cause a Pareto-superior shift in the use of resources.

This paper is not to be interpreted as suggesting that cognitive dissonance is a significant feature of every economic transaction. On the contrary, in the model presented in Section II cognitive dissonance reactions are self-limiting. In most economic transactions there is no gain to rationalizing and cognitive dissonance plays no role. There are, however, special circumstances in which the assumptions mentioned in Section II will apply and cognitive dissonance will play an important role.

Besides safety regulation, we believe cognitive dissonance may be important in understanding innovation, advertising, crime, and Social Security legislation. These applications are potentially of great importance; they are, however, much more speculative than the straightforward application of our model to safety legislation. Section IV explains these applications. Section V then gives conclusions.

II. PSYCHOLOGICAL EVIDENCE FOR THE BASIC PREMISES

Much social psychology is based on the theory of cognitive consistency. At the most abstract level this means that persons are uncomfortable in maintaining two seemingly contradictory ideas. Cognitive dissonance theory is one application of cognitive consistency theory. In practice most cognitive dissonance reactions stem from peoples' view of themselves as 'smart, nice people.' Information that conflicts with this image tends to be ignored, rejected, or accommodated by changes in other beliefs.[4] Among other applications, persons who have made decisions tend to discard information that would suggest such decisions are in error because the cognition that the decision might be in error is in conflict with the cognition that ego is a smart person. Cognitive dissonance theory would suggest that persons in dangerous jobs must decide between two conflicting

---

[4] The description of cognitive dissonance in this paper as well as our choice of which experiments to present owes a great deal to the excellent book by Elliott Aronson (1979).

cognitions. According to one cognition, ego is a smart person who would not choose to work in an unsafe place. If the worker continues to work in the dangerous job, he will try to reject the cognition that the job is dangerous.

The question naturally arises whether the behavior that psychologists label as cognitive dissonance could be considered instead as rational behavior under Bayesian decision theory. Agents with cognitive dissonance reactions have posterior distributions that are unwarranted solely by the information available to them. Their estimate of the state of the world is influenced by their preferences over their state of belief. Using Bayesian decision rules, agents' estimates of the state of the world is only influenced by the information available to them and their preferences over states of the world, but these estimates are independent of their preferences for beliefs per se. The typical psychological experiment motivated by cognitive dissonance theory compares the beliefs of two groups of agents—one a control group and the other a group whose preferences for different beliefs have been changed by the experimenter. The experimenter attempts to change these preferences while no new information is imparted to this second group that could be considered relevant to their estimate of the state of the world. From our examination of the evidence, we find it all but impossible to give a Bayesian interpretation to the results of many of the experiments, because it is all but impossible to give an explanation of the relevance of the differences in information available to the two groups.

This paper relies heavily on our three premises for which there is supporting data from psychological experiments. The presentation of just a bit of this data is useful not only because it lends support to the three premises but also because it shows the types of situations in which cognitive dissonance reactions will be likely to occur. It should be understood, however, that the following paragraphs are merely illustrative. In their brevity, they fail to give the best possible evidence for our three premises and for the theory: that evidence being the great number of experimental results which are easily explained in terms of cognitive dissonance.

Experiments show that groups of persons with the same information have systematically different beliefs that accord with natural theories about their preferences. For example, persons like to view themselves as having made correct decisions. Interviews of bettors at a race track (Robert Knox and James Inkster, 1968) indicate that persons just leaving the betting window place much higher odds on 'their horse' than persons in the queue just prior to their bet. As another example, in an experiment, an investigator (Jack Brehm, 1956) asked women to rate the worthiness of two appliances. They were then allowed to choose between the two appliances, which were given *wrapped* to the women. A few minutes later with the appliances still wrapped the women were asked for a second evaluation. These evaluations systematically changed in favor of the appliance that had been chosen.

Many laboratory examples concern immoral or cruel behavior. One experiment (Keith Davis and Edward Jones, 1960) asked students to watch another student being interviewed and then tell this student he was shallow, untrustworthy, and dull. The students who engaged in such behavior systematically changed their attitudes against the object of their cruelty. In terms of our first two premises, persons prefer to think of themselves as nice people. This self-image can be preserved if they have a low opinion of the object of their cruelty. They revise their opinions accordingly. A similar experiment (David Glass, 1964) reports that students who gave electrical shocks to victims lowered their opinion of their victims.

The cognitive dissonance model not only predicts systematic differences in interpretation of given information but also systematic differences in receptivity to new information according to preferences. In one example (Jerald Jellison and Judson Mills, 1967), some women were first asked to rate a group of products. They were then asked to choose between two of these products of quite different desirability. Before this choice was final, however, one group of these subjects was presented with information on the rejected product and a second group was presented with information on a product that had been similarly rated but had not been one of the possible choices. Curiously, the subjects for whom the information was irrelevant to their decision spent more time reading it than the subjects for whom the information was relevant. This is one of many experiments that purport to show a biased receptivity to new information.

We should not lose sight of our third premise: that the effects of cognitive dissonance on beliefs may be long lasting. It is claimed as one application of cognitive dissonance theory that persons who justify to themselves some difficult undertaking are likely to have a strong and persistent belief that the undertaking is a good one. If an undertaking is difficult and the external reward is small (in comparison to the effort involved), the individual must either justify the undertaking to himself or consider himself stupid to engage in it. Many experiments show such effects over a short time; one particular experiment (Danny Axsom and Joel Cooper, 1980) shows that these effects may be quite long lasting. Two groups of women engaged in two weight-reduction programs, both for four weeks, one involving much effort, the other involving little effort. Over the four weeks, both programs were equally effective in weight reduction. However, a year later the women in the high-effort program had an average weight loss of eight pounds, while those in the low-effort program had on average lost virtually nothing. We consider this as evidence that cognitive dissonance may well have long-lasting effects.

III. A MODEL

A. *General Description of the Model*

This section presents and analyzes a simple model to show the economic consequences of cognitive dissonance. There are two periods. In the first period, workers have a choice between working in a hazardous job or working in a safe job. The worker will choose the job with the highest combined pecuniary and nonpecuniary benefits.

In the first period, workers in the hazardous industry have no choice but to face the possibility of an accident as there is no safety equipment available. If the cost imposed by future wrong decisions is not too great, workers in the hazardous industry will, because of cognitive dissonance, come to believe that the job is really safe.

In the second period, cost-effective safety equipment becomes available. But, because by then workers in the hazardous industry believe the jobs to be safe, they will not purchase the equipment. Safety legislation is needed to restore Pareto optimality since the workers have an incorrect assessment of the marginal rate of substitution between safety equipment and money income.[5]

In this model, both labor markets and product markets are competitive. Also, workers begin with rational expectations. These workers know upon taking a job in the hazardous industry that they will experience cognitive dissonance and alter their estimated probabilities of accident. The purpose of building such a "complete information" model is not realism; we would not expect people to be aware of their future behavior.[6] Rather, the purpose of this assumption is to show that even in a model where workers entering a hazardous job perfectly foresee their future psychological reactions to the unsafe conditions, there may be a welfare-improving role for safety legislation. Such a role is obvious in models without rational expectations in which governments have more information than private agents.

The assumptions of our model are presented in Part B; the model is analyzed in Part C; in Part D the resulting equilibrium is illustrated; in Part E the nature of the equilibrium and the effects of the introduction of safety legislation are discussed; initially, in Parts B, C, D, and E, it is assumed that workers do not make contracts which precommit themselves to the purchase of safety equipment. Part F discusses that assumption and its implications.

B. *Assumptions of the Model*

The assumptions of the model are given in four parts: the description of the demand for labor in the safe industry; the description of the demand for the product of the hazardous industry; the description of the nonpecuniary disadvantages of the hazardous jobs; and the description of the individual worker's psychological choice.

The Labor Market in the Safe Industry. The safe industry is pictured as large relative to the hazardous industry. A job in the safe industry pays a fixed wage, denoted w_s. This wage anchors the wage of workers in the hazardous industry in both periods 1 and 2; that wage is determined by an appropriate equality between the pecuniary plus non-pecuniary benefits in safe and in hazardous jobs.

The Demand for the Product and the Supply of the Product in the Hazardous Industry. The demand for the product of the hazardous industry in each period is given by a downward-sloping demand function $D = D(p_h)$, where D is the demand for the good and p_h is the price of the good. The good is produced by labor alone. One worker produces one unit of the good in each period. The producers are competitive, so that the supply of the good is infinitely elastic at the wage in each period.

---

[5] We assume that workers cannot precommit themselves to buy the safety equipment. That assumption is analyzed in Section III.F.

[6] The implications of models where people are not completely aware of their future behavior are considered in fn. 8.

The Nonpecuniary Disadvantages of Work in the Hazardous Industry. Without safety equipment, all workers in the hazardous industry have a probability q of accident in periods 1 and 2. The cost of an accident to a worker is c_a.

In the first period, no safety equipment is available. In the second period, a worker in the hazardous industry can purchase a new safety device which eliminates the possibility of an accident at a cost c_s. To make this equipment economically relevant, it is assumed that $qc_a > c_s$. We will also assume that workers cannot precommit themselves to purchase this safety equipment. They must decide at the beginning of the second period. The effect of relaxing this assumption and the reasonableness of doing so are considered in Part F. (Note also that in a competitive model it makes no difference whether workers or firms purchase the safety equipment.)

In addition, each worker in the hazardous industry in each period has a psychic cost of fear, equal to $c_f f$, where c_f is the unit cost of fear and f is the level of the worker's fear. (As an expositional convenience the uncomfortable feeling of a worker in a job believed to be unsafe is called 'fear.' This convention should not mask the relevance of our model for the economic consequences of cognitive dissonance. Cognitive dissonance theory has a more complex explanation than animalistic fear for the worker's uncomfortable feeling: he is torn between two cognitions: that he is a smart person; yet he has chosen to work in a hazardous job. The welfare implications and market solution are independent of the precise description of the uncomfortable emotion.)

The Relation between Fear and the Perceived Probability of Accident q^*; and the Worker's Choice of q^*. In general, f will be a function of q^*, the worker's subjective assessment of the probability of an accident occurring during the period. This function is assumed to be of the form

$$f = q^*/q \tag{1}$$

over the range $0 \leq q^* \leq q$. For each worker, prior to his choice between work in the hazardous or safe industry, q^* starts off equal to q, the true probability of an accident. But, cognitive dissonance is modeled by letting each worker choose any value of q^* in the range between 0 and q. However, once that choice has been made, the worker must behave as if the new value of q^* is the true probability of accident. In this model workers are fully aware of the decision environment: they have rational expectations.

C. *Description of the Equilibrium of the Model*

It is easy to analyze the equilibrium of the model by working backwards from period 2. Formal proof that the equilibrium accords with the description given here is available in an appendix on request from the authors. The proof is outlined here. The analysis of the equilibrium proceeds according to four propositions.

Proposition 1: *The wage in the hazardous industry in period 2 is $w_s + c_s$.*

Because real costs of producing in the hazardous industry in the second period are lower than in the first period due to the introduction of the new safety equipment, the price of the good will be lower in the second period, and therefore the demand will be higher. As a result, more of the good will be produced and hence more workers hired in period 2 than in period 1. Of necessity, the marginal worker in period 2 must come from the safe industry. Such a worker believes $q^* = q$ and will therefore purchase the safety equipment. This worker must be compensated for the wage lost from not taking a safe job, w_s, and also for purchasing safety equipment at cost c_s. Such compensation makes the two jobs exactly comparable. Thus the wage in the hazardous industry in period 2 is $w_s + c_s$.

Proposition 2: *A worker in the hazardous industry in period 2 chooses to buy safety equipment if*

$$q^* > qc_s/(qc_a + c_f). \qquad (2)$$

The worker buys safety equipment in period 2 if the perceived cost of fear and the perceived cost of accident exceeds the cost of the safety equipment. The level of fear is q^*/q. The cost of fear is therefore $(q^*/q)c_f$. The perceived cost of accident is q^*c_a. Thus the worker chooses to purchase (or not purchase) safety equipment accordingly as $q^*c_a + (q^*/q)c_f$ is greater than (or less than) c_s. Inequality (2) follows.

Proposition 3: *A worker in the hazardous industry in period 1 chooses*

$$q^* = 0 \qquad (3)$$

if $\quad (qc_a - c_s) < c_s c_f/(qc_a + c_f),$

$$q^* = qc_s/(qc_a + c_f) \qquad (4)$$

if $\quad (qc_a - c_s) > c_s c_f/(qc_a + c_f).$

The variable q^* is chosen by each worker in period 1 to maximize his welfare. The worker correctly perceives that if he chooses q^* below the critical level $qc_s/(qc_a + c_f)$ he will make the wrong decision in period 2 regarding the purchase of safety equipment.

A worker who chooses q^* in the range below the critical level $qc_s/(qc_a + c_f)$ should choose $q^* = 0$, the level which minimizes his fear. The cost to him of fear in this case is 0, but the cost of making the wrong decision in period 2 regarding the purchase of safety equipment is

$$qc_a - c_s \qquad (5)$$

and will be the same for any value of $q^* < qc_s/(qc_a + c_f).$

Alternatively, the worker could maintain q^* sufficiently high so that he will correctly purchase safety equipment. This will occur as long as $q^* > qc_s/(qc_a + c_f)$ according to Proposition 2. And $q^* = qc_s/(qc_a + c_f)$ will minimize the cost of fear.

What value of q^* should the worker choose? To maximize his combined pecuniary and nonpecuniary income he should compare the cost of fear at the level $q^* = qc_s/(qc_a + c_f)$ to the cost of failure to purchase safety equipment at $q^* = 0$. The cost of fear at $q^* = qc_s/(qc_a + c_f)$ is $(q^*/q)c_f$, or

$$c_s c_f/(qc_a + c_f). \tag{6}$$

Accordingly the worker should choose $q^* = 0$ if (6) exceeds (5) and $q^* = qc_s/(qc_a + c_f)$ if (5) exceeds (6).

Proposition 4: *The wage of workers employed in the hazardous industry in period 1 is*

$$w_{h_1} = w_s + qc_a + \min(qc_a - c_s,\, c_s c_f/(qc_a + c_f)). \tag{7}$$

In Case I where the worker chooses $q^* = 0$, he must be compensated for the expected costs due to accidents (qc_a) in period 1 and for the cost of making a wrong decision in period 2. A worker with a safe job in period 2 receives a wage w_s. A worker in the hazardous industry receives a wage $w_s + c_s$. A worker in the hazardous industry who does not purchase safety equipment in period 2 receives total net benefits $w_s + c_s - qc_a$. Thus for a worker in the hazardous industry to receive the same net benefits over the two periods as a worker in the safe industry, he must receive a wage in the first period

$$w_{h_1} = w_s + qc_a + (qc_a - c_s). \tag{8}$$

In Case II, where the worker chooses $q^* = qc_s/(qc_a + c_f)$, he buys safety equipment in period 2 at a cost c_s and he receives a wage $w_s + c_s$. Therefore his net benefits in period 2 are exactly the same as those of a worker in the safe industry. In period 1, however, he has an additional cost of accident equal to qc_a and an additional cost of fear equal to $(q^*/q)c_f$. Thus he must receive additional compensation relative to a worker in the safe industry in amount $qc_a + c_s c_f/(qc_a + c_f)$ so that

$$w_{h_1} = w_s + qc_a + c_s c_f/(qc_a + c_f). \tag{9}$$

Putting together these cases, they yield the proposition.

D *Illustration of the Equilibrium*

Figure 8.1 illustrates this equilibrium. In each period the demand for workers in the hazardous industry exactly equals the demand for the good, because it takes one worker

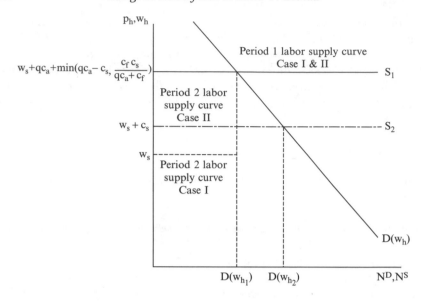

Figure 8.1. *Labor demand and supply in the hazardous industry for periods 1 and 2.*

to produce one unit of the good. In the first period there is an infinitely elastic supply of workers at the reservation wage

$$w_{h_l} = w_s + qc_a + \min(qc_a - c_s, c_s c_f/(qc_a + c_f)). \tag{10}$$

Thus the equilibrium wage in the first period is $w_s + qc_a + \min(qc_a - c_s, c_s c_f/(qc_a + c_f))$. In the second period, there are two possible supply curves for labor. In Case I with $q^* = 0$, workers supply labor up to quantity $D(w_{h_l})$ at wage rate w_s; beyond $D(w_{h_l})$ there is an infinite supply of labor from the safe industry at wage $w_s + c_s$. In Case II with $q^* = qc_s/(qc_a + c_f)$, there is an infinite supply of labor to the hazardous industry at the wage $w_s + c_s$. In both Cases I and II, the equilibrium wage in the second period is $w_s + c_s$ because the demand curve for labor meets each of the two possible supply curves to the right of $D(w_{h_l})$ where labor supply is infinitely elastic at wage $w_s + c_s$.

E. *The Equilibrium Discussed; Introduction of Safety Legislation*

What are the distributional implications of this equilibrium? First, all workers no matter what their employment history will have the same expected pecuniary and nonpecuniary income when summed over the two periods: $2w_s$.[7] When the relative costs of safety, fear, and accidents are such that all workers will choose to buy the safety equipment in the second period, all workers will have an expected income of exactly w_s in each

---

[7] Workers in the safe industry receive a wage of w_s in each period for a total net benefit of $2w_s$.

period. If the parameters of the decision problem are such that workers in the hazardous industry in the first period will choose not to buy the safety equipment in the second period, the situation will be somewhat different. Those workers will perceive themselves as earning $w_s + c_s$ in the second period when in fact their expected income will be

$$w_s + c_s - qc_d < w_s. \tag{11}$$

However, because they foresaw this eventuality at the beginning of the first period, their first-period wages compensated them for this loss. Thus the introduction of the consideration of cognitive dissonance does not change the distribution of utility among workers. What about the distribution between workers and consumers?

We now compare the equilibrium just derived to one with safety legislation. This safety legislation requires the purchase of safety equipment which has been found to be cost effective. In this case the reservation wage for working in the hazardous industry in the first period will be only

$$w'_{h_1} = w_s + qc_d. \tag{12}$$

Since workers know that they will be required to adopt the new safety technology they will always choose $q^* = 0$ and will experience no fear in the first period. Since they will be required to purchase safety equipment in the second period, they will not require compensation for making a wrong decision in period 2 or for keeping fear at a level that will allow them to buy safety equipment when available. With safety equipment, the reservation wage for all workers in the second period will be $w_{h_2} = w_s + c_s$. The wage in the second period will be the same with and without safety legislation:

$$w_{h_2} = w'_{h_2} = w_s + c_s. \tag{13}$$

The net change over the two periods due to safety legislation is a lower wage in the hazardous industry in the first period—hence a lower price of the good produced by this industry.

With safety legislation the workers still have the same expected income summed over both periods, $2w_s$. But, consumers are better off since they pay a lower price for the good of the hazardous industry in the first period. Thus safety legislation causes a Pareto-superior result.[8] If consumers have constant marginal utility of income the welfare gain from safety legislation is equal to the shaded area in Figure 8.2.

---

[8] Customers are the beneficiaries of safety legislation only if workers perfectly foresee their future behavior. If workers are unaware of the impending improvement in safety technology, the effect of fear, or the possibility of changing their beliefs, then the benefit of safety legislation, if any, will go to workers in the hazardous industry. That gain will be $qc_d - c_s$ per worker and will obtain in all cases where workers decide to believe that their jobs are not dangerous during the first period. That would be all situations where the cost of fear is greater than $qc_d - c_s$, and all cases where workers do not know that they may change their beliefs or are unaware of the effect of that choice on their decision to buy safety equipment in the second period. A typescript with a detailed analysis of these possibilities is available from the authors.

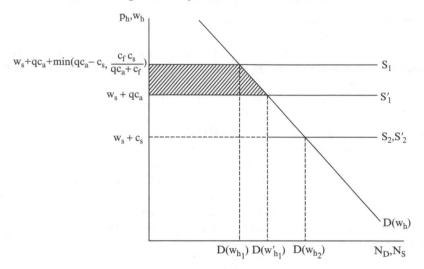

Figure 8.2. *Labor demand and supply in the hazardous industry with and without safety legislation.*
Note: The shaded area illustrates the welfare gain from legislation; the S are supply curves without safety legislation; the S' are supply curves with safety legislation.

F. *Precommitment Contracts*

Jack Hirshleifer has pointed out to us that, in a perfect foresight world, if workers can enter into contracts at the beginning of period 1 which will bind them to purchase safety equipment in the second period, a Pareto-optimal equilibrium can be obtained through the voluntary actions of the workers without government intervention. Whether or not such precommitment contracts are possible depends on the nature of the legal system. If recontracting is allowed in the second period, workers may try to precommit themselves but will want to recontract at the beginning of the second period. Such recontracting must lead to a Pareto-optimal result given the workers' tastes and beliefs *as they stand at the beginning of the second period.* Thus, if workers have taken advantage of their precommitment by allowing themselves to come to believe that their job is safe they will now want to break their contract. If recontracting is allowed, they may do so by paying some amount (less than c_s) to the person with whom they contracted. If the workers have rational expectations and correct perception of the true model in the first period, as we have assumed, they will perceive the futility of precommitment in the presence of possibilities for recontracting and will refrain from trying.

However, in a model where agents acquire reputations from past dealings, precommitments may be viable. Agents who sell safety equipment may not be willing to recontract if by so doing they would jeopardize their reputations, thereby reducing their possibilities for advantageous future precommitment contracts. But, a model in which reputation plays a role ipso facto involves an institutional framework different from the usual competitive model and is likely to have non-Pareto-optimal outcomes.

Finally, if we relax the assumption that workers can foresee their cognitive dissonance reactions, then precommitment contracts become impossible.

IV. POTENTIAL APPLICATIONS

The model described in the last section is illustrative of the use of psychological findings in economic models. In this section we suggest some other possible applications for similar models. Some of these potential applications are directly motivated by cognitive dissonance theory. Others are merely suggested by the economic interpretation we have given that psychological theory.

A. *Sources of Innovation*

Our model describes an economic theory of the choice of beliefs: initially, beliefs are only adopted if the net pecuniary and psychic benefits are positive. Because of cognitive dissonance, beliefs are persistent once adopted. Persons tend to avoid or resist new information that contradicts already established beliefs. As an application, this model yields some insight into the economics of innovation. In the context of the last section, in Case I, the innovators who purchased the new safety equipment in period 2 were not workers familiar by experience with the conditions of the hazardous industry, but, instead, were new workers, who in period 1 worked in the safe industry and then transferred in period 2.

The prediction from the model that innovators are previous outsiders to an activity agrees with two observations. First, in the history of science, Thomas Kuhn (1963) has claimed that the persons who first adopt a new scientific paradigm are predominantly new entrants into the field. In the field of industrial organization, it is believed that industrial laboratories are responsible for much minor innovation, but the major innovations mainly come from outside (Edwin Mansfield, 1968, p. 92). John Jewkes et al. (1959) found that prior to World War II only twelve out of the sixty-one major inventions in their study came from industrial laboratories. Over half came from private individuals. Daniel Hamberg (1963) reports similar findings after World War II.

B. *Advertising*

How does advertising work? Why do companies spend millions of dollars on advertising campaigns and why are people more likely to buy an advertised brand than one which does not advertise, all other things held equal?

This is undoubtedly a complicated question with answers dependent on the particular products and situations. But, the textbooks on advertising emphasize one factor: advertisements convey information about the product. The term 'information,' as used here, does not only refer to facts about the physical attributes of the advertised product. Advertising may also convey information about the social significance of consuming the product and how it may serve the psychological needs of consumers as well as their physical needs.[9]

If the information provided by ads generally allowed people to distinguish the functional or psychological value of a product, then it would be easy to understand how it worked to help determine peoples' choices. But, advertising textbooks admit that there are cases when the information conveyed in ads is irrelevant.

For example, one undergraduate advertising text divides products into three categories: those with significant differences in physical performance, those that differ only in 'design or formulation characteristics' (Weilbacher, p. 174), and 'generic' products or those that are 'if not identical, at least indistinguishable from each other' (Weilbacher, p. 178). When brands in the latter category (and to some degree in the second category) claim a distinction from other brands, the claim is based 'on the pre-emption of a quality or ingredient common to or inherent in all of the individuals in the category or on some abstract or even imagined quality' (Weilbacher, pp. 179, 181). Products that the author sees as belonging in this last category are some of the most heavily advertised. Another book suggests that there are two ways to meet consumers' desires once they have been identified. First, a new product can be created. The authors refer to this as a 'product strategy.' As an alternative they advise their readers that they might want to adopt an 'advertising strategy' with the goal of changing 'the consumers' perceptions' of an existing product so that it would be seen as filling those needs (see David Aaker and John Myers, 1974, p. 158). Finally, although the advertising texts would like to treat peoples' psychological needs as being fully commensurate with the 'overt physical' needs, it is clear that at least with respect to the relevance of the information about the products conveyed by ads, they are not. The trunk size or head room of a car is relevant to someone buying a car if they carry large loads or are tall. A car with a large trunk or high ceiling may be more valuable than one without these attributes. However, the type of toothpaste that an individual uses is going to do little to affect how socially acceptable he may be. Likewise, the type of soft drink one brings usually does not affect the fun of a picnic.

If the information conveyed by ads of this type is of so little value, why would anyone ever pay attention to them?

The theory of belief proposed in this paper suggests an explanation for this phenomenon. As the advertising practitioners point out, people do have needs and tastes and they do buy goods to satisfy them. Some of these needs and tastes are quite obscure or subtle; it may be hard to tell when the needs are being met. In such cases people may *want* to believe that what they have just bought meets their needs. Advertisements give people some external justification for believing just that. People like to feel that they are attractive, socially adept, and intelligent. It makes them feel good to hold such beliefs about themselves. Ads facilitate such beliefs—if the person buys the advertised product.

---

[9] For example, one undergraduate text on advertising suggests that: 'Consumers often expect marketing entities to perform for them, both in an overt physical sense as well as in a psychological sense. Most marketing entities promise some sort of specific psychological satisfaction as well as physical performance' (William Weilbacher, 1979, p. 159).

This formulation also suggests a limitation to the power of advertising. People may be willing to pay a little more for a product with an attractive fantasy attached. However, there are limits to their willingness to pay. When the value of the belief is less than the additional cost of the advertised brand, advertising will fail. Such a view of advertising suggests an approach to the welfare analysis of advertising different from that in the advertising textbooks and also in the economics literature (Richard Schmalensee, 1972).

C. *Social Security*

Another application of this type of model of potential economic importance concerns old age insurance. Social Security legislation is based on the belief that persons left to their own devices tend to purchase too little old age insurance.

If there are some persons who would simply prefer not to contemplate a time when their earning power is diminished, and if the very fact of saving for old age forces persons into such contemplations, there is an argument for compulsory old age insurance. The case, as we see it, is analogous to the case for safety legislation made in the last section. In that model workers found it uncomfortable to contemplate the dangers involved in working in the hazardous industry. For that reason they sometimes failed to have the appropriate marginal rate of substitution between safety and wages. In a similar mode persons may find it uncomfortable to contemplate their old age. For that reason they may make the wrong tradeoff, given their own preferences, between current consumption and savings for retirement.

D. *Economic Theory of Crime*

One application of cognitive dissonance theory is to the economic theory of crime. According to Gordon Tullock (1974), the economists' theory of crime involves a straightforward application of standard price theory:

> Most economists who give serious thought to the problem of crime immediately come to the conclusion that punishment will indeed deter crime. The reason is perfectly simple.... If you increase the cost of something, less will be consumed. Thus, if you increase the cost of committing a crime, there will be fewer crimes. [pp. 104–05]

Psychological experiments motivated by cognitive dissonance theory strongly suggest that Tullock's conclusions are only partially correct. While it may be true that more disobedience will be observed when there is greater deterrence, these experiments show that once the threat of punishment is removed, people who have been threatened with relatively severe punishment are more likely to disobey than those threatened with relatively mild punishment.

In an experiment that has been performed under a variety of conditions, children are told not to play with a very desirable toy. One group is threatened with severe punishment; and another with mild punishment for disobedience. The children are then allowed to play in the room with the toy for some time. Later (in one experiment several weeks later, see Jonathan Freedman, 1965), the children are again put in the room with the toy, only this time without the threat of punishment. Those who have been threatened with the more severe punishment are more likely to play with the forbidden toy than those threatened with mild punishment. It has similarly been shown that children who are punished severely for aggressive behavior at home are more violent in school than those who are mildly punished (see Robert Sears et al., 1953).

The interpretation of these studies is that those who obey rules for which the penalty of violation is relatively small need to create an internal justification for their actions. When they get into a situation where external sanctions for violating the rule are reduced or eliminated, they are less likely to break the rule because they are inhibited by the internal justifications they created in the first situation.

Thus the application of price theory to crime is not so natural as Tullock, and also Becker (1968), would have us believe. Increased punishment may act as a deterrent where its effect is obvious and the probability of apprehension for crime is well understood by the criminal. But most crime is committed with the expectation by the criminal that he will not be caught. Thus self-motivation to obey the law is undoubtedly a key factor in the reduction of crime—and this may decrease with the severity of punishment.

V. CONCLUSION

This paper has provided an example of how psychological theory can be incorporated into theoretical economic models. In particular, a decision model motivated by cognitive dissonance theory has been constructed that is a modification of the usual model of rational decision making.

This model closely follows standard economic analysis insofar as persons are completely informed about the potential consequences of their actions and make their decisions to maximize their own welfare. But, analysis that takes account of cognitive dissonance gives different results from the standard analysis, and, in particular, provides better explanations for some phenomena that are a puzzle according to the standard approach.

For example, the approach in this paper suggests a good reason why noninformational advertising is effective, why Social Security legislation and safety legislation are popular, and also why persons fail to purchase actuarially beneficial flood and earthquake insurance. The explanations do not rely on an assumption that people are basically misinformed—if they believe something other than the truth, they do so by their own choice.

References

Aaker, David A., and Myers, John G., *Advertising Management*, Englewood Cliffs: Prentice-Hall, 1975.

Aronson, Elliot, *The Social Animal*, 3rd edn., San Francisco: W. H. Freeman, 1979.

——., and Carlsmith, J. Merrill, 'Effect of the Severity of Threat on the Devaluation of Forbidden Behavior,' *Journal of Abnormal and Social Psychology*, June 1963, *66*, 584–88.

Axsom, Danny, and Cooper, Joel, 'Reducing Weight by Reducing Dissonance: The Role of Effort Justification in Inducing Weight Loss,' in Elliot Aronson, ed., *Readings for the Social Animal*, 3rd edn., San Francisco: W. H. Freeman, 1980.

Becker, Gary S., 'Irrational Behavior and Economic Theory,' *Journal of Political Economy*, February 1962, *70*, 1–13.

——, 'Crime and Punishment: An Economic Approach,' *Journal of Political Economy*, March/April 1968, *86*, 169–217.

Ben-Horin, Daniel, 'Dying to Work: Occupational Cynicism Plagues Chemical Workers,' *In These Times*, June 27/July 3, 1979, *3*, 24.

Brehm, Jack, 'Postdecision Changes in the Desirability of Alternatives,' *Journal of Abnormal Social Psychology*, May 1956, *52*, 384–89.

Davis, Keith, and Jones, Edward E., 'Changes in Interpersonal Perception as a Means of Reducing Cognitive Dissonance,' *Journal of Abnormal and Social Psychology*, November 1960, *61*, 402–10.

Dickens, William T., 'A Little Learning is a Dangerous Thing . . . ,' mimeo, Berkeley, January 1981.

Freedman, Jonathan, 'Long-term Behavioral Effects of Cognitive Dissonance,' *Journal of Experimental Social Psychology*, April 1965, *1*, 145–55.

Glass, David, 'Changes in Liking as a Means of Reducing Cognitive Discrepancies between Self-Esteem and Aggression,' *Journal of Personality*, December 1964, *32*, 531–49.

Hamberg, Daniel, 'Invention in the Industrial Research Laboratory,' *Journal of Political Economy*, April 1963, *71*, 95–115.

Hirschman, Albert O., 'Obstacles to Development: A Classification and a Quasi-Vanishing Act,' *Economic Development and Cultural Change*, July 1965, *13*, 385–93.

Jellison, Jerald M., and Mills, Judson, 'Effect of Similarity and Fortune of the Other on Attraction,' *Journal of Personality and Social Psychology*, April 1967, *5*, 459–63.

Jewkes, John; Sawers, David; and Stillerman, Richard, *The Sources of Invention*, New York: St. Martin's Press, 1959.

Knox, Robert E., and Inkster, James A., 'Postdecision Dissonance at Post Time,' *Journal of Personality and Social Psychology*, April 1968, Part 1, *8*, 319–23.

Kuhn, Thomas S., *The Structure of Scientific Revolutions*, Chicago: University of Chicago Press, 1963.

Kunreuther, Howard et al., *Disaster Insurance Protection: Public Policy Lessons*, New York 1978.

Mansfield, Edwin, *The Economics of Technological Change*, New York: Norton, 1968.

Schmalensee, Richard L., *The Economics of Advertising*, Amsterdam: North Holland, 1972.

Sears, Robert et al., 'Some Child-Rearing Antecedents of Aggression and Dependency in Young Children,' *Genetic Psychology Monographs*, First Half, 1953, 135–234.

Tullock, Gordon, 'Does Punishment Deter Crime?,' *Public Interest*, Summer 1974, *36*, 103–11.

Weilbacher, William M., *Advertising*, New York: Macmillan, 1979.

9

The Economics of Illusion*

There is a common view that economic theory takes preferences as given while other social sciences—anthropology, psychology, and sociology—are concerned with the nature and formation of those preferences. For example, Debreu describes preferences as abstractly as possible in terms of mathematical axioms (1959, p. 54) while Evans-Pritchard describes preferences as concretely as possible in terms of the Nuers' love of cattle (1940, pp. 16–50). But this popular dichotomy misses the point that these other social sciences are mainly concerned with how people differently conceptualize. A conceptualization concerns more than preferences; it also concerns biased uses of information. Key concepts from anthropology, psychology and sociology (as shall be discussed below) all explain dramatic examples of the role of conceptualizations in the determination of real events. These other social sciences also stress the importance of conceptualizations which are subconscious or, at best, ill-perceived, by the agents who have them.

Traditional economic models of public choice are built in this paper; these models are based on maximization theory and market clearance. There is one major innovation: information is interpreted in a biased way which weights two individualistic goals; agents' desires to feel good about themselves, their activities and the society they live in, on the one hand, and the need for an accurate view of the world for correct decision making, on the other hand. Due to this innovation regarding the way in which information is processed, these models differ dramatically from traditional models with externalities: because any individual's influence on the public choice outcome is close to zero, each individual has an incentive to choose a model of the world which maximizes his private happiness without any consideration of the consequences for social policy. The examples are intentionally chosen to highlight the potential effects of such biased choice of worldview.

* This work was previously published as George Akerlof (1989), 'The Economics of Illusion' *Economics and Politics* 1, 1. Copyright © Blackwell Publishing. Reproduced by kind permission.
† The author would like to thank Laura Nader, Hajime Miyazaki, Joseph Stiglitz and Janet Yellen for valuable help and comments. He would also like to thank the National Science Foundation for generous financial support under research grant number 84-01130, administered by the Institute of Business and Economic Research of the University of California, Berkeley.

Key concepts from the other social sciences which motivate such biased processing of information are *culture* from anthropology, *repression* and *cognitive dissonance* from psychology, and *the definition of the situation* and Durkheimian *structuralism* from sociology. I shall explain at some length how each of these concepts applies to a model in which agents' views of the world are in part chosen subconsciously so as to feel good about themselves and their world.

Culture

The key concept in anthropology is culture. According to Geertz culture is 'an historically transmitted pattern of *meanings*, embodied in *symbols*, a system of inherited *conceptions* expressed in symbolic forms by means of which men communicate, perpetuate and develop their knowledge about and attitudes toward life.' [Geertz (1973, p. 89), italics added]. The words I have italicized, *meanings, symbols* and *conceptions* suggest strongly that culture more concerns ways in which people think about the world than differences in preference relations. It is true that Japanese prefer sushi while Americans prefer hot dogs, but Ruth Benedict's classic on Japanese-American cultural differences, The Chrysanthemum and the Sword, concerns almost exclusively how they differently conceptualize social relations. The classic anthropologist's tale is not one of differences in preferences, it is the tale of cultural misunderstandings. Perhaps the best known such tale is Geertz' story of Cohen, a Jewish trader in Morocco in 1909 whose tent was raided by a Berber tribe with the resultant death of his guest. As compensation he asked for and was granted 500 sheep by the Berber sheikh. The French authorities, thinking he could have only obtained such a settlement by force, took away his sheep and imprisoned him [Geertz (1973, pp. 7–9)]. As Geertz' longer account makes clear this is a tale not of different preferences, but of misperceived meanings, due to the three different conceptions of the world of Cohen, the sheikh, and the French commandant.

The anthropologists' tales of misunderstanding are sufficiently exotic and rare that it is worthwhile giving an example, which demonstrates that biases in perception occur in modern contexts as well as among backward tribes and that these biases also concern central issues. It is often mentioned that two of the leading commentaries on American society have been written by foreigners rather than by Americans, despite the much greater volume of native writings on the subject. In particular I have in mind de Tocqueville's study of American democracy [de Tocqueville (1945 edn.)] and Myrdal's study of the position of American blacks [Myrdal (1962)]. These two examples suggest that what is apparent to an outsider to a culture may not be apparent to insiders; and this can only occur if the insiders have unperceived cultural biases in the way they interpret information.

While it would be possible to give an almost unlimited number of examples of cultural biases and misunderstandings, at the same time it is difficult to see the precise psychological or sociological mechanisms as to why these biases occur. An incident reported by the anthropologist Laura Nader gives a clear-cut example of an elementary event in which a point of view contrary to individuals' culture (or self-image) was repressed. Nader (1981) reports on the taboo of discussing safety by those who work for institutions which are directly or indirectly part of the nuclear power industry. She attended a seminar on breeder reactors at the Lawrence Berkeley Laboratory given by two men from Atomics International as part of the exploration of whether the laboratory should engage in research on breeder reactors. The talk was introduced and motivated by the statement that 'breeder reactors are the way we're going to go.' In the course of the hour presentation safety was not mentioned. Outsiders to the laboratory, professors and graduate students from the local Berkeley campus, asked questions about the obvious safety problem, but no insider from the laboratory asked such a question. Since 'the definition of the situation' had been that breeder reactors were 'the way to go,' questions regarding safety could be construed as against the policy of the laboratory. Curiously, however, the seminar was open to all questions, and, given the professional environment of the laboratory, no scientist at the laboratory would feel constrained in asking any relevant question. The laboratory scientists themselves later explained their own silence regarding safety on the grounds that it was outside their area of expertise. Nader (1981) reported similar responses to the safety issue in another similar environment. Although I shall give other examples from other disciplines the Nader story about the breeder reactor and the safety taboo is the canonical example of this paper: somehow people have an ability to censor their thoughts so as to avoid thinking the deviant or the uncomfortable. And, it turns out, as with the Lawrence Laboratory scientists, they are unaware of these biases.

Psychology

At least two important concepts in psychology, Freudian stage theory and cognitive dissonance, suggest biased information so that people feel good about themselves. One interesting modern interpretation of Freudian stage theory has a direct interpretation in economic terminology. According to Breger (1974) neurosis develops when people have fixations on false views of reality. This fixation occurs because there is too much anxiety associated with giving up the illusions to make any attempts at giving them up worthwhile. In standard economic language the cost of attaining more realism in terms of the anxiety caused exceeds the benefits. Or, in the language of the psychologist, 'The general answer to the question of why certain individuals remain stuck or fixated with dissociative solutions is that excessive anxiety has become connected with the original conflicts, that this anxiety was the original motivation for the dissociation, and that attempts to reopen the area to nondissociative reality-testing rearouses the anxiety.' [Breger (1974, p. 216)].

Irrespective of the precise merits of Freudian stage theory, Freudian psychology leaves us with the general insight that the organism receives an overabundance of information. Unlike a camera film or a filing cabinet, the human mind must 'choose' which stimuli to process and store and which stimuli to ignore or to repress. It is all but inevitable that this choice process involves the aims of the organism, so that its view of the world is all but inevitably biased by its aims.

Lest repression seem a peculiarly Freudian concept, it is worthwhile pointing to its existence in another context. The Wallerstein–Kelly study on the aftermath of divorce

(1980) reports the great frequency of bitter family fights once a decision for divorce has been reached. Presumably, once this decision has been reached the costs relative to the benefits of the repression of marital grievances have abruptly changed and old previously repressed grievances become sources for new conflicts.

Cognitive dissonance theory provides a second psychological model in which information is used selectively according to subjects' desires [Akerlof and Dickens (1982)]. As Elliott Aronson (1979, p. 109) describes cognitive dissonance, individuals want to have a positive self-image as good, smart, or worthwhile. They tend to protect such a positive self-image by rejecting information which tends to lead to the opposite conclusion. This results in a choice of information (which relative to the true state of the world) preserves peoples' good feelings about themselves, but in other ways may lead to foolish decisions.

The social psychologists have also provided a dramatic series of experiments in which, to a surprising degree, people interpret information so as to conform to their wishes. In the Asch experiment [Asch (1951)] subjects are put in a room with a confederate of the experimenter and then asked to match a line to three others, one of which has the exact same length. The task is in no way difficult (with almost 100 percent correct answers when the subjects are alone in the room). In the Asch experiment the confederate is first asked the question and then gives the wrong answer. Surprisingly, when this occurred 30 percent of the subjects also chose the wrong matching line.

Nor can the results be entirely explained by the Bayesian argument that subjects changed their answers because they had the additional information of the confederate's answer: because in trials with varying degrees of privacy of response, subjects gave fewer wrong answers the greater their degree of privacy [Argyle (1957); Mouton, Blake and Olmstead (1956)].

Sociology

Much sociology concerns how 'the definition of the situation' determines outcomes. The description of this concept in the leading sociology text [Broom and Selznick (1977, p. 23)], like Geertz on culture, stresses *unconscious meaning* which is *taken for granted*:

'To define the situation is to give it *meaning* and thus to make it part of the social order. Social order exists when people share the same definition of the situation. They then have similar expectations and know how to orient their conduct. Most of those shared definitions are acquired *unconsciously*. They constitute *a world taken for granted*.' (italics added)

'The definition of the situation' usually refers to micro situations, whereas 'culture' usually refers to a society's grand vision; the definition of the situation is often manipulable by the actors involved. Nevertheless both the anthropologists and the sociologists by somewhat independent routes have discovered aspects of the same phenomenon: that individuals often process information in biased ways because of unclearly perceived assumptions.

Lang's 'File'

An interesting collection of letters and documents published by the mathematician Serge Lang (1981) illustrates the concept, *the definition of the situation*. This collection grew out of an initial letter of protest by Lang concerning a questionnaire sent out by Seymour Martin Lipset and Everett Ladd on 'the opinions of the American professoriate.' Lang, who was aware that his own political opinions differed considerably from those of Lipset, and, suspecting that Lipset's interpretation of the results of the questionnaire would in all likelihood be rather different from his own, wrote a letter of protest regarding the request to fill it out; Lipset replied immediately and in some detail. *The File* was generated as Lang replied to any letter received and contacted any third party mentioned in any letter for confirmation (or denial) of their alleged role regarding the questionnaire, the initial third parties contacted being those mentioned in Lipset's initial reply. Lang's letters and their replies were added to the file along with any relevant material sent to Lang by any third party who had become aware of the growing dispute between Lang and Lipset and Ladd; furthermore, the number of third persons aware of the dispute was growing, as any person who was previously mentioned in *The File* was placed on the 'cc' list of recipients of new material sent to Lang or sent out by him regarding the questionnaire.

Reading *The File* makes clear two points of relevance to this paper. First, answers to questions very frequently are imprecise because respondents often try to answer an alternative question which 'defines the situation' more favorably for the respondent. It is for this reason that *The File* is replete with answers Lang finds unsatisfactory, with the result that a typical reply by Lang to one of his respondents begins: 'Dear Ms Friedman, Thanks for the letter. I shall deal with the points you raise and repeat important points from my previous letter since you did not address yourself to them.' [Lang (1981, p. 405)]. The letter writers including Lang are all trying to define the situation favorably with regard to their own position, and it is rare in approximately five hundred pages of letters to find a question directly answered.

A second implication of *The File* is the difficulty of attaining unambiguous language. There is probably no reason to doubt the intention of Lipset and Ladd that they designed their questionnaire to have as little ambiguity of interpretation as possible. Nor is there reason to doubt the sincerity (or accuracy) of Lipset's complaint against Lang's 'vendetta' [Lang (1981, p. 517)] on the grounds that the problems of his survey were in no way unusual in survey research. Nevertheless, the mathematician Saunders MacLane found that out of 84 questions which were not purely factual, 38 were ambiguous, had different meaning to different people, used loaded words, or had socially approved norms [Lang (1981, pp. 276, 279–288)]. This general problem of ambiguity, etc. occurred despite the use of questionnaire format, which is intended to reduce ambiguity of interpretation to a minimum.

I have described Lang's *File* at some length, partly because Lang's brilliantly intransigent letters (e.g., 'Dear Ms Friedman, . . . I still have two questions unanswered.') uniquely make clear the extent to which disputants try to define situations in their favor, while at the same time the critique of the Lipset–Ladd questionnaire makes clear the extent to which ambiguity appears even where there is attempt to eliminate it.

Durkheimian Structuralism

In the models developed in the next section agents select their view of the world, perhaps subconsciously, so as to maximize their well-being which depends partly on their psychological state and partly on the realism of their actions. In the case of extreme chameleonlike behavior such maximization imposes no problem: individuals could adapt their view of the world to each and every situation so that their desire for a view of the world which promotes their psychological happiness never imposes a constraint on their actions. The Woody Allen movie *Zelig* is instructive in suggesting that such behavior does exist but also that in extreme form such behavior is fairly rare.

Sociologists and anthropologists have asserted that patterns of thought concerning one area are duplicated in other seemingly unrelated areas.[1] For example Durkheim (1915) has asserted that aboriginal Australian natives have the same forms of thought regarding their religion and the organization of society. Subsequent criticism has shown that many of the details in Durkheim's argument are incorrect. Nevertheless the general point that there are patterns of thinking which affect real outcomes is widely believed. The classic ethnographers Malinowski, Mead, Benedict and Evans-Pritchard all attempted to document the patterns of thought in the societies they described. Kroeber's famous textbook (1948) suggests that the frequency of coincidences of great inventions is the result of patterns of thinking in the societies in which the inventions took place. The coincidence of the short skirt and military activity are also argued as examples of events in seemingly unrelated areas of life which are, nevertheless, governed by similar patterns of thought. In a similar vein Goffman argues that in U.S. mental hospitals the 'medical model' carries over into areas of endeavor in which it has no clear relevance; 'it is a perspective ready to account for all manner of decisions, such as the hours when hospital meals are served, or the manner in which linens are folded.' [Goffman (1961, p. 84)].[2]

I. PUBLIC CHOICE MODELS OF ILLUSION

The somewhat lengthy introduction in the last section was intended to show that, unlike economics, other social sciences do not assume unbiased processing of information; on

---

[1] An extreme version of such structuralism is given by Levi-Strauss (1949) who argues that the thought patterns of French peasants in exogamously marrying their daughters and convivially trading wine in cheap restaurants in Southern France are similar.

[2] A similar point has been argued rather abstrusely by Foucault (1979) regarding the relation between the architecture of French hospitals and the way in which French doctors view the practice of medicine. Foucault has argued that their view of medicine as relating almost exclusively to discovering symptoms from the body of the patient (via 'the gaze') led to unnecessarily uncomfortable French hospitals so that doctors could observe their patients.

the contrary, central concerns of anthropology, sociology and psychology are ways in which information processing is unconsciously biased.

A classic problem of externalities and social choice

This section presents a model of externalities and voting behavior which modifies the classic example of overfishing in a depletable pond. Consider the simplest example, which could be standard homework for a microeconomics course, of individuals living around a pond and having utility for fish and leisure

$$U = (\bar{L} - L)^\alpha F^{1-\alpha} \tag{1}$$

where F is their consumption of fish
$\bar{L}$ is their total time available for labor and leisure
L is their labor time in catching fish
$\bar{L} - L$ is their leisure.

The externality in this example occurs because, as more fish are brought out of the pond, there are fewer fish available to the remaining fishermen; and, as a result, the time to catch a fish rises. Or, alternatively stated, in the aggregate there are diminishing returns to fishing. These diminishing returns can typically be brought into the standard homework example by letting fish be produced according to the production function

$$F = L^\beta \tag{2}$$

with $\beta < 1$.

In the absence of taxation the private return to labor is the average product, $L^{\beta-1}$, which is more than the marginal social return to labor, which is $\beta L^{\beta-1}$. A tax t on fish production equal to $(1 - \beta)$ will equate the private return to the marginal social return and will lead to Pareto optimality. Lump sum subsidies can distribute the proceeds from the tax.

In the usual models of voter behavior there should be no trouble in enacting the tax $1 - \beta$, given the unanimity of opinion in this model. Voters understanding the model and knowing the degree of diminishing returns will unanimously prefer tax $t = 1 - \beta$ to any other uniform tax. So standard analysis of externalities with standard social choice theory suggests that taxes will be $1 - \beta$ and Pareto optimality will be restored through the intervention of a collectively approved tax system.

A modification to the classic problem

This classic example will be modified in two ways. First, it will be assumed that work time does not enter the utility function as a complete blank (as in (1)); individuals in the modified utility function get some enjoyment out of their work, although less enjoyment if an hour of work is substituted for an hour of leisure. Additionally, the utility function is modified so that an individual's enjoyment of work depends on the social good he conceives himself as doing. The more the individual feels that his fishing depletes the fish in the pond, and, consequently, makes fishing difficult for others, the less he enjoys fishing. To be more precise, the individual has an estimate of β, which is a parameter which represents the degree of depletion. The lower the individual's estimate of β, the more depletion is estimated to come from fishing, and the less the individual enjoys fishing. The preceding arguments suggest the modified utility function:

$$U = (\bar{L} - L + \hat{\beta}\gamma L)^\alpha F^{1-\alpha} \quad 0 < \alpha < 1, 0 < \gamma < 1 \tag{3}$$

where $\bar{L} - L$ is leisure time

L is time fishing

F is consumption of fish

and $\hat{\beta}$ is the individual's estimate of β.

As can be seen this new utility function (3) conforms with the earlier argument: because γ and $\hat{\beta}$ are less than one an hour of leisure, rather than an hour of fishing, increases utility; and, also, the individual enjoys his work more the higher is $\hat{\beta}$, and consequently the less he conceives his work as depleting the pond.

The second major modification in the preceding classic externality model concerns the individual's estimation of β. It is assumed that the individual knows the structure of the model, including its property, $0 \le \beta \le 1$. Subject to this knowledge there are no constraints on his estimate of β: he can choose $\hat{\beta}$ as he wishes, subject to $0 \le \hat{\beta} \le 1$.

The individual agent with the utility function (3) chooses, L, F and $\hat{\beta}$ to maximize

$$U = (\bar{L} - L + \hat{\beta}\gamma L)^\alpha F^{1-\alpha} \tag{4}$$

subject to the constraint about his knowledge of β, so that

$$0 \le \hat{\beta} \le 1 \tag{5}$$

and subject to his budget constraint

$$F = (1 - t)Lw_F + s \tag{6}$$

where w_F is the average product of an hour's work in terms of fish,

s is the lump sum subsidy in terms of fish,

and t is the tax rate on income earned by fishing.

Solution of the maximization problem (of maximizing (4) given the constraints (5) and (6)) shows that the individual consumer with a wage w_F, a tax rate on fishing of t and a lump sum subsidy of s, will choose

$$L = \frac{(1 - \alpha)L(1 - t)w_F - \alpha(1 - \gamma)s}{(1 - \gamma)(1 - t)w_F} \tag{7}$$

and

$$\hat{\beta} = 1. \tag{8}$$

For society as a whole the subsidy s must meet the balanced budget constraint

$$tw_F L = s. \tag{9}$$

From (7) and (9) it can be calculated that with the tax rate t, and the balanced budget constraint on subsidies,

$$L = \frac{(1 - \alpha)(1 - t)}{(\alpha + (1 - \alpha)(1 - t))(1 - \gamma)} \bar{L}. \tag{10}$$

The individual voter now chooses t to maximize welfare given the behavior of individuals who choose $\hat{\beta}$ according to (8) and L according to (10). In other words the individual voter chooses t to maximize welfare (11)

$$(\bar{L} - L + \gamma \hat{\beta} L)^\alpha F^{1-\alpha} \tag{11}$$

subject to individual maximizing behavior

$$L = \frac{(1 - \alpha)(1 - t)}{(\alpha + (1 - \alpha)(1 - t))(1 - \gamma)} \bar{L} \tag{12}$$

$$\hat{\beta} = 1 \tag{13}$$

and subject to the assumed behavior of the economy

$$F = L^\beta \tag{14}$$

and

$$\beta = \hat{\beta} \tag{15}$$

Solution of this constrained maximization problem yields $t^* = 0$, where t^* is the individual's preferred tax (given his estimate that $\beta = 1$ and given his attempt to see which tax would maximize social welfare).[3]

---

[3] To make this solution feasible it must also be true that $\gamma \leq \alpha/(1 - \alpha)$.

Comments on the preceding model

The usual rational expectations models view individuals as viewing the world with no biases relative to the truth. The purpose of this model is to demonstrate some consequences of an alternative point of view. It shows logically how a standard proposition in social choice theory—that taxes *cum* subsidies will be chosen to reach social optima when there are simple externalities—can be altered when individuals (perhaps subconsciously) choose their beliefs, in part, to feel good about themselves. In this example, if people engage in fishing they have an individual incentive to believe they are not depleting. And if voting behavior is consistent with those beliefs, taxes will be zero. Furthermore, taxes will be zero irrespective of the size of γ (as long as γ is strictly positive) and in that sense independent of the magnitude of the effect of beliefs on the utility function U. The gain in this model from wrong beliefs are private; and all the gains from correct beliefs are public; because each agent has only negligible effect on the public choice decision regarding the level of taxes, he has no reason to select his beliefs to balance his private gain against the gain from better social choice decisions (in terms of better tax-cum-subsidy decisions than occur with $t = 0$). The private gain dominates the choice of $\hat{\beta}$ for that reason.

It is usually assumed that individuals vote in their own best interest. But this best interest may be neither obvious nor pleasant to contemplate. Unless the innate desire to believe the truth is strong or those who know the truth are persuasive, the desire and ability for self-delusion can lead to poor social decisions. This is the leading message of the preceding model. It should be understood, however, that the model is intended as a parable, in the same spirit as the pure exchange economy is usually considered. It is meant to show how the potential modification of chosen self-delusion can dramatically alter the consequences of the textbook model of externalities. For γ arbitrarily small, and therefore for a model arbitrarily close to the standard textbook example, taxes will be chosen equal to zero rather than at their optimal level.

Remark

The model has another feature which is an interesting curiosity, even if of no great economic significance. Suppose a government in the above model could choose $\hat{\beta}$ (perhaps by propaganda), but would nevertheless be constrained by the public's choice of taxes consistent with that value of $\hat{\beta}$. In this model as long as γ is strictly positive the socially optimal $\hat{\beta}$ exceeds the true value β. Why? Because the optimum value of $\hat{\beta}$ puts some weight on knowing the truth, which prevents unrealistic actions, and some weight on an optimistic view of the world, which makes $\hat{\beta}$ as large as possible. As long as the optimal value places some weight on an optimistic view of the world, it will exceed the true value of β. This is the daily stuff of the newspaper advice columns. Dear Abby, should Aunt Jane be told of her problem so that she can act wisely, or should Aunt Jane not be told so she can preserve her self-image?[4]

---

[4] Ibsen wrote about this same problem in 'The Wild Duck', with the same conclusion: the unvarnished truth is not always the social optimum.

II. WARRIORS AND VICTIMS

The provocative book on nuclear strategy by Freeman Dyson has dichotomized the population into two groups: the *warriors* and the *victims* [Dyson (1984, pp. 4–5)]. The warriors are those involved with the military establishment, including both hawks and doves and including scholars of military and international affairs as well as the members of the armed forces, their civilian overseers, and the civilian producers of military hardware. Their dominant characteristic, according to Dyson, is their concentration on detail which is reducible to quantitative calculation. In contrast the victims are the rest of the population, usually depicted as mothers and children. The warriors are the agents for the victims; they speak a technical jargon which makes it difficult for the victims to understand the actions which are taken on their behalf.

Does Dyson's terminology make sense? In a democracy why should the warriors not on the average be the executors of the will of the majority, in this case the so-called *victims*? Why should military strategy and military policy not be the result (perhaps with some chance for error in either direction) of the wishes of the majority? A model is developed here to answer this question, which may apply to professional experts other than the military who are acting as agents for the public. This section for that reason could perhaps have also been titled *professionals* vs. *victims* or *experts* vs. *victims* rather than *warriors* vs. *victims*. I shall use the terms warriors, professionals and experts interchangeably in this section.

The model

There is an economy which produces guns and butter according to the production function

$$G + B = \bar{X} \tag{16}$$

where G is guns

B is butter

and $\bar{X}$ is a technologically determined constant.

The public's preferences are represented by a Cobb-Douglas utility function. Its utility depends on the production of guns and butter and also on its confidence in the incumbent military experts, which is the variable c_{inc}. This utility function is

$$U = A(c_{\text{inc}})G^{\alpha}B^{1-\alpha}. \tag{17}$$

The higher the confidence in the current incumbents the greater is $A(c_{\text{inc}})$ and in turn the greater is U. In this model individuals choose the variable c_{inc} to maximize their utility, while the incumbent experts choose the society's allocation of guns and butter.

Elections are held at which the incumbent experts may be thrown out of office. The voters have a degree of confidence in nonincumbent challengers c^*. This variable is exogenous since it is unaffected by any choices, because it does not enter the utility function. The challengers have a platform which is a proposed allocation of guns and butter. The most threatening platform to the current incumbents would be a division of $\bar{X}$, so that $G = \alpha X$ and $B = (1 - \alpha)X$. That is the platform most preferred by the public.

Voting behavior is as follows: voters will prefer the challenger over the incumbents provided

$$A(c_{\text{inc}})G_{\text{inc}}^{\alpha}B_{\text{inc}}^{1-\alpha} < A(c^*)G_{\text{chal}}^{\alpha}B_{\text{chal}}^{1-\alpha} \tag{18}$$

and will vote for incumbents over the challengers provided

$$A(c_{\text{inc}})G_{\text{inc}}^{\alpha}B_{\text{inc}}^{1-\alpha} \geq A(c^*)G_{\text{chal}}^{\alpha}B_{\text{chal}}^{1-\alpha} \tag{19}$$

where G_{inc} = guns chosen by incumbent
      B_{inc} = butter chosen by incumbent
      G_{chal} = guns chosen by challenger
      B_{chal} = butter chosen by challenger.

The incumbent experts have their own preferences, which are not the same as the preferences of the public at large.

$$U_{\text{inc}} = G^{\beta}B^{1-\beta}. \tag{20}$$

And, presumably, $\beta > \alpha$.

It is, of course, a key assumption that the warriors have a greater preference for guns than the public, which is reflected in the parameter β being greater than α. This bias reflects the usual bias of most experts: they have a bias in favor of resources being used on their own specialty. In the case of warriors, they are responsible for national security. An anthropologist or sociologist could tell complicated stories whereby experts whose careers generally depend on the resources available for their pursuits will tend to want a greater allocation of resources in that area. For the purpose of this example the motivation supplied by such stories should be taken to explain why β is greater than α.

I shall assume that the incumbent experts choose the guns–butter combination according to their preferences, subject to the constraint of their reelection, or mathematically stated, that the incumbent chooses G_{inc} and B_{inc} to maximize

$$U_{\text{inc}} = G_{\text{inc}}^{\beta}B_{\text{inc}}^{1-\beta} \tag{21}$$

subject to

$$G_{\text{inc}} + B_{\text{inc}} = \bar{X} \tag{22}$$

and

$$A(c_{\text{inc}})G_{\text{inc}}^{\alpha}B_{\text{inc}}^{1-\alpha} \geq \max_{G_{\text{chal}}+B_{\text{chal}}\leq\bar{X}} A(c^*)G_{\text{chal}}^{\alpha}B_{\text{chal}}^{1-\alpha} = A(c^*)\alpha^{\alpha}(1 - \alpha)^{1-\alpha}\bar{X}. \tag{23}$$

Constraint (23) is the constraint which assures that the incumbents choose an allocation of resources so that no preferred platform can be offered by challengers. This behavior ensures the incumbent experts continuity of office.

There are two types of solution to the preceding maximization problem. If constraint (23) is not binding, the incumbents will choose to maximize their own utility subject to the production constraint (22) irrespective of the utility of the public. In this case the public's utility will be

$$U = A(c_{\text{inc}})\beta^{\alpha}(1 - \beta)^{1-\alpha}\bar{X}. \tag{24a}$$

On the other hand, if constraint (23) is binding the utility of the public will be

$$U = A(c^*)\alpha^{\alpha}(1 - \alpha)^{1-\alpha}\bar{X}. \tag{24b}$$

Summarizing the binding and nonbinding constraints, it is found in general that the utility of the public is

$$U = \max[A(c_{\text{inc}})/A(c^*), \ \alpha^{\alpha}(1 - \alpha)^{1-\alpha}/\beta^{\alpha}(1 - \beta)^{1-\alpha}]A(c^*)\beta^{\alpha}(1 - \beta)^{1-\alpha}\bar{X}. \tag{25}$$

Formula (25) makes sense. If the experts and the public have the same tastes (i.e., if $\beta = \alpha$), the public attains the maximum obtainable utility, which is $A(c_{\text{inc}})\alpha^{\alpha}(1 - \alpha)^{1-\alpha}\bar{X}$. Also if the public is willing to vote the experts out of office for anything less than the optimal choice of allocation, i.e., if $A(c_{\text{inc}}) = A(c^*)$, then again $U = A(c_{\text{inc}})\alpha^{\alpha}(1 - \alpha)^{1-\alpha}\bar{X}$, which is the maximum attainable utility. If, however, $\beta \neq \alpha$, and $A(c_{\text{inc}}) > A(c^*)$, then less than the maximum physically obtainable utility will occur in the equilibrium. The experts' (rather than the public's) tastes are one factor in the allocation of guns and butter, and public utility will be less than the maximum attainable with experts maximizing the public's utility. This maximum is $A(c_{\text{inc}})\alpha^{\alpha}(1 - \alpha)^{1-\alpha}\bar{X}$. In this sense the public becomes the victim of the experts, *alias* the professionals or the warriors, who are making decisions on their behalf—even though the public has the right to throw those experts out of office.

A further remark

It is worthwhile remarking the consistency of the model in this section with the behavioral experiments by Milgram (1975) on *Obedience and Authority*. In a socio-psychological experiment Milgram found that more than 60 percent of subjects were willing to give 450 volt shocks to confederates of the experimenter on the command of the experimenter. In terms of the preceding model, the subjects have utility for confidence in the experimenter (who is a *professional* or an *expert* in the context of the experiment) so that they are willing to override their own judgment.

III. CONCLUSION

This paper has analyzed in a context of public choice the consequences of choice of belief. This paper has de-emphasized the obvious, that our beliefs are in large part determined by facts, which are sometimes simple and undeniable. Instead it has emphasized those areas, which include most of the questions of public policy debate, where simple undeniable facts alone do not determine what to believe. Where there is such a margin of doubt, individuals have freedom to choose what to believe and, furthermore, in such an environment there is freedom for people to choose beliefs which make them feel good about themselves. In the first model presented (in section I) people chose their beliefs to feel good about what they do. In the second model they chose their beliefs to feel good about failing to delve into the workings of expert bureaucracies, whose judgments can in a well-defined sense make the public the victims of their decisions.

To an economist trained on economic models in which estimations are unbiased predictors of the truth, it seems unnatural to make any other assumption about human behavior. Yet to an acute observer of human behavior, Leonard Woolf, unbiased pursuit of truth is considered a rare trait. He thus describes the philosopher G.E. Moore as 'the only great man whom I have ever met or known in the world of ordinary real life' (1957, p. 131), whose source of greatness was 'a genius for seeing what was important and irrelevant, in thought and in life and in persons...because of the...passion for truth...which burned in him.' (1957, pp. 134–135). This paper has presented economic models in which such pursuit of truth is also unusual rather than the norm—its purposes being to clarify the differences between economic theory and other social sciences, to discover potential pitfalls in the use of economic modeling, and to uncover potentially important reasons for mistakes in public policy.

GEORGE A. AKERLOF
Economics Department
University of California at Berkeley
Berkeley, CA 94720
USA

References

Akerlof, George A. and William T. Dickens, 1973, The economic consequences of cognitive dissonance, *American Economic Review* 72, June, 307–19.

Aronson, Elliot, 1979, *The social animal*, 3rd edn. (W.H. Freeman, San Francisco).

Argyle, Michael, 1957, Social pressure in public and private situations, *Journal of Abnormal and Social Psychology* 54, March, 172–5.

Asch, Solomon E., 1951, Effects of group pressure upon the modification and distortion of judgment, in M H Guetzkow, ed., *Groups, Leadership, and Men* (Carnegie Press, Pittsburgh).

Breger, Louis, 1974, *From instinct to identity: The development of personality* (Prentice-Hall, Englewood Cliffs, New Jersey).

Broom, Leonard and Philip Selznick, 1977, *Sociology*, 6th edn. (Harper and Row, New York).

Debreu, Gerard, 1959, *Theory of value: An axiomatic analysis of economic equilibrium* (John Wiley and Sons, New York).

Deutsch, Morton and Harold B. Gerard, 1955, A study of normative and informational social influence upon individual judgment, *Journal of Abnormal and Social Psychology* 51, Nov., 629–36.

Durkheim, Emile, 1915, *The elementary forms of the religious Life* (George Allen and Unwin, London).

Dyson, Freeman, 1915, *Weapons and hope* (Harper and Row, New York).

Evans-Pritchard, Edward E., 1940, *The Nuer: A description of the modes of livelihood and institutions of a Nilotic people* (Oxford University Press, Oxford).

Foucault, Michel, 1979, *Power/knowledge: Selected interviews and other writings 1972–1977*, Colin Gordon, ed., translated by Colin Gordon, Leo Marshall, John Mepham, and Kate Sopher (Random House, New York).

Geertz, Clifford, 1973, *The interpretation of cultures* (Basic Books, New York).

Goffman, Erving, 1961, *Asylums: Essays on the social situation of mental patients and other inmates* (Doubleday, Anchor Books, Garden City, New York).

Kroeber, Alfred L., 1948, *Anthropology: Revised edition* (Harcourt, Brace and World, New York).

Lang, Serge, 1981, *The file: Case study in correction (1977–1979)* (Springer-Verlag, New York).

Lévi-Strauss, Claude, 1969, The principle of reciprocity, from chapter V, Le principe de reciprocité, in *Les structures élémentaires de la parenté*, 1949 (Presses Universitaires de France, Paris). Abridged and translated by Ruth L. Coser and Grace Frazer, in Lewis A. Coser and Bernard Rosenberg, eds., *Sociological theory, 4th edition* (Macmillan, New York).

Milgram, Stanley, 1975, *Obedience to authority: An experimental view* (Harper and Row, New York).

Mouton, Jane S., Robert R. Blake and Joseph A. Olmstead, 1956, The relationship between frequency of yielding and disclosure of personal identity, *Journal of Personality* 24, March, 339–47.

Myrdal, Gunnar, 1962, *An American dilemma: The negro problem and modern democracy*, with the assistance of Richard Sterner and Arnold Rose, 20th anniversary edition (Harper and Row, New York).

Nader, Laura, 1981, Barriers to thinking new about energy, *Physics Today* 34:2, February, 99–104.

Tocqueville, Alexis de, 1945, *Democracy in America*, The Henry Reeve text as revised by Francis Bowen, further corrected and edited by Phillips Bradley (A.A. Knopf, New York).

Wallerstein, Judith S. and Joan B. Kelly, 1980, *Surviving the breakup: How children and parents cope with divorce* (Basic Books, New York).

Woolf, Leonard, 1975, *Sowing: An autobiography of the years 1880 to 1904* (Harcourt Brace Jovanovich, New York).

10

Richard T. Ely Lecture
Procrastination and Obedience*

BY GEORGE A. AKERLOF[†]

In this lecture I shall focus on situations involving *repeated* decisions with time inconsistent behavior. Although each choice may be close to maximizing and therefore result in
only small losses, the cumulative effect of a series of repeated errors may be quite large.
Thus, in my examples, decision makers are quite close to the intelligent, well-informed
individuals usually assumed in economic analysis, but cumulatively they make seriously
wrong decisions that do not occur in standard textbook economics.

This lecture discusses and illustrates several 'pathological' modes of individual and
group behavior: procrastination in decision making, undue obedience to authority,
membership of seemingly normal individuals in deviant cult groups, and escalation of
commitment to courses of action that are clearly unwise. In each case, individuals choose
a series of current actions without fully appreciating how those actions will affect future
perceptions and behavior. The standard assumption of rational, forward-looking, utility
maximizing is violated. The nonindependence of errors in decision making in the series
of decisions can be explained with the concept from cognitive psychology of undue
salience or vividness. For example, present benefits and costs may have undue salience
relative to future costs and benefits.

Procrastination occurs when present costs are unduly salient in comparison with
future costs, leading individuals to postpone tasks until tomorrow without foreseeing
that when tomorrow comes, the required action will be delayed yet again. Irrational
obedience to authority or escalation of commitment occurs when the salience of an
action today depends upon its deviation from previous actions. When individuals have
some disutility for disobedience and a leader chooses the step sizes appropriately,
individuals can be induced to escalate their actions to extraordinary levels; the social

* This work was previously published as George Akerlof (1991), 'Procrastination and Obedience' *The
Richard T. Ely Lecture, American Economics Association Papers and Proceedings*, 81, 2. Copyright © The American
Economic Association. Reproduced by kind permission.

† Department of Economics, University of California, Berkeley, CA 94720. I thank Glenn Carroll,
Benjamin Hermalin, Daniel Kahneman, David Levine, Andreu Mas Colell, Charles O'Reilly, Christina
Romer, David Romer, Paul Romer, Andrew Rose, Richard Sutch, David Wise, and Janet Yellen for valuable
comments. I gratefully acknowledge support from the Institute for Policy Reform, the Sloan Foundation, and
the National Science Foundation for research support under grant no. SES 90-09051 administered by the
Institute for Business and Economic Research at the University of California–Berkeley.

psychologist Stanley Milgram (1975) led subjects to administer high levels of electrical shock to others in fictitious learning experiments. The subjects were induced into actions that were contrary to their true moral values. In the latter half of the lecture I will give examples to illustrate how sequences of errors, each error small at the time of the decision, cumulate into serious mistakes; these decisions also illustrate how laboratory conditions of isolation, carefully engineered in the Milgram experiment and necessary for the type of behavior he induced, in fact commonly occur in nonexperimental situations. Thus the sequences of errors that are the subject of this lecture are not rare and unusual, only obtainable in the laboratory of the social psychologist, but instead are common causes of social and economic pathology.

Although an analysis of behavioral pathology might initially appear to be outside the appropriate scope of economics, I shall argue that, in important instances, such pathology affects the performance of individuals and institutions in the economic and social domain. Examples include the poverty of the elderly due to inadequate savings for retirement, addiction to alcohol and drugs, criminal and gang activity, and the impact of corporate 'culture' on firm performance. Economic theories of crime, savings, and organizations are deficient and yield misleading conclusions when such behavior is ignored. The behavioral pathologies that I will describe also have consequences for policies toward, for example, savings, substance abuse, and management.

Individuals whose behavior reveals the various pathologies I shall model are not maximizing their 'true' utility. The principle of revealed preference cannot therefore be used to assert that the options that are chosen must be preferred to the options that are not chosen. Individuals may be made better off if their options are limited and their choices constrained. Forced pension plans may be superior to voluntary savings schemes; outright prohibitions on alcohol or drugs may be preferable to taxes on their use reflecting their nuisance costs to others; and an important function of management may be to set schedules and deadlines and not simply to establish 'appropriate' price-theoretic incentive schemes to motivate employees.

I. SALIENCE AND DECISIONS

A central principle of modern cognitive psychology is that individuals attach too much weight to salient or vivid events and too little weight to nonsalient events. Richard Nisbett and Lee Ross (1980) describe the following thought experiment, that they consider the 'touchstone' of cognitive psychology, just as the shifting of a supply or a demand curve is the central thought experiment of economics.

Let us suppose that you wish to buy a new car and have decided that on grounds of economy and longevity you want to purchase one of those stalwart, middle-class Swedish cars—either a Volvo or a Saab. As a prudent and sensible buyer, you go to *Consumer Reports*, which informs you that the consensus of their experts is that the Volvo is mechanically superior, and the consensus of the readership is that the Volvo has the better repair record. Armed with this information, you decide to go and strike a bargain with the Volvo dealer before the week is out. In the interim, however, you go to a cocktail party where you announce your intention to an acquaintance. He reacts with disbelief and alarm; 'A Volvo! You've got to be kidding. My brother-in-law had a Volvo. First, that fancy fuel injection computer thing went out. 250 bucks. Next he started having trouble with the rear end. Had to replace it. Then the transmission and the clutch. Finally sold it in three years for junk.'

[quoted in Nisbett and Ross, p. 15; from Nisbett et al., 1976, p. 129]

The status of this additional information is only to increase the *Consumer Reports* sample by one. Mean repair records are likely to remain almost unchanged. Yet Nisbett and Ross argue that most prospective car buyers would not view the new information so complacently.

An experiment by Eugene Borgida and Nisbett (1977) confirms the intuition that salient information exerts undue influence on decisions. Freshmen at the University of Michigan with a declared psychology major were chosen as subjects. Students were asked to express preferences concerning psychology electives. Before making this decision, a control group was given only mean psychology course evaluations; others were, in addition, exposed to a panel discussion by advanced psychology majors selected so that their course evaluations corresponded to the mean. As in the Volvo thought experiment, vivid information played a greater role than pallid information; compared to the control group, those exposed to the panel chose a higher fraction of courses rated above average. To counter the argument that this bias might be due to thoughtlessness because of the unimportance of the decision, Borgida and Nisbett note that the bias was greater for those who later entered the major than for those who dropped out.

II. PROCRASTINATION

Procrastination provides the simplest example of a situation in which there are repeated errors of judgment due to unwarranted salience of some costs and benefits relative to others. In this case each error of judgment causes a small loss, but these errors cumulatively result in large losses over time and ultimately cause considerable regret on the part of the decision maker.

Let me illustrate with a personal story and then show how such behavior can be modeled. Some years back, when I was living in India for a year, a good friend of mine, Joseph Stiglitz, visited me; because of unexpected limitations on carry-on luggage at the time of his departure, he left with me a box of clothes to be sent to him in the United States. Both because of the slowness of transactions in India and my own ineptitude in such matters, I estimated that sending this parcel would take a full day's work. Each morning for over eight months I woke up and decided that the *next* morning would be the day to send the Stiglitz box. This occurred until a few months before my departure when I decided to include it in the large shipment of another friend who was returning to the United States at the same time as myself.

The preceding story can be represented mathematically in the following way. The box was left with me on day 0. At the end of the year, at date T, the box could be costlessly transported. The cost of sending the box on any day prior to T was estimated at c, the value of a day's work. I estimated Joe's valuation of the use of the contents of the box (which was the same as my value of his use of the contents) at a rate of x dollars per day. I saw no reason to attach any discount rate to his use of the box. However, each day when I awoke, the activities I would perform if I did not mail off the Stiglitz box seemed important and pressing, whereas those I would undertake several days hence remained vague and seemed less vivid. I thus overvalued the cost of sending the box on the current day relative to any future day by a factor of δ. This caused me to procrastinate.

On each day t, until date $T - c/x$, I made the dynamically inconsistent decision that I would not send the box on that day, but would instead send it the very next day. Ultimately, I decided to simply wait and send it costlessly at my departure.

Consider my decision process. On each day t, I awoke and made a plan to send the box on date t^*. I chose t^* to minimize V, the costs net of the benefits of sending the box.

If I sent the box on that day (day t), V would be

$$V = c(1 + \delta) - (T - t^*)x \quad \text{for } t^* = t. \tag{1}$$

The factor δ represents the extra salience of sending the box on that day. If I waited, but sent the box at some later time, other than the time of my departure, V would be

$$V = c - (T - t^*)x \quad \text{for } t + 1 \leq\, < T \tag{2}$$

And if I waited until the end of my stay to send the box, I saw that

$$V = 0 \quad \text{for } t^* = T. \tag{3}$$

On each and every day, up until day $T - c/x$, the time when the costs of sending the box just equaled the benefits of its receipt, I decided to send the box *tomorrow*. Since δc was sufficiently large, at each date t, I set the planned date for sending the box at $t^* = t + 1$. By time $T - c/x$, it was apparent that the costs of sending the box no longer exceeded the benefits, and thus I guiltily decided to ship it at the time of my return. I had procrastinated too long.

Three key features of the situation resulted in procrastination. First, the time between decisions was short. Second, in each period there was a small, but not a minuscule, 'salience cost' to undertaking the job now rather than later. The condition that results in procrastination is $\delta c > x$. The daily benefit from the box, x, is small if the time between decisions is short. δc is significant if there is a significant psychological lump sum cost to doing the project now rather than later. The third key feature of the situation was the dynamic inconsistency in my decision making. Each day I decided to put off the project until tomorrow. I did not have rational expectations, since I did not foresee that when the next day came I would continue to put off the decision for an additional day.

My procrastination was costly. The cumulative loss incurred due to my procrastinating behavior amounted to approximately $Tx - c$.[1] For each day up to the critical day

---

[1] The exact loss is $Tx - c(1 + \delta)$. If I sent the box on date 0, V has value $c(1 + \delta) - Tx$. Since I sent the box at $T, V = 0$. The difference is $Tx - c(1 + \delta)$.

at approximately $T - c/x$, I wrongly decided not to send the box. After the critical time (approximately) $T - c/x$, I made the correct decision to wait to send the box.[2] For every day between 0 and $(T - c/x)$, the loss from the decision made on that day was x, the cost of an extra day's use of the box. The cumulative loss was consequently the product of the daily cost of a delay, x, and the $(T - c/x)$ decisions to delay. This product is $Tx - c$, the total loss from the failure to send the box. In consequence, the cumulative cost of the errors of decision amount to the total loss that occurs over the period. Many wrong decisions all of the same type but of small value cumulated into a significant loss. And yet this loss occurred as a consequence of only a modest amount of irrationality or 'undue salience.'

A numerical example is useful to illustrate the necessary size of the 'salience' premium δ on current relative to future work required for procrastination to occur. Suppose that I valued my time at \$50 per day and Joe Stiglitz' use of his box at 50 cents per day. If δ exceeds .01($= .50/50$), then procrastination will occur for 265($= 365 - 50/.5$) days. We consequently see that in this type of example, where there are significant initial costs relative to the benefits, only small amounts of unwarranted salience on present relative to future action can result in significant delay.

Procrastination with Deadlines. The preceding model of procrastination has the special feature that if the task is not done in a timely fashion, it does not need to be done at all. It is like the referee's report that the editor angrily sends to another reviewer after too long a lapse. However, many tasks have deadlines. For our students, the cost of procrastination involves 'pulling an all-nighter' to get the term paper (conference paper) done on time.

Qualitatively, the same type of results that we have already seen can still occur: small salience costs to beginning projects can result in costly procrastination. Consider what happens if the disutility of a project varies with the square of hours worked per day, and the number of hours to complete a project is fixed. Let the salience cost of beginning a project be a multiple of the disutility of the first day's work. In an example in which the salience cost is 2 percent of the total cost and the length of the project is 100 days, the added cost of completing the project can be calculated at approximately 41 percent.[3]

It may also be worth noting that if the salience value of beginning the project increases with the intensity of the first period's work, a project, such as a reducing

---

[2] The exact critical date is the first day on which the decision maker decides to send at T: i.e., the smallest t such that $c - (T - t - 1)x > 0$.

[3] Let us suppose that the daily utility cost of doing a project varies with the square of the number of hours worked per day, and that the project, without procrastination, would require Th hours of labor. Then we can write the intertemporal utility function as $U = \sum_{t=0}^{T} e_t^2$, where e_t is the number of hours worked on day t. Without procrastination, the total utility cost of the project is $U = Th^2$.

Let us now compare this to the cost borne by a procrastinator. For the procrastinator, current costs are unduly salient in comparison with future costs. The salience premium is δh^2, a multiple of δ of the daily cost of the project if begun on time. The perceived cost of completing the project, if begun at date τ, is thus:

$$V = \delta h^2 + \sum_{t=\tau}^{T} e_t^2.$$

diet, may never be begun, or a task may be begun at the latest possible date at which completion is feasible.

III. PROCRASTINATION: SUBSTANCE ABUSE, SAVINGS, AND ORGANIZATIONAL FAILURES

At first glance, my examples of procrastination may appear to be of no relevance to economics. However, I want to argue that such behavior may be critical in understanding the causes of such varied problems as drug abuse, inadequate savings and some types of organizational failure.

A. *Substance Abuse*

It has often been observed that consumers are knowledgeable about their decisions, and that their decisions are utility maximizing. Ethnographies of drug users suggest that drug use is no exception. Gary Becker and Kevin Murphy (1988) and George Stigler and Becker (1977) have developed the theory of such behavior in their forward-looking models of rational addiction. In these models, use of a good affects the future enjoyment of its consumption, but people correctly foresee these changes in taste. The application of such models, combined with utilitarian ethics, leads to the conclusion that drug use should be legalized with a tax reflecting its nuisance to others.

I do not agree with this conclusion, because I do not agree that the model of forward-looking, rational behavior accurately describes the way in which individuals decide on drug or alcohol intake. Most drug abusers, like most chronically overweight individuals, fully intend to cut down their intake, since they recognize that the long-run cost of their addiction exceeds its benefits. They intend to stop—tomorrow. Individuals following the procrastination model are both maximizing and knowledgeable, and yet their decisions are not fully rational. For example, psychologist Roger Brown describes addictions in the following way.

Actions like smoking a cigarette, having a drink, eating a candy bar, and working overtime to 'catch up' all lead to immediate and certain gratification, whereas their bad consequences are remote in time, only probabilistic, and still avoidable now. It is no contest: Certain and immediate rewards win out over probabilistic and remote costs, even though the rewards are slight and the possible costs lethal.

[1986, p. 636]

In each period, the procrastinator compares the total cost V of the project if begun that day (including the added salience cost δh^2 of that day's input) with the cost of waiting one more day to begin, taking no account that when the next day arrives, it too will have special salience. Behaving in this way, the project is begun with approximately $T\delta^{-1/2}$ days left for its completion. This is a poor approximation for low values of δ because for low values of δ it does not pay to procrastinate. This increases the total cost of the project by a multiple that is the square root of δ. In this example, a small salience cost of beginning a project results in losses from future actions that are a multiple of the cost. For example, if T is 100 days and δ is 2, the salience cost of beginning the project relative to the total nonprocrastinating cost is only .02. But the total cost of completing the project increases by 41 percent ($\sqrt{2} - 1$).

Ethnographies of drug abusers reveal that most are well aware of the long-term consequences of their habit and many have detailed and subtle knowledge of the effects of drugs. (See, for example, Cheryl Carpenter et al., 1988 and Harvey Feldman et al., 1979.) They apply this knowledge to avoid some of the worst potential consequences of drug use. An interview with Don, an 'angel dust' (PCP) user in the Seattle-Tacoma area reveals the knowledge of the long-term effects of drug use, and also an inability to use the knowledge to quit. Don tells his interviewer:

And every time I use the drug and I come down and I am straight, since I do have this heightened form of awareness and perspective, I always tell myself, 'Well, that's the last time I'll use it. I don't need it now.' I can see where this is, what I've got to do, and this is what I want to do and everything falls into place.

[Feldman et al., p. 137]

Later, I will discuss some ways in which the social pressures emanating from group dynamics reinforce individual reasons for addiction.

B. *Savings*

The procrastination model may also pertain to intertemporal savings and consumption decisions. The modern textbook/journal article model of consumption and savings decisions typically views agents as maximizing a time-separable utility function with discount rate δ. This discount is said to parameterize agents' impatience. Curiously, economists who build models with utility functions of this sort consider themselves to be modeling the behavior of *rational* consumers. Yet early discussion of impatience viewed discounting as *irrational* behavior. Irving Fisher regarded such impatience as evidence of lack of foresight or lack of will. In this regard, he writes,

Generally speaking, the greater the foresight, the less the impatience and *vice versa*. . . . This is illustrated by the story of the farmer who would never mind his leaking roof. When it rained he could not stop the leak, and when it did not rain there was no leak to be stopped! Among such persons, the preference for present gratification is powerful because their anticipation of the future is *weak*. [1930, p. 81]

Fisher's example of the farmer fits the model of an agent continually making an inconsistent decision.

A clear moral of the procrastination model is that time-inconsistent behavior is especially apt to occur when there is some fixed cost (perhaps not very great) to beginning a task, the 'periods' are short, and the per period cost of delay is low. Many personal financial decisions satisfy these conditions. A good example concerns the behavior of junior faculty at Harvard. Due to some institutional oddity, university contributions to TIAA/CREF cumulated without payment of interest until the recipient filed a form indicating his desired allocation between the two retirement funds. This could be done at any time and took less than an hour. And yet most junior faculty who left Harvard in the 1970's made this decision only upon their departure. They thus lost hundreds of dollars worth of interest by failing to do an hour's work.[4]

A more serious application of the procrastination model is to savings.[5] Most of the U.S. elderly (those over 65) derive relatively little of their income from financial assets. In 1971, 51 percent of the elderly had no income from financial assets; 78 percent had less than 20 percent of their income from financial assets (Michael Hurd, 1990, p. 571). This stark absence of financial asset income is consistent with the hypothesis that most households would save very little, except for the purchase of their home and the associated amortization of mortgage principal, in the absence of private pension plans. Partly because these additions to financial assets are so small, some seemingly paradoxical results have been obtained. Phillip Cagan (1965) and George Katona (1965), for example, find a *positive* relation between pension plans and private saving. In the life cycle model (up to some limit), $1 of pension savings should lead to $1 reduction of private saving. Steven Venti and David Wise (1986, 1987) report results similar to those of Cagan and Katona. They find no significant relation between ownership of a pension plan and willingness to invest in IRAs. Alicia Munnell's (1976) findings are less extreme. She looked at the savings of a sample of 5,000 men aged 45 to 59 in 1966. She estimated that a $1 private pension contribution caused a reduction in nonpension savings of 62¢ for these men nearing retirement. This is still considerably less than the $1 that would be expected if people were life cycle savers and pension plans did not induce oversaving.[6]

The hypothesis that, in the absence of pension plans, many individuals lack sufficient self-discipline to begin saving for retirement in a timely fashion is consistent with the finding that there were high rates of elderly poverty prior to the rapid, unexpected growth in Social Security payments in the late 1960's and the 1970's. In 1966, the elderly poverty rate was 30 percent, fully double the poverty rate of the non-elderly (David Ellwood and Lawrence Summers, 1986, p. 81).[7]

---

[4] I owe this observation to Janet Yellen.

[5] Richard Thaler and Hersh Shefrin (1981) discuss the role of Christmas Clubs in forcing the scheduling of savings. Their model of saving behavior, and of procrastination, is different from my model in this lecture. Their model discusses two types of decision making: for long-term planning and for maximization of current utility. People may constrain themselves (i.e., may make arrangements such as Christmas Clubs) so that they can then be free to maximize their short-term utility without further constraint. In this way budgets act as mental accounts. The Christmas Clubs relative to my model set clear schedules for saving, which result in penalties if not followed, and thereby prevent procrastination.

[6] It is also low because we might expect those without pension plans to be making up for prior failure to save as they near retirement, just as the procrastinating student has to work especially hard near his term paper deadline.

[7] This high rate may reflect the prior lives of poverty of the elderly population in 1966; this group spent much of their working lives in the Great Depression. But earlier statistics, from such indicators as the fraction of elderly living in poorhouses, show that the elderly had particularly high poverty rates in the 1920's, before both modern pension plans and the Great Depression (Michael Dahlin, 1983).

C. *Organizational Failures*

Procrastination is as prevalant in the workplace as in the home. Procrastination by workers results both in delay in initiating projects that should be begun as well as in delay in terminating projects that should be ended.[8]

In private life, individuals are frequently forced to self-monitor their behavior, as in stopping an addiction, writing a Ph.D. thesis, devising a private asset plan, or sending off referee reports; in such areas procrastination can easily occur leading to serious losses. However, in work situations, outside monitoring is possible, and a major function of management is to set schedules and monitor accomplishment so as to prevent procrastination.

Proper management not only prevents procrastination in project *initiation*; it also prevents procrastination in project *termination*. Psychologists have found tendencies to delay terminations of projects by people who consider themselves responsible for their initiation. Barry Staw (1976) divided a group of 240 undergraduate business students into two groups. One group was asked to decide on investment allocation in a business school case study of the Adams and Smith Corporation. They were then asked to make a further allocation of investment between the division with their initial project and the other division of the firm. In contrast, a control group only had to make the second allocation. Both groups, however, had matched past histories of the firm and the success of the firm's projects. In the case of project failure, those who had made a prior commitment wanted to invest significantly more in that division than the control group with the same matched history who had made no such prior commitment. One explanation matches our model: that failure to terminate the project puts the painful decision off until tomorrow; the pain of admitting a mistake today is salient relative to the pain of having to admit a possibly even bigger mistake tomorrow. This same phenomenon may also be explained, not necessarily inconsistently, by cognitive dissonance. Once people have made decisions, they avoid information that does not support that decision because it is psychologically painful.

Staw and S. McClane (1984) report how the commercial division of a large American bank avoids procrastination in loan cutoff decisions. Loan officers are not penalized for cutting off loans, although they are penalized for failing to foresee possible losses. They are especially penalized if loan losses are discovered by bank examiners before they are reported. Most important, loans with significant difficulties are referred to a separate committee not involved in the initial decision to obtain the maximum salvage value.

In the next section I will discuss how courses of action are reinforced by selective elimination of information contrary to that course of action, so that initial psychological overcommitments are reinforced. Jerry Ross and Staw (1986) examine the history of

---

[8] In their advice book on *Procrastination*, Jane Burka and Lenora Yuen (1983) urge potential procrastinators to set clear and realistic schedules for themselves and then adhere to them. In the preceding Stiglitz-box model, the determination of a schedule that was binding would have resulted in the box being sent on day 1 or day 2. Thomas Schelling (1985, p. 368) has explained in similar terms why parents at the beach may give their children the clear advice not to go in the water at all, even though they do not mind the children getting a little bit wet. In the absence of a clear 'schedule' telling the children when the water is too deep, they may wade ever deeper and end up in danger.

Expo 86 in Vancouver, whose projected losses escalated from a maximum of $6 million to over $300 million. In this case, exit costs reinforced the initial psychological over-commitment: the Prime Minister of British Columbia feared loss of election on termination, contracts would have to be breached, and outside vendors would make losses from investments made in anticipation of the fair.

Staw and Ross (1987) list management practices that limit overcommitment: administrative turnover; low cost to executives for admitting failure; lack of ambiguity in data regarding performance; allowing losses to be blamed on exonerating circumstances; separating termination decisions from initiation decisions; and considering from the beginning the costs and procedures of project termination.

IV. INDOCTRINATION AND OBEDIENCE

Irrational obedience to authority is a second type of 'pathological,' time-inconsistent behavior with important social and economic ramifications. Procrastination occurs when there is a fixed cost of action today and current costs are more salient than future costs. Undue obedience to authority may occur as a form of procrastination if disobedience of an authority is salient and distasteful. In addition, authority may be particularly powerful when yesterday's actions affect the norms of today's behavior. Both such influences (the salience of current disobedience and a shift in the utility of subjects in accordance with their prior actions) are present in Milgram's experiments, which I shall review.

The subjects in the Milgram experiment were adult males, recruited by a mail circular requesting participation in an experiment purportedly concerning the effects of punishment on memory. The subjects were assigned the role of teacher, while an accomplice of the experimenter, a professional actor, played the role of learner. The subjects were instructed to administer shocks to the learner when he gave wrong answers. The shocks were a learner-discipline device. The learner, a trained actor instructed to simulate the appropriate reactions to the shocks administered by the subjects, was visible to the subject through a glass window, and, unbeknownst to the subject, was not wired. Subjects initially gave low voltage shocks (15 volts) with doses increasing 15 volts at a time to a maximum of 450. There are different versions of this experiment, but, in all versions, the learner showed significant response to the shocks. For example, in one version, according to Milgram's description, 'at 75 volts the learner began to grunt and groan. At 150 volts he demands to be let out of the experiment. At 180 volts he cries out that he can no longer stand the pain. At 300 volts he ... [insists] he must be freed' (1965, p. 246, quoted in E. Stotland and L. K. Canon, 1972, p. 6). Despite these protests by the learner, 62.5 percent of the subjects reached the maximum of 450 volts. The experiment has been repeated under a wide variety of conditions, but always with the same result: a significant fraction of the population administers the maximum dosage.

As important as the primary finding from Milgram's experiment that individuals are remarkably obedient is the further finding of their lack of awareness of this trait in themselves and in others. Elliot Aronson (1984, p. 40), a professor of social psychology at UC–Santa Cruz, asks the students in his classes how many would continue to administer shocks after the learner pounds on the wall. Virtually no one responds affirmatively. Milgram conducted a survey of psychiatrists at a major medical school who predicted that most subjects would not administer shocks in excess of 150 volts, and virtually no subjects would administer the maximum 450 volts. This finding supports my central argument: that in appropriate circumstances, people behave in time-inconsistent ways that they themselves cannot foresee, as when they procrastinate or exhibit irrational obedience to authority.

   A Model of Behavior in the Milgram Experiment. Let me present a simple model that is a variant of the previous model of procrastination and which explains the sequential decisions made by the subjects in Milgram's experiment. I shall first assume that current disobedience by the subject is especially painful; it is especially salient. Lee Ross (1988) has argued that special salience is attached to disobedience because there is an implicit contract between the teacher and the experimenter. The experiment defines the situation so that there is no legitimate way for the teacher to terminate.[9] Thus the subject sees the cost of current disobedience as very high, although in an ill-defined way, he may plan to disobey in the future. Second, I shall assume that the subject suffers a loss in utility, not based on the current voltage he administers to the learner, but instead on the deviation of the current voltage from what he last administered. (Alternatively his utility might depend on the deviation from the highest voltage previously administered.) This model is consistent with cognitive dissonance. Once people have undertaken an action, especiallly for reasons they do not fully understand, they find reasons why that action was in fact justified. In this formulation, the subject decides to obey up until time T so as to maximize V_t.

   If he disobeys today at time t, his utility is

$$V_t = -bD(1 + \delta) \tag{4}$$

But if he postpones obeying, his expected utility is

$$V_t = -bD - c\sum_{k=t}^{T-1}(W_k - W_{t-1}) \quad T \geq t + 1 \tag{5}$$

if he first disobeys at time $T \geq t + 1$, where δ is the extra salience attached to today's disobedience, D is the cost of disobedience, W_k is the voltage of the shock administered at time k, and W_{t-1} is the norm for the level of shocks determined by previous actions.

   It can easily be seen in this formulation that at each date, with sufficiently slow expected future escalation of commands the subjects can be led, as in the Milgram experiment, to deliver ever-higher levels of shock. They plan to disobey in the future if

---

[9] Ross suggests that if teachers had a red button to push that would allow them to stop the experiment, very few subjects would have given the maximum dosage. In my model, this would decrease the value of δ, the special salience attached to current disobedience.

the experiment continues, but not currently. While planning future disobedience if escalation continues, at the same time these subjects are continuing to raise the level of shock required to induce them to disobey. The dependence of norms of behavior on previous actions does not just cause continued poor decision making due to postponement, but also causes escalating errors in decisions.

While V may be the function that subjects maximize in the heat of the moment, under the conditions of the Milgram experiment, a more accurate expression of their *true* intertemporal utility function might be

$$V_0 = \sum_k \{ - bD_k - cW_k\} \tag{6}$$

where V_0 is their intertemporal utility and k sums over all the trials.

Such a utility function is reflected in the postexperiment interviews and follow-up questionnaires. Most of the subjects were, in retrospect, extremely regretful of their decisions in the experiment. For example, one subject, who was a social worker, wrote in a follow-up questionnaire a year later:

What appalled me was that I could possess this capacity for obedience and compliance to a central idea, i.e. the value of a memory experiment, even after it became clear that continued adherence to this value was at the expense of the violation of another value, i.e. don't hurt someone else who is helpless and not hurting you. As my wife said, 'You can call yourself Eichmann.'
[Milgram, 1975, p. 54]

The preceding models of procrastination and obedience concern actions that occur because individuals possess cognitive structures of which they are less than fully aware. The assumption that such structures influence behavior is unfamiliar in economics, but central to other social sciences. A major task of psychology is to discover such unperceived behavioral regularities; the concepts of *culture* in anthropology and *the definition of the situation* in sociology both concern cognitive structures only dimly perceived by decision makers.

The Milgram experiment demonstrates that isolated individuals can exhibit remarkably obedient (and deviant) behavior inside the laboratory. In group situations, however, there is evidence that such behavior occurs only when there is near unanimity of opinion. In this regard, the most relevant evidence comes from a variant of the Asch experiment. Solomon Asch (1951, p. 479) found that subjects asked to match the length of a line to a comparison group of lines of different length gave the wrong answer roughly 40 percent of the time if they were preceded by confederates of the experimenter who had previously given the wrong answer. However, in another variant of the experiment, Asch (1952) found that the presence of just a single confederate who gave the right answer in a large group of confederates reduced the number of wrong answers by a factor of two-thirds. This suggests that the presence of like-minded others significantly raises the likelihood of disobedience in situations such as the Milgram experiment. It might be inferred that obedience such as obtained by Milgram could only occur in the laboratory where people are shielded from outside information and influences.

The next four sections will present examples of individuals who participate in groups and make regrettable decisions. In each of the examples, a sequence of small errors has serious ill consequences. Furthermore, in each of the situations described, there is a natural equilibrium in which those who disagree with the actions taken find it disadvantageous to voice their dissent, which is accordingly isolated from the decision-making process.

V. CULTS

A. *Unification Church*

Evidence seems to show that neither members nor inductees into cult groups such as the Unification Church (Moonies) are psychologically very much different from the rest of the population (see Marc Galanter et al., 1979; and Galanter, 1980). The method of induction into the Moonies indicates how normal people, especially at troubled times in their lives, can be recruited into cults and the cult can persist. Membership into the Moonies involves four separate decisions. Potential recruits are first contacted individually and invited to come to a 2-day, weekend workshop. These workshops are then followed by a 7-day workshop, a 12-day workshop, and membership. The potential recruit in consequence makes four separate decisions: initially to attend the 2-day workshop, to continue into the 7-day workshop, and then again into the 12-day workshop, and finally to join the Church. As in the Milgram experiment, the membership decision is achieved in slow stages.

Consider the process from the point of view of the potential recruit. Those who agree to attend the first 2-day workshop must have some predisposition toward the goals of the Church; otherwise they would not have attended. But they are probably surprised on arrival to find so many like-minded persons. In addition, the members of the Church intermingle and apply gentle persuasion in the first 2-day workshop; the inductees' commitment at this point begins to change. Then, continuing with the 7-day workshop, and again with the 12-day workshop, only the most committed continue; those who disagree leave. At each stage the Church members are thus able to increase the intensity of their message. As in the Milgram experiment and other social psychology experiments on conformist behavior, the potential inductee, in the absence of disagreement, is likely to change his opinions. And, as we have seen, because of the self-selection process, there is unlikely to be strong disagreement among the workshop attendees. Galanter's study of eight workshop sequences reveals this gradual attrition according to commitment. Of the 104 guests at the initial 2-day workshops, 74 did not continue. Of the 30 at the 7-day workshops, 12 did not continue (including a few who were rescued by their families, and a few who were told not to continue by the Church). Of the 18 remaining at the 12-day workshops, 9 did not continue to membership. And of the remaining 9, 6 were active church members 6 months later.

The example of the Moonies illustrates a process of conversion. Converts make a sequence of small decisions to accept authority. Ultimately, as a result of this sequence of decisions to obey rather than to rebel, the converts develop beliefs and values very different from what they had at the beginning of the process. This willingness to acquiesce to authority is abetted by self-selection. Those who agree most with the Church self-select into the group. Because those who disagree most exit, the dissent necessary for resistance to escalation of commitment does not develop.

B. *Synanon*

The case of Synanon is possibly the best studied, as well as being, in the end, one of the most horrific of these cult groups. In this group we can see the pressure for obedience to authority operative in the Milgram experiment, as well as the selective exit of would-be dissenters who could break the isolation necessary to maintain this obedience to authority.

Synanon was initially an organization devoted to the cure of drug addicts, but it gradually evolved into a paramilitary organization carrying out the increasingly mani-acal whims of its founder and leader. (My account comes from David Gerstel, 1982.) The leader, Charles Dederich, as well as the other founders of Synanon, adapted the methods of Alcoholics Anonymous for the treatment of drug addiction. At the time, little was known about drug abuse in this country; it was also widely believed that drug addiction was incurable. By proving the contrary, Synanon received considerable favorable publicity. With aggressive solicitation of gifts (especially of in-kind tax deductible gifts) and commercial endeavors such as the sale of pens, pencils, and briefcases with the Synanon logo, it expanded from a houseful of ex-addicts, first to a large residential site in Santa Monica, and, at its peak, to several residential communities in both northern and southern California with more than 1,600 residents (Richard Ofshe, 1980, p. 112).

To understand the path of Synanon from these benign origins into what it eventually became, it is necessary to focus on the methods of control in the organization. The members led dual lives: daytime workday lives, and nighttime lives spent in a pastime called The Game. The daytime lives of members were devoted to hard work, especially for the cause of the community. Members were given virtually no private property and were expected to donate their own resources to Synanon; they had virtually no privacy. Gerstel reports his first impressions of Synanon as amazement at the cleanliness of the buildings, the orderliness of the grounds, and the cheerfulness of the workers. The daytime code of Synanon was to maintain a cheerful positive attitude at all times, exemplified by the song of the trashmen: 'We're your Synanon garbage men./ We don't work for money. Ooooh, we don't work for cash./ We work for the pleasure/Of taking out yo' trash' (Gerstel, p. 5).

At night, however, the unbridled positivism was given up, and members acted out their hostility and aggressions in The Game (adapted from the practices of Alcoholics Anonymous, from which Synanon originated). Participants in The Game were expected to be brutally frank in criticizing any other member who did not live up to the standards expected of Synanon. Because the lives of the members were so open to each other, these criticisms could extend to the smallest detail. Since members had virtually no privacy, this criticism naturally monitored any deviation from the purposes of the organization. The incentives of The Game induced members to strive to maintain the very best behavior.

The Game, however, like any other game, had rules, and those rules led to complete control of this fairly large community by its leader. These rules encouraged the criticism of members by one another, but forbade criticism of the goals of Synanon itself or any shortcomings of its leader. Anyone who criticized the organization or its leadership would be harshly criticized by all (an incentive not to engage in such activity). If that criticism persisted, the offender would be banished from the community.

Under these rules of behavior, Synanon evolved into an organization under the control of a leader who became increasingly insane. In the late 1970's, Dederich insisted that members follow his every whim. That included, to give some examples, enforced dieting (the Fatathon), enforced vasectomies for all males, and an enforced change of partners, first of all for married members of the community, and subsequently for all paired members whether married or not. Those who did not go along with these measures were 'gamed,' that is, criticized vehemently in The Game, beaten up, or evicted. During this period, Dederich was also building up his own armed paramilitary force that reacted against threats both within and outside the community. Within Synanon, dissenters were beaten up. Outside, passersby or neighbors with real or presumed insults aimed at the community were accosted and beaten, often severely. One former member, who was suing for the custody of his child still living there, was beaten to the point of paralysis, never to recover. Dederich was eventually convicted on a charge of conspiracy for murder—for sending unwanted mail to a Los Angeles attorney who was fighting Synanon: two Synanon vigilantes were found leaving a poisonous rattlesnake in his mail box.

The Synanon experience follows closely what Milgram observed in the laboratory. At each move by Dederich, the members were forced individually to decide whether to obey or to disobey. Disobedience involved the present cost of leaving the group and seeking immediately a new way of life with insufficient human and financial resources. Many members in the past had found life outside Synanon painful and had sought refuge there. Thus the consequences of disobedience were immediate and salient. As members chose the course of obedience, their norms of behavior as members of Synanon gradually changed, just as the norms of behavior of Milgram's subjects changed according to the level of punishment they had previously administered. The process was aided, in Synanon as in Milgram's laboratory, by the absence of dissent. In Synanon the absence of dissent was ensured in usual circumstances by The Game and in unusual circumstances by forced expulsions.

VI. CRIME AND DRUGS

Economists modeling crime (see Becker, 1968) and drug addiction have viewed the decisions to engage in these activities as individually motivated. Becker and Murphy, following Stigler-Becker, have even viewed the decision to pursue addictive activities as both rational and forward looking. The Milgram experiment and the behavior of cult groups, if nothing else, serve as warnings. It is inconceivable that the participants in Milgram's experiment were forward looking. These participants could not imagine that anyone (least of all themselves) would behave as they ultimately did. Likewise, the flower children of Synanon of the 1960's could not have conceived of themselves turning into gun-toting toughs in the 1970's. The assumption of forward-looking rationality regarding the change in their consumption capital, to use Stigler-Becker terminology, is totally violated.

The analogy between cult groups and the behavior of teenage gangs, where most criminal activity and drug addiction begin, is fairly complete. A member of a teenage gang typically finds himself (much less frequently herself) in a position very similar to that of a member of Synanon. The typical member of a gang makes a sequence of decisions that results in an escalating obedience to the gang leadership. At each stage of his career as a gang member, he makes the choice whether to obey or to disobey. In extreme cases, disobedience leads to expulsion from the gang. The gang member thus faces the same dilemma as the member of Synanon: whether to forsake friends who are close and in an important respect define his way of life, or to go along with the gang decision. In rising from junior to senior membership in the gang, or in following a leader who himself is becoming deviant, the gang member by obeying increases his commitment to obedience. The situation is exactly analogous to that of subjects in the Milgram experiment.

Furthermore, the isolation from dissent obtained in Milgram's laboratory also naturally occurs in teenage gangs. The major activity of such gangs, according to David Matza (1964) is hanging out, and the major activity while hanging out is insulting other gang members to see how they respond. This activity is called 'sounding,' because it measures the depths of the other member on his response to the insult. The depth probe usually focuses on the manliness of the gang member and/or his commitment to the gang itself. The probing of his commitment to the gang plays the same control function as The Game in Synanon. Those who display less than full commitment to the gang in sounding, or to Synanon in The Game, suffer a form of public censure. Such procedures make members reluctant to voice their disagreements with the goals or activities of the gang, just as members of Synanon found it difficult to display negative attitudes toward the group. Thus members of teenage gangs find themselves in isolated positions, unable to resist the aims of powerful and deviant leaders. The ethnographies we have of such gangs support the importance of sounding and the role of important leaders who play a disproportionate role in planning gang activities (see Jay MacLeod, 1988, and William Whyte, 1943).

Just as the participants in the Milgram experiment 'drifted' into obedience, and members of Synanon drifted into gangsterism, Matza (1964) showed how teenagers 'drift' into delinquency. Matza (1969) likens the process of becoming delinquent to 'religious conversion.' The analogies of *drift* and *conversion* are both consistent with my model of time-inconsistent behavior. Like the cult groups I have just described, delinquent teenage gangs have mechanisms that work to preserve their isolation from outside influences. Should we be surprised that many such gangs with few social constraints engage in harmful deviant activity?

Consider the activities, as chronicled by MacLeod, of the 'Hallway Hangers,' a gang who live in a low-income housing project in a New England city. The major activity of this gang is hanging out in Hallway #13 and sounding each other, with varying degrees of playfulness and malice. While hanging out, the gang ingests a wide variety of stimulants, including beer in vast amounts, a great deal of marijuana, some cocaine, PCP, and mescaline, and occasionally some heroin. The central value of this group is its loyalty to the gang and the other members, just as Synanon's central value from its inception to its end was the loyalty of members to the general community. The ethos of this gang is illustrated by MacLeod's story of Shorty and Slick, when they were caught ripping off the local sneakers factory (as told by Shorty):

See, that's how Slick was that day we were ripping off the sneakers. He figured that if he left me that would be rude, y'know. If he just let me get busted by myself and he knew I had a lot of [. . .] on my head, that's what I call a brother. He could've. I could've pushed him right through that fence, and he coulda been *gone*. But no, he waited for me, and we both got arrested. I was stuck. My belly couldn't get through the [. . .] hole in the fence.

[pp. 32–33]

This same aspect of gang behavior was emphasized 50 years ago in the classic street corner ethnography by Whyte. He explained the lack of social mobility of the most capable corner boys by their unwillingness to adopt a life style that would have sacrificed friendships with peers who would not advance with them. Just as Slick did not run when Shorty got caught in the fence in MacLeod's account, the leader of the 'corner boys' Doc, in Whyte's account, fails to advance himself in school so he can remain with his friends.

Such gangs provide a perfect social environment for regrettable decisions. Gang members find the costs of nonacquiescence especially salient, since such nonacquiescence leads to isolation from the social group to which they are committed. As occurred at Synanon in a similar environment, gang members can then be led step-by-step to escalating levels of crime, drugs, and violence, with each preceding step setting the norm for the next.

The question remains how to alter such behavior by social policy. William Wilson (1987) has argued the importance of the move from the central city to the suburbs of the middle class, which, he says, has resulted in the disappearance of social networks that formerly were the pathways to employment. According to Wilson, the result, especially in the black community, has been a dearth of employed (and therefore eligible) males and a dramatic increase in out-of-wedlock births.

There is, however, another effect of the disappearance of the urban middle class for poor youth left in the central cities. This disappearance has left fewer alternative social groups for those who do not want to acquiesce in the violent acts of their peers, thus making such acquiescence and gang violence more frequent.

Social policy should have the role of recreating, artificially if necessary, the beneficial social networks that have vanished. This would reduce the cost of dissent by gang members to criminal, violent, or drug-prone actions by providing alternatives. In addition, we have seen that just a little bit of dissent, and therefore perhaps just a little bit of information, may stop escalation toward commitment. Lisbeth Schorr (1989) has compiled a long list of social projects that have significantly reduced the problems of the underclass, problems such as teenage pregnancy, school truancy, drug abuse, violence, and alcoholism. In each of these projects, the key to success has been the special effort by social workers involved to gain the trust of their clients. The success of these projects shows that, when isolation can be broken and trust established, small amounts of information can significantly reduce the number of regrettable decisions.[10]

Evidence for the view that social isolation results in high crime rates comes from the positive correlation between crime rates and city size. Smaller cities have less room for specialization in social groups than larger cities—so that isolation from common social norms is more difficult to attain. They also have lower crime rates. Cities with less than 10,000 people have one-fifth the violent crime rates of cities with populations more than 250,000. In 1985, cities with over 250,000 people had 50 percent higher violent crime rates than those cities with populations between 100,000 and 250,000 (U.S. Bureau of the Census, 1987, p. 157).[11]

VII. POLITICS AND ECONOMICS

Economists who have applied the tools of their trade to the political process have studied the workings of democracy and majority rule under individualistic values (see Kenneth Arrow, 1963). They are optimists. The model of cult group behavior, in contrast, is relevant in understanding politics' darker side. I will give two illustrations.

A. *Stalin's Takeover*

My first example concerns Stalin's ascension to power in Russia. The history of the Bolshevik party and the history of Synanon are strikingly similar. (I take the Bolshevik history from Isaac Deutscher, 1949.) Initially, there were the early days of reformist zeal, of meeting secretly in lofts, ware-houses, and other strange places. But, in addition, and most importantly, there was commitment to the organization. To the Bolsheviks, this commitment was of paramount importance. Indeed, it was over the constitutional issue as to whether party members should merely be contributors (either financial or political) or should, in addition, submit to party discipline that split the Russian socialist workers' movement into two parts—the Mensheviks and the Bolsheviks. This loyalty to party discipline, useful in the revolution, ultimately enabled Stalin to take over the party and pervert its ideals. It underlay the acquiescence of his tough comrade revolutionaries in the scrapping of the original principles of Bolshevism: open intraparty debate and dedication to the cause of the workers and peasants. In the 1920's and 1930's, as Stalin collectivized the peasants and tyrannized over dissidents, these old comrades stood by,

---

[10] In the case of the Unification Church, such active intervention frequently occurred as members were captured by relatives and forcibly deprogrammed (Galanter, 1989).

[11] Some of these differences undoubtedly are due to the concentrations of poor people with high crime rates in central cities that are large in size.

perhaps not quite agreeing, but not actively disagreeing either, much like Milgram's passively obedient, passively resistant subjects. Even Trotsky in exile did not unambiguously oppose Stalin until the purges had begun as a series of decisions were made that increasingly brutalized the peasantry and cut off political debate. The exception to the lack of dissent proves the rule. Nadia Alliluyeva was the daughter of one of the founding Bolsheviks and thus an heiress by birth to the ideals of the party. She was also Stalin's wife. When Stalin collectivized the peasantry, moving perhaps 80 million from their farms in six months' time, she voiced her disapproval at a party—he replied savagely. That night she committed suicide.[12] This behavior contrasts with the party leadership who, like Milgram's subjects, had been participating in the decisions that were being taken. At each juncture, they were confronted by the decision whether to break ranks with the increasing brutalization of the peasants and the choking off of dissent, or to remain loyal to the party. By acquiescing step by step to the crescendo of Stalin's actions, they were committing themselves to altered standards of behavior. In contrast, Nadia Alliluyeva, who had withdrawn from the decision-making process to be wife and mother, could feel proper revulsion at the deviation of the party's actions from its prior ideals.

B. *Vietnam War*

A second example of the type of deviant group process I have described occurred in President Johnson's Tuesday lunch group, which was the executive body controlling U.S. military decisions in the Vietnam War (Irving Janis, 1972). Here we see all of the features characterizing our model of salience, authority, and obedience. First, there was the gradual escalation of violence against the Vietnamese. Bill Moyers, reflecting on Vietnam policy after he was out of office, precisely describes how this escalation of commitment happened: 'With but rare exceptions we always seemed to be calculating the short-term consequences of each alternative at every step of the [policymaking] process, but not the long-range consequences. And with each succeeding short-range consequence we became more deeply a prisoner of the process' (Janis, p. 103). The subjects in Milgram's experiments could have said exactly the same thing.

The control of dissension within President Johnson's Tuesday lunch group bore close resemblance to the processes at work in Synanon and the Hallway Hangers. The president would greet Moyers as 'Mr. Stop-the-Bombing'; similar epithets were applied to other dissenters within the group: 'our favorite dove,' 'the inhouse devil's advocate on Vietnam' (Janis, p. 120). A teenage gang would probably consider these soundings mediocre, but their lack of style may not have affected their impact. And the measures within the group which were taken to enforce unanimity ('groupthink' according to Janis) were supplemented by more or less voluntary exit as dissenters at different times came to disagree with the policy: Bill Moyers, George Ball, McGeorge Bundy, and Robert McNamara. Interestingly, since each of these individuals exited fairly soon after

---

[12] An alternative account of Alliluyeva's decision to commit suicide and Stalin's activities on the night before is given by Nikita Khrushchev (1990). The two accounts are not mutually exclusive.

they developed deep reservations about the policy, there was active dissent for only a small fraction of the history of the group.

VIII. BUREAUCRACIES

My examples of obedience to authority, so far, have centered primarily on noneconomic phenomena: religion, crime, drugs, and politics. However, the phenomenon of obedience to authority is also prevalent in bureaucracies that in a modern industrialized society, are the sites of most economic activity.

One function of bureaucracies, following Robert Merton (1968, p. 250) and Weber, is to create specialists. A second function of bureaucracies is 'infusing group participants with appropriate attitudes and sentiments' (Merton, 1968, p. 253). We could interpret the Milgram experiment as a toy bureaucracy, and my model of that experiment as a model of that bureaucracy. In that case, W_{t-1}, the level of voltage that a subject has grown accustomed to giving, constitutes his 'attitudes and sentiments.' In Merton's terms, it defines his bureaucratic personality.

The specialization mentioned earlier can result in bureaucratic personalities that are 'dysfunctional,' to use Merton's terminology. We have already seen such dysfunction in the behavior of the Moonies, Synanon, teenage gangs, drug and alcohol abusers, the Bolshevik party, and President Johnson's Tuesday lunch group. The changes that occurred in individual decision-making behavior were 'latent,' to use another of Merton's terms, since they were not understood by the participants and were unintentional. Furthermore, these changes occur exactly as I have been picturing: in making a sequence of small decisions, the decision maker's criteria for decisions gradually change, with preceding decisions being the precedent for further decisions. Merton gives an example of the consequences of such bureaucratically engendered personalities in the U.S. Bureau of Naturalization concerning the treatment of the request for citizenship of Admiral Byrd's pilot over the South Pole.

According to a ruling of the Department of Labor Bernt Balchen . . . cannot receive his citizenship papers. Balchen, a native of Norway, declared his intention in 1927. It is held that he has failed to meet the condition of five years' continuous residence in the United States. The Byrd antarctic voyage took him out of the country, although he was on a ship carrying the American flag, was an invaluable member of the American expedition, and in a region to which there is an American claim because of the exploration and occupation of it by Americans, this region being called Little America.

The Bureau of Naturalization explains that it cannot proceed on the assumption that Little America is American soil. That would be trespass on international questions where it has no sanction. So far as the bureau is concerned, Balchen was out of the country and technically has not complied with the law of naturalization.

[p. 254, quoted from *The Chicago Tribune*, June 24, 1931, p. 10]

Popular proponents of bureaucratic reform (for example, William Ouchi, 1981, and Thomas Peters and Robert Waterman, 1982) have emphasized the benefits of nonspecialization within firms precisely because they recognize that nonspecialists have a wider range of experience than specialists and thus are less likely to have developed special bureaucratic personalities. Also, as consistent with my secondary theme in earlier examples, nonspecialists by nature are less isolated than specialists. The use of non-specialists may break the isolation necessary for the development of dysfunctional bureaucratic personalities.

Economic models of bureaucracy have typically been based on principal-agent theory. Their purpose is to derive optimal organizational structures, contingent on the technical nature of information flows. (Two excellent examples are Paul Milgrom and John Roberts, 1988, and Bengt Holmstrom and Jean Tirole, 1988). In contrast, my analysis suggests an alternative way in which information affects the performance of a bureaucracy. Bureaucratic structures that make specialized decisions may behave in 'deviant' ways. In special cases such as dedicated scientists in the laboratory, the Green Berets, or the U.S. Forestry Service (see Herbert Kaufman, 1960), this isolation may be beneficial and the deviance quite functional.[13] On the other hand, as we have seen, this same specialization may be dysfunctional. Entirely absent from the principal-agent model is the possibility that behavior changes occur latently in response to obedience to authority. While the theory of bureaucracy must address incentive problems (as in principal-agent problems), it should also consider the need to organize decision making so as to create functional (rather than dysfunctional) changes in personalities.

IX. CONCLUSION

Standard economic analysis is based upon the Benthamite view that individuals have fixed utilities which do not change. Stigler-Becker and Becker-Murphy have gone so far as to posit that these utilities do change, but that individuals are forward looking and thus foresee the changes that will occur. A more modern view of behavior, based on twentieth-century anthropology, psychology, and sociology is that individuals have utilities that do change and, in addition, they fail fully to foresee those changes or even recognize that they have occurred. This lecture has modeled such behavior in sequences of decisions, given examples from everyday life, indicated the situations in which such behavior is likely to occur, and, in some instances, suggested possible remedies. The theory of procrastination and obedience has applications to savings, crime, substance abuse, politics, and bureaucratic organizations.

References

Aronson, Elliot, *The Social Animal*, 4th edn., New York: Freeman, 1984.

Arrow, Kenneth J., *Social Choice and Individualistic Values*, 2nd edn., New Haven: Yale University Press, 1963.

Asch, Solomon E., 'Effects of Group Pressure upon the Modification and Distortion of Judgments' in Harold S. Guetzkow, ed., *Groups, Leadership and Men*, Pittsburgh: Carnegie Press, 1951.

---

[13] In the case of scientists, it may not just be individual but also group psychology under isolation that results in the odd scientific personalities exemplified by the 'mad scientist' image.

Asch, Solomon E., *Social Psychology*, Englewood Cliffs: Prentice-Hall, 1952.

Becker, Gary S., 'Crime and Punishment,' *Journal of Political Economy*, March/April 1968, 76, 169–217.

—— and Murphy, Kevin M., 'A Theory of Rational Addiction,' *Journal of Political Economy*, August 1988, 96, 675–700.

Borgida, Eugene and Nisbett, Richard, 'The Differential Impact of Abstract vs. Concrete Information on Decision,' *Journal of Applied Social Psychology*, July 1977, 7, 258–71.

Brown, Roger, *Social Psychology: The Second Edition*, New York: Macmillan, 1986.

Burka, Jane B. and Yuen, Lenora M., *Procrastination: Why You Do It, What to do About It*, Reading: Addison-Wesley, 1983.

Cagan, Phillip, *The Effect of Pension Plans on Aggregate Saving: Evidence from a Sample Survey*, NBER, Occasional Paper No. 95, New York: Columbia University Press, 1965.

Carpenter, Cheryl et al., *Kids, Drugs and Crime*, Lexington: D.C. Heath, 1988.

Dahlin, Michel R., 'From Poorhouse to Pension: The Changing View of Old Age in America, 1890–1929,' unpublished doctoral dissertation, Stanford University, 1983.

Deutscher, Isaac, *Stalin: A Political Biography*, Oxford: Oxford University Press, 1949.

Ellwood, David T. and Summers, Lawrence H., 'Poverty in America: Is Welfare the Answer or the Problem?,' in Sheldon H. Danziger and Daniel H. Weinberg, eds., *Fighting Poverty: What Works and What Doesn't*, Cambridge: Harvard University Press, 1986.

Feldman, Harvey W., Agar, Michael H. and Beschner, George M., *Angel Dust: An Ethnographic Study of PCP Users*, Lexington: D. C. Heath, 1979.

Fisher, Irving, *The Theory of Interest*, New York: Macmillan, 1930.

Galanter, Marc, 'Psychological Induction Into the Large-Group: Findings from a Modern Religious Sect,' *American Journal of Psychiatry*, December 1980, 137, 1574–1579.

——, *Cults: Faith, Healing, and Coercion*, New York: Oxford University Press, 1989.

—— et al., 'The "Moonies": A Psychological Study of Conversion and Membership in a Contemporary Religious Sect,' *American Journal of Psychiatry*, February 1979, 136, 165–70.

Gerstel, David U., *Paradise, Incorporated: Synanon*, Novato: Presidio Press, 1982.

Hirschman, Albert O., *Exit, Voice and Loyalty: Responses to Decline in Firms, Organizations and States*, Cambridge: Harvard University Press, 1970.

Holmstrom, Bengt R. and Tirole, Jean, 'The Theory of the Firm,' in Richard Schmalansee and Robert Willig, eds., *The Handbook of Industrial Organization*, Amsterdam: North-Holland, 1988.

Hurd, Michael D., 'Research on the Elderly: Economic Status, Retirement, Consumption, and Saving,' *Journal of Economic Literature*, June 1990, 28, 565–637.

Janis, Irving L., *Victims of Groupthink: A Psychological Study of Foreign-Policy Decisions and Fiascoes*, Boston: Houghton Mifflin, 1972.

Katona, George, *Private Pensions and Individual Savings*, Monograph No. 40, SRC, Institute for Social Research, Ann Arbor: University of Michigan, 1965.

Kaufman, Herbert, *The Forest Ranger: A Study in Administrative Behavior*, Baltimore: Johns Hopkins University Press, 1960.

Khrushchev, Nikita S., *Khrushchev Remembers: The Glasnost Tapes*, transl./ed., Jerrold L. Schector with V. V. Luchkov, Boston: Little, Brown, 1990.

MacLeod, Jay, *Ain't No Makin' It*, Boulder: Westview, 1988.

Matza, David, *Becoming Deviant*, Englewood Cliffs: Prentice-Hall, 1969.

——, *Delinquency and Drift*, New York: Wiley & Sons, 1964.

Merton, Robert K., *Social Theory and Social Structure, 1968 Enlarged Edition*, New York: Free Press, 1968.

Milgram, Stanley, *Obedience to Authority: An Experimental View*, New York: Harper and Row, 1975.

Milgram, Stanley, 'Some Conditions of Obedience and Disobedience to Authority,' in I. D. Steiner and M. Fishbein, eds., *Current Studies in Social Psychology*, New York: Holt, Rinehart, and Winston, 1965.

Milgrom, Paul R. and Roberts, John, 'An Economic Approach to Influence Activities in Organizations,' *American Journal of Sociology*, Suppl. 1988, *94*, S154–S179.

Munnell, Alicia H., 'Private Pensions and Savings: New Evidence,' *Journal of Political Economy*, October 1976, *84*, 1013–32.

Nisbett, Richard E. and Ross, Lee, *Human Inference: Strategies and Shortcomings of Social Judgment*, Englewood Cliffs: Prentice-Hall, 1980.

Ofshe, Richard, 'The Social Development of The Synanon Cult: The Managerial Strategy of Organizational Transformation,' *Sociological Analysis*, Summer 1980, *41*, 109–27.

Ouchi, William G., *Theory Z: How American Business Can Meet the Japanese Challenge*, Reading: Addison-Wesley, 1981.

Peters, Thomas J. and Waterman Jr., Robert H., *In Search of Excellence: Lessons from America's Best-Run Companies*, New York: Harper and Row, 1982.

Ross, Jerry and Staw, Barry M., 'Expo 86: An Escalation Prototype,' *Administrative Science Quarterly*, June 1986, *31*, 274–97.

Ross, Lee, 'Review of Arthur G. Miller, *The Obedience Experiments: A Case Study of Controversy in Social Sciences*, New York: Praeger, 1956,' *Contemporary Psychology*, February 1988, *33*, 101–04.

Schelling, Thomas C., 'Enforcing Rules on Oneself,' *Journal of Law, Economics and Organization*, Fall 1985, *1*, 357–73.

Schorr, Lisbeth B., *Within Our Reach*, New York: Doubleday, 1989.

Staw, Barry M., 'Knee-Deep in the Big Muddy: A Study of Escalating Commitment to a Chosen Course of Action,' *Organizational Behavior and Human Performance*, June 1976, *16*, 27–44.

—— and McClane, S., *Throwing Good Money After Bad: Escalation in a Banking Context*, Symposium presentation, Academy of Management, 44th Annual Meeting, Boston, 1984.

—— and Ross, Jerry, 'Behavior in Escalation Situations: Antecedents, Prototypes, and Solutions,' in Larry L. Cummings and Barry M. Staw eds., *Research in Organizational Behavior*, Vol. 9, Greenwich: JAI Press, 1987.

Stigler, George J. and Becker, Gary S., 'De Gustibus Non Est Disputandum,' *American Economic Review*, March 1977, *67*, 76–90.

Stotland, E. and Canon, Lance K., *Social Psychology: A Cognitive Approach*, Philadelphia: Saunders, 1972.

Thaler, Richard H. and Shefrin, Hersh, M., 'An Economic Theory of Self-Control,' *Journal of Political Economy*, April 1981, *89*, 392–406.

Venti, Steven F. and Wise, David A., 'IRAs and Savings,' NBER Working Paper No. 1879, Cambridge, April 1986.

—— and——, 'Have IRAs Increased U.S. Saving?: Evidence from Consumer Expenditure Surveys,' NBER Working Paper No. 2217, Cambridge, April 1987.

Whyte, William F., *Street Corner Society*, Chicago: University of Chicago Press, 1943.

Wilson, William J., *The Truly Disadvantaged: The Inner City, the Underclass and Public Policy*, Chicago: University of Chicago Press, 1987.

U.S. Bureau of the Census, *Statistical Abstract of the United States: 1987*, Washington: USGPO, 1987.

Looting: The Economic Underworld of Bankruptcy for Profit*

GEORGE A. AKERLOF [†]
University of California, Berkeley

PAUL M. ROMER
University of California, Berkeley

During the 1980s, a number of unusual financial crises occurred. In Chile, for example, the financial sector collapsed, leaving the government with responsibility for extensive foreign debts. In the United States, large numbers of government-insured savings and loans became insolvent—and the government picked up the tab. In Dallas, Texas, real estate prices and construction continued to boom even after vacancies had skyrocketed, and then suffered a dramatic collapse. Also in the United States, the junk bond market, which fueled the takeover wave, had a similar boom and bust.

In this paper, we use simple theory and direct evidence to highlight a common thread that runs through these four episodes. The theory suggests that this common thread may be relevant to other cases in which countries took on excessive foreign debt, governments had to bail out insolvent financial institutions, real estate prices increased dramatically and then fell, or new financial markets experienced a boom and bust. We describe the evidence, however, only for the cases of financial crisis in Chile, the thrift crisis in the United States, Dallas real estate and thrifts, and junk bonds.

* This work was previously published as George A. Akerlof and Paul M. Romer (1993), 'Looting: The Economic Underworld of Bankruptcy for Profit', *The Brookings Institution: Brookings Papers on Economic Activity,* *2: 1993.* Copyright © Brookings Institution Press. Reproduced by kind permission.

[†] We would like to give special thanks to James Pierce and William Black. In their capacities as executive director and deputy director of the National Commission on Financial Institutions, Reform, Recovery, and Enforcement, they have been pursuing an independent inquiry into the savings and loan crisis. They have reached many conclusions that we share and they have provided us with much useful corroborating evidence. We are also grateful to Halsey Rogers for invaluable research assistance. Paul Asquith, James Barth, Mark Carey, Roger Craine, Curtis Eaton, Pierre Fortin, Sebastian Edwards, Jeffrey Frankel, Jeffrey Gunther, Bronwyn Hall, Robert Hall, Elhanan Helpman, Richard Lipsey, Ken Rosen, Nate Rosenberg, Edward Safarian, Benjamin Stein, Nancy Wallace, Michael Wolfson, and Janet Yellen gave us useful comments and/or provided us with help in understanding the complexities of unfamiliar areas. None of the assertions we make should be attributed to any of these people, and we alone are responsible for any errors of fact or interpretation. This research was supported by the National Science Foundation, the Canadian Institute for Advanced Research, and the Russell Sage Working Group on Institutions and Development.

Our theoretical analysis shows that an economic underground can come to life if firms have an incentive to go broke for profit at society's expense (to loot) instead of to go for broke (to gamble on success). Bankruptcy for profit will occur if poor accounting, lax regulation, or low penalties for abuse give owners an incentive to pay themselves more than their firms are worth and then default on their debt obligations.

Bankruptcy for profit occurs most commonly when a government guarantees a firm's debt obligations. The most obvious such guarantee is deposit insurance, but governments also implicitly or explicitly guarantee the policies of insurance companies, the pension obligations of private firms, virtually all the obligations of large banks, student loans, mortgage finance of subsidized housing, and the general obligations of large or influential firms. These arrangements can create a web of companies that operate under soft budget constraints. To enforce discipline and to limit opportunism by shareholders, governments make continued access to the guarantees contingent on meeting specific targets for an accounting measure of net worth. However, because net worth is typically a small fraction of total assets for the insured institutions (this, after all, is why they demand and receive the government guarantees), bankruptcy for profit can easily become a more attractive strategy for the owners than maximizing true economic values.

If so, the normal economics of maximizing economic value is replaced by the topsy-turvy economics of maximizing current extractable value, which tends to drive the firm's economic net worth deeply negative. Once owners have decided that they can extract more from a firm by maximizing their present take, any action that allows them to extract more currently will be attractive—even if it causes a large reduction in the true economic net worth of the firm. A dollar in increased dividends today is worth a dollar to owners, but a dollar in increased future earnings of the firm is worth nothing because future payments accrue to the creditors who will be left holding the bag. As a result, bankruptcy for profit can cause social losses that dwarf the transfers from creditors that the shareholders can induce. Because of this disparity between what the owners can capture and the losses that they create, we refer to bankruptcy for profit as looting.

Unfortunately, firms covered by government guarantees are not the only ones that face severely distorted incentives. Looting can spread symbiotically to other markets, bringing to life a whole economic underworld with perverse incentives. The looters in the sector covered by the government guarantees will make trades with unaffiliated firms outside this sector, causing them to produce in a way that helps maximize the looters' current extractions with no regard for future losses. Rather than looking for business partners who will honor their contracts, the looters look for partners who will sign contracts that appear to have high current value if fulfilled but that will not—and could not—be honored.

We start with an abstract model that identifies the conditions under which looting takes place. In subsequent sections, we describe the circumstances surrounding the financial crisis in Chile and the thrift crisis in the United States, paying special attention to the regulatory and accounting details that are at the heart of our story. We then turn to an analysis of the real estate boom in Dallas, the center of activity for Texas thrifts. We construct a rational expectations model of the market for land in which investors infer economic fundamentals from market prices.[1] We then show how the introduction of even a relatively small number of looters can have a large effect on market prices.

In the last section, we examine the possible role of looting at savings and loans and insurance companies in manipulating the prices in the newly emerging junk bond market during the 1980s. In contrast to the Dallas land market, where the movements in prices appear to have been an unintended side effect of individual looting strategies, we argue that in the junk bond market, outsiders could have—and may have—coordinated the actions of some looters in a deliberate attempt to manipulate prices. Evidence suggests that this opportunity was understood and exploited by market participants. By keeping interest rates on junk bonds artificially low, this strategy could have significantly increased the fraction of firms that could profitably be taken over through a debt-financed acquisition.

Before turning to the theoretical model, we will place this paper within the context of the large literature that bears on the issues we address. The literature on the thrift crisis has two main strands: popular accounts[2] and economists' accounts.[3]

In contrast to popular accounts, economists' work is typically weak on details because the incentives economists emphasize cannot explain much of the behavior that took place. The typical economic analysis is based on moral hazard, excessive risk-taking, and the absence of risk sensitivity in the premiums charged for deposit insurance. This strategy has many colorful descriptions: 'heads I win, tails I break even'; 'gambling on resurrection'; and 'fourth-quarter football', to name just a few. Using an analogy with options pricing, economists developed a nice theoretical analysis of such excessive risk-taking strategies.[4] The problem with this explanation for events of the 1980s is that someone who is gambling that his thrift might actually make a profit would never operate the way many thrifts did, with total disregard for even the most basic principles of lending: maintaining reasonable documentation about loans, protecting against external fraud and abuse, verifying information on loan applications, even bothering to have borrowers fill out loan applications.[5] Examinations of the operation of many such thrifts show that the owners acted as if future losses were somebody else's problem. They were right.

Some economists' accounts acknowledge that something besides excessive risk-taking might have been taking place during the 1980s.[6] Edward Kane's comparison of the behavior at savings and loans (S&Ls) to a Ponzi scheme comes close to capturing some of the points that we emphasize.[7] Nevertheless, many economists still seem not to understand that a combination of circumstances in the 1980s made it very easy to loot a

---

[1] For such a model, see Grossman (1976).
[2] The popular books that we have found most useful for understanding the details of what actually took place in several notorious institutions are Adams (1990), Mayer (1990), O'Shea (1991), Pizzo, Fricker, and Muolo (1989), Robinson (1990), and Wilmsen (1991).
[3] See, for example, Kane (1989), White (1991), and Brumbaugh, Carron, and Litan (1989).
[4] See Merton (1978).
[5] Black (1993*b*) forcefully makes this point.
[6] See, for example, Benjamin Friedman's comments on the paper by Brumbaugh, Carron, and Litan (1989).
[7] Kane (1989).

financial institution with little risk of prosecution. Once this is clear, it becomes obvious that high-risk strategies that would pay off only in some states of the world were only for the timid. Why abuse the system to pursue a gamble that might pay off when you can exploit a sure thing with little risk of prosecution?

Our description of a looting strategy amounts to a sophisticated version of having a limited liability corporation borrow money, pay it into the private account of the owner, and then default on its debt. There is, of course, a large literature in corporate finance that emphasizes the strategies that equity holders can use to exploit debt-holders when shareholders have limited liability.[8] We have nothing to add to the analysis of this problem in the context of transactions between people or firms in the private sector. The thrust of this literature is that optimizing individuals will not repeatedly lend on terms that let them be exploited, so if lending occurs, some kind of mechanism (such as reputation, collateral, or debt covenants) that protects the lenders must be at work.

However, this premise may not apply to lending arrangements undertaken by the government. Governments sometimes do things that optimizing agents would not do, and, because of their power to tax, can persist long after any other person or firm would have been forced to stop because of a lack of resources.

AN ABSTRACT MODEL OF LOOTING

A simple three-period model can capture the main points in the analysis of bankruptcy for profit. In this section, we use it to establish three basic results. First, limited liability gives the owners of a corporation the potential to exploit lenders. Second, if debt contracts let this happen, owners will intentionally drive a solvent firm bankrupt. Third, when the owners of a firm drive it bankrupt, they can cause great social harm, just as looters in a riot cause total losses that are far greater than the private gains they capture.

We warn the reader that our approach in setting up the model in this section differs from the approach used in most other examinations of contracts. The typical analysis starts with a description of an economic environment and characterizes efficient contracts. Inefficient contracts are presumed not to arise in the market, or at least not to persist for long.

We start from the assumption that the relevant creditor, the government, agrees to an inefficient contract and can persist in it for some time. We offer no explicit theory of why the government does this. Our goal in the body of the paper is merely to characterize the private sector behavior that the inefficient government contracts and regulations can induce. Only in the conclusion do we hint at the more complicated question of why governments do what they do.

In addition to assuming that contracts are inefficient, our basic model relies on perfect certainty and the presence of legal strategies for looting. Perfect certainty makes the models simpler, but more importantly, it yields a starker contrast between the looting (go broke) strategies that we emphasize and the subsidized risk-taking (go-for-broke) strategies that have so far dominated most previous explanations by economists of the

---

[8] See, for example, Brealey and Myers (1984, pp. 501–03).

S&L crisis.[9] In the first presentation of the model, the assumption that only legal transactions occur is also useful in bringing out the stark contrast between the theory of looting and the theory of go-for-broke. We subsequently show how the essence of the basic model carries over to a model in which owners may actually commit fraud.

Before presenting the three-period model, it is useful to make our basic point in the simplest possible setting and to establish some conventions that simplify our exposition. Let V denote the true value or net worth of a limited liability corporation. Suppose that the government agrees to lend any amount of money to this corporation, subject to the restriction that the owners cannot pay themselves more than M. A single owner/ manager then faces a very simple decision. If M is less than V, the owner operates his corporation according to standard principles of value maximization. The government offer makes no difference to the owner. But if M is greater than V, the owner borrows enough from the government to pay M, knowing full well that the corporation will default on this debt in the future. Worse still, in this case, the owner has no incentive to ensure that the corporation is well managed.

This, in essence, is our story of what happened at many thrifts. The details come in describing the regulations, accounting conventions, and opportunities for illegal payments that created situations in which M exceeded V. Three aspects of this story deserve comment. In what follows, we assume that there is no divergence of interests between managers and owners, unless we explicitly state otherwise. We do this partly to simplify the exposition, but also because it accurately characterizes the situation at many thrifts where the most important abuses took place. A crucial change in the regulations in the 1980s made it possible for a single person to own a thrift or for a parent company to own a thrift as a subsidiary. As one would expect, abusive strategies are easier to implement when ownership is concentrated and managers are tightly controlled by owners. In fact, this is why bank regulators had enforced rules prohibiting concentrated ownership until the 1980s. There were other thrifts with widely dispersed ownership and serious divergences between the interests of managers (who wanted to keep their jobs and reputations) and owners (who would have made much more money if the managers had looted their institutions). They missed out on the action that we try to document.

A second part of this story—that the government is a direct lender to the firm—is a pure convenience. In practice, private individuals lend their deposits to a financial institution and the government guarantees the debts of the institution. For our purposes, this is equivalent to assuming that the depositor holds government debt and that the government lends money directly to the thrift. In either case, the result is the same when the thrift defaults. It is the government that suffers the loss.

The third part of this story—that wealth is shifted from the thrift to the private portfolio of the owner by means of dividend payments—is an expositional shortcut that should not be taken literally. In fact, there are many sweetheart deals whereby an individual or corporate owner of a thrift can extract resources from it. These other ways

---

[9] See Craine (1992) for a recent of a model with uncertainty that can capture the essence of the excessive risk-taking strategy.

are typically illegal, but they can also be difficult to regulate and prosecute. Importantly from the point of view of the owners, they can substantially increase the total amount of wealth that can be extracted from a thrift. One example suggests the range of possibilities. In 1988, the Southmark Corporation exchanged a group of companies for some real estate holdings of San Jacinto Savings and Loan of Houston, Texas, a wholly owned subsidiary of Southmark. Because this was a transaction between affiliated companies, it required regulatory approval. Based on a fairness opinion provided by an investment banking firm that valued the contributed companies at \$140.6 million, regulators approved the trade for a comparable quantity of real estate from San Jacinto. By 1990, it had become clear that the value of the contributed corporations was actually negative.[10]

The General Model

We can now present the abstract model that forms the core of the analysis. It has no uncertainty and only three periods, dated zero, 1, and 2. The given market interest rate is r_1 between periods zero and 1, and r_2 between periods 1 and 2.

A thrift begins life in period zero with an investment by the owners of an amount W_0. The thrift acquires deposit liabilities L_0 and purchases a bundle of assets, A, whose initial value is $A_0 = W_0 + L_0$. The thrift is subject to a net worth or 'capital' requirement imposed by the government. This specifies that the net worth W_0 must be greater than or equal to cA_0 for some constant c. The assets yield a cash payment of $\rho_1(A)$ dollars in period 1 and $\rho_2(A)$ dollars in period 2.

For simplicity, assume that the investment in the assets is not liquid and that the thrift does not purchase any new assets after period zero. In period 1, the thrift receives cash payments $\rho_1(A)$ and pays a dividend Δ_1 to its owners. To accommodate these transactions, the thrift adjusts its deposit liabilities. After these transactions, the deposit liabilities of the thrift will be the deposits from the previous period with accumulated interest, $(1 + r_1) L_0$, minus the cash payment $\rho_1(A)$, plus dividends Δ_1. This means that the thrift can borrow—that is, take in new deposits—to make the dividend payment Δ_1.

In period 2, the investment in the asset makes its final payment and the thrift can be liquidated. The thrift receives payments $\rho_2(A)$. Deposit liabilities from period 1 with accumulated interest will be $(1 + r_2)[(1 + r_1)L_0 - \rho_1(A) + \Delta_1]$. The terminal net worth is the difference between the value of its assets and its liabilities.

If there were no limited liability and no deposit insurance, the decision problem facing the initial investors in the thrift would be to choose the bundle of assets A to maximize the present discounted value of the payments from the thrift. (Because we shall later compare the present value of the optimal stream of earnings V^* to the limit on dividend payments, which is most naturally expressed in period-one units, it also makes sense to express V^* as the period-one present value.) According to the preceding description of the earnings stream,

---

[10] *FDIC v. Milken* (1991, pp. 76–77).

$$V^* = \max_{A,\Delta_1} \frac{\{\rho_2(A) - (1 + r_2)[(1 + r_1)L_0 - \rho_1(A) + \Delta_1]\}}{1 + r_2} + \Delta_1 \tag{1}$$

subject to $0 \leq cA_0 \leq W_0.$

Because the two terms involving the dividend payment in period 1 cancel, the only important choice variable in this maximization problem is the assets purchased in period zero. Because the two terms involving dividends cancel, this equation can be simplified to yield

$$V^* = \max_A [\rho_2(A)/(1 + r_2)] + \rho_1(A) - (1 + r_1)L_0. \tag{2}$$

subject to $0 \leq cA_0 \leq W_0.$

Now suppose that this thrift is a limited liability corporation. Further suppose that the government guarantees the liabilities of the thrift and imposes an upper bound $M(A)$ on the amount of dividends that the thrift can pay to its owners in period 1. As the notation suggests, this upper bound could be a function of the assets that the thrift holds. In this case, the maximization problem facing the owners of the thrift becomes

$$E = \max_{A, \Delta_1, \Delta_2} [\Delta_2/(1 + r_2)] + \Delta_1 \tag{3}$$

subject to

$0 \leq cA_0 \leq W_0,$

$\Delta_1 \leq M(A),$

$\Delta_2 \leq \max\{0, \rho_2(A) - (1 + r_2)[(1 + r_1)L_0 - \rho_1(A) + \Delta_1]\}$

In this expression, we introduce the new symbol E, the value of the owners' equity, because it can differ from the true economic value of the thrift, V^*.

To state the basic result of this section, we need one final definition. Let M^* denote the maximum of $M(A)$ over all choices of A satisfying $0 \leq cA_0 \leq W_0$. M^* is the maximum amount of dividends that can be extracted in period 1.

Proposition

1. *If M^* is less than or equal to V^*—the period 1 maximum value of the thrift's flow of payments—the owners of the thrift choose A to maximize the true value of the thrift.*
2. *If M^* is greater than V^*, the owners of the thrift choose A to maximize $M(A)$. They pay dividends in period 1 equal to M^* and default on the obligations of the thrift in period 2.*

Proof. The economic intuition behind this result is very simple. If the owners cannot pay themselves more than the thrift is worth in period 1, then the net worth of the firm is positive in the second period, and the choice of 0 in the maximum for second period dividends becomes irrelevant. In this case, the maximization problem in equation 3 with limited liability reduces to the maximization problem in equation 1 without limited liability that defines V^*.

If, on the other hand, the owners can pay themselves dividends greater than the true economic value of the thrift, they will do so, even if this requires that they invest in projects with negative net present value. By the adding up constraints, when they can take out more than the thrift is worth, they cause the thrift to default on its obligations in period 2. If they are going to default, the owners do not care if the investment project has a negative net present value because the government suffers all of the losses on the project. As a result, the owners choose A solely with a view toward maximizing the amount of dividends that they can take out in period 1.

(To derive this result formally, substitute the upper bound on dividends in period 2 into the maximand in equation 3 and reverse the order of the two maximization operators.)

Two observations follow immediately from this result. First, if the owners can extract more than the true economic value of the thrift, owners with a positive net worth will voluntarily choose to go bankrupt by extracting resources from it. Bankruptcy for them is a choice, not something that is forced on them by circumstances. Second, when owners choose A to maximize M^*, they may invest in negative net present value projects. If so, the gain to the owners from the looting strategy is strictly less than the payouts by the government. As a result, society incurs a net loss.

These observations illustrate most starkly the difference between the strategy we emphasize—bankruptcy for profit—and the more familiar strategies that depend on excessive risk-taking. According to our strategy, the preferred outcome for the owners of a solvent thrift is the one in which the thrift goes bankrupt. When the owners succeed in extracting more than the true economic value V^*, they will exhibit precisely the kind of indifference to how the thrift is managed that one sees when one examines the daily operations of many bankrupt thrifts. According to the alternative strategy of excessive risk-taking, the preferred outcome for the owners is the one in which the gamble pays off and the thrift remains solvent. If owners were following this strategy, they would be concerned about the quality of their loans and the size of the operating expenses that they incur, because every dollar of loan loss or expense represents a subtraction from their gains if the gamble pays off.

These results also justify our use of the term looting. The bankruptcy for profit strategy can induce large losses to society as a whole because the dependence of M on A can encourage thrift owners to invest in negative net present value projects. The next section shows how these kinds of incentives were created by the regulations in place during the 1980s.

The model so far has assumed that $M(A)$, the limit on payments in period 1, is given only by regulatory and accounting rules, so that all choices made by the thrifts are legal. Our examples of looting, however, preponderantly involve illegal activities. In part, the high proportion of illegal activities relative to legal ones in our examples reflects a bias in our sources, which are mainly derived from evidence in legal proceedings. The looting that was legal or impossible to prosecute never surfaced in court or regulatory proceedings. But, in fact, we believe that the opportunities for legal looting were relatively small relative to the opportunities that include a large variety of ingenious side payments, with varying chances of detection, criminal prosecution, and civil recovery. The model should therefore be extended to include both illegal and legal means of looting.

To do this, let F denote the fraudulent activities undertaken by managers. We make two assumptions about F. First, an increase in F leads to an increase in the expected cost $C(F)$ associated with the risk of being prosecuted or sued by the authorities. These expected costs will depend on the probabilities of losing in court and the cost of losing in a criminal or civil case. They will also depend on the attitudes toward risk of the managers and owners, as well as the reputation costs associated with legal action.

The second effect of an increase in F is an increase in the amount of total resources that could be extracted by owners. Typically, these resources would not take the form of explicit dividend payments, but they still represent reductions in the net worth of the institutions. From the point of view of the true position of the balance sheet of the thrift, they have the same effect as dividend payments. Thus, we can expand our previous expression for the limits on extracted wealth in the first period $M(A)$ and write $M(A, F)$, with the understanding that M is increasing in F.

With these extensions, our model can now be written as follows:

$$E = \max_{A, F, \Delta_1, \Delta_2} \Delta_2 / (1 + r_2) + \Delta_1 - C(F) \tag{4}$$

subject to

$$0 \le cA_0 \le W_0,$$
$$\Delta_1 \le M(A, F),$$
$$\Delta_2 \le \max\{0, \, \rho_2(A) - (1 + r_2)[(1 + r_1)L_0 - \rho_1(A) + \Delta_1]\}.$$

The basic intuition from the previous model carries over into this extended model. A critical value separates the economics of value maximization from the economics of bankruptcy for profit. As above, let V^* denote the maximized value of dividends when there is no scope for looting. In this case, let M^* denote the value of the maximum of $M(A, F) - C(F)$ over A and F. This quantity is the total monetary value that can be extracted from the thrift minus the expected legal cost associated with the chosen level of fraud. If M^* is greater than V^*, owners will loot; that is, they choose A and F to maximize $M(A, F) - C(F)$. If, on the other hand, M^* is less than V^*, they set F equal to zero, choose A to maximize value, and collect V^*.

In summary, when V^* is small, or when the amount that can be extracted from firms with little chance of prosecution is large, looting and illegality are likely to occur. Regulation, proper accounting, and effective enforcement of the law are necessary to ensure that V^* exceeds M^*. There must be limits on legal payments consistent with true economic returns. In addition, accounting and regulatory definitions must make illegal payments easy to detect, prosecute, and recover.

EXAMPLES OF LOOTING

For financial institutions, one rule that limits dividend and other kinds of payouts from a thrift is derived from the requirement that in every period, the net worth of the thrift must exceed the capital specified by regulators. In our three-period example, the dividend limit, M, in period 1 is determined by the requirement that after dividends have been paid, the remaining net worth of the thrift must exceed the constant c times the book value of the asset. Thus in the model where thrifts are operating legally, $M(A)$ can be derived exactly from regulatory constraints and accounting definitions.

Example 1: Inflated Net Worth

We begin with a point about accounting rules that is so obvious that it would not be worth stating had it not been so widely neglected in discussions of the crisis in the savings and loan industry. If net worth is inflated by an artificial accounting entry for goodwill, incentives for looting will be created. Because net worth imposes the critical limit on the ability to extract value from a thrift, each additional dollar of artificial net worth translates into an additional dollar of net worth that can be extracted from the thrift. In particular, if the artificial increase in net worth is bigger than the total required capital, the conditions for looting will be satisfied. This possibility was enhanced because the capital requirement, c, was substantially reduced during the 1980s.

During the 1980s, an artificial increment to regulatory net worth could arise for several different reasons. In circumstances in which one thrift purchased another thrift with a negative net worth, 'goodwill' was created that had exactly the effect of the increment described here. Alternatively, many thrifts were allowed to continue in operation after their true net worth was substantially negative. According to regulatory accounting principles, an artificial increment to net worth was created to remove the legal obligation that regulators would otherwise have had to close such a thrift. (We discuss both goodwill accounting and capital requirements below.)

Overstated net worth by itself does not induce the owners of a thrift to make bad investment decisions, but bankruptcy for profit removes any incentive to manage a thrift carefully. As a result, net losses to society from mismanagement of the thrift are likely.

Example 2: Riding the Yield Curve

Suppose that a thrift is allowed no goodwill in calculating its net worth, but is given the opportunity to invest in assets that generate exaggerated first-period accounting income. Then the thrift will once again be able to pursue bankruptcy for profit.

To use a simple example, consider long bonds. Because there is no uncertainty in the model, arbitrage implies that a two-period long bond issued at par in period zero would have to pay a coupon, r_L, satisfying

$$(1 + r_L) + (1 + r_2)r_L = (1 + r_1)(1 + r_2). \tag{5}$$

Neglecting the cross terms r_2r_L and r_1r_2 gives the usual approximation from a pure expectations theory of the yield curve, $r_L = (r_1 + r_2)/2$. We will be interested in the case where spot rates are increasing over time, so assume that $r_2 > r_L > r_1$.

According to accounting conventions that are still used for a bank or thrift that plans to hold long bonds to maturity, a long bond held in the investment portfolio of a thrift would be valued at par in period 1, even though the market value of the bond would be strictly less than par because interest rates are rising over time. (All that is required for this accounting treatment is an intention by the thrift to hold the bond to maturity.) According to this convention, the accounting return on the investment in the bond is its coupon r_L, which by our assumptions is strictly greater than the true economic return r_1. If the difference is large enough to satisfy

$$r_L - r_1 - c \geq 0,\tag{6}$$

the conditions required to pursue bankruptcy for profit will be satisfied. For many thrifts, the effective value of c could be very small, so that only a small differential between the accounting rate of return r_L and the true economic rate of return r_1 on assets would be needed to make bankruptcy for profit attractive.

Under these circumstances, all a thrift would need to do to exploit bankruptcy for profit is to raise its funds at the prevailing short rate (for example, in the market for certificates of deposit), invest in higher-yielding long bonds, and pay out all of its accounting earnings $(r_L - r_1)A$ as dividends. If $r_L - r_1$ is equal to c, then in the first period, the owners will be able to use artificial profits to extract their initial investment, $W_0 = cA$, without violating the net worth requirements specified by the regulations. If $r_L - r_1$ is greater than c (or if the yield differential persists for several periods in a multiperiod model), the owners can take out more than the value of their initial investment.

When period 2 arrives, the thrift will be obligated to pay a rate of return on its deposits that exceeds the yield on its bonds. If the owners have been able to extract more than the current value of their initial investment, then the thrift will not be able to make good on this commitment and the government will have to take over its obligations.

Note that in contrast to the first example, the rule determining dividend payouts in this example does give thrifts an incentive to purchase a particular kind of asset, but it is not one with a negative net present value. Hence, as in the first example, the accounting rules do not give owners a direct incentive to make a negative net present value investment. As in all cases of bankruptcy for profit, however, the owners have no stake in future gains and losses at a thrift, and therefore will be indifferent to actions that cause social losses.

It is tempting to conclude that this example represents an instance in which a thrift takes a gamble and exposes itself to interest rate risk, but this interpretation is misleading. In this perfect certainty model, there is no risk. The outcome here is perfectly foreseeable. Moreover, as noted above, the outcome that is preferred for the owners is the one in which the thrift is left insolvent, not the one in which it has a positive net worth.

The strategy of riding an upward-sloping yield curve that is illustrated here is not one that was particularly important during the 1980s, but it does illustrate the essence of the point that we are trying to make. If regulations make use of accounting values that differ from true economic or market values, this creates opportunities for abusive behavior that can be consistent with the letter of the law.

Preventing this kind of abuse is also very simple. If all long bonds are marked to market in period 1, no artificial accounting earnings are generated. It is a revealing fact about the regulatory process and about the accounting profession that historical prices may still be used to value government securities that are to be held to maturity.[11]

Example 3: Acquisition, Development, and Construction Loans
For a thrift that is interested in bending accounting rules and overstating net worth, acquisition, development, and construction (ADC) loans are an example of a thrift asset that offered particularly rich opportunities for booking artificial accounting earnings. Real estate investments also created opportunities for owners to make side payments to themselves in a way that was difficult for regulators to monitor and for law authorities to prosecute successfully.

In the most extreme cases, an ADC loan took the following form. A thrift would make a no-recourse loan to a land developer, offering enough money to purchase a tract of land, construct a building, pay the developer a development fee, pay the thrift an initial origination fee on the loan (typically about 2.5 percent of the loan amount), and pay the interest on the loan for the first several years of the project. The thrift could inflate its accounting income for several years by finding an unscrupulous individual with little development experience, and making the following offer. Without putting any money into the project, the developer could borrow money and collect development fees and salary income for several years. In return, the developer would agree to 'pay' the thrift some of its own money in what appeared to be payments on a loan with a very high interest rate. Because the developer would have little or no experience in development, the project would have a negative net present value. This fact alone would be sufficient to ensure an eventual default on the loan by the developer in most cases. The unrealistically high interest rate on the loan would virtually guarantee a default. Because the loan would be a no-recourse loan, the developer could walk away from the project keeping his fees, without putting his personal wealth at stake.

Neglecting for simplicity the origination fees (which technically would generate income in period zero), we can treat this loan as an asset that pays a very high accounting return in period 1 equal to the interest rate on the loan. As in the last example, all that is required for looting to be profitable is that the analog of the inequality in equation 6 be satisfied. The excess accounting profit that the thrift can earn over its cost of funds need only be large enough to exceed the capital requirement, c, which, as we have already noted, could have been quite small.

In contrast to riding the yield curve, this arrangement is very difficult to police because real estate projects that are under construction are inherently difficult to value. Because reserves are created to make the initial interest payments when the loan was taken out, the loan cannot go into default in period 1. If a suspicious regulator or

---

[11] See Floyd Norris, 'Bond-Accounting Shift Is Approved,' *New York Times*, April 14, 1993, p. C1.

accountant challenges the value of the collateral backing up the loan, the thrift owner can arrange for a cooperating appraiser to certify that the value of the project is sufficient to protect against loss on the loan. If necessary, the thrift (or a cooperating thrift) can make a loan to a new developer to purchase the project from the first developer at a profit, 'proving' with a market price the appraisal's validity. In period 2, the developer defaults, the 'highly profitable' thrift suddenly is insolvent, and the government must provide funds to pay off the depositors.

We want to emphasize that an honest developer would not enter into this kind of agreement with the thrift. Even if the developer cannot be held personally responsible for the loan once the project defaults, a default on a major project would damage the reputation of a reputable developer and limit the ability to borrow in the future, especially once the abusive nature of the arrangements becomes clear. As a result, the owners of the thrift have an incentive to seek out the most unscrupulous 'developers,' the ones that it can count on to report grossly overstated interest payments in early years and then to default in subsequent years. Because high dividend payments are likely to attract regulators' attention, other means of extracting money from the thrift are in most cases more profitable, such as no-recourse financing for an overvalued purchase of land from the owners or participation in other sweetheart deals. All of these activities entail some risk of prosecution if they are done flagrantly, but if they are undertaken with care, they are very difficult to prosecute. The perverse incentives created for the owners of the thrift will propagate through the economy, creating misleading price signals and perverse incentives in other parts of the economy. The owners of the thrift pursue bankruptcy for profit, but now, so do the symbiotic developers that it attracts.

In this case, it is clear that bankruptcy for profit fully lives up to our definition of looting. The development projects that are undertaken in this kind of arrangement would typically have a net present value that was substantially negative. In Texas, some of the completed projects that went into default were of such poor quality that the buildings that had been built were simply bulldozed.

The Financial Crisis in Chile

In the previous example of riding the yield curve, the depository institution holds assets that pay a high current yield. Its liabilities, by contrast, have a low current yield. The yield spread results in high current accounting income that can be paid out to shareholders. This current accounting income is, however, not the true economic return on the portfolio, because part of that high current yield merely offsets an expected depreciation in the capital value of the long-lived assets. The anticipated fall in asset values is associated with an expected increase in short-term interest rates.

In this section, we describe a related case, one in which the anticipated decrease in asset values comes from an expected depreciation in exchange rates. In this case, the artificial accounting income can be generated by a mismatch between the currencies in which assets and liabilities are denominated instead of a mismatch in the duration of the assets and liabilities.

To show how a bank can exploit an expected depreciation of the currency under a fixed exchange rate system, suppose that the following four conditions hold. First, the assets of the bank are denominated in the home currency (which we will call pesos). Second, the liabilities of the bank are denominated in the foreign currency (which we will call dollars). Third, there is an expected devaluation of the peso relative to the dollar (that is, an expected fall in the number of dollars offered in exchange for one peso) that is mirrored in a nominal interest rate on peso loans that exceeds the nominal interest rate on dollar loans. Fourth, dollar lenders charge a bankruptcy premium on their loans to the bank that is less than actuarially fair because they have confidence that the peso-issuing government will assume responsibility for the dollar-denominated borrowing by its banks.

Under these conditions, the bank can consider the difference between interest payments in pesos and interest payments in dollars as current profit, and these can be paid out as bank earnings. Of course, this profit is illusory, because the high rate on pesos relative to dollars reflects the expected devaluation. A correct system of accounting would set aside all of the extra earnings from the interest rate premium as a reserve against future losses in asset values arising from changes in the exchange rate. But if the official policy is that no change in the exchange rate will occur, it is difficult for government regulators to insist that firms accrue this kind of reserve.

The preceding outline suggests how fixed exchange rates and misleading accounting can encourage a pattern of bankruptcy for profit that ultimately results in an economy-wide financial crisis. No actual financial crisis will ever be quite this simple because bank regulators will try to stop the bankruptcy for profit scheme that we have just described; furthermore, illegal, as well as legal, means will be used to extract payments. It is therefore useful to review at least one actual devaluation to see whether it is the regulators or the looters who come out ahead. Because there are several excellent accounts of the Chilean financial crisis of 1982 that leave relatively little ambiguity about the facts, we focus on this case.[12]

In 1979, the reformers of the Chilean economy had achieved considerable success. Inflation in the consumer price index (CPI) had fallen to 38 percent per year, from an annual peak of more than 600 percent in 1973. Real gross domestic product had grown by 30 percent over the four-year period from 1975 to 1979.[13] Structural changes involving reduced protection of domestic industry had resulted in a rapid expansion of the manufacturing sector.

Emboldened by these successes, the economic ministers decided to go one step further. They would end inflation by slowing the rate of devaluation of the currency and then fixing the peso–dollar exchange rate. In June 1979, this permanent rate was established at 39 pesos to the dollar.[14] Over the next nine months, restrictions on capital inflows and outflows were greatly relaxed, including restrictions on banks'

---

[12] See Edwards and Edwards (1991), de la Cuadra and Valdes (1992), McKinnon (1991), and Velasco (1991).

[13] Edwards and Edwards (1991, table 2–1, p. 28, and table 1–3, p. 12).

[14] Edwards and Edwards (1991, p. 38).

foreign liabilities. But for reasons mainly outside the operation of the financial sector, the pegging of the exchange rate proved to be unrealistic. Inflation had a momentum of its own and could not be halted immediately. In particular, union wages were fully indexed to past inflation. Thus even if inflation had abruptly stopped (as the planners had hoped), wages would have still risen substantially because of past increases in the CPI. In fact, both wages and the general price level continued to rise even after the exchange rate was pegged. Inflation did indeed decelerate, but from the third quarter of 1979 to the last quarter of 1981, the real exchange rate (in pesos per dollar, adjusted for inflation in each country) appreciated by 50 percent. Blue collar real wages grew by 20 percent from May 1979 to May 1981. For 1981 as a whole, the CPI inflation rate was 9.9 percent.[15]

The peso exchange rate thus became steadily more and more overvalued, and as time passed, there were growing reasons to expect the official policy of a fixed exchange rate to collapse with a devaluation of the peso. There were virtually no restrictions on the flows of capital, so the peso interest rate should have rapidly approached something close to the rate implied by uncovered interest parity—the dollar rate plus the expected rate of depreciation. In the absence of any further regulations on bank behavior, the banks could have borrowed dollars and loaned in pesos, as described above, with the difference between the interest received and the interest paid considered as current income.

Bank regulators were aware of exchange rate risk and required that banks match their dollar assets with their dollar liabilities.[16] Banks responded, in effect, by converting exchange rate risk into credit risk that regulators could not monitor. To see how this is possible, consider a simple example. Suppose that a bank borrows from a major international bank at the London Interbank Offered Rate (LIBOR). The international bank is willing to lend to the Chilean bank without charging a default premium because it is sure that the Chilean government would assume the debts of the bank if it were to fail. Suppose that a firm borrows dollars from the bank and invests the proceeds in peso-denominated financial assets. This firm is now in a position to engage in looting based on the mismatch between the currencies in which its assets and liabilities are denominated. It enjoys a large spread between its current income and its cost of borrowing; it can therefore report substantial current earnings and pay these out as dividends, with the expectation that it will default on its dollar loans when the peso finally depreciates.

Of course, any bank that is trying to maximize economic value will not lend to the firm on terms that would make looting possible; but the bank in our example is willing to do so because it too has an incentive to loot. As in the case of a thrift engaged in ADC lending with a cooperating developer, the bank and the borrower have the same incentive to pursue bankruptcy for profit. To make the example concrete, let us apply our example to the interest rates prevailing from 1979 to 1981, during the period when exchange rates were fixed in Chile. The annual rate on peso loans from Chilean banks was around 50 percent, the rate on dollar loans about 20 percent, and the LIBOR rate roughly 15 percent.[17] Given these rates, the bank in our example can lend dollars to the

---

[15] Edwards and Edwards (1991, table 3–9, p. 75; table 6–7, p. 158; and table 2–1, p. 28).
[16] de la Cuadra and Valdes (1992, pp. 76–77).   [17] McKinnon (1991, table 3–5, p. 39).

firm at a 20 percent annual interest rate, knowing full well that the firm will default on its loans when the currency is realigned. The bank now has dollar liabilities on its books on which it pays 15 percent interest and matching dollar assets (as required by the regulations) on which it collects 20 percent interest. (Banks were presumably limited in their ability to charge higher rates because an implausibly large spread over LIBOR would have been a clear signal that something other than a standard arms-length transaction was taking place.) Until the depreciation takes place, the bank can report strong profits and pay large dividends. At the same time, the firm can report as income the spread between its 20 percent cost of funds on dollar loans and its 50 percent return on its peso loans.

As the yield-curve and ADC examples given above show, this strategy requires that both the bank and the firm be able to report and pay out artificial earnings that are greater than the total equity that the owners have in each corporation. The inequality in equation 6 shows that this will be possible if the yield differential times the holding period (which in this case is the expected time until the depreciation) is greater than the ratio of net worth to total assets. It does not take a big spread between the dollar and peso interest rates for a bank to be able to meet this condition because net worth-to-asset ratios for banks are so small. It was not the case, however, that economic conditions forced all banks into bankruptcy. The conservatively managed Banco del Estado de Chile and the local affiliates of foreign banks did not follow a strategy of bankruptcy for profit and did not become insolvent when the devaluation took place.

If a firm has substantial equity, and regulators can monitor and limit the debt-to-equity ratio for the borrowers from banks, it can take a large interest rate spread to make looting profitable. But for firms that are already on the verge of bankruptcy, it takes virtually no spread at all. In Chile in 1981, there were many such firms. Faced with an appreciating exchange rate, very large rises in real wages, and double-digit real interest rates (that is, peso interest rates minus the peso CPI inflation rate), many Chilean entrepreneurs had little remaining capital in their enterprises. Any such enterprise that could remain alive in the absence of the peso depreciation, but that would fail when the peso depreciated, would have been willing to pay a premium above the dollar rate of interest for a dollar loan. These firms would have preferred dollar loans to peso loans, as long as the dollar rate of interest did not exceed the peso rate of interest. As a result, the banks had a source of demand for dollar loans that induced them to borrow abroad from New York banks, who were anxious to lend to them at little more than the dollar interest rate. Thus, for example, the construction industry increased its dollar-denominated debt by 284 percent in 1981 alone.[18] The increased demand for dollar loans by Chilean banks is shown by a ten-fold increase in their foreign indebtedness from 1978 to 1982, accounting for 70 percent of the total increase in Chilean private indebtedness over this period.[19]

As described, this arrangement gives the bulk of the profits from looting to the firms that can exploit the yield spread. Judging only from the interest rate data, banks

[18] See de la Cuadra and Valdes (1992, p. 86).
[19] See Edwards and Edwards (1991, table 3–8, p. 71).

apparently were able to capture relatively little of the loot. This conclusion, however, is based on the mistaken assumption that the banks were not related to the borrowers. In fact, most large Chilean banks were part of a business *grupo* (or interlocking group of firms like a Japanese *keiretsu*). By having a bank in the group lend to a firm in the same *grupo* and then having the firm lend at the peso rate, the owners could capture the entire spread of 35 percentage points between LIBOR and the domestic peso rate. Retrospective analyses have attached great importance to the role of the banks in such self-dealing between the banks and the firms in the corresponding group.[20] According to James Tybout, *grupo* firms borrowed from their affiliated banks at preferential rates, and purchased equity in affiliated companies to boost share prices, thus transferring gains to their owners through share price appreciation rather than through direct dividend payments.[21] In addition, loans by banks to *grupo* firms were one of the two largest uses of foreign dollar borrowings, matched only by trade financing.

THE LOOTING OF SAVINGS AND LOANS DURING THE 1980S

This section relates the abstract discussion of looting to the facts concerning the savings and loan crisis in the United States. We make three basic points. First, changes in regulations and accounting conventions encouraged the strategies for looting described in the theoretical section. They also increased the amount of wealth that could be extracted by someone who was willing to incur any given level of risk of prosecution. We document the most important changes in regulation and connect them to the models. Second, we examine detailed accounts of the savings and loan crisis for indications that looting did indeed take place. We find abundant evidence of investments designed to yield artificially high accounting profits and strategies designed to pay large sums to officers and shareholders. Third, by adding up the available accounts of looting, it becomes clear that looting could have been a significant contributor to the S&L crisis.

Changes in Regulations

At the beginning of the 1980s, the U.S. savings and loan industry was in deep trouble. As has been widely noted, regulations had induced S&Ls to hold a mismatched portfolio of assets and liabilities that exposed them to significant interest rate risk. By 1980, many honestly run S&Ls had a negative net worth. The industry as a whole was under water by more than $100 billion.[22] The deposit insurance fund did not have enough assets to cover its liabilities.

The federal government had the choice of letting the insurance fund fail, making up the difference with tax revenue, or changing the rules. Letting depositors lose their deposits was unthinkable. Explicitly bailing out the insurance fund was inconvenient. So

---

[20] See Edwards and Edwards (1991, pp. 100–01) and the discussion by McKinnon (1991, p. 40).
[21] Tybout (1986, p. 378).   [22] See Kane (1989, p. 75) and White (1991, p. 77).

the rules were changed. These rules were changed in two principal ways: first, by amending the accounting definition of current income; and second, by changing the definition of net worth or capitalization. These changes were enshrined in the RAP (Regulatory Accounting Procedures), which replaced the GAAP (Generally Accepted Accounting Procedures) as the accounting standards required by regulators. Furthermore, the official policy became one of 'forbearance.'

At the same time, thrifts suddenly found themselves freer to choose their investment activities and set deposit interest rates as they wished. First, the Depository Institutions Deregulation and Monetary Decontrol Act of 1980 and the Garn-St. Germain Depository Institutions Act of 1982 removed many of the restrictions that had previously applied to asset-holdings by thrifts. As thrifts switched from state to federal charters to take advantage of the new opportunities, some states (Texas and California, for example) reacted by adopting even more liberal rules. Second, by eliminating limits on the rates that could be paid on deposits, Garn-St. Germain not only removed the last vestige of franchise value that had helped deter looting in the past, but it also, in effect, gave thrifts an unlimited ability to borrow from the government. To place a new claim on the deposit insurance system, which was implicitly backed by the government, thrifts had only to take in new deposits. Previously, they had been limited to geographically restricted, nonprice competition as a means of attracting deposits. With the removal of interest rate limits, the only constraint on the behavior of thrifts was the severely weakened system of capitalization or net worth requirements. The emergence of a nationwide system of brokers who matched depositors with thrifts was an inevitable response to this change.

The ability to purchase a more diverse set of assets made the valuation of the portfolio held by a thrift more difficult and created opportunities for overvaluation of net worth that could be manipulated by individual thrifts. Increases in the amount that a thrift could lend to one borrower also enhanced the ability of thrift owners and borrowers to collude by funding and carrying out negative net worth projects that generated extractable gains. Traditionally, thrift ownership had to be dispersed among at least 400 shareholders, with no individual shareholder holding more than 10 percent of the equity, and no group holding more than 25 percent. An additional rule change made it possible for a single individual to own his or her own thrift, making it even easier for owners to structure the affairs of the thrift for private benefit.[23]

The strategy of forbearance in dealing with thrifts that could not meet their capital requirements was supplemented by a significant weakening of the capital requirements themselves. At the beginning of the 1980s, capital requirements specified that the book value of equity had to be 5 percent of the book value of an institution's assets. By January 1982, the capital requirement had been reduced to 3 percent.[24] Moreover, new thrifts were given 20 years to reach the required capital levels, so an entrant into the industry needed to maintain only net worth equal to 0.15 percent of assets.[25] Rapidly growing thrifts were also allowed to use an average of assets of the previous four years'

---

[23] See Mayer (1990, p. 63). [24] See Breeden (1990, p. 8). [25] See Breeden (1990, p. 8).

and the current year's (much larger) assets.[26] Thrift owners, who were often land developers, could also deed land or other assets that were difficult to value to their thrift as a contribution to capital.

The new RAP rules, together with generous interpretations of the traditional GAAP rules, created many different ways in which net worth could be overstated. Institutions with significantly negative net worth could then remain open, report profits, and, in most cases, make payouts to managers and owners. S&Ls could value at current market prices some assets that increased in value, yet retain losers on the books at historical cost. Losses on assets that were sold could also be amortized over the maturity of the assets rather than incurred instantaneously, as they should be under any economically rational system of accounting.[27]

Regulators were not, of course, completely blind to the potential problems that their strategy created. For example, when the Federal Home Loan Bank Board, the regulatory agency of the S&Ls, first began to issue 'net worth certificates'—pieces of paper that were treated as increments to the net worth of an insolvent institution—it insisted that the recipients cease dividend payments until the certificates were no longer needed. However, once the pattern of forbearance and stretching of the accounting rules became the norm, the regulators' ability to limit opportunism rapidly diminished.

A particularly important accounting provision concerned the treatment of the intangible assets or 'goodwill' created when one thrift acquired another. Traditional GAAP accounting rules specified that when an acquiring firm paid more for a target than its book value, the difference was identified as an intangible asset that was added to the books of the acquiring firm and depreciated over an appropriate period of time. In the world of value maximization, this is sensible. If someone is willing to pay more than book value, the firm must possess some hidden assets. But in the world of bankruptcy for profit, this procedure can lead to seriously misleading accounting procedures. Traditionally, the Federal Home Loan Bank Board instructed thrifts to limit this period to no more than ten years, but in 1981, this restriction was removed and thrifts could use the absolute upper bound of forty years under GAAP rules.[28]

To illustrate the effects of this decision, consider the following example. Suppose that a troubled thrift had mortgages with a face value of $4 billion but a market value of $3 billion because interest rates had increased. Suppose that it had deposit liabilities of $3.8 billion, and therefore a negative net worth of $800 million. If another thrift acquired this thrift at zero cost by taking over its assets and liabilities, it put $3.8 billion in new deposit liabilities on its books. Because the transaction had a market price of zero, it also put the $3 billion in new mortgage assets on its books, together with $800 million of intangible 'goodwill' assets. From the point of view of the regulators, this paper transaction meant that the measured capital of the industry had increased by $800 million and that an insolvent institution had been resolved. Income at the acquiring thrift would be directly reduced, because the market value of the target was negative. With interest rates of 10 percent, the net reduction in income

---

[26] See Breeden (1990, pp. 8–9).   [27] Breeden (1990, p. 16).
[28] Black (1990, p. 104) and Breeden (1990, pp. 21–25).

would be 10 percent of the difference between $3.8 billion and $3 billion, or $80 million per year.

In the usual world of value maximization, of course, it never makes sense for an acquiring firm to accept $800 million in net new obligations for free. But in the world of bankruptcy for profit, this extravagance made perfect sense because it allowed the acquiring firm to pay out more dividends than would otherwise have been possible. Over time, both the goodwill and the discount from par on the mortgage assets disappear, but the accounting treatment lets this happen at different rates. If the average life of the outstanding mortgages were seven years (a typical value because mortgages are repaid when a house is sold), the acquiring thrift would be allowed to book one-seventh of the discount from par as income each year. In this case, it would generate $143 million ($1 billion/7) in additional accounting income each year. Because the goodwill would be depreciated over forty years, the subtraction from accounting income in each year would be only $20 million. Over the course of the first seven years after the acquisition, this difference would generate $123 million per year in artificial income. Net of the real reduction of $80 million per year, this would imply an additional $43 million in dividends that could be paid out each year for the next seven years. After seven years, the discount from face value would be gone and even accounting earnings would be strictly lower. But in seven years, the current owners would presumably be long gone. Many thrift owners were quick to take advantage of this loophole: in 1982 alone, S&Ls booked $15 billion in goodwill.[29]

Another particularly important accounting provision was the new leniency concerning S&L income from ADC loans to real estate developers. The Garn-St. Germain Act removed the traditional limits on the mortgage loan-to-value ratio,[30] and—even better, from the looters' perspective—allowed the value of the project itself to include interest reserves to pay the interest on the loan for the first several years, as well as a 2 to 4 percent developer's fee that could be taken out at the beginning. This meant that a developer could start a real estate development project with no equity of his own at stake, and pocket a large initial fee. Thanks to the interest reserves, both the developer and the thrift could operate free of any fear of default for years, even if the project being built were completely worthless.[31] The new Regulatory Accounting Procedures also allowed the S&Ls to book as current income an origination fee of up to 2.5 percent of the loan value.[32] While correct accounting would have required loan-loss reserves to be set aside against the risks of loss, practice frequently differed. In Texas, for example, accounting practices allowed both the nominal interest income and the origination fee to be booked as profit—even if the developer never contributed a single dollar of his own wealth to the project.

These accounting arrangements created the perfect opportunity for developers and thrifts to collude in looting by creating overvalued assets, as described earlier. Developers created projects that were initially given artificially inflated accounting valuations and subsequently went bankrupt, with thrifts lending all the funds needed to keep the

---

[29] Breeden (1990, p. 24).   [30] See Kane (1989).   [31] O'Shea (1991, p. 55).
[32] See Breeden (1990, p. 19).

project in business for several years. This scam ultimately became known as the 'Texas strategy' for looting. The effects of this strategy on the real estate market are the subject of the next section.

Among the many provisions reducing the restrictions on asset holdings, the Garn-St. Germain Act of 1982 also allowed thrifts to engage in commercial lending and therefore to purchase junk bonds. Junk bonds offered the same kind of yield spread described in the yield curve example and exploited in Chile. Correct accounting would have required a reserve to offset the high default rate on junk bonds,[33] but lacking adequate supervision requiring risk set-asides, thrifts could report virtually all of the interest income on junk bonds as current income. The implications of this arrangement for the market for junk bonds are discussed later in the paper.

Evidence of Looting

We have seen that the changes in regulations of S&Ls in the early 1980s created opportunities for looting. But did many owners in fact loot their institutions? If they did, did they mainly purchase high-risk assets in the hope that they would sometimes create large positive earnings for their institutions? Or were looting strategies that drained as much income as possible also an important factor in the ultimate cost of the S&L bailout?

Evidence of looting abounds. This evidence is mainly microeconomic rather than macroeconomic in nature, because both looting and highrisk strategies could be used to milk the S&Ls and leave many institutions in deep bankruptcy. To establish a case for looting, it is necessary to show that loans were made, or assets purchased, in circumstances in which no reasonable person could expect a future positive payoff in any future state of the world, but for which the present payoff was very high. An example of this kind would be the loans made by Oakland-based FCA, a rapidly growing thrift that grew to $34 billion in assets before it failed.[34] According to one account, FCA followed a strategy of extremely rapid growth during which it was willing to make loans to any developer willing to pay 20 percent interest plus points, a policy which in the S&L industry was known to attract 'lemons,' projects headed for almost certain default.[35] According to another account, FCA would buy whatever mortgage brokers in the Southwest wanted to sell, and then would unload these mortgages to third parties, lending them the money to buy the mortgages but not forcing the borrowers to keep to their repayment schedules.[36] These policies clearly correspond more closely to a bankruptcy-for-profit strategy than gambling for resurrection as it is difficult to imagine any state of the world in which bankruptcy could have been avoided.

The Texas strategy, first apparent in the examination of Mesquite, a Texas-based Empire Savings and Loan, suggests just as strongly that negative yield, rather than high variance, was the dominant characteristic of the asset portfolios of many thrifts that later

---

[33] That rate was one-third after eleven or twelve years, according to Asquith, Mullins, and Wolff (1989, p. 929).
[34] Stein (1992, p. 206).
[35] See Robinson (1990, pp. 26–27). This adverse selection problem corresponds to the reason for rationing of loans given by Stiglitz and Weiss (1981).   [36] Mayer (1990, p. 111).

failed. This strategy was followed in many different forms by different S&Ls. The first step was to make a loan—often to a developer—for more than the value of the collateral. Various complex systems could be worked out for overvaluing the collateral. In the case of Empire Savings and Loan, for example, a group of colluding developers and thrift owners traded land back and forth in a series of trades at successively higher prices; because their parcels were sufficiently similar, these trades could be used for price evaluations by a friendly appraiser.

Once the development loan was granted, the development itself, as in our model, became a source of generous development fees. The developer would pay a high current return on the loan, often made easier because the loan included payments of interest for the understandably long time until the completion of the project. As a result, the S&L would receive high current payments for some period of time. Furthermore, the developer, whose talents at building had been appreciated and supported by the S&L, might in turn see what a promising future the S&L would have, with its high current earnings and massive growth rate. So the developer and his friends could purchase a sizable bloc of stock in the S&L by contributing overvalued land or projects that could be counted as part of the thrift's capital. The only effective limit on the returns from this strategy was the thrift's ability to find new individuals with reasonably clean criminal records and balance sheets who were willing to play the role of developer, because regulations still put a limit on how much a thrift could lend to any one person or firm. Empire eventually offered finder's fees to anyone who brought in a new potential 'developer.' All that was required was a financial statement that was clean enough to pass muster with the bank examiners.[37]

Table 11.1 contains a list of thrifts for which government investigators considered evidence of fraud to be the strongest. Adding up the resolution costs for those for which we could find cost estimates generates a total cost to the government of $54 billion. This figure is at best an order of magnitude estimate of the potential costs from looting. It will be an underestimate because we lack estimates for some of the thrifts on our list and because estimated resolution costs have typically been underestimates rather than overestimates. In addition, there could have been a great deal of looting that did not attract government attention. On the other hand, it could overstate the losses due to gambling and looting, because some of the total may simply represent losses from the 1970s that were carried forward.

A more direct estimate of the losses due to looting comes from a comparison of the resolution costs of mutual savings banks, which had asset structures similar to that of savings and loans, but were treated as banks rather than thrifts for historical and institutional reasons. As a result, the savings banks were subject to regulatory oversight not by the FSLIC, but by the FDIC, which moved aggressively to limit its exposure to losses from these banks in the early 1980s.[38] Banking authorities did not give the mutuals new powers, liberalize the accounting treatment of their net worth, or encourage them to grow out of their difficulties. Instead, they limited the mutuals' activities, and waited the problem out.

[37] O'Shea (1991, p. 31).   [38] For details, see Mayer (1990, pp. 81–82).

Table 11.1. *Resolution costs at thrifts suspected of fraud present value in millions of dollars*

Savings and loan	State	Resolution cost
American Diversified Savings Bank	CA	798
American Federal of Colorado	CO	339
American S&L	CA	1,699
Ameriway Savings Assoc.	TX	173
Bell Savings Bank	PA	189
Beverly Hills S&L	CA	983
Bexar Savings	TX	483
Brookside Savings	CA	63
Caguas Central FSB	PR	120
Cal America	CA	100
Capital FS&L	AR	23
Caprock S&L	TX	299
Cardinal Savings Bank	NC	34
Carver S&L Association	CA	54
CenTrust Bank	FL	1,705
Century S&L Association	TX	48
Charter Savings Bank	CA	34
City Savings	NJ	1,531
Colonial Federal Savings	NJ	119
Colonial Savings Association	KS	37
Columbia S&L	CA	1,149
Commerce Savings	TX	604
Commodore Savings Association[a]	TX	1,846
Commonwealth[b]	FL	325
Community Federal S&L	MO	372
Community S&L	WI	37
Concordia Federal	IL	90
Continental S&L	TX	678
Cornerstone Savings	TX	24
Creditbanc Savings[a]	TX	1,108
Cross Roads S&L Association	OK	11
Deposit Trust Savings	LA	21
First Atlantic Savings	NJ	247
First California Savings	CA	74
First Federal of Shawnee	OK	56
First Federal S&L	CA	16
First Federal Savings Bank	WY	11
First Network Savings	CA	139
First Savings Assoc. of East Texas	TX	88
First Savings Bank and Trust	MO	3
First State Savings	TX	271
First S&L of Toledo	OH	128

Table 11.1. (*continued*)

Savings and loan	State	Resolution cost
First Texas/Gibraltar Savings[a]	TX	5,034
Franklin Savings (Creditbanc)[a]	TX	...
Freedom S&L Association	FL	349
Frontier Savings[a]	OK	279
General Savings Association	TX	18
Gibraltar	CA	522
Gold River Savings[b]	CA	3
Great West Savings	CO	7
Gulf Federal	LA	176
Hill Financial Savings Association	PA	657
Home Savings	AK	45
Imperial Savings	CA	1,647
Independence Federal	AR	291
Independent American[a]	TX	6,111
Interwest Savings Association (Commodore)[a]	TX	...
Lamar Savings Association[a]	TX	2,115
Liberty Federal	NM	80
Libertyville Federal S&L	IL	9
Lincoln S&L	CA	2,824
MeraBank	AZ	1,023
Mercury Savings	CA	34
Mercury Savings[a]	TX	1,327
Meridian Savings	TX	418
MeritBanc Savings	TX	211
Midwest Federal	MN	826
Mission Savings	TX	65
Multibanc (Independent American)[a]	TX	...
Northpark Savings (Commodore)[a]	TX	...
Odessa Savings[a]	TX	1,490
Otero Savings	CO	257
Paris S&L Association (Mercury)[a]	TX	...
Peoples Bank for Savings	IL	18
Peoples Heritage Federal Savings	KS	958
Peoples Homestead Federal	LA	98
Peoples Savings[a]	TX	343
Phoenix Federal	AL	74
Pima S&L	AZ	319
Resource Savings Association	TX	278
Richardson Savings (Mercury)[a]	TX	...
Royal Palm Savings	FL	154
San Angelo Savings (Odessa)[a]	TX	...
San Jacinto Savings	TX	1,424

(*continued*)

Table 11.1. (*continued*)

Savings and loan	State	Resolution cost
Saratoga Savings	CA	11
Security Savings	TX	468
Skokie Federal	IL	168
Stockton Savings (Lamar)[a]	TX	...
Sun S&L Association	CO	157
Sunbelt Savings of Texas (Independent American)[a]	TX	...
Territory S&L Association	OK	46
TexasBanc	TX	308
Trinity Valley	TX	12
United Savings Association of Texas	TX	1,374
United Savings	NJ	25
United Savings	VA	112
United Savings	WY	147
United Savings of America	FL	26
United Savings Bank	MN	31
Unity Savings	CA	57
Universal Savings	TX	223
University Federal Savings Association	TX	2,557
Victoria Savings	TX	782
Vision Banc	TX	64
Western Savings	AZ	1,728
Western Savings (Independent American)[a,b]	TX	...
Westport Savings	CA	20
Williamsburg Federal S&L	UT	37
Total resolution costs:		53,966

Source: Names on the list are taken from two main sources: a Resolution Trust Corporation (RTC) list of prosecutions already initiated or completed, taken from U.S. Senate (1991); and the RTC's 'Top 100' list of priority cases for prosecution, as leaked in David Johnson, 'S&L Criminal Inquiries Confirmed,' *New York Times*, October 3, 1990, p. D4. We also added two thrifts—United Savings of Texas and Gilbraltar of California—that feature prominently in the FDIC lawsuit against Michael Milken and Drexel Burnham Lambert.

Estimated resolution costs are taken from FSLIC tables in U.S. Senate (1990), from the 1990 and 1991 RTC annual reports, and from an RTC Resolved Conservatorship Report of December 1992. For Cal America, costs are from U.S. House of Representatives (1987). This table includes cases of possible fraud still under consideration that were current at the time that the source documents were published (1990 and 1991). It thus excludes a number of prominent cases—Vernon Savings and Empire Savings in Texas, for example—in which prosecutions came earlier.

[a] Thrifts sold by FSLIC as part of a group of thrifts. If a cost is listed, it is the cost for the entire group, not this thrift alone. If a cost is not listed, the name of the thrift giving the cost for the group appears in parentheses.
[b] The original source carries the cryptic note 'unable to make specific identification.'

In 1982, the savings banks had assets that were 25 percent of the assets at savings and loans.[39] From 1981 to 1986, the FDIC spent about $7 billion to rescue and recapitalize ailing savings banks.[40] If this experience is any guide, the entire thrift crisis could have been solved at a cost of about $28 billion by following a strategy parallel to the one adopted by the FDIC of limiting the activities of insolvent institutions and resolving them over time as reductions in interest rates increased the value of mortgage assets.

Another way to construct an estimate of the losses caused by the combination of the regulatory treatment given to thrifts and the perverse incentives that this created for owners is to compare the resolution costs at stockholder-owned S&Ls with the costs at mutual S&Ls, where the depositors were the legal owners. Because the true owners of the mutuals were more dispersed and faced greater difficulty in controlling the behavior of management and in capturing the gains from looting or gambling in the form of direct payouts, management at the mutuals had much less incentive to pursue strategies that gave shareholders a current gain but that risked their jobs. Consistent with this theory, Benjamin C. Esty has found that stock thrifts failed at three times the rate (26.8 percent) as mutual thrifts (8.1 percent) between 1983 and 1988.[41]

A comparison of the costs at mutual thrifts and stock thrifts similarly suggests that the costs of resolving the thrift crisis could have been in the range of $20–$30 billion. In 1982, mutual S&Ls had about two times as many assets as stock S&Ls. If there had been no incentive to loot, the behavior of the two types of thrifts should have been the same and the costs of resolving the stock thrifts should have been about half the cost of resolving problems at the mutuals. But in fact, the incentives faced by managers in the two different kinds of institutions were quite different; their behavior reflects this difference. While the total quantity of assets held by the mutuals stayed almost constant from 1982 to 1987, assets at the stock thrifts grew more than four-fold.[42] Because losses were incurred on many of the investments made by the stock thrifts during this period of growth, a small problem at the stock S&Ls grew into a very big problem.

To estimate what the resolution costs for the S&Ls would have been if thrift regulators had followed the conservative strategy of the FDIC, we calculated what total resolution costs would have been if all thrifts had behaved like the mutuals after 1982. We used the Treasury bill rate to convert costs incurred in different years into a common unit, 1982 dollars. (Because the thrifts typically had to pay a premium over the Treasury bill rate to attract brokered deposits, the use of this rate makes our estimate of the cost slightly larger than if we used their actual cost of funds. In this sense, our use of the Treasury bill rate is conservative.) If we apply the resulting estimate of the cost per dollar of assets at the mutuals to all assets in the S&L industry, we find that the total cost of resolution would have been $26.8 billion in 1982 dollars.[43]

---

[39] *Federal Reserve Bulletin,* July 1984, p. A26.
[40] Based on personal communication with G. K. Gibbs.   [41] Esty (1992, table 1, panel B).
[42] See Barth (1991, Tables 3–8, p. 57).
[43] The assets and resolution costs of the mutual and stock S&Ls are taken from Barth (1991) and our calculations of resolution costs for 1990 and 1991 from annual reports of the Resolution Trust Corporation. We are grateful to James Barth for providing updated tables of the resolution costs in his book.

Four remarks should be made about this calculation. First, resolving the problem earlier makes the current dollar cost smaller because the resolution cost will grow with the interest rate. If we use the three-month Treasury bill rate to bring a $26.8 billion cost in 1982 forward to 1993, the costs would be slightly less than $60 billion, or (2.15 × $26.8 billion). This number can be compared to an actual cost (that has been converted into 1993 dollars) of $140 billion.

Second, the $26.8 billion total cost of resolving problems in the thrift industry includes looting and excessive risk-taking at mutuals. To make a rough adjustment for this, we calculated the fraction of losses of mutuals from the list of suspect thrifts in table 11.1. Mutuals accounted for 8 percent of the costs in this group. Stock thrifts accounted for the other 92 percent. Using this percentage to calculate an estimate of avoidable losses from 1982 to 1993 at the mutuals reduces our estimate of the cost by about $4 billion in 1982 dollars.

Third, the estimate assumes that mutuals that were converted to stock ownership during this period and that were resolved later had non-negative net worth at the time when they were converted. We think that this is a reasonable assumption. In a conversion, existing depositors are offered the opportunity to purchase shares in the new stock thrift. A dispersed group of investors who do not expect to be able to loot would not pay to invest in a thrift that had a negative net worth. Moreover, the bank board, which had to approve all conversions, required that the net worth of the institution be positive and that the price for the shares in the new institution be fair. These rules, together with restrictions on the amount of equity that could be acquired by insiders, would have made it inconvenient to convert a mutual with a large negative net worth into a stock thrift with the intention of gaining control and looting it.

Fourth, we truncated the resolution costs in 1991, the last year for which data are available. Using the Treasury bill rate to convert costs incurred in different years into costs in 1993, the total resolution costs incurred in the years for which we have data are $140 billion, which is close to the total estimated costs for the bailout of about $150–$175 billion reported by the National Commission on Financial Institution Reform, Recovery, and Enforcement.[44] Thus we expect that our data cover the bulk of total costs that the government will incur. In any case, the comparison of the approximately $60 billion in 1993 costs for thrifts covered in our data versus $140 billion in actual costs is valid. Because the costs at the mutuals tended to be resolved earlier than costs at the stock thrifts, we expect the final totals will primarily reflect additional costs at stock thrifts rather than additional costs at the mutuals. If so, the final tally for the costs of letting the stock thrifts behave as they did will be even higher than our calculations suggest.

Boom and Bust in Dallas

We described earlier how S&Ls could be looted in symbiotic deals with parasitical developers who would also go bankrupt. This section develops a model of this activity

---

[44] National Commission on Financial Institution Reform, Recovery, and Enforcement (1993, p.4).

and shows how a small amount of such looting by S&Ls can be the impulse—through a multiplier—that induces a bubble in building activity and land prices. This bubble will be fueled by honest developers who fail to understand the source of the additional demand caused by looters and parasites. We call these developers copycats because they infer the implicit rents from building by watching the market price for land; they are thus analogous to the investors in the stock market who do not collect fundamental information, but merely purchase the market portfolio.[45] Unfortunately for the copycat developers, when the demand for land expands because of looting, they fail to under-stand the source of the rise in price. The copycats act on the principle that if a crowd is staring at the sky, they too should look, because there must be something to see—otherwise the crowd would not be staring so intently. Most of the time this behavior is correct. When it is wrong, it eventually comes to an abrupt halt.

The Model

We start with a simple model of land prices, and initially, no looters. There are two types of developers. The first, who comprise a fraction $(1 - \beta)$ of the market, have a demand that depends only on a shift parameter, A, and on the price for land, p. Their demand, D_1, is

$$D_1 = (1 - \beta)(A - bp). \tag{7}$$

The shift parameter, A, reflects fundamentals such as the number of people moving into the city or region, the expected incomes of the residents, and other exogenous factors. This first type of developer knows the value of A.

Developers of the second type, who together form a fraction β of the market, do not know the true value of A, but estimate it from signals inferred from the activities of others. Their demand, D_2, is similar to the demand by type 1 developers, but their estimate of the shift parameter is A^e:

$$D_2 = \beta(A^e - bp). \tag{8}$$

In our simple model, parallel to Grossman's fully revealing rational expectations model, we assume that these type 2 developers infer the true value of A from the market price for land.[46] In other words, A^e is estimated from an equation of the form

$$A^e = \delta + \gamma p. \tag{9}$$

We assume that this estimate of A^e is rational, so the parameters δ and γ in this expression must be chosen so that this yields an unbiased estimate for A.

---

[45] For recent models in which agents infer the value of important signals by watching others, see Banerjee (1993), Bikchandani, Hirshleifer, and Welch (1992), Caplin and Leahy (1991), and Romer (1993).

[46] Grossman (1976).

The supply of land to developers, S, which is generated outside the model, is upward-sloping, of the form

$$S = d + ep, \tag{10}$$

where p is the price and d and e are parameters.

Equating supply with demand in this land market yields an equilibrium price for land that is a function of the parameters in the expression for A^e. Matching coefficients so that A^e is equal to A implies that $\delta = d$ and $\gamma = b + e$. With these values substituted in, the demand for land by copycat investors can be written as

$$D_2 = \beta(d + ep). \tag{11}$$

The copycats' reduced-form demand is increasing in price because price increases signal increases in market fundamentals. Moreover, in equilibrium, they purchase a fraction β of all the land that is sold for development. That is, they exactly replicate the behavior of the market as a whole, just as index investors buy their share of the stock market.

This supply and demand system describes a very simple rational expectations equilibrium. Now consider a new equilibrium with a change in regulations, so that looters at S&Ls will offer new loans in the amount N to parasitical developers who are new entrants and who have no interest in making a profit. Initially, before agents adjust the parameters in their expectations function, how will the equilibrium price change? Who will gain and who will lose? And by how much?

To simplify the model, we assume that the parasitical developers take out loans only for building, and that one parcel of land requires B dollars of building. The direct effect of the looting is an increase in the demand for land by an amount $D_3 = N/B$. The new equilibrium equates the new total demand $D_1 + D_2 + D_3$ to the supply S. The looters at the S&Ls and the parasitical developers have every reason to conceal their true intent, so we assume that the honest but uninformed developers do not recognize the parasites as new entrants into this market; these honest developers therefore continue to use the same rule as before to infer the fundamentals from the market price. The informed developers, of course, continue to observe the true value of A. This combination of circumstances will lead directly to a real estate boom and bust. We shall now describe the new equilibrium (and its collapse).

To the copycat developers, it appears that the fundamental shift parameter A has increased by the amount

$$[1/(1 - \beta)](N/B). \tag{12}$$

The price of land increases by

$$[1/(1 - \beta)](N/B)[1/(e + b)]. \tag{13}$$

The quantity of land that is developed increases by the slope coefficient e (from the supply equation) times this price change. Note that these increases vary inversely with the fraction of fundamental developers, $1 - \beta$. If the fundamental developers comprise only 10 percent of the market, the effect of the new demand stemming from the symbiotic relationship between looters and parasites is ten times what it would be if all developers were fully informed.

In the new equilibrium, the fundamental investors withdraw from the market. Given the price increase they observe and the unchanged estimate of the market fundamentals, they reduce their purchases of land by $(1 - \beta)b$ times the price increase. The copycat investors increase their purchases of land by an amount equal to βe times the price increase.

Now suppose that the true value of A is revealed (through persistently high vacancy rates, for example); that the parasitical developments are taken over by regulators and sold on the open market; and that savings and loans are prohibited from engaging in this kind of looting. Because building is irreversible, the price of developed real estate falls below the level before the looters began to finance development. The parasitical developers go bankrupt, as expected. In addition, however, so do some of the fundamental and copycat investors, who take capital losses because of the unexpected price decline. In an extended model of a growing economy, the normal pace of construction activity would be interrupted for several years, with no new building taking place until the local demand had increased to meet the excess supply.

The Evidence

Our model and the sequence of events it portrays describes the building boom of the 1980s in Dallas, the center of activity for the Texas thrifts. The comparison with Houston is illuminating. For both cities, Table 11.2 reports construction activity and vacancy rates for office space. The construction peaks occurred earlier in Houston than in Dallas/Fort Worth, with office construction peaking in 1983 in Houston, but not until 1985 in Dallas/Fort Worth. The timing of these peaks can be explained partly by the differences in the economies of the two cities. Houston's economy is oil-based, while Dallas/Fort Worth's is much more diversified. For example, in Houston 45 percent of office space is occupied by energy-related firms, compared to 10.5 percent in Dallas/Fort Worth.[47] The near-coincidence of the rise and fall in oil prices and construction suggests that oil price changes were the likely cause for the boom and bust in Houston nonresidential and residential construction.

But while the difference in economies may explain why Dallas/Fort Worth peaked later than Houston, it does not explain why significant new construction continued in Dallas/Fort Worth even after high vacancy rates had set in.[48] By 1983, the office

---

[47] Steve Brown, 'City Review: Dallas,' *National Real Estate Investor News*, October 1986, p. 180.

[48] Changes in the deductibility of real estate losses in the Tax Reform Act of 1986 could possibly explain the end of the office building boom. Our problem, however, is not to explain why the boom ended, but rather why with vacancy rates in excess of 20 percent, it continued in Dallas/Fort Worth for so long.

Table 11.2. *Office Construction and vacancy rates for dallas/fort worth and Houston, 1981–90*

Year	Dallas/Forth Worth		Houston	
	Construction[a]	Vacancies[b]	Construction[a]	Vacancies[b]
1981	7,739	8	17,193	6
1982	14,750	11	22,490	8
1983	14,928	20	29,230	20
1984	10,843	19	10,900	24
1985[c]	20,000	23	3,500	24
1986	14,090	32	4,301	32
1987	7,290	32	626	29
1988	2,328	32	756	26
1989	1,807	27	543	24
1990	831	24	837	21

Source: Urban Land Institute (1986, 1990, and 1991).
[a] Thousands of square feet.
[b] Percent of total.
[c] Figures for 1985 are estimates.

vacancy rate in Dallas/Fort Worth had already reached 20 percent, a rate that equaled Houston's. Indeed, from 1986–90, Dallas/Fort Worth vacancy rates were at least as high as those in Houston. Yet significant amounts of building continued until 1988.

The excess of S&L lending is very clear from a comparison with bank lending. Between 1982 and 1986, the assets of Texas commercial banks grew by 27 percent; by contrast, the assets at the Texas S&Ls grew by 99 percent, and those of the notorious 'Texas 40' S&Ls grew by 299 percent,[49] while real estate loans grew almost as fast as total assets.

The after-effects of the building spree are certainly consistent with our model's prediction of widespread bankruptcy after the collapse, even for banks and developers who were not party to looting. In 1987, when the resolution of the crisis was beginning, S&Ls in Texas had a very high delinquency rate of 29 percent on real estate loans, which is unsurprising given the behavior described in our model. But even at Texas banks—which were more tightly regulated—13 percent of the real estate loans were nonperforming, a level that had not been reached since the Great Depression.[50]

Our hypothesis is that many real estate loans were made by the thrifts without serious regard as to whether they would default. It appears to be conventional wisdom among bankers that loans with high rates are very likely to default, as illustrated by the case of FCA discussed earlier. Among Texas thrifts, those that later failed had average mortgage interest rates 76 basis points higher than the mortgage rates of thrifts that remained solvent. Moreover, the S&Ls that grew particularly fast were particularly likely to have high mortgage lending rates. Of the Texas S&Ls that ultimately became insolvent, the

---

[49] U.S. House of Representatives (1990, p. 213).   [50] Short and Gunther (1988, Table 4, p. 5).

thirty-five that grew at rates of more than 50 percent per year between 1980 and 1984 had an average lending rate 148 basis points in excess of the S&Ls that remained solvent.[51] The higher rates were only one of the methods used to loot S&Ls. As noted above, fee income, for which it is more difficult to gather data, was apparently even more important.

The tale we have told can be traced through the city reports on Dallas in the *National Real Estate Investor News* (NREIN). As early as June 1982, developers who seem to correspond to the informed developers in our model realized that something was going on and openly expressed their concern. For example, in a NREIN story subtitled 'Experts Concerned About Huge Supply Pipeline,' Mark Pogue of Dallas' Lincoln Properties said, 'All of us need to be more cautious.... How will this market absorb these millions of square feet?'[52] A year later, in June 1983, Dallas ranked second nationally to Houston in vacant office space.[53] At the same time, paradoxically, it was first in office construction. In October 1983, McDonald Williams of Trammell Crow, one of the county's most successful and respected developers, warned about the overbuilding and put the blame to a considerable extent on 'the push that savings and loans are making into commercial real estate.... They are going to keep us overbuilt, I think.'[54] He also blamed institutional investment funds, which correspond to the copycat suppliers of funds in our model. A year later, with the NREIN reporting that 'old timers in Dallas [were] amazed at the surge in construction,'[55] Dan Arnold of Swearingen Company provided his explanation of the continued activity: 'Financial institutions and lenders have money that must be placed.'[56] Still later, in June of 1985 Wayne Swearingen could not explain why the rising vacancies had not led to a slowdown in office construction. 'We have developers sitting there with empty buildings, and the lenders are giving them money to start another one. I have to blame the lenders. I want them to show me where these builders are going to get cash flow.... *The laws of supply and demand are not governing market behavior.* Continuing construction in the face of high vacancy seems related to the availability of financing for new buildings, rather than need.'[57]

He was speaking just before the crash removed any doubt that there was a problem. Our model suggests that he had the diagnosis exactly right.

Looting, Junk Bonds, and Takeovers

This now leads us to our final question. An even more dramatic development in North America during the 1980s than the boom and bust in real estate was the rise and decline

---

[51] Short and Gunther (1988, table 3, p. 3) and personal communication.

[52] Steven Brown, 'Office Market Outlook: Dallas,' *National Real Estate Investor News*, June 1982, p. 46.

[53] Steve Brown, 'City Review: Dallas,' *National Real Estate Investor News*, June 1983, p. 60.

[54] Steve Brown, 'City Review: Dallas,' *National Real Estate Investor News*, October 1983, p. 127.

[55] Steve Brown, 'City Review: Dallas,' *National Real Estate Investor News*, October 1984, p. 183.

[56] Steve Brown, 'City Review: Dallas,' *National Real Estate Investor News*, October 1984, p. 192.

[57] Steve Brown, 'City Review: Dallas,' *National Real Estate Investor News*, June 1985, pp. 98–100. Italics added.

of junk bonds and debt-financed corporate takeovers. Is there a link between bankruptcy for profit in S&Ls, junk bonds, and takeovers?

At first glance, such a link appears implausible because the value of junk bonds held by S&Ls was small compared to the total junk bond market, and very small compared to the total quantity of assets that changed hands. Even at the peak, S&Ls held only about $13.2 billion of junk bonds,[58] whereas the total outstanding issues of junk bonds exceeded $200 billion by 1989.[59] During the entire decade of the 1980s, the total value of assets changing hands in takeovers was $1.3 trillion.[60] How could a relatively small amount of junk bond purchases by thrifts have had any significant effect on the junk bond market as a whole, and indirectly on the volume of takeovers?

In this section, we suggest that a particular form of S&L looting indeed influenced the timing and volume of takeover transactions. The first part of this argument rests on the assertion, articulated for example by Michael C. Jensen, that the creation of the junk bond market did encourage the takeover wave of the 1980s.[61] The ability demonstrated by Drexel Burnham Lambert in the 1980s to raise billions of dollars in only a few days lent credibility to takeover bids for large firms that never before could have been financed. Even though junk bonds provided only part of the ultimate financing for the totality of takeover transactions, 'high-yield bonds are an important innovation in the takeover field because they help eliminate size as a deterrent to takeover,' as Jensen has argued.[62]

The second part of our argument is that the funds made available by the owners of S&Ls who were interested in looting made it possible to reduce artificially the interest rate on junk debt underwritten by Drexel.[63] Potential purchasers of Drexel debt could observe two key signals concerning the quality of its offerings: the success rate of its underwritings and the default rate on its outstanding issues. Our claim is that relatively small amounts of other people's money could be used to manipulate these two signals and thereby cause Drexel borrowers to pay a lower interest rate than they otherwise would have had to pay.

We will show that unusual circumstances provided an opportunity for successful manipulation of the junk bond market. We will also show that there were many tell-tale signs consistent with the actual occurrence of such market manipulation. Before turning to the details in this argument, we place it in the context of the popular and scholarly literature on takeovers.

Our story of looting and takeovers has nothing to do with the journalistic accounts of a takeover artist who acquires control of a firm and then 'loots' it. Victor Posner is the

---

[58] See Yago (1991, p. 187).

[59] *Investor's Digest Daily,* as cited in Yago (1991, p. 199).

[60] Andrei Shleifer and Robert W. Vishny, 'The Takeover Wave of the 1980s,' *Science* 249, August 17, 1990, p. 745.

[61] Jensen (1988).

[62] Jensen (1988, p. 39).

[63] As far as we know, Benjamin Stein was the first person to emphasize the importance of the links between the savings and loans and the junk bond market. His argument first appeared in a series of articles published in *Barron's* in the late 1980s. For a summary of his case, see Stein (1992).

person most frequently cited as an example of this type of corporate looter, with a personal take from companies under his control reportedly in excess of $23 million in 1984.[64]

The vast bulk of takeover activity cannot be explained in this naive fashion. Detailed accounts of transactions such as the RJR–Nabisco takeover give ample evidence of serious attention to the true economic returns of the deal under consideration.[65] Furthermore, too many sophisticated investors invested in takeovers and had no access to fee income or excessive compensation.[66]

A theory of the takeover wave must therefore be consistent with serious attempts at value-maximization by the investors in takeovers. As noted above, our claim is that looting strategies followed by S&Ls could have led to reduced yields paid on junk bonds, which made debt-financed takeovers more attractive to rational investors.

Market Manipulation

Under normal circumstances, large markets cannot be manipulated for profit by small groups of individuals. Historically, attempts to dominate the U.S. grain, gold, and silver markets have borne out this insight of economic theory. They have led to the downfall, rather than the making, of ambitious speculators. In this section, we argue that conditions in the junk bond market of the 1980s were not normal. Both the structure of information and the availability of other people's money—that is, taxpayers' money controlled by the looters of financial institutions—offered unique opportunities for profitable manipulation of a large-scale market. We wish to show that the evidence is sufficient to give the case for market manipulation its day in court.

The junk bond market of the 1980s was not a thick, anonymous auction market characterized by full revelation of information. To a very great extent, the market owed its existence to a single individual, Michael Milken, who acted, literally, as the auctioneer. Milken created a new securities market that lent funds to firms that had previously been able to borrow only from banks. The market for new issue bonds below investment grade was trivially small prior to the 1980s presumably because of the inherent difficulty in controlling opportunistic behavior when a limited liability corporation borrows money. As we noted above, private lenders face the same difficulties as the government faces in lending to an entity that can declare bankruptcy; borrowers can take the money and run. We also noted that economists presume that opportunistic behavior has somehow been controlled in cases where private lending does take place. An obvious corollary is that opportunistic behavior has not been controlled in cases where apparently profitable lending does not take place. The absence of a large-scale market in securitized risky debt prior to the 1980s presumably reflects an inability to resolve these problems through any institutional arrangement other than bank lending,

---

[64] Stewart (1992, p. 121)   [65] See Burrough and Helyar (1990, pp. 363–66).

[66] For a discussion of the underlying fundamentals that help explain why takeovers were attractive, and why many corporations needed restructuring during the 1980s, see Jensen (1988), Scherer (1988), Shleifer and Vishny (1988), and Andrei Shleifer and Robert W. Vishny, 'The Takeover Wave of the 1980s,' *Science* 249, August 17, 1990, pp. 745–49.

in which the lender and the individual engaged in monitoring the borrower are part of a single organization.

Milken as Loan Broker

The claim that Milken made in the 1980s was, in effect, that he could play the role of both filter and monitor in a securities market for risky debt. He would identify creditworthy borrowers who were willing and able to pay very high yields and he would verify that they did as they promised with the proceeds. (In this second connection, it is puzzling that high-yield bonds in the 1980s typically carried fewer covenants and restrictions than conventional corporate debt,[67] so Milken's control over these firms would presumably have operated through other mechanisms.)

To take advantage of his putative strengths in evaluating and monitoring borrowers, Milken could have had Drexel take the role of a bank, holding the high-yield debt from these firms and earning a spread over Drexel's borrowing costs. But instead of operating like a banker, Milken earned income for himself and for Drexel by charging a commission on all the loans that he arranged between the borrowers and a diverse set of lenders and, allegedly, sharing in the gains from the takeovers made possible by this debt.

In creating this new market for securitized bank loans, Milken faced a serious credibility problem. Loan brokers, who match borrowers and lenders in exchange for a commission, have a deservedly bad reputation. The incentive to match bad credits with gullible lenders and to walk away with the initial fees is very high. It can also take several years for this kind of scheme to be detected because even a bad creditor can set aside some of the initial proceeds from a loan to make several coupon or interest payments. Proponents of junk bonds as 'securitized bank loans' therefore have to argue not only that Milken had unique abilities in evaluating credit risk and making judgments about borrowers, but also that he was somehow able to establish a reputation for competence and reliability with the investors who bought his issues.

In retrospect, it is not easy to make the case that Milken succeeded in establishing his credibility as a loan broker because of an exceptional ability in making judgments about his borrowers. Even at the time, it was clear that Milken made many questionable judgments about borrowers, his initial support and continued backing of Posner being just one particularly salient example.

The most likely explanation for investors' faith in Milken was demonstrated success. Until 1987, when the threat of prosecution became a serious concern, Milken had demonstrated two remarkable kinds of success. The default rate on his junk bonds had been very low compared to the premium over investment grade bonds, and the success rate of his underwritings had been very high. Given the private nature of the junk bond market, these were the only observable signals that an investor could use to judge Milken's performance, and by these measures, he had done extremely well. William Seidman recalls his perceptions at the time:

[67] Asquith and Wizman (1990).

A phenomenon that mystified me when I was dean of the Arizona State University Business School was: How did Drexel Burnham Lambert and its star partner Michael Milken roll up an unparalleled record of successes in selling junk bonds? As far as we could determine, his underwritings never failed and appeared to be marketed successfully, no matter how suspect the company or how risky the buyout deal that was being financed. Other investment houses had some failed junk bond offerings, but Drexel's record was near perfect. We directed our faculty to research the matter.... The faculty came up with no plausible explanation; like so many others they fell back on the thesis of the junk bond king's unique genius.[68]

If we view Milken as someone who invested in a reputation for delivering good returns to purchasers of his debt, it is clear that an unblemished record of delivering on his promises was essential to maintaining this reputational equilibrium. We suggest that Milken may have been able to sustain such a record of successful underwritings and low default rates by manipulating the market.

Purchases by Partnerships

The complaint brought by the FDIC against Milken and his associates gives an explanation of the near-perfect record of underwriting successes.[69] According to the complaint, Milken formed more than 500 different partnerships that purchased securities in public offerings underwritten by his employer. The complaint reports that in the first half of 1988, the partnerships and Drexel insiders made more than 14,000 purchases through 6,000 different accounts from Drexel public offerings. These purchases could serve several purposes. They could ensure that all public offerings were fully subscribed. They could also be used to mark up prices on bonds or strip the equity kicker from a bond before it was sold to the public, thereby hiding from both the issuers and the purchasers the true profits of Drexel and Milken on any deal. Participation in a partnership that was guaranteed to make a profit could also be used as an inducement for managers at mutual funds and savings and loans to buy overvalued or unusually risky junk debt for their institutions.

Jesse Kornbluth reports the details of one transaction that illustrates one way in which large profits could be extracted through the partnerships.[70] When Kohlberg Kravis Roberts (KKR) engaged in its bidding war for Storer Communications, the partnership relied on assurances that Drexel could finance the deal. For KKR to beat its rival, Milken was ultimately forced to raise $1.466 billion in two days to finance a purchase that many professionals thought was too expensive.[71] This was also the first time that Milken had needed to raise sums this large on such short notice. Milken told KKR that it would have to bundle 'equity sweeteners'—warrants—with the debt to be able to finance the deal. Milken had Drexel sell the bundled debt and warrants to various partnerships that he controlled. These partnerships kept the warrants, but sold the debt to outsiders. The warrants on this deal generated about $172 million in profit. Milken-controlled partnerships secretly kept more than 80 percent of these warrants.[72]

[68] Seidman (1993, p. 235).   [69] *FDIC* v. *Milken* (1991).   [70] Kornbluth (1992).
[71] See Bruck (1989, p. 176).   [72] Kornbluth (1992, pp. 323–24).

It is dubious that secret purchases paid by Milken would have been sufficient to manipulate the junk bond market profitably. Someone who wanted to engage in market manipulation would ideally like to have access to large captive pools of financial assets. These assets would provide back-up funds sufficient to ensure that any new issue could be absorbed and moved rapidly from partnership accounts to outside accounts. Furthermore, these captive pools could be used to reduce the observed default rate by having them provide new long-term financing to companies that were truly bankrupt. Outstanding bonds could have been exchanged for new bonds held by the pools of the captive institutions. Or these companies could have been infused with new capital by a junk bond issue.

It is this possibility—that looters at savings and loans helped defer default and reduce observed default rates—that we consider next. Bribes to managers of mutual funds could be used to achieve the same effect, but we will focus on savings and loans because of our interest in the economywide effects of the incentives for looting created by government guarantees.

The Potential Profits from Broker Manipulation

Under normal circumstances, it would not pay a securities broker to use his or her own resources to change default rates in order to increase the demand for his product. The costs of the manipulation would normally overwhelm any recapture through increases in the broker's commissions. However, the late 1980s provided unique opportunities. The availability of S&Ls to be looted made the junk bond market ripe for manipulation.

A comparison of the prospective benefits to buyers of bonds and the prospective increases in commissions to bond brokers shows that a broker cannot normally increase his or her profits by purchasing at par any bonds that are about to go into default and absorbing the losses. This absorption would increase the demand for bonds, which would increase the broker's commissions, but almost invariably by less than the refinance cost to reduce the default rate on previously issued bonds.

The argument goes as follows. The expected benefit to buyers of currently issued bonds from the manipulation of default rates is the expected reduction in future losses. In a steady state, with constant new issues of bonds, the payments made on previously issued bonds will exactly correspond to the reduction in expected future losses on bonds that are currently issued, if buyers' expectations of future default losses are formed by the historical experience of past default losses. Because these expected reductions in losses are in the future but the payments by the broker-manipulator are in the present, the buyers' discounted expected gains will be less than the cost to the manipulator of changing the historical default rates. Only if the number of bonds issued in the past is considerably less than the volume of current issues will the buyers' increased valuation of the bonds exceed the brokers' costs. The broker-manipulator also faces a problem in that he will typically be able to capture only a small fraction of the increase in the market value that his expenditures create.

If buyers extrapolate the artifically low rates of default, faster growth of the market reduces the costs of manipulation relative to buyers' expected gains because it reduces the number of previously issued bonds whose losses must be absorbed relative to currently issued bonds. If the total quantity of bonds outstanding grows at the rate of interest on the junk bonds and if expectations of future default rates are determined by current default rates, the increase in the market value of the newly issued bonds induced by the manipulation will just equal the broker's cost of absorbing default losses. If the market grows faster than the rate of interest, the expected gains in the value of the new bonds will exceed the expected costs to the broker.

Many different circumstances made the junk bond market of the 1980s uniquely manipulable. Drexel and the Milken partnerships were able to capture a significant share of the wedge between the demand curve and supply curve for junk bonds, as earlier illustrated by the Storer deal. Milken and Drexel were not just charging a routine commission. In many cases, they were able take advantage of an unusually large bid-ask spread and to adjust it to extract the maximum possible amount. Accordingly, they could have captured an unusually large share of the increased value of the newly issued bonds that would be caused by manipulation of default rates. So the benefits of such a manipulation would have been unusually large.

Would the costs to the broker of such a manipulation have been low enough to make it worth attempting? Certainly the costs of the manipulation would have been low indeed—zero in fact—if the refinanced issues were not financed by the broker himself, but instead were purchased by S&Ls that were engaged in looting. The high nominal yields of the refinancings would enhance the profit statements of the S&Ls. Additionally the owners and porfolio managers could benefit from favorable terms in the purchase of stock options or shares of Milken's partnerships.

In addition to being able to use other people's money, three additional factors amplified the effectiveness of any portfolio purchases by the S&Ls in reducing the overall default rate. As already discussed, the high-yield securitized debt market was new and growing very rapidly (much faster than the rate of interest during the 1980s), so the volume of old issues whose default losses needed to be manipulated was quite small relative to the volume of newly issued bonds. Second, S&L assets did not need to be used directly to purchase refinancings. It was sufficient for sophisticated investors to understand that the assets of the S&Ls could *later* be used as a guarantee against future losses. In the meantime, these investors could fearlessly pocket the high coupons paid. Third, because the refinancings sold without difficulty and their premiums were so high, copycat investors (that is, investors who inferred asset quality from price) would take a significant fraction of the issues. As in the earlier example of Dallas real estate, copycat investors would multiply the impact of S&L looting.

In sum, the junk bond market of the 1980s provided a unique opportunity for market manipulation. Were these opportunities taken? In the following discussion, we will show that the behavior of the junk bond market is in fact consistent with market manipulation.

The Evidence: Actual Default Rates

We present two kinds of evidence to support the possibility that the kind of manipulation described earlier took place during the 1980s. First, we show that even though

Drexel was believed to have very low default rates, below those of other issuers,[73] in fact the true default rate on its debt was higher than that for other junk underwriters. In particular, the default rate on junk issued to refinance outstanding debt was especially high, as was its debt issued for 'general corporate purposes.' The next section will also review evidence that Milken and his associates engaged in patterns of trading with thrifts consistent with the scheme outlined above.

Paul Asquith, David W. Mullins, and Eric D. Wolff have shown the importance of exchanges in reducing recorded default rates.[74] Of the $14.6 billion of junk bonds issued between 1977 and 1983, $2.2 billion or about 15 percent had already been exchanged by the end of 1988.[75] If these exchanges involved troubled companies that would otherwise have defaulted, the omission of these exchanges from cumulative measured defaults could have substantially altered the observed default rate. There is evidence that these issues did indeed involve unusually troubled companies because refinancings in their short average life up to the end of 1986 had a remarkably high rate of default—39 percent (by quantity) and 33 percent (by value).[76] Because the study by Asquith, Mullins, and Wolff, which is our source for these numbers, was the first to calculate default rates inclusive of these exchanges, there is every reason to believe that they were not taken into account in the junk bond market's halcyon years. Moreover, because this study measured default rates only up to the end of 1988, before the collapse of the junk bond market in 1989 and 1990, the measured default rate as of this point can only underestimate the ultimate default rate.

It should be emphasized that exchanges represented only one way in which defaults could be swept under the carpet. The proceeds from issues for general corporate purposes or perhaps even for mergers and acquisitions could also be used to finance current debt service, thereby preventing default on prior issues.

A more recent analysis by the Bond Investor's Association, which makes use of a comprehensive tabulation of all junk debt, demonstrates an especially high default rate on Drexel-issued refinancings and classifies them according to the stated purpose of the debt issue.[77] As of the end of 1992, the default rate on Drexel bonds issued between 1983 and 1990 to refinance existing bonds was 45.2 percent, compared with 26.0 percent for all other issuers.[78] As the study's author observes, 'These figures lend support to critics who have contended that Drexel concealed the poor quality of many of its issues by refinancings.'[79]

The chronology of events is also consistent with the hypothesis of manipulation. The collapse of the junk bond market quickly followed Milken's indictment in March 1989. Between the end of 1988 and October 1989, the spread between the junk bond yield

---

[73] See George Gilder, 'The War Against Wealth,' *Wall Street Journal*, September 27, 1990, p. A12.

[74] Asquith, Mullins, and Wolff (1989).

[75] Authors' calculations from Asquith, Mullins, and Wolff (1989, Table 1, p. 928, and Table 6, p. 934).

[76] Asquith, Mullins, and Wolff (1989, Table 7, p. 935).

[77] See Lehmann (1993).

[78] Default rates are here calculated by averaging over issues. There were eighty-four refinancings by Drexel and one hundred by other underwriters.

[79] Lehmann (1993, p. 25).

and the yield on ten-year Treasuries rose from 488 basis points to 704. In 1990, the spread rose further, to above 1000.[80] (It has subsequently declined.) These changes in spread are thus much more than the 2 to 3 percent change in yield that might be thought sufficient to make possible a large takeover wave.

Furthermore, over this same period junk bond defaults rose dramatically, by one account from $5 billion in 1988 to $22 billion in 1990. In the first quarter of 1991, they totaled $8.2 billion, compared to only $1.3 billion for the same period in 1988.[81]

Links to Thrifts

Although, as mentioned earlier, S&Ls held only $13.2 billion of junk bonds, these holdings were remarkable for their concentration: 69 percent were held by just eleven institutions, all of which had close ties to Milken. The complaint by the FDIC against Milken on behalf of the Resolution Trust Corporation (RTC) for improprieties in the junk bond market (which was settled for $1.3 billion)[82] makes the general claim that he led a group of 'conspirators' (the so-called Milken Group) who used S&L assets to raise artificially the price of junk bonds.

Beginning at least in 1982, the Milken Group and those acting in concert and conspiracy with it have willfully, deliberately and systematically plundered certain S&Ls. The Milken Group targeted the S&Ls because their deposits provided the S&Ls with an enormous pool of capital. Ready, repeated, easy access to that pool of capital was a necessary part of the Milken Group's scheme to unlawfully inflate the value of junk bonds and to create the illusion that such inflated value could be realized in a liquid market.[83]

Again, lest there be any doubt about its claims, the complaint later reemphasizes them:

Because of the purchases by the Partnership Class [mainly partnerships owned or controlled by the Milken Group] and the other insider accounts, the Milken Group was able to create a false appearance of heavy demand for Drexel-underwritten issues. This deception furthered the scheme by giving apparent credence to the proclamations about the value of junk bonds, and the artificial demand caused the market price for such bonds to increase, enabling the Partnership Class and other insider accounts to reap substantial profits and thus to reward various participants in their schemes.[84]

According to the complaint, many S&L executives variously mismanaged their junk bond purchases. Three of these—Thomas Spiegel of Columbia, Charles Keating of Lincoln, and David Paul of CenTrust—were, along with unknown others, named as co-defendants. According to James B. Stewart, Columbia S&L was one of the 'captive'

---

[80] See First Boston Corporation (1989, 1990), quoted in Black (1993*a*).

[81] See David Gillen, 'Moody's Says Junk Quality Still Sliding; Number of Corporate Defaults Surges,' *The Bond Buyer*, March 15, 1991, p. 3, and Constance Mitchell and Anita Raghaven, 'Junk Bond Prices Hold Steady Despite Report That Defaults Hit a Record in the Latest Period,' *Wall Street Journal*, April 9, 1991, p. 50, quoted in Black (1993*b*).

[82] See Stewart (1992, p. 523) and Seidman (1993, p. 238).   [83] *FDIC* v. *Milken* (1991, p. 38).

[84] *FDIC* v. *Milken* (1991, pp. 44–45).

institutions that allowed Milken to 'freely trade' in their accounts.[85] Columbia was the largest holder of junk bonds by a factor of two, with more than a quarter of all S&L-held junk. Benjamin J. Stein has described how Spiegel was partially rewarded for such cooperation.[86] Stein reports a transaction between Milken and Spiegel involving Columbia's purchase of the shaky bonds and preferred stocks involved in the Storer Communications leveraged buyout described above. A partnership owned by Spiegel family members was reportedly given stock options for equity in Storer for $132,000, with the options sold about a year after the leveraged buyout for $7 million.[87]

The complaint claims that such behavior was part of a general pattern:

> The Milken Group cultivated a group of persons who controlled S&Ls. Each of these persons purchased and sold junk bonds at the bidding of the Milken Group. Each of these persons intended to share in the plunder of their respective institutions and to obtain other benefits the Milken Group provided to those who purchased large quantities of Drexel-underwritten junk bonds. These persons, although not necessarily aware of the scope of or participating in the broad range of illegal activity engaged in by the Milken Group, agreed to follow the bidding of the Milken Group for their own benefit and contrary to the interests of their respective institutions. The persons, in addition to others not now known, include Charles H. Keating, Jr., who controlled Lincoln, David Paul, who controlled CenTrust, and Thomas Spiegel, who controlled Columbia.[88]

According to other sources, such use of other people's money was not confined to S&Ls. According to Stewart and Stein, Fred Carr, the head of First Executive Life Insurance, also gave control of his junk bond portfolio over to Milken. Carr let Milken's group trade the bonds in the First Executive portfolio and send the tickets for confirmation later.[89] The details in this case are relatively well established since the First Executive Companies (the parent), which had presumed assets of $15.2 billion, became massively insolvent and was taken over by authorities in 1991. Roughly one-third of the assets in the life insurance company were invested in junk bonds. By comparison, Metropolitan Life had 1 percent of its portfolio in junk, Aetna had 1 percent, and Prudential, 3 percent.[90]

Milken and Drexel took an active part, apparently, in the transfer of ownership of many of the S&Ls that the complaint describes as captives. In some cases, the connection was indirect, made through close associates. According to the complaint, for example, Executive Life financed the acquisition of 24.9 percent of the equity of Imperial Savings and Loan, while subsidiaries of Columbia took over 8.1 percent of Imperial's common stock.[91] But the relationship was often direct. In the case of Columbia, for example, Drexel acquired 10.3 percent, and a trust for Milken's children acquired 9.9 percent of the S&L's common stock—shares that were sold after Columbia acquired a significant junk bond portfolio.[92] Milken also financed the acquisition of Lincoln Savings and Loan

---

[85] Stewart (1992, p. 521).   [86] Stein (1992).   [87] Stein (1992, p. 105).
[88] FDIC v. *Milken* (1991, p. 32).   [89] See Stewart (1992, p. 521) and Stein (1992).
[90] A.M. Best Company (1990).   [91] FDIC v. *Milken* (1991, p. 62).
[92] FDIC v. *Milken* (1991, p. 56).

by Charles Keating; Ivan Boesky has testified that Milken repeatedly encouraged him to purchase a thrift.

Finally, there is circumstantial evidence that members of the Milken group also tried to manipulate junk bond ratings. According to Stein, the bond rating company Duff & Phelps was taken over by a partnership that had undisclosed ownership shares held by members of the Milken group, including James Dahl, Milken's top salesman in the Beverly Hills office, as well as two of the 'captive' thrifts named in the complaint, Imperial and Columbia. Duff & Phelps subsequently gave favorable ratings to bonds that were issued by Columbia.[93]

Calibrating the Magnitudes

Institutions with close links to Milken and Drexel controlled portfolios that held about $14 billion in junk bonds: about $9 billion at the thrifts named as captives in the complaint and about $5 billion at First Executive. Total defaults on all original issue high-yield bonds with issue dates of 1986 or earlier totaled only $7.6 billion until the end of 1988.[94] If one-quarter of the junk holdings of the so-called 'captive' institutions were used to prevent defaults, this by itself would have reduced the observed default rate by about one-third. If Milken could have persuaded others to purchase some of the bonds of troubled companies, the reduction in the observed default rate would have been greater. One potential source of purchasers was insiders with implicit guarantees that the captives would purchase the bonds before prices fell. Outside investors, behaving like the copycats in Dallas or index investors in the stock market, may also have bought some of these troubled bonds because apparently sophisticated investors were also buying them. Thus junk bond portfolios of the S&Ls were of sufficient size to have had significant impact on perceived default rates in this market.

One more simple calculation suggests how profitable the link with a savings and loan could be. Drexel underwrote the acquisition of Lincoln S&L by Charles Keating's takeover vehicle, American Continental Corporation (ACC), at a cost of $56 million. Over the next five years, Lincoln purchased $2.7 billion of junk bonds.[95] It is easy to verify, with the annual pattern of junk bond purchases reported in the FDIC complaint, that even if Drexel charged at the lower end of its commissions (3 percent) and even if it had a discount rate as high as 15 percent, the commission income alone would have more than paid for the entire purchase price of the thrift—even if Drexel had given the entire $56 million to Keating.

The Role of Manipulation in the Takeover Wave

Whatever the evidence for manipulation of the junk bond market of the 1980s, such manipulation cannot be the whole explanation for the takeover wave of the 1980s. The gain to shareholders of acquired firms between 1977 and 1986 was $346 billion in 1986 dollars.[96] Because this increase is much larger than the total volume of junk

---

[93] Stein (1992, pp. 147–48).   [94] See Asquith, Mullins, and Wolff (1989, table iv, p. 932).
[95] *FDIC* v. *Milken* (1991, p. 64).   [96] Jensen (1988, p. 21).

bonds, no amount of manipulation could have transferred such a sum from holders of junk bonds to shareholders. Thus the manipulation of default rates can, at best, be only a partial explanation for the 1980s takeover wave. Evidence of other transfers (which shows that they also tended to be small relative to total shareholder gains), has been given by Jeffrey Pontiff, Andrei Shleifer, and Michael S. Weisbach on losses to previous bond-holders, Sanjai Bhagat, Andrei Shleifer, and Robert W. Vishny on tax benefits and layoffs, and Alan J. Auerbach and David Reishus on tax benefits.[97] Thus stocks must have been undervalued relative to fundamentals prior to the 1980s, or overvalued thereafter. A full explanation of the takeover wave, irrespective of the role of manipulation of the junk bond market, must explain this departure from fundamental values, which made the takeovers so profitable.

CONCLUSION

This paper has shown how other people's money, typically deposits in financial institutions or insurance funds, can profitably be looted, with the guarantor of the assets, typically the government and its taxpayers, left holding the bag. These opportunities for looting occur when the value of the take net of the cost of prosecution, M^*, exceeds the expected value of the underlying institution, V^*. Under such circumstances, there is special reason for owners of the financial institution to make shady deals with those who make large (perhaps under-the-table) current payments and unkeepable future promises. The large current payments will increase M^*. The unkeepable promises will decrease the value of the institution below V^*.

Furthermore, initial disturbances caused by looting in one market are likely to metastasize with serious multiplier effects into other markets. Thus the looting of S&Ls may result in a construction, or a corporate leveraged buyout, boom and bust. Large multiplier effects are caused by buyers (or sellers) who watch standard signals of market activity to determine their behavior, but who fail to understand that the usual behavior of their signals has been altered by unsuspected looting. The multiplier effects are likely to be particularly large if the actions of the looters can be coordinated in a way that is designed to manipulate market signals.

We examined four historical events in light of our model: the Chilean financial crisis, U.S. S&L regulatory changes, the Dallas/Fort Worth building boom and bust, and the junk bond–financed takeover wave. These illustrations show not only how the looters themselves behave, but also how they interact symbiotically with their accomplices and react to the attempts by the regulators to stop their activities. The historical instances also show, as the theory would predict, that the exact outcome in this game of cat (the regulators) and mouse (the looters) depends very specifically on the constraints faced by the cat and, sometimes, also on its errors.

The theory of looting gives an historical interpretation of what went wrong in the 1980s, and points to other areas that could emerge in the future. Insurance companies,

---

[97] Pontiff, Shleifer, and Weisbach (1990); Bhagat, Shleifer, and Vishny (1990); and Auerbach and Reishus (1988).

especially life insurance companies, are prime targets for looting. The bankruptcy of First Executive Life showed how a life insurance company could be looted through excessive purchase of junk bonds. The case of Coastal States Life Insurance of Georgia, seized in December 1992, shows the difficulty regulators have in controlling portfolios with complicated securities that they do not know how to value.[98] Coastal put almost all of its portfolio into interest-only strips of collateralized mortgage obligations and inverse floaters. After the market value on this supposedly hedged portfolio plunged, it took two years to close Coastal because the owner claimed to have broken no rules. However large the losses to policy holders or the people who will be taxed to make up the losses, Coastal States' owner did not do badly. His life insurance company gave the marketing affiliate he owned $15.5 million of contracts during the few short years of its life. Given the relatively loose structure of insurance supervision, what happened at Coastal can happen at many other insurance firms.

The possibilities to loot pension funds are analogous to the possibilities to loot life insurance companies. Furthermore, where there are pension guarantees, the taxpayers are the ultimate bearers of the burden of underfunded pensions when the sponsor firms go bankrupt. TWA is a case in point. Although its pension fund was one of the country's most underfunded, it offered its workers benefit increases of $100 million while it was in bankruptcy.[99] To avoid such moral hazard, bills have been introduced (but not passed) in Congress to prevent the most underfunded pension plans from increasing pension benefits.[100] One estimate of the uncovered liabilities of the federal government's Pension Benefit Guaranty Corporation is $35 billion.[101]

The currently unfolding scandal on mortgage guarantees backed by the U.S. Department of Housing and Urban Development (HUD) gives a sense of déjà vu because the major features of the S&L scandal are repeated in a new context. The government, for example, is now responsible for the $9.5 million mortgage on a property in Boston, where 'unnecessary costs' were incurred. The board in charge, it was concluded, had 'not always act[ed] in the best interests of the project.'[102] Some $43 billion of such mortgage guarantees have been issued, with defaults expected on $11.9 billion.[103]

Finally, banking crises are endemic to high-inflation countries. In the 1980s, bank stringency occurred in Argentina, Brazil, Chile, Colombia, Costa Rica, Ecuador, Mexico, Peru, and Venezuela, as well as other countries.[104] This paper has shown how attempts to curb the inflation of Latin America can lead to the looting of banks if currency convertibility is one aspect of the disinflation program. Such currency convertibility is now standard advice to countries fighting inflation.[105] The theory and examples of this

---

[98] See Laura Jereski, 'Seized Insurer's Woes Reflect Perils of CMOs,' *Wall Street Journal*, May 12, 1993, p. C1.

[99] See U.S. Congressional Budget Office (1993, p. 12).

[100] U.S. Congressional Budget Office (1993, p. 29).

[101] See U.S. Congressional Budget Office (1993, p. 3).

[102] See Jason DeParle, 'Housing Project Haunted by Ghosts of Noble Ideals,' *New York Times*, September 18, 1993, p. A8.

[103] Price Waterhouse and Company estimate cited in the *Wall Street Journal*, June 21, 1993, p. A12.

[104] See Brock (1992, p. 1).

[105] See Sachs and Larrain (1992, pp. 746–47).

paper warn that the maintenance of such convertibility must be accompanied by careful bank regulation to prevent looting of the kind that occurred in Chile. More generally, it is a safe bet that many developing countries that have far less sophisticated and honest regulatory mechanisms than those that exist in the United States will be victimized by financial market fraud as their financial markets develop.

The S&L fiasco in the United States leaves us with the question, why did the government leave itself so exposed to abuse? Part of the answer, of course, is that actions taken by the government are the result of the political process. When regulators hid the extent of the true problem with artificial accounting devices, when congressmen pressured regulators to go easy on favored constituents and political donors, when the largest brokerage firms lobbied to protect their ability to funnel brokered deposits to any thrift in the country, when the lobbyists for the savings and loan industry adopted the strategy of postponing action until industry difficulties were so large that general tax revenue would have to be used to address problems instead of revenue raised from taxes on successful firms in the industry—when these and many other actions were taken, people responded rationally to the incentives they faced within the political process.

The S&L crisis, however, was also caused by misunderstanding. Neither the public nor economists foresaw that the regulations of the 1980s were bound to produce looting. Nor, unaware of the concept, could they have known how serious it would be. Thus the regulators in the field who understood what was happening from the beginning found lukewarm support, at best, for their cause. Now we know better. If we learn from experience, history need not repeat itself.

References

Adams, James R. 1990. *The Big Fix: Inside the S&L Scandal.* New York: John Wiley.

A.M. Best Company. 1990. *Best's Insurance Reports: Life-Health.* Oldwick, N.J.: A.M. Best.

Asquith, Paul, David W. Mullins, Jr., and Eric D. Wolff. 1989. 'Original Issue High Yield Bonds: Aging Analyses of Defaults, Exchanges and Calls.' *Journal of Finance* 44(4):923–52.

—— and Thierry A. Wizman. 1990. 'Event Risk, Covenants and Bondholder Returns in Leveraged Buyouts.' *Journal of Financial Economics* 27:195–213.

Auerbach, Alan J., and David Reishus. 1988. 'Taxes and the Merger Decision.' In *Knights, Raiders, and Targets: The Impact of the Hostile Takeover,* edited by John C. Coffee, Jr., Louis Lowenstein, and Susan Rose-Ackerman. New York: Oxford University Press.

Banerjee, Abhijit V. 1993. 'A Simple Model of Herd Behavior.' *Quarterly Journal of Economics* (forthcoming).

Barth, James R. 1991. *The Great Savings and Loan Debacle.* Washington: AEI Press.

Bhagat, Sanjai, Andrei Shleifer, and Robert W. Vishny. 1990. 'Hostile Takeovers in the 1980s: The Return to Corporate Specialization.' *BPEA, Microeconomics, 1992:*1–72.

Bikhchandani, Sushil, David Hirshleifer, and Ivo Welch. 1992. 'A Theory of Fads, Fashion, Custom and Cultural Change as Informational Cascades.' *Journal of Political Economy* 100(5):992–1026.

Black, William K. 1990. 'Ending Our Forebearers' Forbearances: FIRREA and Supervisory Goodwill.' *Stanford Law and Policy Review* 2(1):102–16.

——. 1993a. 'Junk Bonds.' *Staff Report 7. San Francisco: National Commission on Financial Institution Reform, Recovery, and Enforcement (April 8).*

——. 1993b. 'The Incidence and Cost of Fraud and Insider Abuse.' Staff report 13. San Francisco: National Commission on Financial Institution Reform, Recovery, and Enforcement (April 12).

Brealey, Richard, and Stewart Myers. 1984. *Principles of Corporate Finance.* New York: McGraw-Hill.

Breeden, Richard C. 1990. 'Concerning Issues Involving Financial Institutions and Accounting Principles Before the Committee on Banking, Housing and Urban Affairs, United States Senate.' Paper prepared for the U.S. Securities and Exchange Commission for testimony before the U.S. Senate Committee on Banking, Housing, and Urban Affairs (September 10).

Brock, Philip L. 1992. 'Introduction.' In *If Texas Were Chile: A Primer on Banking Reform,* edited by Philip L. Brock. San Francisco: ICS Press.

Bruck, Connie. 1989. *The Predators' Ball: The Inside Story of Drexel Burnham and the Rise of Junk Bond Raiders.* New York: Penguin Books.

Brumbaugh, R. Dan, Jr., Andrew S. Carron, and Robert E. Litan. 1989. 'Cleaning Up the Depository Institutions Mess.' *BPEA, 1:1989,* 243–83.

Burrough, Bryan, and John Helyar. 1990. *Barbarians at the Gate: The Fall of RJR Nabisco.* New York: Harper and Row.

Caplin, Andrew, and John Leahy. 1991. 'Business as Usual, Market Crashes and Wisdom after the Fact.' Unpublished paper. Columbia University and Harvard University (December).

Craine, Roger. 1992. 'Fairly Priced Deposit Insurance.' Unpublished paper. University of California, Berkeley (November).

de la Cuadra, Sergio, and Salvador Valdés. 1992. 'Myths and Facts about Financial Liberalization in Chile: 1974–1983.' In *If Texas Were Chile: A Primer on Banking Reform,* edited by Philip L. Brock. San Francisco: ICS Press.

Edwards, Sebastian, and Alejandra Cox Edwards. 1991. *Monetarism and Liberalization: The Chilean Experiment.* Chicago: University of Chicago Press.

Esty, Benjamin C. 1992. 'Organizational Form, Leverage and Incentives: A Study of Risk Taking in the S&L Industry.' Harvard Business School (December 7).

First Boston Corporation. 1989. *High Yield Research, 3rd Quarter Review* (October).

——. 1990. *High Yield Research, 3rd Quarter Review* (October).

Friedman, Benjamin. 1989. 'Comment on "Cleaning Up the Depository Institutions Mess."' *BPEA, 1:1989,* 284–90.

Grossman, Sanford J. 1976. 'On the Efficiency of Competitive Stock Markets Where Traders Have Diverse Information.' *Journal of Finance* 31:573–85.

Jensen, Michael C. 1988. 'Takeovers: Their Causes and Consequences.' *The Journal of Economic Perspectives* 2(1):21–48.

Kane, Edward J. 1989. *The S&L Insurance Mess: How Did It Happen?* Washington: Urban Institute Press.

Kornbluth, Jesse. 1992. *Highly Confident: The Crime and Punishment of Michael Milken.* New York: William Morrow.

Lehmann, Richard. 1993. 'Analyzing Bond Defaults by Proceeds.' *Merrill Lynch: Extra Credit* (January/February):24–28.

Lucas, Robert E. Jr. 1972. 'Expectations and the Neutrality of Money.' *Journal of Economic Theory* 4:103–24.

Mayer, Martin. 1990. *The Greatest-Ever Bank Robbery: The Collapse of the Savings and Loan Industry.* New York: Charles Scribner's Sons.

McKinnon, Ronald I. 1991. *The Order of Economic Liberalization: Financial Control in the Transition to a Market Economy.* Baltimore: Johns Hopkins University Press.

Merton, Robert. 1978. 'On the Cost of Deposit Insurance When There Are Surveillance Costs.' *Journal of Business* 51(3):439–52.

National Commission on Financial Institution Reform, Recovery, and Enforcement. 1993. *Origins and Causes of the S&L Debacle: A Blueprint for Reform.* Washington: The Commission.

O'Shea, James. 1991. *The Daisy Chain: How Borrowed Billions Sank a Texas S&L.* New York: Pocketbooks.

Pizzo, Stephen, Mary Fricker, and Paul Muolo. 1989. *Inside Job: The Looting of America's Savings and Loans.* New York: McGraw-Hill.

Pontiff, Jeffrey, Andrei Shleifer, and Michael S. Weisbach. 1990. 'Reversions of Excess Pension Assets After Takeovers.' *Rand Journal of Economics* 21:600–13.

Robinson, Michael A. 1990. *Overdrawn: The Bailout of American Savings.* New York: Dutton.

Romer, David. 1993. 'Rational Asset Price Movements Without News.' *American Economic Review* (forthcoming).

Sachs, Jeffrey D., and Felipe B. Larrain. 1992. *Macroeconomics in the Global Economy.* Englewood Cliffs, N.J.: Prentice-Hall.

Scherer, Frederic M. 1988. 'Corporate Takeovers: The Efficiency Arguments.' *Journal of Economic Perspectives* 2(1):69–82.

Seidman, William L. 1993. *Full Faith and Credit: The Great S&L Debacle and Other Washington Sagas.* New York: Random House.

Shleifer, Andrei, and Robert W. Vishny. 1988. 'Value Maximization and the Acquisition Process.' *Journal of Economic Perspectives* 2 (Winter):7–20.

Short, Genie D., and Jeffrey W. Gunther. 'The Texas Thrift Situation: Implications for the Texas Financial Industry.' Paper prepared for Financial Industry Studies Department, Federal Reserve Bank of Dallas, Dallas, Texas (September).

Stein, Benjamin J. 1992. *A License to Steal: The Untold Story of Michael Milken and the Conspiracy to Bilk the Nation.* New York: Simon and Schuster.

Stewart, James B. 1992. *Den of Thieves.* New York: Simon and Schuster.

Stiglitz, Joseph E., and Andrew Weiss. 1981. 'Credit Rationing in Markets with Imperfect Information.' *American Economic Review* 71(3):393–410.

Tybout, James. 1986. 'A Firm-Level Chronicle of Financial Crises in the Southern Cone.' *Journal of Development Economics* 24(2):371–400.

Urban Land Institute. Various years. *ULI Market Profiles.* Washington: ULI.

U.S. Congressional Budget Office. 1993. *Controlling Losses of the Pension Benefit Guaranty Corporation.* Washington: Government Printing Office.

U.S. Federal Deposit Insurance Corporation et. al. v. Michael R. Milken et. al. 1991. U.S. District Court, Southern District of New York (January 18).

U.S. House of Representatives. Subcommittee of the Committee on Government Operations. 1987. *Fraud and Abuse by Insiders, Borrowers, and Appraisers in the California Thrift Industry.* Hearing. 100 Cong. 1st sess. Government Printing Office.

U.S. House of Representatives. Committee on Banking, Finance and Urban Affairs. 1990. *Effectiveness of Law Enforcement Against Financial Crime.* Field hearing. 101 Cong. 2 sess. Government Printing Office. Part 1.

U.S. Senate. Committee on Banking, Housing, and Urban Affairs. 1990. *Fraud in America's Insured Depository Institutions.* Hearing. 101 Cong. 2 sess. Government Printing Office.

———. 1991. *Restructuring the Resolution Trust Corporation and the Semiannual report on FIRREA Legislation:1991.* Hearing. 102 Cong. 1 sess. Government Printing Office.

Velasco, Andrés. 1991. 'Liberalization, Crisis, Intervention: The Chilean Financial System, 1975–85.' In *Banking Crises: Cases and Issues,* edited by V. Sundararajan and Tomás J. T. Baliño. Washington: International Monetary Fund.

White, Lawrence J. 1991. *The S&L Debacle: Public Policy Lessons for Bank and Thrift Regulation.* New York: Oxford University Press.

Wilmsen, Steven K. 1991. *Silverado: Neil Bush and the Savings and Loan Scandal.* Bethesda, Md.: National Press Books.

Yago, Glenn. 1991. *Junk Bonds: How High Yield Securities Restructured Corporate America.* New York: Oxford University Press.

PART II

MACROECONOMICS

12

Relative Wages and the Rate of Inflation[*]

GEORGE A. AKERLOF[†]

ESI

E24 E31

I

Monetary theory in the post-Keynesian era has, to a good extent, centered around the question 'is money neutral?'. This is an important question, of course, because the existence of such economic animals as the Phillips Curve may well depend on the answer. Patinkin's famous book argues for the neutrality of money: with different levels of the money supply in a perfectly competitive world all equilibrium *real* variables will be the same.[1] Naturally, in such a world the Phillips Curve cannot exist, but, as Patinkin himself writes, this is more a matter of definition than of empirical fact—for, in the long run, irrespective of the money supply (or its rate of increase), equilibrium is approached; and by definition this equilibrium precludes unemployment.

The question which presents itself is whether Patinkin's results generalize to a world which has 'stickiness' and various 'market imperfections.' Friedman, in his American Economic Association Presidential address, has asserted that it does: the long-run level of unemployment, irrespective of market structure, stickinesses, etc., will be independent of the long-run rate of increase of the money supply.[2] For, his argument goes, in the

[*] This work was previously published as George Akerlof (1969), 'Relative Wages and the Rate of Inflation', *The Quarterly Journal of Economics* LXXXIII, 3. Copyright © The MIT Press. Reproduced by kind permission.

[†] The author would like to thank Bent Hansen, Stephen A. Marglin, William Nordhaus, Albert Fishlow, Giorgio La Malfa and Bagicha Minhas for valuable comments and the Indian Statistical Institute, New Delhi for financial support. All mistakes, however, belong to the author.

[1] D. Patinkin, *Money, Interest and Prices* (2nd edn.; New York: Harper and Row, 1965). It should be stated at the outset that the models here attempt an argument essentially different from the Tobin and Gurley-Shaw portfolio balance type of argument. For this reason the portfolio, or capital investment, decision is intentionally ignored. J. Tobin, 'Money and Economic Growth,' *Econometrica*, Vol. 33 (Oct. 1965); and J. G. Gurley and E. S. Shaw, *Money in a Theory of Finance* (Washington: Brookings Institution, 1960).

[2] M. Friedman, 'The Role of Monetary Policy,' *American Economic Review*, LVIII (Mar. 1968), 7–10. Lindahl foresaw Friedman's argument thirty years ago: '...anticipated changes in the price level have no economic relevance, since they neither influence the relative prices of factors of production and consumption goods, nor the extent and direction of production.' E. Lindahl, *Studies in the Theory of Money and Capital* (London: Allen and Unwin, 1939), p. 148.

long run if a given rate of inflation is universally expected, all persons will hedge against this rate of inflation—and since all bargains are rationally decided by *real* considerations, real transactions (excluding capital formation) will take place as if this rate of inflation did not exist. At first glance Friedman's argument appears perfectly general: but the question remains whether Friedman's logic is still valid if contracts are made according to real considerations, but for the duration of the contract some price variables remain fixed in money terms. The obvious example of such an institution is the union wage bargain with both the union and management aware of the 'real' aspects of the bargain—but with the form of contract restricted so that money wages change at only yearly intervals.[3]

It is quite clear from all historical accounts of hyperinflation that such fixed-money contracts break down as the rate of inflation becomes large.[4] But for the usual Phillips-Curve watcher such cases of hyperinflation are not in the relevant range: rather the question is whether some 'moderate' rate of inflation (say 2 or 3 per cent per annum) is better than none at all.[5] In this range, given the convenience of fixed-money contracts—one of the major reasons itself for the policy goal of price stability—it is not unreasonable to expect the form of contract to remain unchanged.[6]

Of course, it is easy to show the existence and nature of a short-run Phillips Curve with fixed expectations about the future rate of inflation. In the long run if expectations about the rate of inflation are actually realized, the Phillips Curve is far more restricted; but in the models below there is an interpretation whereby such a Phillips Curve exists and the neutrality of money, in turn, is false.[7]

I I

The specific view of the economy which underlies this paper is that of Triffin's *Monopolistic Competition and General Equilibrium Theory*.[8] The economy, as pictured, consists of many monopolists who all compete for a given total level of demand (which is in turn correlated with the level of employment). Perhaps the best way to view the meaning of this model is that the producers in each oligopolistic industry reach a pricing decision not far from the decision that would be reached if the industry were in fact a monopoly. (This process is not dissimilar to what Professor Fellner describes in *Competition Among the Few*.)[9] In turn these industries (acting as monopolies) compete

---

[3] The models presented must be slightly altered to include 'wage drift.'

[4] In particular see C. Bresciani-Turroni, *The Economics of Inflation* (London: Allen and Unwin, 1937).

[5] A. W. Phillips, 'The Relation between Unemployment and the Rate of Inflation in the United Kingdom, 1861–1957,' *Economica*, N.S. XXV (Nov. 1958).

[6] An excellent justification for the convenience of temporarily fixed prices is given by O. Eckstein and G. Fromm, 'The Price Equation,' *American Economic Review*, LVIII (Dec. 1968), 1159–60.

[7] Many besides Friedman have wondered about the relation between the long-run and the short-run Phillips Curve. See especially, R. G. Lipsey, 'The Relation between Unemployment and the Rate of Change of Money Wage Rates in the United Kingdom, 1861–1957: A Further Analysis,' *Economica*, N.S. XXVII, 1960; and E. Kuh, "A Productivity Theory of Wage Levels—an Alternative to the Phillips Curve," *Review of Economic Studies*, XXXIV (Oct. 1967).

[8] Cambridge, Mass.: Harvard University Press, 1940.   [9] New York: Knopf, 1949.

amongst themselves in a Chamberlinian fashion for a fixed level of real aggregate demand.

The natural worry, of course, is that the problem of oligopolistic interdependence has been seriously ignored; but this would be a misunderstanding of the spirit of the argument. Rather monopolistic competition is quite naturally chosen as the simplest example of the imperfect (and interdependent) world we wish to picture—and any of the other classical bargaining solutions might give different results algebraically—but would give the same results qualitatively. Also, Chamberlinian independence is undoubtedly a bad model for the behavior of large firms in many industries; but, on the contrary, it may be a good description of interindustry pricing behavior. As Triffin points out cotton textiles and automobiles may compete as much for a consumer dollar as any two types of cloth or any two types of automobile; but it is also implausible that the automobile manufacturers and the textile producers take account of the mutual interdependence of their pricing decisions.

In this spirit an economy is pictured with only two firms (where this small number of firms is an abstraction of some true multidimensional many-unit economy). And in accord with monopolistic competition theory each firm (or industry) chooses a price level such that marginal cost equals marginal revenue—without taking the other firm's reaction into account. But there is nothing inherent in the approach (except perhaps a desire for algebraic simplicity) which dictates this particular solution to the oligopoly problem.

To give the demand curves form and substance let

$$D_1 = a - p_1/p_2 \tag{1}$$

and let D_2 be, symmetrically,

$$D_2 = a - p_1/p_2 \tag{2}$$

where D and p are demand and prices, where subscripts one and two refer to firms one and two, and where a is a parameter. If $p_1 = p_2$, $D_1 = D_2 = a - 1$. In Chamberlinian language the 'dd' curves of firm one are the demand curves with p_2 fixed. And the 'DD' curve with $p_1 = p_2$ is a vertical line. The parameter a, accordingly corresponds to the level of total output, which is close to the level $2a - 2$. These demand curves are slightly less than ideal for several reasons. (1) Ideally, the demand curves for the two firms should add up to some given constant irrespective of relative prices. But the simplification in algebra made possible by (1) and (2) should justify their choice—at least for expository purposes. It should also be noticed that in the neighborhood of $p_1/p_2 = 1$, $D_1 + D_2 = 2a - 2$, up to second order. (2) An argument is also necessary to justify the use of a as a parameter. If the demand curves were written more generally

$$D_1 = a - bp_1/p_2 \tag{1'}$$

and

$$D_2 = a - bp_2/p_1 \tag{2'}$$

all solutions would depend on the value of a/b—or a parameter which reflects the elasticity of demand. On the other hand, it makes sense to vary a as a proxy to reflect what is happening in another part of the market: as full employment is approached there is a decrease in the elasticity of supply of labor. In the example used in this section, marginal costs are assumed to be zero, to simplify the mathematics. In the next section the supply variable is given the wrong dimensionality (again to simplify the mathematics)—but the artificial device of varying a relative to b gives qualitatively the same results as changing the supply elasticities. A later footnote justifies this procedure rigorously.

Judgment is suspended (until later) about the determinants of a; but two comments must be made now. First of all, a, which corresponds to the level of aggregate demand, is considered a parameter which is, in turn, controlled by the governmental controls of monetary and fiscal policy. Second, quite clearly this is a closed economy—for otherwise a third 'firm' must be added whose pricing behavior is exogenously given. For this reason alone the model described would be a much better picture of the American economy, for example, than of the British.

To continue, the model assumes that firms operate in the following way; they are Chamberlinian monopolistic competitors. That means that each firm sets its price so that $MR = MC$, where marginal revenue represents the change in revenue from selling an additional unit of output—if the competitor leaves *his* price unchanged. It should be emphasized here, as in the next section, that this particular assumption is not in any way essential to the overall point of view.

Temporarily it is assumed that neither firm one nor firm two has any variable costs (or that MC equals zero for both firms). As such this section should be considered a finger exercise for the increasingly complex models of later sections.

The second important element of the model is the nonsynchronization of pricing decisions by firms one and two. By this it is meant that firm one makes a pricing decision each January and firm two makes a pricing decision each July. It is also an important feature of the model that these prices remain constant throughout the year. Measuring time in half-years, firm one makes its price decisions at even times $2t$, and firm two makes its pricing decisions at odd times $2t + 1$, and

$$p_{1,\,2t} = p_{1,\,2t+1} \tag{3}$$

$$p_{2,\,2t+1} = p_{2,\,2t+2}. \tag{4}$$

This constancy of money prices over a two-period interval is the major feature which differentiates our thinking from Friedman's.[10] The justification for this assumption is

---

[10] Friedman, *op. cit.*

that it does describe a real-world form of market imperfection. This assumption becomes considerably more realistic in the next section where the 'price-variables' which are yearly constant are money wages instead of goods prices.

Firms one and two have symmetric demand curves and bargains are made in real terms; with the same expectations about the rate of inflation and a given level of aggregate demand, firm one's view of the world at *even* times will correspond exactly to firm two's view of the world at *odd* times. As a result—which can be rigorously proved—firm one at *even* times will have exactly the same real possibilities as firm two at *odd* times. And the relative price chosen determines the point attained. As a result, the relative price chosen by firm one at even times will be the same as the relative price chosen by firm two at odd times.

At this point, since the model is nearly complete, it is worth-while to pause and summarize the assumptions already made: (A) There are just two firms. (B) Demands are given by (1) and (2). (C) Each firm sets a price once a year, equations (3) and (4). (D) In setting this price each firm maximizes its expected profits over the two-period interval for which this price will be maintained. It fails, however, to take account of the reaction of the other firm in the next period. (E) At least temporarily, the marginal cost of each firm is zero.

The two assumptions of nonsynchronization and the symmetry of the relative pricing decisions can be coupled together:

by the symmetry of (1) and (2) and with identical cost curves and expectations about the rate of inflation,

$$\frac{p_{1,\,2t}}{p_{2,\,2t}} = \frac{p_{2,\,2t+1}}{p_{1,\,2t+1}} = \frac{p_{1,\,2t+2}}{p_{2,\,2t+2}} \tag{5}$$

and together with (3) and (4)

$$
\begin{aligned}
p_{1,\,2t+2} &= \frac{p_{2,\,2t+1}}{p_{1,\,2t+1}} p_{2,\,2t+2} \quad \text{by (5)}\\[2mm]
&= \frac{p_{2,\,2t+1}}{p_{1,\,2t+1}} p_{2,\,2t+1} \quad \text{by (4)}\\[2mm]
&= \frac{p_{1,\,2t}}{p_{2,\,2t}} p_{2,\,2t+1} \quad \text{by (5)}\\[2mm]
&= \left(\frac{p_{1,\,2t}}{p_{2,\,2t}}\right)^2 p_{1,\,2t+1} \quad \text{by (5)}\\[2mm]
&= \left(\frac{p_{1,\,2t}}{p_{2,\,2t}}\right)^2 p_{1,\,2t} \quad \text{by (3)}
\end{aligned}
$$

or, rewriting:

$$\frac{p_{1,\,2t+2}}{p_{1,\,2t}} = \left(\frac{p_{1,\,2t}}{p_{2,\,2t}}\right)^2. \tag{6}$$

Prices rise over the year by a multiple equal to $\left(\frac{p_{1,\,2t}}{p_{2,\,2t}}\right)^2$. Relative prices determine this rate of inflation.[11]

Equation (6) occasions some remarks. It should be clear that it is independent of the particular market behavior: it depends only on symmetry and nonsynchronization. Equation (6) should also make clear that the assumptions both of nonsynchronization and of noncompetitive markets are necessary (as well as sufficient) for this view of inflation.

For nonsynchronization allows the economy to depart from static equilibrium at all times: in this economy firms one and two can only be simultaneously satisfied if the rate of inflation is zero. Later it will be shown that the desired relative price (p_1/p_2) depends on the level of aggregate demand. In the normal case there is only one level of aggregate demand for which the desired relative price is equal to one. Without nonsynchronization any other level of aggregate demand is incompatible with equilibrium—because p_1/p_2 and p_2/p_1 cannot both simultaneously attain their 'desired' values. The level of output for which the desired relative price is one therefore corresponds to Friedman's long-run equilibrium.

The dynamics of this assertion demand a sneak preview of what follows. In Friedman's dynamics, with a given money supply or rate of growth of the money supply, if the desired relative price is larger than one, prices will rise sufficiently to reduce real balances and therefore aggregate demand—and vice versa if the desired relative price is less than one. Friedman's system does not allow—which nonsynchronization does allow—a continued dynamic tension so that relative prices never fully adjust. This is discussed further in Section IV below.

Equation (6) should also make clear the importance of noncompetitive markets. If monopoly power is unimportant, in the presence of unused resources the relative price set by each decision-maker will be very low; with the full use of resources the relative price set by each decision-maker would be high. Thus large changes in the rate of inflation result from small changes in aggregate demand. In the limit this corresponds to the traditional quantity theory point of view.

Returning to the specific model of monopolistic competition and to the demand curves (1) and (2) allows an exact evaluation of the inflationary process. As a Chamberlinian monopolistic competitor, each January the manager of firm one sets the price of the good produced by firm one to maximize revenue for the whole year. There will be some slight differences of behavior if revenue is discounted by a rate of return or the rate of inflation. For the sake of exposition we shall assume for the moment that the revenue maximized is undiscounted.

Revenue is $p_{1,\,2t}D_{1,\,2t} + p_{1,\,2t+1}D_{1,\,2t+1}.D_{1,\,2t+1}$ depends, however, on the unknown price charged by firm two at time $2t + 1$. But suppose that firm one expects this price to rise by a multiple $(\gamma^e)^2$, or that

$p_{2,\,2t+1}^e = \gamma^{e^2} p_{2,\,2t}$ (where '*e*' refers to 'expected'). In this case expected revenue R^e will be:

---

[11] Similar equations can be derived if the demands for firms one and two are not symmetrical and also if the expectations of firms one and two are different.

$$R^e = p_{1,\,2t}\left(a - \frac{p_{1,\,2t}}{p_{2,\,2t}}\right) + p_{1,\,2t+1}\left(a - \frac{p_{1,\,2t+1}}{p^e_{2,\,2t+1}}\right)$$

$$= p_{1,\,2t}\left(a - \frac{p_{1,\,2t}}{p_{2,\,2t}}\right) + p_{1,\,2t}\left(a - \frac{p_{1,\,2t}}{\gamma^{e^2}\,p_{2,\,2t}}\right).$$

Given these expectations firm one chooses $p_{1,\,2t}$ to maximize R^e. Being a monopolistic competitor he maximizes R^e with respect to p_1 as if p_2 were independent of his choice of p_1. This yields the condition that

$$\frac{p_{1,\,2t}}{p_{2,\,2t}} = \frac{a\gamma^{e^2}}{1 + \gamma^{e^2}}$$

If firm two has the same expectations as firm one about the rate of inflation, by (6),

$$\gamma^A = \frac{a\gamma^{e^2}}{1 + \gamma^{e^2}} \tag{7}$$

where $(\gamma^A)^2$ represents the yearly multiple of price change.

Equation (7) gives the actual rate of inflation as a function of the level of aggregate demand and the expected rate of inflation. With given expectations this could be considered a short-run Phillips Curve.

In the long run, however, according to Friedman's argument the expected and the actual rates of inflation should coincide.[12] In functional notation this gives two equilibrium conditions

$$\gamma^A = F(a, \gamma^e) \tag{8}$$

$$\gamma^A = \gamma^e \tag{9}$$

or, rewriting, in equilibrium

$$\gamma = F(a, \gamma), \tag{10}$$

where γ denotes an equilibrium rate of inflation.

The natural question is whether there is a unique $\gamma = \gamma(a)$ for each level of aggregate demand a. Such a function would correspond, of course, to a long-run Phillips Curve.

With only static considerations, there is no such unique γ which can be associated with each a. For $a > 2$ the solutions of (10) are $\gamma = 0$, and $\gamma = \frac{a \pm (a^2 - 4)^{1/2}}{2}$. For $a = 2$ the solutions are $\gamma = 0$ and $\gamma = 1$; and for $a < 2$ the only real solution is $\gamma = 0$.

Considering $a > 2$, there is some reason for choosing the upper roots as the end result of the process described. Figure 12.1 graphs γ^A as a function of γ^e. It is seen that

---

[12] Friedman, *op. cit.*

George A. Akerlof

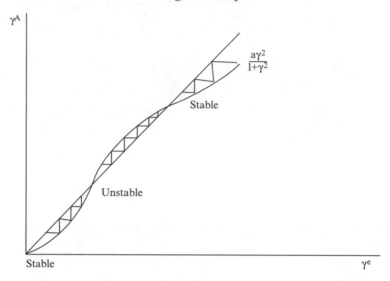

Figure 12.1.

with static expectations, 0 and $(a + (a^2 - 4)^{1/2})/2$ are stable roots (follow the zigzags in Figure 12.1).

Starting with nondeflationary but static expectations about the rate of inflation, with $a > 2$, the upper root will be approached. Choosing this root as '*the solution*' then

$$\gamma = (a + (a^2 - 4)^{1/2})/2 \ a > 2 \tag{11}$$

and $d\gamma/da = 1/2(1 + a/(a^2 - 4)^{1/2}) > 0$; or, the long-run equilibrium of the economy given an initial condition of nondeflationary expectations, is an increasing function of the level of overall aggregate demand. With the restrictions mentioned and the appropriate qualifications (11) can be taken as a long-run Phillips Curve.

While the theory laid down is satisfactory in this stability of the upper roots—and the consequent gravitation toward these upper roots with initial nondeflationary expectations, one fact is particularly unsettling. The double roots are inherent in the problem and depend on the specific nature of neither the cost nor the demand functions. And if $\gamma = 1$ is a solution of system (8) and (9), it will also be a double root. This can be shown formally—but a heuristic argument clarifies the reason for this happening.

The profit-maximizer controlling firm one chooses a relative price x to maximize the sum of its profits in both the early and the later periods. In the noninflationary case the relative price which maximizes profits in the first period and in the second period are exactly the same. With an expected (nonzero) rate of inflation, however, there is a conflict between maximizing profits in the first and in the second periods. If x^1 is the profit-maximizing relative price in the first period, then $x^1\gamma^{e^2}$ is the profit-maximizing relative price in the second period. Since the demand functions are second differentiable and the same weight is placed on both the first and second period, the profit-maximizing solution is approximately (up to second order) to let x be the average of these two relative prices. Therefore, in the neighborhood of $x = 1$,

$$x = \frac{1 + \gamma^{e^2}}{2}, \text{ with the result that}$$

$$\frac{dx}{d\gamma^e} = \gamma^e = 1.$$

At the same time this shows the natural way to elude the double-rootedness problem. A high rate of time discount, which causes the decision-maker to place a low weight on the second period, reduces $dx/d\gamma^e$ and can lead to single-solution results with all the desirable properties. Clearly this is the case in the limit where only the early period is considered and

$$\gamma^e = \gamma^A = p_1/p_2 = a/2.$$

The next step is to add money to the system. This is done in the simplest way. The parameter a, or real demand, is associated with real balances. Suppose that $a = g(M/p)$, or that a is functionally dependent on real balances.

There is a slight problem of representing real balances in our model, because 'the price level' is well defined only if p_1 equals p_2. Therefore real balances are not uniquely well defined. There is the further problem that it is unreasonable to assume that an individual firm considers the effect of its price decision on the level of real balances. All of this suggests that in constructing an example needless complication will be avoided if the demand curve for firm one depends upon M/p_2, where p_2 is interpreted as the price level of 'other' goods and similarly the demand curve for firm two should depend on M/p_1. In this spirit let:

$$D_1 = \frac{M}{p_2} - \frac{p_1}{p_2}$$

$$D_2 = \frac{M}{p_1} - \frac{p_2}{p_1}.$$

Further suppose that the nominal money supply is increasing at a positive rate λ. Given initial nondeflationary price expectations, and, initially M/p_2 and $M/p_1 > 2$, an equilibrium will be approached with λ equal to the rate of inflation. For suppose that p_1 and p_2 are increasing at a rate less than λ, then according to the previous argument a will increase, and therefore the rate of inflation. Similarly if p_1 and p_2 are increasing at a rate greater than λ, real balances (or a) will be decreasing.

As a consequence, in the long run prices and the money supply will be increasing at the same rate. The rate of increase of the money supply determines the level of real balances so that prices and the money supply are increasing at the same rate. The rate of increase of the money supply therefore determines the long-run level of real balances and of real activity.

III

From the last section we preserve the assumption that there are just two firms which act as monopolistic competitors in dividing up a total aggregate demand—and that the demand curves for firms one and two are given by equations (1) and (2) respectively.

But other assumptions are changed: First, the prices of goods are free to adjust in each period. But money wages, in contrast, must remain fixed throughout the year. Second, each firm is given a simple production function—but third, the nature of the wage-bargain must be specified (and therefore given restrictive form). Finally, the framework of this section, being less restrictive, allows easy modification to solve the problem of the dimensionality of a.

To begin, it is assumed that the short-run production function of each firm is

$$Q_1 = E_1$$
$$Q_2 = E_2$$

or, output of each firm is proportional to its employment.

The cost function of each firm can be specified then:

$$C_1 = w_1 Q_1$$
$$C_2 = w_2 Q_2,$$

or the cost of production for each firm is the wage rate of its workers times the level of output.

A bit of algebra shows that if marginal revenue equals marginal cost

$$(a - 2D_1)p_2 = w_1$$
$$(a - 2D_2)p_1 = w_2$$

or, equivalently,

$$p_1 = 1/2(ap_2 + w_1)$$
$$p_2 = 1/2(ap_1 + w_2).$$

Countervailing the oligopoly power of the firms, we picture yearly bargains made between unions and employers. The best justification for this kind of bargaining solution is a desire to incorporate some elements of Professor Galbraith's theory.[13]

---

[13] J. K. Galbraith, *American Capitalism, The Concept of Countervailing Power* (Boston: Houghton Mifflin, 1952).

But different structures, closer to perfect competition, could yield similar results. Specifically in mind are Becker's comments about the returns to specific training costs.[14] It is clear from his argument that the division of the returns to specific training costs, by their nature, involves some sort of bargaining between the employer and the employee. Also several empirical studies of 'learning-by-doing' in specialized tasks give some evidence—although the connection is not necessary—for the importance of specific training.[15]

In our particular model there are just two unions: the union which deals with firm one and the union which deals with firm two. Bargaining occurs yearly—and once a year a money wage is set: this money wage is constant throughout the year. Bargaining for union one occurs every January. Bargaining for the second union occurs every July. Again measuring time in half years, the bargaining between firm one and its union occurs at times $2t$ (for integers t); and bargaining for union two occurs at times $2t + 1$ (for integers t).

One simple example of the union-employer bargaining process is given as follows. Each union realizes that higher wages induce higher prices in its own industry. In turn higher prices lead to less demand and therefore less employment. High wages consequently induce high unemployment rates for the given union; low wages mean the opposite. Thus there may be some level of wages (neither 0 nor ∞) which maximizes total union income. Each union, we say, wishes to maximize its money income over the coming year. (This is based on a model of union behavior suggested by John Dunlop.)[16] The union demands that wage which it thinks will maximize its money income. The firms accede to these demands. Again, it is important to emphasize that the exact nature of the bargaining solution is not important in the phenomenon described.

A similar model is given by assuming that each union maximizes

$$a(u)E + (1 - a(u))\frac{wE}{p},$$

or that the union maximizes some function of employment and real income. As employment rises (or as u the unemployment rate falls) the weight on real income rises. This formulation solves the problem of the artificial nature of the parameter a: we can assume a constant but that a varies with the level of aggregate demand. But another, probably less serious, problem occurs. Since there are two goods, the price level p is not well defined; some device for defining p in terms of p_1 and p_2 is needed before a Phillips Curve can be derived.

---

[14] G. S. Becker, *Human Capital* (New York and London: Columbia University Press, 1964).

[15] See references given by K. J. Arrow, 'The Economic Implications of Learning by Doing,' *Review of Economic Studies*, XXIX (June 1962) and also S. Hollander, *The Sources of Increased Efficiency: A Study of du Pont Rayon Plants* (Cambridge, Mass.: M.I.T. Press, 1965).

[16] J. T. Dunlop, *Wage Determination Under Trade Unions* (New York: Macmillan, 1944), Chap. III.

In the text, however, the original model will be assumed: union one then wishes to maximize $w_{1,\,2t}E_{1,\,2t} + w_{1,\,2t}E_{1,\,2t+1}$ where the period $2t$ represents periods from January to July and $2t + 1$ represents periods from July to January.

Exactly the same problems with the expected and actual rates of inflation occur in the more complex model here that occurred in the last section (and exactly the same analysis can be used). If union one expects $p_{2,\,2t+1}$ to be higher by a multiple γ^e, then

$$E^e_{1,\,2t+1} = 1/2\left(a - \frac{w_{1,\,2t+1}}{p^e_{2,\,2t+1}}\right)$$

$$= 1/2\left(a - \frac{w_{1,\,2t}}{\gamma^e p_{2,\,2t}}\right)$$

(where e refers to 'expected')

and union one chooses its wage to maximize

$$w_{1,\,2t}E_{1,\,2t} + w_{1,\,2t+1}E^e_{1,\,2t+1}, \text{ or },$$

using calculus,

$$\frac{w_{1,\,2t}}{p_{2,\,2t}} = \frac{a\gamma^e}{1 + \gamma^e}.$$

(The difference in γ^e between here and Section II may be noted; this is only a matter of notational convenience).

Also there is an analogue of equation (6). Because of the rationality of economic agents and because the economy is closed, all bargains will occur in real terms, and it can be asserted that

$$w_{1,\,2t} = f(p_{1,\,2t},\, p_{2,\,2t},\, w_{2,\,2t};\gamma^e,\, a)$$
$$p_{1,\,2t} = g(p_{2,\,2t},\, w_{1,\,2t},\, w_{2,\,2t};\gamma^e,\, a)$$
$$p_{2,\,2t} = h(p_{1,\,2t},\, W_{1,\,2t},\, w_{2,\,2t};\gamma^e,\, a).$$

With a given expected rate of price increase, and a given level of aggregate demand, the price of each good or factor (subject to change at a given time) is a linear-homogeneous function of the prices of all other goods and factors.

With $w_{2,\,2t}$ fixed there are three equations and three unknowns. Because all three equations are homogeneous of degree one (in the goods and factor prices), if $(p^0_{1,\,2t},\, p^0_{2,\,2t},\, w^0_{1,\,2t})$ is a solution with $w_{2,\,2t} = w^0_{2,\,2t}$, then $(\lambda p^0_{1,\,2t},\, \lambda p^0_{2,\,2t},\, \lambda w^0_{1,\,2t})$ is a solution with $w_{2,\,2t} = \lambda w^0_{2t,\,2t}$. Therefore, if there is a unique solution of these equations for given γ^e, a and $w_{2,\,2t}$,

$$\frac{w_{1,\,2t}}{w_{2,\,2t}} = \Omega(\gamma^e,\, a).$$

Symmetry dictates with constant γ^e that:

$$\frac{w_{1,\,2t}}{w_{2,\,2t}} = \frac{w_{2,\,2t+1}}{w_{1,\,2t+1}} = \frac{w_{1,\,2t+2}}{w_{2,\,2t+2}}.$$

Combined with nonsynchronization

$$\frac{w_{1,\,2t+2}}{w_{1,\,2t}} = \left(\frac{w_{1,\,2t}}{w_{2,\,2t}}\right)^2. \tag{12}$$

But also $\frac{p_{1,\,2t+2}}{p_{1,\,2t}} = \frac{w_{1,\,2t+2}}{w_{1,\,2t}}$, and therefore the rate of inflation is given by the relative desired wages of the various labor groups.

This is exactly analogous, of course, to the results of the last section.

Also equation (12) is the justification for the title of this paper: the relative wages of labor groups one and two determine the rate of inflation. It should also be mentioned that the wage bargains pictured here correspond closely to the wage determination process of *The General Theory*. At the time when each labor group makes its bargain in *The General Theory* it is either restrained or empowered by the at-least temporary fixity of the wages of other labor groups. Keynes's system of bargaining (which is also his reason for the 'constancy' of the money wage) is much akin to the nonsynchronized procedures assumed here.[17]

There has been some discussion in the literature on inflation of 'leapfrogging,' *alias* 'the wage-wage spiral.'[18] Equation (12) corresponds to such a phenomenon: the changes in relative wages ('leapfrogging') determine the rate of inflation. The rate of this 'wage-wage spiral' is seen below as determined by the level of the parameter a and the structure of the economy: this consists of the demand curves of the firms, the bargainings between the unions and the firms, and the behavior of the firms in setting prices.

It is worth noting that the assumptions necessary to arrive at (12) were symmetry, nonsynchronization and invertibility. Therefore, the particular monopoly and union-bargaining behavior assumed—as important as they may be for particular solutions—are not, by themselves, the keys to the inflationary processes described.

Finally returning, as in the last section, to the specific example, and collecting equations:

$MR = MC$ yields:

$$p_{1,\,t} = 1/2\,(ap_{2,\,t} + w_{1,\,t}) \text{ for all } t \tag{13}$$

$$p_{2,\,t} = 1/2\,(ap_{1,\,t} + w_{2,\,t}) \text{ for all } t. \tag{14}$$

[17] J. M. Keynes, *The General Theory of Employment, Interest and Money* (New York: Harcourt, Brace, 1936), p. 14. 'In other words the struggle about money wages primarily affects the *distribution* of the aggregate real wage among labor groups and not its average amount per unit of employment, which depends, as we shall see, on a different set of forces. The effect of combination on the part of a group of workers is to protect their *relative* wage. The *general* level of real wages depends on the real forces of the economic system.'

[18] See, in particular, W. Fellner, *et al.*, *The Problem of Rising Prices* (Paris: Organization for European Economic Cooperation, 1961), pp. 53–54.

The condition that unions maximize income yields:

$$\frac{w_{1,\,2t}}{p_{2,\,2t}} = a\frac{\gamma^e}{1+\gamma^e} \text{ for all } t \tag{15}$$

$$\frac{w_{2,\,2t+1}}{p_{1,\,2t+1}} = a\frac{\gamma^e}{1+\gamma^e} \text{ for all } t. \tag{16}$$

The condition that bargaining occurs in January for union one gives us:

$$w_{1,\,2t} = w_{1,\,2t+1} \text{ for all } t \tag{17}$$

and that bargaining occurs in July for union two gives us:

$$w_{2,\,2t+1} = w_{2,\,2t+2} \text{ for all } t. \tag{18}$$

Using (13), (14), (17) and (18) equations (15), (16), (17) and (18) can be rewritten as:

$$\frac{p_{1,\,2t}}{p_{2,\,2t}} = az \text{ where } z = \frac{1+2\gamma^e}{2(1+\gamma^e)} \tag{15'}$$

$$\frac{p_{2,\,2t+1}}{p_{1,\,2t+1}} = az \tag{16'}$$

$$2p_{1,\,2t} - ap_{2,\,2t} = 2p_{1,\,2t+1} - ap_{2,\,2t+1} \tag{17'}$$

$$2p_{2,\,2t+1} - ap_{1,\,2t+1} = 2p_{2,\,2t+2} - ap_{1,\,2t+2}. \tag{18'}$$

Solving (15'), (16'), (17') and (18') we find that

$$p_{1,\,2t+1} = \frac{2z-1}{(2-a^2z)z}p_{1,\,2t} \tag{19}$$

$$p_{1,\,2t+2} = \frac{a^2z(2z-1)}{2-a^2z}p_{1,\,2t+1} \tag{20}$$

and, most importantly,

$$\frac{p_{1,\,2t+2}}{p_{1,\,2t}} = \left[\frac{a(2z-1)}{2-a^2z}\right]^2. \tag{21}$$

It is also possible to check that the relative wage $w_{1,\,2t}/w_{2,\,2t}$ is also equal to $a(2z-1)/(2-a^2z)$.

Equation (21) gives the short-run Phillips Curve. This short-run Phillips Curve has the expected properties that:

$$\frac{\partial\left(\frac{p_{1,\ 2t+2}}{p_{1,\ 2t}}\right)}{\partial a} > 0$$

and

$$\frac{\partial\left(\frac{p_{1,\ 2t+2}}{p_{1,\ 2t}}\right)}{\partial \gamma^e} > 0$$

as long as $2 - a^2 z > 0$. This, however, is the relevant range in our model, since otherwise equation (20) would denote inconsistent (negative) price behavior.

But the next question which arises is the nature (or the existence) of a long-run Phillips Curve. In long-run equilibrium, as before, price expectations should be realized. Remembering the definition of γ^e—the expected multiple of increase of p_2 between $2t$ and $2t + 1$—and applying symmetry, it is possible (using (20)) to write γ^A (the actual multiple of inflation of p_2 between $2t$ and $2t + 1$ as a function of the expected inflation γ^e and a.

$$\gamma^A - \frac{a^2 z(2z - 1)}{2 - a^2 z} = \frac{a^2 \gamma^e(1 + 2\gamma^e)}{2(1 + \gamma^e)^2 - a^2(1 + 2\gamma^e)(1 + \gamma^e)} \tag{22}$$

and in equilibrium

$$\gamma^A = \gamma^e. \tag{23}$$

Equation (22) is remarkably similar to our old friend (7). First, for $a = 4/3$, $\gamma^e = 1$ is a double root. This should occasion no surprise—considering the remarks of the last section. Second, for $a > 4/3$, $\gamma^A(\gamma^e)$ has the same shape as the function in Figure 12.1. Upper roots are, therefore, stable; lower roots are therefore unstable. Exactly the same analysis with exactly the same qualifications which applied to the system in the last section can be repeated here. Beginning with nondeflationary static expectations with $a > 4/3$ the system will gravitate to a rate of inflation determined by a. This rate of inflation is locally stable and it increases with higher values of a. In this restricted and qualified sense there is a long-run Phillips Curve.

Money enters just as money entered before. Suppose that aggregate demand is the sum of consumption demand, investment demand, and government demand (assuming that the economy is closed). There will be a relation between a and monetary policy. Static macroeconomic theory shows that this sum will depend on (a) the level of government expenditures, (b) the level and rates of real taxation, and (c) the level of real balances. Suppose that (a) and (b) are fixed; and suppose that the nominal level of the money supply is increasing at a given rate λ. In Figure 12.2, if the rate of employment is larger than $P(\lambda)$, real balances and hence aggregate demand are decreasing. Similarly, if the rate of employment is less than $P(\lambda)$, real balances (and hence aggregate demand) are increasing. $P(\lambda)$ represents the equilibrium rate of employment

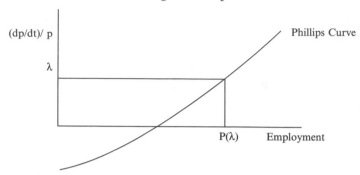

Figure 12.2.

for the rate of increase of the money supply λ—with given policies in real terms for the level of government taxation and expenditure.

But there is one additional warning due: while a rise in real balances can raise demand to any given level, even with negligible real balances, demand may exceed supply. This is one clear element in Bresciani-Turroni's account of the 1923 German hyperinflation: the reduction in demand from the reduction in real balances was not sufficient to allow the government to finance its operations from the expansion of the money supply.[19] The sum of private plus public real demands exceeded the full employment potential of the economy.

In the traditional Keynesian model of inflation[20] and also in Friedman's *Studies in the Quantity Theory of Money*[21] a further complication is added: the aggregate demand relations depend on the rate of price inflation. In the Keynesian view the level of consumption, investment and possibly also government demand depends on the rate of inflation: because the spending today depends on budgets made yesterday. This should not affect the earlier analysis: suppose that the money supply is increasing at the rate λ. In the long run if prices are rising at a rate less than λ, real balances are rising (which shifts the consumption function outward), or if prices are rising at less than λ, real balances are falling. Eventually, as long as the many functions of the economy are stable (the consumption function, investment function, tax function (in real terms) and government expenditure), equilibrium is approached. Friedman, on the other hand, emphasizes the shift of the demand for money due to the rate of inflation. The relevant rate of interest for the holder of money is the nominal rate of interest: the real rate of interest plus the rate of inflation. Again, however, the same logic holds: if the price level increases at a slower rate than the money supply, real balances rise (and hence aggregate demand), and similarly if the price level rises at a faster rate than the money supply, real balances (and hence aggregate demand) decline. The result will be the equilibrium

---

[19] Bresciani-Turroni, *op. cit.* Cagan shows the regularity with which real balances decline in hyperinflation. P. Cagan, 'The Monetary Dynamics of Hyperinflation,' in M. Friedman (ed.), *Studies in the Quantity Theory of Money* (University of Chicago Press, 1956).
[20] J. M. Keynes, *How to Pay for the War* (New York: Harcourt, Brace, 1940).
[21] Chicago University Press, 1956.

previously described—but again the same *caveat* applies: an overambitious program of expenditure (public plus private) will result in hyperinflation—for the aggregate demand curve and the aggregate supply curve may never meet—even at zero real balances.

IV

The theory of the last sections would appear all very special were it not possible to motivate the results in far greater generality. This generalization is provided by Bent Hansen's Chapter IX of *A Study in the Theory of Inflation*.[22]

Following Hansen, a system is considered which has n goods or factors of production. As in *A Theory of Inflation* it is a condition of economic rationality that the demand curves and supply curves of each of these goods or factors be homogeneous of degree zero for a given level of real balances. Therefore we write

$$D_i = D_i(p_1, \ldots, p_n; M/p_1) \quad i = 1, \ldots, n \tag{24}$$

$$S_i = S_i(p_1, \ldots, p_n; M/p_1) \quad i = 1, \ldots, n \tag{25}$$

and in static equilibrium

$$D_i = S_i \tag{26}$$

Each of the n S_i and D_i equations can be considered as equations in relative prices and real balances. Therefore without loss of generality (24), (25) and (26) can be written

$$D_i = D_i\left(1, \frac{p_2}{p_1}, \ldots, \frac{p_n}{p_1}; \frac{M}{p_1}\right) \tag{27}$$

$$S_i = S_i\left(1, \frac{p_2}{p_1}, \ldots, \frac{p_n}{p_1}; \frac{M}{p_1}\right) \tag{28}$$

and, in equilibrium

$$D_i = S_i. \tag{29}$$

And, if nothing unusual occurs, it can be seen (in the so-called normal case) equations (27), (28), and (29) can be solved for the unknowns

$$D_i, \ i = 1, \ldots, n$$
$$S_i, \ i = 1, \ldots, n$$
$$\text{and } p_i/p_1, \ i = 2, \ldots, n \text{ and } M/p_1.$$

---

[22] London: Allen and Unwin, 1951.

This, of course, is the reasoning behind Patinkin's famous volume—and monetary neutrality holds.

But in Sections II and III there is a system of lagged adjustment to price changes. This can be approximated, following Hansen (in turn following Samuelson), by saying that $(dp_i/dt)/p_i = F_i(D_i - S_i)$. The rate of change of the ith price depends on the difference between the demand and the supply of the ith commodity. F_i has the property that $F_i(0) = 0$, $F_i' > 0$: price changes are zero if demand equals supply; and the greater the excess demand the greater the rate of price increase.

In this case, for long-run equilibrium, the rate of change of the price level is equal to the rate of change of the money supply (which was previously called λ). Therefore in the long run it is *not* true that $D_i = S_i$, which would imply that $(dp_i/dt)/p_i$ would be zero. Rather, in the long run

$$D_i = D_i(1, p_2/p_1, \ldots, p_n/p_1; M/p_1, \lambda) \tag{30}$$

$$S_i = S_i(1, p_2/p_1, \ldots, p_n/p_1; M/p_1, \lambda) \tag{31}$$

and

$$F_i(D_i - S_i) = \lambda. \tag{32}$$

It may be possible to solve these equations for the $3n$ unknowns

$$p_i/p_1, i = 2, \ldots, n, M/p_1$$
$$D_i, i = 1, \ldots, n$$

and

$$S_i, i = 1, \ldots, n.$$

And *in general* the real solution to the system will depend on the value of λ (which is the rate of increase of the money supply).[23]

The 'Keynesian' theory of wage adjustment of Section III gives a precise rationale for an adjustment mechanism of the Hansen-Samuelson variety; in turn it leads to the nonneutrality of money—and therefore a Phillips Curve. Reinterpreting the assumptions of Sections II and III, nonsynchronization gives form to the various F_i's—and the presence of noncompetitive markets keeps the F_i's from degeneracy: with the markets

---

[23] Another way to look at this problem is that we have a system of balanced growth equations as in P. A. Samuelson and R. M. Solow, 'Balanced Growth Under Constant Returns to Scale,' *Econometrica*, Vol. 21 (July 1953). Both M. Morishima and F. M. Fisher have suggested that such systems could be used to talk about inflation. See M. Morishima, 'Proof of a Turnpike Theorem: The "No Joint Production Case,"' *Review of Economic Studies*, XXVIII (Feb. 1961); and A. Ando, F. M. Fisher, and H. A. Simon, *Essays on the Structure of Social Science Models* (Cambridge, Mass.: M.I.T. Press, 1963).

assumed, the greater the degree of competition the greater is the slope of the F_i functions; in the limit money is again neutral.

V

Our model differs considerably from most of the standard models of inflation: it has been shown that there are considerable differences from the usual quantity-theory-of-money approach to inflation: in the long run, the rate of increase of the money supply determines the *degree* of full employment.

On the other hand, in the usual demand-pull theories of inflation price rises have a purpose: 'to cheat the slow to spend of their desired shares' of total income.[24] This is the heart of Keynes[25] and Smithies.[26] But in our model inflation occurs without any teleological purpose of destroying aggregate demand—although, as seen in Section III, this can be easily incorporated into the model.

And yet this is not a simple model of cost-push either, for the wage rises would not occur without the price rises just as the price rises would not occur without the wage rises. Rather this is a model of spontaneous inflation in which the chicken and the egg of wage and price rises are mutually the causes of each other. Hansen's Walrasian model of inflation is most similar.[27]

The heart of our system is the gaps between the supply and demand equilibria, whose continued incompatibility is allowed by the nature of the adjustment process. Examples have been given before of systems where the system of adjustment allows a tolerance for continued disequilibrium, with resulting rising prices and wages. The notion of 'leap-frogging' has already been mentioned.[28] J. C. R. Dow has suggested a situation in which unions and firms are each bidding for shares of output, whose sum exceeds unity.[29] Turvey has suggested a similar process.[30] The additional element of the spontaneous inflation here, whatever kind of spiral it may be, is its explicit dependence upon demand and expectations.

Finally, this paper has left us with many exercises unfinished and several questions to be answered. First of all, many different industrial structures could be substituted for the example of monopolistic competition and applied to this framework. Similarly various different bargaining solutions between unions and employers can be substituted. One possible variant on this theme is an economy with a monopolistic and a competitive sector—where the monopolistic sector represents 'industry' and the competitive sector represents 'agriculture.' Such a model could be used to describe inflationary processes in underdeveloped economies.

[24] P. A. Samuelson and R. M. Solow, 'Analytical Aspects of Anti-Inflation Policy,' *American Economic Review*, L (May 1960).

[25] Keynes, *How to Pay for the War, op. cit.*

[26] A. Smithies, 'The Behavior of Money National Income,' this *Journal*, LVII (Nov. 1942).

[27] Hansen, *op. cit.*

[28] Fellner *et al., op. cit.*

[29] J. C. R. Dow, *Oxford Economic Papers*, N.S. Vol. 8 (Oct. 1956).

[30] R. Turvey, 'Some Aspects of the Theory of Inflation in a Closed Economy,' *Economic Journal*, LXI (Sept. 1956).

But more important is the introduction of many grades of labor. For it is important to know the mechanism whereby labor-training programs, etc., shift the Phillips Curve and thereby make more employment possible. In addition it is necessary to have such a macroeconomic view in order to compare the costs and the benefits of such training programs. Similarly, it is important to have models with several types of employers to evaluate the effects of such programs as additional government employment of low-skilled workers.

Further, the high councils of the United States government appear to believe some Phillips-Curve theory.[31] But as Professor Kuh has urged,[32] in a model with heterogeneous labor (and segmented markets) the competition between the 'top' and the 'bottom' of the labor force may be weak. The implication is that unemployment may, in past cycles, be correlated with the bargaining power of wage earners but at the same time it may be structurally independent. If this is the true view of the economy, the Phillips Curve can perhaps be structurally altered; a structure for inflation theory is necessary to decide whether this is in fact the case.

UNIVERSITY OF CALIFORNIA

---

[31] In particular, see *Economic Report of the President*, 1962, p. 44, for an especially clear and authoritative statement of the believed relation between unemployment and inflation.
[32] See Kuh, *op. cit.*

13

The Microeconomic Foundations of a Flow of Funds Theory of the Demand for Money*

E4 1

GEORGE A. AKERLOF[†]

London School of Economics, London WC2A 2AE, England

Received March 9, 1977; revised April 20, 1978

I. INTRODUCTION

Traditional transactions models of the demand for money view money holdings as the resultant of two different types of decisions.[1] The first type of decision concerns payments which shall be denoted *autonomous* because these payments are both in magnitude and in frequency independent of the level of the bank account. The second type of decision concerns a monitoring rule, whereby payments are made to prevent the bank account from becoming too large or too small. Because of their dependence, either in magnitude or in frequency on the level of the bank account, such payments will be denoted as *induced*.

According to the wisdom of the standard IS–LM version of macroeconomics, as, for example, is typically taught in most undergraduate courses in intermediate macroeconomics, monetarists and Keynesians both have similar general models of income determination (e.g., the IS–LM framework) but rather different estimates of the interest elasticity of the demand for money. If money is defined as M_1, which pays no interest, so that interest-bearing time deposits are a dominant asset and Keynes' speculative demand can be ignored, the leading argument for an interest elasticity of the demand for

---

* Reprinted from *Journal of Economic Theory* 18, 1, George Akerlof, 'The Microeconomic Foundations of a Flow of Funds Theory of the Demand for Money', Copyright © 1978, with permission from Elsevier.

† The author would like to thank the National Science Foundation, which supported this research under Grant SOC 75 23076. A revision of this paper was made while the author was Visiting Research Economist, Special Studies Section, Board of Governors of the Federal Reserve System. The author would like to thank Ross Milbourne for valuable comments on an earlier version.

1 See Baumol [2], Fisher [3], Miller and Orr [4], and Tobin [5].

money is that of Tobin [5], Baumol [2], and Miller and Orr [4], who all argue that as interest rates rise bank accounts will be more carefully monitored, so that on average lower money balances will be held.

Irrespective of the empirical importance of this argument for short-run analysis, about which there can be considerable debate, the sources of an interest elasticity of the demand for money are incomplete—since in general the interest elasticity of the demand for money will be determined not just by the interest elasticity of *induced* payments flows which result from changes in the monitoring rules, but also by the interest elasticity of *autonomous* payments flows. Accordingly, this paper examines in a particular model of money holdings how shifts in *autonomous* flows will cause money holdings to shift in turn, the rules for monitoring of bank accounts being taken as constant. Thus income and interest elasticities of the demand for money can be divided into two components: the traditional component from the Baumol/Tobin/Miller–Orr models whereby monitoring rules change in response to autonomous payments flows and interest, and a second component due to shifts in autonomous payments flows as income and interest rates change.

Furthermore, this paper shall attempt to show more than the dependence of average balances on autonomous flows. It also illustrates by example a rule of thumb for discerning what types of changes in flows of funds, under normal circumstances, will increase, decrease, or leave approximately unchanged, the demand for money. By this rule of thumb, increased payments flows from tightly monitored bank accounts to loosely monitored bank accounts increase the demand for money.

This principle has some usefulness in elaborating the sources of the interest elasticity of the demand for money. It is plausible that there is a correlation between the sensitivity of payments flows to the rate of interest and the strictness with which bank accounts are monitored. Those bank accounts which are monitored most strictly so as to economize on foregone interest payments are also likely to belong to those agents whose payments outflows are most likely to be curtailed due to rising interest rates, which yields a flow-of-funds explanation for an interest elasticity to the demand for money.

The role of payments flows in the demand for money will be shown in a model adapted from Miller and Orr [4], which is a generalization of the Baumol–Tobin model. Section 2 will summarize the mathematical behavior of this model; some of this mathematics has been developed by Miller and Orr and some further development is given in the Appendix (along with review of Miller and Orr). Section 3 gives three examples of shifts in payments flows so as to get a broad picture of the types of shifts causing relatively large, and the types of shifts causing relatively small, changes in the demand for money. Section 4 gives two examples, both illustrating the principle that flows from strictly monitored bank accounts to loosely monitored bank accounts tend to increase the demand for money. Section 5 discusses autonomous flows whose shifts might alter this demand. Section 6 gives conclusions.

II. THE MODEL OF PAYMENTS FLOWS AND PROPERTIES OF MONEY DEMAND

A. *The Model*

The model of money holding (adapted from [4]) is described by payments flows and the rule of monitoring.

Payments flows. In each time period, each money holder has three possibilities:

receipt of one unit of money with probability p,
no transaction with probability s, and
payment of one unit of money with probability q.

Since there are only the three possibilities,

$$p + q + s = 1. \tag{1}$$

Monitoring rule. The individual monitors his bank account in the following way. If the bank account reaches an upper threshold (denoted h), the money holder buys $(h - z)$ worth of securities. This returns the bank account to the target z. If the bank account reaches the lower threshold of 0, the money holder sells securities in amount z to restore the bank account to the target z. To focus attention on the major point of this paper, which is the dependence of money holdings on *autonomous* flows (as opposed to dependence on the monitoring rule), h and z will be assumed fixed.

B. *Model as Markov Chain*

Defining the 'state' of the system as the level of money holdings, the preceding model of monitoring of bank accounts and of payments flows describes a finite stationary Markov process, giving the probability of moving from one state of the system to another between time $t - 1$ and time t. In equations, if $f(x, t)$ is the probability of having x units in the bank account at time t, and $f(x, t - 1)$ is the probability of having x units at time $t - 1$, the distribution $f(x, t)$ is given in terms of the distribution $f(x, t - 1)$ by the equations

$$f(x, t) = pf(x - 1, t - 1) + sf(x, t - 1) + qf(x + 1, t - 1),$$
$$1 \leq x \leq h - 1, \ x \neq z, \tag{2}$$

$$f(z, t) = pf(z - 1, t - 1) + qf(1, t - 1) + sf(z, t - 1)$$
$$+ qf(z + 1, t - 1) + pf(h - 1, t - 1), \tag{3}$$

$$f(0, t) = 0, \tag{4}$$

$$f(h, t) = 0, \tag{5}$$

$$\sum_{x=1}^{h-1} f(x, t) = 1. \tag{6}$$

In the steady state, $f(x, t) = f(x, t - 1)$ for all x and, therefore, the longrun, steady-state distribution $f(x)$ is well defined and is given by Eqs. (2′) to (6′).

$$f(x) = pf(x - 1) + sf(x) + qf(x + 1), \quad 1 \le x \le h - 1, x \ne z, \tag{2′}$$

$$f(z) = pf(z - 1) + qf(1) + sf(z) + qf(z + 1) + pf(h - 1), \tag{3′}$$

$$f(0) = 0, \tag{4′}$$

$$f(h) = 0, \tag{5′}$$

$$\sum_{x=1}^{h-1} f(x) = 1. \tag{6′}$$

System (2′) consists of two second-order linear difference equations—from 1 to $z - 1$ and from $z + 1$ to $h - 1$; Equations (3′) to (6′) are four boundary conditions that determine the four arbitrary constants given by (2′). An exact solution to system (2′) to (6′) is given by Miller and Orr, who have also computed the expected value E of this distribution as a function of p/q, h, and z. Defining y as p/q,

$$E = E(y, h, z) = \frac{1}{2} \left\{ \frac{1+y}{1-y} + h + z - \frac{hz(1 - y^{z-h})}{z(1 - y^{z-h}) + (h - z)(1 - y^z)} \right\}. \tag{7}$$

C. *The Properties of E*

The long-run demand for money concerns the function E. Most probably reflecting the vanishing of various numerators and denominators of E for $y = 1$, it is quite difficult to show that E is well behaved, which in fact it is. This good behavior (proofs are given of the less obvious properties in the Mathematical Appendix) is reflected in properties (E1) to (E8).

Property (E1). The function $f(x)$ is independent of s, given p/q, h and z; therefore E is independent of s. (See Appendix AVII.)

Property (E2). $E(y, h, z) + E(1/y, h, h - z) = h$, and therefore $\partial/\partial y \{E(y, h, z) + E(1/y, h, h - z)\} = 0$. (See Appendix AIV.)

Property (E3). $\partial E/\partial y > 0$ for all y, h, z. (See Appendix AV.)

Property (E4). $\partial E/\partial h > 0$ for all y, h, z. (See Appendix AII.)

Property (E5). $\partial E/\partial z > 0$ for all y, h, z. (See Appendix AIII.)

Property (E6). $E(\infty, h, z) = (h + z - 1)/2$.

Property (E7). $E(0, h, z) = (z + 1)/2$.

Property (E8). $E(1, h, z) = (h + z)/3$. (Proof given by Miller and Orr [4].)

III. EXAMPLES OF PAYMENTS SHIFTS WHICH CAUSE LARGE AND SMALL SHIFTS IN MONEY DEMANDED

The question of this paper is how changes in autonomous payments alter the expected value of money holdings. This section explores some examples believed to be indicative of types of shifts which cause large (and small) changes in money demand. Of course, by nature payments flows must affect two bank accounts. If the economy consists of just two individuals denoted A and B, total money demanded is

$$M = E(y_A, h_A, z_A) + E(y_B, h_B, z_B).$$

A shift in autonomous payments which shifts y_A in one direction will shift y_B in the opposite direction. With the probability of remaining stationary, s_A and s_B, equal to zero, since payments to A from B are payments from B to A, $y_A = 1/y_B$, and thus

$$\frac{dM}{dy_A} = \frac{\partial E}{\partial y_A} - \frac{\partial E}{\partial y_B} \frac{1}{y_A^2}.$$

What properties of A relative to B will cause a shift dy_A net of the consequent shift dy_B to result in an increase (or decrease) in money holdings? Two examples in this section show that shifts in payments flows between units which have the same strictness of monitoring will have relatively little effect on money demanded. The third example, whose implications will be further considered in two examples in Section 4, indicates that shifts in autonomous payments between units with different strictness or tightness of monitoring may have significant effects on monetary demand.

EXAMPLE I. Subject to the constraint imposed by the reciprocity of payments between A and B, any values of y_A, h_A, z_A, y_B, h_B and z_B are permissible. But some choices of these parameters relative to one another make greater sense (being more plausible) than others.

This example, by intent, explores the effect of shifts in autonomous payments between equally loosely (or strictly) monitored bank accounts, thus suggesting the assumption $h_A = h_B$. As stated earlier, the condition of reciprocity of payments between A and B yields $y_B = 1/y_A$. We make this assumption regarding the relative values of y_A and y_B.

The choices of z_A and z_B remain. z_A (or z_B) too high or too low will result in too great a frequency of induced payments flows, with resultant high payments for transactions costs. Reasonable values of z_A and z_B will keep these transactions costs relatively small (given h and y). By symmetry

$$D(y, h, z) = D(1/y, h, h - z),$$

where D is the expected length of time between induced payments. (For proof see Appendix AVIII.) For this reason, it makes sense dimensionally to choose

$$z_B = h_A - z_A,$$

given also that $h_B = h_A$ and $y_B = 1/y_A$.

With these relative choices of (y_A, y_B), (h_A, h_B) and (z_A, z_B) a marginal change in autonomous payments dy_A will have an effect on money holdings

$$\frac{\partial}{\partial y_A} \{E(y_A, h_A, z_A) + E(1/y_A, h_A, h_A - z_A)\},$$

which, by (E2), is zero. Consequently, changes in payments flows given these relative values of h, y, and z in the two bank accounts result in no changes in money holding.

EXAMPLE II. In the last example, the relative choice of z_A and z_B was a bit arbitrary. With $y = 1$, Miller and Orr compute the optimal value of z from the maximization of interest earnings net of transactions costs.[2] Remarkably, they find $z = h/3$—independent of the interest rate and cost per transaction in purchase of securities. Using this value of z and Property (E8), for $y_A = y_B = 1$, $h_A = h_B = h$, $z_A = z_B = h/3$,

$$M^D = 8/9h.$$

Now consider the most extreme shift in payments flows between A and B: A becomes a steady payer to B, thus y_A becomes 0 and y_B becomes ∞. Using (E6) and (E7) money demand has become

$$M^D = (h + z - 1)/2 + (z + 1)/2 = 5/6h.$$

The shift in M^D from this extreme shift in payments is $1/18\, h$, or relative to the initial money holdings of $8/9\, h$, there has been a change of $1/16$. We interpret this to mean that, as in example I, even large shifts in payments flows between monitors of equal strictness will have relatively little impact on the total demand for money.

EXAMPLE III. The preceding two examples showed that shifts in autonomous flows between bank accounts with similar levels of monitoring result in relatively small shifts in money demanded. This section gives an indication of the size of shifts in money demanded caused by changes in autonomous payments between bank accounts with different monitoring standards.

---

[2] Professor Martin Weitzman [6] has shown that this optimization result is dependent on the assumption of equal costs per transaction in purchase and sale of securities.

As a starting point, suppose that there are two bank accounts denoted A and B with $y_A = y_B = 1$. The optimization result of Miller and Orr suggests $z_A = h_A/3$, $z_B = h_B/3$ as reasonable values of z_A and z_B. Total money demanded using (E8) will be

$$M^D = 4/9(h_A + h_B).$$

By (E6) and (E7) the most extreme shift in payments flows from A to B will shift M^D to $M^{D'}$:

$$M^{D'} = (z_A + 1)/2 + (h_B + z_B - 1)/2 = h_A/6 + 2/3h_B.$$

At the very most (i.e., $\lim h_B/h_A \to \infty$) M^D will rise to 150% of its original level and at the very least (i.e., $\lim h_B/h_A \to 0$), M^D will decline to three-eights of its former level. The next section will examine in further detail the effects of shifts in payments between bank accounts with unequal standards of monitoring.

IV. EXAMPLE OF SHIFTS IN PAYMENTS FLOWS BETWEEN UNITS OF DIFFERENT SCALE

The last section showed that shifts in payments flows between units with different standards of monitoring will shift the demand for money. Certainly the scale of operation of different units in the economy (for example, households, businesses and government units) is greatly different. Two further examples follow.

EXAMPLE I.   Let there be two types of units in this economy: firms, denoted by the subscript F and in number F; and households, denoted by the subscript H and in number H. Let all payments be between firms and households, with no firm or household receiving from or making payment to more than one other unit in any single period. The equality of outpayments of firms and receipts of households and the equality of receipts of firms and outpayments of households yield the conditions

$$Fp_F = Hq_H \tag{8}$$

and

$$Fq_F = Hp_H \tag{9}$$

and division of (8) by (9) yields $y_F = 1/y_H$.

On reflection, it is clear that s_H and s_F can no longer be chosen independently of each other and also of the previously made assumptions regarding the nature of transactions; for the number of households making receipts or payments in any period must equal the number of firms making receipts or payments in the same period, or

$$(1 - s_F)F = (1 - s_H)H. \tag{10}$$

(For proof of (10) in a somewhat more general context, see Appendix AVI.)

We now choose a numerical example whose relative values we consider of plausible order of magnitude. First, we let there be three times as many firms as households. Second, we let $y_H = y_F = 1$. Mindful of the optimization results of Miller and Orr, we chose z_H equal to $h_H/3$ and z_F equal to $h_F/3$.

It remains to choose h_H and h_F. It is our desire to represent households as being less careful monitors than firms. A household has only one-third the probability of making a receipt or payment as a firm (by (10)) since $H/F = 3$. Since households make receipts or payments with only one-third of the frequency of firms, it also follows (for proof see Appendix AVIII) that with h_H also chosen equal to h_F, households will make induced payments only one-third as often as firms. Again, this seems like a reasonable order of magnitude; accordingly, h_F is chosen equal to h_H.

Letting $h_F = h_H = 9$, for example, what change in M^D will result from a 1% increase in y_H? Straightforward calculation using the formula

$$M^D = FE(y_F, h_F, z_F) + HE(y_H, h_H, z_H)$$

shows that a 1 percent increase in y_H will cause a 0.20% increase in M^D.

EXAMPLE II. The last example was instructive, but this example incorporates one additional feature, which aids in representing the different scale of operations of firms and households. Furthermore, we shall prove in this example a result of some generality.

The function E is useful in that it gives the number of *units* (to be distinguished from the number of dollars) of expected money holdings if one unit is gained with probability p and one unit is lost with probability q in each period. Typically, we might suppose the units involved in transactions by firms are of greater scale than for households. Generally, if a firm gains X_F dollars with probability p_F and loses X_F dollars with probability q_F, has upper threshold $X_F h_F$ and target $X_F z_F$, the firm's expected money holdings will be, in dollars,

$$M_F^D = X_F E(p_F/q_F, h_F, z_F).$$

Similarly, for a household

$$M_H^D = X_H E(p_H/q_H, h_H, z_H),$$

and so total money holdings are

$$M^D = FX_F E(p_F/q_F, h_F, z_F) + HX_H E(p_H/q_H, h_H, z_H).$$

Again choosing $y_H = 1/y_F$, $h_H = h_F$, and $z_H = h_F - z_F$, we can compute how money holdings M^D will react to an increase in y_H. Again as before, assumptions regarding F, H, X_H, X_H, s_F and s_H cannot be totally independent. Appendix AVI shows the generalization of formula (10) where the units for firms and households are of different sizes; this generalization is

$$FX_F(1 - s_F) = HX_H(1 - s_H). \tag{11}$$

We consider it both plausible that $s_H > s_F$ or, equivalently, since the number of households considerably exceeds the number of firms, that $HX_H > FX_H$. As a result

$$
\begin{aligned}
\frac{\partial M^D}{\partial y_H} &= \frac{\partial}{\partial y_H} \{ FX_F E(y_F, h_F, z_F) + HX_H E(y_H, h_H, z_H) \} \\
&= \frac{\partial}{\partial y_H} \left\{ HX_H E \left(\frac{1}{y_H}, h_H, h_H - z_H \right) + HX_H E(y_H, h_H, z_H) \right\} \\
&\quad + \frac{\partial}{\partial y_H} \left\{ (FX_F - HX_H) E \left(\frac{1}{y_H}, h_H, h_H - z_H \right) \right\} \\
&= (HX_H - FX_F) \left(\frac{1}{y_{H^2}} \right) \frac{\partial E}{\partial y_F} (y_F, h_F, z_F);
\end{aligned}
$$

the last expression is positive by the assumption that $HX_H > FX_F$ and also by property (E3). Thus, in this example an increased flow from firms to households, which is to say, from the tight monitors of large scale to the loose monitors of small scale, will increase the demand for money.

V. IMPLICATIONS

Our examples imply that changes in *autonomous* payments will shift the demand for money, just as in the Baumol–Tobin framework changes in monitoring which cause changes in induced payments alter M^D. The net result is a demand for money more complicated and with shifts in it due to many more causes than given by the usual descriptions of M^D and its determinants. Among these determinants, all of which may shift in the short run over the course of the business cycle as well as in the long run, are:

1. flows between households and businesses, among which investment is a determinant of the net inflow into household accounts. Also important are dividend payments and retained earnings.
2. payments made regularly (autonomously) for savings, such as social security payments and life insurance premiums.
3. trade credit. Note that trade credit may be partially induced, since some takers and givers of trade credit may be partially influenced by their money balances. The p-q-s/h-z-0 model must be modified to consider trade credit as probabilistically given or taken, this probability depending on the level of money holdings.
4. the purchase of assets for speculative reasons. This flow is partially dependent on the rate of interest, which influences asset prices.

5. bank loans. Note here that the rationing of bank loans affects autonomous flows and, therefore, may affect M^D. Alternatively, if bank loans are taken as an induced flow, M^D will likewise be affected if induced payments are affected by rationing.
6. sales or accruals of inventories. It is a significant phenomenon that firms with increased inventories find themselves cash-short.
7. consumption. Consumption decisions may shift, resulting in shifts in flows of funds between households and firms.
8. taxes.
9. monitoring decisions.

These nine effects are discussed in greater detail in another paper [1], which chooses different models for discussion—inventory models of money balances with constant payments flows, periodic monitoring, and the use of induced payments for purchases of securities. That paper also finds the demand for money variable as a result of short-run shifts in payments, with income/interest elasticities caused by income/interest elasticities in payments (1) to (8) just mentioned.

VI. CONCLUSION

It has been shown in an inventory–theoretic framework that autonomous payments flows affect the demand for money. It follows automatically that shifts in these flows (and also their income/interest elasticities) impart shifts in money demand (and also income/interest elasticity). We have no desire to reject the now-traditional story whereby money holdings are dependent on the monitoring of bank accounts; rather we wish to make this story richer. As a physical analogy, the height of a river is dependent on the banks and riverbed which monitor its flow and also on the flow of water in it. Similarly, money demand is dependent on the rules used to monitor bank accounts and also on the flows in and out of those accounts.

The main conclusion of this paper, that changes in autonomous payments will affect the demand for money, is robust. There is the singular case of constant thresholds and targets and constant payments inflows or outflows, in which average money holdings are $(h + z)/2$ or $z/2$, according to whether there is a constant inflow or a constant outflow. In that case autonomous payments do not affect average money holdings. This paper has shown that case to be singular: If payments are probabilistic, rather than constant-inflow or constant-outflow, autonomous payments are a determinant of money balances. Furthermore, if the monitoring rule (following Irving Fisher) is periodic (rather than of the constant target–threshold type), autonomous payments are a determinant of money holdings even with constant inflow and constant outflow, as explored by an earlier paper [1] in some detail.

MATHEMATICAL APPENDIX

AI. *Calculation of E(y, h, z)*

This section of the appendix reproduces the appendix to Miller and Orr's 'The Demand for Money by Firms' [4]. The long-run probability distribution ($f(x)$) of holding x units of money is derived—given thresholds h and 0 and target z, and with probability p of gaining one unit in each period and probability $q = (1 - p)$ of losing one unit in each period.

The Model

Assumption 1. With probability p, the money holder gains one unit from payments in each time period. With probability $q = (1 - p)$, the money holder loses one unit from payments in each time period.

Assumption 2. If money holdings reach h, the money holder purchases securities in amount $(h - z)$. Money holdings are returned to the target z. If money holdings reach 0, the money holder sells securities in amount z and money holdings are also returned to the target z.

Denote the probability of holding x units of money at time t by $f(x, t)$. Assumptions 1 and 2 describe the probability of money holding at time $t + 1$ in terms of the probability of money holding at time t by the four equations

$$f(x, t + 1) = pf(x - 1, t) + qf(x + 1, t), \quad 0 \leqslant x \leqslant h, \; x \neq z, \tag{A1}$$

$$f(z, t + 1) = p[f(z - 1, t) + f(h - 1, t)] + q[f(z + 1, t) + f(1, t)], \tag{A2}$$

$$f(0, t + 1) = 0, \tag{A3}$$

$$f(h, t + 1) = 0, \tag{A4}$$

and since f is a probability distribution,

$$\sum_{x=0}^{h} f(x, t + 1) = 1. \tag{A5}$$

In the steady state, $f(x, t) = f(x, t - 1)$ for all x. Define $f(x)$ as the steady-state distribution; then, using (A1)–(A5) and omitting the t's,

$$f(x) = pf(x - 1) + qf(x + 1), \quad 0 \leqslant x \leqslant h, \; x \neq z, \tag{A1'}$$

$$f(z) = p[f(z - 1) + f(h - 1)] + q[f(z + 1) + f(1)], \tag{A2'}$$

$$f(0) = 0, \tag{A3'}$$

$$f(h) = 0, \tag{A4'}$$

$$\sum_{x=0}^{h} f(x) = 1. \tag{A5'}$$

System (A1') to (A5') describes two sets of difference equations (from 1 to $z-1$ and $z+1$ to $h-1$ given by Eq. (A1') and four boundary conditions (Eqs. (A2') to (A5')). For $p \neq q$, Eq. (A1) has the solution

$$f(x) = A + B(p/q)^x, \quad 0 \leqslant x \leqslant z,$$
$$f(x) = C + D(p/q)^x, \quad z \leqslant x \leqslant h. \tag{A6}$$

Since $f(0) = 0$,

$$A + B = 0,$$
$$A = -B. \tag{A7}$$

Since $f(h) = 0$,

$$D = -C(p/q)^{-h}. \tag{A8}$$

Substitution of (A6), (A7), and (A8) into (A2') yields

$$C = A\left[\frac{1-(p/q)^z}{1-(p/q)^{z-h}}\right],$$

$$1 = \sum_{x=0}^{h} f(x) = \sum_{x=0}^{z} A(1-(p/q)^x) + \sum_{z+1}^{h} (1-(p/q)^{x-h})A\left[\frac{1-(p/q)^z}{1-(p/q)^{z-h}}\right],$$

whence

$$A = \frac{1-(p/q)^{z-h}}{z(1-(p/q)^{z-h}) + (h-z)(1-(p/q)^z)}.$$

The distribution of $f(x, y, h, z)$ is

$$f(x, y, h, z) = \frac{(1-y^{z-h})}{z(1-y^{z-h}) + (h-z)(1-y^z)}(1-y^x), \quad 1 \leqslant x \leqslant z, \tag{A9}$$

$$f(x, y, h, z) = \frac{1-y^z}{z(1-y^{z-h}) + (h-z)(1-y^z)}(1-y^{x-h}), \quad z \leqslant x \leqslant h. \tag{A10}$$

Use of the distribution $f(x)$ permits evaluation of the expected value of steady-state cash balances.

$$E(x) = \sum_{x=0}^{b} xf(x) = \sum_{x=0}^{z} xA\left(1 - \left(\frac{p}{q}\right)^x\right) + \sum_{x=z+1}^{b} xC\left(1 - \left(\frac{p}{q}\right)^{x-b}\right).$$

Use of the values of A and C and resort to the identity

$$\sum_{x=1}^{b} x\left(\frac{p}{q}\right)^{x-1} \equiv \frac{d}{d(p/q)} \sum_{x=0}^{b} \left(\frac{p}{q}\right)^x \equiv \frac{1 - (b+1)(p/q)^b + b(p/q)^{b+1}}{[1 - (p/q)]^2}$$

(A11)

yield, after some juggling,

$$E(x) = \frac{1}{2}\left\{\frac{1+y}{1-y} + b + z - \frac{bz(1 - y^{z-b})}{z(1 - y^{z-b}) + (b - z)(1 - y^z)}\right\},$$

where $y = p/q$.

AII. $\partial E / \partial b > 0$

Proof.

$$E = \frac{1}{2}\left\{\frac{1+y}{1-y} + z + \frac{b(b - z)(1 - y^z)}{z(1 - y^{z-b}) + (b - z)(1 - y^z)}\right\}.$$

Consider the expression E_1:

$$E_1 = \frac{b(b - z)}{z(1 - y^{z-b}) + (b - z)(1 - y^z)},$$

$$\text{sgn}\frac{\partial E_1}{\partial b} = \text{sgn}\frac{\partial E}{\partial b}, \quad y < 1,$$

$$\text{sgn}\frac{\partial E_1}{\partial b} = -\text{sgn}\frac{\partial E}{\partial b}, \quad y > 1.$$

Therefore, we wish to show that

$$\partial E_1/\partial b > 0, \quad y < 1,$$
$$\partial E_1/\partial b < 0, \quad y > 1.$$

$$\frac{\partial E_1}{\partial b} = \frac{(2b - z)z(1 - y^{z-b}) + (b - z)^2(1 - y^z) - \log y\, y^{z-b} zb(b - z)}{D^2},$$

where $D = z(1 - y^{z-h}) + (h - z)(1 - y^z)$.

$$\text{sgn}\frac{\partial E_1}{\partial h} = \text{sgn}N,$$

where $N = (2h - z)z(1 - y^{z-h}) + (h - z)^2(1 - y^z) - \log y \, y^{z-h} zh(h - z)$.
It remains to show that

$$N > 0 \quad \text{if } y < 1,$$
$$N < 0 \quad \text{if } y > 1.$$

$N = 0$ if $y = 1$, by direct evaluation.

$$\partial N/\partial y = (h - z)^2 zy^{z-1}(y^{-h} - 1 + \log y \, y^{-h}h).$$

$\therefore$ It remains to show that (see Fig. A1)

$$N_2 < 0, \quad y \neq 1,$$

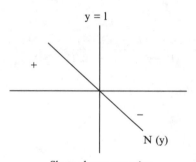

y = 1

+

N (y)

Slope always *negative*

Figure A1

where

$$N_2 = y^{-h} - 1 + \log y \, y^{-h}h.$$
$$N_2 = 0 \quad \text{if } y = 1$$

$$\partial N_2/\partial y = -h^2 \log y \, y^{-h-1}.$$

Therefore,

$$\partial N_2/\partial y > 0, \quad y < 1,$$
$$\partial N_2/\partial y < 0, \quad y > 1,$$

and (see Fig. A2).

$$N_2 < 0, \quad y \neq 1.$$

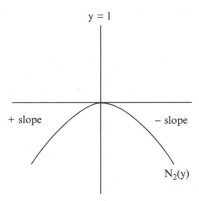

Figure A2

AIII. $\partial E/\partial z > 0$

Proof.

$$E = \frac{1}{2}\left\{\frac{1+y}{1-y} + h + z - \frac{hz(1-y^{z-h})}{z(1-y^{z-h}) + (h-z)(1-y^z)}\right\}$$

$$= \frac{1}{2}\left\{\frac{1+y}{1-y} + h + \frac{-z(h-z)(1-y^{-h})}{hy^{-z} - zy^{-h} - (h-z)}\right\}.$$

Therefore,

$$\frac{\partial E}{\partial z} \text{ has the same sign as } \frac{\partial}{\partial z}\frac{z(h-z)}{hy^{-z} - zy^{-h} - (h-z)}, \qquad y < 1,$$

$$\frac{\partial E}{\partial z} \text{ has the opposite sign from } \frac{\partial}{\partial z}\frac{z(h-z)}{hy^{-z} - zy^{-h} - (h-z)}, \qquad y > 1.$$

$$\frac{\partial}{\partial z}\frac{z(h-z)}{hy^{-z} - zy^{-h} - (h-z)}$$

$$= \frac{[-(h-z)^2 + z^2 y^{-h} + h(h-2z)y^{-z} + h \ \log y \ y^{-z} z(h-z)]}{D^2},$$

where $D = hy^{-z} - zy^{-h} - (h-z)$.

$\therefore \partial E/\partial z$ has the same sign as N,   where $y < 1$,

$\partial E/\partial z$ has the opposite sign from N,   where $y > 1$.

(A12)

$$N = -(b - z)^2 + z^2 y^{-b} + b(b - 2z)y^{-z} + b \ log \ yy^{-z}z(b - z),$$
$$N(1) = 0.$$

(A13)

$$\partial N/\partial y = -bz^2 y^{-z-1}(y^{z-b} - 1 + (b - z) \log y).$$

(A14)

Let

$$N_2(y) = y^{z-b} - 1 + (b - z) \log y,$$
$$N_2(1) = 0.$$

(A15)

$$\partial N_2/\partial y = (1/y)(b - z)(1 - y^{z-b}).$$

$\therefore \partial N_2/\partial y > 0,   y > 1,$

(A16)

$\partial N_2/\partial y < 0,   y < 1.$

(A17)

$\therefore N_2(y) > 0,   y \neq 1,$ using (A15), (A16), and (A17).

$\therefore \dfrac{\partial N}{\partial y} < 0,   y \neq 1.$ by (A14).

$\therefore \{N(y) > 0,   y < 1,$

$N(y) < 0,   y > 1,\}$ using(A13).

$\therefore \left\{ \dfrac{\partial E}{\partial z} > 0,   y < 1, \right.$

$\dfrac{\partial E}{\partial z} > 0,   y > 1,\}$ by(A12).

AIV. $E(y, b, z) + E(1/y, b, b - z) = b.$

Proof.

$$2E(y, b, z) = \frac{1 + y}{1 - y} + b + z - \frac{bz(1 - y^{z-b})}{z(1 - y^{z-b}) + (b - z)(1 - y^z)},$$

$$2E(1/y, b, b - z) = \frac{1 + 1/y}{1 - 1/y} + b + (b - z) - \frac{b(b - z)(1 - y^z)}{(b - z)(1 - y^z) + z(1 - y^{z-b})},$$

whence, by addition, $E(y, b, z) + E(1/y, b, b - z) = b.$

AV. $\partial E/\partial y\ (y, b, z) > 0$ for all $y > 0, y \neq 1.$

Proof. Logically, this theorem can be broken into three parts:

(1) Lemmas 1 and 2 show that $\partial E/\partial y(y, h, 1) > 0$ and $\partial E/\partial y(y, h, h-1) > 0$ for all $y > 0$, $y \neq 1$.

(2) In the theorem (Theorem 1) it is shown that the distribution of x, given y, h, z—denoted $f(x, y, h, z)$—can be broken into two parts: a lower part strictly below the target z and an upper part above and including the target.

The lower part is a multiple of p_1 *independent of x* of the distribution $f(x, y, z, z-1)$. The upper part of the distribution is a multiple p_2 *independent of x* of the distribution of $f(x, y, h-z+1, 1)$.

Thus, computation of $\partial E/\partial y(y, h, z)$ can be divided into computation of $\partial E/\partial y (y, z, z-1)$, $\partial E/\partial y(y, h-z+1, 1)$, $\partial p_1/\partial y$, and $\partial p_2/\partial y$.

(3) The third part of the proof is a computation showing that $\partial p_1/\partial y < 0$ and $\partial p_2/\partial y > 0$. Lemmas 3 and 4 are computations used in the proof that $\partial p_1/\partial y < 0$ and $\partial p_2/\partial y > 0$.

Before Lemma 1, Proposition 1 is presented. It is used in a computation in Lemma 1.

Proposition 1.

$$3 \sum_{x=1}^{h-1} x^2 + \sum_{x=1}^{h-1} x - 2 \sum_{x=1}^{h-1} xh = 0, \ h \geq 2.$$

Proof. The proof proceeds by induction on h. Clearly, the proposition is true for $h = 2$. Assume that the proposition is true for $h - 1$. It shall then be shown to be true for h.

By assumption, $3 \sum_{1}^{h-1} x^2 + \sum_{1}^{h-1} x = 2 \sum_{1}^{h-1} xh$. Then,

$$3 \sum_{1}^{h} x^2 + \sum_{1}^{h} x = 3h^2 + h + 3 \sum_{1}^{h-1} x^2 + \sum_{1}^{h-1} x$$

$$= 2(h^2 + h) + \frac{2(h(h-1))}{2} + 2 \sum_{1}^{h-1} xh$$

$$= 2h(h+1) + 2 \sum_{1}^{h-1} x + 2 \sum_{1}^{h-1} xh$$

$$= 2 \sum_{1}^{h} x(h+1).$$
Q.E.D.

Lemma 1. $\partial E/\partial y (y, h, 1) > 0$, $y > 0$, $y \neq 1$.

Proof.

$$2E(y, h, 1) = \frac{1+y}{1-y} - \frac{h(1 - y^{1-h})}{1 - y^{1-h} + (h-1)(1-y)} + h + 1,$$

by definition of E. By calculation,

$$2\frac{\partial E}{\partial y} = \frac{2}{(1-y)^2} - \frac{b(b-1)(1-by^{1-b}+(b-1)y^{-b})}{(y^{1-b})^2(1-by^{b-1}+(b-1)y^b)^2}.$$

For $y \neq 1$, it suffices to show that

$$\frac{(1-y)^2[b(b-1)/2](1-by^{1-b}+(b-1)y^{-b})}{y^2y^{-2b}(1-by^{b-1}+(b-1)y^b)^2} < 1,$$

or, using (A11), it suffices to show that, for $y \neq 1$,

$$\frac{(1-y)^2 \sum_{x=1}^{b-1} x \sum_{x=1}^{b-1} xy^{-x+1}(1-1/y)^2}{y^{2(1-b)}(\sum_{x=1}^{b-1} xy^{x-1})^2(1-y)^4} < 1.$$

Define the polynomial $P(y)$.

$$P(y) = \left[\sum_{1}^{b-1} xy^{x+1-b}\right]^2 - \left(\sum_{1}^{b-1} x\right)\left(\sum_{1}^{b-1} xy^{-z+1}\right).$$

It suffices to show that $P(y) > 0$ for $y \neq 1$.

P has the following four properties. These properties will be shown in turn.

(P1) $P(1) = 0$.

(P2) $dP/dy|_{y=1} = 0$. Therefore, 1 is a double root of P.

(P3) The coefficients of $P(y)$ have, at most, two changes in sign.

(P4) $P(0) > 0$.

Properties (P1), (P2), (P3), and (P4) show, by DesCartes' rule of signs, that $P(y) > 0$ for $y \neq 1$. These properties will be proved in turn.

Property (P1). Proof is obvious.

Property (P2).

$$\frac{dP}{dy} = 2\left(\sum_{1}^{b-1} xy^{x+1-b}\right)\left(\sum_{1}^{b-1} x(x+1-b)y^{x-b}\right)$$

$$+ \left(\sum_{1}^{b-1} x\right)\left(\sum_{1}^{b-1} x(x-1)y^{-x}\right),$$

$$\frac{dP}{dy}\Big|_{y=1} = \left(2\sum_{1}^{b-1} x(x+1-b) + \sum_{1}^{b-1} x(x-1)\right)\left(\sum_{1}^{b-1} x\right) = 0,$$

by Proposition 1.

Property (P3). The proof of Property (P3) is divided into five parts. Each of these is illustrated in Fig. A3.

(1) The range of coefficients is from $4 - 2h$ to 0.

(2) $C_0 > 0$ (for $h > 2$).

(3) $C_k > 0$, $4 - 2h \leq k \leq 1 - h$.

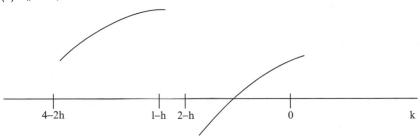

Figure A3. *Plot of coefficients C^k as a function of k described by (1) to (5) below.*

(4) $C_{2-h} < 0$.

(5) $(C_{k+2} - C_{k+1}) - (C_{k+1} - C_k) < 0$, $k \geq 2 - h$.

Therefore the C_k's have declining slopes. Therefore they can change sign at most twice between $k = 2 - h$ and $k = 0$.

Proof. (1) k runs from $4 - 2h$ to 0. This is true by inspection.

(2) $C_0 > 0$, $h > 2$.

Proof. $C_0 = (h - 1)^2 - \sum_1^{h-1} x = (h - 1)(h - 2)/2$.

(3) $C_k > 0$, $4 - 2h \leq k \leq 1 - h$. This is true by inspection.

(4) $C_{2-h} < 0$, $h > 2$.

Proof.
$C_{2-h} = -\sum_1^{h-1} x(h - 1) +$ coefficient of w^{h-2} in the expression

$$(1 + 2w + 3w^2 + \cdots + (h - 1)w^{h-2})$$

$$(1 + 2w + 3w^2 + \cdots + (h - 1)w^{h-2})$$

$$= -\sum_1^{h-1} x(h - 1) + \sum_1^{h-1} x(h - x) = -\sum_1^{h-1} x(x - 1) < 0, \qquad h > 2.$$

(5) Coefficients of C_k change signs *at most once* between $k = 2 - h$ and $k = 0$. This is shown by proving that the second differences of the C_k are negative in this range. In this range,

$$C_k = a_k + b_k,$$

where

$$a_k = \sum_{1}^{h-1} x(-k+1),$$

$b_k =$ coefficient of ω^k in

$$(\omega^{2-h} + 2\omega^{-h+1} + \cdots + (h-1))(\omega^{2-h} + 2\omega^{-h+1} + \cdots + (h-1))$$

$$\text{for } k \geq 2-h$$

$= $ coefficient of ω^{k+2h-2} in

$$(\omega + 2\omega^2 + \cdots + (h-1)\omega^{h-1})(\omega + 2\omega^2 + \cdots + (h-1)\omega^{h-1}) \text{ for } k \geq h.$$

By computation, $(a_{k+2} - a_{k+1}) - (a_{k+1} - a_k) = 0$. Define $d_k =$ coefficient of ω^k in $(\omega + 2\omega^2 + \cdots + h\omega^h)(\omega + \cdots + h\omega^h)$ for $k \geq h+1$. It will be shown that $(d_{k+2} - d_{k+1}) - (d_{k+1} - d_k) < 0$ for $k \geq h+1$. Therefore, $(b_{k+2} - b_{k+1}) - (b_{k+1} - b_k) < 0$ for $2 - h \leq k$.

$$d_k = h(k - h) + (h - 1)(k + 1 - h) + \cdots + (k - h + 1)(h - 1)$$
$$+ (k - h)h,$$

$$d_{k+1} = h(k + 1 - h) + (h - 1)(k + 2 - h) + \cdots + (k + 1 - h)h.$$

By subtraction,

$$d_{k+1} - d_k = \sum_{k-h+1}^{h} x - h(k - h) = \frac{k+1}{2}(2h - k) - (k - h)h.$$

Also,

$$d_{k+2} - d_{k+1} = \frac{k+2}{2}(2h - k - 1) - (k + 1 - h)h.$$

And by computation, $(d_{k+2} - d_{k+1}) - (d_{k+1} - d_k) = -(k+1) < 0$. Therefore, $(C_{k+2} - C_{k+1}) - (C_{k+1} - C_{k+2}) < 0$ for $k \geq 2 - h$. And, therefore, C_k can change sign *at most* twice between $k = 2 - h$ and $k = 0$. But $C_{2-h} < 0$ and $C_0 > 0$. Therefore, C_k changes sign only *once* between $k = 2 - h$ and $k = 0$. Therefore, the coefficients of $P(y)$ change sign only twice.

Property P4. $C_0 > 0$. This property has already been shown (in proof of Property (P3)).

∴ Summing up (P1) to (P4) and applying DesCartes' rule of signs,

$$P(y) > 0 \quad \text{for all } y \neq 1, \, y > 0. \qquad \text{Q.E.D.}$$

Lemma 2. $\partial E/\partial y \, (y, h, h-1) > 0, \, y > 0, \, y \neq 1.$

Proof.

$$E(y, h, h-1) = h - E(1/y, h, 1) \qquad \text{(by Section AIV)}$$

$$\frac{\partial}{\partial y}(E(y, h, h-1)) = \frac{\partial E}{\partial(1/y)}(1/y, h, 1)y^{-2} > 0 \quad \text{by Lemma 1.} \qquad \text{Q.E.D.}$$

Lemma 3. $\partial/\partial y \, [y^{-1}f(2, y, h, 1) + f(h-1, y, h, 1)] < 0, \, y \neq 1.$

Proof. By formula (A10) for $f(x, y, h, z)$,

$$y^{-1}f(2, y, h, 1) + f(h-1, y, h, 1)$$
$$= \frac{[y^{-1}(1 - y^{2-h}) + (1 - y^{-1})][1 - y]}{1 - y^{1-h} + (h-1)(1-y)}, \qquad (A18)$$

$$\frac{\partial}{\partial y} \frac{[y^{-1}(1 - y^{2-h}) + (1 - y^{-1})][1 - y]}{1 - y^{1-h} + (h-1)(1-y)}$$
$$= \frac{\{-1 + (h-1)^2 y^{-h} - 2[(h-1)^2 - 1]y^{1-h} + (h-1)^2 y^{2-h} - y^{2-2h}\}}{D^2}$$

where $D = 1 - y^{1-h} + (h-1)(1-y)$. It remains to be shown that $N < 0 \, y \neq 1$, where

$$N = -1 + (h-1)^2 y^{-h} - 2[(h-1)^2 - 1]y^{1-h} + (h-1)^2 y^{2-h} - y^{2-2h}.$$
$$N(1) = 0.$$

Therefore, it suffices to show that

$dN/dy > 0, \, y < 1,$

$dN/dy < 0, \, y > 1.$

$dN/dy = (h-1)y^{-h-1}N_1,$

where $N_1 = -h(h-1) + 2h(h-2)y + (2-h)(h-1)y^2 + 2y^{2-h}.$
Since $N_1(1) = 0$, it suffices to show that

$dN_1/dy < 0, \quad y \neq 1.$

$dN_1/dy = 2(h-2)N_2,$

where $N_2 = h - (h-1)y - y^{1-h}.$

Since $N_2(1) = 0$, it suffices to show that

$$dN_2/dy > 0, \quad y < 1,$$

$$dN_2/dy < 0, \quad y > 1.$$

$$\frac{dN_2}{dy} = (b-1)(y^{-b} - 1)\begin{cases} > 0, & y < 1, \\ < 0, & y > 1. \end{cases} \qquad\qquad \text{Q.E.D.}$$

Lemma 4. $\partial/\partial y[\, f(1, y, b, b-1) + yf(b-1, y, b, b-1)] > 0$, $y \neq 1$.

Proof. By formula (A9) for $f(x, y, b, z)$,

$$f(1, y, b, b-1) + yf(b-1, y, b, b-1)$$

$$= \frac{[y(1 - y^{b-1}) + (1-y)][1 - y^{-1}]}{(b-1)(1 - y^{-1}) + (1 - y^{b-1})}$$

$$= \frac{(y^{b-1} - y^b)(1 - y^{-1})}{(b-1)(1 - y^{-1}) + (1 - y^{b-1})} + \frac{(1 - y^{b-1})(1 - y^{-1})}{(b-1)(1 - y^{-1}) + (1 - y^{b-1})}$$

$$\frac{\partial}{\partial y} \frac{(1 - y^{b-1})(1 - y^{-1})}{(b-1)(1 - y^{-1}) + (1 - y^{b-1})}$$

$$= \frac{d}{dx} \frac{(1 - x^{-b+1})(1 - x)}{(b-1)(1 - x) + (1 - x^{1-b})} \Big|_{x=1/y} (-1/y^2) > 0$$

by calculation done in Lemma 3 (see (A18)).

$$\frac{\partial}{\partial y} \frac{(y^{b-1} - y^b)(1 - y^{-1})}{(b-1)(1 - y^{-1}) + (1 - y^{b-1})} \quad (\text{using(A11)})$$

$$= \frac{\partial}{\partial y} \left[\frac{y^b(y^{-1} - 1)(1 - y^{-1})}{-y^{b-1} \sum_1^{b-1} x(1/y)^{x-1}(1 - 1/y)^2} \right] \qquad\qquad \text{Q.E.D.}$$

$$= \frac{\partial}{\partial y} \frac{1}{\sum_1^{b-1} xy^{-x}} > 0.$$

Theorem. $\partial E/\partial y(y, b, z) > 0$, $y \neq 1$, $y > 0$.

Proof. Notation. Denote $f(x, y, b, z)$ by $f(x), f(x,y,z,z-1)$ by $f_1(x)$, and $f(x, y, b - z + 1, 1)$ by $f_2(x)$.
  By formulas (A9) and (A10) for f in Section AI,

$$f(x) = A(y, b, z)(1 - y^x), \qquad\qquad\qquad 1 \leqslant x \leqslant z - 1,$$

$$f(x) = C(y, b, z)(1 - y^{x-b}), \qquad\qquad\qquad z \leqslant x \leqslant b,$$

$$f_1(x) = A(y, z, z-1)(1-y^x), \qquad\qquad 1 \leqslant x \leqslant z-1,$$

$$f_2(x) = C(y, b-z+1, 1)(1-y^{x-b+z-1}), \qquad 1 \leqslant x \leqslant b-z.$$

$$\therefore f(x) = \frac{A(y, b, z)}{A(y, z, z-1)} f_1(x) = p_1(y) f_1(x), \qquad 1 \leqslant x \leqslant z-1,$$

where

$$p_1(y) = \frac{A(y, b, z)}{A(y, z, z-1)},$$

$$f(x) = \frac{C(y, b, z)}{C(y, b-z+1, 1)} f_2(x-z+1)$$

$$= p_2(y) f_2(x-z+1), \quad z \leqslant x \leqslant b,$$

where

$$p_2(y) = \frac{C(y, b, z)}{C(y, b-z+1, 1)}.$$

$$\therefore E(y, b, z) = \sum_{1}^{z-1} x p_1(y) f_1(x) + \sum_{z}^{b} x p_2(y) f_2(x-z+1)$$

$$= \sum_{1}^{z-1} x p_1(y) f_1(x) + \sum_{z}^{b} p_2(y)(x-z+1) f_2(x-z+1) \qquad \text{(A19)}$$

$$+ (z-1) \sum_{z}^{b} p_2(y) f_2(x-z+1)$$

$$= p_1(y) E(y, z, z-1) + p_2(y)(z-1)$$

$$+ p_2(y) E(y, b+1-z, 1).$$

Also,

$$\sum_{1}^{b-1} f(x) = \sum_{1}^{z-1} p_1(y) f_1(x) + \sum_{z}^{b} p_2(y) f_2(x-z+1)$$

$$= p_1(y) + p_2(y); \qquad\qquad\qquad\qquad \text{(A20)}$$

$$\therefore 1 = p_1(y) + p_2(y) \text{ for all } y > 0.$$

Using (A19) and (A20),

$$\frac{\partial E(y, b, z)}{\partial y} = \frac{dp_1}{dy} E(y, z, z-1) + \frac{dp_2}{dy}(z-1) + \frac{dp_2}{dy} F(y, b+1-z, 1)$$

$$+ p_1(y) \frac{\partial E}{\partial y}(y, z, z-1) + p_2(y) \frac{\partial E}{\partial y}(y, b+1-z, 1)$$

$$= \frac{dp_2}{dy}[(z - 1 - E(y, z, z - 1)] + \frac{dp_2}{dy} E(y, b + 1 - z, 1)$$

$$+ p_1(y)\frac{\partial E}{\partial y}(y, z, z - 1) + p_2(y)\frac{\partial E}{\partial y}(y, b + 1 - z, 1)$$

≥ 0 if $\dfrac{dp_2}{dy} > 0$ (by Lemmas 1 and 2).

The remainder of the proof consists of showing that $dp_2/dy \geq 0$. By definition, in the steady state, $\sum_1^{z-1} f(x, t) = \sum_1^{z-1} f(x, \quad t - 1)$, or $\sum_1^{z-1}[f(x, t) - f(x, t - 1)]$ $= qf(z) - pf(z - 1) - qf(1) = 0$. Therefore,

$$qf(z) = pf(z - 1) + qf(1),$$
$$f(z) = p_1(y)[yf_1(z - 1) + f_1(1)]. \tag{A11}$$

Similarly,

$$pf(z) = qf(z + 1) + pf(b - 1),$$
$$f(z) = p_2(y)[y^{-1}f_2(2) + f_2(b - z)]. \tag{A22}$$

Hence, dividing (A22) by (A21),

$$\frac{p_1(y)}{p_2(y)} = \frac{y^{-1}f_2(2) + f_2(b - z)}{yf_1(z - 1) + f_1(1)}.$$

But, $d/dy[y^{-1}f_2(2) + f_2(b - z)] < 0$ by Lemma 3, and $d/dy[yf_1(z - 1) + f_1(1)] > 0$ by

Lem**a**. Therefore, $d/dy(p_1(y)/p_2(y)) < 0$, And, using (A20), $dp_2/dy > 0$.   Q.E.D.

AVI.   If $y_F = 1/y_H$, $FX_F(1 - s_F) = HX_H(1 - s_H)$.

Proof.

$$FX_F(p_F - q_F) = HX_H(q_H - p_H), \tag{A23}$$

$$p_H + q_H = 1 - s_H , \tag{A24}$$

$$p_F + q_F = 1 - s_F , \tag{A25}$$

$$p_H - y_H q_H = 0, \tag{A26}$$

$$p_F - y_F q_F = 0. \tag{A27}$$

Using (A24) and (A26),

$$p_H = (1 - s_H)y_H/(1 + y_H), \tag{A28}$$

$$q_H = (1 - s_H)/(1 + y_H). \tag{A29}$$

Using (A25) and (A27),

$$p_F = (1 - s_F)y_F/(1 + y_F),$$ (A30)

$$q_F = (1 - s_F)/(1 + y_F).$$ (A31)

Substituting for p_H, q_H, p_F, and q_F in (A23),

$$FX_F(1 - s_F)\frac{y_F - 1}{1 + y_F} = HX_H \frac{1 - y_H}{1 + y_H}(1 - s_H).$$

Substituting $y_F = 1/y_H$, $FX_F(1 - s_F) = HX_H(1 - s_H)$.   Q.E.D.

AVII.   *The distribution f depends only on p/q independent of s. Therefore, E is independent of s.*

It suffices to show that for $f = f(x, y, h, z)$ given by (A9) and (A10), $f(x) = sf(x) + pf(x - 1) + qf(x + 1)$ for $1 \leqslant x \leqslant h - 1$, $x \neq z$, and $f(z) = sf(z) + pf(z - 1) + qf(z + 1) + pf(h - 1) + qf(1)$. Calculation shows this to be true.   Q.E.D.

AVIII.   **Theorem**   *Denote the duration between transfers as D(y, h, z). For given s, D(y, h, z) = D(1/y, h, h − z), and for given (y, h, z), D(y, h, z) is proportional to $1/(1 − s)$.*
    Proof. $D = [qf(1) + pf(h - 1)]^{-1}$. Using formulas (A28) and (A29) for p and q and formulas (A9) and (A10) for $f(1)$ and $f(h - 1)$,

$$D = \left[(1 - s)\frac{(1 - y)(1 - y^{z-h}) + y(1 - y^{-1})(1 - y^z)}{(1 + y)(z(1 - y^{z-h}) + (h - z)(1 - y^z))} \right]^{-1}, \qquad y \neq 1,$$

whence the theorem follows for $y \neq 1$. It can be checked separately that the theorem is true for $y = 1$.   Q.E.D.

References

1. G. A. Akerlof, 'The Questions of Coinage, Trade Credit, Financial Flows and Peanuts: A Flow-of-Funds Approach to the Demand for Money,' University of California, Berkeley, Working Paper, September 1975.
2. W. J. Baumol, The transactions demand for cash: An inventory theoretic approach. *Quart. J. Econ.* 6 (November 1952).
3. I. Fisher, 'The Purchasing Power of Money,' Macmillan Co. New York, 1911.
4. M. H. Miller and D. Orr, A model of the demand for money by firms, *Quart. J. Econ.* 8 (August 1966).
5   J. Tobin, The interest elasticity of the transactions demand for cash, *Rev. Econ. Statist.* 8 (August 1956).
6. M. Weitzman. A model of the demand for money by firms: Comment. *Quart. J. Econ.* 8 (1968).

14

Irving Fisher on his Head:
The Consequences of Constant
Threshold-Target Monitoring
of Money Holdings[*]

GEORGE A. AKERLOF[†]

I. INTRODUCTION

The monetary theory of Irving Fisher [1911], and also of the inventory theorists, Baumol [1952], Tobin [1956], and Miller and Orr [1966], views money holding as the consequence of two types of decision. The first type of decision concerns payments that are made independent of money holdings and that are, for this reason, denoted *autonomous*. The second type of decision concerns the monitoring rule which determines the payments that are made dependent on the level of the bank account, which payments prevent the bank account from becoming either too high or too low. Because of their dependence on the bank account, such payments will be denoted *induced*.

It makes sense to dichotomize the determinants of money holding in this fashion because these decisions are made for essentially different motives. Autonomous payments are made to take advantage of opportunities for sale or purchase of goods, factors, or securities; the monitoring rule is selected to balance costs relative to benefits of cash holding. Because these two types of decision are made with essentially different motives, they will be made with different lags in response to changes in such variables as income and interest, which affect both decisions in the long run.

[*] This work was previously published as George Akerlof (1979), 'Irving Fisher on his Head: The Consequences of Constant Threshhold-Target Monitoring of Money Holdings', *The Quarterly Journal of Economics* XCIII, 2. Copyright © The MIT Press. Reproduced by kind permission.

[†] The author would like to thank the National Science Foundation for supporting this research under grant number SOC 75-23076, through the Institute of Business and Economic Research, University of California, Berkeley. This paper was revised while the author was Visiting Research Economist, Board of Governors of the Federal Reserve System. The author would also like to thank Janet Yellen, Robert Dorfman, the editor of this *Journal*, and an anonymous referee for valuable comments.

In the model of Irving Fisher the monitoring policy is the average lag with which an induced payment follows an autonomous inpayment. According to Fisher, these average lags will have only a slow response to changes in payment flows and interest, for which reason they may be considered (roughly) constant in the short run.

Baumol, Tobin, and Miller and Orr, on the other hand, explicitly derive the demand for money as the result of the optimal monitoring policy and assumed payments flows. But the returns to complete optimization compared to near optimization in such models can be typically calculated to be small to the point of triviality, even though money holdings in percentage terms may be quite different. For example, consider the Baumol model for a person with an annual income of $12,000, with transactions costs of $10 per transaction, and an annual interest rate of 6 percent. If such a person holds 20 percent more money than prescribed by the Baumol model, he loses only $2 per year, the loss being smaller still if transactions costs are less than $10 per transaction.

The trivial magnitude of the returns from optimization makes a *short-run* model of money holding with constant monitoring rule (in the style of Irving Fisher) preferable to a model of complete optimization (in the style of Baumol, Tobin, and Miller and Orr). Generalizing Fisher permits the demand for money to be written as

$$L = L(P, S), \tag{1}$$

where P is a vector of the probabilities of nonzero autonomous payments and S is a vector representing the policies whereby bank accounts are monitored. The policies S are assumed constant in the short run in this paper, partly because of the preceding argument regarding the magnitude of short-run returns to optimization, but also to contrast the results obtained in this paper with the conventional approach, in which the policies S result from optimal responses to changes in income and interest. Of course, I have no quibble with the notion that in the long run the policies of monitoring are adjusted to be at least roughly consistent with optimization, given the costs of purchasing assets, interest rates, and payments flows. Indeed, some such optimization is seen as historically responsible for the monitoring rules that in the short run are taken as fixed rules of thumb for controlling money holdings.

Irving Fisher's S is a vector of time intervals that represent the average lag with which induced purchases follow autonomous receipts in different bank accounts. According to Fisher, with S constant, a doubling of all autonomous payments causes a doubling of the demand for money. The added assumption that all autonomous payments are proportional to money income yields a quantity theory in the macro sense.

In contrast to Fisher, let S be a vector representing constant targets and thresholds whereby bank accounts are monitored; that is, each bank account, upon exceeding an upper threshold h, is returned to a target z; similarly, upon reaching a lower threshold 0, the bank account is returned to the target z.[1] S is the vector of (h,z) pairs for all bank

---

[1] There is a natural generalization of this monitoring in which money holdings upon exceeding an upper threshold are returned to one target z_h; upon falling below a lower threshold, money holdings are returned to a different target z_l. Boylan [1967] has explored the optimality of such 'multiple (S,s) policies.'

accounts. Let P represent the probability distribution of nonzero autonomous payments and receipts of all bank accounts. In the example below in which bank accounts receive \$1 with probability p, lose \$1 with probability q, and experience no transaction with probability s, P is the vector of different (p,q) pairs (the probabilities of *nonzero* transactions) of all bank accounts. With constant target-threshold monitoring this paper shows that a proportionate increase in the probabilities of all nonzero transactions (e.g., p and q in the example above) results in no change in expected aggregate money holdings. The added assumption that the probabilities of nonzero transactions vary proportionally with income yields a velocity that, rather than being constant, is totally passive.[2] Furthermore, if the *amounts*, rather than the *probabilities* of nonzero transactions, change proportionately with income, with S constant, there is no presumption as to whether the expected demand for money will rise or fall with income. Under special (symmetric) conditions, however, as will be discussed in Section III below, the demand for money will be unchanged.

This passivity of velocity is a phenomenon with a simple explanation. The total expected additions to money holdings in any period are the sum of expected net autonomous payments and expected net induced payments. In equilibrium, with constant money supply, net desired autonomous payments and net induced payments must exactly balance. With constant threshold-target monitoring, a proportionate increase in the probabilities of nonzero autonomous payments produces a proportionate increase in the probabilities of nonzero induced payments. If prior to the increase in the probabilities of autonomous payments expected net autonomous and expected net induced payments exactly balance, then subsequent to the increase the expected values of these two types of payments will continue to balance. A cinematographic analogy makes this proposition clear. A proportionate increase in the probabilities P of nonzero autonomous payments with threshold-target monitoring acts in the same way as if a movie of the payments made in the whole economy were being projected at a proportionately faster speed. If prior to the increase in probabilities the net autonomous and the net induced payments exactly balance, then subsequent to the increase in the 'speed of the movie projector' these two types of payments will continue to balance. No excess demand for money will result, provided, of course, that the targets and thresholds remain unchanged. For this reason velocity will be passive with constant targets and thresholds.

A simple example does not quite capture the generality (or, therefore, the subtleties) in the preceding argument, but it is nevertheless illustrative. Consider an individual bank account with constant inpayments at the rate of x dollars per period. Suppose that every λ periods this bank account is monitored and money holdings are reduced to 0 (by an induced purchase of securities); average money holdings will be $\lambda x/2$ and

---

[2] The basic proposition of this paper, that insofar as probabilities of nonzero transactions are proportional to income, demand for money is independent of income may seem to have limited application, since this proportionality assumption must be violated for income sufficiently great. Otherwise the probabilities of nonzero transactions would exceed unity. It should be remembered, however, that if the unit of time is very short, the probabilities of making any transaction will be correspondingly small. In the limiting continuous case the probability of nonzero transaction in an interval dt is a differential Pdt, while the probability of making no transaction is unity.

velocity will be a constant $2/\lambda$. Suppose, on the contrary, the bank account is monitored so that upon reaching a threshold h, a security is bought, and the bank account is reduced to 0; then the average level of money holdings is $h/2$, independent of x, and velocity will be $2x/h$, exactly proportional to x. In this simple model the change from constant-lag to constant threshold-target monitoring totally changes the behavior of velocity. In the one case, it is constant; in the other, it is exactly proportional to payment flows.

Let Y denote aggregate income, r the rate of interest, and E a vector of exogenous expenditures. Let the probabilities of nonzero transactions depend on Y, r, and E so that $P = P(Y,r,E)$. Then a short-run expected aggregate demand for money function can be written in the form,

$$L = L(Y,\ P(Y,r,E)/Y,S). \tag{2}$$

The first argument denotes the dependence of the demand for money on income insofar as the probabilities of payment are proportional to income; the second argument represents the dependence of the demand for money on payments flows insofar as the probabilities of nonzero autonomous payments are *not* proportional to income.[3]

According to (2) with S constant, $dL/dY | dE = dr = 0$ has two components:

$$\frac{dL}{dY}\Big|_{dE=dr=0} = \frac{\partial L}{\partial Y} + \frac{\partial L}{\partial(P/Y)}\frac{\partial(P/Y)}{\partial Y}; \tag{3}$$

and

$$\frac{dL}{dr}\Big|_{dE=dY=0} = \frac{\partial L}{\partial(P/Y)}\frac{\partial(P/Y)}{\partial r}. \tag{4}$$

With constant-lag monitoring in the style of Irving Fisher and with the probabilities P proportional to Y, the first term of (3) is a positive constant, and (4) vanishes, thus yielding a quantity theory.

In contrast, with threshold-target monitoring the first term of (3) vanishes so that the short-run income elasticity of the demand for money is zero if P is proportional to Y. It is well-known that empirical studies have found low short-run *interest* elasticities of the demand for money. However, these studies cannot be used to infer the ineffectiveness of fiscal policy in the short run, as would be suggested by constant velocity theory; with threshold-target monitoring the short-run income elasticity of the demand for money is also low.

As will be discussed in Section IV, the constant threshold-target model of this paper is at least roughly consistent with the empirical evidence regarding the demand for

---

[3] This paper concentrates its attention on the implications for the demand for money of the proportionality of expected payments flows and income. Two earlier papers, Akerlof [1975] and [1976], examined the consequences for the demand for money of payments flows that are not proportional to income.

money. This evidence shows short-run income elasticities of the demand for money that are an order of magnitude less than the short-run income elasticity of approximately unity predicted by Irving Fisher's theory. As a result, in the usual econometric models fiscal policy is effective in changing aggregate income not because the short-run interest elasticity of the demand for money is high but rather because the short-run income elasticity of the demand for money is low. This low income elasticity has escaped the notice of monetary economists, presumably because Irving Fisher's arguments concerning the proportionality of the transactions demand for money and income have seemed so convincing.[4] According to this paper, those arguments are much more sensitive to the exact nature of Irving Fisher's assumptions than has previously been supposed. A precise explanation for low short-run income elasticity of the demand for money is given.

II. RELATION BETWEEN PAYMENTS FLOWS AND MONEY DEMAND WITH THRESHOLD-TARGET MONITORING

This section presents and analyzes an economy with threshold-target monitoring. It is divided into four parts: Part A, which describes the microeconomic model of payments flows with threshold-target monitoring; Part B, which defines equilibrium in the money market; Part C, which derives the microeconomic consequences of changes in the probabilities of payments; and Part D, which states the consequences of this model for the aggregate demand for money.

A. *Payments Flows and Monitoring*

The model of payments flows and monitoring and its notation is adapted from Miller and Orr. Each bank account, subscripted by the letter i, has an upper threshold h_i, whose attainment triggers an induced purchase of goods or securities in amount $h_i - z_i$, thereby returning the bank account to the target z_i. Similarly, on reaching zero, a sale of either goods or securities in amount z_i is triggered, and the bank account also goes to the target z_i. Autonomous payments in each bank account are probabilistic, with three exhaustive outcomes: an inpayment of \$1 between t and $t + 1$ with probability p_i, no inpayment or outpayment between t and $t + 1$ with probability s_i, and an outpayment of \$1 between t and $t + 1$ with probability q_i.

B. *Nature of Equilibrium: Short Run and Long Run*

If $f_i(m_i,t)$ denotes the probability that bank account i has m_i money holdings at time t, the expected value of money holdings at t, denoted $E(m)_t$, is

$$E(m)_t = \sum_i \sum_{m_i} m_i f_i(m_i,t).$$ (5)

---

[4] For example, Keynes' argument in *The General Theory* [1936] concerning the proportionality of the transactions demand for money and income is a restatement of Irving Fisher's arguments for the constancy of velocity in *The Purchasing Power of Money* [1911].

Let M_t denote the money supply at t, and assume that it is exogenously determined. Assume, also, that the probabilities p_i, q_i, and s_i depend upon endogenous and exogenous variables (such as Y, r, and E). $E(m)_t$ is determined by p_i, q_i, and s_i, given the distributions of money holdings m_i at $t-1$ and given the h_i and z_i.

A short-run equilibrium condition is therefore given by

$$E(m)_t = M_t, \tag{6}$$

where $E(m)_t$ is given by (5); where $f_i(m_i, t-1)$ is given; and where $f_i(m_i,t)$ can be derived from the assumed probabilities of payments and receipts, and the thresholds h_i and targets z_i by equations (7) and (8):

$$f_i(m_i,t) = p_i(\cdot)f_i(m_i-1,t-1) + s_i(\cdot)f_i(m_i,t-1) + q_i(\cdot)f_i(m_i+1,t-1)$$
$$1 \leq m_i \leq h_i-1 \quad m_i \neq z_i; \tag{7}$$

and

$$f_i(z_i,t) = p_i(\cdot)f_i(z_i-1,t-1) + s_i(\cdot)f_i(z_i,t-1)$$
$$+ q_i(\cdot)f_i(z_i+1,t-1) + p_i(\cdot)f_i(h_i-1,t-1).$$
$$+ q_i(\cdot)f_i(1,t-1) \tag{8}$$

Values of the endogenous variables with payments probabilities $p_i(\cdot)$, $q_i(\cdot)$, and $s_i(\cdot)$, such that (5), (6), (7), and (8) are satisfied, cause the money market to be in equilibrium at time t. (Microeconomic Proposition II in the Appendix shows that this equilibrium condition can also be expressed in flow terms: that the expected value of desired autonomous payments between $t-1$ and t plus the expected value of induced payments between $t-1$ and t must equal the change in the money supply.)

Conditions (5), (6), (7), and (8) also yield a long-run equilibrium condition if the money supply is constant. For, if p_i, q_i, and s_i are constant, as they will be in a long-run equilibrium with their functional arguments constant, $f_i(m_i,t)$ will approach a long-run stationary distribution (denoted $f_i(m_i)$), with the property,

$$f_i(m_i, t-1) = f_i(m_i,t) = f_i(m_i). \tag{9}$$

Because of this stationarity property (9), $f_i(m_i)$ is given by the system (10) and (11):

$$f_i(m_i) = p_i(\cdot)f_i(m_i+1) + s_i(\cdot)f_i(m_i) + q_i(\cdot)f_i(m_i+1)$$
$$1 \leq m_i \leq h_i-1 \quad m_i \neq z_i; \tag{10}$$

$$f_i(z_i) = p_i(\cdot)f_i(z_i-1) + s_i(\cdot)f_i(z_i) + q_i(\cdot)f_i(z_i+1)$$
$$+ p_i(\cdot)f_i(h_i-1) + q_i(\cdot)f_i(1). \tag{11}$$

In addition to (10) and (11),

$$f_i(0) = 0 \tag{12}$$

$$f_i(h_i) = 0 \tag{13}$$

$$\sum_{m_i=1}^{h_j-1} f_i(m_i) = 1, \tag{14}$$

so that the system (10) to (14) consists of two second-order difference equations from 1 to $z_i - 1$ and from $z_i + 1$ to $h_i - 1$ (equation (10)), with four boundary conditions, (11) to (14). Miller and Orr [1966, pp. 434–35] have found that

$$f_i(m_i) = \frac{1 - y_i^{z_i - h_i}}{z_i(1 - y_i^{z_i - h_i}) + (h_i - z_i)(1 - y_i^{z_i})}(1 - y_i^{m_i}) \; 0 \leq m_i \leq z_i \tag{15}$$

$$f_i(m_i) = \frac{1 - y_i^{z_i}}{z_i(1 - y_i^{z_i - h_i}) + (h_i - z_i)(1 - y_i^{z_i})}(1 - y_i^{m_i - h_i}) \; z_i \leq m_i \leq h_i, \tag{16}$$

where $y_i = p_i(\cdot)/q_i(\cdot)$.

Consequently, the long-run equilibrium condition in the money market with constant money supply $\overline{M}$ is given by

$$\sum_i \sum_{m_i} m_i \; its \; f(m_i) = \overline{M},$$

where $f(m_i)$ is the distribution defined by (15) and (16).

C. *Basic Microeconomic Propositions*

The definition of long-run equilibrium just given is now used in the statement of the key 'microeconomic propositions' of this paper. These propositions are called microeconomic because the relation between payments probabilities (p_i, q_i, s_i) and endogenous macroeconomic variables remains unspecified. Such a specification will be given in subsection D, which also gives a parallel 'macroeconomic proposition.' (Proofs of these propositions are provided in the Appendix.)

Microeconomic Proposition I. If money holdings in an initial period, denoted $t = 0$, are a random variable with a probability distribution in long-run equilibrium relative to the p_i's, q_i's, s_i's, h_i's, and z_i's in that initial period, as defined by (15) and (16), an equiproportionate change in all p_i's and q_i's will cause no expected change in money holdings, as long as the h_i's and z_i's remain constant.

Proposition I, of course, is the antithesis to the conventional wisdom of the quantity theory. According to Irving Fisher, velocity being constant, an equiproportionate increase in transactions will produce an equiproportionate increase in money holdings. According to Proposition I, an equiproportionate increase in the probabilities of transactions produces no change in money holdings.

Microeconomic Proposition II and III. Microeconomic Propositions II and III verify the two key assertions of the introduction regarding the 'cinematographic' image of payments flows. According to Microeconomic Proposition II, *the expected additions to money holdings of a bank account are the sum of net expected induced payments plus net expected autonomous payments.* Consequently, if the money supply is constant and equal to the expected sum of induced and autonomous flows, these two expectations must also sum to zero. According to Microeconomic Proposition III, *in long-run equilibrium an equipro-portionate increase in the probabilities of nonzero autonomous payments causes an equiproportionate increase in the probabilities of induced payments.* Thus, following the analogy, in long-run equilibrium an increase in the 'speed' of autonomous payments causes an equal increase in the 'speed' of induced payments; and, using Microeconomic Proposition II, since the two flows balance in a long-run equilibrium with constant money supply, so they will continue to balance after an increase in the 'speed' of the autonomous flows; there will be no increase in the demand for money.

D. *Basic Macroeconomic Proposition*

Microeconomic Proposition I has as counterpart its respective macroeconomic proposition.

Macroeconomic Proposition. Let p_i, q_i, and s_i at time t depend upon income Y_t, interest r_t, and other exogenous variables E_t, as $p_i(Y_t,r_t,E_t)$, $q_i(Y_t,r_t,E_t)$, and $s_i(Y_t,r_t,E_t)$. Given the distribution of money holdings in each bank account in an initial period, denoted 0, the expected demand for money, denoted L_t in each subsequent period t is a function of the paths of Y_τ,r_τ,E_τ. In particular, if Y, r, and E are constant between 0 and t, it is possible to write

$$L_t = L_t(Y,r,E).$$

In general, such L_t is of the form,

$$L_t = L_t(p_1(Y,r,E), \ldots, p_N(Y,r,E), \ldots, q_N(Y,r,E);b_1, \ldots,$$
$$b_N,z_1, \ldots, z_N;f_1(1,0), \ldots, f_N(b_N - 1,0)), \tag{17}$$

where there are N bank accounts in the economy.

It follows from Microeconomic Proposition I that (17) can be written in such a way that

$$L_t = L_t(Y,p_1(Y,r,E)/Y, \ldots, p_N(Y,r,E)/Y,q_1(Y,r,E)/Y, \ldots,$$
$$q_N(Y,r,E)/Y;b_1, \ldots, b_N,z_1, \ldots, z_N;f_1(1,0), \ldots, f_N(b_N - 1,0)), \tag{18}$$

and such that, if each $f_i(m_i,0)$ is given by (15) and (16), which is its long-run value, given p_i,q_i,b_i, and z_i, then

$$\frac{\partial L_t}{\partial Y} = 0. \tag{19}$$

Property (19) is, in fact, quite special; it is a precise yet general antithesis to the quantity theory; it states that, except insofar as the probabilities of nonzero transactions change relative to income, the income elasticity of the demand for money is zero; this property is true with constant threshold-target monitoring, provided that prior to the change in income, the distribution of money holdings was in its long-run stationary state.

III. COMMENTS ON THE MODEL

The specificity of the model of the last section makes it easy to pinpoint the most important of the ways in which the model violates reality, of which some are intrinsic and others not. The most glaring violation of reality in the model of the last section occurs in the assumed probability distributions of payments and receipts with no payment or receipt having absolute value more than \$1. This feature of the model, however, is not intrinsic. If there is a probability p_l of receiving l dollars and a probability q_j of paying j dollars, an equiproportionate change in the p_l and q_j for all positive values of l and j and all bank accounts i will still cause no change in the expected value of money holdings, provided that the distributions of money holdings prior to this equiproportionate shift were stationary. This, of course, is the generalization of Microeconomic Proposition I, and it is easy to prove. Also, in addition to having a greater range of payment size, the generalized model should let this payment size depend upon the type of transactions being made; i.e. some purchases (for example, ice cream cones) involve greater probabilities of \$1 payments than other purchases (for example, automobiles) so that each p_l and q_j should depend upon the specific autonomous purchase being made.

A second feature of the last section concerns the nature of the comparative static change; increased nominal income is assumed to induce proportionate increases in the probabilities of receipts and payments, the *size* of those payments being fixed. An alternative representation of changes in nominal income would leave the probabilities of transactions unchanged but let their *size* increase in proportion to income. It is possible to do some analysis of this type of change in transactions probabilities, although the results are a bit less clean than with changes in probabilities. The independence of money demand and income generalizes in the following sense: with constant targets and thresholds, only insofar as the economy deviates from a certain type of symmetry, which will be described, will the demand for money shift as income shifts. Furthermore, there is no presumption in general as to whether increased income will cause increased or decreased demand for money.

Let the size of transactions be uniformly λ dollars so that a bank account receives λ dollars with probability p and loses λ dollars with probability q. Let the targets and thresholds be fixed at z dollars and h dollars, respectively; making the approximation which ignores that h and z are no longer integral multiples of λ, the expected demand for money in terms of units of size λ (following formula (A4) in the Appendix) is $E(y,h/\lambda,z/\lambda)$ and in terms of dollars is

$$E(m) = \lambda E(y,h/\lambda,z/\lambda). \tag{20}$$

Use of (A4) and a particular type of symmetry reveals an economy in which the demand for money is independent of λ. Consider an economy in which bank accounts can be grouped in pairs, so that for a bank account with probability p of gaining λ dollars, probability q of losing λ dollars, with threshold h and target z, there is a dual bank account with probability q of gaining λ dollars, probability p of losing λ dollars, threshold h and target $h - z$. Such a symmetry makes sense because it is possible to think of the two bank accounts as being mutually payer and payee in a single transaction. The relative values of targets and thresholds also make dimensional sense, since both bank accounts have equal average durations between induced transactions. Use of (20) and (A4) shows that the sum of the demand for money of two paired bank accounts is h, independent of λ. Microeconomic Proposition IV, whose proof is given in the Appendix, states that

$$E(y,h,z) + E(1/y,h,h - z) = h$$

where

$$y = p/q.$$

As a result, only insofar as the bank accounts deviate from such symmetric pairing will changes in the size of transactions (i.e., in λ) yield changes in the demand for money. Furthermore, in the absence of such symmetry, increases in λ can result in either increases or decreases in the demand for money. In these two preceding senses the 0-income elasticity of the demand for money with constant targets and thresholds is robust to changes in the specification of the model of the preceding section.

The assumption regarding the independence of payments between different time periods also violates reality, as is evident from the monthly cycle of wage payments and bills, but again it does not appear that this assumption is intrinsic. A separate paper by Ross Milbourne and myself [1977] explores the extent to which periodic autonomous inflows from wage payments with constant targets and thresholds will modify the conclusions of this paper regarding low income elasticities of the demand for money. Constant targets and thresholds will cause bank accounts to be monitored more frequently as income increases. The increased frequency of monitoring tends to reduce money holdings and can more than offset the increased money holdings that occur because of larger payments flows, so that income elasticities of the demand for money, even with periodic payments, might actually be slightly negative.

Finally, of course, threshold-target monitoring is intrinsic for our conclusion. But that is indeed our point. There should be little doubt that an economy with constant threshold-target monitoring will have a low income elasticity of the demand for money.

IV. AGREEMENT WITH EMPIRICAL EVIDENCE

It remains to examine how well the predictions of the short-run constant threshold-target model agree with empirical evidence concerning the demand for money. In this regard, it is worthwhile to compare two possible specifications of money demand; the first of these specifications is consistent with a theory of money demand in which bank accounts are periodically monitored and habits, which are reflected in the periodicity of this monitoring, respond slowly to changes in the costs and benefits of holding cash balances. According to this model (in differential, as opposed to difference, form),

$$\dot{v} = \alpha(v^* - v) \tag{21}$$

where

v is current velocity
v^* is a target (optimum) velocity
and
α is a speed-of-adjustment parameter.
In contrast, the usual equation used in empirical estimates of the demand for money is

$$\dot{m} = \alpha(m^* - m) \tag{22}$$

where

m is real balances demanded
m^* is a targeted (optimum) value of real balances
and
α is again a speed-of-adjustment parameter.
These two possible money-demands behave quite differently in the short run (which in the limit is zero time elapsed since the occurrence of a change). According to (21), velocity is constant in the short run, and money demand is proportional to income; conversely, according to (22), money demand is constant in the short run, and velocity is proportional to income. The model of constant targets and thresholds in the short run is roughly consistent with specification (22), with money demand independent of income; correspondingly, it is inconsistent with equation (21), with constant velocity. Economies in which money demand is described by these two equations are in consequence, quite different in terms of the effectiveness of fiscal policy in the short run. With (21) fiscal policy is totally ineffective in changing income even in the short run; with (22) fiscal policy is quite effective, but not for the usual reason; not because $\partial L/\partial r$ is large but rather because $\partial L/\partial Y$ is small.

Empirical estimates of the demand for money usually use (22) in difference equation form as their specification; in particular such stock adjustment equations have been estimated by Laidler [1966], Chow [1966], and Goldfeld [1973], among others. The famous Goldfeld 'preferred' equation has a one-quarter income elasticity of 0.193, which is considerably less than the elasticity of nearly unity predicted by a theory of the demand for money with constant velocity in the short run. The correctness of this estimate is partly argued by its goodness of fit and also its robustness, as tested by Goldfeld in many ways. Still, the low income elasticity of 0.193 might be at least partially due to the constraint imposed by the stock adjustment equation that the money demand responds to changes in both income and interest with the same speed of adjustment (given by the parameter α). However, estimates of the demand for money (Goldfeld [1973, pp. 598–607]) using Almon lags without a constraint on income and interest elasticities to adjust at the same rate show that these two elasticities do adjust at approximately the same rate. If anything, money demand adjusts slightly more slowly to changes in income than to changes in interest. The one-quarter income elasticity of M_1 with Almon lags is 0.146.

Of course, it has been noticed (Enzler, Johnson, Paulus [1976], Goldfeld [1976]) in recent years that the Goldfeld equation, as estimated from 1952 to 1972 has predicted quite 'badly,' so that the empirical evidence is at least a bit ambiguous. Several explanations have been given for this phenomenon, of which the most convincing is the large increase in the size of the immediately available funds market; the market has grown from $1 billion net purchases by all commercial banks in 1967 to about $35 billion in June 1955.[5] Since Federal Funds are quite liquid and therefore a substitute for money, the dramatically increased importance of this market should alter the demand for money function. Furthermore, the poor predictive powers of the Goldfeld equation should not affect confidence in this paper's prediction of low income elasticities of the demand for money, since the predictions erred on the side of letting money demand follow income too closely.

Finally, of course it should be noted that the behavior of velocity in the short run in the constant target-threshold model explains at least one half of Milton Friedman's dilemma [1959], which is why velocity is covariant with income over the course of the business cycle. The second part of this dilemma, which was to explain why velocity was contravariant with income over the long run, as was observed prior to World War II, can be explained presumably by the adjustments of targets and thresholds by holders of money balances, who weigh the costs and benefits of different targets and thresholds and ultimately choose the optimum.

V. SUMMARY AND CONCLUSION

Economic theorists have usually assumed that the short-run income elasticity of the transactions demand for money is quite large, being approximately unity. The logic behind this supposition is that persons have 'average rates of turnover' that reflect their habits of cash holding. These habits respond slowly to changes in income and interest. This paper shows that if habits are defined differently, in terms of threshold-target

---

[5] See Porter and Mauskopf [1978] and Tinsley and Garrett [1978].

monitoring, velocity is not constant in the short run, but instead is proportional to income. This prediction is, in fact, consistent with the empirical evidence. Thus, fiscal policy is effective in the short run, not for the reason usually given by Keynesians that the interest elasticity of the demand for money is large, but rather because the income elasticity of the demand for money is small.

APPENDIX

MICROECONOMIC PROPOSITION I. If money holdings in an initial period, denoted $t = 0$, are a random variable with a probability distribution in long-run equilibrium relative to the p_i's, q_i's, s_i's, h_i's, and z_i's in that initial period, as defined by (15) and (16), an equiproportionate change in all p_i's and q_i's will cause no expected change in money holdings, as long as the h_i's and z_i's remain constant.

Proof of Microeconomic Proposition I. It will be shown that an equiproportionate rise in the p_i's, q_i's, and $(1 - s_i)$'s, the h_i's and z_i's being constant, causes no change in the distribution of money holdings under the assumed conditions. Therefore, there is no change in expected money holdings.

The proof will proceed by induction.

By definition, $f_i(m_i,0) = f_i(m_i,0)$.

It remains to show that if $f_i(m_i,t) = f_i(m_i,0)$, then $f_i(m_i,t + 1) = f_i(m_i,0)$.

Let p_i, q_i, and s_i be the initial probabilities of autonomously receiving \$1, of autonomously paying \$1, and of making no transaction, respectively.

Let p_i', q_i', s_i' be the corresponding probabilities subsequent to the equiproportionate shift.

By definition, there is a scalar λ, such that

$$p_i' = \lambda p_i \tag{A1}$$

$$q_i' = \lambda q_i \tag{A2}$$

$$s_i' = 1 - \lambda(1 - s_i). \tag{A3}$$

We now make two calculations which show that $f_i(m_i,t + 1) = f_i(m_i,0)$. By (7), for

$$1 \leqq m_i \leqq h_i - 1, \quad m_i \neq z_i,$$

$$f_i(m_i,t + 1) = p_i' f_i(m_i - 1,t) + q_i' f_i(m_i + 1,t) + s_i' f_i(m_i,t);$$

by (A1), (A2), and (A3)

$$= \lambda p_i f_i(m_i - 1,t) + \lambda q_i f_i(m_i + 1,t) + \{1 - \lambda(1 - s_i)\} f_i(m_i,t);$$

by induction assumption

$$= \lambda p_i f_i(m_i - 1, 0) + \lambda q_i f_i(m_i + 1, 0) + \{1 - \lambda(1 - s_i)\} f_i(m_i, 0);$$

by rearrangement of terms

$$= \lambda \{p_i f_i(m_i - 1, 0) + q_i f_i(m_i + 1, 0) + s_i f_i(m_i, 0)\}$$
$$- \lambda f_i(m_i, 0) + f_i(m_i, 0);$$

by stationarity of $f_i(m_i, 0)$ (equation (10))

$$= \lambda f_i(m_i, 0) - \lambda f_i(m_i, 0) + f_i(m_i, 0) = f_i(m_i, 0).$$

Similarly,

$$
\begin{aligned}
f_i(z_i, t + 1) &= p_i' f_i(z_i - 1, t) + q_i' f_i(z_i + 1, t) + p_i' f_i(h_i - 1, t) \\
&\quad + q_i' f_i(1, t) + s_i' f_i(z_i, t) \\
&= \lambda \{ p_i f_i(z_i - 1, 0) + q_i f_i(z_i + 1, 0) \\
&\quad + p_i f_i(h_i - 1, 0) + q_i f_i(1, 0) + s_i f_i(z_i, 0)\} - \lambda f_i(z_i, 0) + f_i(z_i, 0) \\
&= \lambda f_i(z_i, 0) - \lambda f_i(z_i, 0) + f_i(z_i, 0) \\
&= f_i(z_i, 0). \qquad\qquad \text{Q.E.D.}
\end{aligned}
$$

Corollary to Microeconomic Proposition I. If money holdings in an initial period are a random variable with a probability distribution in long-run equilibrium, an equiproportionate change in all p_i's and q_i's will cause no change in the probability distributions of money holdings in subsequent periods, provided the h_i's and z_i's remain constant.

MICROECONOMIC PROPOSITION II. Expected additions to money holdings are the sum of net expected induced payments, plus net expected autonomous payments. (Subscript i will be omitted in Microeconomic Propositions II, III, and IV, since these propositions apply uniformly to all bank accounts.) In symbols,

$$\sum_m mf(m, t + 1) - \sum_m mf(m, t) = -p(h - z)f(h - 1, t) + qzf(1, t) + p - q.$$

Proof.

$$\sum_m mf(m, t + 1) - \sum_m mf(m, t)$$

$$= \sum_{m=1}^{h-1} smf(m, t) + \sum_{m=1}^{h-1} qmf(m + 1, t) + \sum_{m=1}^{h-1} pmf(m - 1, t)$$

$$+ qzf(1, t) + pzf(h - 1, t) - \sum_{m=1}^{h-1} mf(m, t)$$

$$= \sum_{m=1}^{b-1} smf(m, t) + \sum_{m=1}^{b-1} q(m+1)f(m+1, t)$$

$$+ \sum_{m=1}^{b-1} p(m-1)f(m-1, t) - \sum_{m=1}^{b-1} qf(m+1, t)$$

$$+ \sum_{m=1}^{b-1} pf(m-1, t) + qzf(1, t) + pzf(b-1, t) - \sum_{m=1}^{b-1} mf(m, t)$$

$$= \sum_{m=1}^{b-1} smf(m, t) + \sum_{m=1}^{b-1} qmf(m, t) + \sum_{m=1}^{b-1} pmf(m, t)$$

$$- qf(1, t) - p(b-1)f(b-1, t) - \sum_{m=1}^{b-1} qf(m, t)$$

$$+ \sum_{m=1}^{b-1} pf(m, t) + qf(1, t) - pf(b-1, t)$$

$$+ qzf(1, t) + pzf(b-1, t) - \sum_{m=1}^{b-1} mf(m, t),$$

and since $p + q + s = 1$ and $\sum_{m=1}^{h-1} f(m, t) = 1$,

$$= -p(b-z)f(b-1, t) + qzf(1, t) + p - q.$$

MICROECONOMIC PROPOSITION III. An equiproportionate increase in the probabilities of autonomous payments causes an equiproportionate increase in the probabilities of induced payments.

Proof. The probability of a net induced inflow into a bank account in amount z is $qf(1)$. The probability of a net induced outflow from a bank account in amount $(b - z)$ is $pf(b - 1)$. According to the Corollary to Microeconomic Proposition I, an equal increase in p and q leaves $f(1)$ and $f(b - 1)$ unchanged; thus if p and q each change by a factor λ, the probability of an induced inflow in amount z becomes $\lambda qf(1)$ and the probability of an induced outflow in amount $(b - z)$ becomes $\lambda pf(b - 1)$.

Q.E.D.

MICROECONOMIC PROPOSITION IV. Let $E(y, b, z)$ represent the expected value of money holdings of a bank account with upper threshold b, target z and $p/q = y$.

$$E(y, b, z) + E(1/y, b, b - z) = b.$$

Proof. By (15) and (16)

$$E(y, b, z) = \left(\sum_{m=0}^{z} m(1 - y^{z-b})(1 - y^m) + \sum_{m=z+1}^{b} m(1 - y^z) \times (1 - y^{m-b}) \right) /$$
$$\left(z(1 - y^{z-b}) + (b - z)(1 - y^z) \right).$$

A bit of algebraic labor produces the sum (A4):

$$E(y, b, z) = \frac{1}{2} \left\{ \frac{1+y}{1-y} + b + z - \frac{bz(1 - y^{z-b})}{z(1 - y^{z-b}) + (b - z)(1 - y^z)} \right\}. \tag{A4}$$

Use of (A4) with the value of the first argument of E equal to $1/y$, of the second argument equal to b, and of the third argument equal to $b - z$, yields

$$E(1/y, b, b - z)$$
$$= \frac{1}{2} \left\{ -\frac{1+y}{1-y} + 2b - z - \frac{b(b - z)(1 - y^z)}{(b - z)(1 - y^z) + z(1 - y^{z-b})} \right\}. \tag{A5}$$

Addition of (A4) and (A5) yields

$$E(y, b, z) + E(1/y, b, b - z) = b. \qquad\qquad \text{Q.E.D.}$$

LONDON SCHOOL OF ECONOMICS

References

Akerlof, G. A., 'The Microfoundations of a Flow of Funds Theory of Demand for Money,' Working paper, University of California, Berkeley, March 1976.

——, 'The Questions of Coinage, Trade Credit, Financial Flows and Peanuts: A Flow-of-Funds Approach to the Demand for Money,' Working paper, University of California, Berkeley, September 1975.

—— and R. D. Milbourne, 'The Sensitivity of Monetarist Conclusions to Monetarist Assumptions,' Board of Governors of the Federal Reserve System, November 1977.

Baumol, W. J., 'The Transactions Demand for Cash: An Inventory Theoretic Approach,' this *Journal*, LXVI (Nov. 1952), 545–56.

Boylan, E. S., 'Multiple (S,s) Policies and the *n*-Period Inventory Problem,' *Management Science*, XIV (Nov. 1967), 196–204.

Chow, G. C., 'On the Long-Run and Short-Run Demand for Money,' *Journal of Political Economy*, LXXIV (April 1966), 111–31.

Enzler, J., L. Johnson, and J. Paulus, 'Some Problems of Money Demand,' *Brookings Papers on Economic Activity*, 1 (1976), 261–80.

Fisher, I., *The Purchasing Power of Money* (New York: Macmillan, 1911).

Friedman, M., 'The Demand for Money: Some Theoretical and Empirical Results,' *Journal of Political Economy*, LXVII (Aug. 1959), 327–51.

Goldfeld, S. M., 'The Demand for Money Revisited,' *Brookings Papers on Economic Activity*, 3 (1973), 577–638.

——, 'The Case of the Missing Money,' *Brookings Papers on Economic Activity*, 3 (1976), 683–730.

Keynes, J. M., *The General Theory of Employment, Interest and Money* (New York: Macmillan, 1936).

Laidler, D., 'The Rate of Interest and the Demand for Money: Some Empirical Evidence,' *Journal of Political Economy*, LXXIV (Dec. 1966), 543–55.

Miller, M. H., and D. Orr, 'A Model of the Demand for Money by Firms,' this *Journal*, LXXX (Aug. 1966), 413–35.

Porter, R. D., and E. Mauskopf, 'Some Notes on the Apparent Shift in the Demand for Demand Deposits Function,' unpublished manuscript, Board of Governors of the Federal Reserve System, May 1978.

Tinsley, P. A., and B. Garrett, 'The Measurement of Money Demand,' preliminary unpublished manuscript, Special Studies Section, Board of Governors of the Federal Reserve System, April 1978.

Tobin, J., 'The Interest Elasticity of the Transactions Demand for Cash,' *Review of Economics and Statistics*, XXXVIII (Aug. 1956), 241–47.

15

Jobs as Dam Sites[*]

GEORGE A. AKERLOF

London School of Economics

I. INTRODUCTION

Much economic analysis is based on stylized relations between the nature of economic processes and the functions economists use as their tools of analysis. For example, if production processes are duplicable, constant returns to scale production functions are obtained. The student of elementary economics is told that if goods are difficult to substitute, their demand is inelastic; if easy to substitute their demand is elastic. In similar fashion it is the purpose of this paper to categorize the nature of jobs and to show that it has implications for the elasticity of demand for labour with respect to the wage.

We see a job as like a dam site. A dam which under-utilizes a dam site, even though productive in the sense that water is usefully stored or electricity is usefully produced, will nevertheless be costly in the sense that the valuable dam site is wasted. Even at zero cost (and hence a benefit/cost ratio of infinity) it may not pay to use a dam which under-utilizes the site. We picture jobs and workers in the same way. Jobs are pictured as being like dam sites and workers of different skills as being like the potential dams on the dam site. Workers of sufficiently low skills will not be able to get jobs even at zero wages, not because their output on those jobs is negative, but because they under-utilize the jobs themselves. Nor may it matter that the firm will have to pay significantly positive wages to hire skilled workers on its jobs.

This image of the job gives reason for pessimism about the wage elasticity of demand for labour of a given skill, since it says that unskilled workers, no matter how low they bid their wages, may still be unable to bid jobs away from skilled workers.

This has at least five consequences. First, it shows that in a demand downturn, in which prices of final goods and services are below the full employment level, wage flexibility alone will not be sufficient to restore full employment. Skilled workers will receive jobs and positive wages; unskilled workers will not be able to capture jobs even at zero wages.

[*] This work was previously published as George Akerlof (1981), 'Jobs as Dam Sites', *Review of Economic Studies* XLVIII Copyright © 1981 The Society for Economic Analysis Ltd. Reproduced by kind permission of Blackwell Publishing.

Second, the minimum wage is often considered a major cause of unemployment in general and among youth in particular (see Feldstein (1973) for one example). The effects of minimum wages on employment depends critically on the wage elasticity of demand, which is low for unskilled workers if, as in our argument, they cannot capture jobs even at zero wages.

Third, Feldstein among others (1973, pp. 19–26) has argued that wage subsidies should be paid to encourage employees to hire youth in ladder jobs. Feldstein's recommendation rests implicitly on the belief that the elasticity of demand for such youths in such jobs is fairly high—at least in the sense that employers would more than willingly hire such workers with sufficient reduction of the minimum wage. Wage costs thus serve as an upper bound to his estimates of the costs of such programmes. If, on the other hand, jobs are as pictured in this paper, like dam sites, even at a zero wage firms may be quite unwilling to hire unskilled workers in ladder jobs because they may under-utilize the ladder jobs themselves.

The other side to the subsidy issue is manpower training programmes. Such programmes have been strongly criticized in the US for their high cost per worker. Implicit in much of this criticism has been the comparison with on-the-job training on the supposition that the cost of such training must necessarily be less than the wages paid in such jobs. This implicit comparison, however, is invalid according to this paper since the cost of using an unskilled worker in a job is not just the cost of his wages but the cost of his underutilization of the scarce resource, the job itself.

Fourth, the job-as-dam-site view of the labour market explains another well-known phenomenon. The unemployment rates of unskilled labour are always greater than the unemployment rates of skilled labour. There are two common explanations of this phenomenon, to which the dam site model adds a third.[1] One explanation is that money wages for jobs are rigid. When a job is vacant the employer selects from all applicants the most skilled person willing to accept the job at the rigid money wage fixed for the given job. Because of this system of selection less skilled workers do not have the option of underbidding more skilled applicants. The second explanation is Becker's (1964). Workers with greater skills, says Becker, have higher ratios of specific human capital, relative to their wage. As a consequence, in a cyclical downturn, it is suboptimal for a firm to lay off its high-specific-capital workers and potentially lose its investment if they cannot be subsequently rehired. In contrast, in the theory of this paper, skilled workers can always bid the wage for a job below the point where the unskilled worker is willing to compete—unless the unskilled worker is willing to take a negative wage, as sometimes occurs in apprenticeships.

Fifth, economists have long puzzled about the high elasticity of short-run output with respect to employment, as reflected crudely in Okun's law, and less crudely in terms of short-run production functions. It is surprising that the short-run elasticity of output, even with respect to production workers, exceeds unity. The model of this paper

---

[1] A less-known explanation is that of Melvin Reder (1964), who explains this phenomenon as due, at least in part, to promotion ladders. Reder also gives tables that show the comparative unemployment rates by skill level.

gives an explanation why this phenomenon might occur. As the firm goes into the downturn of the business cycle, it may not pay to lay off all workers who produce less output than their wage, because of the loss of specific human capital and, also potentially, because of the effect on the morale of the rest of the work force. On the other hand, the marginal cost of operating the job, even at a zero wage, may exceed the value of the added output, so some workers may be effectively idled in the downturn.

This paper is organized in the following way. Section 2 is an analysis of the key features which result in non-utilization of a resource at zero cost, even though that resource is positively productive. The analogy with low grade land in the Ricardian model is exact, as is the analogy with dam sites.

The third section discusses the nature of jobs. In that section the distinction (new I believe in this paper) between specific technology and specific human capital is made. It is asserted, with at least some empirical backing, that the nature of job organization is a form of specific technology; and, furthermore, that the usual form of such organization causes jobs to have the features which cause low grade complementary factors (e.g. low grade land in the Ricardian model and unskilled labour in our model) to be unutilized even at zero cost when demand is low.

Sections 4 and 5 then are specific examples of jobs as dam sites. They illustrate the low wage elasticity of the demand for unskilled labour. These two sections show that labour, which working with capital has positive marginal product, nevertheless cannot command positive wages when demand is low—because jobs are better utilised by more skilled workers, even though they earn positive wages.

II. COMMON FEATURES IN MODELS OF NON-UTILIZATION AND ANALOGY BETWEEN JOBS AND DAM SITES

This paper is about conditions under which it is unprofitable to hire labour even at zero wages. These conditions occur, it is argued, if labour underutilizes jobs which themselves are valuable resources because of their potential for productivity. There are at least three examples in the economics literature where factors of production are unutilized if the complementary factors are sufficiently scarce: in the putty-clay models, in Ricardian land theory, and in cost-benefit analysis (on the utilization of given projects on fixed dam sites). The discussion of these three examples in this section will reveal their common features which are responsible for the respective factor of production to be unutilized and command a zero return if its complementary factor is sufficiently scarce. Once the common element in these models has been exposed, the analogy between jobs and dam sites appears natural, and hence the argument that unskilled labour even at zero wages may not be profitably employed. In this way a picture of production emerges in which the wage elasticity of demand for labour is quite low.

The first example is the putty-clay model. Although the emphasis of the putty-clay literature has been on the long-run similarity of the putty-clay and the putty-putty models (Akerlof (1967), Bliss (1968), Johansen (1959), Solow (1962, 1963)), the emphasis in this literature could have been quite different. It could have concerned results that are quite special in a more general theory of production, as will be explained presently at some length.

According to this model, λ units of machines of capital-intensity λ use one unit of labour. Insofar as one unit of labour is used with that capital, another unit of labour cannot be so used. According to Solow, there is a distribution of machines of type λ, which produce an output $g(\lambda)$ when using one unit of labour. The perfectly competitive economy will allocate labour over machines in such a way that output is maximized. Thus, the perfectly competitive economy chooses the rate of utilization of machines of type λ, $\mu(\lambda)$ to maximize total output, subject to the constraint that the labour utilized cannot exceed the labour supply.

Letting Λ denote the space of all possible types of machines, and letting $f(\lambda)$ denote the distribution of machines of type λ in the economy, the perfectly competitive economy chooses $\mu(\lambda)$ to maximize

$$\int_{\lambda \in \Lambda} \mu(\lambda) g(\lambda) f(\lambda) d\lambda, \tag{1}$$

subject to the constraint

$$\int_{\lambda \in \Lambda} \mu(\lambda) f(\lambda) d\lambda \leq L, \tag{2}$$

where L is the total quantity of labour in the economy.

The net result of the maximization of (1), subject to the constraint (2) is an aggregate production function that is dependent on the distribution of machines $\{f(\lambda)\}$ and the total supply of labour L. This aggregate production function will have one important qualitative property. Even though labour will have a positive product on low-capital intensity machines, as long as there is a sufficiently large number of highly capital-intensive machines, the addition of low capital-intensive machines will have no effect on aggregate output. The marginal product of such machines (in the production of aggregate output) will be zero. The reason for such zero-marginal products is easy to explain. If machines require labour to be operated, and a labourer who operates a machine must be taken from elsewhere in the economy, a sufficiently labour-intensive machine will, if used, have a negative marginal product, since the opportunity cost of the complementary inputs is greater than the value of its output.

This feature of the putty-clay model is not unique to it, and there are at least two other well-known economic models in which the same principle applies. It is worth discussing (at least briefly) these two other situations, since they will clarify the nature of the job, as described in this paper, and will explain by analogy the results obtained in this paper.

For the first analogy, consider the Ricardian model of land utilization. According to Ricardo, there is land of different grades. Land of grade λ in amount T_λ can be used to produce an output of $Q_\lambda = F_\lambda(T_\lambda, L_\lambda)$ when working with an amount of labour L_λ. Under competitive conditions, there is an aggregate output produced, Q where:

$$Q = \sum_\lambda Q_\lambda = \max \sum_\lambda F_\lambda(T_\lambda, L_\lambda), \tag{3}$$

for given amounts T_λ of each grade of land $\lambda \in \Lambda$ and with L_λ chosen to maximize (3), subject to the constraint (4):

$$\sum_\lambda L_\lambda \leq L. \tag{4}$$

The solution to the maximization of aggregate production (3), subject to the labour constraint (4), shows that, for grades of land λ, such that

$$\partial F/\partial L_\lambda(T_\lambda, 0) < w, \tag{5}$$

$$L_\lambda = 0, \tag{6}$$

where w is the marginal product of labour in the production of aggregate output (i.e. $\partial Q/\partial L$).

In Ricardo's terms, that land which is incapable of producing an output per unit of labour equal to the wage earned elsewhere remains untilled, or in the language of the putty-clay models, is 'scrapped'. One condition which determines whether such scrappage occurs is whether the elasticities of substitution of land for labour in the production functions F_λ are less than unity. If these elasticities of substitution for each λ are uniformly less than one, sufficient abundance of higher-grade land leads to the scrappage of less good land (Matthews (1964)).

Note that, in general, there is an aggregate production function:

$$Q = F(L, T_1, \ldots, T_\Lambda), \tag{7}$$

but this production function has a special property. According to this special property, if the quantity of land of higher grade is sufficiently abundant, land of lower grade will contribute nothing to aggregate output. This scrappage of lower-grade land occurs even though labour and lower-grade land, considered alone, both have positive marginal products. The use of the lower-grade land, however, will require the use of labour, which, in the presence of abundant high-grade land and limited substitutability, has an opportunity cost in excess of its output on the low-grade land. One reason why this result occurs is that labour, insofar as it works with one grade of land, cannot also work with another. In the same way, in the putty-clay model, if labour worked with one type of capital, it was precluded from working with another type of capital.

A job is similar. By nature, insofar as a job is filled by one person, it cannot be filled by another. In the Ricardian model, land of sufficiently poor quality that it could not produce the opportunity cost of the labour tilling it, is untilled. Correspondingly, in the model below, with jobs and with labour of different qualities, labour of such poor quality that it cannot earn the opportunity cost of the jobs it might fill will be unemployed.

A third phenomenon, which is exactly analogous to the scrappage of submarginal land in the Ricardian model, and the idling of low capital-intensive machines in the Johansen–Solow model occurs in cost–benefit analysis. The archetypal cost–benefit problem concerns whether or not to build a dam at a particular dam site. According to the usual cost–benefit analysis, the project selector should choose the project that maximizes the present discounted value of the returns of building the dam net of the costs. Projects that fail to meet this criterion, *even though they have benefit-cost ratios in excess of unity*, should not be built—for a reason that is simple to explain. Only one dam can be built on the dam site. Insofar as one dam is built, another dam cannot be. For this reason, the dam site is a scarce resource. Thus, those dam proposals whose discounted returns are less than the maximum, waste the dam site, even if they have benefit–cost ratios in excess of unity (with the costs calculated exclusive of the imputed rent for the dam site).

The key feature of economic structure in the dam-site example is that the dam site will take only one dam (in the Ricardian example, labour could work with only one grade of land). Insofar as it uses one dam, it cannot use another. As a result, some dams with positive net benefits (exclusive of the imputed rent on the dam site) should not be constructed. According to the title of this paper, jobs are like dam sites, insofar as a job filled by one labourer cannot be filled by another. Consequently, labourers with positive marginal products considered alone may still not be able to earn positive wages (rents), provided they make sufficiently poor use of the job (dam site). In this sense there is a low wage elasticity of demand for such labour.

III. SPECIFIC TECHNOLOGY AND JOBS

The distinction between specific human capital and general human capital is well known (Becker (1964)). Human capital specific to a firm consists of knowledge that raises an individual's productivity to that firm; analogously, human capital specific to an industry raises the individual's productivity in that industry. In contrast, general human capital increases an individual's productivity wherever he works.

Analogous to the distinction between specific and general human capital is the distinction between specific and general technology. Firm-specific technology is technology specific to a particular firm; general technology is technology freely available to all firms. The difference between technology and human capital should be explained because the two concepts, which both refer to the use of knowledge, are in many respects similar.

Suppose that a firm is using a labourer with a given amount of specific human capital. If that labourer withdraws his services and is replaced by another labourer with the same general skills, the output of the firm will decline by the rent on the 'lost' human capital. In contrast, suppose that a firm uses a worker with a given specific technology. If that worker leaves the firm but is replaced by a worker with the same general human capital, the output of the firm will remain the same.

A technology specifies the relation between inputs and outputs. Because returns to labour constitute approximately 75% of all value added, the relation between labour input and material output is of particular importance. One important form of specific technology is the means whereby particular firms relate labour inputs to material outputs.

It is worthwhile to make a list of types of specific technology independent of its use in this paper, because this is an important concept in its own right and worthy of exploration. But making this list also reveals an important feature of specific technology —that much specific technology consists of fixed job descriptions that relate how discrete persons (as opposed to abstract labour units, as in most economic models) relate to each other to accomplish the economic goals of the firm.

The most obvious form of specific technology is specific knowledge of production processes. In its most concrete form, such knowledge is embodied in patents issued. One indication of the order of magnitude of the input into acquiring such specific technology is given by expenditures for research and development by private industry, which, in 1976, in the United States, was $17.4 billion (U.S. Statistical Abstracts, 1979, p. 441). This compares to gross private domestic investment of $243 billion and a gross national product of $1.7 trillion. The very fact that expenditures of this magnitude were incurred by private industry at its own expense is ipso facto evidence for the existence of specific technology in nonnegligible amount.

Knowledge of production processes can be considered as a specific technology type of 'hardware'. In contrast, the other types of specific technology consist of systems of management and are a type of 'software'. There is at least one indication that this type of specific technology is an important determinant of productivity. Pratten (1976) has estimated the relative productivity levels of multinational firms with manufacturing plants in both the U.S. and Great Britain. On a firm-by-firm basis, it was found that productivity per employee was about 50% higher in the U.S. than in the U.K. In contrast, however, for all U.S. manufacturing productivity per employee, measured on a roughly comparable basis, was 116% more than in the U.K. The relatively higher productivity of the multinationals in the U.K. than that of the rest of domestic manufacturing is no doubt partly explained by the use of more inputs per person; more human capital and more capital. But the large difference in the two differentials, 116% compared to 50%, also strongly suggests that there is a large residual, which is explained by the multinationals' use in the U.K. of their specific technology.

Software-specific technology can be classified into three types. The first of these is job descriptions. All firms, either formally or informally, have sets of job descriptions that relate how one person in one job interacts with all persons in all other jobs, and also with the material inputs and outputs.

A second form of specific technology software lies in the knowledge by the personnel of the firm as to how the firm operates. It is commonly believed that such knowledge constitutes either specific human capital, on the one hand—since the worker who leaves the firm takes that knowledge with him—or general technology, in the sense that such knowledge is common. However, it is quite common that specific aspects of a firm's operations are understood by many workers and that such knowledge is also the costless by-product of the normal pursuit of many jobs. If that is the case, it can be said that the firm owns specific technology rather than that the worker owns specific human capital. Such knowledge concerns itself with the firm's internal operations (the interrelations between the firm's work force and special knowledge about the firm's materials and capital stock) and also the firm's external operations (the markets for its goods and its inputs, including governmental interference in those markets).

A third form of software-specific technology lies in the social customs of a firm's employees. Stephen Marglin has related to me a pure example of this phenomenon. He reported visiting two cotton textile mills, one in Northern Yugoslavia, the other in Southern Yugoslavia. The capital equipment in the two factories was exactly the same. Nevertheless, in Northern Yugoslavia, each worker tended four times as many machines as did the workers in Southern Yugoslavia. If Marglin's explanation of this differential is correct, then an interchange of two workers between the north and the south would also result in an interchange of their respective productivities. Leibenstein (1976) would say that the differences in productivities were due to differences in X-efficiency.

One view of the job, as is natural in the 'putty-clay' model, is that a job can be characterized by the use of a fixed number of machines. While I agree that the putty-clay model constitutes one view of the job, it is, I believe, a view more applicable to the textile industry of the nineteenth century, in which each millhand tended a fixed number of machines, than to most modern industry. In my view, most jobs consist of software, which describe the relations of one person in the firm to other persons inside and outside the firm. The key assumption in this paper is that one job could be filled by only one person (rather than, say, two or three or more). There is a reason for this, in that the interrelations of persons in different jobs (which is part of the firm's specific technology) are costly to change except in fairly rare instances or over the longer run. We believe it is costly for firms to change job descriptions to take advantage of relative scarcities of labour and, in most cases, more costly than the advantages to be gained from reacting to flexible wages. There is some empirical support for this point of view. A study of this precise issue by Michael Piore (1968) showed that engineers in U.S. manufacturing do not consciously adjust job descriptions to take advantage of different states of the labour market. The adjustment of job descriptions in U.S. manufacturing, it must be concluded from Piore's study, occurs as a long-run rather than a short-run phenomenon.

IV. A PARTIAL EQUILIBRIUM EXAMPLE

This section illustrates, by an example, the proposition that poor labour cannot outbid good labour for a job, and thus poor labour is always unemployed prior to good labour, if there are flexible wages.

Let a job use one unit of labour of type α, with m_α units of raw materials, to produce q_α units of output. Let p_m be the price of raw materials and p_f the price of final output. Let w_α denote the wage of labour of type α. The profits of the firm in filling this job with labour of type α will be:

$$p_f q_\alpha - p_m m_\alpha - w_\alpha. \tag{8}$$

Similarly, if the firm fills the job with labour of type β, its profits will be:

$$p_f q_\beta - p_m m_\beta - w_\beta. \tag{9}$$

It is now possible to see whether a labourer of type β can underbid a labourer of type α to get the job.

As long as

$$p_f q_\alpha - p_m m_\alpha - w_\alpha > p_f q_\beta - p_m m_\beta - w_\beta, \tag{10}$$

a labourer of type α will be given the job in preference to a labourer of type β; or, alternatively, as long as

$$w_\beta/p_f > -q_\alpha + q_\beta + (p_m/p_f)(m_\alpha - m_\beta) + w_\alpha/p_f, \tag{11}$$

the job will go to labour of type α.

Alternatively stated, if the reservation wage of labour of type β is below the value of the R.H.S. of inequality (11), the type β labourer will not get the job. If a type α labourer is unambiguously more skilled than type β, he or she will both produce more output and use fewer raw materials in the job. In that case, type β's reservation wage would have to be negative if β were to capture the job if w_α/p_f is sufficiently low. In this sense, flexible wages will not guarantee jobs to unskilled labour, even if skilled labour is employed at nonzero wages.

V. A GENERAL EQUILIBRIUM EXAMPLE

A. *Remarks*

The preceding example was only partial equilibrium. It showed that if a type α worker was unambiguously more productive than a type β worker, and if the wages of type α workers were sufficiently low, type β workers would not be employed, unless willing to accept negative wages. The question, however, remained as to why the wages of skilled workers might be so low. The example in this section will show that if demand (in a suitably defined sense) is low, the wages of skilled workers will also be low. Unskilled workers will be unemployed no matter how flexible their wages.

Because the purpose of the example is illustrative, there is no reason for the model to have generality. On the contrary, specificity aids in ease of computation of the equilibrium and in understanding the behaviour of the model.

B. *The Model*

Labour. Let there be two classes of workers: skilled workers and unskilled workers. Let N_{sk} denote the total number of skilled workers and N_{un} denote the total number of unskilled workers. Skilled workers are assumed (for simplicity of the example) to be homogeneous. In contrast, unskilled workers have a distribution of abilities. These abilities, denoted by the index α, are uniformly distributed between a lowest ability of $\alpha = 0$ and a greatest ability of $\alpha = 1$. To model unemployment with perfectly flexible wages, it is assumed that all labourers have a perfectly inelastic supply of labour at any nonnegative wage.

Production. There are two types of jobs. First, there are primary jobs, which, by assumption, can be filled only by skilled workers. By assumption, these primary jobs are not homogeneous—there is a distribution of such jobs. A primary job, filled by a single skilled worker, uses one unit of raw materials and produces q units of output. The outputs have a uniform distribution between an upper bound $\bar{q}$ and a lower bound $\underline{q}$. The total number of jobs in the primary sector is J^{pr}.

In addition to primary jobs, there are secondary jobs. These jobs are all homogeneous and are J^{sec} in number. A skilled worker in one of these jobs produces an output q_{sk}^{sec}. An unskilled worker of grade α (which is uniformly distributed between 0 and 1) produces an output αq_{un}^{sec}. Consistent with the notion that skilled are more productive than unskilled, $q_{sk}^{sec} > q_{un}^{sec}$. No raw materials are used in the production of output in the secondary sector.

Markets. Output is sold in a competitive market at a price p_f and raw materials are purchased at a price p_m. It is convenient to consider these prices as internationally determined, or, alternatively, as determined by a government commodity board which buys all output at p_f and provides raw materials at price p_m. It is also convenient to consider a change in demand, as represented by a change in p_f relative to p_m, with p_f rising relative to p_m as demand rises. It will be demonstrated that as p_f rises relative to p_m, unemployment falls.

C. *Comments on the Model*

The model has many singular features. The reason for most of these singular features is economy of modeling. Two of these singularities, as shall be discussed, are not due to a desire for simplicity of example but, instead, are intrinsic features of the model. These singular features will each be reviewed in turn.

The first singularity concerns the homogeneity of all skilled workers. This assumption is useful, since it avoids a complication. If both jobs and workers are non-homogeneous, it is necessary to work out how non-homogeneous workers are allocated across non-homogeneous jobs. Although this may be a problem of some interest in general, the points of this paper can be most easily illustrated independent of the solution to that problem, by making either jobs or labour homogeneous. We have chosen, with respect to skilled workers, to make the jobs non-homogeneous and the workers homogeneous.

The second assumption is the reverse situation in the secondary sector. All jobs in the secondary sector are homogeneous; unskilled workers, however, are non-homogeneous. Again, the restriction of one category or the other, workers or jobs, to be homogeneous simplifies the programming problem of allocating workers across jobs. With unskilled workers being of continuous grades, it is possible to show how the unemployment rate varies continuously as the marginal worker becomes unemployed with marginal declines in demand.

Third, jobs have fixed coefficients between inputs and outputs. This assumption could be relaxed—at least somewhat. The qualitative behaviour of the model will be unchanged if there is limited substitutability between final output and material input with elasticity of substitution less than unity. In that case, the model will be more difficult to analyze, but in the limit it will behave exactly like the fixed-coefficient model. (See Akerlof (1969) for further comment on this.)

Another singular assumption concerns the use of no raw materials in secondary jobs. Indeed, the unemployment elasticities are increased if raw materials are used in secondary jobs, but skilled workers make better use of those raw materials than unskilled workers. The assumption of *no* raw materials in secondary jobs is useful to illustrate the major point of this paper in a pure way. Even though an unskilled worker has unambiguously positive output net of raw materials used in production in a secondary-sector job, such workers will nevertheless be unemployed if the demand for final output is sufficiently low, because skilled workers become less expensive to use relative to unskilled workers.

There are, however, two fixed-coefficient assumptions that cannot be relaxed if the model is to yield unemployment with perfectly flexible wages. The first of these assumptions is the availability of only a limited number of jobs, J^{pr}, in the primary sector and J^{sec} in the secondary sector. The idea of the model is that as demand contracts, the number of jobs that can be profitably performed in the primary sector contracts. Skilled workers who, in good times, would work in the primary sector, crowd into the secondary sector and compete with unskilled workers. When the total of skilled workers seeking jobs in the secondary sector and unskilled workers exceeds the number of jobs in that sector, unemployment will begin among unskilled workers. As demand contracts further, unemployment of these workers will become continually worse. If unskilled workers could produce output without a job, or if the number of jobs in the secondary sector exceeds the total of all workers (skilled and unskilled), unemployment will never develop.

The second intrinsic singular assumption in the example is the fixity of jobs and workers. If a job is performed by one worker, it cannot be performed by more than one. Insofar as one worker fills a job, another worker can only work elsewhere. This assumption is also intrinsic to the paper: it is because of this property that jobs are viewed as dam sites.

D. *The Analysis of the Model*

Because the model is kinky, its analysis must be divided into separate parts reflecting the six types of possible equilibrium that can occur. With given values of other parameters, the equilibria of the economy can be plotted as a function of the state of aggregate demand as parameterized by p_f/p_m. The parameter space p_f/p_m can be divided into six separate regions (of which one or more may be empty) corresponding to the type of equilibrium. These regions, which will be described presently, are denoted Regions I to VI.

Region I. In Region I, all skilled labour is employed in the primary sector. This type of equilibrium occurs if the net revenue from the marginal job in the primary sector, with all skilled labour working in that sector, exceeds the marginal revenue from employing the first skilled labourer in the secondary sector. This type of equilibrium will occur if the number of jobs in the primary sector exceeds the number of skilled labourers and if the price of final output is sufficiently high relative to the price of raw materials.

Region II. As the price of final output, relative to raw materials, falls, it becomes relatively less profitable to hire skilled labour in the primary sector, relative to the secondary sector. With a fall in p_f/p_m, a point is eventually reached that is the boundary between Regions I and II, where the revenue on the marginal job in the primary sector, net of material costs, equals the marginal revenue product of skilled labour in the secondary sector. For ratios of p_f/p_m less than this boundary,[2] some skilled labour is used in the secondary sector. If the number of unskilled workers is less than the number of secondary-sector jobs, the influx of skilled workers into the secondary sector will not—at least in the beginning—cause any loss of employment, since there are enough jobs to go around. However, as p_f/p_m falls further, there will eventually be a point at which jobs must be rationed between the skilled workers seeking jobs in the secondary sector and the unskilled workers, provided $N_{sk} + N_{un} < J^{sec}$. The level of p_f/p_m at which such rationing begins constitutes the boundary between Region II and Region III.

Region III. In Region III, more workers are seeking jobs in the secondary sector than are available. The jobs go to the most skilled workers, with the least skilled workers unemployed. The marginal product of an employed worker is his output in a secondary-sector job, less the output of the most skilled worker who is unemployed, who would be willing to take his job (given perfectly flexible wages) at a zero wage. As p_f/p_m falls further, production in the primary sector becomes still more uneconomic, and more skilled labourers crowd into the secondary sector. Unskilled labourers become increas-

---

[2] This boundary may be $+\infty$ if $N_{sk} > J^{sec}$.

ingly unemployed. Provided $N_{sk} > J^{sec}$, a point is eventually reached at which all unskilled labourers become unemployed. This point serves as the boundary between Regions III and IV.

Region IV. In Region IV, the use of primary-sector jobs is so uneconomic—because the price of final output has fallen so low, relative to the price of raw materials—that the number of skilled workers seeking employment in the secondary sector exceeds the number of jobs in that sector. All unskilled workers are unemployed. However, the real wage has not yet fallen to zero, but lies between $(q_{sk}^{sec} - q_{un}^{sec})$ and 0, and it equates the total demand for skilled labour in the primary sector and secondary sector to the total supply. Eventually, however, if p_f/p_m falls far enough, the total demand for skilled labour will be less than the total supply, even at a zero wage. The level of p_f/p_m at which this first occurs is the boundary between Regions IV and V.

Region V. In Region V, p_f/p_m is so low that, even at a zero wage, the demand for skilled workers in the primary sector is so low that more skilled workers are released from the primary sector than the total number of jobs in the secondary sector. However, some primary jobs can profitably employ workers at a zero wage.

Region VI. In Region VI, p_f/p_m is so low that no workers at all can be profitably used in the primary sector, even at a zero wage.

E. *A Numerical Example*

Rather than analyze an algebraic example with general parameter values for $J^{pr}, J^{sec}, N_{sk}, N_{un}, \bar{q}, \underline{q}, q_{sk}^{sec}$, and q_{un}^{sec}, we shall, in this section, analyze a particular example with numerical values for the eight parameters. For most randomly chosen examples, one or more of Regions I to VI will be empty. The example chosen, however, has all six regions. It therefore captures the richness of our simple model. The parameters chosen are:

Number of Jobs		Number of Labourers	
Primary sector	$J^{pr} = 10$	Skilled	$N_{sk} = 8$
Secondary sector	$J^{sec} = 6$	Unskilled	$N_{un} = 4$

Output on most productive job in primary sector $= \bar{q} = 15$
Output on least productive job in primary sector $= \underline{q} = 10$
Output of skilled labour in secondary sector $= q_{sk}^{sec} = 8$
Output of highest grade unskilled labour $= q_{un}^{sec} = 5$

Region I. If all skilled labour is used in the primary sector, output on the marginal job is 11. The net revenue product of this marginal job is therefore:

$$11p_f - p_m. \tag{12}$$

In contrast, the revenue product of the first skilled worker in a secondary job is $8p_f$. As long as

$$11p_f - p_m > 8p_f, \tag{13}$$

all skilled labour is used in skilled jobs; it will receive a wage equal to $11p_f - p_m$. Unskilled labour will be hired in secondary jobs; since unskilled labour exceeds the number of those jobs (6 compared to 4), such labour will receive a real wage equal to their total output in such jobs, and no unemployment will occur.

   Region II. If

$$11p_f - p_m < 8p_f, \tag{14}$$

the marginal product of the marginal skilled worker is greater in the secondary sector than in the primary sector and, therefore, some marginal skilled workers work in the secondary sector. This point is reached when

$$p_f/p_m = \frac{1}{3} \tag{15}$$

No unemployment occurs, however, until more than two skilled workers seek employment in the secondary sector. This point will occur when

$$12p_f - p_m = 8p_f, \tag{16}$$

or

$$p_f/p_m = \frac{1}{4} \tag{17}$$

Hence, for $\frac{1}{4} < p_f/p_m < \frac{1}{3}$, the wage rate for skilled labour is $8p_f$; the wage rate of unskilled labour of grade α, $0 \lessgtr \alpha \lessgtr 1$, is $5\alpha p_f$. All labour is employed.

   Region III. For $p_f/p_m < \frac{1}{4}$ there is some unemployment. The wage of a skilled worker is his output, less the output of the marginal worker α_{min} who would alternatively take his place in a secondary sector job. Thus, if $\alpha_{min} < 1$, his wage is:

$$w_{sk} = 8p_f - 5\alpha_{min}p_f. \tag{18}$$

Simultaneously, we can compute α_{min}. With a wage of skilled labour of w_{sk}, the marginal job in the primary sector has an output of q_{min}, where:

$$p_f q_{min} = w_{sk} + p_m. \tag{19}$$

Employment in the primary sector (given the density of jobs in that sector) and given (18) and (19), will be:

$$E_{sk}^{pr} = 2(15 - q_{min}) \tag{20}$$

$$= 2(15 - (w_{sk} + p_m)/p_f) \tag{21}$$

$$= 2(15 - 8 + 5\alpha_{min} - p_m/p_f). \tag{22}$$

Thus, the number of skilled workers seeking jobs in the secondary sector is:

$$N_{sk} - E_{sk}^{pr} = 8 - 2(15 - 8 + 5\alpha_{min} - p_m/p_f). \tag{23}$$

But, knowing the number of skilled workers in the secondary sector, it is possible to compute the number of secondary jobs left over for unskilled workers, which will be:

$$J^{sec} - \{N_{sk} - E_{sk}^{pr}\} = 6 - [8 - 2\{15 - 8 + 5\alpha_{min} - p_m/p_f\}]. \tag{24}$$

The number of jobs filled by unskilled workers is, according to the definition of α_{min},

$$(1 - \alpha_{min})N_{un} = (1 - \alpha_{min})4. \tag{25}$$

Hence,

$$(1 - \alpha_{min})4 = 6 - [8 - 2\{15 - 8 + 5\alpha_{min} - p_m/p_f\}]. \tag{26}$$

Solving for α_{min} yields:

$$\alpha_{min} = 1/7(p_m/p_f - 4). \tag{27}$$

Equation (27) yields the unemployment rate for unskilled workers for p_f/p_m in the range where $0 \leq \alpha_{min} \leq 1$, or in the range

$$\frac{1}{11} \leq p_f/p_m \leq \frac{1}{4}.$$

Region IV. In this region, $\frac{1}{13} \leq p_f/p_m \leq \frac{1}{11}$, the wage earned by skilled workers is such as to equate the supply equal to the demand. At a wage, $0 \leq w_{sk} \leq 3p_f$, the demand for skilled workers in the primary sector is:

$$2(15 - (w_{sk} + p_m)/p_f), \tag{28}$$

and the demand for skilled workers in the secondary sector corresponds to the number of jobs, which is 4. Consequently, the wage w_{sk} which equates the demand of skilled workers to the supply is given by:

$$2(15 - w_{sk}/p_f - p_m/p_f) + 4 = 8, \tag{29}$$

so that the equilibrium wage is:

$$w_{sk}/p_f = 13 - p_m/p_f. \tag{30}$$

For $p_f/p_m < \frac{1}{13}$, the supply of skilled labour exceeds the number of jobs at a zero wage and, consequently, $p_f/p_m = \frac{1}{13}$ is the boundary point between Regions IV and V.

Region V. $\frac{1}{15} \leqq p_f/p_m \leqq \frac{1}{13}$. It is easily checked that, for p_f/p_m in this region, the demand for labour at a zero wage is less than the supply. At a zero wage, some primary jobs have a positive revenue product, as do all secondary jobs. However, for $p_f/p_m = \frac{1}{15}$, even the most productive job in the primary sector has zero marginal product. For this reason, $p_f/p_m = \frac{1}{15}$ is the boundary between Regions V and VI.

Region VI. In Region VI, $p_f/p_m < \frac{1}{15}$. All skilled labour works in the secondary sector and wages are zero.

VI. SUMMARY AND CONCLUSION

According to this paper, firms own jobs. The key property of a job is that it can be filled by only one worker, just as a dam site can be filled by only one dam in our analogy. If the price of skilled workers is low enough, unskilled workers no matter how flexible their wages, cannot bid away jobs from the skilled workers. An example was given, in which declines in demand caused the real wages of skilled workers to decline and, as a result of the competition from skilled workers, unskilled workers became unemployed. This image of production, in which job descriptions only change slowly is naturally associated with a low wage elasticity of demand for unskilled workers. The introduction listed some of the many important consequences of pessimism regarding the size of this elasticity.

First version received July 1978; *final version accepted August* 1980 *(Eds.).*
The author would like to thank Sanford Grossman, Oliver Hart, Mervyn A. King, Hajime Miyazaki, Janet L. Yellen, and a referee for this journal for valuable comments, and the U.S. Department of Labour for financial assistance under Small Grant No. 91-06-78-27 and the National Science Foundation under Research Grant SOC 75-23076, administered by the Institute of Business and Economic Research of the University of California, Berkeley. A previous incarnation of this paper bore the title, 'A Theory of Involuntary Unemployment'.

References

Akerlof, G. A. (1967), 'Stability, Marginal Products, Putty, and Clay', in Shell, K. (ed.), *Essays on the Theory of Optimal Economic Growth* (Cambridge, Mass.; London: MIT Press), 281–294.

Akerlof, G. A. (1969), 'Structural Unemployment in a Neoclassical Framework', *Journal of Political Economy*, 77, 399–407.

Becker, G. S. (1964), *Human Capital: A Theoretical and Empirical Analysis, with Special Reference to Education* (New York: Columbia University Press).

Bliss, C. J. (1968), 'On Putty-Clay', *Review of Economic Studies*, 35, 105–132.

Feldstein, M. S. (1973) *Lowering the Permanent Rate of Unemployment*, U.S. Congress, Joint Economic Committee (Washington: Government Printing Office).

Johansen, L. (1959), 'Substitution Versus Fixed Production Coefficients in the Theory of Economic Growth: A Synthesis', *Econometrica* 27, 157–176.

Leibenstein, H. (1976) *Beyond Economic Man: A New Foundation for Microeconomics* (Cambridge, Mass: Harvard University Press).

Matthews, R. C. O. (1964), 'The New View of Investment: Comment', *Quarterly Journal of Economics*, 78, 164–172.

Piore, M. J. (1968), 'The Impact of the Labor Market upon the Design and Selection of Productivity Techniques within the Manufacturing Plant', *Quarterly Journal of Economics*, 82, 602–620.

Pratten, C. F. (1976), *Labor Productivity Differrentials within International Companies* (Cambridge: Cambridge University Press).

Reder, M. W. (1964), 'Wage Structure and Structural Unemployment', *Review of Economic Studies*, 31, 309–322.

Solow, R. M. (1962), 'Substitution and Fixed Proportions in the Theory of Capital', *Review of Economic Studies*, 29, 207–218.

Solow, R. M. (1963), 'Heterogeneous Capital and Smooth Production Functions: An Experimental Study', *Econometrica*, 31, 623–645.

U.S. Department of Commerce, Bureau of the Census. (1979) *Statistical Abstract of the United States* Vol. 99 (Washington: Government Printing Office). 1978.

16

Labor Contracts as Partial Gift Exchange*

GEORGE A. AKERLOF[†]

I. INTRODUCTION

In a study of social relations among workers at a utility company in the eastern United States, George Homans [1953, 1954] observed that a small group of young women (doing a job called 'cash posting') exceeded the minimum work standards of the firm by a significant margin (i.e., on average by 15 percent). Most of these women neither desired nor expected promotion in the firm in return for their troubles. Why did they do it?

Section II shows that the standard neoclassical model cannot simultaneously explain both the behavior of the firm and the behavior of the cash posters. But, as shown in Section III, application of a standard sociological model does explain the behavior of both the young women and their employer. According to this model, in their interaction workers acquire sentiment for each other and also for the firm. As a consequence of sentiment for the firm, the workers acquire utility for an exchange of 'gifts' with the firm—the amount of utility depending upon the so-called 'norms' of gift exchange. On the worker's side, the 'gift' given is work in excess of the minimum work standard; and on the firm's side the 'gift' given is wages in excess of what these women could receive if they left their current jobs. As a consequence of worker sentiment for one another, the

* This work was previously published as George Akerlof (1982), 'Labor Contracts as Partial Gift Exchange', *The Quarterly Journal of Economics*, XCVII, 4. Copyright © The MIT Press. Reproduced by kind permission.

† The author would like to thank William Dickens, Brain Main, Hajime Miyazaki, Janet L. Yellen, and two referees for invaluable help. He would also like to thank the National Science Foundation for generous financial support under Research Grant SOC 79-05562, administered by the Institute of Business and Economic Research of the University of California, Berkeley.

firm cannot deal with each worker individually, but rather must at least to some extent treat the group of workers with the same norms, collectively.

Norm–gift-exchange models have been used in many sociological studies to explain the behavior of workers. And these explanations are simple; properly understood, they are in tune with everyone's personal experiences of human behavior, so that they can be taken to have considerable generality. For that reason I feel confident in extrapolating such behavior beyond the narrow and particular instance of the 'cash posters' to concern wage bargains and work conditions in some generality. Sections IV and V verbally explore the consequences of such behavior for wage determination; Sections VI and VII build formal mathematical models; and Section VIII gives conclusions.

This model of the microeconomics of the labor market is used to explain two phenomena that have not been successfully analyzed by more conventional economic theory. First, in most other analyses of unemployment, such as that of search theory [Phelps *et al.*, 1970], all unemployment is voluntary. In my analysis there are primary labor markets in which unemployed workers are unable to obtain jobs at the prevailing market wages. Second, the theory of dual labor markets [Doeringer and Piore, 1971] brings up the question as to which markets will be primary and which markets secondary. In the formal models developed in this paper, it is endogenously determined whether a market will be primary or secondary. Primary markets are those in which the gift component of labor input and wages is sizeable, and therefore wages are not market-clearing. Secondary labor markets are those in which wages are market-clearing.

The major feature of the usual model of implicit contracts due to Azariadis [1975] and Baily [1974] is risk-sharing agreements by the contracting agents over a span of time. These models have been taken as a vehicle for Okun's [1981, p. 133] description of labor and customer markets. This paper offers an alternative microfoundation for implicit contracts. Its emphasis is sociological. It focuses on the gift-exchange nature of employment arrangements, where the exchange is based partially on norms of behavior that are endogenously determined. This dependence of implicit contracts on *norms* of behavior (rather than on risk sharing) captures important aspects of Okun's description [1975, 1981] that have not been analyzed in the Azariadis-Baily framework.

According to this paper, norms of work effort are a major determinant of output. In emphasizing effort, it carries further the work of Leibenstein [1976] on X-efficiency. The focus on effort could also be expressed in Marxian terminology via the distinction between *labor power* and *labor* as in Edwards' recent book [1979] on the inevitable conflict between labor and management over the use of labor power.[1] In Edwards' terms this paper gives equilibrium models of the resolution of this conflict. Finally, it should be mentioned, Hirschman's concepts of *Exit*, *Voice*, and *Loyalty* [1970] can be expressed in terms of norms and gift exchange.

---

[1] For a review of the Marxian literature on this distinction, also see Edwards [1979].

II. THE NON-NEOCLASSICAL BEHAVIOR OF THE CASH POSTERS OR OF THE EASTERN UTILITIES CO.

Economists usually assume that labor is hired as a factor of production and is put to work like capital. There is, however, one fundamental difference between labor and capital that is ignored by this assumption. Once a capitalist has hired capital, he is, over a fairly wide latitude, free to use it (or abuse it) as he wishes. However, having hired a laborer, management faces considerable restriction on how it can use its labor. Not only are there legal restrictions (such as OSHA regulations, child labor laws, etc.), but the willing cooperation of labor itself must usually be obtained for the firm to make the best use of the labor services.

Of course, standard economic theory does describe the nature of contracts when there are many possible standards of performance. According to standard theory, when a firm hires a laborer, there is an understanding by both parties that certain minimum standards of performance must be met. Furthermore, the contract may be *implicit* in the sense that workers need not be currently rewarded for their current performance but may earn chances for promotion with higher pay in the future in return for good performance in their current jobs. If this is the case, the firm need not have tight rules regarding work and compensation that very carefully specify the *quid pro quo* of pay for work, since injustices in the present can be compensated later. So standard theory can serve as a good approximation to reality even where very specific contracts relating effort or output to compensation would be quite expensive.

Against this background let us consider the study by Homans of 'The Cash Posters.' In this study a group of ten young women working as cash posters for a utility company in a New England city were interviewed and closely observed over a period of six months. The duty of a cash poster at Eastern Utilities was to record customers' payments on ledger cards at the time of receipt. The company's standard for such cash posting was 300 per hour, and careful records were made of the speed at which individual cash posters variously worked. Anyone who worked below the rate of 300 per hour received a mild rebuke from the supervisor. Table 16.1 adapted from Homan's article, 'The Cash Posters,' shows both the number of cash postings per hour of different workers and their rate of error.

Note from Table 16.1 that the average number of cash postings per hour (353) was 17.7 percent greater than the standard set by the company. The simple neoclassical theory of contracts cannot simultaneously explain why the faster persons did not reduce their speed to the standard; or, alternatively, why the firm did not increase the speed expected of its faster workers. The possibility that the faster workers worked harder than the standard for either increased pay or promotion was belied by the uniformity of wage for all cash posters and by the refusal of promotion by two cash posters. When promotion did occur, it was normally to a job considered more responsible than cash posting, but nevertheless paying the same wage. In addition, voluntary quits among the cash posters were quite frequent (with most of the young women leaving to be married), so that in most cases promotion was not a relevant consideration. Since pay was not

Table 16.1 *Work performance of individual cash posters*

	Age in years	Time on job in years-months	Mean cards per hour	Mean errors per hour
Asnault	22	3–5	363	0.57
Burke	26	2–5	306	0.66
Coughlin	20	2–0	342	0.40
Donovan	20	1–9	308	0.79
Granara	21	1–3	438	0.65
Lo Presti	25	−11	317	0.03
Murphy	19	−7	439	0.62
Rourke	17	−4	323	0.82
Shaugnessy	23	−2	333	0.44
Urquhart	18	−2	361	0.49
Average	21.1	1–4	353	0.55

dependent on effort and promotion was rarely a consideration, the standard economic model of contract would predict that workers set their work habits to meet the company's minimum standards of performance as long as they have marginal disutility for work at that level. On the other hand, if workers do have positive utility for work at this level, the lack of incentives for effort given by the firm should lead them to choose to work to the point where the marginal disutility of additional effort is just zero. But in that case the firm could increase its profits by increasing work standards for the faster workers. Unless their utility function is discontinuous, they would still prefer their current jobs to what they could obtain elsewhere at somewhat faster speeds of work.

Since output is easily observable, it is at least a bit surprising from the point of view of the neoclassical theory of contracts that workers are not paid wages proportional to their outputs. This constitutes another puzzlement regarding the system of industrial relations among the cash posters at Eastern Utilities, although a potential answer has been suggested by Etzioni [1971]. According to Etzioni, workers find pecuniary incentives, such as piece rates, 'alienating.'

The mysterious behavior of the cash posters and of Eastern Utilities in terms of neoclassical theory can be posed a bit more formally. Suppose for whatever reason (perhaps Etzioni's) that the firm has decided to pay the same wage $w = \bar{w}$ to all cash posters. Further, suppose that workers have a utility function $u(w,e)$, where w is the wage rate and e is effort. Workers, mindful of the firm's work rules, should choose their effort e to maximize

$$u(w,e), \tag{1}$$

subject to the constraints,

$$w = \bar{w} \tag{2}$$

$$e \gtreqless e_{\min}, \tag{3}$$

where $\bar{w} = 1.05$ per hour, the wage fixed for all cash posters, and e_{min} is the minimum effort necessary to accomplish the required 300 cash postings per hour.

Solution of this trivial maximization problem yields

$$e = e_{\min} \tag{4}$$

as long as $u_e < 0$ for $e \gtreqless e_{\min}$. On the assumption that utility is convex, there are two potential types of solutions. Each poses an empirical problem. If $u_e(\bar{w}, e_{\min}) < 0$, the question arises—why did the workers not reduce their effort to 300 per hour? On the other hand, if $u_e(\bar{w}, e_{\min}) > 0$, so that workers choose $u_e = 0$, why did the firm not raise the minimum standards for different workers above the point where $u_e = 0$? In either case the observation obtained is inconsistent with the neoclassical model.[2]

Of course, each cash poster may have a different utility function, and for some reason the firm may find it optimal to set the same minimum standard for all workers. For example, the rate perhaps cannot be set higher than 300 per hour in deference to the two workers who find the standard a bit onerous (as shown by Burke's and Donovan's performance in Table 16.1, only 2 percent above the 300 minimum). But the question of why the same standard should be set for all workers can be answered only in terms of the interactions of workers among themselves and also with the firm. It is precisely in such terms that the next section poses the solution to the cash poster mystery.

Other potential objections such as the non-observability of output and risk aversion by workers can be all but ruled out. Workers kept records of their outputs so output was easily observable; and workers did not work faster than the minimum out of fear of being sacked for falling below the minimum; as already mentioned, falling below the minimum occasioned no more than mild rebuke.

An explanation for either the firm's behavior or the workers' behavior must depend either on maximization of something other than profits by the firm or on interaction of the workers with each other and with the firm that alters their utility functions. It is to such a theory that we now turn.

III. SOCIOLOGICAL EXPLANATION OF CASH POSTERS'–EASTERN UTILITIES' BEHAVIOR

The previous section showed behavior by the cash posters inconsistent with a simple neoclassical theory of worker utility maximization and firm profit maximization. I do not doubt that there is some neoclassical model involving turnover costs or difficulty of

---

[2] The argument is just a bit subtle. If a worker with convex utility and positive marginal product for effort has a positive utility for wage income and zero disutility for added effort, the firm can increase his compensation and force him to work harder, to the advantage of both. If the worker was satisfied with his job before this additional trade, he will be even more satisfied afterwards, and therefore less willing to quit.

observation[3] which can explain the behavior of the firm and the cash posters, but given the failure of the simple model, the adequate model must of necessity be complicated. In contrast, this section presents a simple sociological explanation of the joint behavior of the cash posters and the Eastern Utilities Company.

According to a prominent school of sociological thought, the determinant of workers' effort is the norm of the work group. According to Elton Mayo [1949, p. 70], referring to the famous studies at the Hawthorne plant in the Bank Wiring Observation Room, 'the working group as a whole actually determined the output of individual workers by reference to a standard, predetermined but clearly stated, that represented the group's conception of a fair day's work. The standard was rarely, if ever, in accord with the standards of the efficiency engineers.'

According to an alternative, but equivalent, view of the cash posters' performance, they give a *gift* to the firm of work in excess of the minimum work required of 300 per hour. Offhand, it may seem absurd to view the worker as giving the firm a gift of any part of his work. Of course, the worker does not strictly give his labor as a gift to the firm; he expects a wage in return and, if not paid, will almost certainly sue in court. Likewise, the firm does not give the wage strictly as a gift. If the worker consistently fails to meet certain minimum standards, he will almost surely be dismissed. But above these minimum standards the worker's performance is freely determined. The norm (or 'standard' as Mayo termed it) for the proper work effort is quite like the norm that determines the standards for gift giving at Christmas. Such gift giving is a trading relationship—in the sense that if one side of the exchange does not live up to expectations, the other side is also likely to curtail its activities.

The classic anthropological literature on the gift, particularly the essay by Marcel Mauss [1954], emphasizes this reciprocal nature of gift-giving.[4] Mauss points out that, in the two major branches of Western European languages, the root for *poison* is the same as the root for *gift*, since in ancient German the word *gift* means both gift and poison, and the Greek word δόσιϛ for poison, which is the root of the English *dose*, has the same root as the Greek word to *give*. The reason for the close association of the words for *gift* and *poison* in these ancient languages comes from the obligatory nature of reciprocity of a gift, or, equivalently, the threat of harm that was believed to befall a recipient who failed to reciprocate. Although the magic has gone out of the sanctions behind repayment of most gifts, there are probably few in modern times who have never received a gift they did not want or who have not given a gift they considered to be inadequately appreciated.[5]

---

[3] For an interesting explanation of unemployment due to imperfect information, see Stoft [1980]. Solow [1980] supports the view that involuntary unemployment must be explained by sociological models of behavior.

[4] A good, although not recent, review of the anthropology and sociology of gift exchange is Belshaw [1965]. See also Titmuss [1971].

[5] It has been suggested to me by one referee that the analysis of labor contracts as partial gift-exchange relates to the Freeman-Medoff argument [1979] on trade unions as collective voice. Reciprocal gift-giving induces union formation because discontented workers find it more difficult to quit and find another job with gift-giving than without. As in Mauss' analysis it is suggested that reciprocal gift-giving, i.e., mutual benevolence and dependence, go together with mutual hostility and militancy.

Why should there be any portion of labor that is given as a gift by the firm or of treatment of the worker by the firm that can be considered a gift? The answer to this question is at once trivial and profound. Persons who work for an institution (a firm in this case) tend to develop sentiment for their co-workers and for that institution; to a great extent they anthropomorphize these institutions (e.g., 'the friendly bank'). For the same reasons that persons (brothers, for example) share gifts as showing sentiment for each other, it is natural that persons have utility for making gifts to institutions for which they have sentiment. Furthermore, if workers have an interest in the welfare of their coworkers, they gain utility if the firm relaxes pressure on the workers who are hard pressed; in return for reducing such pressure, better workers are often willing to work harder.

The giving of gifts is almost always determined by norms of behavior. In most cases the gift given is approximately in the range of what the recipient expects, and he reciprocates in kind. The norms of gift-giving are determined by the relationship between the parties; thus, for example, it is expected that an increase in workers' productivity will be rewarded by increased wages to the workers. Much of union wage negotiations concerns the question of what constitutes a *fair* wage. To an economist who believes that wages are market-clearing or only determined by the relative bargaining power of the contractual parties, long discussions about the 'fair wage' should have no bearing on the final settlement. But this notion neglects the fact that the average worker works harder than necessary according to the firm's work rules, and in return for this donation of goodwill and effort, he expects a fair wage from the firm.

This view of wages-effort as mutually reciprocal *gifts* leaves several unanswered questions. The firm decides not only work rules but also wages for each and every worker. Why should not Eastern Utilities set high standards of minimum effort and terminate all workers who are not capable of meeting or who are not willing to meet that standard (for example, Burke and Donovan in Table 16.1)? Again there is a simple answer. In working together, workers acquire sentiment for each other. An increase in minimum standards that would put pressure on Burke and Donovan might easily be considered by the group as a whole as failure by the firm to reciprocate the group's collective donation of productivity 17.7 percent in excess of the minimum requirements. Indeed, although the details are unclear in Homans' account, there is indication that such a situation had arisen with respect to the cash posters. As Homans reports, 'a couple of years before, when relations between the posters and a former division head were strained, there may have been some restriction on output.'

In a different context, that of a soldier in basic training in World War II, it is revealed most clearly why better workers come to the aid of their fellows:

If one is so favored by nature or training that he gets much more done, or done better, than his neighbor, he shows up that neighbor. The neighbor then gets rebukes or extra work. One cannot do this to any decent fellow who is trying his best, especially when you have to live side by side with him and watch his difficulties and sufferings. Therefore, the superior person—if he has any heart at all and if he is sensitive to the attitudes of his barracks mates—will help his less able neighbor to get along [Stouffer *et al.*, 1949, Vol. 2, p. 414].

Of course, the cash posters were working under less extreme conditions. Nevertheless, they undoubtedly could have expressed their own reasons for helping each other in similar terms.

I have indicated the nature of the trade between firms and workers that is exemplified in the case study of the cash posters and that gives a consistent and plausible explanation for the behavior of both the firm and the workers; this explanation tells why workers exceed the minimum standards of work on the one hand, and why the firm does not raise these minimum standards on the other hand. But work standards are only one dimension of the treatment of workers. Another dimension is wages. For reasons similar to why minimum work standards are not necessarily set at the limit that workers will bear before leaving the firm, the optimal contract may not set wages at the minimum acceptable: if part of worker effort is a *gift*, likewise, part of wages paid should be a *gift*.

IV. REFERENCE GROUPS

With the cash posters (or any other work group whose effort is determined not by the work rules but by the group's norms) the question arises: What does the group receive in return for working more than prescribed by the work rules? In the first place the worker may receive leniency in the work rules. Even if the worker habitually works at a speed in excess of work rules, he still benefits from leniency in two ways. First, he derives positive utility from the *gift* by the firm of potential leniency should he slacken his pace; second, as already mentioned, if he has sympathy for other members of the work group, he derives utility from the firm's generous treatment of other members of the group for whom the work rules are a binding constraint. Additionally, the firm may give remuneration in excess of that needed to obtain another worker of similar skills. Thus, excess remuneration and leniency of work rules constitute the major gifts by the firm to its workers.

Presumably, the gift of the worker to the firm, effort in excess of the work rules is linked to the gift of the firm to the worker. Following Mauss and others, reciprocity is a major feature of gift exchange (as also of market exchange).

The *quid pro quo* in gift exchange is, however, established at least slightly differently from market exchange. The norms for effort are established according to the conception of a fair day's work. (Note that Mayo described the work standard in precisely those terms.) In return the workers expect to be treated 'fairly' by the firm. The conception of fair treatment has been the subject of considerable work by social psychologists and sociologists. For the most part it is not based on absolute standards, but, rather, on comparison of one's own situation with that of other persons.

According to Festinger [1954], persons have an innate psychological need to compare their actions and treatment with those of others. Persons use comparison with others as a guide to how they ought to behave or how they ought to be treated. The point should be clear to any parent with a young child. Consider the young child who has fallen but not hurt himself/herself. Such situations usually produce that momentary pause before the child decides whether s/he should cry. If the surrounding adults act as if the situation calls for crying, the child is likely to behave accordingly; however, if adults act as if s/he should not cry, the child is likely not to do so. In the context of this paper I wish to note that the child's behavior is not determined by the real phenomenon of being hurt, but rather by the social definition of the situation given by the norms of the surrounding adults. In this way the child calibrates his/her actions by the social standards set by others.[6]

How do people decide that they are fairly treated? There is no natural measure (just as there is no natural language). Merton [1957] has constructed a theory of how people determine the fairness of their treatment by reference to the treatment of reference individuals and treatment of reference groups.

In World War II the Research Branch of the Information and Education Division of the U.S. Department of War conducted a large number of surveys of soldiers' attitudes. Some of these attitudes appear paradoxical from a purely individualistic, utilitarian point of view. For example, in the Army Air Force, in which promotion rates were much higher than in the rest of the army, soldiers were much less satisfied with their chances of promotion than elsewhere. Or, as a second example, although all soldiers abroad showed strong desire to return to the United States, noncombat soldiers abroad showed little more dissatisfaction with army life than soldiers stationed in the United States. Merton [1957] explains these seemingly paradoxical findings (as well as many others) with the concept of the reference group. The soldier in the Air Force felt unsatisfied with his chances of promotion precisely because the promotion rate was high in the Air Force, thereby enabling him to compare himself with other personnel who had been promoted (and causing him to feel relatively deprived). Noncombat soldiers abroad felt relatively satisfied given their objective conditions because they compared their lot to that of combat soldiers abroad, whereas the soldiers in the United States felt relatively unsatisfied (relative to their objective conditions) because they compared their lot to that of civilians at home. In each of these cases the seemingly paradoxical behavior is quite natural when the soldiers' attitudes are explained in terms of their deprivation relative to that of the appropriate reference group.

At the same time that *The American Soldier* [1949, Volumes 1 and 2] shows how attitudes toward fairness are formed (e.g., through reference to the relative deprivation of the appropriate reference group), it also contains evidence consistent with our hypothesis that *group norms* determine performance (as we have suggested is the case with respect to the cash posters and had been found earlier in the studies by Mayo [1949] and Roethlisberger and Dickson [1947]). In this regard three specific findings are worthy of particular note.

First, the Research Branch chose to measure performance of combat units by the percentage of *nonbattle casualties*. This statistic is equivalent to the percentage of combat men who became ineffective for reasons other than wounds or other battle injuries. This statistic was chosen as the best proxy for the quality of the unit, since it is almost independent of the group's battle environment. It is, as well, unambiguously related to the quality of discipline in the unit: presumably, better organized units would lose

---

[6] For this point of view of social interaction, see Coser [1971] on Park, Mead, and Cooley. The idea of the 'definition of the situation' is due to William I. Thomas.

smaller fractions of persons outside of battle. An excellent correlation was obtained [Stouffer, 1949, Vol. 2, p. 11] on a company-by-company basis between relatively favorable attitudes toward army life in interviews taken before the Normandy landing and the rate of nonbattle casualties following the Normandy landing in the three tested army divisions. This correlation of performance and attitude is a useful indicator that satisfaction in the job leads to improved job performance, justifying one aspect of our view that the firm will be willing to give a *gift* to the worker to increase his job satisfaction, so as, in turn, to increase his job performance.

There is one other noteworthy statistic from the same study. For one regiment (the Thirty-seventh Regiment of the Ninth Division) a graph was made plotting the percentage of nonbattle casualties of soldiers with and without previous combat experience in the same company. The graph shows a clear relation: in those companies in which the combat veterans had high rates of nonbattle casualties, the new recruits also had high rates (and vice versa). The correlation between the two statistics (taken across companies) was 80 percent [Stouffer, 1949, Vol. 2, p. 27]. This statistic is consistent with the hypothesis that members of a work group tend to take on the *group* norms, the companies with group norms more favorable to army life having fewer casualties among both new recruits and veterans. However, this conclusion follows of necessity only if the Research Branch was correct in its judgment that nonbattle casualties were independent of the environment; otherwise, such a correlation could be obtained because veterans and new recruits respond alike in their nonbattle casualties to changes in the environment.

Finally, there is the study by the Research Branch on the attitudes of soldiers in the Caribbean. It was hypothesized that there would be correlation between dissatisfaction and comfort. Perhaps surprisingly, at least to a very utilitarian view of motivations, the evidence showed at most only weak relation between dissatisfaction and the quality of soldiers' living conditions. This finding is useful in supporting our view that the morale of the working group (and indirectly its norms of work behavior) will depend largely on deprivation relative to that of reference individuals and reference groups, rather than depending on objective conditions alone.

This behavior of the American soldier is exactly consistent with our hypotheses concerning the behavior of the cash posters. We hypothesized (1) that the cash posters worked harder than required because of favorable work attitudes; (2) these attitudes, following Mayo *et al.*, were not just individual but also attitudes of the work group; (3) these attitudes depended in part upon workers' sense of fair treatment, where fairness was measured by comparison with persons similarly situated. In exact parallel *The American Soldier* shows (1) favorable attitudes were correlated with lower percentages of nonbattle casualties, both on a group-by-group basis and also on an individual basis. (2) The company-by-company correlation between performances of recruits and combat veterans demonstrates that performances were not randomly distributed over individuals but in fact varied systematically over groups. (There is considerable research in social psychology that shows how such patterns occur.) (3) Finally, attitudes of groups of soldiers toward the army can be systematically explained under the hypothesis that soldiers form their attitudes by comparing their situations to that of reference individuals or reference groups. I take the fact that the same model seems to apply to both the cash posters and the American soldier to be an indication of its universality.

V. THE FAIR WAGE

The gift of the firm to the worker (in return for the worker's gift of hard work for the firm) consists in part of a wage that is fair in terms of the norms of this gift giving. Using reference-individual–reference-group theory, the fairness of this wage depends on how other persons in the worker's reference set are similarly treated. Although, persons do sometimes have reference groups, or reference individuals who are dissimilar [Hyman, 1942], in matters of fairness it is probably safe to suppose that most persons compare themselves to persons who are *similar*. In that case one argument of the perceived fairness of the wage will be the wages received by other similar workers. Such workers, of course, include workers who are employed; but, in addition, it includes workers in the reference set who are unemployed. While empirically unemployment at any moment is a fairly small fraction of the labor force, flows in and out of unemployment are large, and most workers have many friends and close relatives. The probability that a whole reference set be free of unemployment for a significant period (say a year) is not large for most persons.

There is one other argument to the reference wage. To the psychologist or sociologist, to say that persons compare their own behavior or treatment with that in the past is probably neither useful nor profound. But persons certainly do that, and some economic theory (for example, the Modigliani–Duesenberry peak income hypothesis) does depend on such behavior. Thus, one additional argument to the reference wage, in addition to the remuneration of similar employed and unemployed persons and their respective weights in the reference set, is past wages.

Consistent with this observation is the role of past wages in all labor negotiations. Labor disputes often concern the level of past wages, which are the benchmark for current negotiations. To cite a case in point, consider the General Motors strike of 1970. In the 1967–1970 contract wages were indexed, but an eight-cent-per-hour limit was placed on raises due to increases in the cost of living. The cost of living increased relative to wages by considerably more than eight cents per hour with a resultant level of wages twenty-six cents below the fully indexed level [Pearlstine, 1970]. The union claimed that the corporation had already received a windfall gain for the three years of the contract during which period wages were not fully indexed, and the negotiations should concern growth of the real wage from the fully indexed level; the company claimed negotiations should concern growth from the actual 1970 level. This matter was the most contentious issue in the settlement of a long strike.

Summing up all our discussion of the fair wage, the fair wage received by the worker depends on the effort he expends in excess of the work rules, the work rules themselves, the wages of other workers, the benefits of unemployed workers, as well as the number of such workers, and the worker's wages received in previous periods. Our theory of reference-group behavior thus yields a fair wage that looks very much like the wage paid in a Phillips curve:

$$w^f_{i,t+1} = f(w_{i,t}, w_0, b_u, u, e_i, e_0) \tag{5}$$

where

$w^f_{i,t+1}$	is the perceived fair wage of individual i at $t + 1$
$w_{i,t}$	is the actual wage of individual i in previous period(s)
w_0	is the wage paid of others in the individual's reference set in current and previous periods
b_u	is unemployment benefits of individuals in the reference set in current and previous periods
u	is the number of unemployed in the reference set in current and previous periods
e_i	is the individual's work rules in current and previous periods
e_0	is the work rules of persons in the individual's reference set in current and previous periods.

Equation (5) is, of course, the basis for a Phillips curve of the traditional sort. It is important to note, however, that contrary to the Phillips relations obtained from search theory [Phelps *et al.*, 1970], (5) is not derived from market-clearing considerations. In general, there can be workers willing to enter gift relations with a firm, but no firms willing to enter gift relations with the workers. The next two sections model this occurrence. Our models are based upon the preceding discussion of reference groups and of the cash posters.

VI. A MODEL

This section and the next develop formal models that capture to some degree of accuracy most of the gift-giving idea in wage contracts. The ingredients of this model are spelled out in this section as follows.

1. *Norms* of effort on the part of workers in the work group. These norms depend on the work rules of the firm, the average wage paid by the firm, the incentive system of the firm (in terms of the different wages paid for different levels of output or effort), and the utility of co-workers in the firm who are part of the work group and for whom each worker has sympathy. All of these variables are endogenous to the firm. Exogenous to the firm, the norms depend on the returns to other persons in the workers' reference sets. In terms of our model these variables can be summarized by wages received by workers at other firms, the unemployment rate, and unemployment benefits. The model is considerably simplified by assuming only one time period. I do not see that this assumption takes anything away from the argument; it can be easily modified.

We thus summarize norms by the equation,

$$e_n = e_n(\{w(e, \varepsilon)\}, e_{min}, u_1, \ldots, u_j; w_0, u, b_u), \tag{6}$$

where

$\{w(e,\varepsilon)\}$ is the function that relates wages of a worker of type ε to his effort; this is the remuneration system of the firm

e_{min} is the work rules

u_j is the utility of the *j*th worker in the firm

w_0 is the wage paid by other firms (perhaps a vector)

u is the unemployment rate

b_u is the unemployment benefit.

2. *Workers.* Each worker has a utility function. A worker who has been offered employment must decide on his level of effort and whether or not to accept employment at the terms offered. The utility of each worker depends on the norms for effort, the effort itself, and the wage rate if employed; it depends on the unemployment benefit if unemployed. A worker makes two choices. If offered employment (i.e., if the firm offers to 'exchange gifts'), he must decide whether or not to accept the offer, and, if accepted, he must decide the size of the reciprocal gift. Thus, a worker of trait ε has a utility of working for the firm of

$$u\left(e_n,e,w,\varepsilon\right), \tag{7}$$

and if not working for the firm, of

$$u\left(b_u,\varepsilon\right).$$

If working for the firm, the worker chooses the level of effort e, which maximizes utility u, subject to the condition necessary to maintain his employment, that effort should exceed the firm's minimum requirement, $e \geqq e_{min}$. Accordingly, the worker chooses a job, if offered, in preference to unemployment accordingly as

$$\max_{e \geqq e_{min}} \; u\left(e_n,e,w,\varepsilon\right) \tag{8}$$

is greater than or less than

$$u\left(b_u,\varepsilon\right). \tag{9}$$

If a worker has more than one offer from different firms, he chooses the offer that maximizes his utility.

Across workers there is a distribution of tastes ε; we call this distribution function $f(\varepsilon)$.

3. *Firms.* We are, finally, left with firm behavior. Firms have an output that depends on the work effort of the workers. This output q is

$$q = f(e_1, e_2, \ldots, e_J),\tag{10}$$

where J is the number of workers hired. e_j is the effort of worker j.

Firms pay wages in general according to type of worker ε and effort, so that $w = w(e, \varepsilon)$.

Thus, wage cost is, accordingly,

$$\sum_{j=1}^{J} w\left(e_j, \varepsilon_j\right),$$

where e_j is the effort of worker j and ε_j is the tastes of worker j.

The firm chooses the wage function $w(e, \varepsilon)$, work rules, $e_{\min}$, and the number of workers it wishes to hire to maximize profits, which are

$$pf(e_1, \ldots, e_J) - \sum_{j=1}^{J} w\left(e_j, \varepsilon_j\right),\tag{11}$$

where p is the price of output. The firm's behavior is subject to the constraint that a worker chooses whether or not to join the firm according to whether or not the firm is making the worker his best offer (including unemployment as an alternative); the firm also views e_n as endogenously determined.

Models may differ regarding the firm's knowledge of workers' tastes ε; in the models of the next section, where this is relevant, we assume that the probability that it chooses a worker of given tastes ε from the unemployment pool is random. That assumption, while convenient, could be modified.

The general model just described of norms-workers-firms is enough taken across all workers and firms to describe aggregate supply for a whole economy. Two such examples are explored in some detail in the next section. These examples describe major features of models with such norm-determined firm-worker interaction.

VII. TWO EXAMPLES

According to the standard neoclassical model of the labor market, the firm purchases labor services in an optimal amount, *given the market wage.* This statement does not completely describe the firm's choice set, although in the *neoclassical* model the inaccuracy is of no importance. The neoclassical firm can purchase all the labor services it wishes if it pays a wage *at least as great as* the market wage. The firm chooses the wage and its purchases of labor services subject to this constraint. If the firm chooses a wage below the market-clearing level, it receives no labor. As far as its choice is concerned, it would be making the same decision if it demanded no labor and paid the market wage; and there is no advantage to choosing a wage in excess of the market rate. The firm's choice of wage therefore is always at the boundary: it will choose the optimal quantity of labor at the market-clearing wage.

However, once labor contracts are viewed in the context of gift exchange, it is not necessarily true that the firm will always choose wages on the boundary. In gift exchange, the usual norm is that gifts should be more than the minimum required to keep the other party in the exchange relationship. In terms of the labor market this means that the worker who does no more than necessary to keep his job is the subject of at least some slight loss of reputation; reciprocally, the firm that pays its workers no more than the minimum necessary to retain them will also lose some reputation. In the neoclassical model the firm *never* chooses to pay more than the market-clearing wage because there is no advantage to doing so. In the gift-exchange model, however, the interior solution, in which the firm finds it advantageous to pay a wage in excess of the one at which it can acquire labor, may occur because there are some benefits (as well as costs) from paying a higher wage. Doubtless, this interior solution need not occur. Where it does occur, the labor market is primary. A worker entering the labor market will not automatically find work at the wage received by equally qualified employed persons. If the boundary solution occurs, in contrast, the labor market clears; the market is secondary, and a person in that market can readily obtain work at the wage received by current employees of similar qualifications.

The purpose of this section is to demonstrate by two specific examples the characteristics of the labor market in which gift exchange occurs in the sense that the workers' norm for effort depends upon their treatment by the firm. One example assumes that the firm's work rules are fixed, and with this assumption the equilibrium wage and unemployment are derived. The second example assumes that the real wage is fixed and demonstrates that work rules do not equilibrate supply and demand for labor in the sociological model (with norms) as they do in the neoclassical model. This model is specifically constructed with the behavior of the cash posters in mind.

Example I.   Wages

Rather than present a model and show that there will be equilibrium unemployment, we work in reverse. All the parameters and functions of the model are chosen with the exception of the size of the labor force. It is then shown that appropriate particular choice of the size of the labor force will yield an equilibrium with unemployment rate u_0.

Let $\bar{l}$ workers per firm be the supply of labor. $\bar{l}$ will later be chosen to have a particular value to conform to the unemployment rate u_0, but that choice is at the end, not at the beginning of the story.

Let output q be a function of effort e and labor n according to the production function,

$$q = (en)^{\alpha}. \tag{12}$$

Let effort e of all workers be at the norm e_n. And let all workers be the same so that

$$e = e_n. \tag{13}$$

Let the effort norm be a function of the wage of the firm relative to the reference wage as

$$e_n = -a + b(w/w_r)^{\gamma}, \quad \gamma < 1. \tag{14}$$

(Two considerations explain the particular choice of $e_n - w$ function (14). First, the firm chooses w to maximize the number of labor efficiency units per dollar spent. Solow [1979] has shown that such an internal maximum occurs where the elasticity of w with respect to e is equal to unity. And to insure that this choice of w yields the maximum effort per dollar of expenditure, the $e_n - w$ elasticity must be declining. The function (14) has been chosen accordingly with a declining $e_n - w$ elasticity. A second consideration is responsible for the negative intercept of $-a$. If positive effort is obtained at a 0 wage, a 0 wage [with infinite effort per dollar] is optimal.)

Let the reference wage w_r be the geometric mean,

$$w_r = w_0^{1-u} b_u^u, \tag{15}$$

where

u is the unemployment rate,
w_0 is the wage paid by other firms, and
b_u is the level of unemployment benefits.

Since the firm in question is the typical firm, it also follows that the employment by the firm n is the average number of employed persons per firm, or

$$n = (1 - u)\bar{l}. \tag{16}$$

Furthermore, again because the firm in question is the typical firm, its wage is the same as the wage of other firms, or

$$w = w_0. \tag{17}$$

Suppose that u is u_0. It will be shown that with appropriate choice of the parameter $\bar{l} = l_0$, the profit-maximizing firm will choose to hire an amount of labor $n = (1 - u_0)\bar{l}$ if its wage w is the same as the wage of other firms w_0. Consequently, u_0 is an equilibrium rate of unemployment with labor supply l_0.

The firm behaves in the following fashion. With unemployment at $u_0 > 0$, it can obtain all the workers it wants at any wage. Consequently, it chooses n and w to maximize profits, or

$$\prod = (en)^{\alpha} - wn \tag{18}$$

subject to the constraints

$$e = e_n \tag{19}$$

$$e_n = -a + b\left(w/w_r\right)^{\gamma} \tag{20}$$

$$w_r = w_0^{1-u} b_u^u. \tag{21}$$

This maximization problem together with the condition $w = w_0$ yields the demand for labor n^d as a function of the unemployment rate u_0:

$$n^d = \left(\alpha^{-1} b_u \left(\frac{a\gamma}{1-\gamma}\right)^{-\alpha} \left(\frac{a}{b(1-\gamma)}\right)^{1/\gamma u_0}\right)^{1/(\alpha-1)}. \tag{22}$$

If n^d is consistent with the unemployment rate, then the supply of labor, which is as yet an unchosen parameter of our model, must be

$$\bar{l} = l_0 = \frac{n^d}{1-u_0} = (1-u_0)^{-1} \left(\alpha^{-1} b_u \left(\frac{a\gamma}{1-\gamma}\right)^{-\alpha} \left(\frac{a}{b(1-\gamma)}\right)^{1/\gamma u_0}\right)^{1/(\alpha-1)}. \tag{23}$$

With $\bar{l}$ chosen in this fashion according to the right-hand side of (23), our model has an equilibrium at the rate of unemployment u_0, where $0 < u_0 < 1$. Note that the unemployed would be willing to work at the wage paid employed workers, but firms will be unwilling to hire them at that wage, or one which is lower.

Moreover, it is also easy to construct an example in which the firm's choice of w is not interior. After all, if the coefficient $b = 0$ and $a < 0$, the example exactly corresponds to the neoclassical model verbally analyzed at the beginning of this section in which all markets cleared. In our analysis the property, whether or not markets clear, or, alternatively stated, whether labor markets are secondary or primary is endogenous.[7]

Example II.   Work Standards

The first example illustrated the possibility (and the accompanying discussion partially characterized that possibility) that the relation between work norms and wages will cause an economy-wide (or labor-market-wide) equilibrium with nonmarket-clearing prices because firms themselves find it advantageous to set wages above the minimum at which they can freely obtain labor.

Our discussion of the cash posters, however, was not concerned with wages but rather with work rules. According to the standard neoclassical model, even if for some reason wages are not fixed at market-clearing levels, still firms should adjust work rules to the point where supply and demand for labor are equal (*even at a nonequilibrial wage*). This section gives an example in which the work rules will not equilibrate labor supply

---

[7] Just because some markets clear does not mean that there is no unemployment. Unemployed workers may be waiting for an opportunity to take a primary sector job. See Hall [1975].

and demand. It is not the simplest example—partly because of our desire to make the model a faithful representation of the cash posters, and partially also because the reaction of workers to norms inherently involves a great deal of behavior that cannot easily be represented by simple linear functions.

Because in the standard neoclassical model, work standards would equate demand and supply for labor even at a fixed nonequilibrating wage rate, we start with the assumption that the wage rate $\bar{w}$ is fixed. Although artificial, we could assume that the government has controlled wages. Certainly this occasionally happens when the government imposes certain forms of incomes policy.

Recall that among the cash posters some workers worked much above the work standard set by the firm (45 percent for Granara and Murphy) while some workers were quite close to the margin (only 2 percent above for Burke and Donovan).

To represent a model in which some workers are above the margin while other workers are at the margin, it is necessary to have at least two types of workers. For that reason our model has two groups of workers with different tastes. Poor workers form a fraction p of the work force. Good workers form a fraction $1 - p$.

In the story behind our model the firm is capable of identifying the tastes of workers only after they have joined the firm, but not before. In terms of the cash posters, who could have predicted that the almost equally outgoing and gregarious Murphy and Burke would have work records which were polar opposites? Homans hints that this difference may have occurred in part because Burke socialized primarily with a group of 'ledger posters,' while the rest of the cash posters socialized mainly among themselves. Certainly no personnel officer could have predicted such an occurrence.

Although the firm can measure performance easily once workers are hired, it is assumed that it cannot fire them without a reduction in the work norms. As a result, in the model constructed labor effort is observable ex post but not predictable ex ante.

Worker Behavior

Among the two types of workers, good workers who work for the firm have utility, denoted U^+, where

$$U^+ = A - B(e - (e_n + \varepsilon))^2 \tag{24}$$

The parameter A depends on wages, but since they are assumed fixed, we have suppressed that dependency. Poor workers who work for the firm have utility, denoted U^-, where

$$U^- = A - B(e - (e_n - \varepsilon))^2. \tag{25}$$

The parameters A and B are both positive, e_n is the norm of work effort, e is actual effort by the individual worker, and ε is a parameter reflecting the type of worker. U^+ and U^- are the utilities of good workers and bad workers, respectively, when working for the firm. Workers have the option of working for the firm with effort e and also the option of quitting and being unemployed. In that case their utility is assumed to be 0.

A worker who works for a firm maximizes his utility subject to abiding by the work rules of the firm. Thus, a good worker with utility function U^+ chooses e to maximize

$$A - B(e - (e_n + \varepsilon))^2, \tag{26}$$

subject to the constraint

$$e \geq e_{min}^+, \tag{27}$$

where e_{min}^+ is the minimum work standard set by the firm for good workers. Accordingly, for such a worker if U^+ working for the firm is positive, the worker chooses to work with effort e^+:

$$e^+ = max\,(e_{min}^+, e_n + \varepsilon). \tag{28}$$

Similarly, if U^- working for the firm is positive, a poor worker chooses to work with effort e^-:

$$e^- = max\,(e_{min}^-, e_n - \varepsilon). \tag{29}$$

Norms. The norms of behavior depend upon the work rules,

$$e_n = e_n(e_{min}^-, e_{min}^+). \tag{30}$$

Later it will be assumed that e_{min}^- and e_{min}^+ have an effect on norms only insofar as they are a binding constraint on workers' effort.

Firm Behavior

On its side, the firm takes into account the reaction of the workers' effort to the norms and the reaction of the norms to work rules. In the case of excess supply of labor, where labor is freely available as long as U^+ and U^- are positive, the firm chooses e_{min}^+, e_{min}^-, and n to maximize profits, or

$$(\bar{e}(e_{min}^-, e_{min}^+)n)^\alpha - \bar{w}n, \tag{31}$$

where $\bar{e}(\ )$ is the function combining (28), (29), and (30) with the appropriate weights to account for the dependence of average effort on work rules.

Accordingly, at an interior maximum the firm that can obtain all the labor it wishes will choose e_{min}^- and e_{min}^+ to maximize $\bar{e}(e_{min}^-, e_{min}^+)$, and its demand for labor according to the marginal product condition,

$$\alpha \bar{e} \left(e_{min}^{-*}, e_{min}^{+*} \right)^{\alpha} n^{\alpha-1} = \bar{w}. \tag{32}$$

As long as n so chosen by the typical firm is less than $\bar{l}$, the demand for labor is less than the supply, and the assumption that the firm can obtain all the labor it wishes is justified.

Problems with obtaining an interior maximum. The question, however, arises, how there can be an interior maximum for e_{min}^{+} or e_{min}^{-}. After all, why should the firm not increase e_{min}^{+} just up to the point where all good workers are on the verge of quitting? (In so doing, it also may have the added dividend of screening out the poorer workers.) In the real world workers usually apply sanctions against such behavior by the firm. For example, in the case of the cash posters, remember that Homans recorded a work slowdown in a previous dispute with a supervisor. In our model this is represented by the fact that as the work rules force workers to work sufficiently in excess of the norms, they quit.

Let the fraction p of poor workers be $\frac{1}{2}$. Let the tastes parameter ε be 1. And let the parameters A and B in (24) and (25) be 2 and $\frac{1}{2}$, respectively, so that

$$U^{+} = 2 - \frac{1}{2}(e - (e_n + \varepsilon))^2 \tag{33}$$

$$U^{-} = 2 - \frac{1}{2}(e - (e_n - \varepsilon))^2. \tag{34}$$

Good workers, who maximize U^{+}, will choose

$$e = e_n + \varepsilon \tag{35}$$

as long as they are unconstrained by the work rules. Similarly, if unconstrained, poor workers, who maximize U^{-}, will choose

$$e = e_n - \varepsilon. \tag{36}$$

We assume that the work rules have an effect on the effort norm if and only if they are binding. Accordingly, the norm depends on $max(e_{min}^{+} - (e_n + \varepsilon), 0)$ and $max(e_{min}^{-} - (e_n - \varepsilon), 0)$. Furthermore, it is assumed that the norms are egalitarian in that a difference between the work rules for the two types of workers will have a negative effect on the norms.

Accordingly, the norm in this example follows the formula,

$$e_n = 6 - 0.8 max(e_{min}^{+} - (e_n + \varepsilon), e_{min}^{-} - (e_n - \varepsilon), 0) - 20|e_{min}^{+} - e_{min}^{-}|. \tag{37}$$

The second term of (37) reflects the decline in the norm of effort as the work rules become increasingly binding on the workers' choice of effort. The third term reflects the effect on the norm of an inequality in the treatment of the two types of workers.

It is easy to check that the firm which wishes to maximize $\bar{e}$ will choose

$$e^+_{min} = e^-_{min} \overset{\leq}{=} 5, \tag{38}$$

and at this maximum $\bar{e} = 6$.

I will sketch the proof. First, inequality in e^+_{min} and e^-_{min} causes such a large reduction in e_n (the coefficient of the last term of (37) being 20) that the firm always finds it advantageous to set $e^+_{min} = e^-_{min}$. In that case the formula for e_n (37) can be simplified to

$$e_n = 6 - 0.8\max(e_{min} - (e_n - \varepsilon), 0). \tag{39}$$

A bit of algebra shows that with $\varepsilon = 1$ (39) can be rewritten as

$$e_n = 6 \quad e_{min} \overset{\leq}{=} 5 \tag{40A}$$

$$e_n = 30 - 4e_{min} - 4 \quad e_{min} \overset{\geq}{=} 5. \tag{40B}$$

It is easy to check using (34), (40A), (40B) and the value of $\varepsilon = 1$ that U^- is positive if $e_{min} < 5.4$ and negative if $e_{min} > 5.4$. Similarly, U^+ is positive if $e_{min} < 5.8$ and is negative for $e_{min} > 5.8$.

Thus, in the range $0 \overset{\leq}{=} e_{min} < 5.4$ both good and bad workers are working. For $0 \overset{\leq}{=} e_{min} \overset{\leq}{=} 5$ work rules are binding on neither good nor bad workers, and therefore

$$\bar{e} = \tfrac{1}{2}(e_n + \varepsilon) + \tfrac{1}{2}(e_n - \varepsilon) = e_n = 6, \quad 0 \overset{\leq}{=} e_{min} \overset{\leq}{=} 5. \tag{41}$$

For $5 < e_{min} < 5.4$ work rules are binding on poor workers but not on good workers. U^- and U^+ are both positive so both good and bad workers are at work. Hence

$$\bar{e} = \tfrac{1}{2}(e_n + \varepsilon) + \tfrac{1}{2}e_{min} \quad 5 < e_{min} < 5.4 \tag{42}$$

$$= 13.5 - 1.5e_{min} < 6 \quad 5 < e_{min} < 5.4. \tag{43}$$

By design of the example, for $e_{min} > 5.4$ U^- is negative; also by (40B) for $e_{min} > 5.4$, $e_n + \varepsilon < e_{min}$, so work rules are binding on good workers. U^+ is positive for $e_{min} < 5.8$. Consequently, in the range $5.4 < e_{min} < 5.8$ only good workers are at work, and since their effort is constrained by work rules,

$$\bar{e} = e_{min} \qquad 5.4 < e_{min} < 5.8. \tag{44}$$

For $e_{min} > 5.8$ $\bar{e}$ is indeterminate, since U^+ and U^- are both negative. The number of workers willing to work is, however, 0. Hence $\bar{e}$ is maximized according to (41), (43), and (44) at $\bar{e} = 6$ with $e^+_{min} = e^-_{min} \overset{\leq}{=} 5$.

To obtain an example with unemployment rate u_0, it is only necessary to choose $\bar{l} = l_0$ consistent with u_0 and the marginal productivity condition for labor demand so that

$$\bar{l} = l_0 = (1 - u_0)^{-1}(\alpha^{-1}6^{-\alpha}\bar{w})^{1/(\alpha-1)}. \tag{45}$$

Remark. This example corresponds exactly to cash poster behavior. The firm paid the same wage to all workers. One group of workers (a minority) worked at the work standard, or very close to it. Other workers worked above that standard. For reasons unspecified by Homans, but which are consistent with our model, the firm did not raise standards on either good workers or poor workers. At the equilibrium unemployment is involuntary.

VIII. CONCLUSION

This paper has explored the idea that labor contracts are partial gift exchanges. According to this idea, at least in part, wages are determined by, and in turn also influence, the norms of workers' effort; similarly, workers' effort is determined, at least in part, by these norms. A relation between the terms of exchange and norms is in our view what differentiates gift exchange from pure market exchange.

Indeed, while the norms may be greatly influenced by the same things as market prices, there is still a major difference between pure market exchange and gift exchange. In pure market exchange the maximum price at which a buyer is willing to purchase a commodity or factor service is the minimum at which the respective commodity or factor service is obtainable. Obversely, the minimum price at which a seller is willing to sell a commodity or factor service is the maximum at which the respective commodity or factor service can be sold. In gift exchange buyers may be willing to pay more than the minimum at which they can purchase a commodity or factor service because of the effect of the terms of exchange on the norms. Similarly, sellers may be willing to accept less than the maximum at which they can sell a commodity or factor service because of the effects of the terms of exchange on the norms. It has been shown that due to this behavior with gift exchange markets need not clear. Thus, the gift-exchange economy and the neoclassical economy differ in at least one fundamental respect. Future papers will explore further differences between the two models of exchange.

UNIVERSITY OF CALIFORNIA, BERKELEY

References

Azariadis, C., 'Implicit Contracts and Unemployment Equilibria,' *Journal of Political Economy*, LXXXIII (Dec. 1975), 1183–1202.

Baily, M. N., 'Wages and Employment Under Uncertain Demand,' *Review of Economic Studies*, XLI (Jan. 1974), 37–50.

Belshaw, C. S., *Traditional Exchange and Modern Markets* (Englewood Cliffs, NJ: Prentice-Hall, 1965).

Coser, L. A., *Masters of Sociological Thought: Ideas in Historical and Social Context* (New York: Harcourt Brace Jovanovich, 1971).

Doeringer, P. B., and M. J. Piore, *Internal Labor Markets and Manpower Analysis* (Lexington, MA: D. C. Heath & Co., 1971).

Edwards, R., *Contested Terrain: The Transformation of the Workplace in the Twentieth Century* (New York: Basic Books, 1979).

Etzioni, A. W., *Modern Organizations* (Englewood Cliffs, NJ: Prentice-Hall, 1971).

Festinger, L., 'A Theory of Social Comparison Processes,' *Human Relations*, VII (1954), 117–40; reprinted in *Readings in Reference Group Therapy*, Herbert H. Hyman and Eleanor Singer, eds. (New York: The Free Press, 1968).

Freeman, R. L., and J. L. Medoff, 'The Two Faces of Unionism,' *The Public Interest*, No. 57 (Fall 1979), 69–93.

Hall, R. E., 'The Rigidity of Wages and the Persistence of Unemployment.' *Brookings Papers on Economic Activity*, III (1975), 301–49.

Hirschman, A. O., *Exit, Voice and Loyalty* (Cambridge: Harvard University Press, 1970).

Homans, G. C., 'Status Among Clerical Workers,' *Human Organization*, XII (Spring 1953), 5–10; reprinted in G. C. Homans, *Sentiments and Activities* (New York: Free Press of Glencoe, 1962).

——, 'The Cash Posters,' *American Sociological Review*, XIX (Dec. 1954), 724–33; reprinted in G. C. Homans, *Sentiments and Activities* (New York: Free Press of Glencoe, 1962).

Hyman, H. H., 'The Psychology of Status,' *Archives of Psychology*, No. 269 (1942); reprinted in part in *Readings in Reference Group Theory*, Herbert H. Hyman and Eleanor Singer, eds. (New York: The Free Press, 1968).

Leibenstein, H., *Beyond Economic Man: A New Foundation for Microeconomics* (Cambridge, MA: Harvard University Press, 1976).

Mauss, M., *The Gift: Forms and Functions of Exchange in Archaic Societies*, translated by Ian Cunnison (London: Cohen and West, 1954).

Mayo, E., *The Social Problems of an Industrial Civilization* (London: Routledge and Kegan Paul, 1949).

Merton, R. K., *Social Theory and Social Structure*, revised and enlarged edition (Glencoe, IL: The Free Press, 1957).

Okun, A., 'Inflation: Its Mechanics and Welfare Costs,' *Brookings Papers on Economic Activity*, II (1975), 366–73.

——, *Prices and Quantities: A Macroeconomic Analysis* (Washington, D.C.: The Brookings Institution, 1981).

Pearlstine, N., 'Auto Pact Tension Eases; Strike Chances Viewed as Tied to Chrysler, GM Parleys,' *Wall Street Journal*, CLXXVI, No. 48 (Sept. 4, 1970), 5, column 2.

Phelps, E. S. *et al.*, *The Microeconomic Foundations of Employment and Inflation Theory* (New York: Norton, 1970).

Roethlisberger, F. J., and W. J. Dickson, *Management and the Worker: An Account of a Research Program Conducted by the Western Electric Company, Hawthorne Works, Chicago* (Cambridge, MA: Harvard University Press, 1947).

Solow, R. M., 'Another Possible Source of Wage Stickiness,' *Journal of Macroeconomics*, I (Winter 1979), 79–82.

——, 'On Theories of Unemployment,' *American Economic Review*, LXX (March 1980), 1–10.

Stoft, S., 'Cheat-Threat Theory,' University of California Thesis Prospectus, August 1980.

Stouffer, S. A., E. A. Suchman, L. C. de Vinney, S. A. Star, and R. M. Williams, Jr., *The American Soldier: Adjustment During Army Life*, Vol. 1 (Princeton, NJ: Princeton University Press, 1949).

Stouffer, S. A., A. A. Lumsdaine, M. H. Lumsdaine, R. M. Williams, Jr., M. B. Smith, I. L. Jarvis, S. A. Star, and L. S. Cottrell, Jr., *The American Soldier: Combat and its Aftermath*, Vol. 2 (Princeton, NJ: Princeton University Press, 1949).

Titmuss, R. M., *The Gift Relationship: From Human Blood to Social Policy* (New York: Random House, 1971).

17

The Fair Wage–Effort Hypothesis and Unemployment*

GEORGE A. AKERLOF AND JANET L. YELLEN [†]

I. INTRODUCTION

This paper explores the consequences of a hypothesis concerning worker behavior, which we shall call the fair wage–effort hypothesis.[1] According to this hypothesis, workers have a conception of a fair wage; insofar as the actual wage is less than the fair wage, workers supply a corresponding fraction of normal effort. If e denotes effort supplied, w the actual wage, and w^* the fair wage, the fair wage–effort hypothesis says that

$$e = \min(w/w^*, 1), \tag{1}$$

where effort is denoted in units such that 1 is normal effort. This hypothesis explains the existence of unemployment. Unemployment occurs when the fair wage w^* exceeds the market-clearing wage.[2] With natural specifications of the determination of w^*, this

* This work was previously published as George A. Akerlof and Janet L. Yellen (1990), 'The Fair Wage–Effort Hypothesis and Unemployment', *The Quarterly Journal of Economics* CV, 2. Copyright © The MIT Press. Reproduced by kind permission.

[†] We would like to thank Samuel Bowles, Daniel Kahneman, David Levine, John Pencavel, David Romer, and Lawrence Summers for helpful comments and discussions. We also gratefully acknowledge financial support from the Sloan Foundation (for the first author), from the Guggenheim Foundation (for the second author), from the Institute for Industrial Relations, and from the National Science Foundation under grant numbers SES 86-005023 and SES 88-07807 administered by the Institute for Business and Economic Research at the University of California, Berkeley.

[1] Akerlof and Yellen [1988] contains a summary of the results obtained in this paper.

[2] For evidence of discrepancies between lay theories of fair wages and market-clearing wages, see Kahneman, Knetsch, and Thaler [1986].

hypothesis may explain why skill and unemployment are negatively correlated. In addition, it potentially explains wage differentials and labor market segmentation.[3]

The motivation for the fair wage–effort hypothesis is a simple observation concerning human behavior: when people do not get what they deserve, they try to get even. The next section will present five types of evidence for the fair wage–effort hypothesis. *First*, it will draw on psychology, where the fair wage–effort hypothesis corresponds to Adams' [1963] theory of equity. Numerous empirical studies have tested this theory. They are, on balance, strongly supportive. *Second*, in sociology the fair wage–effort hypothesis corresponds to the Blau-Homans [1955, 1961] theory of social exchange. Sociological studies, including studies of work situations, show that equity usually prevails in social exchange. *Third*, the fair wage–effort hypothesis accords with common sense. It appears frequently in literature; it is considered obvious by personnel textbooks; and it explains commonly observed taboos regarding discussion of wages and salaries. *Fourth*, the fair wage–effort hypothesis explains wage compression among individuals with different skills. *Fifth*, simple models of the fair wage–effort hypothesis potentially explain empirically observed unemployment-skill correlations; they also explain why unemployment has not fallen with the rise in education despite lower unemployment of more educated workers.

Having reviewed the evidence for the fair wage–effort hypothesis, Sections III and IV construct models using this hypothesis. These models differ in the determination of the fair wage w^*. In Section III w^* is exogenous. In Section IV w^* depends on *relative* wages as well as on market forces. These models provide efficiency wage explanations for unemployment. Yet they are not subject to the criticism that bonding schemes or complicated contracts will reduce or eliminate involuntary unemployment.[4] If such bonds are considered unfair, then they will not be optimal. In relations where fairness is important, grudges due to past events lead to potential future reprisals. In the existing literature this model most closely resembles Summers' [1988] relative wage-based efficiency wage theory. In Summers' model workers compare their own compensation with that of comparable groups in other firms; in our model, in contrast, workers compare their pay with that of coworkers in the same firm.

II. MOTIVATION FOR THE FAIR WAGE–EFFORT HYPOTHESIS

A. *Equity Theory*

Adams [1963] hypothesized that in social exchange between two agents the ratio of the perceived value of the 'inputs' to the perceived value of the 'outcomes' would be equal. In a labor exchange the 'input' of the employee is the perceived value of his labor, and the 'outcome' is the perceived value of his remuneration. On the firm's side the input is

---

[3] Levine [1990] has offered a similar explanation for these phenomena based on worker cohesiveness.

[4] For reviews of this literature and the problems with efficiency wage models, see Akerlof and Yellen [1986], Katz [1986], Stiglitz [1987], and Yellen [1984].

the perceived value of the remuneration, and the outcome is the perceived value of the labor.

In the context of a wage contract, Adams' formula says that the perceived value of the labor input will equal the perceived value of the remuneration. This formula can be translated into economic notation to say that the number of units of effective labor input (denoted e for effort) times the perceived value of a unit of effective labor (denoted w^*) will equal the perceived value of remuneration (denoted w). In other words,

$$e = w/w^*.$$

We wish to emphasize that w^*, the perceived value of a unit of labor, will be the *fair* wage, and not the market-clearing wage.

According to psychologists, with both w and w^* fixed, workers who do not receive a fair wage for input of effort $e = 1$ may change *actual* effort e, or they may change their *perceived* effort. Similarly, they may change their perceived level of remuneration (by redefining the nonpecuniary terms of the job). In the theory below, we shall assume that when wages are underpaid workers adjust actual rather than perceived efforts or the perceived value of the nonpecuniary returns to the job.

Psychological experiments have mainly concentrated on discovering whether individuals who are *overpaid* will increase their effort input since psychologists consider this the surprising prediction of Adams' theory. They consider it obvious that agents who feel underrewarded will supply correspondingly *fewer* inputs [Walster, Walster, and Berscheid, 1977 p. 42]. As might be expected, overreward experiments yield ambiguous results. It has been suggested [Walster, Walster, and Berscheid, 1977, p. 124] that this ambiguity occurs because it is less costly for overpaid agents to increase the psychological evaluation of their labor inputs than to increase actual input. These experimental results are consistent with the hypothesis that overpayment does not increase input, and thus that $e = 1$ for $w > w^*$.

While much less work has been done on underpaid subjects, several studies have obtained supportive results.[5] In one revealing study Lawler and O'Gara [1967] compared the performance of workers who were paid the 'going' rate of 25 cents per interview with the performance of interviewers who were seriously underpaid at the rate of 10 cents per interview. The underpaid interviewers conducted far more interviews that were on average of significantly lower quality. Psychologically the lower paid interviewers also had reduced self-esteem—suggesting that workers adjust not only the amount of effort but also their perception of the quality of the labor input when equity is not realized.

In a clever experiment Pritchard, Dunnette, and Jorgenson [1972] hired men to work for a fictitious Manpower firm they realistically set up for their experiment. After the workers had been at work for three days, the firm announced a change in their method of pay. Subjects' earnings were variously adjusted upward or downward. Those subjects

---

[5] Reviewers consider this implication of equity theory obvious; some experiments have yielded contradictions of the theory, but in all cases there are easy alternative explanations [Goodman and Friedman, 1971].

with downward adjustments expressed considerable job dissatisfaction on a question-naire and also performed less well in their work after the change. In a similar experiment Valenzi and Andrews [1971] hired workers at $1.40 per hour, but then announced that, due to the budgetary process involving their grant from the National Institute of Mental Health, some workers would receive more than the stipulated $1.40, and some would receive less. Twenty-seven percent of those who were given the lower wage of $1.20 quit immediately—a result consistent with an upward sloping labor supply curve but also explained by the workers' anger at their unfair treatment.

In what is probably the most revealing experiment, Schmitt and Marwell [1972] gave workers a choice: whether to work cooperatively in pairs or to work alone. When pay was equal, workers chose to work in pairs. However, workers were willing to sacrifice significant earnings to work alone when the pay in pairs was unequal.

B. *Relative Deprivation Theory*

The economic consequences of the fair wage–effort hypothesis depend on how the fair wage is determined.[6] According to relative deprivation theory, peoples' conceptions of fairness are based on comparisons with salient others. Psychological theory, however, offers little guide as to which reference groups will be salient. There are three natural possibilities: individuals may compare themselves with others in similar occupations in the same firm, with those in dissimilar occupations in the same firm, or with individuals in other firms. In the model constructed in Section IV below, workers compare themselves with others in the same firm. If workers compare themselves with similar others who are 'close substitutes,' we find that equilibrium will be segregated and workers of different abilities will work in different firms. Labor is allocated inefficiently, but there is no unemployment. If workers, however, compare themselves with others who are 'dissimilar' or 'complements' in production, equilibrium is characterized by unemployment for low-skill workers or by dual labor markets with pay disparities for low-skill workers.

Although the behavioral consequences of relative deprivation have been hard to document (for natural reasons), there is very good evidence that relative deprivation generates feelings of dissatisfaction. (This corresponds exactly to the model proposed in Section IV.)

Martin [1981] has done an ingenious experiment in a near-field situation which shows that workers are likely to experience feelings of relative deprivation when there are unequal wages. Technicians at a factory were asked to imagine themselves in the position of a technician earning the average pay in a firm similar to their own. They were first asked which pay level—highest or lowest pay of technicians; highest, average, or lowest pay of supervisors—they would most like to know for comparison to their own wage. Most technicians wanted to know the pay of the highest level of techni-cians which is consistent with our model that people work less hard if they are paid

---

[6] Most experiments make an implicit assumption regarding the wage considered fair: either some stated wage, a previously received wage, or wages received by others.

less than they deserve but not harder if they receive more than they deserve. Those people who receive less are of comparatively little interest (and therefore have little positive influence on work); whereas those people who are paid more are of considerable interest and, if the ratio is deemed inequitable, can have considerable negative impact.

The second part of Martin's experiment is of further importance for our model. After workers had made their comparison choice, they were then given a pay plan and asked to rate it on the basis of being dissatisfying, expected, or just. When the difference in pay of the supervisors and technicians was large, the technicians found the pay levels to be dissatisfying and unjust. This gives an empirical basis for the assumption in Section IV that low paid workers will feel relatively deprived when workers of other groups receive high wages.

C. *Social Exchange Theory*

Sociologists, as well as psychologists, have developed a version of equity theory. Blau's model of exchange [1955] hypothesizes that there will be equivalent rewards net of costs on both sides of an exchange. Blau's model was motivated by his empirical study [1955] of the helping behavior of agents in a government bureaucracy. The agents who did investigative work would consult with other agents concerning difficult problems. Although consultation with other agents, rather than with the supervisor, was against the official rules of the agency, and its existence was denied by the supervisor, on average, agents had five contacts with other agents per hour, most of which were consultations. In this agency agents varied in expertise. Blau noticed that agents of average expertise would consult agents with the greatest expertise only infrequently. In contrast, agents of equal ability consulted with each other frequently. This suggested a puzzle to Blau: why did the average agents not ask for more help from the experts? According to his explanation, the average agents refrained from consulting the experts more because they found it difficult to reciprocate. They were able to pay each expert with gratitude and respect; but there were diminishing returns to the experts from receiving gratitude. The exchanges between the average agents and the experts, Blau concluded, were not carried beyond the point where the two sides of the exchange were of equal value.

Homans [1961] has proposed a similar theory, based on his own observations, Blau's study, and on work on conformity by social psychologists led by Festinger. The Blau-Homans theory is a general theory of social exchange. Homans develops a key proposition regarding social exchange when the subjective equalities are not met on the two sides of an exchange: 'The more to a man's disadvantage the rule of distributive justice fails of realization, the more likely he is to display the emotional behavior we call anger' [Homans, 1961, p. 75]. In simple English, if people do not get what they think they deserve, they get angry. It is this simple proposition that underlies our model. Workers whose wage is less than the fair wage w^* will be angry. The consequence of this anger is to reduce their effective labor input below the level they would offer if fully satisfied. This relation is given the simple, natural, functional form $e = w/w^*$ for $w < w^*$.

D. *Empirical Observations of Work Restriction in the Workplace*

Sociologists have documented the existence of output restriction in the workplace. In his classic study of 1930, Mathewson [1969] records 223 instances of restriction in 105 establishments in 47 different locations. These observations were recorded from his work experiences as a participant observer, interviews with workers, and from the letters of six colleagues, who were also participant observers. According to Mathewson, 'occasionally workers have an idea that they are worth more than management is willing to pay them. When they are not receiving the wage they think fair, they adjust their production to the pay received.' This is an exact statement of the fair wage–effort hypothesis. The following, from the bulletin board of a machine shop, expresses the fair wage–effort hypothesis poetically:

> I am working with the feeling
> That the company is stealing
> Fifty pennies from my pocket every day;
> But for ever single pennie [sic]
> They will lose ten times as many
> By the speed that I'm producing, I dare say.
> For it makes one so disgusted
> That my speed shall be adjusted
> So that nevermore my brow will drip with sweat;
> When they're in an awful hurry
> Someone else can rush and worry
> Till an increase in my wages do I get.
>
> No malicious thoughts I harbor
> For the butcher or the barber
> Who get eighty cents an hour from the start.
> Nearly three years I've been working
> Like a fool, but now I'm shirking—
> When I get what's fair, I'll always do my part.
> Someone else can run their races
> Till I'm on an equal basis
> With the ones who learned the trade by mining coal.
> Though I can do the work, it's funny
> New men can get the money
> And I cannot get the same to save my soul [Mathewson, 1969, p. 127].

In the introduction to the reprinted edition of Mathewson, Donald Roy, a sociologist known for his own worker participant observations of restriction in a machine shop, relates a story from his own experience [1952]. A machine crew were discontent because of what they considered an unfair ratio between wages and profits. A laminating machine in this factory apparently had extremely odd performance: it would operate perfectly for a long time and then go mysteriously awry. Sheets of heavy paper in the process of lamination would suddenly tear and stick to the machine's rollers, necessitating difficult and sticky work to unwrap the material. The crew operating the machine was putting too much stress on it, causing the paper to tear and stick. Despite the necessity of cleaning the rollers (an unpleasant job relative to tending the working machine) they considered this operation worthwhile to redress their grievances [Roy, 1969, p. xxiv]. The preceding story illustrates that workers reduce their effective labor power if they feel they are getting less than they deserve. It also indicates that they may feel that they deserve a wage higher than that required to induce them to be physically present at their jobs; further, the remuneration of dissimilar agents—in this case the profit earners— enters their calculation of their fair wage.

Studies by Mathewson and Roy are examples of the work of the human relations school of organization. According to this school of thought, workers have considerable control over their own effort and output. This ability of workers to exercise control over their effort, and their willingness to do so in response to grievances, underlies the fair wage–effort hypothesis.

A recent report in *The New York Times* [Salpukas, 1987] concerns the problems generated by two-tier wage systems. Despite the considerable savings in labor costs, many of the companies that adopted such systems are now phasing them out due to the resentment of employees on the job as well as the high turnover generated by the low wages. These wage systems have 'produced a resentful class of workers who in some cases are taking their hostility out on customers' [Salpukas, 1987, p. 1]:

'The attitude on the airplane can be a big problem,' said Pat A. Gibbs, the head of the Association of Professional Flight Attendants, which represents the attendants at American [Airlines]. 'You can tell that the anger is there.' Robert L. Crandall, American's chairman and chief executive, acknowledged in a recent speech that quality of service has suffered because of the pressures that deregulation has brought to cut labor costs.

The lower-paid workers often do just what is required and no more, and sometimes refuse to help the higher-paid workers.... 'Having people work side by side for different pay is difficult' said Mr. Olson of Giant Foods. About half of the supermarket chain's workers are in the lower pay tier [Salpukas, 1987, p. D22].

E. *Literature, Jealousy, and Retribution*

Jealousy and retribution, the relation between equity and performance, are not recent discoveries of psychologists and sociologists: they are part of everyone's experience. Literature offers many excellent examples, such as the story of Joseph [*Bible*, Genesis, 37–50]. Joseph's father, Jacob, loved him more than all his children and made him a coat of many colors. When Joseph's brothers saw that their father loved him most of all, they hated him. One day when Joseph was in the countryside they threw him into a pit, from which he was fortuitously rescued and sold into slavery. When Jacob heard of Joseph's presumed death, he wept inconsolably. This sad story of Jacob, Joseph, and his brothers is an example of management failure made worse by inequitable rewards.

F. *Personnel Management Texts*

Textbooks on personnel management regard the need for equitable treatment of workers as obvious. By way of illustration Dessler [1984, p. 223] writes:

The need for equity is perhaps the most important factor in determining pay rates.... Externally, pay must compare favorably with those in other organizations or you'll find it hard to attract and retain qualified employees. *Pay rates must also be equitable internally in that each employee should view his or her pay as equitable given other employees' pay rates in the organization.* (Emphasis in last sentence added.)

Kochan and Barocci, who view equity as most important in 'experts'' opinions of compensation systems, quote approvingly from a War Labor Board project (by William H. Davis): 'There is no single factor in the whole field of labor relations that does more to break down morale, create individual dissatisfaction, encourage absenteeism, increase labor turnover and hamper production than obviously unjust inequalities in the wage rates paid to different individuals in the same labor group within the same plant' [Kochan and Barocci, 1985, p. 249].

Carroll and Tosi [1977, p. 303] write: 'Pay satisfaction is influenced by what an individual gets as compared to what he wants and considers fair. The fairness of pay (perceived equity of pay) is determined largely by an individual's comparison of himself and his pay to other reference persons and theirs [sic].'

G. *Wage-Salary Secrecy*

Most employees do not openly discuss their wages and salaries except with close friends. Organizations often have a policy of secrecy in regard to wages and salaries. These practices of silence and secrecy are evidence that others' pay is not a matter of indifference to most workers. Personnel textbooks recommend openness about compensation schedules (e.g., Henderson [1982], pp. 444–46) but also caution at the same time the need for an active program to explain wage and salary payments. The need for such a program is another indication of the common concern about others' pay.

Explaining the equity of a compensation system may not be easy. Most workers believe that remuneration should be according to performance (see Dyer, Schwab, and Theriault [1976] for a survey of managers which documents this belief). However, most workers view their own performance as superior. In four separate surveys taken by Meyer [1975], between 68 percent and 86 percent of workers considered their own performance in the top quartile. In the model of Section IV there is wage compression: wages have less dispersion than their market-clearing levels. Such low dispersion may be partly attributed to workers' positively biased estimation of their own performance: if pay accorded with performance, workers would view the scale as inequitable.

H. *Wage Patterns*

The models in Section IV predict wage patterns that are consistent with empirical findings. These findings constitute additional evidence in favor of our model.

Many studies have documented consistent wage differentials across industries. Slichter [1950] found a correlation between the wages of skilled and unskilled workers by industry. Dickens and Katz [1986], with a far more detailed classification of occupation than skilled and unskilled, find similar correlations across industries; those industries which have high wages for one occupation also have high wages for other occupations. Krueger and Summers [1988] find industry wage differentials in longitudinal regressions controlling for individual characteristics; this suggests that such differentials are not just due to unobserved differences in labor quality. When a given worker moves from one industry to another his or her wage tends to change according to the industry wage differentials. Krueger and Summers show that these industry wage differentials also appear when adjustments have been made for the quality of employment, suggesting that differentials persist above and beyond what can be explained by compensating wage differentials. While no evidence will ever be totally definitive, since each individual has special characteristics and since each job has its own peculiar attributes, these findings clearly point to the existence of different wage scales across industries.

What explains the phenomenon of industry-wide wage differentials? The explanation offered in this paper is based on fair wages. If firms must pay a high wage to some groups of workers—perhaps because they are in short supply or perhaps to obtain high quality—demands for pay equity will raise the general wage scale for other labor in the firm, who would otherwise see their pay as unfair. Frank [1984] has also documented compression of wages relative to skills. Although he has another interpretation (due to status considerations), his data are consistent with the fair wage–effort hypothesis.

Lazear [1986] and Milgrom and Roberts [1987] have proposed interesting alternative explanations for wage compression. A wage scale with high dispersion gives employees incentives to withhold information from managers in order to increase their influence [Milgrom and Roberts] or to undermine the reputations of other workers [Lazear]. But fair wage–effort models offer better explanations for wage compression among occupations between which there is low mobility, as found by Slichter and Dickens and Katz. If a secretary has no expectation of becoming a manager, the Lazear–Milgrom-Roberts models would not predict compression of the manager-secretary wage differential.

The behavior of union-nonunion wage differentials is also consistent with the fair wage–effort hypothesis. According to Freeman and Medoff [1984], when plants are unionized, white-collar workers receive boosts in fringe benefits, although their wages do not increase significantly. In 1982 when General Motors negotiated wage concessions with its union employees and thereafter announced bonuses for its executives, the loss of morale amid the ensuing uproar forced a retraction of the proposed bonuses. GM and the UAW subsequently negotiated an 'equality of sacrifice' agreement that required white-collar and blue-collar workers to share equally in reductions or increases in pay.[7]

---

[7] See Freeman and Medoff [1984].

Table 17.1 *Unemployment and skill*

Unemployment rates by occupation, April 1987[a]	
Managerial and professional specialty	2.1
Technical, sales, and administrative support	4.3
Service occupations	7.6
Precision production, craft, and repair	6.5
Operators, fabricators, and laborers	9.8
Unemployment rates by education, 1985[b]	
Less than 5 years	11.3
5 to 8 years	13.0
1 to 3 years of high school	15.9
4 years of high school	8.0
1 to 3 years of college	5.1
4 years or more of college	2.6

[a] *Source*: U. S. Department of Labor, *Employment and Earnings*, 34 (May 1987), p. 21, Table A-12.
[b] *Source*: Summers [1986], Table 4, p. 350.

I. *Patterns of Unemployment*

As a general rule, unemployment is lower for occupations with higher pay and for workers with greater education and skill. These facts are illustrated in Table 17.1.[8] Most efficiency wage models offer no natural explanation for these unemployment-skill correlations. Skilled work is probably more difficult to monitor than unskilled work. Worker-discipline models (in the style of Bowles [1985], Foster and Wan [1984], Shapiro and Stiglitz [1984], and Stoft [1982]) would thus predict higher unemployment for skilled than for unskilled labor, unless shirking yields significantly greater utility to unskilled than to skilled workers. In contrast, the fair wage–effort model provides a potential explanation of these correlations.

III. A RUDIMENTARY MODEL OF UNEMPLOYMENT WITH THE FAIR WAGE–EFFORT HYPOTHESIS

A. *The Model*

This section presents the simplest model of unemployment embodying the fair wage–effort hypothesis. It is assumed that there is a single class of labor with an exogenously determined fair wage w^*. The assumption that the fair wage is exogenous will be relaxed in Section IV. The effort e of a given type of labor, according to the fair wage–effort hypothesis, is (equation (1), repeated here):

[8] Also see Reder [1964].

$$e = \min(w/w^*, 1), \tag{1}$$

where w is the wage paid and w^* is the exogenously determined fair wage. If the worker receives more than the fair wage, he contributes full effort of 1. If the worker receives less than the fair wage, he reduces effort proportionately (to maintain the balance between inputs and outcomes).

There are a large number of identical firms, so that the product market is perfectly competitive. The production function is of the form

$$Q = \alpha eL, \tag{2}$$

where Q is output, e is average effort of laborers hired, and L is the labor hired.

Finally, there is a fixed supply of labor, $\bar{L}$, which will work independent of the wage rate.

B. *Equilibrium*

In the competitive equilibrium of this model, the unemployment rate is either unity, with no labor hired, if α is less than w^*, or zero, with all labor hired at the wage α, if α exceeds w^*. This occurs because, under the fair wage–effort hypothesis, the marginal cost to the firm of a unit of effective labor is at least as large as w^*, whereas the marginal product of a unit of effective labor is α.

The quantity of effective labor input is the product of e, the average effort of the workforce, and L, the number of workers hired. From the production function, the marginal product of a unit of effective labor is a constant, α. The marginal cost of a unit of effective labor to the firm is w/e—the wage per unit of effort. According to the fair wage–effort hypothesis, (1), this marginal cost is w^* for all wages less than or equal to w^*, and w for wages in excess of w^*. The firm's demand for labor depends on the relationship between the marginal cost and marginal product of effective labor. There are two cases.

Case I: $\alpha < w^*$. If $\alpha < w^*$, the marginal cost of effective labor is at least as large as w^*, regardless of the wage paid by the firm. Since the marginal cost of effective labor exceeds its marginal product, the firm cannot operate profitably. In this case, the demand for labor is zero, and the unemployment rate is unity.

Case II: $\alpha > w^*$. If the aggregate supply of labor exceeds the aggregate demand for labor so that there is unemployment, the firm is free to set its wage at any level. It will choose the wage that minimizes w/e, the marginal cost of effective labor.[9] If the firm chooses to pay any wage between zero and w^*, the marginal cost of effective labor is w^*. Since the marginal cost of effective labor is lower than labor's marginal product, α, every firm should hire an infinite amount of labor, resulting in aggregate excess demand for

---

[9] According to the fair wage–effort hypothesis, this wage is not unique. Any wage between zero and w^* results in the same effective cost of labor—w^*. Later, we shall assume that in cases of indifference, the firm chooses to pay the fair wage, w^*.

labor. Under these circumstances, competition for workers will force firms to pay wages in excess of w^*. The demand for labor will also be infinite for any wage between w^* and α, since the marginal product of a unit of effective labor continues to exceed its marginal cost. In contrast, if the wage paid exceeds α, marginal cost exceeds the marginal product of effective labor, and the demand for labor is zero. Since the demand for labor is infinitely elastic at the wage $w = \alpha$, equilibrium is characterized by full employment with all firms paying the 'market-clearing' wage, $w = \alpha$.

C. *Discussion*

This rudimentary model describes an equilibrium in which employment and the distribution of income are partially determined by the usual economic fundamentals of tastes, technology, and endowments. But in the unemployment case, conceptions of fairness, embodied in the parameter w^*, also affect the equilibrium. In a trivial sense w^* could be said to reflect tastes; insofar as $w < w^*$, workers prefer to provide proportionately lower effort; but this is not the conventional use of the word tastes. We have assumed that workers reduce effort, not because they are better off doing so in any objective sense, but rather because they are mad. People who are mad (in the American use of the term as well as in the English use of the term) are likely to engage in acts that do not maximize their utility.

Because the model is so very simple and completely linear, the unemployment rate is either zero or one. There are many natural remedies for this. If the production function has diminishing returns, the equilibrium unemployment rate could lie between zero and one. If there are different classes of labor, each with its own value of α and w^*, those laborers with $\alpha > w^*$ will be employed, and those with $\alpha < w^*$ will be unemployed. For each class of labor the unemployment rate would be zero or one, but the aggregate unemployment rate would lie between zero and one. If w^* depends monotonically on the unemployment rate, with w^* (0) being infinity and w^* (1) being zero, there will also be an equilibrium unemployment rate between zero and one. Such a dependence makes sense. At high unemployment rates people may be grateful to be employed so they consider the fair wage low; at low unemployment rates they are unlikely to consider themselves lucky to be employed, and so the fair wage may be high.

Many assumptions in the preceding model call for generalization. For example, w^* should be endogenized. w^* may depend on the wages of other workers who are salient in the worker's life, the profits accruing to the firm's owners,[10] or the worker's past wage history. The production function may be nonlinear; labor of different types may be complements or substitutes; and effort may not enter the production function multiplicatively. The next section explores the consequences of several such complications.

---

[10] The introduction of profits as a determinant of the fair wage explains the finding of Dickens and Katz [1987] and Krueger and Summers [1987] that industry wage premiums are correlated with industry concentration and profitability. It also provides an additional reason, based on fairness, why the premiums paid to different occupations within an industry are positively correlated.

IV. A RELATIVE DEPRIVATION MODEL OF THE FAIR WAGE

This section develops a model with two labor groups, both of which behave according to the fair wage–effort hypothesis. Various outcomes are possible. In one type of equilibrium all firms hire both kinds of labor. In this case, the group with the lower wage experiences some unemployment, while the group with the higher wage rate is fully employed. Thus, skill, as endogenously defined by earnings, and unemployment are negatively correlated. Equilibria are also possible in which there is a primary and a secondary labor market. Low-skill workers in such an equilibrium experience no unemployment, but there is a wage differential between jobs in the two sectors, and primary sector jobs are rationed. Although not explicitly modeled, wait unemployment could naturally occur. Finally, equilibria also occur in which the two types of labor do not work together. Such equilibria are inefficient.[11]

A. *Assumptions*

The key behavioral assumptions concern *endowments, tastes, technology,* and *fairness*.

Endowments. The total supply of labor of types 1 and 2 are $\bar{L}_1$ and $\bar{L}_2$, respectively.

Tastes. Each worker supplies his or her total labor endowment to the market.

Technology and Market Structure. There are a fixed number of identical, perfectly competitive firms. Each firm has a neoclassical production function F, which is adequately approximated by a quadratic form in the effective labor power of the two types of labor:

$$F = A_0 + A_1(e_1 L_1) + A_2(e_2 L_2) - A_{11}(e_1 L_1)^2 + A_{12}(e_1 L_1)(e_2 L_2) - A_{22}(e_2 L_2)^2, \qquad (3)$$

where L_1 and L_2 are the labor inputs of types 1 and 2 and e_1 and e_2 are their respective levels of effort.[12]

Fairness. The key assumptions of the model concern fairness. In this regard there are three assumptions. The first is the fair wage–effort hypothesis. The second defines the fair wage in a natural way. And the third says that in cases of indifference to profits firms choose to pay fair wages.

(i) *The fair wage–effort hypothesis.* According to the fair wage–effort hypothesis,

$$e_1 = \min(w_1/w_1^*, 1); \qquad (4)$$

$$e_2 = \min(w_2/w_2^*, 1). \qquad (5)$$

---

[11] Romer [1984] has considered a model with heterogeneous productivities and a common just wage and has reached similar conclusions.

[12] We assume that A_1, A_2, A_{11}, and A_{22} are positive. A_{12} may be positive, in which case the two labor types are termed complements, or A_{12} may be negative, in which case the labor types are termed substitutes.

(ii) *Fair wages: determination of* w^*. In the introductory section we motivated the idea of the reference wage. We shall assume here that one determinant of the fair wage w^* is the wage received by other members of the same firm. Thus, the fair wage of group 2 depends on the wages received by group 1, and symmetrically, the fair wage of group 1 depends on the wages received by group 2.

We also assume that market conditions influence fair wages. Workers in low demand, all else equal, view their fair wage as lower than workers in high demand. While the study of lay theories of fairness by Kahneman, Knetsch, and Thaler [1986] shows that people's views of fairness do not correspond exactly to market clearing, it clearly reveals that market forces have some impact on the prices and wages that people consider fair. Accordingly, we shall here assume that a second determinant of w^* is the market-clearing wage.

Combining the two arguments, we posit that the fair wage w^* of a group is a weighted average of the wage received by the reference group and the market-clearing wage.[13] Accordingly, we write

$$w_1^* = \beta w_2 + (1 - \beta)w_1^c \tag{6}$$

$$w_2^* = \beta w_1 + (1 - \beta)w_2^c, \tag{7}$$

where w_1^c and w_2^c are the 'market-clearing wages' of groups 1 and 2, respectively.

We define the market-clearing wages, w_1^c and w_2^c, as those wages that would clear the market for labor of a given type in a simple neoclassical economy where workers exert full effort regardless of the wage they are paid. Fixing $e_1 = e_2 = 1$, the quadratic production function (3) yields labor demand functions of the simple form,[14]

$$L_1 = a_1 - b_1 w_1 + c_1 w_2 \tag{8}$$

$$L_2 = a_2 + b_2 w_1 - c_2 w_2. \tag{9}$$

We assume that 'own' wage effects are stronger than 'cross' wage effects so that $b_1 > c_1$ and $c_2 > b_2$.[15]

The *Marshallian* definition of the market-clearing wage would be

$$w_1^c = w_1 - (\bar{L}_1 - L_1)/b_1; \tag{10}$$

---

[13] Alternatively, we could assume that the fair wage depends inversely on the unemployment rate of the group. This assumption yields similar results.

[14] In terms of the parameters of the production function F:

$$a_1 = (A_2 A_{12} + 2A_1 A_{22})/\blacktriangle; \quad b_1 = (2A_{22})/\blacktriangle; \quad c_1 = -A_{12}/\blacktriangle;$$

$$a_2 = (A_1 A_{12} + 2A_2 A_{11})/\blacktriangle; \quad b_2 = -A_{12}/\blacktriangle; \quad c_2 = (2A_{11})/\blacktriangle,$$

$$where \blacktriangle = 4A_{11}A_{22} - A_{12}^2 > 0.$$

[15] In terms of the production function, this means that $2A_{22} + A_{12} > 0$ and $2A_{11} + A_{12} > 0$.

$$w_2^c = w_2 - (\bar{L}_2 - L_2)/c_2. \tag{11}$$

The Marshallian market-clearing wage is that wage which, with the other wage held constant, is just enough lower to induce the hiring of the total labor supply of $\bar{L}_1$ or $\bar{L}_2$, respectively.[16] In contrast, we define the *Walrasian* market-clearing wages as those that *jointly* clear both markets.[17]

In summary, the fair wages of types 1 and 2 labor are weighted averages of the wages of the other labor group and its respective Marshallian market-clearing wage ((6) and (7)).

(iii) *Fair Wages Paid When Indifferent.* Finally, we assume that firms have some small preference for paying fair wages. As a result, when their profits are unaffected by payment of fair wages, they prefer to do so.

This model possesses three classes of equilibria. In one type of equilibrium, which is emphasized in the discussion below, all firms hire both types of workers, and some 'low-pay' workers are unemployed. We call this the *integrated* equilibrium, since both types of labor work for all firms. In addition, *segregated* equilibria may occur. In *partially segregated* equilibrium some firms hire only low-pay workers, while other firms hire labor of both types. Such an equilibrium has no unemployment, but there are wage differentials for low-pay labor between primary sector (integrated) firms and secondary sector (segregated) firms. In an augmented model such pay differentials could result in 'wait' unemployment as workers queue for the better paying jobs. In *fully segregated* equilibrium some firms hire only low-pay workers, while other firms hire only high-pay workers. Both classes of workers are fully employed. Each of these equilibria will be described in turn.

B. *Integrated Equilibria*

An integrated equilibrium in this model is characterized by some unemployment for 'low-pay' workers and full employment for 'high-pay' workers. 'Low-(high-) pay' workers are endogenously defined as the labor group that receives lower (higher) pay in equilibrium. Low-pay workers receive their fair wage, which is in excess of market clearing. Their employment is determined by firms' demand at this wage. In contrast, 'high-pay' workers receive their market-clearing wage, which is in excess of their fair wage.[18] The structure of pay in equilibrium exhibits wage compression due to

---

[16] The reader may wish to note that payment of such a wage while keeping the other wage fixed implies disequilibrium in the other labor market. The Walrasian equilibrium concept of jointly market-clearing wages produces similar results.

[17] These wages satisfy the two demand conditions, equations (8) and (9), with $L_1 = \bar{L}_1$ and $L_2 = \bar{L}_2$.

[18] This assumes that the parameters of the model are such that the Walrasian 'market-clearing' wages of the two groups differ. In the singular case in which the Walrasian wages of the two groups are identical, there is no unemployment. In this special case equilibrium coincides exactly with the Walrasian equilibrium without considerations of fairness.

considerations of fairness; the higher is β, the lower is the wage differential. Integrated equilibria are likely to occur when there is significant complementarity in production between high- and low-pay workers. This characterization of the equilibrium is straightforward to justify.

First, *there cannot be an equilibrium in which both groups are fully employed and work at full effort* (except in the razor's edge case in which the Walrasian market-clearing wages of both groups are identical). In such an equilibrium both labor groups would receive wages equal to their respective full employment marginal products.[19] Such an equilibrium cannot prevail, however, because workers with lower pay would consider their wage unfair; as a consequence, these workers would reduce effort below the normal level ($e = 1$). Such a reduction in effort raises the marginal cost of effective labor; in equilibrium, 'low-pay' workers experience unemployment because the marginal cost of effective labor of this type exceeds their marginal product.

Second, *equilibrium cannot be characterized by unemployment for the more highly paid group.* Suppose that the more highly paid group experiences unemployment. The firm could unambiguously profit from cutting the wage of these workers. Since workers consider it fair to receive lower pay than the other labor group if they are unemployed, the more highly paid workers must be earning a wage in excess of their fair wage. This group accordingly works at full effort ($e = 1$), and the marginal cost of effective labor services (w/e) for this labor type is equal to the wage w. Now consider the consequences of a cut in the pay of this group. The marginal cost of effective labor (w/e) for this group declines. In addition, this wage cut lowers the pay that the other labor group deems fair, potentially raising the effort that these 'coworkers' supply, and lowering the marginal cost of *their* services to the firm as well.

Third, *the 'low wage' group is paid its fair wage in equilibrium.* Since low-wage workers experience unemployment, firms can set their wage to minimize the effective cost of their labor services. This is the appropriate objective for profit-maximizing firms because the wage that is paid to low-wage workers has no spillover effect on the marginal cost of effective labor services of high-wage workers. High-wage workers are paid in excess of their fair wage and work at full effort. The marginal cost of 'high-wage' labor services is thus equal to the (high) wage irrespective of the wage paid to low-wage workers. The cost of an effective unit of labor from the 'low-wage' group is $w^* = w/e$ if the firm pays any wage between zero and w^* and w if the firm pays in excess of w^*. The 'cost-minimizing' wage is nonunique, with the firm's minimum cost of effective labor for the 'low-wage' group being w^*. It can achieve minimum cost per effective labor unit by paying any wage between zero and w^*. We have assumed that when profits are unaffected by the firm's wage choice, it will prefer to pay the fair wage. If this assumption is relaxed, there can be 'work sharing' equilibria in which a larger number of workers receive less than fair wages and work at less than full efficiency. The equilibrium utilization of 'effective' labor services from 'low-wage' workers will,

---

[19] With all workers operating at full effort, the firm's demand for labor would be determined by the labor demand functions (8) and (9). The equilibrium wage rates would be determined by the 'market-clearing' condition that the demand and supply be equal for labor of each type.

however, be identical whether firms pay fair or unfair wages. There could also be equilibria in which different firms pay different wages between zero and w^* to 'low-wage' workers.

Fourth, *the 'high-wage' group is paid its market-clearing wage in equilibrium.* One might imagine that considerations of fairness could lead to equilibria with shortages of skilled labor, with such 'high-wage' workers receiving less than the market-clearing wage; however, such equilibria are not possible in our model due to the assumption of perfectly competitive labor markets. In a situation of skilled labor shortage, any individual firm unable to hire its desired level of skilled labor could raise profits by paying an infinitesimally higher wage than its competitors. Such an increase in wages, however small, would allow this firm to hire as much skilled labor as it wished, thereby increasing profits noninfinitesimally. Profits would increase even if higher wages paid to skilled workers necessitate raising the pay of low-skill workers to maintain fairness.

In order to compute the wages of high and low paid workers and the unemployment rate of low paid workers in equilibrium, it is necessary to identify the 'high-pay' group. It follows from the propositions above that the 'high-pay' or 'skilled' group is the group that would receive higher pay in the corresponding Walrasian equilibrium without fairness effects on efficiency. In the discussion that follows we assume that group 1 is the 'high-wage' *skilled* group and group 2 the 'low-wage' *unskilled* group. The equilibrium values of w_1 and w_2 and the aggregate employment of the unskilled labor group 2 are determined by three equilibrium conditions:

$$w_2 = w_2^* = w_1 - ((1 - \beta)/\beta c_2)(\bar{L}_2 - L_2) \tag{12a}$$

$$L_2 = a_2 + b_2 w_1 - c_2 w_2 \tag{12b}$$

$$w_1 = ((a_1 - \bar{L}_1)/b_1) + (c_1 w_2/b_1). \tag{12c}$$

According to (12a), the wage of unskilled workers is their fair wage as defined by (7) and (11). For the profit-maximizing firm, workers should be hired to the point where the marginal product of effective labor is equal to its marginal cost. Accordingly, (12b) gives the demand for unskilled workers. Since these workers work at full effort, this is given by the labor demand function (9).[20] Similarly, equation (8) describes the demand for skilled workers. Equation (12c) shows the equilibrium wage of skilled workers, w_1, which equates the demand for these workers, given by (8), with their supply.

The equilibrium is portrayed graphically in Figure 17.1. The downward sloping line in Figure 17.1 shows how the demand for unskilled labor, given by (12b), varies as w_2 changes, when w_1 adjusts endogenously according to (12c) to maintain full employment for skilled labor. That is, this 'labor demand' schedule is a partial 'reduced form' of (12b) and (12c). The upward sloping line in Figure 17.1 is the 'fair wage constraint' or 'labor supply' schedule for unskilled labor. This curve is analogous to the 'no shirking constraint' described by Shapiro and Stiglitz [1984]. It shows how the fair (= actual)

---

[20] We ignore the possibility that (12b) may not be satisfied with equality for any positive value of L_2, in which case there is a corner solution with $L_2 = 0$.

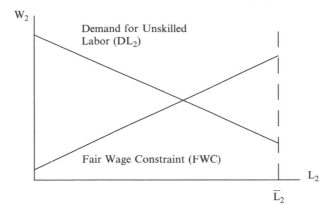

Figure 17.1.

wage of unskilled workers varies as their employment changes when w_1 again adjusts endogenously according to (12c) to maintain full employment for skilled labor. The 'fair wage constraint' is a partial reduced form of (12a) and (12c) and is upward sloping because unskilled workers deem it fair to earn more as their employment rate rises or their unemployment rate falls. The slope of this constraint depends critically on β, which is the weight that workers attach to peer comparisons as opposed to market-clearing wages in determining fair wage norms. In the extreme case in which $\beta = 1$, the fair wage constraint is horizontal, and the fair (= actual) wage paid to unskilled workers is equal to w_1 and independent of the unskilled unemployment rate. In contrast, if $\beta = 0$, so that workers deem it fair to earn the market-clearing wage, the fair wage constraint is vertical at $\bar{L}_2$.

C. *Comparative Statics: Labor Supply and Productivity Shocks*

The system—(12a), (12b), and (12c)—generates predictions concerning the compara-tive static effects of labor supply and productivity shocks on wages and unemployment. We characterize a productivity shock by a uniform shift in the marginal productivity of type 1 or 2 labor, parameterized as a change in A_1 or A_2 in the production function (3). The complete comparative statics of the model are summarized in Table 17.2. The most interesting results concern the impact of various shocks on unskilled unemployment. Movements in unskilled unemployment in this model hinge on the shock's impact on the Walrasian equilibrium differential between skilled and unskilled wages. Shocks that raise the Walrasian wage differential are 'resisted' by unskilled workers and thus cause higher unemployment, while shocks that reduce the Walrasian differential between skilled and unskilled wages permit unskilled unemployment to fall.

An increase in the supply of skilled labor *unambiguously* lowers the unemployment of unskilled workers because it reduces the Walrasian wage differential between skilled and unskilled wages. Unskilled employment rises even in the case where skilled and unskilled labor are substitutes; in this instance, the increase in skilled labor supply

Table 17.2 *Comparatative Static Effects of Labor Supply and Productivity Shocks*

	Effect on:		
Change in:	w_1	w_2	L_2
$\bar{L}_1$	< 0	$\gtreqless 0$ if $\left[1 + \frac{b_2(1-\beta)}{c_2\beta}\right] \lesseqgtr 0$	> 0
$\bar{L}_2$	$\lesseqgtr 0$ if $A_{12} \gtreqless 0$	< 0	$0 < \frac{dL_2}{d\bar{L}_2} < 1$
$\bar{A}_1$	> 0	> 0	< 0
$\bar{A}_2$	$\lesseqgtr 0$ if $A_{12} \gtreqless 0$	$\lesseqgtr 0$ if $\frac{(1-\beta)}{\beta c_2}(b_1 c_2 - b_2 c_1) - c_1 \gtreqless 0$	> 0
$\bar{A}_1 \text{ and } \bar{A}_2 (d\bar{A}_1 = d\bar{A}_2)$	> 0	> 0	0

produces a downward shift in the demand for unskilled labor, as depicted in Figure 17.2. Nevertheless, the employment of unskilled workers rises because the 'fair wage constraint' shifts down by even more. The wage deemed fair by unskilled workers falls by an amount that is equal to the wage cut suffered by skilled workers.

As might be expected, an increase in the supply of unskilled labor leads to an increase in unskilled unemployment. Graphically, this shock shifts the fair wage constraint to the right by the amount of the increase in unskilled labor. An increase in the size of a labor force group is commonly believed to result in increases in the unemployment rate of that group. Our model is thus consistent with the observation that the unemployment of teen-agers and highly educated people has increased as these groups have increased their share of the labor force.

A simple way of parameterizing productivity shocks is by a uniform shift in the respective marginal products of the two types of labor. In terms of the production

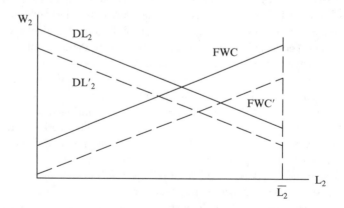

Figure 17.2.

function (3), this corresponds to changes in A_1 and A_2, respectively.[21] Such an increase in the productivity of skilled labor raises the Walrasian wage differential: the Walrasian equilibrium wage of skilled labor rises, and the Walrasian equilibrium wage of unskilled workers remains unchanged. The consequence is an increase in unemployment of unskilled workers who 'resist' any widening of the wage differential. Graphically, this shock leaves the demand for unskilled workers unchanged but shifts the fair wage constraint up; unskilled workers consider it fair to receive higher wages when skilled workers receive pay hikes. According to this model, productivity increases of skilled workers produce an uneven pattern of gains. Both skilled and unskilled workers achieve wage gains; but unskilled workers experience an increase in unemployment.

An increase in the productivity of unskilled labor (an increase in A_2) lowers the Walrasian differential between skilled and unskilled wages, and causes an unambiguous reduction in unskilled unemployment.

The model can also be used to analyze the impact of a simultaneous increase in the productivity of skilled and unskilled labor, as might occur if education levels rise across the board. While increases in A_2 lead to a reduction in unskilled unemployment, increases in A_1 have the opposite effect. Our model provides one possible explanation of why unemployment rates in the United States have not fallen in the face of a general increase in education. Summers [1986, p. 348] has calculated that with constant education-specific unemployment rates, increases in education between 1965 and 1985 should have caused a 2.1 percent reduction in unemployment. In our model, as people upgrade their own skill through increased education, they decrease their own probability of unemployment but increase the probability of unemployment of those with less skill. An across-the-board increase in education consequently may not decrease aggregate unemployment. Indeed, in our model an equal increase in the productivity of skilled and unskilled labor leaves unemployment absolutely unchanged.

The discussion above assumes that the equilibrium of the system is symmetric and integrated, with all firms behaving identically and hiring both types of labor. Asymmetric equilibria are also possible, however, in which firms pursue different hiring strategies but earn identical profits. The system consisting of equations (12a), (12b, and (12c), describes an equilibrium only if two further conditions are satisfied. First, no firm can profitably switch from hiring both types of labor to hiring only low paid labor. Second, firms that hire high-pay workers must also find it optimal to hire some low-pay workers. If the first condition is violated, equilibrium, if it exists, will be asymmetric and segregated: some firms will hire *only* low-pay workers. Two types of segregated equilibria—partially and fully segregated—are possible. We shall discuss these in turn.

D. *Partially Segregated Equilibria*

Partially segregated equilibrium may occur because, even if the three key equilibrium conditions in equation (12) are satisfied, a firm adopting a 'deviant' strategy may earn

---

[21] Other possible parameterizations of productivity shocks, such as labor-augmenting neutral changes that alter the effective labor power of a given labor type in the production function (3), lead to less clearcut results.

higher profits. Deviant firms would take advantage of the availability of low-pay, unemployed labor who are willing to work at their reservation wage. In our model, with a vertical labor supply schedule, this wage is zero. Deviant firms hiring only low-pay workers need not be concerned with fairness. The condition under which such deviation is profitable is conceptually simple: starting from a potential equilibrium satisfying (12), a firm hiring only low-pay labor at a zero wage must make greater profit than the firm that hires both types of labor at the fair wage equilibrium. The condition for profitable deviation can easily be described in terms of producer surplus: if the surplus achieved by a firm hiring both types of labor at the integrated equilibrium exceeds the surplus of a firm hiring only low-pay workers at their reservation wage, then no deviation is profitable. A deviant strategy will *not* be profitable if high- and low-pay labor are sufficiently complementary in production. A deviant strategy will *always* be profitable if the two types of labor are perfect substitutes in production.

If deviation is profitable, then exit by deviants would occur. As deviant firms are established, unemployment of low-pay workers is eliminated, and the wage of low-pay workers in segregated firms is bid up to the point where segregated and integrated firms earn identical profits. A partially segregated equilibrium, provided that it exists, has the following properties: high-pay workers are fully employed at integrated firms; low-pay workers are fully employed but divided between integrated and segregated firms; integrated and segregated firms earn identical profits; 'low-pay' workers earn more at integrated than at segregated firms. The equilibrium corresponds to standard descriptions of the dual labor market; jobs for 'low-skill' workers occur in both a primary and secondary sector. Good jobs for low-skill workers in the primary sector are rationed. If pay disparities cause 'wait' unemployment as workers queue for jobs in the primary sector[22] (a simple modification of our model), then the partially segregated equilibrium would also exhibit unemployment.

E. *Fully Segregated Equilibria*

The profitable entry of deviant firms, which destroys the potential equilibrium satisfying (12), may lead to an interesting 'corner' solution. The fair wage of low-skill workers depends inversely on their unemployment. As deviant firms hire low-pay workers, their unemployment falls, and the fair wage rises.[23] In consequence, integrated firms will reduce their employment of low-pay workers. This process may lead to equilibrium at a corner in which firms with high-pay labor are unwilling to hire *any* low-pay workers at their fair wage. If the two types of labor are perfect substitutes in production, only fully segregated equilibria can occur. Firms hiring high-pay workers are unwilling to hire any low-pay workers, since the marginal product of the first unit of low-pay labor at such firms is less than the fair wage of low-pay workers. Firms hiring low-pay workers are similarly unwilling to hire any high-pay workers. In the absence of integration in the

---

[22] See, for example, Hall [1975].

[23] In a more complicated model the fair wage would also depend on the wage differential between the two sectors.

workplace, low-pay workers work at full effort since considerations of fairness do not apply. The introduction of any high-pay workers into a segregated low-pay workplace potentially causes a significant reduction in effort by the low-pay workforce as considerations of fairness become relevant to their effort on the job.

The fully segregated equilibrium has full employment of both types of labor with no wage differentials, full effort, and market-clearing wages for each group of labor. Still, fairness significantly affects the allocation of resources and efficiency in production, except in the limiting case in which both types of labor are perfect substitutes. In a fully segregated equilibrium considerations of fairness prevent firms from combining labor in the production process, even though it is almost always efficient to do so.

VI. CONCLUSION

This paper has presented a theory whereby effort depends on the relation between fair and actual wages. This framework easily generates involuntary unemployment and rationalizes wage compression. The theory conforms to common sense, and also to sociological and psychological theory and observation.

Like all real efficiency wage models, the equilibrium of our model exhibits neutrality: if all exogenous nominal variables change proportionately, then all endogenous nominal variables also change in proportion; and real variables such as the unemployment rate remain unchanged. As a consequence, this model might be regarded as irrelevant to an explanation of cyclical fluctuations in unemployment. Plausibly, however, the level of nominal wages perceived to be fair does not rapidly change in proportion to shifts in nominal aggregate demand. In this instance, our model predicts that aggregate demand shocks will produce cyclical variations in unemployment, thus yielding demand-generated business cycles.

University of California, Berkeley

References

Adams, J. Stacy, 'Toward an Understanding of Inequity,' *Journal of Abnormal and Social Psychology*, LXVII (November 1963), 422–36.

Akerlof, George A., and Janet L. Yellen, 'Introduction,' in George A. Akerlof and Janet L. Yellen, eds., *Efficiency Wage Models of the Labor Market* (Cambridge, England: Cambridge University Press, 1986).

——, and ——, 'Fairness and Unemployment,' *American Economic Review, Papers and Proceedings*, LXXVIII (May 1988), 44–49.

The Holy Bible: King James Version (New York: New American Library, 1974).

Blau, Peter M., *The Dynamics of Bureaucracy: A Study of Interpersonal Relations in Two Government Agencies* (Chicago: Chicago University Press, 1955).

Bowles, Samuel, 'The Production Process in a Competitive Economy: Walrasian, Neo-Hobbesian and Marxian Models,' *American Economic Review*, LXXV (March 1985), 16–36.

Carroll, Stephen J., and Henry L. Tosi, *Organizational Behavior* (Chicago: St. Clair Press, 1977).

Dessler, Gary, *Personnel Management*, 3rd edn. (Reston, VA: Reston Publishing Co., 1984).

Dickens, William T., and Lawrence F. Katz, 'Interindustry Wage Differences and Industry Characteristics,' in Kevin Lang and Jonathan S. Leonard, eds., *Unemployment and the Structure of Labor Markets* (New York: Basil Blackwell, 1987), pp. 48–89.

——, and ——, 'Industry Wage Patterns and Theories of Wage Determination,' mimeo, University of California, 1986.

Dyer, Lee, Donald P. Schwab, and Roland D. Theriault, 'Managerial Perceptions Regarding Salary Increase Criteria,' *Personnel Psychology*, XXIX (Summer 1976), 233–42.

Foster, James E., and Henry Y. Wan, Jr., 'Involuntary Unemployment as a Principal-Agent Equilibrium,' *American Economic Review*, LXXIV (June 1984), 476–84.

Frank, Robert H., 'Are Workers Paid Their Marginal Products?,' *American Economic Review*, LXXIV (September 1984), 549–71.

Freeman, Richard B., and James L. Medoff, *What Do Unions Do?* (New York: Basic Books, 1984).

Goodman, Paul S., and Abraham Friedman, 'An Examination of Adams' Theory of Inequity,' *Administrative Science Quarterly*, XVI (September 1971), 271–88.

Hall, Robert E., 'The Rigidity of Wages and the Persistence of Unemployment,' *Brookings Papers on Economic Activity* (1975:2), 301–35.

Henderson, Richard I., *Compensation Management: Rewarding Performance*, 3rd edn. (Reston, VA: Reston Publishing Co., 1982).

Homans, George C., *Social Behavior: Its Elementary Forms* (New York: Harcourt Brace Jovanovich, 1961).

Kahneman, Daniel, Jack Knetsch, and Richard Thaler, 'Fairness as a Constraint on Profit Seeking: Entitlements in the Market,' *American Economic Review*, LXXVI (September 1986), 728–41.

Katz, Lawrence F., 'Efficiency Wage Theories: A Partial Evaluation,' in Stanley Fischer, ed., *NBER Macroeconomics Annual 1986* (Cambridge, MA: MIT Press, 1986).

Kochan, Thomas A., and Thomas A. Barocci, *Human Resource Management and Industrial Relations* (Boston: Little Brown, and Company, 1985).

Krueger, Alan B., and Lawrence H. Summers, 'Reflections on the Interindustry Wage Structure,' in Kevin Lang and Jonathan S. Leonard, eds., *Unemployment and the Structure of Labor Markets* (New York: Basil Blackwell, 1987), pp. 17–47.

——, and ——, 'Efficiency Wages and the Inter-Industry Wage Structure,' *Econometrica*, LVI (March 1988), 259–93.

Lawler, Edward E., and Paul W. O'Gara, 'The Effects of Inequity Produced by Underpayment on Work Output, Work Quality and Attitudes Toward the Work,' *Journal of Applied Psychology*, LI (October 1967), 403–10.

Lazear, Edward P., 'Pay Inequality and Industrial Politics,' Hoover Institution, Palo Alto, CA, mimeo, 1986.

Levine, David, 'Cohesiveness and the Inefficiency of the Market Solution,' *Journal of Economic Behavior and Organization* (1990), forthcoming.

Martin, Joanne, 'Relative Deprivation: A Theory of Distributive Injustice for an Era of Shrinking Resources,' in Larry L. Cummings and Barry M. Staw, eds., *Research in Organizational Behavior: An Annual Series of Analytical Essays and Critical Reviews*, volume 3 (Greenwich, CT: JAI Press, 1981).

Mathewson, Stanley B., *Restriction of Output Among Unorganized Workers*, 2nd edn. (Carbondale, IL: Southern Illinois University Press, 1969).

Meyer, Herbert, 'The Pay for Performance Dilemma,' *Organizational Dynamics*, III (Winter 1975), 39–50.

Milgrom, Paul, and John Roberts, 'Bargaining and Influence Costs and the Organization of Economic Activity,' Working Paper 8731, Department of Economics, University of California, Berkeley, 1987.

Pritchard, Robert D., Marvin D. Dunnette, and Dale O. Jorgenson, 'Effects of Perceptions of Equity and Inequity on Worker Performance and Satisfaction,' *Journal of Applied Psychology Monograph 56* (February 1972), 75–94.

Reder, Melvin W., 'Wage Structure and Structural Unemployment,' *Review of Economic Studies*, XXXI (October 1964), 309–22.

Romer, David, 'The Theory of Social Custom: A Modification and Some Extensions,' *Quarterly Journal of Economics*, IC (November 1984), 717–27.

Roy, Donald F., 'Quota Restriction and Goldbricking in a Machine Shop,' *American Journal of Sociology*, LVII (March 1952), 427–42.

——, 'Introduction to this Edition,' x–lii, in Stanley B. Mathewson, *Restriction of Output Among Unorganized Workers*, 2nd edn. (Carbondale, IL: University of Southern Illinois Press, 1969).

Salpukas, Agis, 'The 2-Tier Wage System is Found to be 2-Edged Sword by Industry,' *The New York Times*, CXXXVII (July 21, 1987), 1 and D22.

Schmitt, David R., and Gerald Marwell, 'Withdrawal and Reward Allocation as Responses to Inequity,' *Journal of Experimental Social Psychology*, VIII (May 1972), 207–21.

Shapiro, Carl, and Joseph E. Stiglitz, 'Equilibrium Unemployment as a Worker Discipline Device,' *American Economic Review*, LXXIV (June 1984), 433–44.

Slichter, Sumner, 'Notes on the Structure of Wages,' *Review of Economics and Statistics*, XXXII (February 1950), 80–91.

Stiglitz, Joseph E., 'The Causes and Consequences of the Dependence of Quality on Price,' *Journal of Economic Literature*, XXV (March 1987), 1–48.

Stoft, Steven, 'Cheat Threat Theory: An Explanation of Involuntary Unemployment,' mimeo, Boston University, May 1982.

Summers, Lawrence H., 'Why Is the Unemployment Rate So Very High Near Full Employment?' *Brookings Papers on Economic Activity* (1986: 2), 339–83.

——, 'Relative Wages, Efficiency Wages, and Keynesian Unemployment,' *American Economic Review, Papers and Proceedings*, LXXVIII (May 1988), 383–88.

Valenzi, Enzo R., and I. Robert Andrews, 'Effects of Hourly Overpay and Underpay Inequity When Tested with a New Induction Procedure,' *Journal of Applied Psychology*, LV (February 1971), 22–27.

Walster, Elaine, G. William Walster, and Ellen Berscheid, *Equity: Theory and Research* (Boston: Allyn and Bacon, 1977).

Yellen, Janet L., 'Efficiency Wage Models of Unemployment,' *American Economic Review*, LXXIV (May 1984), 200–05.

18

A Near-Rational Model of the Business Cycle, with Wage and Price Inertia*

GEORGE A. AKERLOF AND JANET L. YELLEN[†]

I. INTRODUCTION

This paper offers an explanation of why changes in the nominal supply of money are not neutral in the short run. It shows that aggregate demand shocks can cause significant changes in output and employment if agents adjust wages and prices in ways which are 'insignificantly' suboptimal from their individual standpoints. Alternatively, very small transaction costs of decision making or changing prices could account for large fluctuations in real economic activity.

The argument proceeds in six steps.

1. The property of nonneutrality is shown to be important for business cycle theory.
2. The concept of near-rationality is introduced. Near-rational behavior is nonmaximizing behavior in which the gains from maximizing rather than nonmaximizing are small in a well-defined sense.
3. It is argued that in a wide class of models—those models in which objective functions are differentiable with respect to agents' own wages or prices—the cost of inertial money wage and price behavior as opposed to maximizing behavior, is small when a long-run equilibrium with full maximization has been perturbed by a shock. If wages and prices were initially at an optimum, the loss from failure to adjust them will be smaller, by an order of magnitude, than the shock.

* This work was previously published as George A. Akerlof and Janet L. Yellen (1985), 'A Near-Rational Model of the Business Cycle, with Wage and Price Inertia', *The Quarterly Journal of Economics* C, Supplement. Copyright © The MIT Press. Reproduced by kind permission.
   † This is a revised version of Akerlof and Yellen [1983]. The authors would like to thank Andrew Abel, Alan Blinder, Richard Gilbert, Hajime Miyazaki, John Quigley, James Tobin, and James Wilcox for helpful conversations. The research for this paper was supported by National Science Foundation Grant No. SES 81-19150 administered by the Institute for Business and Economic Research of the University of California, Berkeley.

4. The economic meaning of objective functions differentiable in agents' own prices and wages will be explained. Profit functions do *not* have this property when there is perfect competition in the labor and product markets. But in a wide class of models, including those with imperfect competition, objective functions *do* have this property.
5. Some intuition will be provided to explain why nonmaximizing behavior that results in only second-order losses to the individual nonmaximizers will nevertheless have first-order effects on real variables.
6. An example will be presented of a model in which inertial price and wage behavior causes first-order changes in real activity but imposes only insignificant losses on nonmaximizing agents. In this model the typical firm's profits are a continuous, differentiable function of the price it charges and the wage it offers. The model assumes imperfect competition in the product market and a relationship between wages and labor productivity leading to 'efficiency wage' payments in the labor market. It will be argued that the assumption of efficiency wages is appealing because it rationalizes one important stylized view of the economy—the dual labor market—and because it provides a coherent explanation of persistent involuntary unemployment.

The Need for a Model without Money Neutrality

As is well-known, *anticipated* changes in aggregate demand cause no fluctuations in employment or output in neoclassical models with market clearing (see Sargent [1973]). The insensitivity of employment and output to aggregate demand shifts generalizes, however, beyond such neoclassical models. As long as a model postulates behavior that is rational—i.e., derived from maximization of objective functions that depend only on real variables—there is no reason why anticipated demand shocks should have any effect on real output. Thus, recent models in which involuntary unemployment can be rationalized as a result of staggered or implicit contracts, imperfect information, labor turnover, or efficiency wages still leave unanswered the question of how changes in the money supply, unless unanticipated, can affect real output.

In the Keynesian model, changes in aggregate demand cause fluctuations in real output because of agents' inertia in changing money wages and prices. There is abundant empirical evidence for the phenomenon of wage and price sluggishness (see, for example, the discussion in Okun [1981]). Nevertheless, the reasons why prices and wages do not adjust quickly to changes in aggregate demand remain mysterious. In the standard Keynesian model with competitive markets, there are substantial gains to be made by agents who do adjust wages and prices quickly; so inertial behavior, in that model, is both irrational and costly. In partial answer to this problem, the new classical macroeconomics has proposed models in which money is neutral with full information but is nonneutral insofar as unanticipated money shocks fool agents who are imperfectly informed about wage and price distributions. The applicability of this model has been the subject of considerable debate. This paper suggests an alternative.

Near-Rational Behavior

The alternative explanation of nonneutrality offered in this paper is based on the idea that inertial wage-price behavior by firms may not, in fact, be very costly; it may be near-rational. Firms that behave suboptimally, adjusting prices and wages slowly, may suffer losses from failure to optimize, but those losses may be very small. Near-rational behavior is behavior that is perhaps suboptimal but that nevertheless imposes very small individual losses on its practitioners relative to the consequences of their first-best policy. Technically, *very small* is defined as being second-order in terms of the policy shocks that create a disturbance from a long-run, fully maximizing equilibrium. This paper argues that inertial wage and price behavior which is near-rational, in the sense that it causes only second-order losses to its practitioners, can nevertheless cause first-order changes in real activity. As a result, changes in the money supply can cause first-order changes in employment and output if agents are near-rational. In sum, this paper argues that a small amount of nonmaximizing behavior can cause a significant business cycle in response to money supply shocks that would be neutral in the absence of such inertial behavior.

The Crucial Requirement for the Near-Rationality of Inertial Behavior: Differentiability of Objective Functions in Agents' Own Wages and Prices

Consider a shock that perturbs an equilibrium in which all agents are maximizing. Sticky wage and price behavior will be near-rational for any agent whose objective function is differentiable as a function of *his own wages and prices*. The error in wages or prices caused by inertial behavior will result in losses to the agent that are second-order in terms of the policy shock, since at the equilibrium prior to the shock, the agent chose prices (wages) so that the marginal benefits of higher prices (wages) was just offset by the marginal costs. An error in wages and prices therefore has a second-order effect on the value of the objective function. This is just an application of the envelope theorem (see Varian [1978]).

The Assumption of Differentiability

The condition that the objective function is differentiable in an *agent's own wages and prices* requires explanation. This assumption does not hold in a competitive model. Consider firms' profits in a competitive model. In this model a firm that individually pays a wage lower than the market wage can hire no labor. At the market wage, labor availability jumps discontinuously and consequently so do profits. With the firm's own wage higher than the market-clearing, profits decline proportionately with the excess of the wage over the market-clearing level. Accordingly, profit as a function of the firm's wage is not differentiable at the optimum wage, which is the market-clearing wage. A similar story is true with regard to prices. If the firm charges a price above the market-clearing level, a competitive firm has no sales. Profits jump discontinuously when a firm's own price falls to the market-clearing level because the firm can then have all the sales it wants. And at prices lower than the market-clearing level, profits decline proportionately to the gap between the market-clearing price and the firm's own price. In the competitive model lower prices or higher wages than the market-clearing levels confer no benefits on the firm.

In contrast, there are many models of price and wage setting in which profits are a differentiable function of the firm's own price or wage. In models with imperfect information by buyers, monopoly or oligopoly in the product market, or monopolistic competition with differentiated products, a firm's profits vary *differentiably* with its own price because its sales do not fall to zero as its price departs marginally from the prices charged by other firms. In these models, price reductions by firms result in marginal benefits due to increased sales, as well as the marginal cost of less revenue per unit of output sold.

Similarly, there are models of the labor market in which profits are a differentiable function of the firm's own wage offer. This occurs in models where workers have imperfect information, which confers at least temporary monopsony power on firms, and in monopsonistic and oligopsonistic labor markets.[1] In most models of staggered contracts, the profit function is differentiable with respect to the *timing* of wage changes. Finally, in the efficiency wage model of unemployment, as will be presently described, profits are a differentiable function of wages because the higher labor costs per employee that result from higher wage offers are at least partially offset by a reduction in labor cost due to increased productivity.

Thus, there is a wide class of models in which firms' profits are a differentiable function of wage and price variables. In any such model inertial wage or price-setting behavior in response to a shock, starting from a long-run equilibrium with full maximization, will impose only small losses on nonmaximizing agents.

First-Order Consequences of Sticky Wages and Prices for Real Variables

It has now been seen that in a wide class of models, the effect of wage and price stickiness on agents' objective functions is second-order in terms of the magnitude of a shock starting from a long-run equilibrium in which all agents maximize. Nevertheless, such wage and price stickiness commonly has a first-order effect on equilibrium values of real variables following the shock. Although this property must be checked in any particular variant of the model proposed, there is a general intuition why it usually occurs.

If *all* agents maintain sticky prices following a change in the money supply by a fraction ε, there would be a change in real balances by the same fraction. The change in real balances would clearly be of the same order of magnitude as the shock; and in most

---

[1] In an implicit contract model without severance pay and with money, it is possible to show the existence of near-rational contracts in which money is nonneutral. If firms alter their short-run hiring when the money supply changes on the false assumption that unemployment benefits are fixed in money terms rather than in real terms, their policies are near-rational. But the effect of these policies on equilibrium employment and output are first-order in states of the world where there was some unemployment in the long-run equilibrium prior to the money supply shock. Thus, changes in aggregate demand can have a first-order effect on equilibrium in implicit contract models, if contracts are near-rational.

models all other real variables would change by the same order of magnitude. The property that most real variables change by the same order of magnitude as the shock continues to hold, although the argument is more subtle, in models of short-run equilibrium when only a fraction of agents have sticky prices or wages while the remainder of agents maximize.

The Example Chosen

The next section presents a specific model that illustrates the proposition that near-rational wage and price stickiness can account for business cycle fluctuations. The model presented has three basic features. The first of these is sticky wage and price behavior. By that we mean that following a shock to a long-run equilibrium in which all agents exactly maximize, a fraction β of agents maintain the same nominal prices and wages, while the remaining agents are full maximizers.

The second feature of the model guarantees that *price* stickiness is a near-rational policy in response to a shock of a long-run equilibrium with full maximization. We assume that firms are monopolistic competitors with their sales dependent on the level of real aggregate demand and the firm's own price relative to the average prices charged by other firms. For simplicity, we assume that real aggregate demand is proportional to real balances. As the logic of the previous discussion should indicate, price stickiness in such a model is near-rational. Even with a market-clearing labor market, such price inertia suffices to explain how money supply changes could cause proportional changes in real variables.

It is the intent of this paper to present an example that shows not only how monetary nonneutrality can result from near-rational behavior, but also how equilibria can be characterized by involuntary unemployment. Involuntary unemployment occurs in our model because the productivity of workers is assumed to depend on the real wage they receive, inducing firms to set wages above the market-clearing level. Because such efficiency wage models may be unfamiliar, they will be briefly described, with some comments on why we consider them to be a realistic basis for a model of nonclearing labor markets.

Efficiency Wage Models of Unemployment

There is now a burgeoning literature[2] that explains involuntary unemployment in developed countries as the result of *efficiency wages*. According to the efficiency wage hypothesis, real wage cuts may harm productivity. If this is the case, each firm sets its wage to minimize labor cost per efficiency unit, rather than labor cost per worker. The wage that minimizes labor cost per efficiency unit is known as the efficiency wage. The firm hires labor up to the point where its marginal revenue product is equal to the

---

[2] See, for example, Akerlof [1982]; Bowles [1981, 1983]; Calvo [1979]; Foster and Wan [1984]; Malcomson [1981]; Miyazaki [1984]; Salop [1979]; Schlicht [1978]; Shapiro and Stiglitz [1984]; Stoft [1982a, 1982b]; Weiss [1980]; and Weisskopf, Bowles, and Gordon [1983].

real wage it has set. And it easily happens that the aggregate demand for labor, when each firm offers its efficiency wage, falls short of labor supply, so that there is involuntary unemployment.

There are three basic variants of this model (see Yellen [1984] for a survey). In one case, firms pay higher wages than the workers' reservation wages so that employees have an incentive not to shirk. In a second version, wages greater than market-clearing are offered so that workers have an incentive not to quit and turnover is reduced. In a third version, wages greater than market-clearing are paid to induce loyalty to the firm.

Although there are potential problems with these models (e.g., complicated contracts in some cases will be Pareto-superior and eliminate equilibrium unemployment; these models may exhibit countercyclical, rather than procyclical productivity), nevertheless, with modification, they have real promise as an explanation of involuntary unemployment. Furthermore, any model of the *dual labor market* must explain why primary-sector firms pay more than the market-clearing wage, and such an explanation can only come from an efficiency wage theory.

II. A MODEL OF CYCLICAL UNEMPLOYMENT

As motivated in the Introduction, this section constructs a model in which changes in the money supply will cause changes of the same order in the level of employment in near-rational short-run equilibrium. As indicated earlier, the model is based on monopolistic competition and efficiency wage theory.

The Model

Assume a monopolistically competitive economy with a fixed number of identical firms. In the initial equilibrium each firm sets its price and wage to maximize profits, under the assumption that changes in its own price will have no effect on the prices charged by rivals or on the average price level. In this sense, each firm is a Bertrand maximizer. There are two different types of firms. One type, which is a fraction β of all firms, sets its price and wage according to a rule of thumb in the short run. The variables pertaining to such firms are denoted n, since these are *non*maximizing firms. The remaining fraction $(1 - \beta)$ of the total are short-run maximizers, as well as long-run maximizers. They set their price and wage at the levels that maximize profits, on the Bertrand assumption that the prices charged by competitors (and the average price level) will be unaffected by their decision. Variables relating to these firms are denoted m, since they are *maximizing* firms.

Accordingly, let the demand curve facing each firm be

$$X = (p/\bar{p})^{-\eta}(M/\bar{p}) \quad \eta > 1, \tag{1}$$

where X = output of the firm, p = the price of the firm's output, $\bar{p}$ = the average price level, and M = the money supply per firm. The parameter η is chosen to be greater than one, so that each firm has increasing revenues as its own price falls. $\bar{p}$, the average price level, is given as the geometric mean of the prices charged by all firms. In long-run equilibrium all firms charge the same price, $p = \bar{p}$, and so the system of demand equations (1) is consistent with a quantity theory:

$$\bar{p}X = M. \tag{2}$$

Firms produce output according to the production function:

$$X = (eN)^{\alpha} \quad 0 < \alpha < 1, \tag{3}$$

where $e =$ average effort of laborers hired and $N =$ number of laborers hired.

Effort e is assumed to depend on the real wage paid ω, according to the function, $e = e(\omega)$. $e(\omega)$ is assumed to be a function whose elasticity with respect to ω is less than one at high ω and is greater than one at low ω. An example of such a function is

$$e(\omega) = -a + b\omega^{\gamma} \quad 0 < \gamma < 1, \quad a > 0, \quad b > 0. \tag{4}$$

In most efficiency wage theories, e realistically depends not only on ω but also on the unemployment rate and the wages paid by other firms. The dependence of e on unemployment plays an important role in these models: through this dependence, increases in the supply of labor cause more workers to be hired in equilibrium. An increase in labor supply, in the absence of any other repercussions, causes unemployment to rise. This rise in unemployment causes a rise in e, which in turn, causes firms to increase their demand for labor. (Other repercussions will also follow, as the equilibrium real wage and other things also change.) Our example omits the dependence of e on unemployment and other wages with the result that equilibrium employment is independent of labor supply. The peculiarity of this outcome should not be disturbing, since this is not an essential property of efficiency wage models. Our goal is to illustrate, in the simplest fashion, how first-order changes in welfare can occur because of inertial wage and price behavior whose individual cost is second-order. Since that property does not turn on the dependence of e on unemployment or other wages, and since such dependence considerably complicates the model, we have adopted the simpler assumption: $e = e(\omega)$.

Long-Run Equilibrium

The production function and demand function can be used to compute the profit function for each firm, which is revenue (price times output sold), net of factor costs (money wages times labor hired). The profits of each firm are accordingly

$$\Pi = p\left(\frac{p}{\bar{p}}\right)^{-\eta}\frac{M}{\bar{p}} - \left(\frac{p}{\bar{p}}\right)^{-\eta/\alpha}\left(\frac{M}{\bar{p}}\right)^{1/\alpha}\omega(e(\omega))^{-1}\bar{p}. \tag{5}$$

In long-run equilibrium each firm chooses the price of its own output and the wage paid its own workers, so as to maximize profits (provided that the demand for labor is less than the supply), on the assumption that the average price level $\bar{p}$ is unaffected by that decision.

For notational convenience, denote the price level in the initial period as p_0; this is the average price level, the price of maximizing firms, and the price of nonmaximizing firms. With an initial money supply $\bar{M}_0$, the first-order condition for profit maximization and the condition $p = \bar{p}$ yields an equilibrium price of

$$p_0 = k\bar{M}_0, \quad \text{where } k = \left(\frac{\eta\omega^*}{\alpha(\eta - 1)e(\omega^*)}\right)^{\alpha/(1-\alpha)} \tag{6}$$

The real wage ω is chosen at the optimizing level ω^*, where the elasticity of effort with respect to the real wage is unity. (This is a standard result in such models [Solow, 1979] and represents the condition that the firm chooses the real wage that minimizes the unit cost of a labor efficiency unit.)

With this choice of real wage ω^*, the demand for labor is

$$N_0 = k^{-1/\alpha}/e(\omega^*). \tag{7}$$

The total supply of labor per firm $\bar{L}$ is assumed to exceed total labor demanded (which is the right-hand side of (7)). In this case, there will be unemployment, and the firm will be able to obtain all the labor it wants at its preferred real wage ω^*.

Assumptions Concerning Short-Run Equilibrium

This characterization of the initial (long-run) equilibrium lays the foundation for determining how much employment will change if there is a change in the money supply when some of the firms are nonmaximizers in the short run. Also to be calculated is the difference between the actual profits of a nonmaximizing firm and its expected profits if it were to continue setting its prices and wages in the Bertrand-maximizing fashion.

The description of short-run behavior follows. Suppose that the money supply changes by a fraction ε, so that $M = M_0(1 + \varepsilon)$. Suppose also that there are two groups of firms which behave differently in the short run. The m-firms, which are the short-run maximizers, set both the price of their output and the wage paid their workers at those levels that exactly maximize profits, on the assumption that the average price level is unaffected by their individual decisions. The n-firms, which follow a rule of thumb, continue to charge the same price for output and to pay the same money wage. This assumption corresponds to the common finding that money wages are sticky over the business cycle, and also that prices are a constant markup over normal average unit cost. (See Nordhaus and Godley [1972] and Nordhaus [1974] for such a model of pricing and further references; this behavior of wages corresponds to any standard Phillips curve.) An increase in the money supply induces the nonmaximizing firms to hire more labor—to an extent dependent on the reduction in the relative price of output, the increase in aggregate real balances, and the number of laborers needed to produce output according to the production function.

The Nature of Short-Run Equilibrium

The first key task, with respect to this short-run model, is to compute the difference between the profit of a typical nonmaximizing firm, and its profits if it were to abandon its rule-of-thumb behavior and adopt, instead, the Bertrand behavior of the maximizing firms. It will be shown that, for ε equal to zero, the derivative of this difference with respect to ε is zero. In this sense, the prospective loss in profits to the nonmaximizing firms, due to their *individual* nonmaximizing behavior is a second-order effect. The second key task is to calculate the derivative, with respect to ε, of the ratio between the total employment and initial employment. This derivative is positive for ε equal to zero.

In short-run equilibrium the key endogenous variables are determined by (8) to (12):

$$p^n = p_0 \tag{8}$$

$$\omega^m = \omega^* \tag{9}$$

$$p^m = p_0(1 + \varepsilon)^\theta, \tag{10}$$

where

$$\theta = \frac{(1 - \alpha)/\alpha}{\beta(\eta/\alpha - \eta + 1) + (1 - \beta)((1 - \alpha)/\alpha)} \leq 1$$

$$\bar{p} = p_0(1 + \varepsilon)^{(1-\beta)\theta} \tag{11}$$

$$\omega^n = \omega^*(1 + \varepsilon)^{-(1-\beta)\theta}. \tag{12}$$

$p^n = p_0$:   it is obvious, by assumption, that $p^n = p_0$.

$\omega^m = \omega^*$:   setting the derivative of the profit function (5) with respect to ω equal to zero yields the optimizing condition that the elasticity of effort, with respect to the real wage ω^m be unity. It follows that, in equilibrium, ω^m is unchanged from its long-run value of ω^*.

$p^m = p_0(1 + \varepsilon)^\theta$:   setting the derivative of the profit function with respect to p^m equal to zero, with $\omega = \omega^*$, yields the optimizing p^m as a function of $\bar{p}$ and M. Remembering that $\bar{p}$ is a geometric mean of prices, so that $\bar{p} = (p^n)^\beta (p^m)^{1-\beta}$, and setting $p^n = p_0$ and $M = \bar{M}_0(1 + \varepsilon)$ yields $p^m = p_0(1 + \varepsilon)^\theta$.

$\bar{p} = p_0(1 + \varepsilon)^{(1-\beta)\theta}$: this follows directly from the definition of $\bar{p} = (p^n)^\beta (p^m)^{1-\beta}$ and the values of $p^n = p_0$, $p^m = p_0(1 + \varepsilon)^\theta$.

$\omega^n = \omega^*(1 + \varepsilon)^{-(1-\beta)\theta}$: the money wage paid by the nonmaximizing firm is unchanged at its initial value w_0. The real wage is, accordingly, $w_0/\bar{p}$, which can be rewritten as the product $(w_0/p_0)(p_0/\bar{p})$. The first term of this product is ω^*, and the second is $(1 + \varepsilon)^{-(1-\beta)\theta}$.

Calculation of p^n, ω^m, p^m, p, and ω^n

Each of these will be explained in turn.

Now, consider the position of nonmaximizing firms. Their actual profits $\prod^n$ in the short-run equilibrium are given by the profit function (5), evaluated with $p^n = p_0$, $\bar{p} = p_0(1 + \varepsilon)^{(1-\beta)\theta}$, $\omega^n = \omega^*(1 + \varepsilon)^{-(1-\beta)\theta}$, and $M = \bar{M}_0(1 + \varepsilon)$. Whether or not it is reasonable for these firms to follow rule-of-thumb behavior, we assume, depends upon the difference between their maximum expected profits and their actual profits. The optimum price for any nonmaximizing firm to charge, on the assumption of constant $\bar{p}$, is just the price being charged by the maximizing firms, which is $p^m = p_0(1 + \varepsilon)^\theta$. The maximum expected profits of any nonmaximizing firm are thus identical with the actual profits $\prod^m$ being earned by the typical maximizing firm. $\prod^m$ is found by substituting $p^m = p^m(\varepsilon) = p_0(1 + \varepsilon)^\theta$, $\bar{p} = p_0(1 + \varepsilon)^{(1-\beta)\theta}$, $\omega^m = \omega^*$, and $M = \bar{M}_0(1 + \varepsilon)$ into the profit function (5). Accordingly, $\prod^n$ and $\prod^m$ can be written, respectively, as functions of ε:

$$\prod^n = (p_0)^{1-\eta} f(\varepsilon) - (p_0)^{-\eta/\alpha} g(\varepsilon) h(\varepsilon) \omega^* [e(h(\varepsilon)\omega^*)]^{-1} \tag{13}$$

$$\prod^m = (p^m(\varepsilon))^{1-\eta} f(\varepsilon) - (p^m(\varepsilon))^{-\eta/\alpha} g(\varepsilon) \omega^* (e(\omega^*))^{-1}. \tag{14}$$

The precise functional forms of $f(\varepsilon)$ and $g(\varepsilon)$ are unimportant. What is crucial is their similar role in the $\prod^n$ and $\prod^m$ functions. They can be calculated explicitly by substituting $p_0(1 + \varepsilon)^{(1-\beta)\theta}$ and $M_0(1 + \varepsilon)$ for $\bar{p}$ and M, respectively, into the profit function (5). Similarly, $h(\varepsilon)$ can be found as $(1 + \varepsilon)^{-(1-\beta)\theta}$, since $\omega^n = \omega^*(1 + \varepsilon)^{-(1-\beta)\theta}$. $h(\varepsilon)$ has the property that $h(0) = 1$.

$\prod^n$ and $\prod^m$ are not very different. Their first and second terms have the common factors $f(\varepsilon)$ and $g(\varepsilon)$, respectively. The derivative of $\prod^m$, with respect to p^m, is zero, since that variable is chosen to maximize that function. And the derivative of $\prod^m$ with respect to ω is equal to zero for $\omega = \omega^*$. These properties are useful in showing that the derivative of the difference between $\prod^m$ and $\prod^n$ with respect to ε vanishes for $\varepsilon = 0$.

The derivative of $\prod^m - \prod^n$ with respect to ε can be grouped into four separate terms, each one corresponding to one set of curly brackets in (15):

$$\frac{d(\prod^m - \prod^n)}{d\varepsilon} = \left\{ (1-\eta)(p^m(\varepsilon))^{-\eta} f(\varepsilon) + \left(\frac{\eta}{\alpha}\right)(p^m(\varepsilon))^{-\eta/\alpha-1} g(\varepsilon)\omega^*(e(\omega^*))^{-1} \right\} \frac{dp^m}{d\varepsilon}$$

$$+ \left\{ \omega^*[e(h(\varepsilon)\omega^*)]^{-1} - h(\varepsilon)\omega^{*2} e'(h(\varepsilon)\omega^*)[e(h(\varepsilon)\omega^*)]^{-2} \right\} \cdot \frac{dh}{d\varepsilon}(p_0)^{-\eta/\alpha} g(\varepsilon)$$

$$+ \left\{ (p^m(\varepsilon))^{1-\eta} f'(\varepsilon) - (p^m(\varepsilon))^{-\eta/\alpha} \omega^*[e(\omega^*)]^{-1} g'(\varepsilon) \right\}$$

$$- \left\{ (p_0)^{1-\eta} f'(\varepsilon) - (p_0)^{-\eta/\alpha} h(\varepsilon)\omega^*[e(h(\varepsilon)\omega^*)]^{-1} g'(\varepsilon) \right\}. \tag{15}$$

The first term in curly brackets in (15) is zero because of the first-order condition for p^m as the maximand of the profit function $\prod^m$. The second term in curly brackets vanishes for ε equal to zero, since $h(0) = 1$, and since ω^* has been chosen to maximize profits. (This causes $\omega^* e'(\omega^*)[e(\omega^*)]^{-1}$ to equal unity.) Thus, the first two terms in curly brackets in (15) are zero for ε equal zero because of the optimizing choice of the respective variables, p and ω. The third and fourth terms in curly brackets cancel for ε equal to zero, because $p^m(0) = p_0$ and $h(0) = 1$. These terms reflect the common effect of ε on $\prod^m$ and $\prod^n$. Since all four terms in curly brackets either vanish or cancel for ε equal zero, it follows that

$$\left. \frac{d(\prod^m - \prod^n)}{d\varepsilon} \right|_{\varepsilon=0} = 0. \tag{16}$$

This is a key result of this paper. It says that the loss to the nonmaximizers over their maximum possible profits in this model is second order with respect to ε. It also follows trivially that this loss in percentage terms is equal to zero for ε equal zero and has a derivative of zero.

Employment

The elasticity of total employment, with respect to changes in the money supply is not zero. For ε equal zero, this elasticity can be calculated as

$$\frac{d(N/N_0)}{d\varepsilon} = \frac{1}{\alpha}(1 - (1-\beta)\theta) + \beta(1-\beta)\theta. \tag{17}$$

Two comments are in order about (17). First, since θ is less than one, an increase in the money supply causes an increase in employment. Also, since $\theta = 1$ for $\beta = 0$, the elasticity of employment with respect to changes in the money supply vanishes as

Table 18.1 *Percentage loss in profits due to nonmaximizing behavior for different percentage changes in employment, elasticity of output with respect to labor input (α), elasticity of demand (η), and proportion of nonmaximizers (β)*

	5% Change in employment			10% Change in employment		
	$\beta = 0.25$	$\beta = 0.5$	$\beta = 0.75$	$\beta = 0.25$	$\beta = 0.5$	$\beta = 0.75$
$\alpha = 0.25$						
$\eta = 1.5$	0.084	0.023	0.011	0.309	0.088	0.043
$\eta = 3.0$	0.220	0.059	0.028	0.808	0.226	0.107
$\eta = 5.0$	0.298	0.079	0.036	1.090	0.303	0.142
$\eta = 20.0$	0.408	0.107	0.049	1.496	0.410	0.189
$\eta = 100.0$	0.443	0.116	0.052	1.623	0.442	0.203
$\alpha = 0.5$						
$\eta = 1.5$	0.088	0.024	0.012	0.330	0.092	0.045
$\eta = 3.0$	0.295	0.080	0.038	1.109	0.306	0.146
$\eta = 5.0$	0.459	0.122	0.057	1.726	0.471	0.222
$\eta = 20.0$	0.768	0.201	0.091	2.892	0.774	0.356
$\eta = 100.0$	0.888	0.231	0.104	3.343	0.889	0.405
$\alpha = 0.75$						
$\eta = 1.5$	0.046	0.012	0.006	0.175	0.045	0.021
$\eta = 3.0$	0.207	0.054	0.025	0.796	0.209	0.097
$\eta = 5.0$	0.397	0.103	0.048	1.533	0.402	0.186
$\eta = 20.0$	0.974	0.251	0.114	3.769	0.979	0.447
$\eta = 100.0$	1.304	0.334	0.151	5.046	1.304	0.591

$a = 1.0$, $b = 2.0$, $\gamma = 0.5$.

the fraction of nonmaximizers approaches zero. Such a result should be expected, since as β approaches zero, the model approaches one of monetary neutrality.

Simulations

We did some simulations of the preceding model of unemployment for various values of the elasticity of output with respect to labor input (α), the elasticity of demand for each firm (η), and the fraction of nonmaximizers (β). The parameters of the wage–effort function, a, b, and γ, were chosen equal to 1.0, 2.0 and 0.5, respectively, so that $\omega^*[e(\omega^*)]^{-1}$ would conveniently equal one.[3]

For each set of parameter values, Table 18.1 reports the percentage difference between the profits of maximizers and nonmaximizers for changes in the money supply, which, respectively, produce 5 percent and 10 percent increases in employment. For 5 percent changes in employment, all values but one, even for values of η (the elasticity of demand) as large as 100, are less than 1 percent. For changes in employment of 10

[3] Another choice of the a, b, γ parameters showed negligible differences from the results reported in Table 18.I.

percent, these differences are mainly below 1 percent for low values of η, and, at the maximum value in the table, for $\alpha = 0.75$, $\eta = 100$, and $\beta = 0.25$, only reaches 5.05 percent. Although this loss in profits is extreme in the table, it is not beyond the bounds of possibility. Quite conceivably, over the course of the business cycle, a quarter of all firms could fail to correct a policy that caused a 5 percent loss in profits.

III. CONCLUSION

In conclusion, a model has been presented in which changes in aggregate demand cause significant changes in equilibrium output. This model meets Lucas' criterion that there are 'no \$500 bills lying on the sidewalk.' There is a class of maximizers in this model who are ready to take advantage of *any* profitable opportunity; and those agents who are not maximizing can make at most only small gains from altering their behavior.

The model presented also satisfies the condition that there is involuntary unemployment. This occurs because of the assumption that wages are determined in excess of market-clearing according to the efficiency wage criterion of minimization of cost per labor efficiency unit.

As the introduction may have made clear, the basic method applied in this paper to show the short-run nonneutrality of money should be applicable in a wide range of models, of which the monopolistic-competition, efficiency-wage model of the last section was only one example.

UNIVERSITY OF CALIFORNIA, BERKELEY

References

Akerlof, George A., 'Labor Contracts as Partial Gift Exchange,' this *Journal*, XCVII (Nov. 1982), 543–69.

——, and Janet Yellen, 'The Macroeconomic Consequences of Near-Rational Rule-of-Thumb Behavior,' mimeo, September 1983.

Bowles, Samuel, 'Competitive Wage Determination and Involuntary Unemployment: A Conflict Model,' mimeo, University of Massachusetts, May 1981.

——, 'The Production Process in a Competitive Economy: Walrasian, Neo-Hobbesian and Marxian Models,' mimeo, University of Massachusetts, May 1983.

Calvo, Guillermo, 'Quasi-Walrasian Theories of Unemployment,' *American Economic Review Proceedings*, LXIX (May 1979), 102–07.

Foster, James E., and Henry Y. Wan, Jr., ' "Involuntary" Unemployment as a Principal-Agent Equilibrium,' *American Economic Review*, LXXIV (June 1984).

Malcomson, James, 'Unemployment and the Efficiency Wage Hypothesis,' *Economic Journal*, XCI (Dec. 1981), 848–66.

Miyazaki, Hajime, 'Work Norms and Involuntary Unemployment,' this *Journal*, XCIV (May 1984), 297–312.

Nordhaus, William D., 'The Falling Share of Profits,' *Brookings Papers on Economic Activity*, 1 (1974), 169–208.

——, and Wynne A. H. Godley, 'Pricing in the Trade Cycle,' *Economic Journal*, LXXXII (Sept. 1972), 853–82.

Okun, Arthur M., *Prices and Quantities: A Macroeconomic Analysis* (Washington, D. C.: The Brookings Institution, 1981).

Salop, Steven, 'A Model of the Natural Rate of Unemployment,' *American Economic Review*, LXIX (March 1979), 117–25.

Sargent, Thomas J., 'Rational Expetations, the Real Rate of Interest and the Natural Rate of Unemployment,' *Brookings Papers on Economic Activity*, 2 (1973), 429–80.

Schlicht, Ekkehart, 'Labor Turnover, Wage Structure and Natural Unemployment,' *Zeitschrift für die Gesamte Staatswissenschaft*, CXXXIV (June 1978), 337–46.

Shapiro, Carl, and Joseph E. Stiglitz, 'Equilibrium Unemployment as a Worker Discipline Device,' *American Economic Review*, LXXIV (June 1984).

Solow, Robert M., 'Another Possible Source of Wage Stickiness,' *Journal of Macroeconomics*, I (Winter 1979), 79–82.

Stoft, Steven, 'Cheat-Threat Theory,' Unpublished Ph.D. thesis, University of California, Berkeley, 1982a.

——, 'Cheat-Threat Theory: An Explanation of Involuntary Unemployment,' mimeo, Boston University, May 1982b.

Varian, Hal, *Microeconomic Analysis* (New York: Norton, 1978).

Weiss, Andrew, 'Job Queues and Layoffs in Labor Markets with Flexible Wages,' *Journal of Political Economy*, LXXXVIII (June 1980), 526–38.

Weisskopf, Thomas, Samuel Bowles, and David Gordon, 'Hearts and Minds: A Social Model of Aggregate Productivity Growth in the U. S., 1948–1979,' *Brookings Papers on Economic Activity*, 2 (1983), 381–441.

Yellen, Janet L., 'Efficiency Wage Models of Unemployment,' *American Economic Review Proceedings*, LXXIV (May 1984), 200–05.

/ US /

19

The Macroeconomics of Low Inflation*

GEORGE A. AKERLOF[†]

Brookings Institution and University of California, Berkeley

WILLIAM T. DICKENS AND GEORGE L. PERRY

Brookings Institution

The concept of a natural unemployment rate has been central to most modern models of inflation and stabilization. According to these models, inflation will accelerate or decelerate depending on whether unemployment is below or above the natural rate, while any existing rate of inflation will continue if unemployment is at the natural rate. The natural rate is thus the minimum, and only, sustainable rate of unemployment, but the inflation rate is left as a choice variable for policymakers. Since complete price stability has attractive features, many economists and policymakers who accept the natural rate hypothesis believe that central banks should target zero inflation.

We question the standard version of the natural rate model and each of these implications. Central to our analysis is the effect of downward nominal wage rigidity in an economy in which individual firms experience stochastic shocks in the demand for their output. We embed these features in a model that otherwise resembles a standard natural rate model and show there is no unique natural unemployment rate. Rather, the rate of unemployment that is consistent with steady inflation itself depends on the inflation rate. In the long run, a moderate steady rate of inflation permits maximum employment and output. Maintenance of zero inflation measurably increases the sustainable unemployment rate and correspondingly reduces the level of output. We show that these effects are large, not negligible as some previous studies have claimed.

The view that unemployment will settle at a fixed natural rate if *any* steady rate of inflation is maintained is presumably the rationale for the Economic Growth and Price

* This work was previously published as George A. Akerlof, William T. Dickens, George L. Perry (1996), 'The Macroeconomics of Low Inflation', *The Brookings Institution: Brookings Papers on Economic Activity*, *1: 1996.* Copyright © Brookings Institution Press. Reproduced by kind permission.

† We would especially like to thank Neil Siegel, Justin Smith, and Jennifer Eichberger for invaluable research assistance. We are also grateful to Pierre Fortin, Harry Holzer, and Christina Romer for providing us with data, and to John Baldwin, Paul Beaudry, Bryan Caplan, Bradford De Long, Erica Groshen, Peter Howitt, Shulamit Kahn, Kenneth McLaughlin, Craig Riddell, David Romer, Paul Romer, Charles Schultze, Lars Svensson, Robert Solow, and Michael Wolfson for their help and comments. George Akerlof also expresses his gratitude for the financial support of the Canadian Institute for Advanced Research and of the National Science Foundation under research grant SBR-9409426.

Stability Act of 1995, proposed by Senator Connie Mack. According to the preamble of this bill, 'because price stability leads to the lowest possible interest rates and is a key condition to maintaining the highest possible levels of productivity, real incomes, living standards, employment, and global competitiveness, price stability should be the primary long-term goal of the Board of Governors of the Federal Reserve System.'[1] But as our results show, a target of zero inflation will impose permanent real costs on the economy rather than the real benefits this preamble describes.

Although the appealing simplicity of the assumptions underlying natural rate models has put them in the forefront of macroeconomic modeling, there is ample precedent for our attention to downward wage rigidity and efficient employment levels, not only among labor economists but also in earlier macroeconomic models of inflation. James Tobin stressed their importance in his 1971 presidential address to the American Economic Association, in which he presented a model based on nominal rigidity that 'implies a long-run Phillips curve that is very flat for high unemployment and becomes vertical at a critically low rate of unemployment.' Indeed, in the first Phillips curve paper written in the United States, Paul Samuelson and Robert Solow had noted that 'downward inflexibility keeps prices from falling.... The result is an upward drift in average prices—with the suggestion that monetary and fiscal policies restrictive enough to prevent an average price rise would have to be so very restrictive as to produce a considerable level of unemployment and a significant drop in production.' They, in turn, were reflecting on the 'demand shift' theory of Charles Schultze, who stressed that 'creeping inflation is associated with the dynamics of resource allocation.'[2]

The plan of the paper is as follows. We start with a review of ethnographic evidence that points to reasons why rational firms would want to avoid cutting nominal wages, and then provide a range of evidence establishing empirically that nominal wage cuts are rare, except when firms are under extreme financial strain. This evidence includes comprehensive data on U.S. manufacturing establishments, data on both Canadian and U.S. union wage settlements, employers' reports from special studies, and our own telephone survey of individuals in the Washington, D.C., area. We also examine recent studies based on panel data that measure wage changes as the first difference in reported wage levels from consecutive survey years. These estimates of wage changes suggest that wage cuts are frequent, seemingly contradicting the findings from other sources. However, we show that the apparent frequency of wage cuts in the panel data is spurious, because many of the apparent wage cuts arise from errors in reported wage levels.

Having established the empirical importance of downward wage rigidity, we present a formal model that reflects optimizing behavior of firms that explicitly allows for downward wage rigidity under all but extreme circumstances and takes account of heterogeneous wage setting by firms. Relative to previous attempts to assess the consequences of downward wage rigidity, our innovations multiply the calculated losses in employment and output from low inflation policies in three ways. First, our

---

[1] Quoted in U.S. Congress, Joint Economic Committee, 'Statement by Connie Mack on the Economic Growth and Price Stability Act,' news release, September 20, 1995.

[2] Tobin (1972, p. 11); Samuelson and Solow (1960, p. 182); Schultze (1959, p. 134).

interpretations of the evidence on wage rigidity lead us to model nominal wage cuts as much less likely than do other authors. Second, we show that the effects of constraints are cumulative in a heterogeneous dynamic model, where firms that raise wages in response to favorable shocks in one period are more likely to be constrained by downward rigidity in subsequent periods. And third, we provide a general-equilibrium solution in which the impact on wages of downward wage constraints acts like a real cost shock, which the constrained firms pass on, in terms of higher prices.

General-equilibrium and partial-equilibrium analyses produce very different estimates of the consequences of targeting zero inflation. Both analyses begin with an estimate of the shift in the aggregate supply of labor because of nominal wage rigidity. Partial-equilibrium analysis then multiplies the shift between the real wage with and without nominal wage rigidity by the elasticity of demand for labor to obtain the impact of downward wage rigidity on the level of employment. Typically, this elasticity of demand is assumed to be fairly low—less than one.

General-equilibrium analysis follows the impact of downward wage rigidity beyond the labor demand of the individual firms with downward wage constraints. The special case of constant product elasticities of demand is not essential to the argument, but makes it easy to highlight the difference between general-equilibrium and partial-equilibrium analysis. Firms whose nominal wages are raised by constraints pass on their increased costs in higher prices. The markup is constant, because of constant elasticity of demand, and so the average real wage will be unchanged by the impact of wage constraints. The real average wage has two components. The first component is the unconstrained real wage that results from labor supply and demand or bargaining, and is a function of the unemployment rate. The other component of real wages is due to downward wage rigidity. When this component increases, unemployment must increase by enough to lower the unconstrained component equally, to keep average real wages constant. The increase in the component due to downward rigidity can be thought of as a permanent cost shock. Typically, it takes a 2 percent increase in unemployment to offset such a 1 percent cost shock. Our analysis produces such a multiplier.

We develop a stochastic simulation based on our general-equilibrium model. This simulation is calibrated to conform to data on the U.S. economy. We use it to examine the performance of the economy at alternative steady rates of inflation. We calibrate the model to have an unemployment rate of 5.8 percent at 3 percent inflation because this seems to be the typical estimate of the present natural rate. But performance changes nonlinearly as the steady inflation rate approaches zero, and at zero inflation the sustainable unemployment rate is noticeably higher. In a large number of simulations using different parameter values, the change in the sustainable unemployment rate is rarely less than 1 percentage point.

We also develop a version of the model that is suitable to estimation with time-series data. It embeds the features of the simulation model in an otherwise conventional natural rate model of inflation, allowing for parameters to be estimated from time-series data. When the model is fit to postwar data, the estimated parameters are reasonably consistent with the counterpart concepts in the simulation model, and the calculated values of sustainable unemployment rates vary with inflation rates in much the same way as they do in the simulation model. We then show that a dynamic simulation of the model fit to postwar data closely tracks price changes during the Great Depression, a period that notoriously defies explanation with conventional natural rate models.

Evidence on Downward Rigidity

Our own reading of the evidence, and the fundamental assumption of the model that we develop below, is that nominal wages are downward rigid, except when firms are under extreme duress. Twenty-five years ago, that hypothesis would have been widely accepted and could have been employed in a macroeconomic model without specific empirical support. Since then, it has come to be ignored in theoretical macroeconomic models, and its empirical importance has recently been questioned by some authors on the basis of panel data on wage changes. We present a range of evidence demonstrating that downward rigidity is an important feature of wage behavior, and then show that contrary results from panel data are spurious, because they arise from errors made by respondents in reporting their wage levels. But first we discuss various studies that suggest why downward wage rigidity is likely to be a feature of wage setting.

Ethnographic Evidence

Ethnographic observation by Truman Bewley and William Brainard provides direct evidence on the attitudes of employers toward wage cuts.[3] In 1992, Bewley and Brainard interviewed businesspeople and others professionally involved in the job market in Connecticut, inquiring specifically about the reluctance to cut wages and the reasons behind the wage cuts that do occur. They discovered that pay cuts were only an infrequent response to declines in sales, and that managers were much more fearful of the effects on morale caused by a cut in pay than by a wage freeze, which leaves real wages declining by the rate of inflation. The previous two years had been difficult for firms in the region, and the authors did find instances of wage cuts. In their sample of sixty-one firms, five had initiated cuts for some or all of their workers in the recent past, while the managers of six more firms could remember cuts during the last ten years. An additional eleven firms had initiated wage freezes. Of the eleven firms that reported cutting wages at some time in their history, most, but not quite all, had done so in response to serious problems. And in two cases, the cuts had been rescinded within six months.

Looking at the circumstances surrounding the pay cuts, Bewley and Brainard describe one firm that cut wages as having had losses for three years, another as doing so in 1991 in response to losses that began in 1989, another in response to 'cash flow problems,' another because its sales suddenly 'fell off a cliff,' and yet another because it was 'in danger of going out of business.' These firms instigated nominal wage cuts, and workers accepted them, only when the firms faced the prospect of bankruptcy. In two

---

[3] Bewley and Brainard (1993); Bewley (1994).

other instances, wages were cut because they were perceived as having gotten permanently out of line. One store had allowed its sales force to build up the base rate of pay as an incentive to achieve high volume, with the result that incentive pay for sales had become too low. It used the recession as an opportunity to reestablish the balance between commissions and base pay. The other readjustment of long-term wages occurred when a raider took over a plant in the South. The previous owner had maintained parity between this plant, which was not unionized, and its other, unionized establishments. The new owner took advantage of the disparity between union wages and competitive wages to make a 15 percent wage cut at the time of take-over. Overall, Bewley and Brainard paint a picture in which firms cut wages only reluctantly.

The attitudes of employers that Bewley and Brainard report support the well-known study of popular conceptions of fairness by Daniel Kahneman, Jack Knetsch, and Richard Thaler. They show that most people feel that nominal pay cuts are unfair, except in unusual circumstances such as the near-bankruptcy of their employers. Respondents were asked whether they viewed a number of different actions as fair or unfair. Sixty-two percent considered that it would be unfair for a company making a small profit to decrease wages by 7 percent if inflation were zero. In contrast, if inflation were 12 percent, only 22 percent of respondents thought that a raise of only 5 percent would be unfair.[4] Eldar Shafir, Peter Diamond, and Amos Tversky produce similar findings in their study of money illusion.[5] Their questions show that interviewees do not like wage cuts; they prefer situations in which nominal wages rise, even though the real consequences are the same.

A recent study by Carl Campbell and Kunal Kamlani examines the reasons why firms are reluctant to reduce wages in recessions.[6] Compensation professionals at larger firms and wage setters from smaller firms were asked to evaluate the importance of different reasons for the reluctance to make wage cuts in recessions. They gave the most weight to the potential loss of the most productive workers (who, presumably, were receiving lower wages relative to productivity than their coworkers) and the effect on the motivation of workers who received wage cuts. Confirming the earlier findings of Kahneman, Knetsch, and Thaler, the respondents thought that workers whose wages were cut at firms with losses would decrease their efforts by less than their counterparts at firms earning profits. Those who might expect that norms against nominal wage cuts only apply to blue collar workers would be surprised to learn that these compensation professionals thought that the effect on productivity would, in fact, be more significant for white collar workers.

Bewley and Brainard directly document the importance attached to avoiding nominal wage cuts, except as an extreme measure, when a firm is in serious trouble. Kahneman, Knetsch, and Thaler and Campbell and Kamlani provide reasons why rational employers would behave in this way. We now turn to quantitative evidence on the importance of downward rigidity in nominal wages.

---

[4] Kahneman, Knetsch, and Thaler (1986, p. 731, questions 4A and 4B).
[5] Shafir, Diamond, and Tversky (1994).
[6] Campbell and Kamlani (1995).

Wage Changes in Manufacturing

From 1959 to 1978, the Bureau of Labor Statistics (BLS) collected data on the distribution of general wage changes in manufacturing establishments. These data are confined to production and related workers in establishments that make general wage changes, but in other respects are quite broad, covering establishments of all sizes and wages for both unionized and nonunionized workers. The results, summarized in Table 19.1, show that in any given year a considerable fraction of firms gave no general nominal wage increase in the low-inflation period of the early 1960s, and among nonunion establishments, many gave no general increase even during the inflationary 1970s. But in no year did a nontrivial fraction of these manufacturing establishments cut wages. The data show a pronounced asymmetry; the part of the tail of the distribution of wage changes below zero is almost completely truncated. These data are not available for the early 1980s, a period when wage concessions were reported in some conspicuously troubled industries.

Table 19.1. *General wage changes in manufacturing, 1959–78*
Percent, production and related workers

	Union			Nonunion		
Year	Increase	No change	Decrease	Increase	No change	Decrease
1959	87.0	12.9	0.0	68.6	31.4	0.0
1960	87.1	12.8	0.1	59.0	41.0	0.0
1961	83.3	16.6	0.1	54.0	45.6	0.4
1962	72.8	27.1	0.1	52.9	47.1	0.0
1963	77.8	22.0	0.2	69.6	30.2	0.2
1964	76.1	23.9	0.1	56.2	43.8	0.0
1965	87.3	12.7	0.0	75.4	24.6	0.0
1966	80.9	19.1	0.0	77.8	22.2	0.0
1967	90.6	9.4	0.0	81.1	18.9	0.0
1968	93.7	6.3	0.0	87.6	12.4	0.0
1969	93.2	6.8	0.0	75.5	24.5	0.0
1970	94.8	5.2	0.0	77.6	22.4	0.0
1971	92.0	8.0	0.0	70.2	29.4	0.4
1972	92.9	7.1	0.0	83.2	16.8	0.1
1973	95.9	4.1	0.0	90.1	9.9	0.0
1974	97.8	2.2	0.0	89.1	10.7	0.3
1975	97.3	2.7	0.0	84.7	15.3	0.0
1976	96.9	3.1	0.0	88.4	11.6	0.0
1977	96.1	3.9	0.0	84.8	15.2	0.0
1978	96.6	3.4	0.0	89.3	10.7	0.0

Source: Bureau of Labor Statistics, 'Current Wage Developments,' various issues.

Union Settlements

BLS data for 1970 through 1994 on union settlements for private workers that involved more than one thousand workers provide another look at the frequency of wage cuts, and also at the unusual developments of the early 1980s. In this period, wage cuts were common only in 1983, when 15 percent of all settlements had negative changes in the first year. Even in this year there was considerable evidence of downward rigidity, in that 22 percent of all contracts had no wage change. In the preceding year, 42 percent of new contracts had freezes and 2 percent had wage cuts. This episode supports our view that downward rigidity is broken when firms are under extreme duress. The 1981–82 recession was particularly severe; unemployment peaked at over 10 percent, the highest level since the end of the Great Depression. Excluding 1983 from our sample, an average of only 1.7 percent of workers were involved in negative wage settlements in the first year of a contract, and this overstates the frequency of wage cuts in any given year, since there were fewer negative changes over the life of the contract than in the first year. Assuming an average contract life of two years, and if all wage cuts occur in the first year, the proportion of workers with negative changes in any one year would be only 0.9 percent. Most recently, from 1990 through 1994, only 2.2 percent of workers covered by new settlements took wage cuts, despite inflation in the CPI averaging only 3.6 percent.

A further check on the frequency of negative wage changes under conditions of very low inflation and high unemployment comes from Canadian data analyzed by Pierre Fortin.[7] From 1992 to 1994, Canada averaged 1.2 percent inflation (as measured by the CPI) and 11.0 percent unemployment. Fortin's tabulation of wage settlements in large collective agreements without COLA clauses shows that only 5.7 percent of such agreements had cuts, while 47.2 percent called for unchanged wages. This huge mass at zero demonstrates the undeniable importance of wage rigidity in Canadian contracts. In somewhat better times there were yet fewer cuts in base pay. From 1986 to 1988, for example, with 4.2 percent inflation and 8.8 percent unemployment, only 0.25 percent of such contracts had wage cuts, while 12.6 percent had wage freezes.

Historical Evidence on Wage Rigidity

Although evidence on wage rigidity before World War II is much harder to come by, some authors have tackled the job. Daniel J. B. Mitchell, in his study of changing wage flexibility, compares the postwar behavior of manufacturing wages discussed above with evidence on manufacturing wages from establishment surveys in the 1920s. Although he expresses reservations about the reliability of these early surveys, he concludes that downward wage rigidity was less characteristic of the 1920s, and suggests that it became prominent as a result of legal and institutional changes, especially the development and acceptance of modern labor relations practices, which, he argues, have their roots in the Great Depression. Anthony O'Brien, however, using information from trade and industry

---

[7] Personal communication from Pierre Fortin, University of Quebec at Montreal, August 13, 1995.

sources, establishes the existence of downward rigidity in the 1920s. He shows that employers were even reluctant to cut wages during the onset of the Great Depression, before the legal and institutional changes cited by Mitchell occurred, and he finds that this reluctance was overcome only after economic conditions worsened in the early 1930s. Christopher Hanes finds evidence of nominal wage rigidity in the recession that began in 1893, as well as in the early stages of the Great Depression. All three authors are testing modern theories of why firms would be reluctant to cut wages; none finds reason to question that firms had been reluctant to do so, even before the postwar period.[8]

A Survey of Wage Changes

In order to get direct evidence on wage changes for individuals, in the summer of 1995 we conducted a telephone survey of the Washington, D.C. area. In particular, we wanted to ask directly about wage changes in order to be able to compare our results with those of the Panel Study of Income Dynamics (PSID), which asks about wage levels. We judged that although many workers might not report accurately the amount of their base wage or salary each year, they would be able to recall whether their wage had changed in the last twelve months and, if so, whether it had increased or decreased. When respondents did report negative wage changes, we requested further information about the circumstances. If individuals are frequently moved into lower positions, it might be rare to see a wage reduction for a job classification, even though individuals correctly report that they have taken wage cuts. The questionnaire was designed to detect such a possibility.

In the core of the survey, respondents were first asked about their employment status, and, if employed, whether they had the same employer as one year ago. Those who had stayed with the same employer were then asked if their job title or classification had changed over the past year, and whether they were performing substantially the same duties as they had been a year ago. After the method of pay (for example, hourly wage, annualized salary) had been ascertained, respondents were asked, 'Excluding overtime, commissions, and bonuses, has your base rate of pay changed since a year ago today?' Affirmative responses were followed with 'Did it increase or decrease? By how much?' Additional demographic information, including age, race, and sector of employment, was then solicited.

We contacted a total of 569 individuals. Of the 409 respondents who had not changed employers and who were wage or salary earners, seven reported wage or salary cuts with no change in the circumstances of their job. Four of these were workers for the District of Columbia government, which then and now confronts a budget crisis; one was a construction worker who speculated that his employer had reduced wages and substituted illegal aliens for native-born workers; one was a railroad worker who was paid by the run and reported the rate had been reduced because of cutbacks; and one acted sufficiently intoxicated that the interviewer doubted whether any of the questions were being understood, before the respondent abruptly hung up. In addition to these

[8] Mitchell (1985); O'Brien (1989); Hanes (1993, 1996).

seven, four other respondents reported a change in circumstances that resulted in a lower individual wage or salary, but not necessarily lower overall compensation, for the same job. Of these, two had been promoted from part-time to full-time employment over the course of the year; one explained that she had taken a decrease in wages but was more than compensated by an increase in benefits. The other two said that they had changed jobs within the firm.

The survey results, summarized in Table 19.2, show that only 2.7 percent of respondents who had stayed at the same job had received wage cuts. This result does not depend on the large number of federal workers in the Washington area. In fact, only 2.4 percent of private sector workers reported wage cuts. Admittedly, the survey is not a representative sample of the national population, as it is confined to the Washington area and biased toward people who answered the telephone and were willing to answer our questions. Nonetheless, it suggests that the fraction of workers who receive wage cuts in any given year is small; with double the survey fractions, the numbers are still small. This conclusion is supported by the answers to another question on our survey: whether respondents personally knew anyone who had ever taken a cut in pay while on the same job. The meaning of these answers depends upon the universe of friends, relatives, and acquaintances of the respondents and on their memories. Nevertheless, if pay cuts were fairly common, we would expect that they could easily dredge up some instances. Yet only 14.7 percent of respondents recalled personal knowledge of a pay cut.

Recent Panel Studies

Four recent studies, by David Card and Dean Hyslop, David Lebow, David Stockton, and William Wascher, Shulamit Kahn, and Kenneth McLaughlin, have used data from the PSID to analyze wage change for individuals.[9] In each case, the authors compute wage change as the difference between reported wage levels in consecutive years. All find evidence of asymmetry in the histograms of wage changes, and some bunching at zero change. But the histograms also show that in any year, a noticeable fraction of workers receive wage or salary cuts. If true, such a finding would greatly reduce the economic significance of downward rigidity. However, we show that the crude data cannot be interpreted in this way. Most of these negative changes are spurious; they arise because errors in the reporting of wage levels greatly exaggerate the actual frequency of wage cuts. All four studies are aware of the importance of reporting error. But, except for McLaughlin, the authors make no attempt to correct for the errors that we find important, and we find that McLaughlin's correction does not go nearly far enough.[10]

---

[9] Card and Hyslop (1996); Lebow, Stockton, and Wascher (1995); Kahn (1995); McLaughlin (1994).

[10] McLaughlin presents corrected measures of the standard deviation of wage changes, and then infers the impact of the correction for the frequency of negative wage changes, using the empirical distribution of wage changes in the PSID. However, this is inappropriate if the underlying true distribution is asymmetric, as the distribution of wage changes appears to be. For example, suppose that the true distribution of wage changes contained no negative values. If a normal measurement error was added to the true values, a large number of

Table 19.2. *Job stayers reporting changes in base pay in previous year*
Percent, except where indicated

| | Reported change | | | Number of respondents |
	Negative	None	Positive	
Total	2.7	30.8	66.5	409
Private	2.4	34.0	63.6	250
Public	3.1	25.8	71.1	159
Wage earners	5.8	39.8	54.4	103
Private	4.0	41.9	54.1	74
Public	10.3	34.5	55.2	29
Salaried and other	1.6	27.8	70.6	306
Private	1.7	30.7	67.6	176
Public	1.5	23.8	74.6	130

Source: Authors' calculations from 1995 Washington area telephone survey, as described in text.

Validation studies of wage surveys similar to the PSID show that reporting errors are quite large. For example, the January 1977 validation study of the Current Population Survey (CPS) shows an estimated standard deviation of 0.167 in the difference between log wages reported by household respondents and those reported by their employers.[11] With such a standard deviation, response error alone could easily account for all the observations of wage cuts in the PSID. We compare the findings using the PSID with other evidence to show this is, in fact, the case.[12]

Armed with our survey results, we check whether the PSID-generated data could have arisen from a population that resembles our survey, making appropriate allowance for reporting error in the PSID. To this end, we 'dirty' our data by adding random errors corresponding to observed distributions of response errors in the CPS, in which questions about wages are quite similar to those in the PSID. To estimate the distribution of the response error in wage changes, we need to know not only the distribution of response error for wage levels in a single survey, but also the autocorrelation of those response errors across surveys and the frequency with which people report their wages correctly. The distribution of these response errors is generated with the help of three

false negative wage changes would be recorded. Simply reducing the variance of the empirical distribution by a mean-preserving reduction in the spread equal to the variance of the measurement error, as McLaughlin does, will reduce the frequency of false negatives but will not eliminate them. It is impossible to reconstruct the true underlying distribution in this fashion. Kahn recognizes the presence of errors but does not attempt to correct for them because doing so would only strengthen her conclusions about the presence of downward rigidity.

[11] Mellow and Sider (1983, p. 335, n. 6) report that 'the estimated variance of the difference in log wage is 0.167.' Our calculations, based on regression estimates that they present, suggest approximately this figure for the standard deviation.

[12] A validation survey for the PSID shows large errors in reported income, but since the plant chosen for the survey did not pay straight time wages, the accuracy of the PSID question on hourly earnings cannot be assessed (see Duncan and Hill, 1985).

separate statistics. In the 1977 CPS validation survey, workers' wage responses are matched against responses of their employers and, as mentioned above, have a standard deviation of 0.167 in the difference between log wages reported by individuals and log wages reported by their respective employers. The CPS–Social Security match survey shows the autocorrelation of differences between earnings reported by CPS respondents and their individual earnings as reported to the Social Security Administration.[13] These parameters would be sufficient to generate a normal distribution of response error, but one final consideration suggests that the errors are not normal: some respondents—in fact, 44.2 percent—report their wages or salaries exactly right. So we generate the error distribution under the assumption that 44.2 percent of respondents make no error in either year and the rest make normally distributed autocorrelated errors.

The alternative distributions of wage change are compared in Figure 19.1. The upper left panel shows the histogram of wage changes in our Washington area survey. The histogram when our wage survey is dirtied as just described is shown in the upper right panel. And the lower right panel shows the histogram of wage changes calculated from the PSID of 1988, a year in which wage inflation was comparable to the average wage increase in our sample. The dirtied histogram shows a much fatter left tail and even more instances of negative wage change than the PSID, implying that an error-free distribution of wage changes from the PSID would show an even smaller proportion of wage cuts than our survey.

Our conclusion that most negative wage changes in the PSID are due to measurement error is robust to various changes we made in generating the error term. We performed various checks. For example, since our data on wage changes probably also contain some measurement error, it should not be surprising that the standard deviation of our dirtied distribution is greater than that of the PSID. As a conservative alternative to the previous comparison, we assume a response error small enough to make the variation in our data plus this response error just conform to the PSID data for 1988. This yields approximately the same proportion of negative wage changes as that reported by Kahn. The lower left panel in Figure 19.1 shows this alternative hypothetical distribution.

Comparing Union Settlement Data with the PSID

John Shea has examined the measurement errors for unionized workers in the PSID directly and reports his results in a discussion of the Card and Hyslop study.[14] Shea matches individual PSID households to the provisions of particular union contracts by relating PSID information on individuals' industry, occupation, union affiliation, and county of residence to information from other sources about employers' locations and bargaining outcomes. For the period from 1981–82 through 1986–87, this procedure yields 379 observations for which Shea has contract data to compare with responses from employees in the PSID. He calculates that only 1.3 percent of his sample have received nominal wage cuts according to their contracts, while over the same period,

---

[13] Bound and Krueger (1991).   [14] Shea (1996).

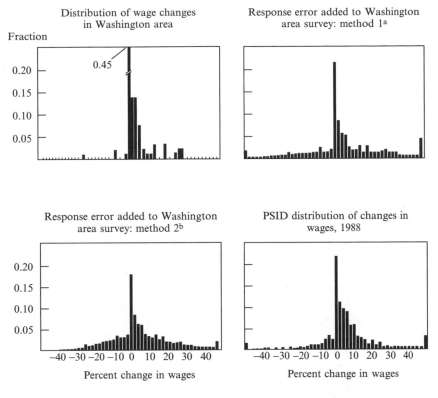

Figure 19.1. *Distribution of wage changes for job stayers.*

Source: Data for the upper left panel are from the authors' survey; for the lower right panel, from the Panel Study of Income Dynamics (PSID); and for the other panels, from the authors' calculations as described in text.

[a] With correlation of correct responses in consecutive years of 1.0, and standard deviation of response error of 0.167.

[b] With correlation of correct responses in consecutive years of 0.5, and standard deviation of response error calculated so that standard deviation of distribution equals standard deviation of wage changes in the PSID.

21.1 percent report wage levels in consecutive years of the PSID that, when subtracted, imply wage cuts.

As a further check on the PSID-based results, we compare the incidence of wage cuts calculated from the PSID data with the incidence of cuts in new union contracts discussed above. Kahn reports that, on the average, 11.8 percent of changes in nominal wages were negative for union workers in the PSID for the years 1976 to 1988.[15] Given that only 3.5 percent of workers in large bargaining sessions took a pay cut in the first year of a new contract, this implies that a minimum of 70 percent of the negative wage changes from the PSID are spurious; recognizing that wage cuts are concentrated in the first year

[15] Kahn (1995, Table 2, p. 17).

of multiyear contracts raises the proportion to 85 percent, on the assumption that any cuts occurred in the first year of two-year contracts. If the wages of workers involved in smaller settlements behave more like those in the nonunionized sector, the foregoing figures would overstate wage cuts if nonunion workers have a lower incidence of wage cuts than union workers. In fact, Kahn shows that in the PSID from 1976 to 1988, the incidence of negative wage changes for nonunionized workers is 20 percent lower than for unionized workers (9.45 percent as compared to 11.77 percent).[16]

Comparing the PSID with Employers' Wage Reports

We also have evidence about wage changes from employers' records to compare with the PSID data on wages of new hires. As a by-product of his study of the hiring and jobs of less-educated workers, Harry Holzer has obtained employer data on wages. He interviewed a random sample of employers in four cities: Atlanta, Detroit, Boston, and Los Angeles. All of these employers were asked about the work conditions of new hires, including the last person hired. Weighting the data by employer size, Holzer shows that one year after a vacancy had been filled, only 4.8 percent of new hires had taken a wage cut.[17] These numbers are larger than those implied by our survey, and are also larger than the recent figures for union givebacks, but they are still quite small and, considering that they refer only to new hires, are not inconsistent with the other data. By contrast, the PSID data shows that 13.6 percent of new hires experience wage cuts in their first year on the job.[18]

Other Ways to Cut Wage Costs

Some may object that our attention to downward wage rigidity ignores other ways in which employers can reduce wage costs and so avoid the employment effects that we associate with this phenomenon. Firms could cut nonwage benefits, but we suspect that the scope for doing so is limited. Workers would object to cuts in benefits, just as they object to cuts in pay. Many companies have recently asked workers to pay a larger share of the cost of health insurance, but since health costs have, on average, been rising quite rapidly, in most cases such increases will only partly defray the companies' increasing costs for this benefit.

Firms could also hire new workers at wages below those paid to existing workers. While firms certainly have some freedom to adjust the wages of new hires, it is doubtful that this is important to our overall findings. First, the cost of new labor will not matter to a firm that is laying off workers. Second, a firm that is recovering from a negative shock that has resulted in a nominal constraint on its wage setting may well hire back laid-off workers, who will be paid their old wage. Finally, even a growing firm does not

---

[16] Kahn (1995, Table 2, p. 17).

[17] Personal communication from Harry J. Holzer, Michigan State University, East Lansing, Mich., April 20, 1995, and Holzer (1996).

[18] This is the fraction of job stayers with one to two years of tenure that reports lower wages in 1992 than in 1991.

have complete freedom in how it sets its entry wages. Consider the controversy that arose in the early 1980s when a very few firms adopted 'two-tier' salary systems that allowed newly hired workers to be paid less than those already on the job. The fact that this practice was newsworthy suggests that it is infrequent, and the worker resistance to the plans that was reported at that time suggests why.

More subtly, firms may avoid the customary wage increases associated with merit and seniority. In a firm that is maintaining its size or growing while undergoing normal turnover, such increases will lead to a reduction in labor costs. On the other hand, in a shrinking or stable firm with low turnover, the necessity of granting some merit increases, or increases with seniority or promotion, can add an upward drift to labor costs. Data from the PSID for average wage levels by age cohort, which are not sensitive to the reporting errors that we discuss above, permit us to estimate the size of normal wage gains of this type. Measured as the average annual wage change for a cohort of job stayers relative to the mean wage increase of all workers in the economy, these averaged 1.2 percent a year between 1970 and 1992. Freezing all the wage increases normally associated with merit, promotion, and seniority could provide savings in unit labor costs of about this amount.

We allow for all these effects in two ways. First, both the simulation model and a version of the time-series model presented below allow for a drift of individual wages relative to the economy mean wage, to capture the possibility that firms erode nominal wage constraints in the ways just discussed. Second, both models allow firms that are in distress to lower wages to desired levels.

Summary

To conclude, data on changes in wages and salaries that are relatively free of error strongly confirm the existence of downward nominal wage rigidity. The results of different studies are summarized in Table 19.3. All show an asymmetry of wage changes about the mean, and all but the PSID show that negative wage changes are quite rare. We show that reporting errors in the PSID cause wage changes calculated from that data to greatly exaggerate the actual frequency of wage declines. Indeed, reporting error in the PSID is sufficiently large to explain the difference between the distribution of wage changes constructed from the PSID and the other sources that we have described.

Despite the pervasive evidence, some model builders reject downward wage rigidity on the grounds that it implies money illusion. Some who might accept the idea that wage cuts are rare because they violate implicit contracts between firms and workers might, nonetheless, insist that the rigidity must apply to real rather than nominal wages. Having already provided direct evidence that downward rigidity is, in fact, widespread and applies to nominal wages, there is not much about wages that we can add in response. However, we would point to the existence of money illusion in another familiar context, the payment of dividends. Our computations using CRSP data show a pattern that strongly resembles that observed for nominal wage changes. Dividends are rarely cut, and the distribution of changes in nominal dividends is asymmetric and bunched at zero.

Table 19.3. *Evidence on nominal wage and salary rigidity*

Source	Nature of data	Summary
Bureau of Labor Statistics	Changes in wages by employers making general wage changes, 1959–78	Negligible fractions of both union and nonunion employers making negative changes
Authors' survey of Washington area	Phone survey of respondents' wage changes in previous year, 1995	1.7 percent with negative pay changes and no change in job characteristics; additional 1 percent with changes in job characteristics
Bureau of Labor Statistics	Contract settlements involving more than 1,000 workers	2.3 percent of contracts with negative changes in first year, average 1970–94
Pierre Fortin	Canadian labor contracts without COLAs	0.25 percent with wage cuts during 1986–88; 5.7 percent with cuts and 47.2 percent with wage freezes during 1992–94
Panel Study of Income Dynamics	Difference between consecutive responses of job stayers on wages and salary	10.6 percent of wage earners and 24.3 percent of salary earners with pay cuts
Harry Holzer four-city study	Changes in wages of new employees reported by firms hiring noncollege graduates	4.84 percent of new employees with wage cuts
O'Brien, Hanes, and others	Historical data	Considerable wage rigidity in prewar recessions

Source: Authors' summary of studies described in text.

SIMULATION MODEL

In this section we present a formal model calibrated to the major stylized facts concerning wage change, job change, and estimates of the lowest sustainable rate of unemployment in the U.S. economy. This model rests on three pillars: monopolistic competition, large heterogeneous demand and supply shocks to different firms, and downward wage rigidity.

These three characteristics of the economy produce a nonlinear relation between long-run inflation and unemployment. Supply and demand shocks are heterogeneous: they affect firms that are monopolistically competitive. For a variety of reasons, workers share in the effects of firm-specific shocks. For example, a positive demand shock to a firm will result in a rise in the wages of the workers at that firm, and also in an increase in employment. These job shocks thus cause both job creation and job destruction, and dispersion in wage changes. With this heterogeneity, money wage rigidity will act as a constraint on the wage changes of some firms, even when wages in the economy as a whole are rising. The binding effect of downward wage rigidity raises real wages and decreases employment. The number of constrained firms and the effects of the constraint will be nonlinear with inflation.

Our simulation exercises are informed by empirical findings about these features of the U.S. economy. We have already documented from many sources the extent of downward rigidity in money wages. We now look briefly at the other two features.

MONOPOLISTIC COMPETITION. Monopolistic competition is a pervasive feature of our economy. Very few prices are set in auction markets and virtually all firms have some discretion in determining the prices they charge. Robert Hall and Mark Bils both use the cyclical nature of the U.S. economy to infer the existence of extensive monopolistic competition from the observation that small changes in employment result in large changes in output.[19] An elasticity of demand of -3.8 in our simulation model yields a labor share of 0.73, as observed in the U.S. economy in 1994.

HETEROGENEITY OF WAGE AND EMPLOYMENT CHANGES. The third pillar of the model is heterogeneity in shocks to demand and supply. The U.S. economy displays considerable firm-level heterogeneity in wage and employment changes. The simulation model has sufficient firm-level demand and supply shocks to generate these observations.

Jonathan Leonard and Steven Davis, John Haltiwanger, and Scott Schuh have documented that each year, on average, growing firms increase employment by an amount equal to about 11 percent of total employment, while shrinking firms contract employment by only slightly less.[20] These numbers change a little over the course of the business cycle, but whatever the unemployment rate, gross job creation and gross job destruction are much larger than the corresponding net changes.

There is also ample evidence of significant heterogeneity in both the level and change of wages across individuals and firms. We have described a number of studies that attempt to measure the distribution of individuals' wage changes.[21] However, the standard deviation of average wage changes for firms will be smaller than that for individuals. Using the BLS data for general wage increases for manufacturing establishments cited above, we computed what the standard deviation would be if the left half of the distribution were symmetrical with the right half. This approximates what the standard deviation would be in the absence of downward rigidity. For 1964–78, but excluding the oil shock years of the early 1970s, this procedure gives a median standard deviation of 2.8 percentage points. This is probably lower than the variation in the change in the average wage across firms, since demand conditions may force firms to pay more or less for specific types of labor and this may affect average wages. Also, we compute that the standard deviation of negotiated first-year wage changes for the Canadian contract data described above ranges from 2 to 4 percentage points, depending on the year.

---

[19] Hall (1988); Bils (1987)

[20] Leonard (1987); Davis, Haltiwanger, and Schuh (1996).

[21] McLaughlin (1994) presents several estimates of the standard deviation of percentage real wage growth across individuals who stay on the same job. These estimates are corrected for measurement error, and none is less than 9.5 percentage points.

We believe the distribution of observed wages and wage changes reflects market forces and the desires of firms and workers. We further believe that if firms are forced to pay higher wages, they will hire less labor.[22] The heterogeneity of wage changes may reflect changes in the demand and supply of idiosyncratic skills in small geographic or occupational markets. Alternatively, if wages are set to satisfy wage norms and such norms depend on profitability, or if wages reflect explicit or implicit bargaining, wage changes will depend on firm demand. Our simulation model allows for either interpretation.

Deriving the Simulation Model

The simulation model is presented in two parts. First, we describe the underlying representative firm model of monopolistic competition and wage setting. We then show how the simulation model is constructed from this model, by allowing a large number of simulated firms to face different supply and demand conditions and downward money wage rigidity. Without downward wage rigidity and heterogeneity, our simulated economy has unique equilibrium real wage and unemployment rates. The behavior of this economy can be summarized by the price setting and wage setting behavior of the monopolistically competitive firms.

PRICE DETERMINATION. Given monopolistically competitive firms, each with its own market niche, the demand for a firm's output (D) will be

$$D = [(M/\bar{p})(p/\bar{p})^{-\beta}]/n, \tag{1}$$

where M is the money supply, p is the price of the firm's output, $\bar{p}$ is the average price in the economy, and n is the number of firms. The first factor, $M/\bar{p}$, for simplicity, represents aggregate demand. The second factor in equation 1, $(p/\bar{p})^{-\beta}$, gives the downward slope to the demand for the firm's product. For a representative firm that is charging the average price, this term will be equal to one, since p will be equal to $\bar{p}$. Nonetheless, the presence of this term affects the equilibrium output and pricing in the economy, since each firm takes $\bar{p}$ as given and sets prices to equate marginal cost and marginal revenue.

Each firm produces output (Q) in proportion to labor input (L):

$$Q = L. \tag{2}$$

It is useful to normalize the labor force to equal one. So, letting the unemployment rate be u, output will be $1 - u$.[23]

---

[22] See Dickens (1994) for a discussion of the theoretical and empirical evidence on whether labor demand responds to negotiated changes in wages; and Dickens (1986) for a discussion of the employment effects of wage changes in firms where bargaining is implicit or the threat of collective action forces them to pay higher wages.

[23] With labor productivity (G_t) changing, we assume that $Q = G_t L$. Also, with changes in productivity, we assume that fixed costs are proportional to full employment output, so they are proportional to G_t, and that s, the value of leisure, is also proportional to labor productivity.

Given the level of their wages, firms will choose prices to maximize profits. This maximization will determine individual firms' prices, p, and also the average level of all prices, $\bar{p}$. Once firms' prices are given, their demand is given according to equation 1, and so the level of output is also determined.

WAGE DETERMINATION. In the absence of any constraint against money wage cuts, the wage is assumed to result from an implicit or explicit bargain between the firm and its workers. We call the result of this bargain the notional wage, since it is the wage that would be set in the absence of any constraint due to nominal rigidities.

Consistent with the idea that the notional wage is the consequence of an implicit or explicit bargain between the firm and the workers, it is a weighted average of two factors. This is the generalized Nash solution: the surpluses of firms and workers, geometrically weighted according to bargaining power, are maximized with respect to the real wage. The firms' surplus consists of total revenues net of the wages paid to the workers and fixed costs. The workers' surplus is their wages net of their opportunity costs—their expected returns if they looked for jobs elsewhere.

The bargained real notional wage, ω^n, per efficiency unit is given by the formula[24]

$$\omega^n = a[(pD - \bar{p}f)/\bar{p}L] + (1 - a)[(1 - u)\bar{w}/\bar{p} + u\,s], \tag{3}$$

where $\bar{w}$ is the average nominal wage, u is the unemployment rate, a is an index of workers' bargaining power that takes values between zero and one, s is the value of the workers' time while unemployed, and f is the ratio of the fixed costs of the firm to the value of output at full employment.[25] When worker bargaining power is equal to zero, wage setting becomes competitive, with the real wage equal to the opportunity cost of time.

Analysis of the Representative Firm Model

The equilibrium of the representative firm model occurs at the intersection of an aggregate demand equation resulting from pricing behavior, and an aggregate supply

---

[24] Such a wage equation can be easily derived as the generalized Nash solution when firms and workers bargain over wages but not employment. If workers receive a wage from the firm of w^n, the surplus per worker left to the firm in nominal terms will be

$$S_f = p - \bar{p}(f/L) - w^n,$$

where f represents the fixed costs of production. We assume that the capital of the firm is firm-specific, so it has no alternative use.

A worker's surplus for working for the firm is

$$S_w = w^n - w_o,$$

where w_o is the worker's opportunity cost. This value of the worker's alternative is, in turn, a weighted average. If the worker must seek employment elsewhere, with probability u he or she will be unemployed and the value of staying at home will be denoted by s, which includes the unemployment benefit; and with probability $(1 - u)$ that he or she will be employed and will, on average, receive the average wage in the economy. If w^n is chosen to maximize the geometric mean of the firms' surplus and the workers' surplus—that is, to maximize $S_f^{1-a}S_w^a$—the wage will be given by the bargaining equation (equation 3).

[25] We assume that s and profits rise with productivity, and therefore, productivity affects the notional real wage in a multiplicative fashion.

equation resulting from the wage setting model. Both of these relationships depend only on the real wage. The aggregate demand curve is the result of monopolistically competitive pricing. Each firm chooses its own price to maximize revenues net of payments to labor, taking the money wage and the aggregate price level as fixed. A firm whose demand curve has constant elasticity, as in equation 1, and with the production function of equation 2, will set its nominal price, p, as a constant markup over the nominal unit labor cost. So the aggregate demand curve will be of the form

$$\omega = (\beta - 1)/\beta, \tag{4}$$

where ω is the notional real wage.

Equation 4 conforms to our reading of the character of the real wage—it varies little with the cycle. Some have argued that the real wage is procyclic; others have argued that it is countercyclic. Equation 4, which results from the constant elasticity of demand function, equation 2, is embraced as a compromise between these two possible readings of the evidence. In Figure 19.2, AA represents equation 4. It gives the response of prices, relative to wages, as a function of the level of demand (or employment). Because the real wage is constant, AA is a horizontal line.

If the price equation, which is set taking wages as constant, is perceived as the aggregate demand equation, its counterpart, the aggregate supply curve, will be given by the wages that result from the wage determination process, which are set with constant price expectations. Thus the aggregate supply curve, which relates notional wages and unemployment, will come out of equation 3. Noting that in equilibrium $p = \bar{p}$, $D/L = 1$, $L = 1 - u$, and $\bar{w}/\bar{p} = (\beta - 1)/\beta$ equation 3 will yield

$$\omega^n = d[(1 - f)/(1 - u)] + (1 - a)[(1 - u)(\beta - 1)/\beta + us]. \tag{5}$$

This is curve SS in Figure 19.2. It slopes upward because the value of workers' alternative uses of their time rises—as do profits—as unemployment falls.[26] Along this curve, as employment rises the bargained real wage rises. As employment increases, unemployment declines, assuming constant labor supply.

LSRU not NAIRU

The equilibrium unemployment and real wage rates in this economy occur at the intersection of the AA and the SS curves. We call this level of unemployment the LSRU (lowest sustainable rate of unemployment).

In the absence of downward wage rigidity, the LSRU would constitute the NAIRU ('nonaccelerating inflation' rate of unemployment) of the model, the level of unemployment at which inflation remains constant. With downward wage rigidity, however, higher sustained rates of unemployment accompany very low rates of sustained inflation, and a unique NAIRU does not exist.

---

[26] As long as s, the value of leisure, is less than the real wage, $(\beta - 1)/\beta$, SS will slope upward.

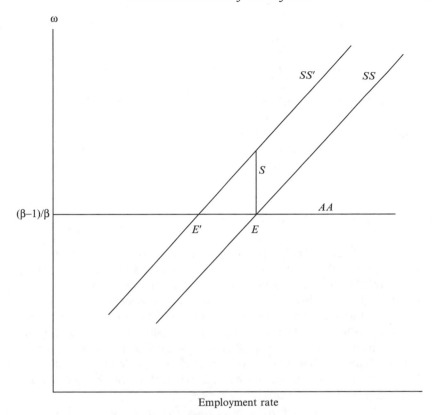

Figure 19.2. *Reduced-form price and wage equations.*
Source: Author's model as described in text.

Adding Heterogeneity and Wage Rigidity

We now add firm-level heterogeneity and nominal wage rigidity to the model of the representative firm to obtain the simulation model.

DEMAND AND SUPPLY HETEROGENEITY. Heterogeneity is introduced by the addition of a random term, ε, to the demand for each individual firm. The demand equation, equation 1, becomes

$$D = (M/\bar{p})(p/\bar{p})^{-\beta} e^{\varepsilon}/n. \qquad (1a)$$

The expected value of e^{ε} is one because it represents the shocks specific to individual firms. We also assume that ε is serially correlated—following a simple AR(1) process. The innovations to ε are assumed to be normal with constant variance.

We also add heterogeneity to the wage bargains with a supplementary random term, η. The bargaining equation, equation 5, becomes

$$\omega^n = a[(pD - \bar{p}f)/\bar{p}L] + (1 - a)[(1 - u)(\beta - 1)/\beta + us] + \eta. \tag{5a}$$

The term η is an AR(1) process with mean zero and constant variance normal innovations. It can be thought of as reflecting idiosyncratic variation in bargaining power or change in labor supply conditions.

Further realism is added by letting the bargained wage respond autoregressively to levels of current variables, such that

$$\begin{aligned}
\omega^n = (1 - z)\omega_{-1} &+ z\{a[(pD - \bar{p}f)/\bar{p}L] \\
&+ (1 - a)[(1 - u)(\beta - 1)/\beta + us]\} + \eta.
\end{aligned} \tag{5b}$$

MONEY WAGE RIGIDITY. It remains to describe in detail the nature of money wage rigidity in the simulation model. Complete money wage rigidity is too stark. Our survey and the interviews by Bewley and Brainard suggest that wage cuts are quite rare; nevertheless, sometimes they do occur. Bewley and Brainard suggest that firms are likely to make wage cuts after a second year of losses. The interviews of Kahneman, Knetsch, and Thaler show that most respondents would view reductions in money wages as fair if a firm was losing money. In this spirit, our simulation allows firms with two years of consecutive losses to cut wages to their notional level. When they do this, we also give those firms with negative ε an increase in that term that leaves ε partway between its former value and zero.

There are two possible interpretations of these features of the model. On the one hand, releasing the wage constraint could be viewed as an adjustment deemed fair by the existing workers after two years of losses. In this case, the increase in the firms' ε reflects reorganizing for greater efficiency as they cut wages. Alternatively, one might view the firms as going out of business. The workers in those firms find employment in new firms with no wage history to constrain wage setting. In this case, keeping ε negative would reflect the disadvantages experienced by new firms relative to established firms.

There are further reasons to relax the downward wage constraint. We discussed above how firms might try to find alternative ways to reduce labor costs if money wages cannot fall. This will only partly offset the effects of downward wage rigidity in unit labor costs, because either existing employees will resist changes, such as cuts in benefits, or the employer will be forced to adopt less efficient employment arrangements. The simulation allows for all these ways in which employers can circumvent downward wage rigidity, by assuming that constrained firms will be able to reduce their labor costs at the rate of 1 percent per year.

To summarize the treatment of downward wage rigidity: the nominal wage paid will be a fraction (0.99) of the previous money wage or the nominal notional wage, whichever is greater, except in the case of firms with two consecutive periods of losses.

For those firms, the nominal wage will be the notional wage for a firm with the demand shift, ε, decreased by a fraction of its value (if negative).

INTUITIVE WORKING OF THE SIMULATION MODEL. The effects of nominal wage rigidity in this model can also be seen in Figure 19.2. Nominal wage rigidity shifts up the wage setting equation (supply equation) in Figure 19.2 from *SS* to *SS'*. The amount of the shift depends on the rate of inflation. The resulting real wage and employment level can be found at the intersection of the aggregate demand curve and the shifted aggregate supply curve. With a horizontal *AA* curve, the real wage is unchanged and all the effect of the shift is in employment. We describe below in greater detail the dynamics of this shift.

Parameterization of Model and Simulation Results

We now simulate the model to determine the effect on employment and output of targeting zero inflation. The procedure also provides evidence on the robustness of our results. Our simulation model has ten parameters. Three come from the demand equation, six from the wage setting equation, and one determines the behavior of firms that have two periods of negative profits. The parameters from the demand equation are the elasticity of demand (β), the standard deviation (σ_ε) of the innovation in ε, and the first-order autocorrelation of ε. Parameters from the wage setting equation include the bargaining power of labor (a), the level of fixed costs (f), the value of time spent unemployed (s), the degree of autoregression in the wage setting equation (z), the standard deviation (σ_η) of the innovation in η, and the first-order autocorrelation of η.

Prior knowledge does not allow us to specify with confidence the values of all these parameters. A commonly used alternative approach is to pick a number of characteristics of the economy equal to the number of parameters, and choose the parameter values so that the simulated values for those characteristics match the values for the actual economy. However, our simulation model is meant to characterize the behavior of the economy along many fewer dimensions than the number of parameters. So we simulate the performance of the economy for a large number of different combinations of parameter values, where each combination must match only three important character-istics of the economy: an equilibrium rate of unemployment at 3 percent inflation, the rate of job creation and destruction, and the standard deviation of firm wage changes. To do this, we divide the parameters into two groups: seven parameters chosen randomly, and three parameters that we use as instruments to hit our three targets. For those parameter combinations that permit the model to converge, we simulate the effect of reducing inflation from 3 percent to zero.

We choose the equilibrium rate of unemployment at 3 percent inflation as 5.8 percent, in accord with our perception that this is the median of existing natural rate estimates, and because the behavior of inflation over the last year and a half, when the unemployment rate has varied between 5.4 percent and 6 percent, suggests an equilib-rium value in that range. We choose job creation and destruction to fit the observations of Leonard and Davis, Haltiwanger, and Schuh cited earlier, that about 11 percent of jobs are created, and slightly fewer destroyed, over the course of a year.[27] Finally, we choose to make the standard deviation of wage change equal to 2.8 percent, the number cited above from manufacturing data.

Simulation Procedure

Given the three characteristics of the real economy that we want our simulation to display, computational strategy determines how the ten parameters of our model are divided into two groups: three instruments and seven parameters to be chosen randomly, s, σ_ε, and σ_η are chosen as the instruments because we know that the equilibrium unemployment rate is substantially affected by s, while the amount of churning in firm size and the standard deviation of wage changes are most directly affected by σ_ε and σ_η, respectively.

The remaining parameters are chosen uniformly in their relevant ranges. The two autocorrelation parameters are chosen between 0 and 1. The weight on the share of profits is chosen between 0 and 1. The elasticity of demand is chosen between 2 and 6, comfortably encompassing the value of 3.8 which is consistent with labor's share in the U.S. economy. Fixed costs (times n) are chosen between 0.0 and 0.3, so as to keep total fixed costs below capital's share, which is less than 0.3. The extent of reversion of the demand shock for reorganizing firms (those with two periods of negative profits) is chosen between 0 and 1. Finally, the bargaining power of labor (a) is allowed to take any value between 0 and 1.

For each attempted simulation, the seven random parameter values are chosen first. Then the program, through an iterative process, moves the instruments so as to match the three simulated characteristics to their target values—unemployment of 5.8 percent, a job creation rate of 0.11, and a standard deviation of wage changes of 2.8 percent. The value of time while unemployed (s) is restricted to exceed 0 in this exercise. In over 80 percent of the cases, it is impossible to hit the targets given the values of the randomly chosen parameters and the restriction on s.[28] When the program is able to find values for the three instrumental parameters that allow the simulation to hit the three targets, it then simulates the effect of reducing the inflation rate from 3 percent to zero and records the results. The process is repeated to obtain a reasonable number of simulation trials.

---

[27] The churning of employment between firms is a mechanism by which nominal rigidity is overcome in the economy, and by embodying this feature we capture this mechanism in the simulation. Constrained firms will tend to shrink, and workers who lose employment at high wage constrained firms may find reemployment at low wage unconstrained firms.

[28] We checked a number of these cases to be sure that the failure to find acceptable parameter values for so many cases is due to their nonexistence and does not represent a failure of our search algorithm. Doing a grid search by hand, we were unable to find values of our instrumental parameters that allowed our simulation to hit the three calibration targets. The failure is due to the wide range of values that we allow the randomly chosen parameters to take. In experiments where the ranges are sharply restricted, the search algorithm is able to calibrate the simulation in the majority of cases.

Long-Run Simulation Results

With 432 successful runs of the simulation, the median increase in the equilibrium unemployment rate associated with operating with zero rather than 3 percent inflation is 2.1 percentage points. The minimum value obtained is 0.6 percentage points. The tenth percentile of the distribution of unemployment changes is 1 percentage point, and the ninetieth percentile is 5.7 percentage points. The range containing 90 percent of the simulated values runs from 0.8 percentage points to 8.5 percentage points.

To examine the long-run relation between inflation and unemployment, we choose benchmark parameters to look at a typical case, and then adjust them slightly to hit our three targets. We choose the elasticity of demand (β) as 3.8 to yield a labor share of 0.73, and we set the bargaining power of labor (a) at 0.2, the fraction of fixed costs (f) at 0.15, and the value of time spent unemployed (s) at 0.38. We set the standard deviation of demand shocks at 0.25 and the standard deviation of shocks to the wage equation at 0.02. We set the autocorrelation coefficients for the two error processes to 0.75 and the smoothing coefficient for wage bargaining (z) to 0.75. Finally, we reset the $\in$ of firms with two periods of negative profits to half its former value (when, as in the great majority of cases, it was negative).

The long-run Phillips curve corresponding to these parameter values is pictured in Figure 19.3. The LSRU is, by assumption, 5.8 percent. At 3 percent inflation, unemployment is 5.9 percent, only 0.1 point above the LSRU. Equilibrium unemployment increases at an accelerating rate as inflation is held below 3 percent. At 2 percent inflation, it rises to 6.1 percent; at 1 percent, to 6.5 percent; and at zero inflation to 7.6 percent. Deflation is yet worse: with 1 percent deflation, the equilibrium unemployment rate rises to 10.0 percent.

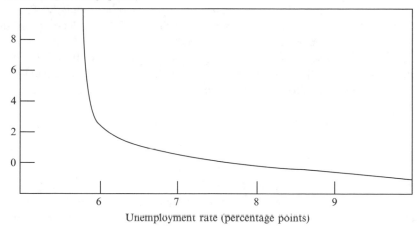

Figure 19.3. *Long-run Phillips Curve, simulation model.*
Source: Authors' calculations from simulation model.

A HEURISTIC EXPLANATION. The higher unemployment associated with zero inflation should be no surprise. Define S as the difference between average actual and average notional wages, divided by the expected price level. The increase in S associated with going from 3 percent to zero inflation acts like a permanent real cost shock, which producers will try to pass on to their customers. Notional real wages must fall sufficiently to offset this real cost shock. And lower notional real wages require higher unemployment. Any attempt—for example, through stabilization policy—to maintain employment at its former level but with the cost shock equal to S, would require prices higher than expected prices. This disequilibrium expectation only goes away as higher inflation takes S back to its initial level.

Figure 19.2 helps in understanding this change in the equilibrium level of unemployment. The wage setting curve, SS, and the actual wage curve at zero inflation, SS', will differ by S. This difference will be the consequence of downward wage rigidity. Since the AA curve is flat, the increase in unemployment—the shift from E to E'—will be the product of S and the slope of the wage setting equation. For example, in the benchmark case, S increases from almost zero to 1 percent of wages as long-term inflation falls from 3 percent to zero. Calculation shows that with the benchmark parameters, the slope of the wage setting equation is about two, and therefore the change in the unemployment rate is, likewise, approximately 2 percentage points.

The argument why the slope of the wage setting equation with respect to the unemployment rate will be the appropriate multiplier of the increase in wages due to downward rigidity follows in three steps. First, each level of steady-state inflation is associated with a given constant value of S. Second, for any such value of S, there will be only one employment level with constant inflation. This is so because in each period with an expected price level p^e, the average nominal wage will be set equal to $p^e(\omega^n + S)$, where ω^n is the notional wage. The price will be set as the markup over this actual wage, $[\beta/(\beta - 1)]p^e(\omega^n + S)$. If $(\omega^n + S)$ exceeds $(\beta - 1)/\beta$, actual prices will exceed expected prices and there will be accelerating inflation. Similarly, if $(\omega^n + S)$ is less than $(\beta - 1)/\beta$, p will be less than p^e and there will be decelerating inflation. As a result, the only point in the diagram where there is a constant inflation rate of zero, and where the value of S corresponds to zero inflation, will be E'. Third, if a constant level of zero inflation is to be maintained, as in the diagram, the unemployment rate must exceed the LSRU (which is unemployment at E) by S times the slope of SS.

The slope of this wage settlement equation can be estimated fairly robustly. It is the inverse slope of the Phillips curve with respect to the unemployment rate. In our estimations reported below, it is very close to two.

PROPORTION OF FIRMS CONSTRAINED. The nonlinear response of unemployment to inflation is mirrored in the fraction of constrained firms, as shown in Table 19.4. As inflation falls from 3 percent to zero, the fraction of constrained firms rises from 5 percent to 33 percent. The fraction of firms making readjustments as a result of two periods of negative profits rises as inflation falls, but this change is small. This behavior occurs because, following Leonard and Davis, Haltiwanger, and Schuh, we set the rate of job creation and destruction very high, even at the LSRU. This means that a

Table 19.4. *Unemployment and firms constrained and reorganizing, by rate of inflation (in percent)*

Inflation	Unemployment	Firms constrained in wage setting	Firms reorganizing
10	5.8	0	3.1
7	5.8	0.2	3.1
5	5.8	1	3.2
4	5.8	2	3.2
3	5.9	5	3.3
2	6.1	10	3.4
1	6.5	19	3.6
0	7.6	33	3.9
−1	10.0	53	4.3

Source: Authors' calculations from simulation model.

considerable fraction of businesses will be making readjustments even at high and moderate rates of inflation, and their number will not increase much as inflation falls and unemployment rises.

Checks for Robustness

The simulation is most sensitive to three parameters: the value of time unemployed (s), the bargaining power of labor (a), and the standard deviation of the innovation to the wage bargain (σ_ε). Figure 19.4 plots the simulated change in the equilibrium unemployment rate between 3 percent and zero inflation for different values of s. This parameter is chosen to obtain an unemployment rate of 5.8 percent at a simulated inflation rate of 3 percent, given the values of the seven randomly chosen parameters. When those randomly chosen parameters dictate a value of s that is close to the average real wage, employment becomes very sensitive to small changes in the wage, exacerbating the effect of nominal rigidity. For values of s below 0.45, there are no simulations where the increase in unemployment is greater than 5 percentage points.

When the bargaining power of labor (a) is small, demand shocks have little or no effect on wages. To reach the target standard deviation of wage changes, the simulation increases the variation of the innovation to the bargaining equation (σ_η). The responsiveness of unemployment to a zero inflation target depends on the nature of the variation in wages. Figure 19.5 shows that as the bargaining power of labor increases, the effects of zero inflation decline considerably.

The other parameters have much smaller effects on the change in the unemployment rate. Higher values of the autocorrelation coefficient in the wage determination process (z) and the error process in the wage bargaining equation are associated with increases in the change in the unemployment rate of about 1.5 percentage points over their ranges. Other parameters are associated with still smaller differences.

Change in unemployment (percentage points)

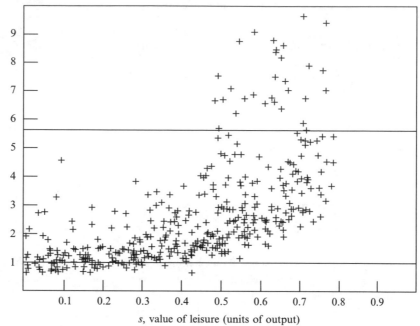

s, value of leisure (units of output)

Figure 19.4. *Simulated changes in unemployment vs. the value of leisure (s)*[a]

Source: Authors' simulations.
[a] Calculating the change in unemployment associated with operating at zero rather than 3 percent inflation.

In a very large fraction of the cases in which we are unable to calibrate the simulation, the reason is that the only value of time spent unemployed (*s*) that would yield an unemployment rate of 5.8 percent was negative. We experiment with allowing a lower bound of −1 for this parameter, instead of 0. When we do this the median change in the unemployment rate declines to 1.3 percentage points and the minimum value observed in 722 trials is 0.3 percentage points. The fifth percentile of the distribution is 0.4 percentage points.

Finally, the simulation is predictably sensitive to the assumption about the conditions under which firms are allowed to reduce their wages. We conduct a number of runs in which we allow firms to escape the constraint of nominal wage rigidity when profits have been negative for only one period, rather than two. When we do this for 289 simulation runs, there are a couple in which there is no measurable change in the equilibrium unemployment rate between 3 percent and zero inflation. The median change drops to 1.5 percentage points and the fifth percentile of the distribution is 0.2 percentage points.

Change in unemployment (percentage points)

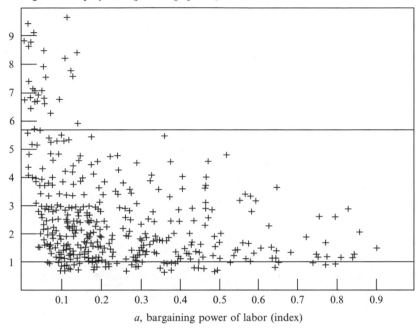

Figure 19.5. *Simulated changes in unemployment vs. workers' bargaining power (a)*[a]

Change in unemployment (percentage points)

Source: Author' simulations.

[a] Calculating the change in unemployment associated with operating at zero rather than 3 percent inflation.

A Model for Estimation

A model derived as an approximation to the simulation model yields an equation for inflation that can be estimated by nonlinear least squares. We add a term reflecting the effects of downward wage rigidities to the standard accelerationist Phillips curve (for example, as estimated by Robert Gordon).[29] We denote this additional term S_t because it is the *shift* in expected unit labor costs arising from downward wage rigidity. S_t is defined as the gap between the average level of expected real actual and notional wages deflated by labor productivity (G_t): $S_t = (\bar{w}_t - \bar{w}_t^n)/p_t^e G_t$. The shift in unit labor costs because of downward wage rigidity should have the same effect on the Phillips curve as a change in unit labor costs for any other reason. As a consequence, S_t enters the price Phillips curve linearly, as if it were a shift to the wage setting equation.

S_t is determined by the behavior of its two components, the actual wage and the notional wage. The notional wage is determined by the wage setting equation, and will therefore depend on the level of unemployment. Because of downward wage rigidity, the actual wage of each firm this period is either the notional wage of this period or the actual wage of last period, whichever is greater. Thus actual wages depend on past wages, and hence S_t depends on its own past value. We derive how S_t enters the Phillips curve, and then explain the recursion in which S_t is a function of S_{t-1} and other variables. (Further details of these derivations are provided in Appendix A.)

The Augmented Phillips Curve

In this intermediate model, S_t enters as an additional linear variable in an otherwise conventional Phillips curve. To understand why this is so, it is useful to consider how a price Phillips curve can be derived from a wage setting equation. In the absence of nominal wage rigidities, expected real wages for this period will be the real notional wage. Thus the nominal wage will be the product of the expected price level and the notional real wage:

$$w_t = p_t^e \omega_t^n. \tag{6}$$

Today's price will be the product of the markup factor (m) and unit labor cost, so that

$$p_t = m p_t^e \omega_t^n / G_t. \tag{7}$$

The usual Phillips curve is derived by taking the natural log of equation 7, subtracting the natural log of p_{t-1} from both sides, and expressing the natural log of ω_t^n in terms of its arguments. The equation that we estimate is derived by exactly the same process. But because of nominal wage rigidity, the average wage will be higher than $p_t^e \omega_t^n$ by $p_t^e G_t S_t$, and thus, with the markup, the price level will be higher by $m p_t^e S_t$. Thus with nominal rigidity, the current wage and the current price for a representative firm are given by the modified equations

$$w_t = p_t^e (1 + S_t G_t / \omega_t^n) \omega_t^n \tag{6a}$$

and

$$p_t = m p_t^e (1 + S_t G_t / \omega_t^n) \omega_t^n / G_t, \tag{7a}$$

respectively. The estimation equation is obtained by taking the natural log of each side of equation 7a and subtracting the natural log of p_{t-1} from both sides of the equation. Because the difference between the notional wage and the actual wage will be small in equilibrium, ω_t^n / G_t can be approximated as $(\beta - 1)/\beta$ and therefore, the natural log of $(1 + S_t G_t / \omega_t^n)$ is approximately equal to $[\beta/(\beta - 1)]S_t$. We also approximate the wage setting equation (equation 5) as a loglinear function of unemployment. This yields as the equation to be estimated

$$\pi_t = \pi_t^e + c - au_t + \frac{\beta}{\beta - 1} S_t, \tag{8}$$

where π_t is the rate of price inflation and π_t^e is the expected rate of price inflation.

Equation 8 is the usual accelerationist Phillips curve with the addition of the term $[\beta/(\beta - 1)]S_t$. It remains to determine a recursion equation for S_t, which is otherwise unknown, so that it can be jointly estimated with the other terms in this augmented Phillips curve.

The Recursive Nature of S_t

In the recursion equation, S_t depends on its past values and other variables. To begin the derivation, recall the definition $S_t = (\bar{w}_t - \bar{w}_t^n)/p_t^e G_t$. Because of downward wage inflexibility, the wage of each firm will be the maximum of the notional wage and the nominal wage of the previous period. Thus S_t can be inferred from the joint distribution of w_{t-1} and w_t^n.

We assume that for each firm, w_{t-1} and w_t^n have a bivariate normal distribution, and that the means of this distribution vary over time but the standard deviations and the covariance, when normalized by the expected price level (p_t^e) and by trend productivity (G_t), are constant. This makes sense as an approximation, since in the long run nominal wages will be proportional to both productivity and prices. We choose the expected rather than the actual price for the normalization of the standard deviation, since S_t is the difference between notional and actual wages, which are set on the basis of expected rather than actual prices.

Given that for each firm w_t is simply the maximum of w_{t-1} and w_t^n, the difference between $\bar{w}_t$ and w_t^n will equal the expected value of $(w_{t-1} - w_t^n)$ when $(w_{t-1} - w_t^n)$ is greater than zero, multiplied by the probability that $(w_{t-1} - w_t^n)$ is greater than zero. Define the new variable, $v_t = [\bar{w}_{t-1} - \bar{w}_t^n]/p_t^e G_t$. If w_{t-1} and w_t^n have a bivariate normal distribution, their difference will have a normal distribution, and the expected value of the truncated normal will be

$$S_t = \frac{E((w_{t-1} - w_t^n)|(w_{t-1} - w_t^n) > 0)Pr(w_{t-1} - w_t^n > 0)}{p_t^e G_t} \tag{9}$$
$$= \sigma_0 \phi(v_t/\sigma_0) + \Phi(v_t/\sigma_0)v_t,$$

where ϕ and Φ are, respectively, the standard normal density function and the cumulative normal distribution function (see appendix A for the proof).

Equation 9 expresses S_t as a nonlinear function of v_t. To obtain the recursion for our estimation, one needs to express v_t as a function of S_{t-1} and current and past values of other variables. This comes from the decomposition of v_t as the difference of two components,

$$v_t = \frac{\bar{w}_{t-1} - \bar{w}_{t-1}^n}{p_t^e G_t} - \frac{\bar{w}_t^n - \bar{w}_{t-1}^n}{p_t^e G_t}. \tag{10}$$

The first term of the decomposition is a multiple of S_{t-1}: $p^e_{t-1}G_{t-1}/p^e_t G_t$. The second term of the decomposition is the same multiple of the product: $[\bar{w}^n_{t-1}/G_{t-1}p^e_{t-1}]$ $[\bar{w}^n_t - \bar{w}^n_{t-1}/\bar{w}^n_{t-1}]$. The first factor of this product is approximated from the markup equation as $(\beta - 1)/\beta$; the second factor, the percentage change in the notional wage, $p^e_t \omega^n_t$, is approximated as $\pi^{ee}_t + g_t - a(u_t - u_{t-1})$, where π^{ee}_t is the rate of change of price expectations and g_t is the growth of productivity. Hence the recursion formula for v_t in terms of S_{t-1} is

$$v_t = \frac{S_{t-1} - [(\beta - 1)/\beta][\pi^{ee}_t + g_t - a(u_t - u_{t-1})]}{1 + \pi^{ee}_t + g_t} \tag{11}$$

(see Appendix A for greater detail). In terms of expected and actual price inflation, π^{ee}_t is given by

$$\pi^{ee}_t \cong \ln p^e_t - \ln p^e_{t-1} \cong \pi^e_t + \pi_{t-1} - \pi^e_{t-1}, \tag{12}$$

where

$$\pi^e_t = \alpha\pi_{t-1} + (1 - \alpha)\pi_{t-2}. \tag{13}$$

The estimation equation must also take account of the feature of the simulation model whereby firms under extreme duress are allowed to reduce their wages. We introduce this feature into the equation by assuming that v_t will decline if there is a drop in the profit share of GDP, denoted r. This yields the final element of the equation that we estimate:

$$v_t = \frac{S_{t-1} - [(\beta - 1)/\beta][\pi^{ee}_t + g_t - a(u_t - u_{t-1})]}{1 + \pi^{ee}_t + g_t} + d(r_t - r_{t-1}), \tag{14}$$

where r_t is the share of profits in GDP.

We estimate the augmented Phillips curve of equation 8 jointly with the formula for S_t in terms of v_t (equation 9), v_t in terms of S_{t-1} (equation 14), and the formation of price expectations (equations 12 and 13). We estimate the five parameters: c and a in equation 14, σ_0 in equation 9, d in equation 14, and α in equation 13. The parameter β is unidentified and is assumed to equal 3.8—as in the benchmark simulation. Changing this value does not affect the impact of nominal constraints.

Explanation of the Recursion Formula for S_t

First, it is important to understand why S_t should depend on v_t; v_t represents the gap between the average wage of last period and the average notional wage of this period.

To gain an intuitive appreciation for these equations, it is useful to see how S_t responds to different values of v_t according to equation 9. Consider first two extremes.

When almost all firms are constrained, v_t will be very large. In this case, the first term in equation 9 will be zero. The second term will be equal to v_t. From the definitions of S_t and v_t, wages in this period will be exactly equal to wages last period, which is what should happen if all firms are constrained. On the other hand, if v_t is very negative, as it would be with very high inflation, no firms will be constrained; and there will be no difference between notional and actual wages. This corresponds to a value of S_t that is close to zero. Both the first term and the last term of equation 9 will be zero. By the definition of S_t, the actual wage will be equal to the notional wage, as should be the case without binding wage constraints. Between these two extremes, the second term of equation 9 determines the extent to which formerly constrained firms continue to be constrained, while the first term represents the effects on firms that did not have binding constraints last period, but whose wage constraints have become binding in this period. At low levels of inflation and productivity growth, this term will cause S_t to grow.

It remains to explain the arguments and the form of equation 11, for v_t. Consider that v_t and S_{t-1} differ in their numerators by the difference $\bar{w}_t^n - \bar{w}_{t-1}^n$, while the denominators differ by a factor $p_t^e G_t / p_{t-1}^e G_{t-1}$. It should therefore be no surprise that equation 11, which expresses v_t as a function of S_{t-1}, should have as arguments the growth of inflationary expectations, the growth of productivity, and the change in the unemployment rate, which are the major determinants of the change in the notional wage.

The economic reasons why each of these three arguments will affect S_t should be clear. Productivity growth and inflation will raise the notional wage and therefore narrow the gap between actual and notional wages. A rise in the unemployment rate, on the other hand, will reduce the notional wage and therefore will increase the gap between actual and notional wages. The exact form of the relation between v_t and S_{t-1} as a function of these change variables (equation 11) reflects the weights that must be attached to these change variables as a result of the form of the difference between v_t and S_{t-1}.

In sum, equation 9 modulates the change in S_t according to the number of firms that face wage constraints. Operating jointly, equations 9 and 14 give the appropriate weights to inflation, productivity growth, and changes in unemployment in changing S_t. By raising the notional wage, inflation and productivity growth erode the gap between the actual and the notional wage, whereas increases in unemployment decrease the notional wage, and therefore increase that gap. This behavior should be kept in mind in our examination of prices and the predictions of S_t in the Great Depression.

Time-Series Estimation

We fit our model to annual time-series data using the log change in the GDP deflator to measure inflation. We use the aggregate unemployment rate because we want to predict historical periods out of sample, for which only the aggregate rate is available. And we use the ratio of corporate profits to GDP, with the 1954–84 trend removed, to measure the change in the profit share. For comparison, we also fit a standard natural rate model to the same data by omitting S_t from the regression. The first two columns of Table 19.5

Table 19.5. *Regression estimates of phillips curve models of inflation*[a]

| | Period of estimation and model | | | | |
| | 1954–95 | | 1929–42 | Combined sample | |
Independent variable	Standard (5-1)	Downward rigidity (5-2)	Downward rigidity (5-3)	Standard (5-4)	Downward rigidity (5-5)
Constant	0.031 (0.008)	0.026 (0.010)	0.027 (0.018)	−0.003 (0.008)	0.033 (0.004)
Inflation $t - 1$	0.68 (0.16)	0.83 (0.22)	1.16 (0.16)	1.06 (0.14)	0.97 (0.11)
Inflation $t - 2$	0.32	0.17	−0.16	−0.06	0.03
Unemployment	−0.52 (0.13)	−0.50 (0.13)	−0.59 (0.24)	0.04 (0.08)	−0.62 (0.03)
Parameters of S					
σ_0^b		0.029 (0.012)	0.013 (0.085)		0.029 (0.008)
Profit rate coefficient		0.53 (1.36)	0.24 (0.19)		0.33 (0.11)
Summary statistic					
R^2	0.82	0.84	0.87	0.45	0.88
N	42	42	14	56	56
Addendum					
LSRU	5.9	5.2	4.6	...	5.3

Source: Authors' regressions using data described in appendix A. Standard errors are shown in parentheses.
[a] The dependent variable is the log change in the GDP deflator.
[b] σ_0 is the standard deviation of the gap between lagged wages and notional wages, $(w_{t-1} - w_{t-1}^n)/p_t^e G_t$.

give the regression estimates for the postwar years 1954–95: equation 5-1 is the natural rate model and equation 5-2 is our downward rigidity model.[30]

The estimates in equation 5-1 are unremarkable and the implied minimum sustainable rate of unemployment, the LSRU here, is 5.9 percent, which is typical of natural rate estimates for such models. Equation 5-2 fits the data slightly better. Inflation enters with a shorter lag than in the standard model and the implied LSRU is 5.2 percent. In the parameters estimated in forming S_t, the standard deviation of the desired change in real productivity adjusted wages is 2.9 percent, which is very near the value that we estimate for the distribution of general manufacturing wage changes, discussed above. The profits term has the expected sign and a magnitude that would make its effect noticeable in providing some relief from wage constraints. We are not surprised that the estimate has a high standard error, since we did not expect, and do not find, much variation in S_t

[30] Our treatment of productivity growth, oil shocks, and wage and price controls is explained in Appendix A.

during the postwar years. This lack of variation is apparent from the bottom panel of figure 19.6, and is the reason why there is little basis for choosing between the conventional model and our model in postwar time series.

The top panel of Figure 19.6 gives the values of S_t for the Great Depression, as generated in a dynamic simulation of equation 5-2, described below. The variations of S_t during this period are an order of magnitude larger than the variations in the postwar years. And as we show, the significance of the new model becomes apparent when equations 5-1 and 5-2 are used to predict out of sample the developments in the Great Depression.

The Great Depression

Understanding the performance of the economy in the Great Depression of the 1930s has long been a challenge to economists. Most conspicuously, theories of inflation based on the natural rate of unemployment are unable to account for developments after 1933 because the historically high unemployment rates that prevailed between that year and World War II predict accelerating deflation in natural rate models. Schultze's Brookings paper, and Gordon's discussion of that paper, both infer that in conventional models fit to the Great Depression, effects from the level of unemployment on inflation are absent and only change effects matter.[31] The Great Depression thus provides a strong test of the model developed here.

OUT-OF-SAMPLE PREDICTIONS FOR THE GREAT DEPRESSION. We use equation 5-2, which has been fit to the 1954–95 period, to produce a dynamic simulation of price changes during the Great Depression. For this purpose, S_t is constructed by assuming a value of zero in 1924 and using actual values of inflation up to 1929, when the dynamic simulation begins. For years after 1929, the model-generated values of inflation are used to compute inflationary expectations, both in generating S_t and in the conventional part of our inflation equation. No attempt is made to predict the years between 1942 and 1954, which comprise World War II and the Korean War, and the associated price controls. A new dynamic simulation is begun in 1954, with S_t constructed by assuming a value of zero in 1947 and using actual values of inflation until 1954.

The predicted and actual values of inflation are given in Figure 19.7, where they are compared with values from equation 5-1, the conventional natural rate equation. The model with downward nominal rigidity captures the price movements remarkably well, both during the onset of the Great Depression and, more important, during the recovery years and the sharp second collapse later in the 1930s.

The severity of the downturn that started in 1929 destroyed corporate profits. In 1930 such profits fell to one-third of their 1929 levels, and the following two years produced aggregate losses. Our model predicts that under these conditions, downward rigidity would give way in many firms, and as shown in Figure 19.6, S_t declines to its minimum value of zero in 1930–31 and the model predicts falling prices. In these early years of the decade, our model and the conventional model predict about equally well. Subsequently,

---

[31] Schultze (1981); Gordon (1981).

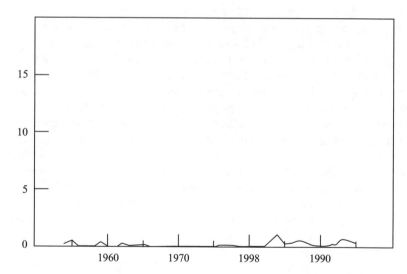
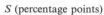
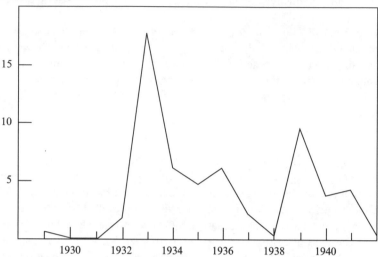

Figure 19.6. *Wage constraint term, S*

Source: Authors' estimates for equation 5-2 of Table 19.5, using data described in Appendix A.

Model with downward rigidity
Inflation (percentage points)

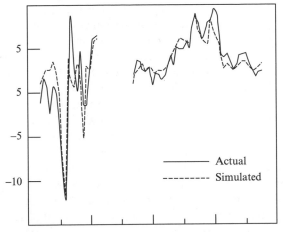

Standard natural rate model

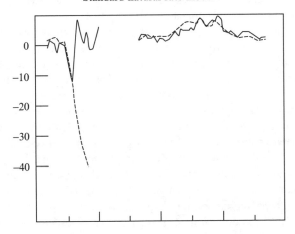

Figure 19.7. *Dynamic simulations of inflation, 1929–42 and 1954–95[a].*

Source: Authors's dynamic sillulations, using equation19.2 for the model with downward rigidity and equation 19-1 for the standard model; both equations are found in Table 19.5. Data used are described in appendix A.

[a] Model fit to data for 1954–95

the negative inflation rates begin to overwhelm other effects; S_t becomes slightly positive in 1932 and very large by 1933, indicating that downward rigidity is acting strongly against the deflation predicted by the conventional variables. For 1933, the conventional model predicts price declines of over 20 percent, while our model predicts inflation. Once profits turn up in 1934, our model tracks the remainder of the decade reasonably well, including the period of sharp contraction and recovery later on, when the variations in S_t resemble those of the early 1930s, but with a smaller amplitude.

Additional Estimates and Tests

We examine the robustness of the findings based on equation 5-2 in a number of ways. Equation 5-3 estimates the model for the Depression years alone. Considering the very few degrees of freedom available, the estimates of coefficients and parameters of S_t are remarkably close to those in equation 5-2. An F test fails to reject the hypothesis that the structure for the postwar period and the Great Depression are the same. Equations 5-4 and 5-5 combine the data for the two periods. As expected, the standard model, equation 5-4, fits very poorly and estimates no unemployment effect. Our downward rigidity model yields estimates not far from those for either subperiod, though the parameters are estimated more precisely. This is not surprising, since the Great Depression provided much more variation relevant to estimating the parameters of S_t.

We conduct several other experiments for robustness that are not reported in Table 19.5. The change in the unemployment rate is often included in Phillips curve models. However, it is insignificant when we add it to our model for any of the periods, and has no impact on the estimates of other parameters. We also test the idea that there would be a significant amount of leakage from nominal wage constraints as a result of job switching by workers, which would eliminate wage increases normally associated with seniority, or other mechanisms that would not actually violate downward wage rigidity for individual job slots. To test for such effects, which would show up as a drift in average wages relative to the wage setting captured in our model, we adjust the model by adding a constant term to the equation for v_t. However, that parameter is estimated to be near zero and insignificant, and has no effect on the rest of the estimates.

Since the functional form for the inclusion of profits in our model is chosen arbitrarily and is not derived from the microeconomic model in the same way as the other terms, we experiment with a number of alternative specifications. The postwar estimates of the role of profits are sensitive to our choice of specification. However, the ability to track the general characteristics of the Great Depression in out-of-sample forecasts is preserved in all the models that we try. Furthermore, the estimates using the combined pre- and postwar data are remarkably robust to these changes. We also test the effect of dropping the constraint that the coefficient on expected inflation equals 1.0 (the constraint that enforces the natural rate hypothesis). Without this constraint, the freely estimated coefficients are not far from 1.0 and there is no substantial change in the other parameters of the model.

Finally, the basic results reported here are also obtained with a form of the microeconomic model that allows the price-wage margin to vary in response to shocks received by firms. Such a model was used in the draft of this paper that was presented at the Brookings Panel meeting. Because that earlier version resulted in procyclical variations in the price-wage margin, and because such cyclical variation is not an agreed upon characteristic of the economy, we have modified the model as presented here. The earlier version produced all the qualitative results reported here, including the tracking of the Great Depression and the consistency of the coefficient estimates across periods.

Ideally, we would check the model against wages and hourly compensation, as well as price behavior during the Great Depression. However, the available data refer to manufacturing alone and, as the informal table below shows, their behavior is suspect, at least for our examination of aggregate inflation. The table shows the increase in real compensation and in productivity for the nonfarm business sector. The thirteen-year interval 1929–42 spans the Great Depression, ending in the first year in which the unemployment rate stayed below 10 percent. The adjoining thirteen-year intervals are shown for comparison:[32]

Period	Real compensation (percent increase)	Productivity (percent increase)
1916–29	29.6	36.8
1929–42	70.3	25.6
1942–55	44.3	39.3

According to these data, real compensation in manufacturing rose by an astounding 70 percent over the course of the Great Depression, alongside a rise of just 26 percent in productivity. In the prosperous adjoining periods, real compensation rose by far less, while productivity rose by substantially more. Perhaps the compensation data are accurate and measure a historic increase in relative compensation for the manufacturing sector. Some increase is consistent with the growing strength of manufacturing unions during the period, although the magnitude still seems large. But regardless of whether the data are accurate for the manufacturing sector, they cannot be useful to our inquiry about aggregate inflation. So our quantitative exploration is confined to explaining price inflation.

Alternative Stabilization Paths

The empirical success with time-series estimation lends important support to the simulation model and to its demonstration that maintaining complete price stability increases the economy's sustainable rate of unemployment. We now use the empirical model to illustrate this point, by comparing economic performance under alternative inflation targets pursued by the monetary authority. In Figure 19.8, the economy starts with both unemployment and inflation at 6 percent. Then policy is set to reduce the inflation rate by 1 point a year until it reaches its target level. In one case the target is zero inflation, and in the other it is 3 percent inflation. Productivity growth is set at 1.5 percent a year, which is about 0.5 percent faster than the disappointing trend that has held since the 1970s, but is still only about one-half the trend achieved in the first thirty postwar years. Because we have no way to generate changes in profits for this projection, the two paths are calculated from equation 5-2, holding profits constant in forming S_t.

For the first three years, inflation declines by the targeted 1 point a year and unemployment rises. In the fourth year, the two paths for unemployment diverge

[32] U.S. Department of Commerce (1966, series B72, pp. 202–03, and series A164, pp. 190–91).

² Model fit to data for 1954–95.

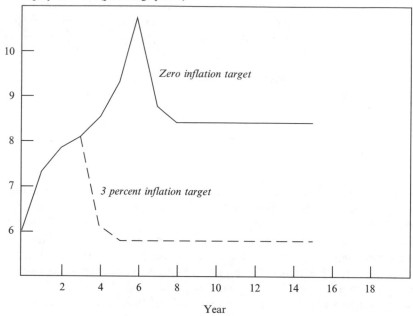

Unemployment rate (percentage points)

Figure 19.8. *Alternative stabilization paths, zero and 3 percent inflation targets*[a].

sharply as the target inflation rates also diverge. In the case of steady 3 percent inflation, the target has been reached and unemployment declines. By year five, the steady state is nearly achieved at a sustainable unemployment rate of 5.8 percent.

With a target of zero inflation, unemployment continues to rise after the third year. Moreover, the effects of wage rigidity mount as inflation approaches zero, increasing the incremental unemployment cost of reducing inflation further. The zero inflation rate target is not reached until the sixth year, at which point unemployment has reached 10.8 percent. Unemployment declines gradually from that point, nearing its steady-state rate of 8.4 percent after a decade. Comparing the two paths, the sustainable rate of unemployment is 2.6 percentage points higher in the long run with the zero inflation target, a result broadly consistent with the steady-state results from the simulation model presented above.

Conclusions and Implications

We demonstrate the prevalence of downward wage rigidity in the U.S. economy and model its significance for the economy's performance. Downward rigidity interferes with the ability of some firms to make adjustments in real wages, leading to inefficient reductions in employment. With trend growth in productivity near recent rates, as the rate of inflation approaches zero, the number of firms constrained and the degree of their constraints increase sharply, as does this inefficiency and shortfall in employment. The difference in the sustainable rate of unemployment between operating with a steady 3 percent inflation rate and a steady zero percent inflation rate is estimated as 1 to 2 percentage points in our simulation model, and 2.6 percentage points in the empirical time-series model. The main implication for policymakers is that targeting zero inflation will lead to a large inefficiency in the allocation of resources, as reflected in a sustainable rate of unemployment that is unnecessarily high.

Some might argue that the behavior that we model characterizes a regime that will change, that a determined zero inflation policy would break down wage rigidity. We have several thoughts about this. We suspect that wage rigidity is deeply rooted, not ephemeral or characteristic of a particular set of institutions or legal structures, although these may well help to codify it and expand the relations to which it applies. The psychological studies that we cite treat as fundamental the notions of fairness and worker morale that appear to underlie nominal rigidity. Historical studies find downward rigidity present well before the existence of modern labor market laws and institutions, although whether to the same degree cannot be established from the available evidence. We observe that rigidity breaks down at the firm level when firms are under extreme duress, a condition that employees can observe and are willing to respond to; and we account for this behavior in our model. But this does not imply that rigidity in the aggregate is susceptible to a permanent regime change following analogous macroeconomic conditions. In the Great Depression, when extreme duress became widespread, downward rigidity initially gave way, but it did not break down permanently. Eventually laws and institutions were strengthened to reinforce downward rigidity. The idea that rigidity represents a particular regime that will disappear if the appropriate policies are sustained would seem to have the sign wrong.

There is a further question of whether one should want to eliminate downward rigidity, even if one could do so. We have not addressed this question in our analysis, but observe that downward rigidity provides a brake against runaway deflation. It is a feature of labor markets that stabilizes the economy against extreme outcomes by reducing deflationary expectations and permitting real interest rates to fall, thus preventing the bankruptcies that accompany debt deflation. Rather than either denying its importance, which our analysis establishes, or anticipating that it will give way under some policy regime, we conclude that policy should be framed recognizing the existence and implications of downward rigidity.

Finally, our analysis of the macroeconomics of low inflation has a direct bearing on the public finance literature that evaluates the distortions in the tax system that arise from nonzero inflation rates. In that literature, moving to zero inflation reduces distortions that exist in a nominally defined tax system. A widely used simplification compares the present value of permanently removing these distortions with the one-time unemployment cost of getting inflation to zero. In such a comparison, even small permanent benefits outweigh large one-time costs. But our analysis shows that such a comparison is invalid. The unemployment costs are not one-time but, rather, permanent and substantial. Comparing low inflation rates with a zero inflation rate, we are convinced that the unemployment costs outweigh the costs of tax distortions. We fully appreciate the benefits of stabilizing inflation at a low rate, and advocate that as an appropriate target for monetary policy. But the optimal inflation target is not zero.

APPENDIX A

Derivation of the Estimation Equation and Specification of the Estimation and Dynamic Simulations

THIS APPENDIX presents the derivation of the estimated equations in the text, equations 8, 9, and 14, and explains the estimation procedure and the dynamic simulations reported.

Derivation

The derivation has two parts. The first part shows how S_t, which is the average increase in unit labor costs due to downward wage rigidity, will enter an augmented Phillips curve. The second part shows the derivation of the recursion relation of S_t. S_t is defined as the average gap between expected actual and notional real wages adjusted for productivity: $S_t = (\bar{w}_t - \bar{w}_t^n)/p_t^e \ G_t$. This *shift* in expected real unit labor costs has the same effect on the Phillips curve as an increase in the notional wage relative to productivity. We first show that it will enter the Phillips curve in exactly the same way as the determinants of the notional wage from the wage setting equation.

Because the current wage, w_t, for each firm depends upon last period's nominal wages, downward nominal wage rigidity will cause S_t to have a recursive component.

DERIVATION OF THE AUGMENTED PHILLIPS CURVE. We use the equations of the simulation model, modified to account for productivity growth, to show how the standard price-inflation Phillips curve is derived from price equations and wage setting equations in the presence of wages constrained by downward rigidity.

The demand function for each firm is exactly the same as in the simulation model:

$$D_t = [(M_t/\bar{p}_t)(p_t/\bar{p}_t)^{-\beta}]/n. \tag{A1}$$

The production function is altered to reflect the rate of trend productivity growth, so that

$$Q_t = G_t L_t, \tag{A2}$$

where G_t is labor productivity.

Profit maximization by the firm yields the price, p_t, as a markup over unit labor costs:

$$p_t = \frac{\beta w_t}{(\beta - 1)G_t}. \tag{A3}$$

We now change the wage setting equation to account for long-term growth in productivity. We assume that the average real wage at other firms grows with productivity, as does s, the value of time when unemployed. Under these assumptions, equation 5 for the determination of the notional real wage can be approximated in exponential form for a representative firm as

$$\omega_t^n = exp\,(h - au_t)G_t,\tag{A4}$$

where u_t is the economywide unemployment rate.

From the definition of S_t, the average nominal wage is the sum of the notional wage and the difference between the nominal and the notional wage due to wage ridigity, such that

$$\bar{w}_t = \bar{w}_t^n + G_t p_t^e S_t,\tag{A5}$$

and since w_t^n is equal to $p_t^e \omega_t^n$ (given that the nominal notional wage at t will be set with expectations about the price level at t),

$$\bar{w}_t = p_t^e(\bar{\omega}_t^n + S_t G_t)\tag{A6}$$

or,

$$\bar{w}_t = p_t^e\left(1 + \frac{S_t}{(\bar{\omega}_t^n/G_t)}\right)\bar{\omega}_t^n.\tag{A7}$$

Because $p_t = [\beta/(\beta - 1)]w_t/G_t$ by equation A3, the notional real wage divided by productivity can be approximated by $(\beta - 1)/\beta$. As a result,

$$\bar{w}_t \cong p_t^e\left(1 + \frac{S_t}{(\beta - 1)/\beta}\right)\bar{\omega}_t^n.\tag{A8}$$

Using (A3) for the relation between p_t and $\bar{w}_t$ yields

$$p_t \cong \frac{\beta}{\beta - 1}p_t^e\left(1 + \frac{S_t}{(\beta - 1)/\beta}\right)(\bar{\omega}_t^n/G_t).\tag{A9}$$

Taking the natural log of both sides of the equation and using equation A4 as the approximation for ω_t^n yields

$$ln\,p_t \cong ln\,\frac{\beta}{\beta - 1} + ln\,p_t^e + \frac{\beta}{\beta - 1}S_t + h - au_t.\tag{A10}$$

Subtracting the natural log of p_{t-1} from both sides of (A10), and noting that inflation, π_t, is approximately equal to $ln\,p_t - ln\,p_{t-1}$ and expected inflation, π_t^e, is approximately equal to $ln\,p_t^e - ln\,p_{t-1}$, yields the standard expectations augmented Phillips curve, modified by the presence of downward rigidity, S_t:

$$\pi_t = \pi_t^e + c - au_t + \frac{\beta}{\beta - 1} S_t, \tag{A11}$$

where $c = h + ln(\beta/(\beta - 1))$. For our nonlinear estimation, it remains to derive the recursion relation of S_t.

The Recursion Relation

The current nominal wage depends on the nominal wage in the past as well as on the current notional wage. Since the current notional wage is a parametric function of the current unemployment rate (according to equation A4), we can express S_t as a function of its past value and the unemployment rate. We begin with the definition of S_t:

$$S_t = \frac{(\bar{w}_t - \bar{w}_t^n)}{p_t^e G_t}. \tag{A12}$$

It is now necessary to express $\bar{w}_t$ as a function of $\bar{w}_{t-1}$ and $\bar{w}_t^n$. Because w_t is equal to $max\,(w_{t-1},\, w_t^n)$,

$$\bar{w}_t - \bar{w}_t^n = E(w_{t-1} - w_t^n \,|\, (w_{t-1} - w_t^n) \geq 0)\, Pr\,((w_{t-1} - w_t^n) \geq 0). \tag{A13}$$

We now derive the preceding result. The main argument resumes after equation A18.

$$\bar{w}_t = E(w_t^n \,|\, w_t^n > w_{t-1})\, Pr\,(w_t^n > w_{t-1}) + E(w_{t-1} \,|\, w_{t-1} \geq w_t^n)\, Pr\,(w_{t-1} \geq w_t^n). \tag{A14}$$

Equation A14 can be written as

$$\begin{aligned}
\bar{w}_t = &\int_{-\infty}^{\infty} \int_{w_{t-1}}^{\infty} w_t^n B(w_t^n,\, w_{t-1})\, dw_t^n\, dw_{t-1} \\
&+ \int_{-\infty}^{\infty} \int_{w_t^n}^{\infty} w_{t-1} B(w_t^n,\, w_{t-1})\, dw_{t-1}\, dw_t^n,
\end{aligned} \tag{A15}$$

where B is the bivariate density of w_t^n and w_{t-1}. Equation A15, in turn, can be rewritten as

$$\begin{aligned}
\bar{w}_t = &\int_{-\infty}^{\infty} \int_{w_{t-1}}^{\infty} w_t^n B(w_t^n,\, w_{t-1})\, dw_t^n\, dw_{t-1} \\
&+ \int_{-\infty}^{\infty} \int_{w_t^n}^{\infty} w_t^n B(w_t^n,\, w_{t-1})\, dw_{t-1}\, dw_t^n \\
&+ \int_{-\infty}^{\infty} \int_{w_t^n}^{\infty} (w_{t-1} - w_t^n) B(w_t^n,\, w_{t-1})\, dw_{t-1}\, dw_t^n,
\end{aligned} \tag{A16}$$

or,

$$
\begin{aligned}
\bar{w}_t = \; & E(w_t^n | w_t^n > w_{t-1}) Pr(w_t^n > w_{t-1}) \\
& + E(w_t^n | w_{t-1} \geq w_t^n) Pr(w_{t-1} \geq w_t^n) \\
& + E(w_{t-1} - w_t^n | w_{t-1} \geq w_t^n) Pr(w_{t-1} \geq w_t^n).
\end{aligned}
$$

(A17)

As a result,

$$
\bar{w}_t - \bar{w}_t^n = E(w_{t-1} - w_t^n | (w_{t-1} - w_t^n) \geq 0) Pr((w_{t-1} - w_t^n) \geq 0).
$$

(A18)

We assume that w_t^n and w_{t-1} have a joint normal distribution, so their difference has a normal distribution and (A13) can be written as

$$
\bar{w}_t - \bar{w}_t^n = \sigma_t \phi \left(\frac{\bar{w}_{t-1} - \bar{w}_t^n}{\sigma_t} \right) + \Phi \left(\frac{\bar{w}_{t-1} - \bar{w}_t^n}{\sigma_t} \right) (\bar{w}_{t-1} - \bar{w}_t^n),
$$

(A19)

where ϕ is the standard normal density function, Φ is the cumulative distribution, and σ_t is the standard deviation of $w_{t-1} - w_t^n$. Making the further assumption, as an approximation, that the variances and co-variances of the joint distribution of w_{t-1} and w_t^n are all proportional to the square of $p_t^e G_t$,

$$
\sigma_t = \sigma_0 p_t^e G_t.
$$

(A20)

This normalization of σ_t makes sense, as wages must grow with productivity and this period's wage is determined by expected prices for this period. As a result, we find that

$$
S_t = \frac{\bar{w}_t - \bar{w}_t^n}{p_t^e G_t} = \sigma_0 \phi \left(\frac{v_t}{\sigma_0} \right) + \Phi \left(\frac{v_t}{\sigma_0} \right) v_t,
$$

(A21)

where

$$
v_t = \frac{\bar{w}_{t-1} - \bar{w}_t^n}{p_t^e G_t}.
$$

(A22)

Recursion occurs because v_t can be expressed as a function of S_{t-1} and other variables. This function is obtained by first decomposing $\bar{w}_{t-1} - \bar{w}_t^n$, the numerator of v_t, into two terms: $[\bar{w}_{t-1} - \bar{w}_{t-1}^n] - [\bar{w}_t^n - \bar{w}_{t-1}^n]$. The first term is the numerator of S_{t-1}, while the second term, the change in the notional wage, can be expressed as a function of the determinants of that change. Accordingly, the next step is to note the decomposition

$$v_t = \frac{\bar{w}_{t-1} - \bar{w}_{t-1}^n}{p_{t-1}^e \ \ G_{t-1}} \frac{p_{t-1}^e \ G_{t-1}}{p_t^e G_t}$$
$$- \frac{\bar{w}_t^n - \bar{w}_{t-1}^n}{\bar{w}_{t-1}^n} \frac{\bar{w}_{t-1}^n}{p_{t-1}^e G_{t-1}} \frac{p_{t-1}^e G_{t-1}}{p_t^e G_t}. \tag{A23}$$

We now make four substitutions or approximations:

—By definition, $S_{t-1} = [\bar{w}_{t-1} - \bar{w}_{t-1}^n]/p_{t-1}^e G_{t-1}$.

—$p_{t-1}^e G_{t-1}/p_t^e G_t$ is approximately $(1 + g_t + \pi_t^{ee})^{-1}$, where g_t is the growth of productivity and π_t^{ee} is the growth of price expectations.

—The term $[(\bar{w}_t^n - \bar{w}_{t-1}^n)/\bar{w}_{t-1}^n]$ is the rate of change of $p_t^e \bar{\omega}_t^n$, which is approximated as $g_t + \pi_t^{ee} - (au_t - au_{t-1})$, using equation A4.

—Since $p_t = [\beta/(\beta - 1)][w_t/G_t]$ by equation A3, we approximate $[\bar{w}_{t-1}^n/p_{t-1}^e G_{t-1}]$ as $(\beta - 1)/\beta$.

$$v_t \cong \frac{S_{t-1} - [(\beta - 1)/\beta][\pi_t^{ee} + g_t - a(u_t - u_{t-1})]}{1 + \pi_t^{ee} + g_t}, \tag{A24}$$

where

$$\pi_t^{ee} \cong \ln p_t^e - \ln p_{t-1}^e \cong \pi_t^e + \pi_{t-1} - \pi_{t-1}^e. \tag{A25}$$

And by assumption, inflationary expectations are formed by

$$\pi_t^e = \alpha \pi_{t-1} + (1 - \alpha)\pi_{t-2}. \tag{A26}$$

To this point, the model does not incorporate the feature of our simulation that relaxes the constraint against wage cuts for firms under extreme duress. To do so, we allow S_t to decline when the share of profits (r) falls, by adding $d(r_t - r_{t-1})$ to equation A24 to yield

$$v_t \cong \frac{S_{t-1} - [(\beta - 1)/\beta][\pi_t^{ee} + g_t - a(u_t - u_{t-1})]}{1 + \pi_t^{ee} + g_t}$$
$$+ d(r_t - r_{t-1}). \tag{A27}$$

Equations A11, A21, A27, A25, and A26 describe the model that we estimate.

Estimation

We estimate this model on annual data for the United States from 1954 to 1995. The profit rate is constructed as the ratio of domestic profits and IVA to GDP from the National Income and Product Accounts (NIPA). The 1947 to 1984 trend is removed from the series, since it is thought that it mainly reflects an increased reliance on debt financing by U.S. firms, rather than the declining health of individual firms. The equation that we estimate is equation A11, with an error term added to reflect errors of approximation and omitted factors. We assume that expected inflation is a moving average of the previous two years' inflation. We also assume that the error in equation A11 is i.i.d. with mean zero, except in the years of the Nixon price controls and the supply shocks of 1973 and 1979. We include dummy variables for those years to allow the error to have a nonzero mean. The Nixon price control dummies are *NIXON*, which is equal to 0.25 in 1971 (because the controls were introduced in the fall), 1 in 1972 (when the controls were fully operational), and 0.5 in 1973 (because in that year the controls were being eroded and exceptions were regularly allowed), and *NIXOFF*, which is equal to 1 in 1974, the year in which the price controls were fully removed.

We compute inflation as the log change in the GDP deflator, and use the total civilian unemployment rate. Taking the average annual change, we measured trend productivity as 2.96 percent per year from 1954 to 1973, and 0.90 percent per year between 1973 and 1995. We smooth the transition between these two periods by allowing it to occur in equal steps over the five years centered in 1973.

The model is estimated by nonlinear least squares, which allows for the simultaneous estimation of the parameters of the Phillips curve and S. Thus the time series of S_t is itself generated by the estimation process. In the estimation procedure, the history of S_t is reconstructed for each evaluation of the objective function. S_t is assumed equal to zero in 1947, and is computed using equations A21 and A27 for subsequent years. The parameters estimated are a and c from equation A11, σ_0 from equation A21, d from equation A27, the coefficients on the dummy variables, and the coefficient of lagged inflation α in equation A26.

Dynamic Simulation

We conduct dynamic forecasts of the model for the postwar period and the Great Depression. For the postwar period, S_t is set equal to zero in 1947 and then constructed using actual values of all variables until 1954. For years after 1954, the predicted values of inflation are used to form inflationary expectations and to construct S_t.

For the dynamic simulations of the Great Depression, we use Stanley Lebergott's (1964) unemployment series. GNP and the GNP deflator are taken from the NIPA, and profit rates are calculated from that data using pretax profits. For years before 1929, which are used to obtain start-up values, the GNP deflator constructed by John Kendrick (1961) is used in log change form to measure inflation, and profit rates are assumed unchanged. The trend rate of productivity growth was calculated as 2.1 percent for the entire prewar period. S_t is constructed by using actual values of its determinants until 1929, after which the dynamic predictions of inflation are used to construct inflationary expectations. The results of both exercises are described in the text.

References

Ball, Laurence, and N. Gregory Mankiw. 1994. 'Asymmetric Price Adjustment and Economic Fluctuations.' *Economic Journal* 104(423): 247–61.

Bewley, Truman. 1994. 'A Depressed Labor Market, as Explained by Participants.' Book manuscript. Yale University, Department of Economics.

——. and William Brainard. 1993. 'A Depressed Labor Market, as Explained by Participants.' Unpublished paper. Yale University, Department of Economics (February).

Bils, Mark. 1987. 'The Cyclical Behavior of Marginal Cost and Price.' *American Economic Review* 77(5): 838–55.

Bound, John, and Alan B. Krueger. 1991. 'The Extent of Measurement Error in Longitudinal Earnings Data: Do Two Wrongs Make a Right?' *Journal of Labor Economics* 9(1): 1–24.

Campbell, Carl M., and Kunal Kamlani. 1995. 'The Reasons for Wage Rigidity: Evidence from a Survey of Firms.' Unpublished paper. Colgate University, Department of Economics (February).

Card, David, and Dean Hyslop. 1996. 'Does Inflation Grease the Wheels of the Labor Market?' Paper prepared for Monetary Policy and Low Inflation Conference. National Bureau of Economic Research, Cheeca Lodge, Islamorada, Florida (January 11–13).

Davis, Steven J., John C. Haltiwanger, and Scott Schuh. 1996. *Job Creation and Job Destruction.* Cambridge, Mass.: MIT Press (forthcoming).

Dickens, William T. 1986. 'Wages, Employment and the Threat of Collective Action by Workers.' Working Paper 1856. Cambridge, Mass.: National Bureau of Economic Research (June).

——. 1995. 'Do Labor Rents Justify Strategic Trade and Industrial Policy?' Working Paper 5137. Cambridge, Mass.: National Bureau of Economic Research (May).

Duncan, Gregory J., and Daniel H. Hill. 1985. 'An Investigation of the Extent and Consequences of Measurement Error in Labor-Economic Survey Data.' *Journal of Labor Economics* 3(4): 508–32.

Feldstein, Martin. 1996. 'The Costs and Benefits of Going from Low Inflation to Price Stability.' Working Paper 5469. Cambridge, Mass.: National Bureau of Economic Research (February).

Gordon, Robert J. 1981. 'Comment.' *BPEA, 2:1981,* 581–88.

——. 1993. *Macroeconomics,* 6th edn. New York: Harper Collins.

——. 1994. 'Inflation and Unemployment: Where is the NAIRU?' Paper prepared for Meeting of Academic Consultants, Board of Governors of the Federal Reserve System (December).

Hall, Robert E. 1988. 'The Relation between Price and Marginal Cost in U.S. Industry.' *Journal of Political Economy* 96(5): 921–47.

Hanes, Christopher. 1993. 'The Development of Nominal Wage Rigidity in the Late Nineteenth Century.' *American Economic Review* 83(4): 732–56.

——. 1996. 'Firm Characteristics and Nominal Wage Rigidity in the Down-turns of 1983, 1929, and 1981.' Unpublished paper. University of Pennsylvania, Department of Economics (February).

Holzer, Harry J. 1996. *Employers, Jobs and Hiring of Less-Educated Workers.* New York: Russell Sage Foundation.

Kahn, Shulamit. 1995. 'Evidence of Nominal Wage Stickiness from Micro-data.' Unpublished paper. Boston University, School of Management.

Kahneman, Daniel, Jack L. Knetsch, and Richard Thaler. 1986. 'Fairness as a Constraint on Profit Seeking: Entitlements in the Market.' *American Economic Review* 76(4): 728–41.

Kendrick, John W. 1961. *Productivity Trends in the United States.* Princeton, N.J.: Princeton University Press.

Lebergott, Stanley. 1964. *Manpower in Economic Growth: The American Record since 1800.* New York: McGraw-Hill.

Lebow, David E., David J. Stockton, and William L. Wascher. 1995. 'Inflation, Nominal Wage Rigidity, and the Efficiency of Labor Markets.' Finance and Economics Discussion Series

94–45. Washington: Board of Governors of the Federal Reserve System, Division of Monetary Affairs (October).

Leonard, Jonathan S. 1987. 'In the Wrong Place at the Wrong Time: The Extent of Frictional and Structural Unemployment.' In *Unemployment and the Structure of Labor Markets*, edited by Kevin J. Lang and Jonathan S. Leonard. New York: Basil Blackwell.

Lucas, Robert E., Jr. 1972. 'Econometric Testing of the Natural Rate Hypothesis.' In *The Econometrics of Price Determination*, edited by Otto Eckstein. Washington: Board of Governors of the Federal Reserve System and Social Science Research Council.

McLaughlin, Kenneth J. 1994. 'Rigid Wages?' *Journal of Monetary Economics* 34(3): 383–414.

Mellow, Wesley, and Hal Sider. 1983. 'Accuracy of Response in Labor Market Surveys: Evidence and Implications.' *Journal of Labor Economics* 1(4): 331–44.

Mitchell, Daniel J. B. 1985. 'Wage Flexibility: Then and Now.' *Industrial Relations* 24(2): 266–79.

O'Brien, Anthony Patrick. 1989. 'A Behavioral Explanation for Nominal Wage Rigidity during the Great Depression.' *Quarterly Journal of Economics* 104(4): 719–35.

Romer, Christina D. 1996. 'Inflation and the Growth Rate of Output.' Working Paper 5575. Cambridge, Mass.: National Bureau of Economic Research (May).

Samuelson, Paul A., and Robert M. Solow. 1960. 'Problems of Achieving and Maintaining a Stable Price Level: Analytical Aspects of Anti-inflation Policy.' *American Economic Review, Papers and Proceedings* 50(2): 177–94.

Sargent, Thomas J. 1971. 'A Note on the "Accelerationist" Controversy.' *Journal of Money, Credit, and Banking* 3(3): 721–25.

Schultze, Charles L. 1959. 'Recent Inflation in the United States.' Study Paper 1. Joint Economic Committee, 86 Cong. 1 sess. (September).

———. 1981. 'Some Macro Foundations for Micro Theory.' *BPEA, 2:1981*, 521–92.

Shafir, Eldar, Peter Diamond, and Amos Tversky. 1994. 'On Money Illusion.' Unpublished paper. Princeton University, Department of Psychology (February).

Shea, John. 1996. 'Comment on "Does Inflation Grease the Wheels of the Labor Market?" by David Card and Dean Hyslop.' Prepared for Monetary Policy and Low Inflation Conference. National Bureau of Economic Research, Cheeca Lodge, Islamorada, Florida (January 11–13).

Shiller, Robert J. 1996. 'Why Do People Dislike Inflation?' Working Paper 5539. Cambridge, Mass.: National Bureau of Economic Research (April).

Tobin, James. 1972. 'Inflation and Unemployment.' *American Economic Review* 62(1): 1–18.

U.S. Department of Commerce. 1966. *Long Term Economic Growth, 1860–1965*. Washington: Department of Commerce.

———. 1973. *Long Term Economic Growth, 1860–1970*. Washington: Department of Commerce.

20

Behavioral Macroeconomics and Macroeconomic Behavior*

BY GEORGE A. AKERLOF[†]

Think about Richard Scarry's *Cars and Trucks and Things That Go*.[1] Think about what that book would have looked like in sequential decades of the last century had Richard Scarry been alive in each of them to delight and amuse children and parents. Each subsequent decade has seen the development of ever more specialized vehicles. We started with the Model T Ford. We now have more models of backhoe loaders than even the most precocious four-year-old can identify.

What relevance does this have for economics? In the late 1960's there was a shift in the job description of economic theorists. Prior to that time microeconomic theory was mainly concerned with analyzing the purely competitive, general-equilibrium model based upon profit maximization by firms and utility maximization by consumers. The macroeconomics of the day, the so-called neoclassical synthesis, appended a fixed money wage to such a general-equilibrium system. 'Sticky money wages' explained departures from full employment and business-cycle fluctuations. Since that time, both micro- and macroeconomics have developed a Scarry-ful book of models designed to incorporate into economic theory a whole variety of realistic behaviors. For example, 'The Market for "Lemons"' explored how markets with asymmetric information operate. Buyers and sellers commonly possess different, not identical, information. My paper examined the pathologies that may develop under these more realistic conditions.

For me, the study of asymmetric information was a very first step toward the realization of a dream. That dream was the development of a behavioral macroeconomics in the

---

* This work was previously published as George Akerlof (2001), 'Behavioral Macroeconomics and Macroeconomic Behavior' *Nobel Prize for Economics Lecture, December 8, 2001*. Copyright © The Nobel Foundation 2001. Reproduced by kind permission.

George A. Akerlof delivered the lecture on which this chapter is based in Stockholm, Sweden, on December 8, 2001, when he received the Bank of Sweden Prize in Economic Sciences in Memory of Alfred Nobel. The article is copyright © The Nobel Foundation 2001 and is published here with the permission of the Nobel Foundation.

† Department of Economics, University of California, Berkeley, CA 94720-3880. I thank Janet Yellen for extraordinarily helpful discussions and editorial assistance. I also thank Henry Aaron, William Dickens, Ernst Fehr, William Gale, and Robert Shiller for invaluable comments and the Canadian Institute for Advanced Research for generous financial support.

[1] See Scarry (1974).

original spirit of John Maynard Keynes' *General Theory* (1936). Macroeconomics would then no longer suffer from the 'ad hockery' of the neoclassical synthesis, which had overridden the emphasis in *The General Theory* on the role of psychological and sociological factors, such as cognitive bias, reciprocity, fairness, herding, and social status. My dream was to strengthen macroeconomic theory by incorporating assumptions honed to the observation of such behavior. A team of people has participated in the realization of this dream. Kurt Vonnegut would call this team a *kerass*, 'a group of people who are unknowingly working together toward some common goal fostered by a larger cosmic influence.'[2] In this lecture I shall describe some of the behavioral models developed by this *kerass* to provide plausible explanations for macroeconomic phenomena which are central to Keynesian economics.

For the sake of background, let me take you back a bit in time to review some history of macroeconomic thought. In the late 1960's the New Classical economists saw the same weaknesses in the microfoundations of macroeconomics that have motivated me. They hated its lack of rigor. And they sacked it. They then held a celebratory bonfire, with an article entitled 'After Keynesian Macroeconomics.'[3] The new version of macroeconomics that they produced became standard in the 1970's. Following its neoclassical synthesis predecessor, New Classical macroeconomics was based on the competitive, general-equilibrium model. But it differed in being much more zealous in insisting that all decisions—consumption and labor supply by households, output, employment and pricing decisions by producers, and the wage bargains between both workers and firms—be consistent with maximizing behavior.[4] New Classical macroeconomics therefore gave up the assumption of sticky money wages. To account for unemployment and economic fluctuations, New Classical economists relied first on imperfect information and later on technology shocks.

The new theory was a step forward in at least one respect: price and wage decisions were now based upon explicit microfoundations. But the behavioral assumptions were so primitive that the model faced extreme difficulty in accounting for at least six macroeconomic phenomena. In some cases, logical inconsistency with key assumptions of the new classical model led to outright denials of the phenomena in question; in other cases, the explanations offered were merely tortuous. The six phenomena are:

1. *The existence of involuntary unemployment:* In the New Classical model, an unemployed worker can easily obtain a job by offering to work for just a smidgeon less than the market-clearing salary or wage; so involuntary unemployment cannot exist.
2. *The impact of monetary policy on output and employment:* In the New Classical model, monetary policy is all but ineffective in changing output and employment. Once

---

[2] See ⟨http://www.gibbsonline.com/gibbsbooks.html⟩.

[3] See Robert E. Lucas, Jr. and Thomas Sargent (1979).

[4] Most of these puzzles were dormant at the time; they were inherent in the literature, but there was no active discussion of them. Probably the most active research program in macroeconomics during the late 1960's was the development of large-scale macroeconometric models. The models of search unemployment by Edmund S. Phelps et al. (1970) appeared in the late 1960's to answer the question: what is the meaning of unemployment? But they adopted a framework of search unemployment, which was, by nature, voluntary.

changes in the money supply are fully foreseen, prices and wages change proportionately; real wages and relative prices are constant; and there is no impact on the real economy whatsoever.

3. *The failure of deflation to accelerate when unemployment is high:* The New Classical model produces an accelerationist Phillips curve with a unique natural rate of unemployment. If unemployment falls below this natural rate, inflation accelerates. With unemployment above the natural rate, inflation continually decelerates.

4. *The prevalence of undersaving for retirement:* In the New Classical model, individuals decide how much to consume and to save to maximize an intertemporal utility function. The consequence is that privately determined saving should be just about optimal. But individuals commonly report disappointment with their saving behavior and, absent social insurance programs, it is widely believed that most people would undersave. 'Forced saving' programs are extremely popular.

5. *The excessive volatility of stock prices relative to their fundamentals:* New Classical theory assumes that stock prices reflect fundamentals, the discounted value of future income streams.

6. *The stubborn persistence of a self-destructive underclass:* My list of macroeconomic questions to be explained includes the reasons for poverty because I view income distribution as a topic in macroeconomics. Neoclassical theory suggests that poverty is the reflection of low initial endowments of human and nonhuman capital. The theory cannot account for persistent and extreme poverty coupled with high incidence of drug and alcohol abuse, out-of-wedlock births, single-headed households, high welfare dependency, and crime.[5]

In what follows I shall describe how behavioral macroeconomists, incorporating realistic assumptions grounded in psychological and sociological observation, have produced models that comfortably account for each of these macroeconomic phenomena. In the spirit of Keynes' *General Theory*, behavioral macroeconomists are rebuilding the

---

[5] I have left out two important questions whose microfoundations have been developed since the late 1960's. First, why might credit be rationed? Donald R. Hodgman (1960, p. 258) makes clear that the economic theory of the early 1960's found credit rationing to be an unexplained puzzle: 'Economists of a more analytical persuasion have been reluctant to accept [credit rationing] at face value because of their difficulty in providing a theoretical explanation for the phenomenon which is consistent with the tenets of rational economic behavior. Why should lenders allocate by non-price means and thus deny themselves the advantage of higher interest income?' He attributes such views to Paul Samuelson as revealed in Congressional testimony. Asymmetric information provides an excellent reason for credit rationing. (See especially Dwight Jaffee and Thomas Russell [1976] and Joseph E. Stiglitz and Andrew Weiss [1981].) A second question relating to microfoundations concerns the reasons for leads and lags in macroeconomic variables, such as durable consumption, money demand, and prices. *S-s* models with lumpy costs to making changes can explain such leads and lags (unless the variable in question is either always decreasing or always increasing). Pioneering work on the effects of *S-s* pricing has been done especially by Robert J. Barro (1972) and Katsuhito Iwai (1981). Ricardo Caballero (see, for example, 1993) has compared the leads and lags in such models with a situation with no costs of adjustment. Andrew F. Caplin and Donald F. Spulber (1987) and Caplin and John Leahy (1991) have also looked at the implications of *S-s* policy for the relation between the shifts in the ideal price and the actual price being charged. See Akerlof (1973, 1979) for analysis of the effects of target-threshold monitoring on the short-run income and interest elasticity of the demand for money.

microfoundations that were sacked by the New Classical economics. I shall begin my review by describing one of my earliest attempts in this field, which led to the discovery of the role of asymmetric information in markets.

I. ASYMMETRIC INFORMATION

I first came upon the problems resulting from asymmetric information in an early investigation of a leading cause for fluctuations in output and employment—large variations in the sales of new cars.[6] I thought that illiquidity, due to the fact that sellers of used cars know more than the buyers of used cars, might explain the high volatility of automobile purchases.[7] In trying to make such a macroeconomic model, I got diverted. I discovered that the informational problems that exist in the used car market were potentially present to some degree in all markets. In some markets, asymmetric information is fairly easily soluble by repeat sale and by reputation. In other markets, such as insurance markets, credit markets, and the market for labor, asymmetric information between buyers and sellers is not easily soluble and results in serious market breakdowns. For example, the elderly have a hard time getting health insurance; small businesses are likely to be credit-rationed; and minorities are likely to experience statistical discrimination in the labor market because people are lumped together into categories of those with similar observable traits. The failure of credit markets is one of the major reasons for underdevelopment. Even where mechanisms such as reputation and repeat sales arise to overcome the problem of asymmetric information, such institutions become a major determinant of market structure.

To understand the origins of the economics of asymmetric information in markets, it is useful to reflect on the more general intellectual revolution that was occurring at the time. Prior to the early 1960's, economic theorists rarely constructed models customized to capture unique institutions or specific market characteristics. Edward Chamberlin's monopolistic competition and Joan Robinson's equivalent[8] were taught in graduate and even a few undergraduate courses. However, such 'specific' models were the rare exception; they were presented not as central sights, but instead as excursions into the countryside, for the adventurous or those with an extra day to spare.[9] During the early 1960's, however, 'special' models began to proliferate as growth theorists, working slightly outside the norms of standard price-theoretic economics, began to construct models with specialized technological features: putty-clay, vintage capital, and learning by doing. The incorporation into models of such specialized technologies violated no established price-theoretic norm, but it sowed the seed for the revolution that was to come. During the summer of 1969, I first heard the word *model* used as a verb, and not

---

[6] See Akerlof (1970).

[7] Frederic S. Mishkin (1976) later developed the ideas that set me on this course initially. He showed why the demand for automobiles is more volatile because cars are illiquid due to asymmetric information.

[8] See Robinson (1942) and Chamberlin (1962).

[9] For example, I could well imagine a graduate student being unaware of Harold Hotelling's (1929) model of spatial competition. I cannot remember it in the graduate curriculum and remember finding it tucked away as an appendix to Chamberlin's *Monopolistic Competition*.

just as a noun.[10] It is no coincidence that just a few months earlier 'The Market for "Lemons"' had been accepted for publication.[11] The 'modeling' of asymmetric information in markets was to price theory what the 'modeling' of putty-clay, vintage capital, and learning by doing had been to growth theory.[12] It was the first application of a new economic orientation in which models are constructed with careful attention to realistic microeconomic detail. This development has brought economic theory much closer to the fine grain of economic reality. Almost inevitably, the analysis of information asymmetries was the first fruit of this new modeling orientation. It was the ripest fruit for picking. In the remainder of this essay, I shall discuss the payoffs of this new orientation for the new field of behavioral macroeconomics.

II. INVOLUNTARY UNEMPLOYMENT

I once had an economist friend who said that he *could not* sell his house, a complaint that I reiterated sympathetically to one of his colleagues. The colleague responded that there was only one problem: the house was unreasonably priced. At a lower price the house would sell, perhaps instantly.

New Classical economics views involuntary unemployment as a logical impossibility, like my friend's inability to sell his house. Could not an unemployed worker obtain a job if only she were willing to reduce her reservation wage? The New Classical answer is yes: unemployed workers are those searching for work (hence unemployed, rather than out of the labor force) but rejecting jobs that are available because they had expected better pay. The unemployed may be unhappy that they cannot sell their labor at the wage or salary that they would ideally like, but except for those affected by the minimum wage or union bargaining, they are voluntarily, not involuntarily, unemployed. Everyone can get a job at the market-clearing wage. In New Classical theory, periods of declining employment—business-cycle downturns—may be caused by an unexpected decline in aggregate demand, which leaves workers mistakenly holding out for nominal wages that exceed the new market-clearing level.[13] Alternatively, declining employment may be due to negative supply shocks, which cause workers to withdraw from the labor force and eschew the jobs which are available. Any account of the business cycle based on voluntary variations in job-taking faces a significant empirical difficulty—to explain why quits decline in cyclical downturns. If higher unemployment results from workers' rejection of the poor returns from work, quits should rise along

---

[10] Conversation with Michael Rothschild in Cambridge, Massachusetts, summer of 1969. I remember the usage just as many people today may remember the first time they heard someone say they would 'grow the economy.'

[11] I do not have the exact date of the acceptance of this article, but I remember that it took slightly more than a year between acceptance and publication.

[12] See Robert M. Solow (1959, 1962) and Kenneth J. Arrow (1962).

[13] This theory suffers from a further theoretical difficulty. Since aggregate unemployment is readily observable with a short lag, workers should condition their expectations of prevailing wage distributions on the aggregate unemployment rate. Such conditioning would eliminate serial correlation in unemployment.

with unemployment. But there are fewer quits, not more, when unemployment rises. The procyclic behavior of quits is indisputable.[14]

Instead of denying the very existence of involuntary unemployment, behavioral macroeconomists have provided coherent explanations. Efficiency wage theories, which first appeared in the 1970's and 1980's, make the concept of involuntary unemployment meaningful.[15] These models posit that, for reasons such as morale, fairness, insider power, or asymmetric information, employers have strong motives to pay workers more than the minimum necessary to attract them.[16] Such 'efficiency wages' are above market clearing, so that jobs are rationed and some workers cannot obtain them. These workers are involuntarily unemployed. In the next section I will extend this reasoning to explain why involuntary unemployment varies cyclically.

The pervasive empirical finding of a wide spread of earnings for seemingly similar workers is strongly suggestive of the near ubiquity of efficiency wages. Long before the efficiency wage was a gleam in the eye of macroeconomists, labor economists had documented wide dispersion in earnings across seemingly similar jobs and among workers with apparently identical characteristics.[17] Analysis of panel data indicates that workers of the same quality receive different wages depending upon their place of work. Moreover, data show that workers who switch industries receive wage changes that are correlated with the respective wage differentials between the industries.[18] Industries with higher pay (conditional on characteristics) also have lower quit rates, suggesting that pay differences are not simply compensating differentials due to different working conditions or benefits.[19] It thus appears that there are 'good jobs' and 'bad jobs.'

The existence of good jobs and bad jobs makes the concept of involuntary unemployment meaningful: unemployed workers are willing to accept, but cannot obtain, jobs identical to those currently held by workers with identical ability. At the same time, involuntarily unemployed workers may eschew the lower-paying or lower-skilled jobs that are available. The definition of involuntary unemployment implicit in efficiency wage theory accords with the facts and agrees with commonly held perceptions. A meaningful concept of involuntary unemployment constitutes an important first step forward in rebuilding the foundations of Keynesian economics.

---

[14] This question was raised by James Tobin (1972). For some data on the countercyclical behavior of quits, see Akerlof et al. (1988). Kenneth J. McLaughlin (1991) has attempted to reconcile the procyclicality of quits with New Classical economics as follows: He defines quits as employee-initiated separations, and layoffs as firm-induced separations. In McLaughlin's model a positive productivity shock causes more workers to ask for wage increases. Since some requests are rejected, quits rise as unemployment declines. But why should firms' wage offers lag behind worker demands in the face of a positive productivity shock?

[15] An excellent concise summary of this literature is given by Janet L. Yellen (1984).

[16] The inclusion here of insider-outsider models is taking an especially broad interpretation of the concept of efficiency wages.

[17] See John T. Dunlop (1957).

[18] See William T. Dickens and Lawrence F. Katz (1987) and Alan B. Krueger and Lawrence H. Summers (1988). Note that these studies are for the United States in a period when unionization was quite weak; it is thus unlikely to be the major factor in such wage differentials. In contrast, Dunlop's wage differentials may have been mainly the result of differentials in union power.

[19] See Krueger and Summers (1988).

But why do firms pay wages above rock bottom? In my view, psychological and sociological explanations for efficiency wages are empirically most convincing.[20] Three important considerations are: reciprocity (gift exchange theory from anthropology), fairness (equity theory from psychology), and adherence to group norms (reference group theory in sociology and theory of group formation in psychology). In the earliest 'sociological' version of efficiency wage theory based on gift exchange, firms give workers above market-clearing wages and workers reciprocate in their commitment to the firm.[21] The payment of above-market-clearing wages may also be motivated by considerations of fairness: in accordance with the psychological theory of equity, workers may exert less effort insofar as their wage falls short of what is considered fair.[22] Group norms typically determine the conceptions workers form about how gifts should be reciprocated and what constitutes a fair wage. In the laboratory, Ernst Fehr and his coauthors have established the importance both of reciprocal behavior and social norms for worker effort in experimental settings.[23] My favorite version of efficiency wages is the insider-outsider model, whereby insider workers prevent the firm from hiring outsiders at a market-clearing wage lower than what the insiders are currently receiving.[24] This theory implicitly assumes that insiders have the ability to sabotage the inclusion of new workers into a firm. A detailed study by Donald Roy of an Illinois machine shop reveals the dynamics by which this may occur: In Roy's machine shop, insiders established group norms concerning effort and colluded to prevent the hiring of rate-busting outside workers. Workers who produced more than the level of output considered 'fair' were ostracized by others.[25] Collusion by insiders against outsiders is a compelling motive for many firms to pay wages that are above market clearing.

An alternative version of efficiency wage theory, grounded in asymmetric information, views above-market-clearing wages as a disciplinary device. In the Shapiro-Stiglitz model, firms pay 'high' wages to reduce the incentive of workers to shirk. The attempt of all firms to pay 'above-average' wages, however, pushes the average level of wages above market clearing, creating unemployment. Unemployment serves as a disciplinary device, because workers who are caught shirking and fired for lack of effort can become reemployed only after a period of unemployment.[26]

---

[20] See Katz (1986) and Alan S. Blinder and Don H. Choi (1990). Blinder and Choi find strong evidence in favor of morale considerations for paying high wages as well as mixed evidence in favor of efficiency wages as a worker discipline device. Truman Bewley (1999) concludes that morale is an important reason for failure to make wage cuts. Carl M. Campbell III and Kunal S. Kamlani (1997) report that morale is a major reason firms do not make money wage cuts, but so is concern over quits by the best workers.

[21] See Akerlof (1982) and Matthew Rabin (1993).

[22] See Akerlof and Yellen (1990) and David I. Levine (1991).

[23] See, for example, Fehr et al. (1993), Fehr et al. (1996), and Fehr and Armin Falk (1999).

[24] See Assar Lindbeck and Dennis J. Snower (1988).   [25] See Roy (1952).

[26] See Steven Stoft (1982), James E. Foster and Henry Y. Wan, Jr. (1984), Carl Shapiro and Stiglitz (1984), and also Samuel Bowles (1985). The worker-discipline model captures a slice of reality, but as the whole explanation for involuntary unemployment it suffers from both theoretical and empirical difficulties. Theoretically, in jobs where supervision is imperfect and workers can determine their own effort, firms with good reputations could demand that workers post bonds. These bonds would be forfeited in the event that a worker is caught shirking. As long as they remain employed by the firm, workers would receive wages augmented by the interest on the bond; the principal would be returned at retirement. This payment scheme solves the incentive problem facing the firm and is cheaper for the firm than above-market-clearing efficiency wages.

The worker-discipline model fits the standard logic of economics more comfortably than approaches grounded in sociology and psychology. But sociological and psychological models, including the insider–outsider model, that rely on elements outside the standard economic box, probably yield a better overall explanation for involuntary unemployment. These behavioral models capture Keynes' emphasis, in the initial chapters of the *General Theory*, on equity and relative wage comparisons.

III. EFFECTIVENESS OF MONETARY POLICY

A central proposition of the New Classical economics is that monetary policy, as long as it is fully perceived, can have no effect on output or employment. Perfectly foreseen changes in the money supply induce rational wage and price setters to raise or lower nominal wages and prices in the identical proportion leaving output and employment constant.[27] This New Classical hypothesis conflicts, however, with empirical evidence on the impact of monetary policy and the widespread popular belief in the power of central banks to affect economic performance.

A major contribution of behavioral macroeconomics is to demonstrate that, under sensible behavioral assumptions, monetary policy *does* affect real outcomes just as Keynesian economics long asserted. Cognitive psychology pictures decision makers as 'intuitive scientists' who summarize information and make choices based on simplified mental frames.[28] Reliance on rules of thumb that omit factors whose consideration have only a small effect on profit or utility is an implication of such cognitive parsimony. In the wage-price context, simple rules cause inertia in the response of aggregate wages (and prices) to shocks—the exact 'sticky wage/price' behavior that New Classical economists had so scornfully derided. In the New Classical critique, the inertial wage behavior hypothesized in the 'neoclassical synthesis' is irrational, costly for workers and firms, hence implausible. Behavioral economists have responded by demonstrating that rules of thumb involving 'money illusion' are not only commonplace but also sensible— neither foolhardy nor implausible: the losses from reliance on such rules are extremely small.

In joint work with Janet Yellen, I first demonstrated this result in the context of a model with efficiency wages and monopolistic competition. We assumed that some price setters follow the rule of thumb of keeping prices constant following a shock to demand (caused by a change in the money supply). We showed that the losses to the 'rule-of-thumb' firms from their failure to readjust prices following a change in

---

Gary S. Becker and George J. Stigler (1974) make this precise suggestion. In their scheme the worker receives the bond back when he leaves the job in good standing. (Other ways to reduce wages to market clearing in similar spirit have been pointed out by Lorne Carmichael [1985] and Kevin M. Murphy and Robert J. Topel [1990].) Empirically, the discipline-device theory fails to explain why industry wage differentials are so highly correlated across occupations, so that some industries offer 'good jobs' to workers in all occupations, including those where there is little scope to shirk. (See Dickens and Katz, 1987.)

[27] This logic is clearly spelled out by Donald Patinkin (1956).
[28] See Richard Nisbett and Lee Ross (1980).

the money supply are *second-order* (or *small*),[29] whereas the impact on output of a monetary shock in this economy is *first-order* (or *significant*) relative to the size of the shock.[30] We dubbed the rule-of-thumb strategies employed by firms with inertial price setting 'near-rational' since the losses they suffer from their departure from complete optimization are *second-order* (or *small*).

The logic of the key result—that near-rational price stickiness is sufficient to impart significant power to monetary policy—is simple. With monopolistic competition, each firm's profit function is second-differentiable in its own price so that the profit function is flat in the neighborhood of the optimum own-price. In consequence, any deviation from the profit-maximizing price causes a loss in profits that is small—second-order with respect to the size of those deviations. But if the deviations from the optimum of a large number of firms are similar—for example, if they are all slow to adjust their prices following a change in the money supply—then real balances (the money supply deflated by the price level) change by a first-order amount relative to a situation with fully optimizing price-setting behavior. This first-order change in real balances, in turn, causes first-order changes in aggregate demand, output, and employment. For example, suppose that the money supply increases by a fraction ε and a fraction of firms keep their prices unchanged. Each firm's losses, relative to fully optimizing behavior, are approximately proportional to the square of ε. If ε is 0.05, for example, its square is quite a small number, 0.0025, so the losses from price stickiness are apt to be small. However, assuming money demand is proportional to income, the change in real output is first-order—proportional to ε. (With fully maximizing behavior by all firms, the change in the money supply leaves output unchanged.) Thus, small deviations from complete rationality—indeed small and *reasonable* deviations from complete rationality—reverse the conclusion that expected changes in the money supply have no effect on real income and output.[31]

Rule-of-thumb pricing behavior takes many forms. For example, staggered price (wage) models, in which firms keep nominal prices (wages) fixed for a period of time, correspond closely to descriptions of price-(wage-) setting processes.[32] In the Taylor staggered contract model, during each period, half of all firms set a nominal price which they maintain for the succeeding two-period interval.[33] A variant of the staggered contract model, due to Guillermo A. Calvo, assumes instead that a fixed nominal price is reset at randomly varying intervals.[34] New Classical economists object to both

---

[29] In this context *second-order* is the mathematical representation of the concept *small*. Correspondingly, *first-order* is the mathematical representation of the concept *significant in size*.

[30] See Akerlof and Yellen (1985*a*, *b*), N. Gregory Mankiw (1985), Michael Parkin (1986), and Olivier Blanchard and Nobihiro Kiyotaki (1987).

[31] The same results hold in a number of alternative frameworks. For example, if firms set profit-maximizing efficiency wages, nominal wage stickiness is a form of rule-of-thumb behavior with similar consequences: the losses to the firm holding wages constant are second-order, but shocks to the money supply change real variables by a first-order amount. In Mankiw's formulation small 'menu costs,' which are fixed costs for making a price change, inhibit price changes with effects on equilibrium output that are an order larger than the menu cost.

[32] Especially see Carlton (1986).

[33] See Akerlof (1969), Stanley Fischer (1977), and John Taylor (1979).

[34] See Calvo (1983).

renditions of the model, on the grounds that such price setting is not maximizing.[35] Of course, they are right: instead of keeping nominal prices unchanged during a fixed interval, Taylor's and Calvo's firms would do better by establishing prices that vary within the interval in accordance with the firm's expectations of the money supply (aggregate demand). Such profit-maximizing behavior would again render money supply changes neutral. However, price-setting (wage-setting) strategies of the Taylor/Calvo type are near-rational: the small amount of nominal rigidity that characterizes these models is sufficient to allow monetary policy to be stabilizing, yet the losses relative to a strategy that varies prices within the pricing interval are second-order.[36] There are many other forms of near-rational rule-of-thumb behavior that render monetary policy efficacious.[37]

Near-rational, rule-of-thumb models solve the great puzzle posed by Lucas regarding the effectiveness of monetary policy with rational expectations.[38] New Classical economics finds it difficult to explain more than a fleeting relation between money and output. The new behavioral economics, with a variety of plausible near-rational behaviors, yields a robust relation between changes in the money supply and changes in output.

[35] See Barro (1977) for this complaint about staggered contract models.

[36] See Akerlof and Yellen (1991). Technically, it turns out that the amplitude of the business cycle, as measured by the standard deviation of (log) income rises due to Taylor's staggered contracts by an amount that is proportional to the standard deviation of the pricing 'error' made by Taylor's firms. Monetary policy can offset this price stickiness and reduce business-cycle volatility. But the losses realized by firms from the use of Taylor-type staggered contracts are second-order, proportional to the variance of shocks to the system. In this sense, staggered pricing has a first-order effect on both the size of the business cycle and the stabilizing properties of monetary policy. But the nonmaximizing behavior which allows monetary policy to stabilize the economy results in losses that are second-order.

[37] For example, Mankiw and Ricardo Reis (2001) have recently suggested that the response of income to monetary shocks is better explained by a 'near-rational' model in which prices (and/or wages) respond slowly to new information than by near-rational, staggered price models in the Taylor/Calvo style. Slow response to new information may result from the considerable managerial costs involved in gathering, processing, and sharing information involved in the price-setting process. (See Zbaracki et al. [2000], quoted in Mankiw and Reis.) The Mankiw-Reis formulation resolves three paradoxes present in rational expectations staggered price models. Sticky information yields the empirically observed long lags of response of income to changes in monetary policy (Milton Friedman [1968] and Christina D. Romer and David H. Romer [1989]); it is consistent with the surprisingly slow response of inflation to shocks found in estimates of Phillips curves (Robert J. Gordon, 1997); and it fails to yield the theoretical perversity in rational expectations staggered contract models of deflationary policies that lead to increases, not decreases, in output (Lawrence J. Ball, 1994).

Experimental evidence suggests that the coordination problems involved in reaching a new equilibrium may be external as well as internal to the firm. Fehr and Jean-Robert Tyran (2001) conducted experiments in which price setters were given payoffs derived from a near-rational model with monopolistic competition. They found that negative changes in the money supply caused considerable output reductions when payoffs were denominated in nominal terms. Subjects acted as if other price setters suffered from money illusion, making them, in turn, reluctant to cut prices. (A new approach to the dependence of monetary policy on coordination failure is implicit in Peter Howitt and Robert Clower, 2000.) This paper suggests that the reaction of prices to money supply changes involves the formation of expectations concerning the response of other price setters to the same shock. Fehr and Tyran's (2001) experiment points to yet another form of near-rational behavior: price setters may fully maximize, but on the assumption that other firms follow sticky, rule-of-thumb pricing behavior. Again, monetary policy is effective in changing output and employment.

[38] See Lucas (1972).

IV. THE PHILLIPS CURVE AND THE NAIRU

Probably the single most important macro-economic relationship is the Phillips curve. The 'price-price' Phillips curve relates the rate of inflation to the level of unemployment, the expected rate of inflation, and variables affecting aggregate supply, such as the price of oil or food. The trade-offs between inflation and unemployment implicit in this relation define the 'feasible set' for monetary policy and thus play a decisive role in its formulation. The Phillips curve was first estimated for Britain,[39] then subsequently for the United States[40] and many other countries.[41]

The basis of the Phillips curve is supply and demand. Phillips posited that when demand is high and unemployment low, workers can bargain for higher nominal wage increases than when demand is low and unemployment high. Firms' pricing policies translate wage inflation (adjusted for productivity) into price inflation. For policy makers, therefore, a durable trade-off exists between inflation and unemployment.

In the late 1960's, Friedman (1968) and Phelps (1968) added an important new wrinkle. They argued that workers care about and bargain for real, not nominal, wage gains: workers routinely expect and receive compensation for expected inflation, then bargain from there, demanding higher expected real wage gains at lower rates of unemployment. Again, pricing policies translate wage inflation into price inflation. The consequence of this small shift in assumption—that workers bargain for real, not nominal, wage increases—is enormous: instead of a durable unemployment-inflation trade-off, there is now just a unique 'natural' unemployment rate consistent with stable inflation. With 'real-wage' bargaining, the long-run Phillips curve—the unemployment/inflation combinations consistent with equality between actual and expected inflation—is vertical because there is one and only one unemployment rate: the 'natural rate'—at which actual and expected inflation match.

To see why the long-run Phillips curve must be vertical, imagine that a central bank attempts via monetary policy to hold unemployment below the natural rate. With labor markets abnormally tight, workers demand nominal wage increases in excess of expected inflation (plus normal real wage cum productivity gains). Firms, in turn, pass the associated cost increases into prices, so that inflation exceeds what workers initially anticipated when they bargained. With unemployment below the natural rate, actual inflation therefore exceeds expected inflation. *Ex post*, workers have been fooled. So, over time, inflationary expectations, and inflation in turn, accelerates. With unemployment held below the natural rate, the consequence is ever accelerating *inflation*. Similarly, the Friedman-Phelps model predicts that a central bank attempting to hold unemployment above the natural rate indefinitely eventually causes accelerating *deflation*. Only the natural rate of unemployment yields steady inflation.

Economists accepted the natural rate hypothesis remarkably quickly after it was first proposed by Friedman and Phelps in the late 1960's. Three things conspired in its

---

[39] See A. W. Phillips (1958) and Richard G. Lipsey (1960).

[40] See Robert J. Gordon (1970) and George L. Perry (1970) for some early estimates for the United States.

[41] To give just one example, Robert J. Flanagan et al. (1983) estimated the Phillips curve for many different countries.

favor. First, it seemed to explain remarkably well the inflation-unemployment experience of the 1960's and 1970's. At the low unemployment rates of the late 1960's, inflation rose, which apparently drove up inflationary expectations, shifting the short-run unemployment inflation trade-off outward. Thus the 1970's began with a much less favorable unemployment inflation trade-off than the 1960's. (Analysts ignored the equally plausible explanation that as inflation increased, as it did in the late 1960's, wage bargains and price setting began to take inflationary expectations, which had previously been ignored, into account.)[42] Second, empirical estimates of the Phillips curve yielded coefficients on past inflation whose sum was not statistically different from unity. The inference was drawn that the lagged inflation terms in such estimates correspond to expected inflation, which is an autoregressive weighted average of past inflation, and that the coefficient on expected inflation in determining current inflation is one.[43] Finally, there is a bias for economists to accept rationally, based null hypotheses, even though accepted only by tests with relatively low power.[44]

Economists should not have accepted the natural rate hypothesis so readily. There are both theoretical and empirical reasons to be highly suspicious. Theoretically, the natural rate hypothesis reminds me of a common diet book rule of thumb. According to that rule of thumb for every 3,200 calories extra that we eat, we gain a pound. For every 3,200 calories less, we lose a pound. This always makes me imagine twin brothers. One of these twin brothers eats just enough to keep his weight even. The other twin eats one more 100-calorie cookie per day. If the rule of thumb is right, after one year the cookie eater is 11 pounds heavier than his brother. After a decade he is 110 pounds heavier. Fifty years later, should he live so long, he would be 550 pounds heavier. Just as expected, the rule of thumb does break down when extrapolated over long time periods: more accurate renditions of the relationship between weight and calories show that the maintenance of higher weight requires extra caloric intake. Happily the twins' weights will not diverge forever. Similarly, my guess is that for at least some band of unemployment rates, inflation would asymptote to a constant value rather than accelerate or decelerate indefinitely. Such a priori reasoning could be wrong, but the error from overextrapolation of the diet book rule of thumb warns us that the natural rate hypothesis is rather odd. At very low unemployment rates, the Friedman/Phelps prediction of accelerating inflation seems quite possibly reasonable and empirically relevant.[45] But I am suspicious about the theory's applicability when unemployment is high.

---

[42] This alternative explanation was given by Otto Eckstein and Roger Brinner (1972), but did not make it into the mainstream.

[43] We should here note Thomas J. Sargent's (1971) criticism that the coefficient on lagged inflation will not equal one in an accelerationist model if the process generating inflation is stable, without a unit root.

[44] We shall see an example of such bias below when we review Summers' criticism of the acceptance of the random walk hypothesis based on failure to reject by tests with very low power against alternative hypotheses.

[45] The occurrence of hyperinflation with low unemployment maintained sufficiently long is one prediction of the theory. The frequent occurrence of hyperinflation seems to support the theory. But these hyperinflations have occurred when governments have lost fiscal credibility (and could only pay their deficits by seigniorage). It may be the loss of fiscal credibility, not the maintenance of low unemployment, which is the cause of the hyperinflation.

My suspicions regarding the natural rate hypothesis are supported by an empirical fact, which reveals that its applicability is not *universal*. Unemployment in the United States for the whole of the 1930's was indisputably in excess—surely *greatly* in excess—of any plausible natural rate. According to the natural rate hypothesis, price deflation should have accelerated for the whole decade. That did not happen. Prices fell for a time, but deflation stopped after 1932; there was no significant deflation for the next ten years, despite extremely high unemployment. This evidence suggests that, at least after some time, at high levels of unemployment and low inflation rates, the natural rate hypothesis breaks down. Such a failure would not be terribly serious for a theory derived from empirical observation, but it constitutes a serious flaw for a relationship derived from a priori principles, principles that are accepted because they are supposed to be always and everywhere true.

The evidence of the 1930's is not unique. Modern economies display similar characteristics. For example, Pierre Fortin estimates that from 1992 to 2000, the Canadian economy experienced almost 12 points of unemployment in excess of a very conservative, 8-percent estimate of NAIRU.[46] During that same period, inflation averaged a very low $1\frac{1}{2}$ percent per year. According to natural rate theory, core inflation should have declined by roughly 6 percentage points, since a typical estimate of the Phillips curve slope is $\frac{1}{2}$. Instead, inflation declined over that period by only 0.1 percent.

Econometric evidence further suggests that the natural rate theory rests on shifty sand rather than bedrock. Time-varying estimates of the natural rate show that it changes over time; but, even with allowance for such shifts, estimates of the natural rate possess high standard errors. Douglas Staiger et al. (1997) compute a 95-percent confidence interval for the U.S. natural rate which exceeds 5 percentage points; this is more than three times the standard deviation of the U.S. monthly unemployment rate over the last 50 years.

In recent papers, William Dickens, George Perry, and I have explored two behavioral hypotheses that, contrary to the natural rate model, produce a stable trade-off between unemployment and inflation at sufficiently high unemployment and low inflation rates. The first hypothesis is 'pure Keynes': workers resist, and firms rarely impose, cuts in nominal pay. The second hypothesis concerns the role of inflationary expectations in wage bargains: we argue that, at very low inflation, a significant number of workers do not consider inflation sufficiently salient to be factored into their decisions. However, as inflation increases, the losses from ignoring it also rise, and therefore an increasing number of firms and workers take it into account in bargaining.

Keynes' assumption that workers resist nominal wage cuts was consistent with his intuitive understanding of psychology. The assumption also coincides with psychological theory and evidence. Prospect theory posits that individuals evaluate changes in their circumstances according to the gains or losses they entail relative to some reference point. The evidence suggests that individuals place much greater weight on avoiding losses than on incurring gains. Daniel Kahneman and Amos Tversky (1979) have demonstrated that many experimental results which are inconsistent with expected

---

[46] Observation due to Fortin in Fortin et al. (2001).

utility maximization can be rationalized by prospect theory. Downward wage rigidity is a natural implication of prospect theory if the current money wage is taken as a reference point by workers in measuring gains and losses. In support of this view, Eldar Shafir et al. (1997) found in a questionnaire study that individuals' mental frames are defined not just in the real terms hypothesized by classical economists but also exhibit some money illusion.

Numerous empirical studies document that money wages are, in fact, downward sticky. Using panel data, David Card and Dean Hyslop (1997) and Shulamit Kahn (1997) found that distributions of nominal wage changes are asymmetric around zero. Fortin found a remarkable pileup of wage changes at zero in Canadian data. From 1992 to 1994, when Canadian inflation was 1.2 percent and the unemployment rate averaged 11.0 percent, only 5.7 percent of non-COLA union agreements had first-year wage cuts, whereas 47 percent had wage freezes.[47] In detailed interviews in Connecticut, Bewley found that managers are willing to cut nominal wages only as a last resort.[48] To investigate whether firms cut total compensation through benefit cuts as opposed to money wage cuts, David E. Lebow et al. examined the individual industries covered by the Employment Cost Index: they found that benefit cuts are only a minor substitute for nominal wage cuts.[49] Using Swiss data, Fehr and Lorenz Goette found that even a seven-year period of low inflation and low productivity growth did not increase the frequency of money wage cuts.[50]

At low inflation there is a long-run trade-off between output and inflation if there is aversion to nominal pay cuts. Unlike the Friedman-Phelps model, in which such a trade-off is transitory, long-term increases in inflation (if it is close to zero) result in significantly less employment and more output.[51] The logic goes as follows. In both good times and bad, some firms and industries do better than others. Wages need to adjust to accommodate these differences in economic fortunes. In times of moderate inflation and productivity growth, relative wages can easily adjust. Unlucky firms can raise the wages they pay by less than the average, while the lucky firms can give above-average increases. However, if productivity growth is low (as it was from the early 1970's through the mid-1990's in the United States) and there is no inflation, firms that need to cut their real wages can do so only by cutting the money wages of their employees. Under realistic assumptions about the variability and serial correlation of demand shocks across firms, the needed frequency of nominal cuts rises rapidly as inflation declines. An aversion on the part of firms to impose nominal wage cuts results in higher permanent rates of unemployment. Because the real wages at which labor is supplied are higher at every level of employment when inflation is low, the unemployment rate consistent with stable inflation rises as inflation falls to low levels. Spillovers produce an aggregate employment impact which exceeds the employment changes in those firms that are constrained by their inability to cut wages. Thus, a benefit of a little inflation is that it 'greases the wheels of the labor market.'

---

[47] See Fortin (1995, 1996).   [48] See Bewley (1999).
[49] See Lebow et al. (1999).   [50] See Fehr and Goette (2000).   [51] See Tobin (1972).

Simulations of a model with intersectoral shocks and aversion on the part of firms to nominal wage cuts suggests that, with realistically chosen parameters, the trade-off between inflation and unemployment is severe at very low rates of inflation, when productivity growth is low. For example, a permanent reduction in inflation from 2 percent per year to zero results in a permanent increase in unemployment of approximately 2 percentage points.[52] Estimation of a Phillips curve for the United States after World War II, corresponding to the simulation model just described, gives similar results. When the Phillips curve thus estimated is used to simulate the inflation experience of the 1930's, the fit is shockingly close to actual U.S. inflation experience during the depression.[53] A comparable simulation of the standard natural rate model, in contrast, counterfactually, shows accelerating deflation throughout the 1930's.

An alternative behavioral theory also generates a permanent trade-off between inflation and unemployment at low inflation. This theory is based on the idea that because inflation is not salient when it is low, anticipated future changes in the price level are ignored in wage bargaining.[54] With monopolistic competition and efficiency wages such ignorance of inflation when it is low is near-rational.[55] The psychology of just noticeable differences and cognitive psychology both suggest that people tend to ignore variables that are unimportant to their decisions.[56] Econometric estimates of the Phillips curve which allow for the possibility that past inflation has a different impact on current inflation when inflation is high than when it is low are consistent with this hypothesis: at high inflation, the sum of coefficients on past inflation is close to one.[57] At low inflation, this sum of coefficients is much closer to zero. Similarly, regressions using survey measures of expected inflation as an independent variable yield much higher coefficients on the expected inflation term at high inflation than at low inflation.[58] Not surprisingly then, when periods of low and high inflation are combined to estimate a nonlinear model of the influence of inflationary expectations we find that their impact depends on the recent history of inflation.

The demonstration by behavioral macroeconomics that very low inflation has the cost of permanently high unemployment and low output, has important implications for monetary policy. Most of us think of central bankers as cautious, conservative, and safe.

---

[52] See Akerlof et al. (1996).

[53] This is done by sequentially feeding in the simulated inflation of the previous period to derive adaptively the next period's inflationary expectations. The fit is so excellent that there must be a component of luck.

[54] Past inflation is incorporated indirectly because wage bargains take into account the wages paid by competitors.

[55] See Akerlof et al. (2000).

[56] This formulation is also influenced by the public's mental frame regarding inflation. Robert J. Shiller (1997*a*, *b*) has elicited the differences in mental frame between the public and economists by questionnaire responses.

[57] One is not, however, necessarily the magic number for the reasons noted earlier by Sargent (1971).

[58] Such regressions address the problem suggested by Sargent that the natural rate model should produce coefficients on expected inflation that correspond to the money supply rule, and those coefficients need not be equal to unity. If expectations are observed without error, the coefficient on expected inflation with natural rate theory should be unity. Error in the expectations data should bias its coefficient downward, but it should not, as observed, result in changes in the coefficient, unless there are also changes in the error of observation between periods of high and low inflation.

But I consider many to be dangerous drivers: to avoid the oncoming traffic of inflation, they drive on the far edge of the road, keeping inflation too low and unemployment too high. During the 1990's, Canada had very low inflation and an unprecedented unemployment gap—close to 4 percentage points—with the United States.[59] Europe has also had high unemployment and very low inflation. Japan has gone much further, allowing deflation. Central bankers who accept the textbook version of the natural rate hypothesis should follow the advice of Oliver Cromwell to the General Assembly of the Church of Scotland: 'I beseech you in the bowels of Christ, think it possible you may be mistaken.' It is no coincidence that the leading survey of cognitive psychology uses this citation to demonstrate a common perceptual error: overconfidence.[60]

V. UNDERSAVING

It is common wisdom that people save too little. To compensate for this failure, most developed country governments heavily support the elderly in retirement. In addition, a very large number of employers require and subsidize pension contributions of their employees. Many forms of saving receive tax advantage. Even with these legs up, the common wisdom is that financial assets of most households still fall considerably short of what they need to maintain their consumption in retirement.[61]

For New Classical economics, saving too little or too much, like involuntary unemployment, is an impossibility, a straightforward contradiction of the assumptions of the model. Since saving is the result of individual utility maximization, it must, absent externalities, be just right. Behavioral macroeconomics, in contrast, has developed theoretical tools and empirical strategies to advance understanding of such time-inconsistent behavior.

A key theoretical innovation permitting systematic analysis of time-inconsistent behavior is the recognition that individuals may maximize a utility function that is divorced from that representing 'true welfare.' Once this distinction is accepted, 'saving too little' becomes a meaningful concept. The idea can be illustrated by the ancient myth of the lemmings, who every few years are said to converge in a death march, which ends

---

[59] 3.8 percent from 1990 to 1999, according to the *Economic Report of the President* (2000, Table B-107).

[60] See Nisbett and Ross (1980). This book is one of the leading primers for the psychology of behavioral macroeconomics. Curiously, cognitive psychologists have a much more empirical basis for their theories than economists.

[61] Eric M. Engen et al. (1999, p. 97) reach the opposite conclusion. They compare the actual wealth with that derived in a calibrated optimization model. Their preferred calibration has a rate of time preference of 3 percent. With data from the U.S. Health and Retirement Survey with a broad definition of wealth to include all home equity, 60.5 percent of households have more than the median optimal wealth in the calibrated model. But I would focus on an alternative result from their simulations. If we exclude home equity investment in spendable financial capital, and assume a zero rate of intertemporal time discount, only 29.9 percent of households reach the preretirement age of 60 or 61 with more than the optimal median wealth for someone of their age (p. 99, Table 5). Like the discussants, both for empirical and a priori reasons, I view a zero rate of discount as more correct. This conforms to people's stated preference for nondeclining consumption at a zero rate of interest (see below) and it weights utility at different ages on a one-for-one basis. My choice to exclude home equity capital assumes that retirees should not have to leave their homes for financial reasons, or to reverse-mortgage them, as they get older.

with their final plunge into the sea.[62] The alleged behavior of those lemmings reveals a distinction common among psychologists, but rare for economists. Unless the lemmings experience an unusual epiphany in that final plunge, their utility or welfare is given by one function; yet they maximize another.

Think about it: the popular view of saving, that people undersave, is similarly described. Determining whether people save too much or too little involves asking whether people, like the lemmings, have one (intertemporal) utility function which describes their welfare, but maximize another.[63] Such evidence as there is suggests potentially large difference between the two concepts. High negative rates of time discount are necessary to explain actual wealth-earnings ratios.[64] Yet, questionnaire responses on the consumption-saving trade-offs that people think they *ought to make* reveals an intertemporal discount rate that is on average slightly positive.[65]

The hyperbolic discount function, which has been used to study intertemporal savings choices, can be used to formalize the distinction between the utility function that describes actual saving behavior and the utility function that measures the welfare resulting from that behavior. The hyperbolic function captures the difficulty people have in exercising self-control. In contrast to the constant discount rates that are standard in neoclassical theory, the hyperbolic function assumes that the discount rates used to evaluate trade-offs between adjacent periods decline as the time horizon lengthens: individuals use high discount rates to evaluate options that require an immediate sacrifice for a future reward and lower discount rates when the same sacrifice is deferred into the future. Thus, they are patient in making choices requiring gratification delays when those sacrifices are deferred; but impatient in delaying gratification in the short run. Because present consumption is more salient than future consumption, individuals procrastinate about saving. The hyperbolic function accords closely with experimental findings: Human and animal subjects are far less willing to delay gratification immediately than to commit to such delays in the future.[66]

Two forms of procrastination may result from hyperbolic discounting. 'Naive procrastination' occurs when an individual assumes incorrectly that her utility function will be different in the future. She mistakenly projects that, although today is salient, tomorrow will be different. She fails to see that tomorrow's self will be different from today's self, so that tomorrow will be just as salient as today once it has moved one step closer. The naive procrastinator mistakenly believes that she will save (diet, exercise, quit smoking, etc.) tomorrow, although she has not done so today, and is surprised that

---

[62] My 1946 version of *The Encyclopedia Britannica* describes as fact the march of the lemmings, which 'never ceases until they reach the sea, into which they plunge and are drowned.'

[63] This difference is made explicit in David I. Laibson (1999).

[64] See Engen et al. (1999, pp. 157–58).

[65] See Robert S. Barsky et al. (1995, p. 34).

[66] See Robert H. Strotz (1956), Phelps and Robert A. Pollak (1968), George Ainslie (1992), George Loewenstein and Drazen Prelec (1992), Laibson et al. (1998), and Laibson (1999). In Akerlof (1991) I was regrettably unaware of earlier work on intertemporal inconsistency. In economics this includes Strotz (1956), Phelps and Pollak (1968), Richard H. Thaler (1981), and Loewenstein (1987). Loewenstein and Thaler (1989) give an excellent early review of the previous literature on dynamic inconsistency including the psychological experiments and theory. See also Ainslie (1992).

the sacrifices deferred today are also deferred again tomorrow. More sophisticated procrastination takes the form of preproperation, according to the terminology of Ted O'Donoghue and Rabin (1999). The preproperator has fully rational expectations about who her future self will be. She says to herself: there is no reason to save today if tomorrow is going to be especially salient. If tomorrow is especially salient then I will spend whatever savings I have laid aside today when it was also especially salient. So I should not make the sacrifice today.

Laibson has used hyperbolic discounting as the basis of a research program on saving behavior and policy. With coauthors Andrea Repetto and Jeremy Tobacman (1998) he has simulated the effects of different tax incentive programs in a world in which consumers preproperate. They estimate that large positive welfare effects result from small changes in incentives to save which reduce the amount of preproperation. Because of this work the regulations regarding tax-advantaged 401(k) savings plans have been changed. If firms so choose, workers may now be automatically enrolled with an automatic default contribution. Adoption of such plans significantly increases plan participation and many workers maintain their contributions at the level of the default.[67]

Besides the popularity of social security and other programs that 'force' consumers to save, the best evidence of undersaving is probably the observation that, upon retirement, individuals, on average, reduce consumption substantially.[68] In fact, consumption at retirement declines discontinuously.[69] Those with more wealth and higher income replacement reduce their consumption by much less. This finding is difficult to explain with the standard life cycle, exponential discounting model.[70]

Thaler and Shlomo Benartzi (2000) have devised a savings plan to overcome workers' tendency to procrastinate and have tested it on an experimental basis at a mid-size manufacturing firm: employees were invited to join a savings plan allowing them to elect, in advance, the fraction of wage or salary increases to be set aside for savings. Consistent with hyperbolic discounting, but not with the standard exponential model, workers chose relatively modest saving out of current income but committed to save large fractions of future wage and salary increases. Within a short period of time, the average savings rate had doubled.[71]

---

[67] See Brigitte C. Madrian and Dennis F. Shea (2001).

[68] See James Banks et al. (1998) and B. Douglas Bernheim et al. (2001).

[69] Such declines might occur if retirement is associated with negative income shocks. Bernheim et al. (2001, p. 854) suggest that such an adjustment is relatively minor.

[70] Retirees, of course, obtain greater leisure, and thus one might expect a reduction in consumption as leisure is substituted for consumption. It is difficult, but not impossible, to explain, in addition, why such substitution varies systematically both with the level of wealth and with the income replacement ratio. This could occur if those with a particular taste for leisure in retirement have by choice high income replacement ratios and have accumulated high levels of savings.

[71] From 4.4 percent to 8.7 percent. This behavior is also explained by prospect theory by Kahneman and Tversky (1979). According to prospect theory the framing of decision-making is important and people resist taking losses. In this context these employees do not want to take losses in their consumption.

VI. ASSET MARKETS

Keynes' *General Theory* was the progenitor of the modern behavioral finance view of asset markets. In Keynes' metaphor 'professional investment may be likened to those newspaper competitions in which competitors have to pick out the six prettiest faces from a hundred photographs, the prize being awarded to the competitor whose choice most nearly corresponds to the average preferences of the competitors as a whole.'[72] Thus stock markets are too volatile and also too responsive to news. This view of the stock market contrasts with the efficient markets model in which stock prices measure the present value of future returns adjusted for risk.

In the early 1980's Robert Shiller conducted a direct test of the Keynesian excess volatility hypothesis. He reasoned that if stock prices really are the predicted value of expected future returns, they should vary less than the discounted returns themselves. Shiller's insight was a direct application of a simple statistical principle: a good forecast should have lower variance than the variable being forecast. If the weather forecast has greater variance than the actual weather, the weather forecaster should be fired.[73] Using 100 years of U.S. data on stock prices and dividends, Shiller (1981) compared the variance of detrended stock prices to the variance of the detrended present discounted values of dividends.[74] He found just what Keynes would have expected: the standard deviation of (detrended) stock prices is five times larger than the standard deviation of (detrended) discounted dividends. These results have been confirmed in more sophisticated tests that properly allow for the nonstationarity of both stock prices and the present discounted values of dividends.[75]

The results of variance-bounds tests notwithstanding, belief in efficient markets was sustained by empirical results such as the finding of insignificant serial correlation in returns in monthly data.[76] Rejection of the hypothesis that returns are serially correlated suggests that the stock market follows something close to a random walk. In response, Summers (1986) showed in a model of 'fads'—with serially correlated deviations from

---

[72] Keynes (1936, p. 156).

[73] For example, drawing from a normal distribution, the forecast that yields the smallest squared deviation between the actual draw and the forecast is the mean of the distribution, which is a constant with no variance at all.

[74] He extrapolated future dividends for times beyond his period of observation. For a similar test also see Steven F. LeRoy and Richard Porter (1981).

[75] See John Y. Campbell and Shiller (1987). Although Shiller's tour de force initially seemed to clinch the case, two technical problems cast a shadow of doubt. The first problem is that detrending potentially introduces a serious bias into Shiller's procedure: neither stock price series nor dividends are stationary and a nonstationary series does not even possess a variance. The second problem relates to the shortness of Shiller's sample and his extrapolation of future dividends beyond the present. Allan W. Kleidon (1986) showed in simulated data that the difference between the variance of Shiller's detrended stock price and of his dividend series is not large enough to confidently reject the efficient market null hypothesis when returns follow a random walk. The Campbell-Shiller test allows for the nonstationarity of stock prices and dividends, provided the two series are cointegrated. This test is also valid even if firms smooth dividends.

The high volatility of stock prices could also be explained by a high frequency cycle in the expected real rate of return on stocks. But such a cycle is inconsistent with most standard classical models of the economy, where real returns are mainly determined by the state of technology, and the capital–labor ratio. In the standard classical model both technology and the capital–labor ratio change slowly.

[76] Where not insignificant in the statistical sense, such correlation seemed insignificant in magnitude.

perfect markets—that serial correlation tests have very low power: the power of such tests is so low as to require 5,000 years worth of data before it could discriminate 50 percent of the time between the random walk hypothesis and a fad which would drive stock prices more than 30 percent away from fundamentals 35 percent of the time.[77]

Beyond establishing the existence of excess volatility, Shiller has also examined its possible causes. In *Irrational Exuberance* (2000), he reviews the news coverage of the stock market bubble of the 1990's and explains how the idea of a 'new era' both in financial markets and the real economy was propagated. As stock prices rose, the 'new economy' mantra was transmitted from person to person; individual investors acted on the opinions of the media, which exaggerated the effects of economic fundamentals such as the internet on productivity. Such stock market bubbles are common; they have occurred in many other countries and frequently over the course of history. Indeed, Kindleberger's accounts of manias and panics and Galbraith's history of the *Great Crash* of 1929 are distinguished predecessors to *Irrational Exuberance.*

A second major empirical finding that casts doubt on the rationality of the stock market is the equity premium puzzle. Over the last 200 years, the return on equity has been significantly higher than the return on bonds. For example, from 1802 to 1998 the real return on a value-weighted market equity index was 7.0 percent per annum compared to 2.9 percent for a relatively riskless security.[78] Over the last 75 years, 1926–2000, the real returns were 8.7 percent on equity versus 0.7 percent on bonds, a gap of 8.0 percent. A gap of this size is huge: Jeremy J. Siegel and Thaler (1997) calculate that a $1,000 investment made 75 years ago would have yielded $12,400 in bonds and $884,000 in stocks. This gap is so large that rejection of rationality is duck soup: With intertemporal maximization of utility, the marginal utility of consumption today should equal the expected extra utility tomorrow from forgoing one unit of consumption today. With a constant relative risk-aversion utility function, this condition implies that the expected equity premium should equal the product of the coefficient of risk aversion and the covariance between the growth of consumption and the return on stock prices. For reasonable values of the coefficient of risk aversion, however, this product is much smaller than the equity premium, thus rejecting rational consumption behavior. This rejection is known as the equity premium puzzle.[79]

Further evidence of the irrationality of stock prices comes from cross-section data. Similar to Shiller's time-series finding of excess volatility coupled with reversion to the mean in price/dividends ratios, Werner F. M. De Bondt and Thaler (1985) find reversion to the mean of stock returns in a cross section: successive portfolios formed by the previous five years' 50 most extreme winners considerably underperform the

---

[77] Kenneth D. West (1988) similarly demonstrated the low power of Kleidon's efficient markets test using Shiller's detrended data.

[78] See Rajnish Mehra (2001, p. 1).

[79] It is remarkable that even this weak test leads to rejection, since most theories of consumption, whether maximizing or not, would suggest considerable correlation between the rate of return on stocks and the rate of growth of consumption. For example, such a correlation occurs if consumers have a consumption function which naively depends on their wealth, or, alternatively, if the same optimism that leads to high returns in the stock market also leads to consumption binges. Jonathan A. Parker (2001) suggests a possible resolution of the equity premium puzzle.

market average, while portfolios of the previous five years' 50 worst losers perform better than the market average. Other stock market anomalies, such as a 20-percent one-day decline in stock prices in October 1987 in the absence of any significant news also cast doubt on the efficient markets hypothesis.[80]

Asset markets are not only important for their own sake, they are also important because they affect the macroeconomy, through at least three channels. First, the value of assets affects wealth and, in turn, consumption. Second, the price of existing assets relative to the price of new capital—Tobin's q ratio—affects investment since investment can be viewed as an arbitrage between new capital stock and claims to similar existing assets.[81] Finally, asset values affect the chances that firms will go bankrupt. Firms close to bankruptcy find it difficult, if not impossible, to borrow, and thus commonly forgo profitable investment opportunities.[82]

VII. POVERTY AND IDENTITY

If income distribution is a topic in macroeconomics, as many have professed, then behavioral economics also offers insight on the most enduring macroeconomic problem facing the United States: the disparity in income and social condition between the majority white population and the African-American minority. As a legacy both of slavery and the Jim Crow discrimination that followed it, poverty weighs especially heavily on African-Americans. The black poverty rate of 23.6 percent in 2000 was roughly triple the white rate of 7.7.[83] Despite comprising only about one-eighth of the population, African-Americans have almost one-fourth of all U.S. poverty.[84] The reality is yet more disparate than these statistics indicate because the problems of the poorest African-Americans go beyond mere poverty. They include extraordinarily high rates of crime, drug and alcohol addiction, out-of-wedlock births, female-headed households, and welfare dependency. Statistics on incarceration indicate that even the worst of these problems affect a significant fraction of African-Americans. Thus, for example, about 4.5 percent of black males are either in jail or in prison.[85] The black male incarceration rate exceeds the white male rate by a factor of eight to one.[86] And the lifetime chances of a black male youth entering prison exceeds one-fourth.[87]

---

[80] See Romer (1993, p. 1112).

[81] See the literature on q theory, especially including Tobin (1969), Summers (1981), Andrew B. Abel (1982), and Fumio Hayashi (1982).

[82] See Stewart C. Myers (1974); Michael C. Jensen and William H. Meckling (1976). Owen Lamont (1995) shows how dual equilibria may occur because of such dependence.

[83] Hispanics have a similar but less extreme history of discrimination.

[84] See <http:// www.census.gov/Press-Release/www/2000/ cb00-158.html>.

[85] In 1996 there were 530,140 black male prisoners and 213,100 black non-Hispanic and 80,900 Hispanic jail in-mates of both sexes. There were 462,500 male and 55,800 female inhabitants of jails. Extrapolating the black Hispanic rate at 0.3 and the male/female rate for black as the same as white yields 211,814 black males in jail in 1996. The black male population was about $1/2(30 + 0.6 \times 4.7)$ million $= 32.282/2 = 16.141$ million. The net result is about 4.5 percent of the African-American male population in prison or jail. Source of incarceration rates: Correctional populations of the U.S. 1996, U.S. Department of Justice, Table 5.7, p. 82. Source: <http:// www.census.gov/statab/www/ part 1a.html>.

[86] See <www.hrw.org/ reports/2000/usa/Table3.pdf>.

[87] This is an estimate based on incarceration rates in 1993.

Because standard economic theory, in our view, is incapable of explaining such self-destructive behavior, Rachel E. Kranton and I have developed models, based upon sociological and psychological observation, to understand the persistence of African-American disadvantage (2000). Our theory stresses the role of identity and the decisions that individuals make about who they want to be. In our theory of minority poverty, dispossessed races and classes face a Hobson's choice. One possibility is to choose an identity that adapts to the dominant culture. But such an identity is adopted with the knowledge that full acceptance by members of the dominant culture is unlikely. Such a choice is also likely to be psychologically costly to oneself since it involves being someone 'different'; family and friends, who are also outside the dominant culture are likely also to have negative attitudes toward a maverick who has adopted it. Thus individuals are likely to feel that they can never fully 'pass.' A second possibility is to adopt the historically determined alternative identity, which, for many minorities, is an oppositional culture. Each identity is associated with prescriptions for ideal behavior. In the case of the oppositional identity, these prescriptions are commonly defined in terms of what the dominant culture is *not*. Since the prescriptions of the dominant culture endorse 'self-fulfillment,' those of the oppositional culture are self-destructive. The identity of the oppositional culture may be easier on the ego, but it is also likely to be economically and physically debilitating.

This identity-based theory of disadvantage is consistent with a considerable body of evidence. For example, it captures the central findings of studies by authors such as Franklin Frazier (1957), Kenneth Clark (1965), William E. B. Du Bois (1965), Ulf Hannerz (1969), Lee Rainwater (1970), William J. Wilson (1987, 1996), and Elijah Anderson (1990). Read any African-American biography: the uncomfortable dance between acceptance and rejection invariably takes center stage.

The identity theory of minority poverty has social policy implications that depart from those derived from standard neoclassical theory. For example, the standard economic theory of crime and punishment implicitly argues for combating crime by deterrence: raise the stakes high enough, as California did with its 'three strikes and you're out' law, and the potential criminal will think twice. But the prisons are full and crime has not stopped. An identity-based theory suggests, in contrast, that large negative externalities from incarceration may offset the short-run gains from deterring criminal activity through tougher incarceration policies.[88] Prison itself is a school for counter-cultural identity, and thus the breeding ground for future crime. Moreover, externalities in identity formation argue for programs to allay crime before it has occurred. These include, for example, effective, easily accessed drug treatment and rehabilitation programs and public jobs for innercity youth. Identity theory suggests that the benefits of increased expenditures for schools in African-American neighborhoods with high poverty rates are likely to be substantial: African-American children have been found to be particularly responsive to differences in teacher quality and class size.[89] It may take

---

[88] See Steven D. Levitt (1996).
[89] See Ronald F. Ferguson (1998) on the effect of teacher quality and Krueger and Diane M. Whitmore (1999) on the effect of class size.

the extraordinary teacher and close personal attention to sort through student issues concerning identity in addition to covering the standard curriculum.[90] Finally, the externalities involved in identity formation argue for affirmative action, because it is a symbol of welcome for African-Americans into the white society that has rejected them for so long.[91]

VIII. CONCLUSION

It is now 30 years since the revolution which began in growth theory and then swept through microeconomics. The new microeconomics is standard in all graduate programs, half of a two-course sequence. Adoption of the new macroeconomics has been slower, but the revolution is coming here as well. If there is any subject in economics which should be behavioral, it is macroeconomics. I have argued in this lecture that reciprocity, fairness, identity, money illusion, loss aversion, herding, and procrastination help explain the significant departures of real-world economies from the competitive, general-equilibrium model. The implication, to my mind, is that macroeconomics *must* be based on such behavioral considerations.

Keynes' *General Theory* was the greatest contribution to behavioral economics before the present era. Almost everywhere Keynes blamed market failures on psychological propensities (as in consumption) and irrationalities (as in stock market speculation). Immediately after its publication, the economics profession tamed Keynesian economics. They domesticated it as they translated it into the 'smooth' mathematics of classical economics.[92] But economies, like lions, are wild and dangerous. Modern behavioral economics has rediscovered the wild side of macroeconomic behavior. Behavioral economists are becoming lion tamers. The task is as intellectually exciting as it is difficult.

References

Abel, Andrew B. 'Dynamic Effects of Permanent and Temporary Tax Policies in a q Model of Investment.' *Journal of Monetary Economics*, May 1982, *9*(3), pp. 353–73.

Ainslie, George. *Picoeconomics*. Cambridge, U.K.: Cambridge University Press, 1992.

Akerlof, George A. 'Relative Wages and the Rate of Inflation.' *Quarterly Journal of Economics*, August 1969, *83*(3), pp. 353–74.

——. 'The Market for "Lemons": Quality Uncertainty and the Market Mechanism.' *Quarterly Journal of Economics*, August 1970, *84*(3), pp. 488–500.

——. 'The Demand for Money: A General-Equilibrium Inventory-Theoretic Approach.' *Review of Economic Studies*, January 1973, *40*(1), pp. 115–30.

——. 'The Economics of "Tagging" as Applied to the Optimal Income Tax, Welfare Programs, and Manpower Planning.' *American Economic Review*, March 1978, *68*(1), pp. 8–19.

---

[90] See Lisa Delpit (1995).

[91] Glenn C. Loury (1995) has suggested that affirmative action may also have the opposite effect: it may exacerbate blacks' sense of exclusion and make them feel that they are viewed as not belonging even when they do achieve.

[92] See John R. Hicks (1937) and Patinkin (1956).

——. 'Irving Fisher on His Head: The Consequences of Constant Threshold-Target Monitoring of Money Holdings.' *Quarterly Journal of Economics*, May 1979, *93*(2), pp. 169–87.

——. 'Labor Contracts as Partial Gift Exchange.' *Quarterly Journal of Economics*, November 1982, *97*(4), pp. 543–69.

——. 'Procrastination and Obedience.' *American Economic Review*, May 1991 (*Papers and Proceedings*), *81*(2), pp. 1–19.

——. Dickens, William T. and Perry, George L. 'The Macroeconomics of Low Inflation.' *Brookings Papers on Economic Activity*, 1996, (1), pp. 1–59.

——. 'Near-Rational Wage and Price Setting and the Long-Run Philips Curve.' *Brookings Papers on Economic Activity*, 2000, (1), pp. 1–44.

—— and Kranton, Rachel E. 'Economics and Identity.' *Quarterly Journal of Economics*, August 2000, *115*(3), pp. 715–53.

——; Rose, Andrew K. and Yellen, Janet L. 'Job Switching and Job Satisfaction in the U.S. Labor Market.' *Brookings Papers on Economic Activity*, 1988, (2), pp. 495–582.

—— and Yellen, Janet L. 'A Near-Rational Model of the Business Cycle, with Wage and Price Inertia.' *Quarterly Journal of Economics*, Supp., 1985*a*, *100*(5), pp. 823–38.

——. 'Can Small Deviations from Rationality Make Significant Differences to Economic Equilibria?' *American Economic Review*, September 1985*b*, *75*(4), pp. 708–20.

——. 'The Fair Wage-Effort Hypothesis and Unemployment.' *Quarterly Journal of Economics*, May 1990, *105*(2), pp. 255–83.

——. 'How Large Are the Losses from Rule-of-Thumb Behavior in Models of the Business Cycle?' in William C. Brainard, William D. Nordhaus, and Harold W. Watts, eds., *Money, macroeconomics, and economic policy: Essays in honor of James Tobin*. Cambridge, MA: MIT Press, 1991, pp. 59–78.

Anderson, Elijah. *StreetWise: Race, class, and change in an urban community*. Chicago: University of Chicago Press, 1990.

Arrow, Kenneth J. 'The Economic Implications of Learning by Doing.' *Review of Economic Studies*, June 1962, *29*(3), pp. 155–73.

Ball, Lawrence. 'Credible Disinflation with Staggered Price-Setting.' *American Economic Review*. March 1994, *84*(1), pp. 282–89.

Banks, James; Blundell, Richard and Tanner, Sarah. 'Is There a Retirement-Savings Puzzle?' *American Economic Review*, September 1998, *88*(4), pp. 769–88.

Barro, Robert J. 'A Theory of Monopolistic Price Adjustment.' *Review of Economic Studies*, January 1972, *39*(1), pp. 17–26.

——. 'Long-Term Contracting, Sticky Prices, and Monetary Policy.' *Journal of Monetary Economics*, July 1977, *3*(3), pp. 305–16.

Barsky, Robert S.; Kimball, Miles S.; Juster, F. Thomas and Shapiro, Matthew. 'Preference Parameters and Behavioral Heterogeneity: An Experimental Approach in the Health and Retirement Survey.' National Bureau of Economic Research (Cambridge, MA) Working Paper No. 5213, August 1995.

Becker, Gary S. and Stigler, George J. 'Law Enforcement, Malfeasance, and the Compensation of Enforcers.' *Journal of Legal Studies*, January 1974, *3*(1), pp. 1–18.

Bernheim, B. Douglas; Skinner, Jonathan and Weinberg, Steven. 'What Accounts for the Variation in Retirement Wealth Among U.S. Households?' *American Economic Review*, September 2001, *91*(4), pp. 832–55.

Bewley, Truman. *Why wages don't fall during a recession*. Cambridge, MA: Harvard University Press, 1999.

Blanchard, Olivier Jean and Kiyotaki, Nobihiro. 'Monopolistic Competition and the Effects of Aggregate Demand.' *American Economic Review*, September 1987, *77*(4), pp. 647–66.

Blinder, Alan S. and Choi, Don H. 'A Shred of Evidence on Theories of Wage Stickiness.' *Quarterly Journal of Economics*, November 1990, *105*(4), pp. 1003–15.

Bowles, Samuel. 'The Production Process in a Competitive Economy: Walrasian, Neo-Hobbesian, and Marxian Models.' *American Economic Review*, March 1985, *75*(1), pp. 16–36.

Caballero, Ricardo. 'Durable Goods: An Explanation for Their Slow Adjustment.' *Journal of Political Economy*, April 1993, *101*(2), pp. 351–84.

Calvo, Guillermo A. 'Staggered Prices in a Utility-Maximizing Framework.' *Journal of Monetary Economics*, September 1983, *12*(4), pp. 383–98.

Campbell, Carl M. III and Kamlani, Kunal S. 'The Reasons for Wage Rigidity: Evidence from a Survey of Firms.' *Quarterly Journal of Economics*, August 1997, *112*(3), pp. 759–89.

Campbell, John Y. and Shiller, Robert J. 'Cointegration and Tests of Present Value Models.' *Journal of Political Economy*, October 1987, *97*(5), pp. 1062–88.

Caplin, Andrew F. and Leahy, John. 'State-Dependent Pricing and the Dynamics of Money and Output.' *Quarterly Journal of Economics*, August 1991, *106*(3), pp. 683–708.

—— and Spulber, Daniel F. 'Menu Costs and the Neutrality of Money.' *Quarterly Journal of Economics*, November 1987, *102*(4), pp. 703–25.

Card, David and Hyslop, Dean. 'Does Inflation "Grease the Wheels" of the Labor Market?' in Christina D. Romer and David H. Romer, eds., *Reducing inflation: Motivation and strategy*, NBER Studies in Business Cycles, Vol. 30. Chicago: University of Chicago Press, 1997, pp. 195–242.

Carmichael, Lorne. 'Can Unemployment Be Involuntary? Comment.' *American Economic Review*, December 1985, *75*(5), pp. 1213–14.

Chamberlin, Edward. *The theory of monopolistic competition: A re-orientation of the theory of value.* Cambridge, MA: Harvard University Press, 1962.

Clark, Kenneth. *Dark ghetto.* New York: Harper & Row, 1965.

De Bondt, Werner F. M. and Thaler, Richard H. 'Does the Stock Market Overreact?' *Journal of Finance*, July 1985, *40*(3), pp. 793–805.

Delpit, Lisa. *Other people's children: Cultural conflict in the classroom.* New York: New Press, 1995.

Dickens, William T. and Katz, Lawrence F. 'Inter-industry Wage Differences and Industry Characteristics,' in Kevin Lang and Jonathan S. Leonard, eds., *Unemployment and the structure of labor markets.* New York: Blackwell, 1987, pp. 48–89.

Du Bois, William E. B. *The souls of black folk.* Greenwich, CT: Fawcett Publications, 1965.

Dunlop, John T. 'The Task of Contemporary Wage Theory,' in John T. Dunlop, ed., *The theory of wage determination.* New York: St. Martin's Press, 1957, pp. 3–27.

Eckstein, Otto and Brinner, Roger. 'The Inflation Process in the United States.' Joint Economic Committee of the Congress of the United States, Washington, DC, 1972.

Economic Report of the President. 2000.

Engen, Eric M.; Gale, William G. and Uccello, Cori E. 'The Adequacy of Household Saving.' *Brookings Papers on Economic Activity*, 1999, (2), pp. 65–187.

Fehr, Ernst and Falk, Armin. 'Wage Rigidity in a Competitive Incomplete Contract Market.' *Journal of Political Economy*, February 1999, *107*(1), pp. 106–34.

——; Gachter, Simon and Kirchsteiger, Georg. 'Reciprocal Fairness and Noncompensating Wage Differentials.' *Journal of Institutional and Theoretical Economics*, December 1996, *152*(4), pp. 608–40.

—— and Goette, Lorenz. 'Robustness and Real Consequences of Nominal Wage Rigidity.' Institute for Empirical Research in Economics (University of Zurich) Working Paper No. 44, May 2000.

——; Kirchsteiger, Georg and Riedl, Arno. 'Does Fairness Prevent Market Clearing? An Experimental Investigation.' *Quarterly Journal of Economics*, May 1993, *108*(2), pp. 437–59.

—— and Tyran, Jean-Robert. 'Does Money Illusion Matter?' *American Economic Review*, December 2001, *91*(5), pp. 1239–62.

Ferguson, Ronald F. 'Can Schools Narrow the Test Score Gap?' in Christopher Jencks and Meredith Phillips, eds., *The black-white test score gap*. Washington, DC: Brookings Institution Press, 1998, pp. 318–74.

Fischer, Stanley. 'Long-Term Contracts, Rational Expectations, and the Optimal Money Supply Rule.' *Journal of Political Economy*, February 1977, *85*(1), pp. 191–205.

Flanagan, Robert J.; Soskice, David W. and Ulman, Lloyd. *Unionism, economic stabilization and incomes policies: European experience*. Washington, DC: Brookings Institution Press, 1983.

Fortin, Pierre. 'Canadian Wage Settlement Data.' Mimeo, Université de Québec à Montréal, April 1995.

——. 'The Great Canadian Slump.' *Canadian Journal of Economics*, November 1996, *29*(4), pp. 761–87.

——; Akerlof, George A.; Dickens, William T. and Perry, George L. 'Inflation, Unemployment, and Macroeconomic Policy in the United States and Canada: A Common Framework.' Mimeo, Université de Québec à Montréal, June 2001.

Foster, James E. and Wan, Henry Y., Jr. 'Involuntary Unemployment as a Principal-Agent Equilibrium.' *American Economic Review*, June 1984, *74*(3), pp. 476–84.

Frazier, Franklin. *The black bourgeoisie: The rise of the new middle class in the United States*. New York: Free Press, 1957.

Friedman, Milton. 'The Lag in Effect of Monetary Policy.' *Journal of Political Economy*, October 1961, *69*(5), pp. 447–66.

——. 'The Role of Monetary Policy.' *American Economic Review*, March 1968, *58*(1), pp. 1–17.

Gordon, Robert J. 'The Recent Acceleration in Inflation and Its Lessons for the Future.' *Brookings Papers on Economic Activity*, 1970, (1), pp. 8–41.

——. 'The Time-Varying NAIRU and Its Implications for Economic Policy.' *Journal of Economic Perspectives*, Winter 1997, *11*(1), pp. 11–32.

Hannerz, Ulf. *Soulside: Inquiries into ghetto culture and community*. New York: Columbia University Press, 1969.

Hayashi, Fumio. 'Tobin's Marginal q and Average q: A Neoclassical Interpretation.' *Econometrica*, January 1982, *50*(1), pp. 213–24.

Hicks, John R. 'Mr. Keynes and the "Classics": A Suggested Interpretation.' *Econometrica*, April 1937, *5*(1), pp. 147–59.

Hodgman, Donald R. 'Credit Risk and Credit Rationing.' *Quarterly Journal of Economics*. May 1960, *74*(2), pp. 258–78.

Hotelling, Harold. 'Stability in Competition.' *Economic Journal*, March 1929, *39*(153), pp. 41–57.

Howitt, Peter and Clower, Robert. 'The Emergence of Economic Organization.' *Journal of Economic Behavior and Organization*, January 2000, *41*(1), pp. 55–84.

Iwai, Katsuhito. *Disequilibrium dynamics: A theoretical analysis of inflation and unemployment*. New Haven, CT: Yale University Press, 1981.

Jaffee, Dwight M. and Russell, Thomas. 'Imperfect Information and Credit Rationing.' *Quarterly Journal of Economics*, November 1976, *90*(4), pp. 651–66.

Jensen, Michael C. and Meckling, William H. 'Theory of the Firm: Managerial Behavior, Agency Costs and Ownership Structure.' *Journal of Financial Economics*, October 1976, *3*(4), pp. 305–60.

Kahn, Shulamit. 'Evidence of Nominal Wage Stickiness from Microdata.' *American Economic Review*, December 1997, *87*(5), pp. 993–1008.

Kahneman, Daniel and Tversky, Amos. 'Prospect Theory: An Analysis of Decision under Risk.' *Econometrica*, March 1979, *47*(2), pp. 263–92.

Katz, Lawrence F. 'Efficiency Wage Theories: A Partial Evaluation,' in Stanley Fischer, ed., *NBER macroeconomics annual 1986*. Cambridge, MA: MIT Press, pp. 235–76.

Keynes, John Maynard. *The general theory of employment, interest and money*. New York: Macmillan, 1936.

Kleidon, Allan W. 'Variance Bounds Tests and Stock Price Valuation Models.' *Journal of Political Economy*, October 1986, *94*(5), pp. 953–1001.

Krueger, Alan B. and Summers, Lawrence H. 'Efficiency Wages and the Inter-industry Wage Structure.' *Econometrica*, March 1988, *56*(2), pp. 259–93.

Krueger, Alan B. and Whitmore, Diane M. 'The Effect of Attending a Small Class in the Early Grades on College Test-Taking and Middle School Test Results: Evidence from Project STAR.' Mimeo, Industrial Relations Section, Princeton University, September 1999.

Laibson, David I. 'The Adequacy of Household Saving: Comments and Discussion.' *Brookings Papers on Economic Activity*, 1999, (2), pp. 174–77.

——; Repetto, Andrea and Tobacman, Jeremy. 'Self-Control and Saving for Retirement.' *Brookings Papers on Economic Activity*, 1998, (1), pp. 91–172.

Lamont, Owen. 'Corporate-Debt Overhang and Macroeconomic Expectations.' *American Economic Review*, December 1995, *85*(5), pp. 1106–17.

Lebow, David E.; Saks, Raven E. and Wilson, Beth Anne. 'Downward Nominal Wage Rigidity: Evidence from the Employment Cost Index.' Board of Governors of the Federal Reserve System, Finance and Economics Discussion Series: 99/31, July 1999.

LeRoy, Stephen F. and Porter, Richard. 'The Present Value Relation: Test Based on Implied Variance Bounds.' *Econometrica*, May 1981, *49*(3), pp. 555–74.

Levine, David I. 'Cohesiveness, Productivity, and Wage Dispersion.' *Journal of Economic Behavior and Organization*, March 1991, *15*(2), pp. 237–55.

Levitt, Steven D. 'The Effect of Prison Population Size on Crime Rates: Evidence from Prison Overcrowding Litigation.' *Quarterly Journal of Economics*, May 1996, *111*(2), pp. 319–51.

Lindbeck, Assar and Snower, Dennis J. *The insider-outsider theory of employment and unemployment*. Cambridge, MA: MIT Press, 1988.

Lipsey, Richard G. 'The Relation between Unemployment and the Rate of Change of Money Wage Rates in the United Kingdom, 1862–1957: A Further Analysis.' *Economica*, New Series, February 1960, *27*(1), pp. 1–31.

Loewenstein, George. 'Anticipation and the Valuation of Delayed Consumption.' *Economic Journal*, September 1987, *97*(387), pp. 666–84.

—— and Prelec, Drazen. 'Anomalies in Intertemporal Choice: Evidence and an Interpretation.' *Quarterly Journal of Economics*, May 1992, *107*(2), pp. 573–97.

—— and Thaler, Richard H. 'Anomalies: Intertemporal Choice.' *Journal of Economic Perspectives*, Autumn 1989, *3*(4), pp. 181–93.

Loury, Glenn C. *One by one from the inside out*. New York: Free Press, 1995.

Lucas, Robert E., Jr. and Sargent, Thomas J. 'After Keynesian Macroeconomics,' in Federal Reserve Bank of Boston, *After the Philips curve: Persistence of high inflation and high unemployment*, Conference Series No. 19, 1979, pp. 49–72.

Madrian, Brigitte C. and Shea, Dennis F. 'The Power of Suggestion: Inertia in 401(k) Participation and Savings Behavior.' *Quarterly Journal of Economics*, November 2001, *116*(4), pp. 1149–87.

Mankiw, N. Gregory. 'Small Menu Costs and Large Business Cycles: A Macroeconomic Model.' *Quarterly Journal of Economics*, May 1985, *110*(2), pp. 529–38.

—— and Reis, Ricardo. 'Sticky Information versus Sticky Prices: A Proposal to Replace the New Keynesian Phillips Curve.' Mimeo, Harvard University, February 2001.

McLaughlin, Kenneth J. 'A Theory of Quits and Layoffs with Efficient Turnover.' *Journal of Political Economy*, February 1991, *99*(1), pp. 1–29.

Mehra, Rajnish. 'The Equity Premium Puzzle: Why Is It a Puzzle?' Mimeo, University of Chicago, May 2001.

Mishkin, Frederic S. 'Illiquidity, Consumer Durable Expenditure, and Monetary Policy.' *American Economic Review*, September 1976, *66*(4), pp. 642–54.

Murphy, Kevin M. and Topel, Robert J. 'Efficiency Wages Reconsidered: Theory and Evidence,' in Yoram Weiss and Gideon Fishelson, eds., *Advances in the theory and measurement of unemployment*. New York: MacMillan, 1990, pp. 204–40.

Myers, Stewart C. 'Interactions of Corporate Financing and Investment Decisions—Implications for Capital Budgeting.' *Journal of Finance*, March 1974, *29*(1), pp. 1–25.

Nisbett, Richard and Ross, Lee. *Human inference: Strategies and shortcomings of social judgment.* Englewood Cliffs, NJ: Prentice-Hall, 1980.

O'Donoghue, Ted and Rabin, Matthew. 'Doing It Now or Later.' *American Economic Review*, March 1999, *89*(1), pp. 103–24.

Parker, Jonathan A. 'The Consumption Risk of the Stock Market.' *Brookings Papers on Economic Activity*, 2001, (2), pp. 279–348.

Parkin, Michael. 'The Output-Inflation Trade-off When Prices Are Costly to Change.' *Journal of Political Economy*, February 1986, *94*(1), pp. 200–24.

Patinkin, Donald. *Money, interest, and prices: An integration of monetary and value theory.* Evanston, IL: Row, Peterson, 1956.

Perry, George L. 'Changing Labor Markets and Inflation.' *Brookings Papers on Economic Activity*, 1970, (3), pp. 411–41.

—— 'Money-Wage Dynamics and Labor-Market Equilibrium.' *Journal of Political Economy*, August 1968, *76*(4), Part 2, pp. 678–711.

——. 'The New Microeconomics in Inflation and Employment Theory.' *American Economic Review*, May 1969 (*Papers and Proceedings*), *59*(2), pp. 147–60.

Phelps, Edmund S. and Pollak, Robert A. 'On Second-Best National Saving and Game-Equilibrium Growth.' *Review of Economic Studies*, April 1968, *35*(2), pp. 185–99.

—— et al. *Microeconomic foundations of employment and inflation theory.* New York: W. W. Norton, 1970.

Phillips, A. W. 'The Relationship between Unemployment and the Rate of Change of Money Wages in the United Kingdom, 1861–1957.' *Economica*, New Series, November 1958, *25*(100), pp. 283–99.

Rabin, Matthew. 'Incorporating Fairness into Game Theory and Economics.' *American Economic Review*, December 1993, *83*(5), pp. 1281–302.

Rainwater, Lee. *Behind ghetto walls: Black families in a federal slum.* Chicago: Aldine, 1970.

Robinson, Joan. *The economics of imperfect competition.* London: Macmillan, 1942.

Romer, Christina D. and Romer, David H. 'Does Monetary Policy Matter? A New Test in the Spirit of Friedman and Schwartz,' in Olivier Jean Blanchard and Stanley Fischer, eds., *NBER macroeconomics annual, 1989*. Cambridge, MA: MIT Press, 1989, pp. 121–70.

Romer, David H. 'Rational Asset-Price Movements without News.' *American Economic Review*, December 1993, *83*(5), pp. 1112–30.

Roy, Donald. 'Quota Restriction and Goldbricking in a Machine Shop.' *American Journal of Sociology*, March 1952, *57*(5), pp. 427–42.

Sargent, Thomas J. 'A Note on the "Accelerationist" Controversy.' *Journal of Money, Credit, and Banking*, August 1971, *3*(3), pp. 721–25.

Scarry, Richard. *Richard Scarry's cars and trucks and things that go*. New York: Golden Books, 1974.

Shafir, Eldar; Diamond, Peter and Tversky, Amos. 'Money Illusion.' *Quarterly Journal of Economics*, May 1997, *112*(2), pp. 341–74.

Shapiro, Carl and Stiglitz, Joseph E. 'Equilibrium Unemployment as a Worker Discipline Device.' *American Economic Review*, June 1984, *74*(3), pp. 433–44.

Shiller, Robert J. 'Do Stock Prices Move Too Much to be Justified by Subsequent Changes in Dividends?' *American Economic Review*, June 1981, *71*(3), pp. 421–36.

——. 'Why Do People Dislike Inflation?' in Christina D. Romer and David H. Romer, eds., *Reducing inflation: Motivation and strategy*, NBER Studies in Business Cycles, Vol. 30. Chicago: University of Chicago Press, 1997a, pp. 13–65.

——. 'Public Resistance to Indexation: A Puzzle.' *Brookings Papers on Economic Activity*, 1997*b*, (1), pp. 159–211.

——. *Irrational exuberance*. Princeton, NJ: Princeton University Press, 2000.

Siegel, Jeremy J. and Thaler, Richard H. 'Anomalies: The Equity Premium Puzzle.' *Journal of Economic Perspectives*, Winter 1997, *11*(1), pp. 191–200.

Solow, Robert M. 'Investment and Technical Progress,' in Kenneth J. Arrow, Samuel Korbin, and Patrick Suppes, eds., *Mathematical methods in the social sciences*. Stanford, CA: Stanford University Press, 1959, pp. 89–104.

——. 'Substitution and Fixed Proportions in the Theory of Capital.' *Review of Economic Studies*, June 1962, *29*(3), pp. 207–18.

Staiger, Douglas; Stock, James H. and Watson, Mark W. 'How Precise Are Estimates of the Natural Rate of Unemployment?' in Christina D. Romer and David H. Romer, eds., *Reducing inflation: Motivation and strategy*, NBER Studies in Business Cycles, Vol. 30. Chicago: University of Chicago Press, 1997, pp. 195–242.

Stiglitz, Joseph E. and Weiss, Andrew. 'Credit Rationing in Markets with Imperfect Information.' *American Economic Review*, June 1981, *71*(3), pp. 393–410.

Stoft, Steven. 'Cheat-Threat Theory: An Explanation of Involuntary Unemployment.' Mimeo, Boston University, May 1982.

Strotz, Robert H. 'Myopia and Inconsistency in Dynamic Utility Maximization.' *Review of Economic Studies*, January 1956, *23*(3), pp. 165–80.

Summers, Lawrence H. 'Taxation and Corporate Investment: A *q*-Theory Approach.' *Brookings Papers on Economic Activity*, 1981, (1), pp. 67–127.

——. 'Does the Stock Market Rationally Reflect Fundamental Values?' *Journal of Finance*, July 1986, *41*(3), pp. 591–601.

Taylor, John. 'Staggered Wage Setting in a Macro Model.' *American Economic Review*, May 1979 (*Papers and Proceedings*), *69*(2), pp. 108–13.

Thaler, Richard H. and Benartzi, Shlomo. 'Save More Tomorrow: Using Behavioral Economics to Increase Employee Saving.' Mimeo, University of Chicago, November 2000.

Tobin, James. 'A General Equilibrium Approach to Monetary Theory.' *Journal of Money, Credit, and Banking*, February 1969, *1*(1), pp. 15–29.

——. 'Inflation and Unemployment.' *American Economic Review*, March 1972, *62*(1), pp. 1–18.

West, Kenneth D. 'Bubbles, Fads and Stock Price Volatility Tests: A Partial Evaluation.' *Journal of Finance*, July 1988, *43*(3), pp. 639–56.

Wilson, William J. *The truly disadvantaged*. Chicago: University of Chicago Press, 1987.

——. *When work disappears: The world of the new urban poor*. New York: Knopf, 1996.

Yellen, Janet L. 'Efficiency Wage Models of Unemployment.' *American Economic Review*, May 1984 (*Papers and Proceedings*), *74*(2), pp. 200–05.

Zbaracki, Mark J.; Ritson, Mark; Levy, Daniel; Dutta, Shantanu and Bergen, Mark. 'The Managerial and Customer Costs of Price Adjustment: Direct Evidence from Industrial Markets.' Mimeo, Emory University, 2000.

Index

Index